OXFORD EU LAW LIBRARY

General Editors: David Anderson, QC
Barrister at Brick Court Chambers and
Visiting Professor of Law at King's College London.
Piet Eeckhout, Professor of European Law
and Director of the Centre of European Law at King's College London.

EU EXTERNAL RELATIONS LAW

Second Edition

OXFORD EU LAW LIBRARY

The aim of this series is to publish important and original studies of the various branches of EU law. Each work provides a clear, concise, and original critical exposition of the law in its social, economic, and political context, at a level which will interest the advanced student, the practitioner, the academic, and government and Community officials. Formerly the Oxford European Community Law Library Series.

Other Titles in the Library

EU Justice and Home Affairs Law
Third edition
Steve Peers

The European Union and its Court of Justice
Second edition
Anthony Arnull

The General Principles of EU Law
Second edition
Takis Tridimas

EU Company Law
Vanessa Edwards

EU Anti-Discrimination Law
Fifth edition
Joanna Goyder and Albertina Albors-Llorens

EU Agriculture Law
Second edition
J.A. Usher

Intellectual Property Rights in EU Law
Vol 1: Free Movement and Competition Law
David T. Keeling

EU Customs Law
Second edition
Timothy Lyons, QC

EC Employment Law
Third edition
Catherine Barnard

Directives in EU Law
Second edition
Sacha Prechal

The Law of Money and Financial Services in the EU
Second edition
J.A. Usher

Workers, Establishment, and Services in the European Union
Robin C.A. White

EU External Relations Law

Second Edition

PIET EECKHOUT

OXFORD
UNIVERSITY PRESS

OXFORD
UNIVERSITY PRESS

Great Clarendon Street, Oxford OX2 6DP

Oxford University Press is a department of the University of Oxford.
It furthers the University's objective of excellence in research, scholarship,
and education by publishing worldwide in

Oxford New York

Auckland Cape Town Dar es Salaam Hong Kong Karachi
Kuala Lumpur Madrid Melbourne Mexico City Nairobi
New Delhi Shanghai Taipei Toronto

With offices in

Argentina Austria Brazil Chile Czech Republic France Greece
Guatemala Hungary Italy Japan Poland Portugal Singapore
South Korea Switzerland Thailand Turkey Ukraine Vietnam

Published in the United States
by Oxford University Press Inc., New York

First published 2011

British Library Cataloguing in Publication Data
Data available

Library of Congress Cataloging in Publication Data
Data available

Typeset by SPI Publisher Services, Pondicherry, India
Printed and bound by
CPI Group (UK) Ltd,
Croydon, CR0 4YY

ISBN 978–0–19–960663–4

3 5 7 9 10 8 6 4 2

Series Editor's Foreword

The foreign policy ambitions of the European Union are evident from Articles 3(5) and 21 of the TEU and from the fact that, as Professor Eeckhout aptly puts it, there now appear to be virtually no significant areas of international law-making in which the Union cannot participate.

In this respect at least, the Union is not obviously out of step with the popular will. The pooling of national sovereignty over external trade seems barely to feature on the standard eurosceptic list of complaints, in recognition perhaps of the influence that comes with being part of one of the world's largest trading blocs. Almost two thirds of those questioned in a 2010 Eurobarometer survey said that they favoured a common foreign policy for the 27 Member States of the European Union, as against 25 per cent who were opposed. Imperfect as the reality may be, the principle of common external action appears to have a fair degree of support.

The emergence of the Union as a fully-fledged actor on the international stage has, however, been attended by almost constant legal conflict over competence, the major protagonists being the European Commission on the one hand and Member States on the other. This book functions, in part, as a definitive military history of that forty years' war, ranging from the dramatic early breakthroughs of *ERTA* and *Opinion 1/76* and the set-piece battles of *Opinion 1/94* and *Open Skies* to more recent skirmishes over such vitally important matters – to those involved – as whether it is open to a Member State to propose a pollutant for regulation in an international forum where the Commission is also represented.

More interesting still is the author's analysis of the effects of international law in the Union's legal order. He defends the Court of Justice against the fashionable charge of parochialism, in relation to both its refusal to accord direct effect to the WTO (though he draws the line at the Court's failure to give effect to WTO dispute resolution decisions) and its treatment of the UN Charter in the first *Kadi* case – to which he made a decisive contribution on Mr Kadi's behalf before the Court of Justice. His verdict that the Union is an exporter of international co-operation will not find favour everywhere but is soundly argued. It will be interesting to see what happens when, perhaps in an ECHR context, the Court of Justice is asked for the first time to accept that it is bound by the ruling of another supranational court.

Impressive, to the practitioner, is the author's shrewdness in identifying future *causes célèbres*. What to make of the reference to fair as well as free trade in Article 5 TEU? What will happen to 1200 bilateral investment treaties, now that some of the matters they regulate fall within the exclusive competence of the Union? Is shared competence the new exclusive competence? Should the degree of protection accorded to those whose assets are frozen depend on the underlying justification for the sanction? Will the attempt to make a judge-free Alsatia of the Common Foreign and Security Policy survive the exercise of the Court's power in Article 40 TEU to patrol its borders?

Such questions will no doubt be addressed as the Lisbon Treaty beds down. In the meantime, it is a pleasure to welcome the second edition of this essential book, its range and utility amply reflected in its new title.

David Anderson
February 2011

Contents

Part II—International Foundations: Treaties and International Law

Part III—Policies

Table of Cases

Chronological

Germany

United Kingdom

United States

International Court of Justice

World Trade Organization

Table of Legislation

Directives

Joint Actions

Regulations

European Treaties

United Kingdom

Other international instruments

UN Resolutions

List of Abbreviations

General

ACP	Africa, Caribbean and Pacific Group of States
AETR	European Agreement concerning the Work of Crews of Vehicles Engaged in International Road Transport
AFSJ	Area of Freedom, Security and Justice
BITs	bilateral investment treaties
CAP	Common Agricultural Policy
CCT	Common Customs Tariff
CFI	Court of First Instance of the European Union, now the General Court
CFSP	Common Foreign and Security Policy
cif	cost, insurance, and freight included
CN	combined nomenclature, with reference to the CCT (see above)
Coreper	Committee of Permanent Representatives of the Member States
CSDP	Common Security and Defence Policy
DSU	Dispute Settlement Understanding (WTO)
EAEC	European Atomic Energy Community
EAEC Treaty	Treaty establishing the European Atomic Energy Community
EBRD	European Bank for Reconstruction and Development
ECAA	European Common Aviation Area
ECB	European Central Bank
ECHR	European Convention on Human Rights
ECJ	European Court of Justice
ECOWAS	Economic Community of West African States
ECSC	European Coal and Steel Community
ECT	Energy Charter Treaty
ECtHR	European Court of Human Rights
EDF	European Development Fund
EEA	European Economic Area

EEAS	European External Action Service
EFTA	European Free Trade Area
EIB	European Investment Bank
EMU	Economic and Monetary Union
EPC	European Political Co-operation (the predecessor to the CFSP)
ESCB	European System of Central Banks
EUMC	European Union Military Committee
EUMS	European Union Military Staff Organization
FAO	Food and Agriculture Organization (UN)
FRY	Federal Republic of Yugoslavia
FYROM	Former Yugoslav Republic of Macedonia
GATS	General Agreement on Trade in Services
GATT	General Agreement on Tariffs and Trade
GSP	generalized tariff preferences
ICCPR	International Covenant on Civil and Political Rights
ILC	International Law Commission
ILO	International Labour Organization
IMF	International Monetary Fund
IMO	International Maritime Organization
ITLOS	International Tribunal for the Law of the Sea
LMOs	living modified organisms
Marpol	International Convention for the Prevention of Pollution from Ships
MFN	most favoured nation
OECD	Organization for Economic Co-operation and Development
OPAC	Proscribed Organizations Appeal Commission (UK)
PFOS	perfluoroctane sulfonates
PIC	prior informed consent
PNR	passenger name record
POPs	persistent organic pollutants
PSC	Political and Security Committee
SPS	Agreement on Sanitary and Phytosanitary Measures (WTO)
TBT	Agreement on Technical Barriers to Trade (WTO)
TEU	Treaty on European Union
TFEU	Treaty on the Functioning of the European Union

TRIMs	Agreement on Trade-Related Investment Measures (WTO)
TRIPs	Agreement on Trade-Related Aspects of Intellectual Property Rights (WTO)
UNCLOS	United Nations Convention on the Law of the Sea
UNCTAD	United Nations Conference on Trade and Development
VCLT	Vienna Convention on the Law of Treaties
WTO	World Trade Organization

Publications

CDE	Cahiers de Droit européen
CLJ	Cambridge Law Journal
CML Rev	Common Market Law Review
EFA Rev	European Foreign Affairs Review
EIoP	European Integration online Papers
EJIL	European Journal of International Law
ELJ	European Law Journal
ELR	European Law Review
ICLQ	International Comparative Law Quarterly
IOLR	International Organizations Law Review
JCMS	Journal of Common Market Studies
JIEL	Journal of International Economic Law
JWT	Journal of World Trade
JWTL	Journal of World Trade Law
LIEI	Legal Issues of Economic Integration
Nord J Int L	Nordic Journal of International Law
NYIL	Netherlands Yearbook of International Law
OJLS	Oxford Journal of Legal Studies
RGDIP	Revue générale de droit international public
RMCUE	Revue du marché commun et de l'union européenne
RSCAS	Robert Schuman Centre for Advanced Studies
RTDE	Revue trimestrielle de droit européen
UNYB	Yearbook of United Nations Law
YEL	Yearbook of European Law

1

Introduction

Constitutional moment

The first edition of this book was written in 2003, a year of great constitutional moment for the EU's role on the world stage. It was not, however, a moment of universal euphoria over unquestionable progress. At one level the Convention on the Future of Europe was debating the constitutionalization of the EU, charting a course for a proper external projection of the EU phenomenon by constructing the constitutional and institutional foundations for an effective European foreign policy. It proposed abolishing the pillar structure, whose stone-faced mysteries had resisted and confused all conceptual understanding, and had led to much expenditure of ineffective political and institutional energy. It proposed express confirmation of the Union's legal personality, which is in effect an international legal personality. It proposed an assembly of all Treaty provisions on EU external relations, gleaned from the various treaties, renovated, and expanded, in a vital Title of Part III of the new constitution. It proposed a solution for resolving inter-institutional tension between the Commission and the Council, namely the creation of a double-hatted Minister for Foreign Affairs. It proposed, not least, an ambitious, some might say Utopian,[1] formulation of the principles and objectives of the Union's external action. At the outset of this book that formulation, which later became Article 21 of the TEU, as amended by the Treaty of Lisbon, is worth quoting:

1. The Union's action on the international scene shall be guided by the principles which have inspired its own creation, development and enlargement, and which it seeks to advance in the wider world: democracy, the rule of law, the universality and indivisibility of human rights and fundamental freedoms, respect for human dignity, the principles of equality and solidarity, and respect for the principles of the United Nations Charter and international law.

The Union shall seek to develop relations and build partnerships with third countries, and international, regional or global organisations, which share the principles referred to in the first subparagraph. It shall promote multilateral solutions to common problems, in particular in the framework of the United Nations.

[1] R Kagan, *Of Paradise and Power: America and Europe in the New World Order* (Alfred Knopf, 2003).

2. The Union shall define and pursue common policies and actions, and shall work for a high degree of co-operation in all fields of international relations, in order to:

(a) safeguard its values, fundamental interests, security, independence and integrity;
(b) consolidate and support democracy, the rule of law, human rights and the principles of international law;
(c) preserve peace, prevent conflicts and strengthen international security, in conformity with the principles of the United Nations Charter, with the principles of the Helsinki Final Act and with the aims of the Charter of Paris, including those relating to external borders;
(d) foster the sustainable economic, social and environmental development of developing countries, with the primary aim of eradicating poverty;
(e) encourage the integration of all countries into the world economy, including through the progressive abolition of restrictions on international trade;
(f) help develop international measures to preserve and improve the quality of the environment and the sustainable management of global natural resources, in order to ensure sustainable development;
(g) assist populations, countries and regions confronting natural or man-made disasters; and
(h) promote an international system based on stronger multilateral co-operation and good global governance.

...

If Europe, with all its political, economic, and intellectual resources, could realize only a segment of all this, the world might truly become a better place. The Convention, which clearly appreciated that its work on EU external action was central to its own constitutional moment, might in some measure earn its lofty denomination evoking the best episode of the American dream, and prove that the Age of Enlightenment is not dead.

Yet at the very same time Europe was facing one of its gravest political crises in the form of its inability to speak with one voice about the approach towards the Hussein regime in Iraq. In the corridors of the Convention there were arguments about the futility of the constitution-drafting exercise, in particular as regards EU external action, in the face of such fundamental cleavages between the Member States. The Common Foreign and Security Policy (CFSP), then in existence for ten years, but rarely if ever noticed by the general public, might as well be abandoned, notwithstanding opinion polls showing strong public support for a united European foreign policy.

Institutions and the law are quite resistant to such radical solutions. The Convention continued its work, attempting to create an adequate constitutional and institutional framework whilst recognizing that it could not itself supply the political will required to make Europe's foreign policy work. Its final product, the Constitutional Treaty, did not come to pass. But much of its substance, including in the sphere of external relations, was kept, and incorporated in the changes to the founding Treaties which the Treaty of Lisbon put on the EU's statute book. Not, however, without also in this area abandoning some of the constitutional terminology, such as the office of the Minister for Foreign Affairs—instead we continue to have a 'mere' High Representative.

All this might suggest to those unfamiliar with the EU that its foreign policy is still in its infancy. Such an assessment would be wholly unjustified. In her book on the intergovernmental pillars of the EU, Denza describes the foreign and security relations of a single sovereign State as supported and realized through a range of powerful instruments:[2]

> The State by its nature has international legal personality; it may conclude treaties, become a member of international organizations, send and receive diplomatic and consular missions, defend its external interests by domestic legislation and its physical and political integrity by armies and weapons. By exploiting its natural and human resources it has money at its disposal which may be used for internal as well as external purposes.

Denza employs this description to contrast, at least to some extent, the sovereign State with the EU's CFSP. However, it is in fact striking that the EU already possesses and uses most, if not all, of those 'powerful instruments'. Whether the EU, as distinct from the EC, had international legal personality was a matter of debate for some time, but the Treaty of Lisbon ended that debate by providing, in Article 47 TEU, for such overall EU legal personality. Article 281 EC had always provided that the Community had legal personality, and as early as 1971 the Court of Justice, in the seminal *AETR* ruling, construed this provision as confirming international legal personality.[3] Such personality is not a theoretical construction, as the EU is a party to hundreds of international agreements covering many areas of international law-making and establishing links with countries in all corners of the globe. The EU is also a member of a number of other international organizations, a rather unique phenomenon, even if still of limited scope. The EC did not send formal diplomatic and consular missions, but that lacuna was more apparent than real in the light of the important role played by European Commission delegations in third countries. Those delegations are now, after Lisbon, 'European Union delegations' (see Articles 32 and 35 TEU). The EU has the capacity to enact legislation; indeed in matters of external trade it has exclusive competence, and has wholly replaced the individual Member States. The EU has significant financial resources, an important part of which is spent on external action, often in conjunction with Member States' expenditure (e.g. development co-operation). Finally, the current EU even has a military component, and engages in military operations.[4]

[2] E Denza, *The Intergovernmental Pillars of the European Union* (OUP, 2002) 85–6.

[3] See Ch 3. [4] See Ch 11.

Subject matter and methodology

This book explores the legal foundations of the EU's foreign policy, or external relations as is the prevailing denomination. It brings together the various strands of EU external action,[5] focusing on both the external policies outlined in the TFEU (the former 'First Pillar') and the CFSP (the former 'Second Pillar').

The aims of the project which led to this book were the collection, organization, and presentation of the many different aspects and developments of external relations law; to give access to practice, case law, and academic literature linked to external relations; to advance our understanding (or at least this author's understanding) of the role of law in EU external policies; and to offer introduction, survey, analysis, and reflection. The academic approach is largely doctrinal, but with attention to historical development, political and institutional context, and in narrative form. The attempt is to be true to this series' aim of providing 'a clear, concise, and critical exposition of the law in its social, economic, and political context'. The book may also serve as a basis for further and deeper academic reflection on specific aspects of EU external relations law. Indeed, the author finds it rewarding to see how, subsequent to the publication of the first edition, a younger generation of scholars has published important treatises on the subject,[6] and how the structure of the first edition has been influential as a template for other studies.[7]

Academic literature on EU law has generally tended to concentrate on the case law of the European Courts, in particular that of the Court of Justice. There are a number of obvious reasons for this, which need not be explored here. There has also been contestation of Court-centred analysis. Academic lawyers have rightly become more critical of the Court, and more attention is devoted to non-judicial actors and developments. Law does not invariably develop through case law, and judicial proclamations may conceal rather than reveal the problems which the polity and society face, and may create legal illusions.

This book none the less devotes a lot of attention to the case law. The rulings by the EU Courts offer a rich record of problems, questions, and issues concerning external relations. Case law has contributed to shaping the constitutional foundations of external action as well as some of the actual policies. It exposes the inter-institutional struggle which explains a lot of basic features, including the old pillar structure itself. It is the meeting place for true encounters between EU law and international law, as parties to litigation put the two systems in confrontation. In-depth study of the case law allows one to develop a richer and more nuanced, focused, and calibrated legal discourse on EU external relations.

[5] The Treaty of Lisbon speaks of external action instead of external relations.

[6] R Holdgaard, *External Relations of the European Community—Legal Reasoning and Legal Discourses* (Kluwer, 2008) and G De Baere, *Constitutional Principles of EU External Relations* (OUP, 2008).

[7] P Koutrakos, *EU International Relations Law* (Hart Publishing, 2006).

The most challenging dimension of the project was to find an overall framework of analysis, which would allow for the selection of relevant topics. It was soon realized that the book could not cover all external policies and all international agreements. External EU policies are not confined to 'inherent' domains of external relations such as trade, development co-operation, and foreign and security policy. Most, if not all, of the EU's 'internal' policies have a significant external dimension. Environmental policy is possibly the best example: the EU's environmental policy is perhaps as much constructed through participation in international environmental law-making as through internal legislation. Accordingly, a study of all external policies could not be undertaken in this book. The same is true for the treaty-making practice, in particular as regards the variety of agreements, in terms of concepts and subject matter, and as regards the specific features of relations with third countries or groups of third countries. The EU has concluded association, partnership, and co-operation agreements, of some form or other, with so many third countries. Each of those agreements forms the basis for a particular bilateral relationship. Again, a study of those agreements could not be undertaken, and this book does not provide an analysis, as such, of treaty relations between the EU and third countries.

So what does the book cover? It aims to identify the legal, and indeed constitutional, foundations of external relations. What are the bases in the founding treaties for the EU's external relations? What competences have been conferred on the EU to act in the international sphere? How does the EU conclude international agreements and become a member of international organizations? What is the role of the various EU institutions in the conduct of external relations? What is the relationship between EU law and international law? What are the effects of international law, and in particular international agreements, in the EU's legal order? These are all fundamental questions the answers to which this book attempts to unravel.

The book is organized in three parts. The first is entitled Constitutional Foundations: Competences and Objectives. It is wholly devoted to the Treaty foundations (both TFEU and TEU) for external relations and external policies. It concentrates on the Treaty provisions which confer competence to conclude international agreements, which are the core of external action. Ever since the creation of the EEC this has been a big legal battlefield, due to the reluctance, resistance, and inhibitions of the Member States to cede sovereignty to the EU, in particular as regards external relations. Chapter 2 examines the EU's competences in matters of commercial policy, which formed the basis in the original EEC Treaty for external action. From the 1970s onwards the Court of Justice has played a pivotal role in defining the scope and nature of competence as regards external trade. Chapter 3 complements that analysis by concentrating on the doctrine of implied powers, equally foundational for the EU's external action, and equally contested. Partly on the basis of the analysis in those two chapters, Chapter 4 looks more generally at external competences under the TFEU in the main areas of EU policy-making. Chapter 5 concludes Part I by looking at external competences for the conduct of the CFSP, under the TEU.

The title of the second part of the book is International Foundations: Treaties and International Law. It contains four chapters on the relationship between international law and treaties, and EU law. Chapter 6 explores the life cycle of international agreements, analysing the EU procedures for negotiation, conclusion, suspension, and termination of treaties and agreements. Such analysis reveals the role of the various EU institutions in the conduct of external relations, and throws up constitutional questions of division of powers, democracy, accountability, and legitimacy. Chapter 7 concentrates on mixed agreements and membership of international organizations. Mixed agreements, i.e. agreements with third countries or international organizations to which both the EU and its individual Member States are parties, are a hallmark of EU external relations, again reflecting the resistance to cession of sovereignty. They give rise to many questions and problems which the chapter aims to analyse. It also focuses on membership of international organizations, for purposes of convenience—even though that is a subject of its own, the issues to which it gives rise are often the same as in the case of mixed agreements, because EU membership is invariably combined with Member States' membership. Furthermore, the concept of an international organization is not easy to define, as many international agreements (often mixed agreements in terms of EU participation) provide for some type of institutional framework. Chapter 8 looks at the role of the European Courts in the interpretation and application of agreements concluded by the EU. It examines the main heads of jurisdiction of those courts, aiming to identify in what way such jurisdiction extends to international agreements. It also offers an analysis of methods of interpretation of such agreements. Chapter 9, lastly, the longest chapter of this book, examines the effects of international agreements and international law in the EU legal order.

There is a third part of the book, even though Parts I and II could be regarded as sufficient for a book on the legal foundations of EU external relations. This third part concentrates on a few external policies. It is much more selective than Parts I and II, because there are many established and developing external policies which are not analysed. It first focuses on the common commercial policy (Chapter 10), which is historically at the heart of the EU's external relations. Chapter 11 studies the actors and instruments of the CFSP. Chapter 12, lastly, explores the links between trade policy and foreign policy in the area of economic and financial sanctions. That chapter offers a form of case study of those links. The purpose of this third part on external policies is to put some flesh on to the bones of constitutional and institutional developments, and to improve the understanding of those developments. Issues of external competence or legal effects of international agreements should not be studied in isolation, because the way in which the law develops is clearly influenced by the substantive policies which are projected and conducted. The analysis of actual policies also further clarifies the role of the various institutions, and throws up additional questions of constitutionalism.

Second Edition and Treaty of Lisbon

Much has happened in the field of EU external relations law since the first edition of this book was published. The most prominent development is of course the entry into force of the Treaty of Lisbon. That Treaty, in substance not dissimilar to the Constitution for Europe, made many important changes to the conduct of EU external relations—now officially termed 'external action'. Although, at the time of writing, the Treaty has been in force for close to one year, it is still early days for determining and describing its effects on EU external relations law. The institutional innovations, in particular, are still in their infancy, and it will take a number of years for commentators to be in a position to see what the various changes really mean for this area of EU policy-making. Accordingly, this second edition does not aim to offer anything like a definitive treatment of the Lisbon changes. The law is very much in motion here, and this book can only attempt to offer a snapshot.

However, it is not only the basic treaties which have been amended. Questions of EU external relations law are the subject of litigation in the EU Courts with an ever increasing frequency. The case law which developed between 2003 and 2010 is impressive, and this second edition aims to analyse it in substantial depth. The aim has also been, though, not to expand the book too much, in order to continue to offer a sufficiently concise treatment. Something has got to give, therefore. The chapter on the EU's external human rights policy has been abandoned, primarily because that policy has not developed much in recent years, and appears less important (unfortunately) than the other external policies analysed in Part III. Also, the EU's sanctions policy, studied in Chapter 12, throws up a host of human rights issues. Commentators of the first edition have also pointed out that an analysis of the EU's external policies connected to the Area of Freedom, Security, and Justice (AFSJ) merit deeper analysis. The author could not agree more. As, however, a new edition of Steve Peers' magisterial analysis of the legal dimension of the AFSJ has just been published, in this Series, the author would kindly refer the reader to that volume.[8] Lastly, the author has cut some sections of the first edition, throughout the book, which were regarded as no longer so vital in the light of the way in which the law has evolved.

It was also decided to shorten the title of the book to *EU External Relations Law*, which is sufficient to reflect its ambition and content.

Through this book the author hopes to show the importance of this subject, not only in its own right, but for the developing identity of the EU as a whole. The organization of the external relations of the EU and its Member States is crucial for the unique type of federalism which Europe is constructing.[9]

[8] S Peers, *EU Justice and Home Affairs Law* (3rd edn, OUP, 2011).

[9] Cf JHH Weiler, *The Constitution of Europe* (CUP, 1999) 186–7.

Part I

Constitutional Foundations: Competences and Objectives

2

Competence in matters of commercial policy

Introduction

The European Union, as it developed out of the European Communities, has some of its legal origins in the General Agreement on Tariffs and Trade (GATT). After World War II, GATT was negotiated with a view to establishing a multilateral legal framework for trade liberalization. It reflected prevailing economic theory on the benefits of free trade, and was centred on the concept of non-discrimination, as a response to the beggar-thy-neighbour policies of the 1930s. Article I GATT spells out the most-favoured-nation principle (MFN), which requires equal treatment of trading partners. If that principle were unqualified, it would not be possible to set up forms of regional economic integration based on preferential terms of trade within the region concerned. GATT tolerates derogations from MFN for integration purposes, however, provided they take the form of either a customs union or free-trade area and comply with the requirements of Article XXIV GATT. Again this was based on economic theory, which recognizes the potential benefits flowing from closer integration,[1] even though it must be added that the theoretical support is qualified.[2]

When the EEC was set up, it was decided to establish a customs union, the most advanced form of trade integration, since there was the further aim of building a common market, with free movement of factors of production. Accordingly, (current) Article 28(1) TFEU provides that:

> The Union shall comprise a customs union which shall cover all trade in goods and which shall involve the prohibition between Member States of customs duties on imports and exports and of all charges having equivalent effect, and the adoption of a common customs tariff in their relations with third countries.

The customs union is at the core of the internal market, and establishing the customs union was among the first major policies which the EEC implemented, in the 1960s, together with the Common Agricultural Policy. The abolition of customs

[1] J Viner, *The Customs Union Issue* (Carnegie Endowment for International Peace, 1950).

[2] See e.g. J Bhagwati, *The World Trading System at Risk* (Harvester Wheatsheaf, 1991) ch 5.

duties in internal trade is now largely of historical (and constitutional[3]) interest, and the common customs tariff is discussed in Chapter 10. However, it was clear to the drafters of the EEC Treaty that a common external tariff was only one segment of a common external trade policy, and that indeed the latter was required if the customs union and the common market were to work well. They therefore wrote a chapter on the common commercial policy which the EEC was to set up and conduct.

The original EEC Treaty chapter on the common commercial policy was short, and the current title in the TFEU is even shorter due to the repeal of some provisions. The title on the common commercial policy is now part of Part V of the TFEU, which concerns external action by the Union, and contains only two provisions. It opens by identifying the aims of this policy: by establishing a customs union, the Union shall contribute, in the common interest, to the harmonious development of world trade, the progressive abolition of restrictions on international trade and on foreign direct investment, and the lowering of customs and other barriers (Article 206 TFEU). Then follows Article 207, which further describes the measures to be adopted in the framework of this policy:

> 1. The common commercial policy shall be based on uniform principles, particularly with regard to changes in tariff rates, the conclusion of tariff and trade agreements relating to goods and services, and the commercial aspects of intellectual property, foreign direct investment, the achievement of uniformity in measures of liberalization, export policy and measures to protect trade such as those to be taken in the event of dumping or subsidies. The common commercial policy shall be conducted in the context of the principles and objectives of the Union's external action.

The article also sets out the role of the various institutions and the procedure to be followed for the adoption of such measures, and was in this respect substantially amended by the Treaties of Amsterdam, Nice, and Lisbon. At this stage, it is important to note that, where prior to Lisbon the Commission and the Council were the leading institutions, the European Parliament has now become a full co-legislator. It must also be emphasized, for the purpose of further analysis in this chapter, that the original version of the paragraph quoted above did not include services, the commercial aspects of intellectual property, and foreign direct investment. The former two were gradually added by Amsterdam, Nice, and Lisbon, whereas foreign direct investment has only been part of the common commercial policy since Lisbon.

In the course of the 1960s, the young EEC was successful in removing internal customs duties and adopting the common customs tariff. The latter required common action in the framework of GATT, to which all the Member States were contracting parties. As the Treaty empowered the Commission to conduct trade

[3] It was in this area that the ECJ delivered its foundational ruling in Case 26/62 *Van Gend en Loos v. Nederlandse Administratie der Belastingen* [1963] ECR 1.

negotiations, the Commission effectively replaced the Member States in GATT dealings, in a pragmatic arrangement characteristic of the then GATT.[4]

In the 1970s, however, the EEC lost much of its pristine state, and at the level of trade policy it soon became clear that developing a truly uniform external trade policy, over and above the customs union, was going to be more difficult than had been envisaged. Achieving such uniformity in fact required the abolition of long lists of import restrictions which individual Member States still operated. In a period of economic stagnation and crisis that proved impossible to achieve, and it was only by 1994, twenty-four years after the due date, that complete uniformity of import conditions was reached.[5] In the light of such difficulties in establishing what is in effect the core of any external trade policy, it will come as no surprise that there was soon also a legal debate on the exact scope of the common commercial policy. When, as will be seen, the Court of Justice decided that the EEC's powers to conduct this policy were exclusive of those of the Member States, the legal stakes became even higher. The scene had been set for a series of turf battles, mostly between the Commission and the Council. This chapter aims to analyse and portray those battles, and the case law and treaty amendments they gave rise to.[6] It aims to do that from a historical perspective, in the sense of discussing both internal and external events which throw light on how the law on trade policy powers developed. The chapter also aims to show the significant political dimension of these legal battles, so closely interwoven with the classic struggle between supranationalism and intergovernmentalism. In fact, they may be the epitome of this struggle, because of the potent mix of external relations, exclusive competences, and qualified majority voting—a threesome of political sensitivities.

Opinion 1/75 and the notion of exclusivity

The first case in which the ECJ showed awareness of the significance of the transfer of trade policy powers from the Member States to the EEC was *Hauptzollamt Bremerhaven v. Massey-Ferguson*.[7] In issue was the validity of a regulation on the valuation of goods for customs purposes. The regulation had been adopted on the basis of (current) Article 352 TFEU, and it was argued that this legal basis was incorrect. The Court disagreed, but it did point out that the proper functioning of the customs union justified a wide interpretation of the Treaty provisions on the customs

[4] For an account see Joined Cases 21 to 24/72 *International Fruit Company v. Produktschap voor Groenten en Fruit* [1972] ECR 1219.

[5] See Ch 10.

[6] See also C Kaddous, *Le droit des relations extérieures dans la jurisprudence de la Cour de justice des Communautés européennes* (Helbing & Lichtenhahn, 1998) 181–218; P Koutrakos, *EU International Relations Law* (Hart Publishing, 2006) ch 2; R Holdgaard, *External Relations Law of the European Community—Legal Reasoning and Legal Discourses* (Wolters Kluwer, 2008) ch 3.

[7] Case 8/73 *Hauptzollamt Bremerhaven v. Massey-Ferguson* [1973] ECR 897.

union and the common commercial policy, and of the powers which these provisions conferred on the institutions to allow them thoroughly to control external trade by measures taken both independently and by agreement.[8]

That statement was no more than a first indication, but a few years later the Court was to decide its first Opinion on an envisaged international agreement, pursuant to (current) Article 218(11) TFEU. That provision establishes a procedure enabling the Court to rule on the compatibility of an envisaged agreement with the Treaty, also as regards matters of competence.[9] If it had not existed, there might not have been nearly as many external competence cases, for it is politically and legally much more difficult to challenge the lawfulness of an international agreement once it has been concluded. The procedure of a request for an Opinion allows the institutions and the Member States to ensure that the envisaged agreement indeed comes within the Community's competence and is adopted under the correct Treaty provision. In practice, however, the procedure has often been used for opposite reasons, particularly by the Commission, namely to disprove Member State competence through the assertion of exclusive Community competence. As will be seen throughout this chapter and the next, those attempts have rarely been wholly successful.[10]

Opinion 1/75 concerned a draft 'Understanding on a Local Cost Standard' which had been drawn up under the auspices of the OECD.[11] This 'Understanding' concerned export credits. The participating governments essentially agreed not to finance or cover credit, in respect of local costs related to export transactions (in effect, payment of the purchase price), for more than 100 per cent of the value of the goods and services exported. The Commission asked whether the Community had the power to conclude the 'Understanding' and, if so, whether that power was exclusive. Thus phrased, the question identified the two vital components in EU external competences claims: the scope of those competences, and whether or not they are exclusive of the competences of Member States.[12] In both respects, *Opinion 1/75* contains important statements.

As regards the scope of the Community's competences,[13] the Court pointed out that (current) Article 207 TFEU referred to export policy, and thus necessarily covered systems of aid for exports, particularly export credits. It identified the relevant measures as constituting an important element of commercial policy, and stated that that concept had the same content whether it was applied in the context of the international action of a State or to that of the Community. This rather cryptic statement was to return in later case law, and indicates that international practice

[8] Ibid, para 4. [9] See Ch 8.

[10] Cf T Tridimas and P Eeckhout, 'The External Competence of the Community and the Case-Law of the Court of Justice: Principle versus Pragmatism' (1994) 14 YEL 143.

[11] *Opinion 1/75 re Understanding on a Local Cost Standard* [1975] ECR 1355.

[12] A Dashwood and C Hillion, 'Introduction' in A Dashwood and C Hillion (eds), *The General Law of E.C. External Relations* (Sweet & Maxwell, 2000) v–vi.

[13] *Opinion 1/75* (n 11 above) 1362–3.

in the area of trade policy is one factor for determining the scope of the common commercial policy. The Court also referred to directives concerning credit insurance, which expressly recognized the important role played by export credits in international trade, as a factor of commercial policy. It concluded that the subject matter of the 'Understanding' came within the scope of (current) Article 207 TFEU.

The Court then specifically considered the power to conclude international agreements on commercial policy, as envisaged by the relevant Treaty provisions. It stated that a commercial policy was made up by the combination and interaction of internal and external measures, without priority being taken by one over the others. It further developed that idea, indicating, *inter alia*, that the common commercial policy was above all the outcome of a progressive development based upon specific measures which could refer without distinction to 'autonomous' and external aspects of that policy, and which did not necessarily presuppose the existence of a large body of rules, but combined gradually to form that body. The Court was thus pointing out that the common commercial policy could be built gradually, through both the adoption of internal legislation and the conclusion of international agreements.

Reading the Opinion up to that point, one might have expected the Court, in the second part, to characterize the Community's competence as shared with the competence of Member States. That might have seemed more logical in the light of the Court's references to the gradual development of this policy. But the Court did not adopt that approach. It described the nature of the Community's competences in the following terms.[14] The common commercial policy was conceived in the context of the operation of the common market, for the defence of the common interests of the Community, within which the particular interests of the Member States had to endeavour to adapt to each other. This conception was clearly incompatible with the freedom to which the Member States could lay claim by invoking a concurrent power, so as to ensure that their own interests were separately satisfied, at the risk of compromising the effective defence of the common interests. Any unilateral action on the part of the Member States would lead to disparities in the conditions for the grant of export credits, calculated to distort competition between undertakings of the various Member States in external markets. Such distortion could be eliminated only by means of a strict uniformity. Concurrent powers therefore could not be accepted, and the Treaty provisions on concluding agreements of commercial policy showed clearly that the exercise of concurrent powers was impossible. To accept the contrary would amount to recognizing that, in relations with third countries, Member States could adopt positions which differed from those which the Community intended to adopt, and would thereby distort the institutional framework, call into question the mutual trust within the Community, and prevent the latter from fulfilling its task in the defence of the common interest.

[14] Ibid, 1363–4.

On a further point, no doubt elicited by the fact that the 'Understanding' concerned export credits granted by the Member States from their own resources, the Court considered that it was of little importance that the obligations and financial burdens inherent in the execution of the agreement envisaged were borne directly by the Member States. The 'internal' and 'external' measures adopted by the Community within the framework of the common commercial policy did not necessarily involve a transfer to the institutions of the Community of the obligations and financial burdens which they could involve. Those measures were solely concerned to substitute for the unilateral action of the Member States a common action based upon uniform principles on behalf of the whole Community.

The Court's analysis contained various reasons for the exclusive nature of trade policy competences. They deserve brief comment, particularly as the Court never returned to the subject.

The Court's first reason was that the defence of the Community's common interests required exclusivity. It is certainly true that trade policies often concern significant economic interests, and that it would be very difficult to map out a meaningful common policy if the Member States were allowed to continue to pursue their own trade policies. Yet it is clear that this is essentially a political argument, which may also be valid for other common policies. One may think of the common transport policy, also prescribed by the then EEC Treaty, but in this field the Court never recognized exclusive powers.

A second, but related argument is more persuasive. The Court referred to the distortions of competition between undertakings established in the Community which were likely to arise in the absence of uniform export credit conditions. It is indeed not difficult to see the scope for such distortions: the whole purpose of the OECD 'Understanding' was to limit excessive competition in the grant of export credits. However, the argument is of much broader scope, and connects the common commercial policy as a whole, as regards both imports and exports, with the internal market. Indeed the EU internal market, characterized as it is by strong integration and generalized free movement of products, persons, capital, and companies, could hardly function effectively in the absence of a common external trade policy, which uniformly lays down the external terms of trade. As the common commercial policy took some time actually to be completed in certain sectors, there are numerous examples to illustrate that. To mention just one, it took until the 1990s to create a uniform import regime for Japanese cars. Previously, a number of Member States operated restrictions on imports of such cars, evidently to protect their domestic manufacturers. Yet the latter were also in competition with other European car manufacturers, established and with a large market share in Member States which did not operate such restrictions. The distortion of competition was evident.[15]

[15] For further details, also as regards other sectors, see P Eeckhout, *The European Internal Market and International Trade—A Legal Analysis* (OUP, 1994) ch 6.

As will be seen below, the concept of distortion of competition may be complemented with the notion of deflections of trade. In the absence of a uniform external trade policy, particularly as regards imports, deflections of trade are likely to occur: imports will tend to go to the Member State with the most liberal policy, and will then, by virtue of the internal market, find their way to the less liberal Member States. Such trade deflections could only be avoided through the erection of barriers to intra-EU trade, but those are anathema to a genuine internal market.[16]

It is worth adding that the notions of competition distortion and trade deflection have their counterparts in the Court's case law on the EU's 'internal' competences to harmonize national laws with a view to establishing the internal market. In the important Tobacco Advertising Directive case, for example, the Court examined whether the directive was aimed at eliminating distortions of competition or obstacles to trade or free movement.[17] The latter notion is the internal counterpart of deflections of trade. Thus it can be seen that essentially the same economic risks justify internal legislative powers and external exclusive competence.

The Court's third reason for exclusivity in *Opinion 1/75* was based on the principle of Member States' loyalty towards the Community and its institutions. That reason is not very persuasive: it does not follow from the fact that certain powers are shared between the EU and the Member States that the latter will act contrary to the EU's interests, or will disregard common decisions.[18]

In support of exclusivity, the Court could also have referred to the international legal basis for the customs union. GATT defines a customs union as the substitution of a single customs territory for two or more customs territories, so that substantially the same duties *and other regulations of commerce* are applied by each of the members of the union to the trade of territories not included in the union.[19] This conjunction of the external tariff and other external trade policies is obvious from an economic perspective and, as the EEC Treaty clearly opted for a single common customs tariff and a uniform common commercial policy, the Court's ruling in favour of exclusive commercial policy powers, which followed the adoption of the common tariff, made eminent sense.

None the less, from a constitutional perspective the Court's decision continues to be remarkable. It may be that it was also in part the child of a particular period in the Court's case law. Waelbroeck has demonstrated that in the early 1970s the case law on competence, not only in the field of commercial policy but also in other fields such as agriculture, wavered between what he called a federalist-conceptualist

[16] See further Ch 10.

[17] Case C–376/98 *Germany v. European Parliament and Council* [2000] ECR I–8419. See also, most recently, Case C–58/08 *The Queen on the application of Vodafone and Others v. Secretary of State for Business, Enterprise and Regulatory Reform*, judgment of 8 June 2010.

[18] See further M Cremona, 'Defending the Community Interest: the Duties of Co-operation and Compliance' in M Cremona and B De Witte (eds), *EU Foreign Relations Law—Constitutional Fundamentals* (Hart Publishing, 2008) 127.

[19] Art XXIV(8)(a) GATT, emphasis added.

approach, where Community competence is construed as being necessarily exclusive, and a pragmatic approach, where concurrent powers are recognized. In particular, the period 1973–5, when *Opinion 1/75* was delivered, is characterized by Waelbroeck as a period of hesitation between those approaches.[20]

But if that was the case, it must be emphasized that the Court never hesitated to confirm the exclusive nature of the Community's trade policy competences. None the less, as will be seen below as well as in Chapter 10, the Court did not interpret the principle of exclusivity in a strict way, and left considerable scope for a gradual implementation of the common commercial policy and for some measure of recognition of Member States' powers, provided their exercise was regulated by Community law.

The Treaty of Lisbon, whose amendments set out the nature of the EU's various competences, confirmed this exclusive competence. According to Article 3(1) TEU the Union shall have exclusive competence in the areas of the customs union and the common commercial policy. Article 2(1) TFEU describes the characteristics of exclusivity:

> When the Treaties confer on the Union exclusive competence in a specific area, only the Union may legislate and adopt legally binding acts, the Member States being able to do so themselves only if so empowered by the Union or for the implementation of acts of the Union.

We will return to this provision when examining, below, the scope of the new powers in matters of foreign direct investment.

The rise of UNCTAD and the broad conception of 'trade'

In the light of the principle of exclusivity one might have expected the Court to interpret the scope of the common commercial policy somewhat narrowly. Exclusive competences are exceptional in the EU constitutional order, and politically sensitive, in particular where external relations are involved. The Court did not, however, adopt such an approach in the 1970s and 1980s. It took a broad view of the notion of trade, against the backdrop of increased worldwide questioning of the free-trade model, especially as regards its effects on developing countries. In 1964, UNCTAD had been established, an organization built on the link between trade and development, and it soon came to be seen as a rival to GATT. Its activities were geared towards establishing preferential terms of trade for developing countries, which implied forms of trade regulation rather than trade liberalization. In 1976, UNCTAD established an 'Integrated Programme for Commodities', designed

[20] M Waelbroeck, 'The Emergent Doctrine of Community Pre-emption—Consent and Re-delegation' in T Sandalow and E Stein (eds), *Courts and Free Markets* (OUP, 1982) 551, 556–61.

to improve the conditions for trade in certain commodities which were of particular interest to developing countries. The programme provided that in respect of eighteen such commodities negotiations were to be opened for introducing international arrangements between producer and consumer countries. Within that framework, a 1978 conference negotiated a draft International Agreement on Natural Rubber. The main feature of the draft agreement was the creation of a buffer stock system designed to stabilize natural rubber prices. The Commission had proposed to the Council that it be given a mandate to conduct the negotiations, since it considered that the draft agreement came within the scope of (current) Article 207 TFEU. The Council had rejected that view, and had decided that the negotiations were to be conducted by a Community delegation and by delegations from Member States, which were to act on the basis of a common standpoint. The Commission then went to the Court of Justice and requested an Opinion on the scope of the Community's competence.[21] This is a classic scenario which, as will be seen, often returns, and which features no real disagreement as to the actual negotiating position to be adopted from the European side, but is more concerned with the respective roles of the Commission, the Council, and delegations from Member States.

Opinion 1/78 is a long and complex judicial text, which analyses and describes the objectives and features of the draft agreement at considerable length. As regards the scope of (current) Article 207 TFEU, however, the Court discussed the relevant principles in just three paragraphs, which became a classic in EU external relations law.[22]

The Court first referred to the link between the various agreements on commodities: as an increasing number of products which were particularly important from the economic point of view were concerned, it was clear that a coherent commercial policy would no longer be practicable if the Community were not in a position to exercise its powers also in connection with a category of agreements which were becoming, alongside traditional commercial agreements, one of the major factors in the regulation of international trade.

The Court developed this concern in the next paragraph, concentrating on the new type of trade regulation and management which UNCTAD advocated. It would, in the Court's opinion, no longer be possible to carry on any worthwhile common commercial policy if the Community were not in a position to avail itself also of more elaborate means devised with a view to furthering the development of international trade. (Current) Article 207 TFEU was not to be interpreted so as to restrict the common commercial policy to the use of instruments intended to have an effect only on the traditional aspects of external trade to the exclusion of more highly developed mechanisms. Such a 'commercial policy' would be destined to become nugatory in the course of time. Although it might have been thought

[21] *Opinion 1/78 re International Agreement on Natural Rubber* [1979] ECR 2871.

[22] Ibid, paras 43–45.

that at the time of Treaty drafting, liberalization of trade was the dominant idea, the Treaty nevertheless did not form a barrier to the Community's developing a commercial policy aiming at a regulation of the world market for certain products rather than at a mere liberalization of trade.

In the third paragraph the Court confirmed this from the perspective of the text of (current) Article 207 TFEU. That provision empowered the Community to formulate a commercial 'policy', based on 'uniform principles', thus showing that the question of external trade had to be governed from a wide point of view and not only having regard to the administration of precise systems such as customs and quantitative restrictions. The same conclusion was deduced from the fact that the enumeration in Article 207 of the subjects covered by commercial policy was conceived as a non-exhaustive enumeration which could not close the door to any other process intended to regulate external trade. A restrictive interpretation, the Court concluded, would risk causing disturbances in intra-Community trade by reason of the disparities which would then exist in certain sectors of economic relations with non-member countries.

The concern underlying the Court's reasoning in those paragraphs is obvious and was at the time no doubt justified. Despite the fact that the draft rubber agreement employed novel conceptions regarding trade relations between developing and developed countries, it was clearly an international agreement on trade in rubber. The decision of principle which the Court thus reached was that the Community had exclusive competence to enter into the agreement. However, at the time of delivering the Opinion it was not yet clear whether the buffer stock, central to the operation of the agreement, was to be financed from the Community budget or by the Member States. The Court considered that this was an important point. It stated that the financing of the buffer stock constituted an essential feature of the whole scheme, and that, if the financing was to be undertaken by the Member States, that would imply their participation in the decision-making machinery or, at least, their agreement with regard to the arrangements for financing envisaged. That in turn would require that the Member States participate in the agreement together with the Community, and the 'exclusive competence of the Community could not be envisaged in such a case'.[23]

Opinion 1/78 is thus more mixed than is sometimes thought. On the one hand, the Court took a broad view of the concept of common commercial policy, recognizing extended exclusive Community competences. On the other hand, it allowed for Member State participation, and thus mixed action, through the financing arrangements. That aspect of the ruling has been criticized on the ground that it was inconsistent with *Opinion 1/75*, where the Court decided that the financial side was irrelevant, and on the ground that it put the cart before the horse: instead of allowing finance to determine exclusivity, exclusivity should have determined

[23] Ibid, para 60. The political outcome was that commodity agreements were concluded as mixed agreements: see Ch 7.

finance.[24] It is none the less possible to distinguish *Opinions 1/75* and *1/78*. In the former, the 'Understanding' purported to impose a cap on export credit expenditure by the participating States, and in no way required such expenditure. In the latter, the contracting parties had to finance the operation of the agreement, and in effect such financing amounted to development aid, a matter which clearly did not come within the scope of the common commercial policy, even though at the time there were no other express Treaty provisions on such aid.[25] In any event, *Opinion 1/78* remains significant for its emphasis on a broad interpretation of (current) Article 207 TFEU and the commercial policy concept which it embodies.

The bipolar world of *Commission v. Council*

In the course of the proceedings leading up to *Opinion 1/78*, the Commission and the Council submitted different views on the scope of the common commercial policy in attempts to lay down general criteria for the concept of commercial policy. The Commission argued that a measure of commercial policy had to be assessed primarily by reference to its specific character as an instrument regulating international trade (the so-called 'objective/instrumental' approach).[26] The Council, on the other hand, considered that any measure the aim of which was to influence the volume or flow of trade had to be regarded as a commercial policy measure (the so-called 'subjective/purposive' approach).[27] Of those contrasting approaches, the former was probably the broader one, whereas the latter left considerable room for manoeuvre for the Council, then chief legislator in this field, through the definition and description of the aims of the measures which it adopted. At one stage the debate on those theories acquired near scholastic dimensions. It was very much a lawyers' debate, with participation by academics and by lawyers from the legal services of the Commission and the Council,[28] and it may be doubtful whether the institutions themselves and the Member States' governments felt well entertained by such discussions. The practice as regards the conclusion of international agreements was not in any event greatly affected. The EEC at the time often concluded 'trade and economic co-operation' agreements, and as such agreements contained

[24] JHH Weiler, 'The External Legal Relations of Non-Unitary Actors: Mixity and the Federal Principle' in D O'Keeffe and HG Schermers (eds), *Mixed Agreements* (Kluwer Law and Taxation Publishers, 1983) 72; JHH Weiler, *The Constitution of Europe* (CUP, 1999) 174; PJG Kapteyn and P VerLoren van Themaat, *Introduction to the Law of the European Communities* (3rd edn, by LW Gormley, Kluwer Law International, 1998) 1281.

[25] See Ch 4.

[26] *Opinion 1/78* (n 21 above) 2883–4.

[27] Ibid, 2887–8.

[28] See e.g. C-D Ehlermann, 'The Scope of Article 113 of the EEC Treaty', in *Mélanges offerts à Pierre-Henri Teitgen* (Pedone, 1984) 150–1; JHJ Bourgeois, 'The Common Commercial Policy—Scope and Nature of the Powers' in ELM Völker (ed), *Protectionism and the European Community* (2nd edn, Kluwer, 1986) 1–16; J Steenbergen, 'Annotation Case 45/86' (1987) 24 CML Rev 73.

a non-trade dimension, they were concluded on the basis of (current) Articles 207 and 352 TFEU.[29]

The Court of Justice never looked at the scope of the common commercial policy in such general terms.[30] Views differed on which thesis was most vindicated in *Opinion 1/78*, but the truth is probably that neither was and that the Court opted for judicial economy, aiming to resolve the problem before it rather than developing an abstract formula for capturing the scope of the common commercial policy.

The Commission and the Council had a re-run of *Opinion 1/78* in 1987, in a case on the correct legal basis for the adoption of generalized tariff preferences (GSP).[31] The Community GSP system was developed in the 1970s, upon recommendation by UNCTAD. It is a unilateral system of tariff reductions for imports from developing countries, and thus again links trade and development.[32] Since 1971, the Council had adopted the relevant EEC regulations without making express reference to the EEC Treaty provisions considered to form the legal basis. It acted by unanimity. The Commission, by contrast, had consistently proposed that the regulations be adopted under (current) Article 207 TFEU—requiring qualified majority. Before the Court, the Council declared that the regulations were in fact based on (current) Articles 207 and 352 TFEU, the latter requiring unanimity. Commission and Council again presented their theories on the scope of the common commercial policy, but the Court stood firm in its refusal to be drawn into scholastics. It noted the Council's explanation that the use of both (current) Articles 207 and 352 TFEU was required because the contested regulations not only had commercial-policy aims, but also major development-policy aims. The Court based its analysis on the principle that in the context of the organization of the powers of the Community, the choice of legal basis for a measure could not depend simply on an institution's conviction as to the objective pursued, but had to be based on objective factors which were amenable to judicial review.[33] It thus clearly rejected a purely subjective 'subjective/purposive' approach.[34] The Court then pointed out that (current) Article 352 TFEU could only be used if there was no other Treaty provision conferring competence.[35] Consequently, the Court examined whether (current) Article 207 alone was a sufficient legal basis. Here it referred to the language of that provision, which spoke of 'changes in tariff rates'. It then recalled its statement in *Opinion 1/75* on the concept of commercial policy having the same content whether it was applied in the context of the international action of a State or in that of the Community. The Court considered that the link between trade and

[29] E.g. K Lenaerts and E De Smijter, 'The European Community's Treaty-Making Competence' (1996) 16 YEL 23.

[30] K Lenaerts and P van Nuffel, *Constitutional Law of the European Union* (R Bray (ed) and trans, Sweet & Maxwell, 1999) 622.

[31] Case 45/86 *Commission v. Council* [1987] ECR 1493.

[32] See Ch 10.

[33] *Commission v. Council* (n 31 above) paras 10–11.

[34] There is an analogy with *Germany v. European Parliament and Council* (n 17 above) para 85.

[35] *Commission v. Council* (n 31 above) para 13.

development had become progressively stronger in modern international relations, as recognized in the contexts of both UNCTAD and GATT. It was against that background that the model was evolved on which the Community's GSP system was based; that system reflected a new concept of international trade relations in which development aims played a major role. The Court then returned to the text of the Treaty, considering that, in defining the characteristics and the instruments of the common commercial policy, the Treaty took possible changes into account. It pointed in particular to the reference 'to the harmonious development of world trade'. Lastly, the Court recalled its statements on the broad scope of the common commercial policy in *Opinion 1/78*. It concluded that (current) Article 207 TFEU was the correct legal basis, and annulled the regulations.[36]

After *Opinion 1/78*, the judgment in *Commission v. Council* cannot have come as much of a surprise. The Court essentially reiterated its views on a modern commercial policy requiring the inclusion of trade measures with development aims.[37] Whilst there may in this context indeed be more emphasis on the instrument used than on the aims pursued, the judgment did not provide unqualified support for the Commission's thesis. The Court also looked at the aims of the measure, but took the view that development aims were integral to a modern commercial policy. From the perspective of international developments in trade policy since the 1960s, that view was clearly correct.

The internal market and external trade

Opinion 1/75 rightly referred to the link between the unity of the common market (now internal market) and a uniform common commercial policy. The Court considered that this was an argument for exclusive competence, but a moment's thought will clarify that it may also serve to delimit the scope of this competence. If indeed potential distortions of competition or deflections of trade in the internal market justify trade policy powers, then those concepts may amount to some form of test for the competence calculus. Where a Member State adopts a measure which bears some relation to external trade, could that measure give rise to distortion of competition or deflection of trade, threatening the unity of the internal market? If so, the measure would in principle have to come within the scope of the EU's exclusive competences.

There are a number of potential measures which are obvious trade measures and clearly fit the bill of the above calculus. An import quota is one of them. However, trade restrictions may just as easily result from measures whose objectives are

[36] Ibid, paras 14–21.

[37] Cf J Raux, 'Politique de coopération au développement et politique commerciale commune' in M Maresceau (ed), *The European Community's Commercial Policy after 1992: The Legal Dimension* (Martinus Nijhoff, 1993) 157–95.

wholly unrelated to trade. What about a decision to prohibit the marketing of a particular food product, because it is considered harmful for public health? Such a decision, where taken by a Member State, will almost invariably affect domestic products, imports from other Member States, *and* imports from third countries. Is it then, in so far as it affects non-EU imports, a trade policy measure coming within the powers of the EU?

Such questions reveal an important characteristic of modern trade measures: often those measures are taken in order to achieve non-trade objectives. Those objectives may range from protection of the environment, protection of public health, consumer protection, and international security, to protection of human rights. Indeed, the new version of Article 207(1) TFEU provides that the common commercial policy is to be conducted in the context of the principles and objectives of the Union's external action. Where those objectives are pursued through measures which affect international trade, and, in the EU context, the unity of the internal market, should one simply conclude that a trade measure exists in EU law terms, with the resulting transfer of competences from the Member States to the EU?

In academic literature the link between the internal market and the common commercial policy was further explored in the second half of the 1980s, particularly as regards general market regulation. This investigation coincided with the internal market programme, put on the rails by the 1985 Commission White Paper[38] and the 1986 Single European Act. That programme generally raised the question of the external dimension of this enormous legislative endeavour, in terms of both substance and legal form. As regards the latter, the question was whether all external policies relating to the establishment and completion of the internal market came within the scope of the Treaty's common commercial policy. That question may sound abstract and legalistic, but in a number of areas it was clearly crucial for the actual direction of future policy. For example, in the field of air transport the reply to the question would determine whether or not the Community acquired sole negotiating authority over air traffic agreements with non-member countries. If external trade in air transport services came within the scope of the common commercial policy, then the Community would have exclusive competence as regards such agreements.[39] This of course presupposed that trade *in services* could be covered by Article 207.[40]

One of the most interesting proposals for the interpretation of (current) Article 207 TFEU was made by Timmermans.[41] He suggested that the interpretation should dovetail the rule-of-reason approach towards (current) Article 34 TFEU, set

[38] *Completing the Internal Market*, COM(85)310 final, June 1985.

[39] Eeckhout (n 15 above) ch 3.

[40] Note that transport is at present expressly excluded from the scope of the common commercial policy, see Art 207(5) TFEU.

[41] CWA Timmermans, 'La libre circulation des marchandises et la politique commerciale commune' in P Demaret (ed), *Relations extérieures de la Communauté européenne et marché intérieur: aspects juridiques et fonctionnels* (Story, 1986) 91, 96–9.

in motion by the *Cassis de Dijon* judgment.[42] Under this rule of reason, Member States are entitled to regulate the market on the basis of 'mandatory requirements', an open-ended list of non-economic concerns of public policy. Timmermans noted that these 'mandatory requirements' in effect recognized Member State competence from an internal market perspective, and that it would make little sense if such non-trade measures, when applied in an external trade context, were to be regarded as coming within the Community's exclusive competence. He therefore proposed to read the rule of reason into the interpretation of (current) Article 207 TFEU: also in external trade, Member States would continue to be entitled to adopt measures based on 'mandatory requirements' or on the express exceptions in (current) Article 36 TFEU. Such measures, when proportionate, were not to be considered trade policy measures. From a perspective of internal market unity, Timmermans further argued, such a rule of reason was clearly defensible: there was no risk of deflections of trade in the products concerned, as Member States could in any event, also as regards internal trade, erect barriers conforming to the rule of reason.

Timmermans' proposal was welcome and continues to deserve consideration. Where a Member State regulates its market with a view to protecting the environment, its consumers, or public health, and does so in a proportionate manner, without discrimination against imported products, it makes sense (a) not to consider this as an unlawful barrier to trade in so far as imports from other Member States are concerned, and (b) not to consider this as an external trade measure in so far as imports from non-member States are involved. If the EU considers that such regulation unduly fragments the market, it has competence, for example, under Article 114 TFEU to harmonize the laws of the Member States.

A weakness of Timmermans' proposal was perhaps that it did not address 'non-trade measures' (in the sense of measures not pursuing commercial or economic aims) which none the less concern only external imports or exports. In 1990, the Court of Justice was confronted with such a measure in the *Chernobyl I* case. Shortly after the nuclear accident in Chernobyl, Ukraine, the Council had adopted a regulation laying down maximum levels of radioactive contamination as regards agricultural products imported from Central and Eastern Europe. Although clearly aimed at protecting public health within the Community, the regulation had been adopted on the basis of (current) Article 207 TFEU, and the Court accepted that.[43] There is, however, a better opportunity to examine the judgment below in the section on trade and environment.

The Uruguay Round and Maastricht

Important as the precise delimitation of the scope of the EU's powers over external trade in goods may be, at the time there were a number of more hotly debated questions.

[42] Case 120/78 *Rewe v. Bundesmonopolverwaltung für Branntwein* [1979] ECR 649.
[43] Case C–62/88 *Greece v. Council* [1990] ECR I–1527.

In 1986, the GATT contracting parties initiated a new round of multilateral trade negotiations, the so-called Uruguay Round, which was to be much more innovating than any previous GATT round. The negotiating agenda identified three new topics: trade in services, trade-related aspects of intellectual property rights, and trade-related investment measures. Particularly as regards the first two, services and intellectual property, a debate developed on whether they were covered by the Treaty provisions on the common commercial policy. The answer to those questions was to be of huge political and institutional, if not constitutional, significance, for it would determine whether or not the Community had sole authority to negotiate and conclude the wide-ranging international agreements which were the subject of the Uruguay Round. Yet, interestingly, the debate was again academic in more than one sense. While it was being conducted, the negotiations went ahead unperturbed, in a pragmatic arrangement with the Commission as European negotiator, closely supervised by the Council and representatives of Member States.[44] Even when the competence issue came to a head, when the agreements had to be signed and concluded, and the Commission went to Court, claiming that the Community had exclusive competence, there remained an awkward gap between legal principle and practice. The Uruguay Round had resulted in the establishment of a new World Trade Organization, and whereas the Commission in its request for an Opinion argued for exclusive competence, it referred, in its third question, to an 'agreement already reached that [the Member States] will be original Members of the WTO'.[45] The Commission never clarified how exclusive Community competence could be reconciled with such membership.

But before analysing *Opinion 1/94*, it is worth saying a little more about some political developments leading up to the court battle.

In the course of 1991, more than halfway through the Uruguay Round, the Treaty on European Union was negotiated. In the framework of those negotiations the Commission proposed far-reaching changes to the Community's external competences, no doubt against the backdrop of the ongoing Uruguay Round. It suggested that competences be transferred to the newly established European Union to pursue a 'common external economic policy', which was to include trade, and economic and commercial measures involving services, capital, intellectual property, investment, establishment, and competition. Community competences over all those matters were to be exclusive, but it would be possible to authorize Member States to take some of these measures within certain prescribed limits and conditions. Such authorizations would be granted by the Commission itself.[46]

It is not clear whether the Commission ever really considered that its proposals would form the basis for a serious negotiation between the Member States.

[44] P van den Bossche, 'The European Community and the Uruguay Round Agreements' in JH Jackson and AO Sykes (eds), *Implementing the Uruguay Round* (OUP, 1997) 25–6.

[45] *Opinion 1/94 re WTO Agreement* [1994] ECR I-5267, 5283.

[46] See M Maresceau, 'The Concept "Common Commercial Policy" and the Difficult Road to Maastricht' in Maresceau (n 37 above) 6–10.

The intergovernmental conference rejected them out of hand, and confined the debate on amendments to (current) Article 207 TFEU to a possible extension to 'services directly related to trade'.[47] But even that modest proposal did not survive the negotiations, and in the end the scope of the common commercial policy was left unmodified. It is an episode which is worth bearing in mind, as it formed the basis for the 'defence' of the Council and some Member State governments in the *Opinion 1/94* battle: the Commission was accused of seeking the implementation, by means of judicial interpretation, of proposals which were rejected at the Maastricht negotiations.[48]

The joint competence settlement of *Opinion 1/94*

The Uruguay Round negotiations ended in early 1994. The Agreement establishing the WTO, which brought together nearly all the results of the multilateral negotiations in one single international agreement, was signed at Marrakesh on 15 April 1994. By that time, the legal dispute on competence between the Commission (supported only by the Belgian government) and the Council (supported by most other Member States) was in full swing. The political sensitivity of the issue is perhaps best illustrated by a skirmish at the GATT Ministerial Conference at Marrakesh. As regards the signing of the WTO Agreement, the Commission had suggested that its representative and the Member State ministers should sign as a group under the collective rubric of the EU. Yet even though the order of signing is a matter of pure protocol, with no effect whatsoever on the legal distribution of powers or on the commitments entered into, the Member State governments refused and insisted that the overall alphabetical order of the list of GATT delegations be followed.[49]

On 6 April 1994, the Commission submitted its request for an Opinion to the Court. Essentially, the Commission asked whether the Community had exclusive competence[50] to conclude the WTO Agreement, on the basis of the then Treaty provisions on the common commercial policy, or in combination with implied powers pursuant to (current) Articles 114 and 352 TFEU. The Court's analysis of implied powers is considered in the next chapter, and the reader is also referred to those pages for a complete view of *Opinion 1/94*.[51]

[47] Ibid, 10–11.

[48] *Opinion 1/94* (n 45 above) 5306. There may be an analogy here with *Opinion 2/94 re accession to the ECHR* [1996] ECR I–1759, where the Council may have intended to achieve through judicial interpretation what it could not achieve through internal political negotiation.

[49] *Financial Times*, 14 April 1994.

[50] The Commission's actual questions did not refer to exclusivity, but that was clearly the tenor of its arguments, in the interpretation of the Court: *Opinion 1/94* (n 45 above) paras 13–14.

[51] Other specific analyses include JHJ Bourgeois, 'The EC in the WTO and Advisory Opinion 1/94: An Echternach Procession' (1995) 32 CML Rev 763; M Hilf, 'The ECJ's Opinion 1/94 on the WTO—No Surprise, but Wise?' (1995) 6 EJIL 245; J Dutheil de la Rochère, 'L'ère des compétences

As regards the scope of the common commercial policy, it is somewhat ironic to see that the Commission was effectively compelled to rely on the 'subjective/purposive' approach previously advocated by the Council. The Commission did not expressly refer to that theory, but it is clear that it essentially argued for exclusive Community competence on grounds of the clear trade policy *objectives* of all the WTO agreements.

The Court's ruling on joint or shared competence has now been superseded by the amendments to (current) Article 207 TFEU, which make agreements on trade in services and on the commercial aspects of intellectual property fully part of the common commercial policy. The Opinion continues to be a milestone in EU external relations law, however, and thus to deserve analysis.

Trade in goods

The Court first looked at the multilateral agreements on trade in goods, in Annex 1A of the WTO Agreement. Even though it was generally accepted that the bulk of those agreements came within the Community's trade policy powers, questions had arisen over coal and steel products; the Agreement on Agriculture and the Agreement on Sanitary and Phytosanitary Measures (SPS Agreement); and the Agreement on Technical Barriers to Trade (TBT Agreement). The discussion on coal and steel products concerned the interrelationship between the ECSC Treaty and the EC Treaty, and is only of historical interest after the expiry of the former.

As regards the Agriculture and SPS Agreements, the Council contended that the Treaty provisions on agriculture were the appropriate legal basis, and not those on the common commercial policy. The Court conceded that it had held that the agriculture provisions were the appropriate legal basis for a directive laying down uniform rules on the conditions under which products, including imported ones, could be marketed.[52] However, that directive was intended to achieve one or more of the Treaty's agricultural policy objectives, which was not the case for the Agreement on Agriculture, whose objective was to establish a fair and market-oriented agricultural trading system. The fact that the Agreement required internal measures to be adopted on the basis of the Treaty provisions on agriculture did not prevent the international commitments themselves from being entered into pursuant to the Treaty commercial policy provisions alone. The same conclusion was reached for the SPS Agreement, which, according to its preamble, was confined to establishing a multilateral framework for minimizing the negative effects of SPS measures on trade.[53]

partagées' (1995) 390 RMCUE 461; T Tridimas, 'The WTO and OECD Opinions' in A Dashwood and C Hillion (eds), *The General Law of EC External Relations* (Sweet & Maxwell, 2000) 48–60; A Burnside, 'The Scope of the Common Commercial Policy Post Opinion 1/94: Clouds and Silver Linings' in Dashwood and Hillion (above) 152–9.

[52] Case C–131/87 *Commission v. Council* [1989] ECR I–3764, para 27.

[53] *Opinion 1/94* (n 45 above) paras 28–31.

As regards the TBT Agreement, the Court considered that it was merely designed to ensure that technical regulations and standards, and conformity assessment, did not create unnecessary obstacles to international trade.[54]

The Court concluded that all the WTO agreements on trade in goods came within the Community's commercial policy competence. Even if the Court's analysis was succinct, this is an important dimension of *Opinion 1/94*. With respect to goods, the Court confirmed the broad conception of 'trade', in line with international developments in trade policy. It is also obvious that here the Court did indeed primarily rely on the trade objectives of the various agreements, and considered that their effect on internal legislation, at Community and Member State level, as well as the need for implementation through internal legislation, did not stand in the way of conclusion on the basis of the Treaty's provisions on the common commercial policy.

Trade in services

The Court then turned to Annex 1B of the WTO Agreement, the General Agreement on Trade in Services (GATS). Much more was at stake here, as there were diametrically opposing views on whether trade in services was covered by the Treaty provisions on a common commercial policy, and in the light of the debate which had taken place at the Maastricht intergovernmental conference. GATS is an agreement which aims to achieve liberalization of international trade in services through the application of basis legal concepts (such as non-discrimination and market access) and liberalization mechanisms (such as schedules of concessions/commitments) borrowed from GATT. Its logic is that neoliberal economic theory on the benefits of free trade is equally valid for trade in services. GATS also provides for some form of definition of trade in services, a phenomenon much more difficult to capture than trade in goods. In Article I(2) GATS trade in services is defined as comprising four modes of supply: (1) cross-frontier supplies not involving any movement of persons; (2) consumption abroad, which entails the movement of the consumer into the territory of the WTO member country in which the supplier is established; (3) commercial presence, i.e. the presence of a subsidiary or branch in the territory of the WTO member country in which the service is to be rendered; (4) the presence of natural persons from a WTO member country, enabling a supplier from one member country to supply services within the territory of any other member country. That definition is intended to be as comprehensive and inclusive as possible, and the modes of supply are used for structuring the specific commitments entered into by WTO members. Those commitments entail the granting of market access (Article XVI) and national treatment (or non-discrimination, Article XVII) in specific services sectors for the various modes of supply.[55]

[54] Ibid, paras 32–33.

[55] See further S Lester, B Mercurio, A Davies, and K Leitner, *World Trade Law—Text, Materials and Commentary* (Hart Publishing, 2008) ch 15. For a comparison with EU law on services, see P Eeckhout, 'Constitutional Concepts for Free Trade in Services' in G de Búrca and J Scott (eds), *The EU and the WTO—Legal and Constitutional Issues* (Hart Publishing, 2001) 211–35.

The Court tackled the issues straight on. It summarized the Commission's argument in one paragraph, and then proceeded to consider, first, services other than transport. The Court referred to *Opinion 1/75*, where it had decided that the common commercial policy covered credits for the financing of local costs linked to export operations.[56] It pointed out that those local costs concerned expenses incurred for the supply of both goods and services, but that the Court had nevertheless recognized exclusive competence, without distinguishing between goods and services. The Court then harked back to its pronouncements in *Opinion 1/78* on the broad interpretation of the common commercial policy. It referred to the Commission's assessment that in certain developed countries the services sector had become the dominant sector of the economy and that the global economy had been undergoing fundamental structural changes: the trend was for basic industry to be transferred to developing countries, whilst the developed economies had tended to become exporters of services and of goods with a high value-added content. This trend, the Court noted, was borne out by the WTO agreements, which were the subject of a single process of negotiation covering both goods and services. The Court's conclusion was that, having regard to this trend in international trade, it followed from the open nature of the common commercial policy that trade in services could not immediately,[57] and as a matter of principle, be excluded from the scope of the common commercial policy.[58]

If the Court had stopped there, the Commission would have won an important victory. But the Court went on, considering that its conclusion had to be made more specific, taking into account the definition of trade in services given in GATS, so as to see whether the overall scheme of the EC Treaty was not such as to limit the extent to which trade in services could be included in the common commercial policy. The Court then described the four modes of supplying services. As regards cross-frontier supplies, it noted that neither the supplier nor the consumer moved, and that this was not unlike trade in goods. There was thus no particular reason why such a supply should not fall within the concept of common commercial policy. However, the same could not be said of the other three modes, namely consumption abroad, commercial presence, and the presence of natural persons. The Court pointed out that, as regards natural persons, it was clear from then Article 3 EC, which distinguished between 'a common commercial policy' and 'measures concerning the entry and movement of persons', that the treatment of nationals of non-member countries on crossing the external frontiers of Member States could not be regarded as falling within the common commercial policy. More generally, the Court continued, the existence in the Treaty of specific chapters on the free movement of natural and legal persons showed that those matters did not fall within the common commercial policy.[59]

The Court's reasoning, concise as it may have been, was not difficult to understand. The Court was of the opinion that, in so far as GATS commitments had

[56] N 11 above. [57] The French version uses the term '*d'emblée*'.
[58] *Opinion 1/94* (n 45 above) paras 36–41. [59] Ibid, paras 42–46.

an effect on cross-border movement of natural and legal persons, they could not come within the notion of commercial policy as encapsulated in the EC Treaty.[60] The reason was not so much that that notion is inherently incapable of extending to movement of persons, but rather that such an approach did not conform to the structure and organization of the then EC Treaty, which looked at such movement, both internally and externally, under different chapters. If anything, that perspective was strengthened with the changes made by the Amsterdam Treaty, inserting into the EC Treaty the new Title IV on visas, asylum, immigration, and other policies related to the free movement of persons. It was indeed incontrovertible that the EC Treaty distinguished between external trade policy and immigration policy.

Notwithstanding the above, the Court's reasoning was not entirely persuasive. As has been noted,[61] GATS is not intended to be an instrument of immigration policy. It is of course true that GATS commitments may have an effect on immigration. Where a WTO member commits itself to full market access for a particular type of service, provided through commercial presence or the movement of natural persons, it has to allow companies or persons from other WTO members providing such services free access to its territory. Similarly, where market access through consumption abroad is granted, there will have to be free entry by consumers (e.g. tourists). The question, however, is whether that was sufficient to exclude GATS from the scope of the common commercial policy. Provisions on external trade in goods may also have an effect on non-trade policies, as the Court itself recognized in the first part of *Opinion 1/94*. The fact that the Agreement on Agriculture would affect EC common market organizations did not put that agreement outside the scope of the common commercial policy. GATS indeed affected immigration, but it did that only through the prism of ensuring market access and non-discrimination for internationally traded services.

It is also notable that the Opinion did not refer to the unity of the internal market. The Court did not analyse the risk of deflections of trade or distortions of competition created by non-uniform external trade policies as regards services. Yet such risk is self-evident, in particular as regards distortion of competition.[62] For example, in an integrated and liberalized internal financial services market, different policies by Member States on access and treatment of foreign financial services companies seeking to operate on that market are just as much likely to distort competition as are different policies on imports of goods. The unity of the internal market in services thus requires a uniform external trade policy.

Perhaps the Court was also influenced by the fact that much of the regulation of services industries continued to be in the province of the Member States rather than that of the EU, and that GATS directly interfered with certain aspects of such regulation, as can be seen when browsing through the GATS commitments of the EU and its Member States. The Court may have been reluctant to effect, through

[60] Tridimas (n 51 above) 51. [61] Tridimas and Eeckhout (n 10 above) 161–2.
[62] For an example of deflections of trade in services, see Eeckhout (n 15 above) 25–6.

judicial pronouncement rather than political consensus, what it perhaps saw as a significant transfer of competences from the Member States to the Community, particularly in the light of the exclusive nature of trade policy competences. In any event, the result of the Court's ruling was that the EC's and the Member States' powers to regulate international trade in services were, at least in so far as GATS was concerned, indivisibly linked. The Community's competence over cross-border services was exclusive, and the Member States generally retained competence over the other modes of supplying services.[63] As any meaningful GATS negotiation encompasses all modes of supply, the EC and its Member States were compelled to act in common. Politically, then, the difference between exclusive and shared competence was reduced to the decision-making: shared competences required unanimous action by the EC and its Member States, whereas EC trade policy competences were exercised by the Council deciding by qualified majority.

Transport

As the Treaty contained a specific chapter on the common transport policy, the Court examined transport services separately. The Commission clearly attached great importance to its claim that international agreements of a commercial nature in relation to transport (as opposed to those relating to safety rules) fell within the common commercial policy: if correct, the Community would have gained exclusive competence to negotiate such agreements, for example in the air transport sector.[64] By contrast, competence under the common transport policy was shared;[65] thus there was more political discretion where a common external policy was to be constructed under such competence. Note also that transport services could be regarded as cross-border services in the meaning of Article I(2) GATS.

The Court was not impressed by the Commission's submission.[66] It referred to its case law on implied powers, in particular the *AETR* judgment, where it had held that competence to conclude international agreements could flow implicitly from certain Treaty provisions.[67] That judgment concerned transport policy, and the idea underlying it, the Court pointed out, was that international agreements in transport matters were not covered by the common commercial policy. The distinction which the Commission attempted to draw between agreements on safety rules and those of a commercial nature was rejected, as the *AETR* judgment drew no such distinction and as the later ruling in *Opinion 1/76*, confirming implied external transport powers, concerned an economic agreement.[68]

[63] But see Ch 3 as regards implied powers.
[64] See Ch 3 for recent case law regarding air transport.
[65] See Ch 3; see now Art 4(2)(g) TFEU.
[66] *Opinion 1/94* (n 45 above) paras 48–52.
[67] Case 22/70 *Commission v. Council* [1971] ECR 263, para 16; see Ch 3.
[68] *Opinion 1/76 re Inland Waterways* [1977] ECR 741.

The Commission had also referred to precedent, in the sense that a number of trade embargoes which the EC had adopted on the basis of the Treaty's commercial policy provisions involved the suspension of transport services. The Court regarded those precedents as inconclusive: as the embargoes related primarily to the export and import of products, they could not have been effective without at the same time suspending transport services. Such suspension was therefore a necessary adjunct to the principal measure. In any event, the Court continued, mere practice of the Council could not derogate from the rules laid down in the Treaty and could not, therefore, create a precedent binding on Community institutions with regard to the correct legal basis.

Intellectual property

As regards the TRIPs Agreement, the Court started its analysis by stating that the Commission's argument for exclusive Community competence was essentially that the rules concerning intellectual property rights were closely linked to trade in the products and services to which they applied. It then looked at section 4 of Part III of TRIPs, on enforcement measures to be applied at border crossing points. The Court pointed out that that section of TRIPs had its counterpart in an EC regulation on measures to prohibit the release for free circulation of counterfeit goods,[69] which had been based on the Treaty's commercial policy provisions. That was indeed the correct legal basis, the Court reasoned, because the regulation concerned measures to be taken by the customs authorities at the external frontiers of the Community. Since measures of that type could be adopted autonomously by the Community within the context of the common commercial policy, it was for the Community alone to conclude international agreements on such matters.[70]

However, the above TRIPs provisions formed but a small section of the Agreement, and the Court did not accept the Commission's claim for the remainder. It admitted that there was a connection between intellectual property and trade in goods, in that intellectual property rights enabled those holding them to prevent third parties from carrying out certain acts. The power to prohibit the use of a trade mark, the manufacture of a product, the copying of a design, or the reproduction of a book, a disc, or video cassette, the Court illustrated, inevitably had effects on trade. Intellectual property rights were moreover specifically designed to produce such effects, but that was not enough to bring them within the scope of the common commercial policy: intellectual property rights did not relate specifically to international trade, but affected internal trade just as much as, if not more than, international trade.[71]

[69] Council Regulation 3842/86 laying down measures to prohibit the release for free circulation of counterfeit goods [1986] OJ L357/1.

[70] *Opinion 1/94* (n 45 above) paras 54–55.

[71] Ibid, para 57.

The Court then further examined the TRIPs Agreement and its relationship with intra-Community harmonization of intellectual property law. It pointed out that the primary objective of TRIPs was to harmonize the protection of intellectual property on a worldwide scale. As TRIPs laid down rules in fields in which there were no Community harmonization measures, the conclusion of the agreement would achieve such harmonization and contribute to the establishment and functioning of the common market. If such conclusion were based on the commercial policy provisions alone, it would enable the Community institutions to escape the internal constraints in relation to procedures and voting which normally applied in the case of harmonization (see current Articles 114 and 352 TFEU).[72]

As a third element in its analysis, the Court did not accept that institutional practice in relation to autonomous measures or external agreements adopted on the basis of the Treaty's commercial policy provisions altered this conclusion.

The Court's analysis of TRIPs was convincing. Notwithstanding the reference in its name to trade-related aspects, the TRIPs Agreement is indeed primarily concerned with intellectual property protection as such, and not with any specific effects on international trade of such protection. Indeed, it is noteworthy that a particularly significant trade issue resulting from the application and enforcement of intellectual property rights is not addressed by TRIPs: the issue of exhaustion of rights.[73] The question whether rights are exhausted in an international trade context where the intellectual property right holder markets or consents to marketing its own products, is left to the discretion of WTO members.[74] TRIPs could thus only be regarded a trade agreement if it were sufficient that its overall objective was to affect trade (but not necessarily promote it), by ensuring general protection of intellectual property. Clearly, in the Court's opinion that overall objective was insufficient to bring the agreement within the Community's exclusive trade policy powers.

The Court's general conclusion in *Opinion 1/94* was that the Community and its Member States were jointly competent to conclude both GATS and TRIPs. There will be opportunity to consider the implied powers dimension of the Opinion in Chapter 3. The discussion of this episode may be concluded by referring to two subsequent rulings, in which the Court confirmed the *Opinion 1/94* approach.

In *Opinion 2/92*, which was in fact requested by the Belgian government one-and-a-half years before the Commission's request for *Opinion 1/94*, and which was before the Court at the same time as *Opinion 1/94*, the Court looked at an OECD decision on national treatment of foreign undertakings. It described this national treatment rule as concerning mainly the conditions for the participation of

[72] Ibid, paras 58–59.

[73] Art 6 TRIPs provides that 'for the purposes of dispute settlement ... nothing in this Agreement shall be used to address the issue of the exhaustion of intellectual property rights'.

[74] On the EU approach in the field of trade marks see e.g. D O'Keeffe and B Keane, 'The Shadow of *Silhouette*' (1999/2000) 19 YEL 139.

foreign-controlled undertakings in the internal economic life of the Member States in which they operated. It recognized that the rule also applied to the conditions of those undertakings' participation in trade between the Member States and non-member countries, conditions which were the subject of the common commercial policy. However, so far as the participation of foreign-controlled undertakings in intra-Community trade was concerned, such trade was governed by the Community's internal market rules and not by the rules of the common commercial policy. It followed that the national treatment rule related only partially to international trade, and that it affected internal trade to the same extent as international trade, if not more so. Therefore, the Treaty provisions on the common commercial policy did not confer exclusive competence.[75]

In *Parliament v. Council* the Court considered a challenge to Council decisions, based on the Treaty provisions on the common commercial policy, whose effect was to extend the benefits of EC public procurement rules to US undertakings. As that extension covered services, the Court recalled that in the then state of Community law only cross-border services came within the scope of the common commercial policy. Since the extension also related to supplies made thanks to a commercial presence or the presence of natural persons, the Council decisions were wrongly based, and were annulled.[76]

Trade and foreign policy

As mentioned above, many different types of measures may affect international trade. Also, trade measures may be taken for the purpose of pursuing policies which are not economic or commercial in nature. One such interface concerns trade and general foreign policy. If one reflects on this a little further, one notices the awkwardness of the EU's dichotomy between trade policies, devised and implemented under the TFEU, and general foreign and security policy, which forms the subject of gradual co-ordination within the framework of the EU's Common Foreign and Security Policy (CFSP). From a legal perspective, trade policy appears to dominate. It predates the CFSP, and comes within the exclusive competence of the EU, a competence exercised by supranational institutions capable of adopting legal acts which are directly effective and supreme. Under the CFSP, by contrast, there are no exclusive EU powers, the approach is intergovernmental, and the precise dimensions and effects of legal acts are vague and uncertain.[77] From a political perspective, however, this state of affairs appears to make no sense. How can trade issues be dissociated from general foreign policy? If one looks at the practice of third countries,

[75] *Opinion 2/92 re Third Revised Decision of the OECD on national treatment* [1995] ECR I–521, paras 24–28.

[76] Case C–360/93 *Parliament v. Council* [1996] ECR I–1195.

[77] See further Chs 5 and 11.

it is clear that their position and participation in international trade relations form part of a broader foreign policy, and that decisions on trade matters may be guided by such broader policy.

It is, for example, clear that the EU's support for China's WTO accession, some years ago, was not only inspired by trade policy considerations, but formed part of a broader policy, pursued by the EU and its Member States. It would be interesting to analyse the EU's trade policy against the broader canvas of international politics. At an aggregate level, this state of affairs poses no particular problems for the EU's exclusive trade policy competences. Those competences are in any event exercised by political institutions, one of them, the Council, representing national governments, and the policy directions there adopted are a matter of political rather than legal concern. When one speaks at a general level of trade relations with third countries forming part of a broader foreign policy, there appear to be no particular problems for the scope and nature of the EU's common commercial policy. However, matters become more complex when one focuses on certain types of more individualized trade measures which are taken for foreign policy or even external security reasons. It is in such a context that the awkwardness of the dichotomy becomes apparent.

From the 1980s onwards, the EC developed a practice of adopting various types of economic sanctions, particularly in the trade field.[78] Trade restrictions and embargos are indeed a preferred instrument for exercising political and economic pressure on countries and regimes, and they may be decreed by the UN Security Council. Even though the reasons behind such measures may be wholly disconnected from commercial policy as such, it is difficult to see them as anything but trade measures, given their marked effects on trade. However, the authority to adopt trade sanctions would then appear to come within the EU's exclusive competences. Somewhat surprisingly perhaps, the EU's practice confirmed this, and the Council adopted such sanctions by way of regulations based on (current) Article 207 TFEU; not, however, without combining this with 'political' decisions taken, at first, under the heading of European Political Co-operation and subsequently under its successor, the CFSP. The Treaty on European Union then codified this practice through the introduction of (then) Articles 301 and 60 EC. This acceptance and confirmation of EC involvement were no doubt also inspired by the advantages which regulations offered as a legal instrument: the procedure for their adoption was straightforward (particularly as the European Parliament was not involved), and they applied directly and uniformly in the laws of the Member States.

From a legal perspective, this approach towards economic sanctions raised delicate and difficult issues of interrelationship between the CFSP and other EU external policies. Those issues are discussed in Chapters 5 and 12. But what about the powers of the Member States in those cases where there is no common policy? Are the Member States entitled to restrict trade for foreign policy reasons, or is

[78] See for an early overview PJ Kuijper, 'Trade Sanctions, Security and Human Rights and Commercial Policy' in Maresceau (n 37 above) 387. See further Ch 12.

that not possible in light of the EU's exclusive competence to conduct a common commercial policy?

Those questions came up in two cases which German courts referred to the Court of Justice.[79] Both cases concerned the lawfulness, under Community law, of German legislation which was applied to control the export of so-called dual-use goods.[80] In *Werner v. Germany* the German authorities had refused a licence for the export to Libya of a vacuum induction, smelting, and cast oven, as well as induction spools for that oven, on the grounds that the products could be used for the production of missiles.[81] In *Leifer and Others* a number of people were criminally prosecuted for having exported to Iraq between 1984 and 1988 plant, parts of plant, and chemicals without the requisite export licence. The authorities considered that those products were used in Iraq's chemical weapons programme.[82] The German legislation enabled the authorities to curtail contracts and activities in the sphere of foreign trade in order to guarantee Germany's security, prevent a disturbance of peaceful coexistence, or prevent the external relations of Germany from being seriously disrupted. In both cases the German courts asked the Court of Justice whether the export controls and restrictions in issue were compatible with the Community's exclusive competence under (current) Article 207 TFEU.

The Court's analysis in these judgments was almost identical.[83] The Court started by stating that the question was whether the common commercial policy solely concerned measures which pursued commercial objectives, or whether it also covered commercial measures having foreign policy and security objectives. It recalled the text of (current) Article 207 and referred to the principle of a non-restrictive interpretation of the common commercial policy concept, so as to avoid disturbances in intra-Community trade by reason of the disparities which would then exist in certain sectors of economic relations with non-member countries, a principle established in *Opinion 1/78*.[84] So, the Court continued, measures whose effect was to prevent or restrict the export of certain products could not be treated as falling outside the scope of the common commercial policy on the ground that they had foreign policy and security objectives. The specific subject matter of commercial policy, which concerned trade with non-member countries and, according to (current) Article 207, was based on the concept of a common policy, required that a Member State should not be able to restrict its scope by freely deciding, in the light of its own foreign policy or security requirements, whether a measure was covered by (current) Article 207.

[79] In an earlier judgment, Case C–367/89 *Richardt and 'Les Accessoires Scientifiques'* [1991] ECR I–4621, the Court had analysed the issues purely from an internal market perspective.

[80] I.e. goods which may be used for both civil and military purposes.

[81] Case C–70/94 *Werner v. Germany* [1995] ECR I–3189.

[82] Case C–83/94 *Leifer and Others* [1995] ECR I–3231.

[83] *Werner v. Germany* (n 81 above) paras 7–11; *Leifer and Others* (n 82 above) paras 7–11.

[84] *Opinion 1/78* (n 21 above).

In these cases the Court again displayed a principled approach to the interpretation of (current) Article 207. However, one should not jump to the conclusion that the Court considered *ultra vires* (and thus unlawful) attempts by Member States autonomously to control exports of dual-use goods on foreign or security policy grounds. In both judgments the Court in the end accepted that the German legislation conformed to EC legislation on exports, which enabled Member States to adopt restrictions on public security grounds. The legislation thus benefited from a specific Community authorization, which was sufficient to render it compatible with the principle of exclusive Community competences.[85]

The Court returned to the relationship between commercial and foreign policy in *Centro-Com*.[86] That case concerned a trade embargo against the Federal Republic of Yugoslavia (Serbia and Montenegro), decreed by the UN Security Council and implemented through an EC regulation.[87] There was an exception for supplies of medical products and foodstuffs, and Centro-Com, an Italian company, had benefited from that exception and exported pharmaceutical goods and blood-testing equipment to Montenegro. When it sought payment through a bank account held by the National Bank of Yugoslavia with Barclays in London, the Bank of England refused release of the funds, in implementation of a new government policy permitting payment only for exports from the United Kingdom. The policy had been adopted in order to combat circumvention of the sanctions. Centro-Com challenged the refusal in the UK courts, and the Court of Appeal referred the case to the Court of Justice, asking, *inter alia*, whether the refusal to release the funds was compatible with the common commercial policy, and with (current) Article 207 TFEU in particular.

The Court took care to clarify the relationship between measures of foreign and security policy and the common commercial policy.[88] Indeed, one of the UK's arguments was that the measures at issue had been taken by virtue of its national competence in the field of foreign and security policy and that performance of its obligations under the UN Charter and under Security Council resolutions came within that competence. The United Kingdom further argued that the validity of those measures could not be affected by the Community's exclusive competence or by the relevant sanctions regulation, which did no more than implement at Community level the exercise of Member States' national competence in the field of foreign and security policy. The Court accepted that the Member States had indeed retained their competence in the field of foreign and security policy. None the less, the powers retained by the Member States had to be exercised in a manner consistent with Community law. Similarly, the Member States could not treat

[85] See also Ch 12.

[86] Case C–124/95 *The Queen, ex parte Centro-Com v. HM Treasury and Bank of England* [1997] ECR I–81.

[87] Council Regulation 1432/92 prohibiting trade between the European Economic Community and the Republics of Serbia and Montenegro [1992] OJ L151/4.

[88] *Centro-Com* (n 86 above) paras 23–30.

national measures whose effect was to prevent or restrict the export of certain products as falling outside the scope of the common commercial policy on the ground that they had foreign and security objectives. Consequently, while it was for Member States to adopt measures of foreign and security policy in the exercise of their national competence, those measures nevertheless had to respect the provisions adopted by the Community in the field of the common commercial policy provided for by (current) Article 207 TFEU. It was indeed, the Court continued, in the exercise of their national competence in matters of foreign and security policy that the Member States expressly decided to have recourse to a Community measure, which became the above-mentioned sanctions regulation, based on (current) Article 207. As the preamble to the regulation showed, it ensued from a decision of the Community and its Member States which was taken within the framework of political co-operation and which marked their willingness to have recourse to a Community instrument. It followed that, even where measures such as those in issue in the main proceedings had been adopted in the exercise of national competence in matters of foreign and security policy, they had to respect the Community rules adopted under the common commercial policy. The Court then examined whether the UK measure was compatible with the relevant regulations, and found that it was not. That substantive analysis need not concern us here.[89]

The Court's statements on competence were persuasive and consistent with previous rulings, yet at the same time unable to bridge the gap between the exercise of exclusive trade policy powers and foreign and security policy decisions. It is true that the Court pointed to the link between the political co-operation decision and the regulation, but it did so in a descriptive rather than prescriptive manner. If no political co-operation (or currently CFSP) decision were taken, one should think that the EU would still have full, exclusive competences to adopt trade measures which pursue foreign and security policy objectives. The conclusion to be drawn is that the political subordination of the EU's trade policy is not matched by any legal subordination. More generally, the above judgments confirm that trade measures are trade measures, whatever the objectives pursued. Import and export measures come within the scope of (current) Article 207 TFEU, even if their purpose is wholly unrelated to commercial or economic considerations.

Chapters 5 and 12 look further into the relationship between trade and foreign policy, by focusing on the scope of the CFSP and on the EU's evolving sanctions policy.

Trade and environment

There are several types of linkages between international trade and environmental protection, and a lot of reflection on those linkages is taking place, at official levels,[90]

[89] See Ch 12.

[90] See e.g. the WTO's Committee on Trade and Environment.

and in various academic disciplines.[91] One of those connections is that trade measures can be used to pursue certain environmental protection policies. Perhaps a few non-exhaustive examples may be given. A State may regulate production processes or the marketing of certain products or services in a manner which affects international trade. A State may also have concerns over importing products which contribute to environmental degradation when used or consumed. Or it may wish not to export such products, for fear of causing such degradation abroad. A State may further be reluctant to participate in the trade in environmentally valuable goods, such as a threatened species. Or it may not wish to trade in products whose production processes cause excessive environmental harm, locally, regionally, or at the level of the global commons. And it also happens that a State uses trade as a means of persuading other States to provide for higher environmental protection, by conditioning its willingness to import upon a certain level of protection. States can do all of that, either through autonomous action or in the framework of international agreements on environmental protection.

In the context of the WTO there is an important debate, fed by case law, on the lawfulness of such measures, and on the link between WTO free-trade rules and multilateral environmental agreements.[92] That is a debate on the legal substance of trade and environment policies, but in EU law the debate has a formal, jurisdictional counterpart. Where does competence lie to take action in the field of trade and environment? Do all environmental measures affecting trade come within the EU's exclusive competence? Or does that depend on the centre of gravity of the measure; whether it is primarily a trade measure or an environmental measure?[93]

Before looking at the Court's case law on such questions,[94] it is useful to point out that, since the Single European Act 1986, the EEC Treaty has provided for a Community policy on the protection of the environment (see, currently, Articles 191 to 193 TFEU). The powers conferred upon the Community in this field extend to external relations, as Article 191(4) provides that, within their respective spheres of competence, the Union and the Member States shall co-operate with third countries and with the competent international organizations. It further provides that the arrangements for Union co-operation may be the subject of agreements between the Union and the third parties concerned. Therefore, the question of the proper competence location of trade-and-environment measures is not so much concerned with whether the EU has any powers at all, but rather with whether the

[91] For a general treatment see e.g. E-U Petersmann, *International and European Trade and Environmental Law after the Uruguay Round* (Kluwer Law International, 1995); J Wiers, *Trade and Environment in the EC and the WTO—A Legal Analysis* (Europa Law Publishing, 2002); E Vranes, *Trade and the Environment—Fundamental Issues in International Law, WTO Law and Legal Theory* (OUP, 2009).

[92] Ibid.

[93] For an in-depth, albeit no longer recent, examination, see P Demaret, 'Environmental Policy and Commercial Policy: The Emergence of Trade-Related Environmental Measures (TREMs) in the External Relations of the European Community', in Maresceau (n 37 above) 305–86.

[94] See also Holdgaard (n 6 above) 43–50.

EU's competence is exclusive (under the common commercial policy) or shared with the Member States (under the EU's environmental policy). It may further be noted that Article 11 TFEU provides that environmental protection requirements must be integrated into the definition and implementation of all the Union policies and activities, in particular with a view to promoting sustainable development (the so-called principle of integration).[95]

In *Chernobyl I*, the Court for the first time looked at trade and environment through the prism of external competence.[96] Following the accident at the Chernobyl (Ukraine) nuclear power station in April 1986, the Member States immediately took action to block imports of contaminated agricultural products from Central and Eastern Europe. Within a couple of weeks the Community got involved and the Council of Ministers adopted a regulation on such imports, based on (current) Article 207 TFEU. Greece did not agree with that course of action, and challenged a successor regulation,[97] arguing that in the light of the public health objective of the measure the legal basis was incorrect. Thus, the case did not concern environmental protection in a strict sense, but the Treaty provisions on environmental policy were referred to in argument: Greece claimed that the regulation should have been based on Articles 130r and 130s EEC (now, with amendments, Articles 191 and 192 TFEU), possibly in conjunction with (current) Article 352 TFEU, or on Article 31 of the EAEC Treaty. The analysis can therefore be fully transposed to pure trade-and-environment measures.

The Court's reasoning was as follows.[98] It first referred to the principle it had established in the *GSP* case,[99] i.e. that in the context of the organization of the powers of the Community the choice of legal basis for a measure had to be based on objective factors which were amenable to judicial review. It then analysed the objective of the regulation, as expressed in its preamble, where it was indicated that 'the Community must continue to ensure that agricultural products and processed agricultural products intended for human consumption and likely to be contaminated are introduced into the Community only according to common arrangements', and that those 'common arrangements should safeguard the health of consumers, maintain, without having unduly adverse effects on trade between the Community and third countries, the unified nature of the market and prevent deflections of trade'. The Court further pointed out that the regulation established uniform rules regarding the conditions under which agricultural products likely to be contaminated could be imported into the Community from non-member

[95] See on that principle D McGillivray and J Holder, 'Locating EC Environmental Law' (2001) 20 YEL 152.

[96] *Greece v. Council* (n 43 above).

[97] Council Regulation 3955/87 on the conditions governing imports of agricultural products originating in third countries following the accident at the Chernobyl nuclear power station [1987] OJ L371/4.

[98] *Greece v. Council* (n 43 above) paras 13–20.

[99] *Commission v. Council* (n 31 above).

countries. Having thus examined the objective and content of the regulation, the Court concluded that it was intended to regulate trade between the Community and non-member countries, and that it came within the common commercial policy. The fact that maximum permitted levels of radioactive contamination were fixed in response to a concern to protect public health and that the protection of public health was one of the objectives of Community action in environmental matters could not remove the regulation from the sphere of the common commercial policy. (Current) Articles 191 and 192 TFEU were intended to confer powers on the Community to undertake specific action on environmental matters, but they left intact the powers held by the Community under other provisions of the Treaty, even if the measures taken under those provisions pursued at the same time any of the objectives of environmental protection. That interpretation was confirmed by the principle of integration, which implied that a Community measure could not be part of Community action on environmental matters merely because it took account of environmental protection requirements.

At the time, commentators felt that the Court had accepted too broad an interpretation of (current) Article 207,[100] yet from the perspective of safeguarding the unity of the internal market the judgment made sense. This is well expressed in the Opinion of Darmon AG, where he stated that, in order to avoid any change in patterns of trade and any distortion of competition in dealings with non-member countries, the Community had to be able, under the common commercial policy, to adopt uniform rules regarding the conditions under which products from non-member countries could be imported into its territory. In the Advocate General's conception, those conditions could include, in particular, compliance with maximum permitted levels of radioactivity without the measure in question thereby being of a different nature or not capable of adoption under (current) Article 207. The contested regulation seemed to him by its very nature to come within the common commercial policy.[101] One could add that the judgment essentially adopted the same approach as the above cases on trade and foreign policy: trade measures are trade measures, whatever the objectives pursued.

The Court was again confronted with trade and environment from an external competence perspective when it had to rule on a request for an Opinion concerning the appropriate legal basis for the Cartagena Protocol on Biosafety.[102] The main difference from *Chernobyl I* is that the Cartagena Protocol is much less clearly concerned with trade, so that the above approach was inappropriate.

The Cartagena Protocol is a protocol to the Convention on Biological Diversity, a mixed agreement to which both the EU and its Member States are parties. The legal basis for conclusion was (current) Article 192 TFEU.[103] The Convention aims

[100] ELM Völker, *Barriers to External and Internal Community Trade* (Kluwer, 1993) 186–8.
[101] *Greece v. Council* (n 43 above) para 32 of the Opinion.
[102] *Opinion 2/00 re Cartagena Protocol on Biosafety* [2001] ECR I-9713.
[103] Council Decision 93/626 [1993] OJ L309/1.

at 'the conservation of biological diversity, the sustainable use of its components and the fair and equitable sharing of the benefits arising out of the utilization of genetic resources'. Article 19(3) of the Convention provides for the negotiation of a protocol 'in the field of the safe transfer, handling and use of any living modified organism resulting from biotechnology that may have adverse effect on the conservation and sustainable use of biological diversity'. That provision formed the basis for the negotiation of the Cartagena Protocol. It is also worth mentioning that Article 34 of the Convention allows for conclusion of the Convention and any Protocol by States and by regional economic integration organizations. Where such organizations become parties together with their member States, the organization and its member States shall decide on their respective responsibilities for the performance of obligations, and they shall not be allowed to exercise rights concurrently. Further, the relevant organization must declare the extent of its competence.

The Cartagena Protocol was negotiated between 1997 and 2000, and was signed on behalf of the Community and its Member States on 24 May 2000. At that occasion, there was a divergence in the views of the Commission and the Council. The Commission had proposed that the decision authorizing signature be based on (current) Articles 207 and 191(4) TFEU, but the Council unanimously adopted the decision on the basis of Article 192(1) alone. The Commission then requested the Court's Opinion, essentially asking whether its proposal had been correct. It pointed out that there would have to be a declaration regarding the Community's competence, and took the view that the Court's Opinion would ensure a framework of legal certainty for managing the Protocol, in particular when voting rights were exercised. The Commission was thus mainly concerned with the future management of the Protocol, in terms of representation of and decision-making by the Community and its Member States. It accepted that the Protocol would become a mixed agreement, but considered that there was preponderant Community competence under (current) Article 207 TFEU, which should be reflected in future implementation.

Article 1 of the Cartagena Protocol states that its objective is:

> ... to contribute to ensuring an adequate level of protection in the field of the safe transfer, handling and use of living modified organisms resulting from modern biotechnology that may have adverse effects on the conservation and sustainable use of biological diversity, taking also into account risks to human health, and specifically focusing on transboundary movements.

In accordance with Article 4, and without prejudice to certain specific provisions, the Protocol 'shall apply to the transboundary movement, transit, handling and use of all living modified organisms' that may have the above-mentioned adverse effects. Article 2(2) provides that 'the Parties shall ensure that the development, handling, transport, use, transfer and release of any living modified organisms are undertaken in a manner that prevents or reduces the risks to biological diversity, taking also into account risks to human health'. To that end, the Protocol sets up various control procedures, such as the informed agreement procedure (Articles 7 to 10 and 12), the procedure for living modified organisms intended for direct use as food or feed, or for processing (Article 11), and a simplified procedure (Article 13). Article 20 creates a Biosafety Clearing-House.

In its Opinion the Court examined whether the conclusion of the Protocol should be based on (current) Article 207 TFEU. It first pointed to settled case law that the choice of legal basis for a measure, including one adopted in order to conclude an international agreement, did not follow from its author's conviction alone, but had to rest on objective factors—in particular the aim and content of the measure—which were amenable to judicial review. The Court then introduced a principle, novel as regards external competence claims, but derived from case law on the legal basis of 'internal' acts. It stated that, if examination of a Community measure revealed that it pursued a twofold purpose, or that it had a twofold component, and if one was identifiable as the main or predominant purpose or component, whereas the other was merely incidental, the measure had to be founded on a single legal basis, namely that required by the main or predominant purpose or component.[104] By way of exception, the Court emphasized, if it was established that the measure simultaneously pursued several objectives which were inseparably linked without one being secondary and indirect in relation to the other, the measure could be founded on the corresponding legal bases.[105] Since interpretation of an international agreement was in issue, the Court also recalled that under Article 31 VCLT 'a treaty shall be interpreted in good faith in accordance with the ordinary meaning to be given to the terms of the treaty in their context and in the light of its object and purpose'.[106]

Having thus done the groundwork, the Court identified the question in issue as being: (a) whether the Protocol, in the light of its context, its aim, and its content, constituted an agreement principally concerning environmental protection which was liable to have incidental effects on trade in living modified organisms (LMOs); (b) whether, conversely, it was principally an agreement concerning international trade policy which incidentally took account of certain environmental requirements; or (c) whether it was inextricably concerned both with environmental protection and with international trade.[107]

As regards the context of the Protocol, the Court recalled its link with the Convention on Biological Diversity, an instrument indisputably falling within the field of environmental protection. As regards purpose, it was clear beyond doubt that the Protocol pursued an environmental objective, highlighted by its reference to the precautionary principle, a fundamental principle of environmental protection

[104] The Court referred to Case C–155/91 *Commission v. Council* [1993] ECR I–939, paras 19 and 21 (*Waste Directive* judgment); Case C–42/97 *Parliament v. Council* [1999] ECR I–869, paras 39–40; and Case C–36/98 *Spain v. Council* [2001] ECR I–779, para 59.

[105] Here the Court referred to Case C–300/89 *Commission v. Council* [1991] ECR I–2867, paras 13 and 17 (the *Titanium Dioxide* judgment), and to *Parliament v. Council* (n 104 above) para 38.

[106] *Opinion 2/00* (n 102 above) paras 22–24.

[107] Ibid, para 25.

included in (current) Article 191(2) TFEU. The title of and preamble to the Protocol confirmed this. As regards content, finally, there was a clear reflection of the Protocol's environmental aim in the fundamental obligation to prevent or reduce the risks to biological diversity in the development, handling, transport, use, transfer, and release of any LMO. Article 4 of the Protocol, defining its scope as applying to all LMOs that could have adverse effects on biological diversity, also showed that the Protocol intrinsically concerned environmental protection. Further confirmation was found in the type of control procedures which the Protocol set up. It followed from this examination that the Protocol's main purpose or component was the protection of biological diversity against the harmful effects which could result from activities that involved dealing with LMOs, in particular from their transboundary movement.[108]

The Court did not stop there, but also rebutted the Commission's arguments regarding the common commercial policy. In essence the Commission had relied on a broad interpretation of (current) Article 207 TFEU, and had pointed out that the Protocol applied to transboundary movements of LMOs, and that the control procedures would specifically relate to such movements, which included trade in LMOs. The Court accepted that, but did not consider that this modified the Protocol's character as an instrument intended essentially to improve biosafety and not to promote, facilitate, or govern trade. First, the Protocol covered any form of movement of LMOs between States, whether or not commercial. Likewise the juxtaposition of the terms 'transfer', 'handling', and 'use' of LMOs indicated the parties' wish to cover any manner in which LMOs were dealt with. Secondly, the Commission's interpretation would effectively render the specific Treaty provisions concerning environmental policy largely nugatory, since, as soon as it was established that Community action was liable to have repercussions on trade, the envisaged agreement would have to be regarded as coming within the common commercial policy. Thirdly, the practical difficulties associated with the implementation of mixed agreements were irrelevant when selecting the legal basis for a Community measure.[109]

The Court thus decided that conclusion of the Protocol on behalf of the Community had to be founded on a single legal basis, specific to environmental policy. It also decided that (current) Article 192(1) TFEU provided such a basis, and not Article 191 TFEU, which only defined the objectives to be pursued in the context of environmental policy.[110]

Did *Opinion 2/00* inaugurate a new, more restrictive reading of (current) Article 207 TFEU, and, correspondingly, a broader reading of the Community's external competences in matters of environmental policy? Did the Opinion bury the conception that trade measures are trade measures, no matter which objectives they pursue? The reply to those questions need not be affirmative. As was mentioned, the Cartagena Protocol on Biosafety is much less obviously a trade measure than the import

[108] Ibid, paras 26–34. [109] Ibid, paras 35–41. [110] Ibid, paras 42–44. See further Ch 4.

restrictions in issue in *Chernobyl I*, or than the export restrictions in *Werner*, *Leifer*, and *Centro-Com*. At first glance, one may be tempted to identify transborder movement with trade, but the Court was right to look at the Protocol more closely, and to detect that the notion of transborder movement is wider than the notion of international trade; that the Protocol not only regulates such movement, but also other issues; and that there is generally no significant trade or economic dimension to the Protocol. Thus, the fact that the application of the Protocol will no doubt affect trade was insufficient for bringing it within the scope of (current) Article 207 TFEU. The Court could have added that the Protocol could just as much affect trade between Member States, a matter for the internal market, as it could affect external trade.

The Opinion also reflected the Court's overall approach to trade-and-environment issues. For example, in the case law on the free movement of goods, policies for the protection of the environment have been raised almost to the level of an express exception to the prohibition of quantitative restrictions and measures having equivalent effect.[111] In that case law, one also finds indications of the Court's reluctance to protect a principle of free trade in environmentally harmful products, such as waste.[112] Similarly, the case law on the delimitation of the EU's competence to harmonize national laws for the purpose of establishing an internal market and its competence to pursue environmental policies also betrays a reluctance to regard the circulation of environmentally harmful products as an internal market matter.[113] *Opinion 2/00* is in a sense the external competence counterpart of those developments in the case law.

That *Opinion 2/00* did not introduce a more restrictive reading of (current) Article 207 TFEU is confirmed by a subsequent judgment, *Commission v. Council*, on the Energy Star Agreement.[114] In 1992, the United States Environmental Protection Agency set up a voluntary labelling programme for office equipment and other appliances, called the Energy Star programme, focused on energy-saving features. The Energy Star logo was introduced for the labelling of equipment which adhered to certain rules concerning energy consumption. After observing that the Energy Star programme already established the standard for office equipment sold on the American market and the Energy Star requirements were becoming the standard worldwide, including in the Community, the Commission decided that, rather than developing a separate labelling programme, the better course was to introduce the Energy Star programme in the Community. To that effect the Community negotiated and signed the Agreement between the Government of the United States of America and the European Community on the co-ordination of energy-efficient labelling programmes for office equipment.[115]

[111] Case C–379/98 *PreussenElektra v. Schleswag* [2001] ECR I–2099.
[112] E.g. Case C–2/90 *Commission v. Belgium* [1992] ECR I–4431.
[113] Case C–155/91 *Commission v. Council* [1993] ECR I–939.
[114] Case C–281/01 *Commission v. Council* [2002] ECR I–12049.
[115] See [2001] OJ L172/1.

According to the preamble to the agreement, the contracting parties wish 'to maximize energy savings and environmental benefits by stimulating the supply of and demand for energy-efficient products'. Article I provides for the use of a common set of energy-efficiency specifications and a common logo, the latter for the purpose of identifying qualified energy-efficient product types. Under Article V manufacturers, vendors, or resale agents can enter the Energy Star labelling programme by registering with either the Commission or the US Environmental Protection Agency, which are designated as management entities responsible for implementation of the agreement. Articles VI, VII, and VIII deal with co-ordination of the Energy Star labelling programme between the contracting parties, registration of the Energy Star marks in the Community, and monitoring by each management entity of compliance with the provisions on the proper use of the Energy Star marks.

The Council concluded the agreement on the basis of (current) Article 192(1) TFEU.[116] The Commission challenged that decision, arguing that the agreement should have been concluded on the basis of (current) Article 207 TFEU.

The Court, broadly following the Opinion of Alber AG, agreed with the Commission. It first referred to its statements in *Opinion 2/00* concerning measures pursuing a twofold purpose or having a twofold component. It was not in dispute that the Energy Star Agreement was designed to co-ordinate energy-efficient labelling programmes for office equipment. Such co-ordination necessarily facilitated trade inasmuch as manufacturers needed to refer to just one standard and to comply with just one registration procedure. That co-ordination therefore undoubtedly constituted a commercial policy measure. However, it was also clear that the labelling programme in question was intended to promote energy savings and therefore in itself constituted an environmental policy measure. It followed that the agreement simultaneously pursued a commercial-policy and an environmental-protection objective, and it therefore had to be established whether either objective was the agreement's main or predominant aim, or whether the objectives pursued were inseparable without one being secondary and indirect in relation to the other.[117]

The Court then pointed out that it was clear from the terms in which the agreement was couched that the programme was essentially intended to enable manufacturers to use, in accordance with a procedure for the mutual recognition of registrations, a common logo to identify for consumers certain products complying with a common set of energy-efficiency specifications which they intended to sell on the American and Community markets. An instrument having a direct impact on trade in office equipment was therefore involved. It was true that in the long term, depending on how manufacturers and consumers in fact behaved, the programme should have a positive environmental effect. However, that was merely an indirect and distant effect, in contrast to the effect on trade in office equipment that was direct and immediate. Furthermore, the agreement did not itself contain new

[116] Council Decision 2001/469, in ibid.

[117] *Commission v. Council* (n 114 above) paras 34–39.

energy-efficiency requirements. The commercial policy objective therefore had to be regarded as predominant.[118] The Court also rejected a number of objections against that conclusion,[119] and annulled the Council decision in issue.

The Court's judgment was in line with its analysis of the TBT Agreement in *Opinion 1/94*. Technical regulations, standards, and the labelling of products, in a context of international trade, appear to have a predominant trade character.[120] If one contrasted the judgment with *Opinion 2/00*, the conclusion was clearly that the Court was reluctant to accept a dual legal basis, and preferred to establish the predominant purpose or component of an agreement (or of an autonomous measure).

The judgment in *BAT* also reaffirmed the principles concerning acts having a twofold purpose or component.[121] In issue was the validity of a directive on the approximation of the laws, regulations, and administrative provisions of the Member States concerning the manufacture, presentation, and sale of tobacco products.[122] According to the eleventh recital of the preamble, the directive would have consequences for tobacco products exported from the Community. Under Article 3(2) the provisions on maximum yield of cigarettes as regards tar, nicotine, and carbon monoxide also applied to cigarettes manufactured within, but exported from, the Community. In the light of this provision, the directive had been adopted on the basis of both (current) Articles 114 and 207 TFEU. BAT challenged this recourse to a dual legal basis. The Court examined whether such recourse was necessary or possible. It first recalled the above principles, and considered that in their light the directive could not simultaneously have (current) Articles 114 and 207 TFEU for a legal basis. Without there being any need to consider whether, in its provisions affecting tobacco products exported to non-member countries, the directive also pursued an objective linked to the implementation of the common commercial policy under (current) Article 207 TFEU, that objective was in any event secondary in relation to the aim and content of the directive as a whole, which was primarily designed to improve the conditions for the functioning of the internal market. The Court also accepted that the directive could, on the basis of (current) Article 114, regulate the manufacture of cigarettes for export with a view to avoiding circumvention of its provisions through illicit re-importation.[123]

Exceptionally, however, the Court may establish that the trade and environment objectives or components are indissociably linked, and that an act requires a dual legal basis. It did so in two parallel judgments delivered in early 2006.[124] The cases concerned the Rotterdam Convention on the prior informed consent procedure

[118] Ibid, paras 40–43. [119] *Commission v. Council* (n 114 above) paras 44–47.

[120] See also Ch 4.

[121] Case C-491/01 *The Queen v. Secretary of State for Health, ex parte British American Tobacco* [2002] ECR I-11453.

[122] Directive 2001/37 [2001] OJ L194/26.

[123] *British American Tobacco* (n 121 above) paras 81–98.

[124] Case C–94/03 *Commission v. Council* [2006] ECR I–1 and Case C–178/03 *Commission v. European Parliament and Council* [2006] ECR I–107.

for certain hazardous chemicals and pesticides in international trade;[125] and Regulation 304/2003 concerning the import and export of dangerous chemicals.[126] That regulation transposes the Rotterdam Convention, but also goes further than its provisions. In both cases the Commission had proposed that (current) Article 207 TFEU be indicated as the legal basis, but the Council had rejected that proposal, and had based the decision to conclude the convention, and the regulation, on (current) Article 192(1) TFEU. The Commission challenged the relevant Council acts. The reasoning of both Kokott AG and the Court was similar in the two cases. The analysis below focuses on the *Rotterdam Convention* case.[127]

Kokott AG started her assessment by pointing out that the choice of the correct legal basis was of considerable practical and institutional, indeed constitutional importance: it determined not only the applicable legislative procedure, but also whether the Community's competence was exclusive or shared.[128] She referred to the principles concerning the centre of gravity of a measure, as primarily resulting from *Opinion 2/00* and from the Energy Star Agreement case. She observed that, to draw a line between (current) Articles 207 and 192 TFEU, the Court had developed the criterion of 'direct and immediate effect'. If an international agreement with environmental policy aims had no direct and immediate effects on trade, it was to be based on (current) Article 192 TFEU. The direct and immediate effects did not have to consist in promoting or facilitating trade. Also instruments which were intended essentially to govern trade came within the scope of (current) Article 207 TFEU. The examination therefore had to focus on the centre of gravity of the Rotterdam Convention, in terms of its content, purpose, and context, and on whether any effects the convention could have on trade were direct and immediate.[129]

As regards the content of the convention, the Advocate General agreed with the parties that the prior informed consent (PIC) procedure constituted the nucleus of the convention. That procedure, which applied to international trade in certain chemicals, classified as hazardous, essentially provided for the mutual provision of information by the contracting parties on their individual import practices. Parties also undertook to pass the information thus received on the import practices of other parties on to economic operators within their jurisdiction, and to ensure that those practices were observed. Kokott AG noted that, as the Court held in *Opinion 2/00*, such a PIC procedure was a typical instrument of environmental policy. International trade was merely the external point of reference of the PIC procedure. The subject matter of the convention was not primarily the promotion, facilitation, or even the regulation of trade in hazardous chemicals, but only the exchange of information on import practices. The PIC procedure could at most indirectly contribute to transparency and thus possibly facilitate trade. It could

[125] [2003] OJ L63/27. [126] [2003] OJ L63/1.

[127] See also P Koutrakos, 'Legal Basis and Delimitation of Competence in EU External Relations' in M Cremona and B De Witte (eds), *EU Foreign Relations Law—Constitutional Fundamentals* (Hart Publishing, 2008) 177–80.

[128] *Commission v. Council* (n 124 above) para 24 of the Opinion. [129] Ibid, paras 30–31.

also make trade more expensive. Apart from such indirect effects, the convention essentially had no commercial policy rules as its subject matter. It did not lay down common rules for imports and exports and did not determine the conditions for importation. Nor did it provide for mutual recognition.[130]

As regards the objectives of the convention, the Advocate General considered that both Article 1 of and the preamble to the convention showed the emphasis on environmental policy concerns. It was true that the preamble also referred to international trade, but trade was more a point of attachment for the real environmental policy aims of the convention, and had no substantive position of its own among those objectives. The convention was an environmental agreement with commercial policy references, not a commercial policy agreement with environmental references. The context in which the convention was situated confirmed this analysis: the convention was based on the work of the United Nations Environment Programme and of the FAO, and showed links with the 1992 Rio Conference on Environment and Development.[131]

Kokott AG therefore concluded that the convention's centre of gravity was in the sphere of environmental policy. Its consequences for international trade were more indirect than direct.[132]

The Court, in its judgment, started by recalling the centre of gravity principles. It then stated that it could not be denied that the protection of human health and the environment was the most important concern in the mind of the signatories of the convention. This was apparent, not only from the preamble but also from the convention's actual text, in which several provisions unequivocally confirmed the importance of that objective.[133] The Court then described and analysed those provisions.

However, the Court did not leave it there. It could not be inferred from the preceding analysis that the commercial component of the convention was purely incidental. A reading of the convention and, more particularly, of its articles concerning the PIC procedure, prompted the conclusion that the convention also contained rules governing trade in hazardous chemicals and having direct and immediate effects on such trade. The Court referred to Article 1 of the convention and to the Council decision to conclude the convention, which referred respectively to 'international trade' and 'the international regulation of trade'. It was clearly therefore through the adoption of measures of a commercial nature that the parties to the convention sought to attain the objective of protecting human health and the environment. Although the PIC procedure was a typical instrument of environmental policy, its implementation under the convention was governed by provisions which directly regulated the trade in the products that it covered. The convention only applied to certain hazardous chemicals and pesticides which were traded internationally. Such an explicit link between trade and the environment was lacking in the Cartagena Protocol examined in *Opinion 2/00*. The Rotterdam Convention's

130 Ibid, paras 35–39.
131 Ibid, paras 42–44.
132 Ibid, para 45.
133 Ibid, paras 34–37 of the judgment.

PIC procedure involved a number of measures that had to be classified as measures 'governing' or 'regulating' international trade in the products concerned, and therefore falling within the scope of the common commercial policy. The Court referred to the convention's provisions on import regimes, and highlighted Article 10(9). That provision required parties that had decided not to consent to the import of a specific chemical or to consent thereto only under certain conditions, simultaneously to prohibit or to make subject to the same conditions, both the import of the chemical from any source and domestic production of the chemical for domestic use. This provision was particularly indicative of the close links in the agreement between commercial and environmental policies. In so far as that article was also concerned with domestic production, it was undeniable that it fell within the scope of the policy of protecting human health and the environment. At the same time, however, the clear commercial aspect could not be denied, since a ban or restriction imposed by the contracting parties had to apply to any imports of the products concerned, whatever their provenance. Countries not having signed the convention were therefore also covered by that provision, which was liable to have a direct impact on trade from or to those countries.[134]

The Court concluded that the convention included, both as regards the aims pursued and its contents, two indissociably linked components, neither of which could be regarded as secondary or indirect as compared with the other. The decision approving the convention should therefore have been based on (current) Articles 207 and 192(1) TFEU. That conclusion was not excluded by operation of the rule that recourse to a dual legal basis is not possible where the procedures are incompatible, or where the use of two legal bases is liable to undermine the rights of the Parliament. The relevant Treaty provisions both provided for qualified majority voting, and the right of the Parliament to be consulted was not encroached upon by using the Treaty's commercial policy provisions as a legal basis.[135] It was finally important to note that by employing a dual legal basis the Community was also giving indications to the other parties to the convention both with regard to the extent of the Community's competence and with regard to the division of competences between the Community and its Member States.[136]

In the parallel *Chemicals Regulation* case, relating to Regulation 304/2003 concerning the export and import of dangerous chemicals,[137] the Court considered that, in so far as the regulation implemented the Rotterdam Convention, the same Treaty provisions had to be used as a legal basis, given the clear convergence of the provisions of the two measures.[138] Moreover, the provisions of the regulation which went beyond those of the convention also justified recourse to (current) Articles 207 and 192(1) TFEU.[139]

[134] Ibid, paras 42–47.

[135] The legal position has changed here, as both Arts 192 and 207 TFEU now provide for the ordinary legislative procedure.

[136] *Commission v. Council* (n 124 above) paras 51–55.

[137] N 126 above.

[138] *Commission v. European Parliament and Council* (n 124 above) paras 45–47.

[139] Ibid, paras 50–51.

These two judgments showed that it is not inconceivable that the centre-of-gravity test leads to the finding that there are two indissociably linked purposes or components—commercial policy and environmental policy—and that a dual legal basis is required. The Court, however, emphasized that this is exceptional, and this may be seen to be confirmed by its latest ruling on external competence in trade and environmental matters.

Commission v. European Parliament and Council of 2009 concerned Regulation 1013/2006 on shipments of waste.[140] The facts will sound familiar by now: the regulation had been adopted on the basis of (current) Article 192(1) TFEU, but the Commission argued that (current) Article 207 TFEU should also be used as a legal basis. The regulation succeeded and updated the provisions of Regulation 259/93 on the supervision and control of shipments of waste within, into and out of the European Community.[141] That regulation was in turn adopted on the basis of (then) Article 130s EEC, which later became current Article 192 TFEU. It aimed to implement obligations under the 1989 Basel Convention on the control of transboundary movements of hazardous wastes and their disposal.[142] The challenged regulation (1013/2006) applied to shipments of waste: between Member States, within the Community, or with transit through third countries; imported into the Community from third countries; exported from the Community to third countries; or in transit through the Community, on the way from and to third countries.[143] Title II of the regulation concerned shipments of waste within the Community. The basic scheme consisted of subjecting such shipments to a procedure of prior written notification and consent. Title III concerned shipments of waste exclusively within Member States, and required that the latter establish an appropriate system for supervision and control, which took into account the need for coherence with the Community system. Title IV of the regulation concerned the scheme for exports to third countries. Certain exports of waste were prohibited, and for others the provisions of Title II applied, *mutatis mutandis*. Title V governed imports of waste from third countries, and again prohibited certain imports, as well as applying the scheme of Title II to those imports which were allowed. Title VI laid down the rules applicable to the transit of waste through the Community from and to third countries. The Commission argued that (current) Article 207 TFEU constituted the correct legal basis for Titles IV to VI.

Maduro AG first examined whether the exceptional use of a dual legal basis could be allowed in a case such as this, where one of the Treaty provisions conferred on the Community exclusive competence and where the other conferred merely shared competence. He referred in particular to the scope for Member States to continue to act in matters of environmental policy, for example pursuant to Article

[140] Case C–411/06 [2009] ECR I–7585. The regulation is published in [2006] OJ L190/1.

[141] [1993] OJ L30/1.

[142] The Basel Convention was approved on behalf of the Community by Decision 93/98 [1993] OJ L39/1.

[143] Art 1(2).

193 TFEU.[144] The question therefore had to be asked whether the competence for adopting a given measure could be of an exclusive and shared nature simultaneously. The Advocate General then looked at the *Rotterdam Convention* and the *Chemicals Regulation* cases, but emphasized that the judgments had to be read carefully. The Court was able, in his opinion, to adopt the dual legal basis approach only because it was possible to draw a clear distinction between what in those measures fell within the exclusive competence of the Community provided for by (current) Article 207 TFEU, and what fell within the shared competence conferred by (current) Article 192 TFEU. However, precisely how the Court drew that distinction, Maduro AG did not clarify. He nevertheless considered that one and the same issue could not fall within exclusive competence and shared competence. In the present case, though, the Commission had identified the provisions which it contended should be adopted on the basis of (current) Article 207 TFEU: Titles IV to VI of the regulation.[145]

Maduro AG then examined the Commission's plea, and rejected it. It was clear both from an examination of the object and aim of the regulation and from its context that its environmental dimension was predominant. He drew attention to the preamble, which already in recital 1 confirmed that 'the main and predominant objective and component of this Regulation is the protection of the environment'. Other recitals confirmed this focus on environmental protection. The object of the regulation was to impose obligations of notification, procedure, and control on shipments of waste, so that such shipments took place in conditions suitable for ensuring environmental protection. Those obligations extended to imports and exports of waste, in so far as they were not altogether prohibited. The prior written notification and consent procedure was very similar to the prior authorization procedures which the Court had termed typical instruments of environmental policy in *Opinion 2/00* and in the *Rotterdam Convention* case. The Advocate General further noted that there was an inconsistency in the Commission's argument, in so far as the Commission accepted that the provisions of the regulation on shipments of waste within the Community were correctly based on (current) Article 192 TFEU: logic would require that the regulation's scheme was intended to ensure the free movement of waste and should therefore be based on (current) Article 114 TFEU. Furthermore, the fact that the control procedures of the regulation were applicable to commercial trade in waste, and therefore liable to affect that trade, did not mean that their object was to promote, facilitate, or govern that commercial trade. If the Commission's interpretation were accepted, the Treaty provisions relating to environmental protection would be rendered largely meaningless since, as soon as it was established that a Community action was liable to affect commercial trade,

[144] Art 193 TFEU provides: 'The protective measures adopted pursuant to Article 192 shall not prevent any Member State from maintaining or introducing more stringent protective measures. Such measures must be compatible with the Treaties. They shall be notified to the Commission.'

[145] *Commission v. European Parliament and Council* (n 140 above) paras 12–14 of the Opinion.

the measure envisaged would have to fall within the scope of the common commercial policy.[146]

Nor did the Advocate General consider that the *Rotterdam Convention* and *Chemicals Regulation* cases assisted the Commission's argument. He acknowledged that there was a contradiction between the Court's approach in those cases, and its ruling in *Opinion 2/00*. A closer reading, however, showed that this was mere appearance. In the *Rotterdam Convention* case the Court emphasized the explicit link established by that convention between trade and the environment. The control procedure provided for in the convention applied only to certain hazardous chemicals and pesticides which were traded internationally and the implementation thereof was governed by provisions which directly regulated trade in goods. Such a link was lacking in the Cartagena Protocol. In the case under consideration the prior written notification and consent procedure did not govern only extra-Community shipments of waste, but concerned first and foremost intra-Community shipments.[147]

The Court followed the Advocate General's Opinion. It found that the objective and components of the regulation relating to the protection of the environment had to be regarded as being the main or predominant objective and component. As regards the objectives, the Court noted the various references in the preamble to environmental protection, and observed that the preamble did not make any reference to the pursuit of objectives falling within the common commercial policy.[148] As regards the content of the regulation, the Court analysed the regulation's principal instrument: the prior written notification and consent procedure. It established that, like the PIC procedure established by the Cartagena Protocol on Biosafety, the procedure provided for by the contested regulation could be described as a typical instrument of environmental policy. The Court noted that the procedure also applied to shipments of waste between the Community and third countries in cases where exports or imports of waste were not prohibited. The Court further pointed to Article 49 of the regulation, which imposed an obligation on those involved in the shipment of waste to take 'the necessary steps to ensure that any waste they ship is managed without endangering human health and in an environmentally sound manner . . . '. That obligation, general in nature, applied to all shipments, including those between the Community and third countries. The Court also pointed out that the prior written notification and consent procedure clearly pursued an environmental protection purpose in the field of shipments of waste between the Member States, and was therefore correctly based on (current) Article 192(1) TFEU. It would not be coherent to consider that the same procedure, when it applied to shipments of waste between Member States and third countries with the same environmental protection objective, was in the nature of an instrument of common commercial policy.[149]

[146] Ibid, paras 16–24. [147] Ibid, paras 27–30.
[148] Ibid, paras 49–54 of the judgment. [149] Ibid, paras 55–63.

An examination of the legislative context of the regulation confirmed that analysis. The regulation replaced Regulation 259/93, which had been based on Article 130s EEC (the predecessor to current Article 192 TFEU), a choice of legal basis which the Court had endorsed.[150] The regulation further aimed to implement the Basel Convention, which had a clear environmental purpose. The fact that the regulation went beyond the Basel Convention by extending to non-hazardous waste and to waste intended for recovery did not make it commercial or weaken its environmental dimension, since waste, of whatever type, was inherently harmful to the environment.[151]

The Court concluded its examination by rejecting Commission arguments to the effect that waste constituted goods which could be the object of commercial transactions, and that the notion of commercial policy should be interpreted broadly. The Court pointed out that the regulation defined the terms 'shipment' and 'import' and 'export' in a neutral manner, thereby emphasizing the carriage of waste with a view to its treatment rather than carriage for commercial purposes. A broad interpretation of the concept of common commercial policy did not call into question the finding that the regulation was an instrument falling principally under environmental policy: a Community act could fall within that area, even if the measures provided for by that act were liable to affect trade. A Community act fell within the exclusive competence in the field of the common commercial policy only if it related specifically to international trade in that it was essentially intended to promote, facilitate, or govern trade and had direct and immediate effects on trade in the products concerned. The Court also rejected the argument that it should follow the same approach as in the *Chemicals Regulation* case. That regulation contained components of commercial policy absent from the regulation on shipments of waste.[152]

How should one assess the case law since *Opinion 2/00*? The core principles have not changed: the centre-of-gravity test emphasizes the predominant purpose and component, and it is only exceptionally that a dual legal basis is justified. The exception is not, however, mere theory, as the *Rotterdam Convention* and *Chemicals Regulation* judgments show. In addition, the Court now also looks at whether an act relates specifically to international trade in that it is intended to promote, facilitate, or govern trade and has direct and immediate effects on trade in the products concerned.[153]

These are helpful clarifications. On the other hand, the judgments show that the line between commercial policy and environmental policy is ever more difficult to draw. Essentially one and the same mechanism, the PIC procedure is at the heart

[150] Case C–187/93 *Parliament v. Council* [1994] ECR I–2857.

[151] *Commission v. European Parliament and Council* (n 140 above) paras 64–67.

[152] Ibid, paras 68–76.

[153] See also Case C–347/03 *ERSA v. Ministero delle Politiche Agricole e Forestali* [2005] ECR I–3785, para 75.

of the legal instruments in *Opinion 2/00*, the *Rotterdam Convention* and *Chemicals Regulation* judgments, and the *Shipments of Waste* judgment. And yet the Court decides that in one set of cases, the legal acts were rightly adopted on the basis of (current) Article 192(1) TFEU, whereas in the other set it was necessary to base the acts also on (current) Article 207 TFEU. That is not to say that the Court was incorrect in finding a commercial component in the Rotterdam Convention and in the Chemicals Regulation. It is true that those instruments have a stronger trade focus, as they apply to actual international trade in chemicals. The Cartagena Protocol and the Shipments of Waste Regulation, by contrast, apply to all types of movement and shipment, and their effect on trade may therefore be seen to be more indirect. However, to some degree this is a matter of formulation, legislative technique, and product scope. The Rotterdam Convention and the Chemicals Regulation could also be drafted as applying to all 'movements', and not just 'trade', without thereby becoming fundamentally different instruments. All four legal acts which were the subject of the four rulings referred to have the same basic purpose—to protect the environment. They use very similar techniques and mechanisms to attain that objective, and they all have effects on trade. Precisely how 'direct' or 'indirect' those effects are, is difficult to determine. There appears to be a fine line between an act which has predominant environmental objectives and components, and only incidental effects on trade, and an act in which environmental policy and commercial policy are indissociably linked.

The question may be asked whether it really matters if that line is drawn. In terms of legislative procedure the Treaty of Lisbon aligns the common commercial policy with environmental policy: Articles 192 and 207 TFEU both provide for the ordinary legislative procedure. The procedure for concluding international agreements in these respective areas of policy-making is very similar.[154] For procedural purposes it will no longer be significant to distinguish between commercial policy and environmental policy. That only leaves the distinction between exclusive and shared competences. This is emphasized by Kokott AG and Maduro AG,[155] and the Court alludes to it in the *Rotterdam Convention* judgment when it states that a dual legal basis gives indications to the other parties to the convention both with regard to the extent of Community competence and with regard to the division of competences between the Community and its Member States.[156] Maduro AG rightly points out that the nature of the EU's competence has a considerable effect on the residual competence of the Member States. Exclusive competence precludes any legislative action by the Member States, except where they act as trustees of the common interest to avoid a legislative lacuna. But where competence is shared, the Member States remain free to legislate as long as their measures do not interfere

[154] See Art 218 TFEU, and the special provisions of Art 207(3) and (4) TFEU as regards the common commercial policy; see further Ch 6.

[155] Respectively, *Commission v. Council* (*Rotterdam Convention* case, n 124 above) para 24 of the Opinion; and *Commission v. European Parliament and Council* (*Shipments of Waste* case, n 124 above) para 12 of the Opinion.

[156] *Commission v. Council* (n 124 above) para 55.

with the effectiveness of EU rules.[157] Indeed, in theoretical terms the distinction between exclusive and shared competences is fundamental. However, whether it matters so much in practice in cases such as those under discussion may be more doubtful. These are not cases where the question is whether the EU must act, or whether the Member States can act on their own. The decision in favour of an EU act has been taken, and the issue concerns the correct legal basis in the Treaties. Also in the sphere of environmental policy, Member States are often precluded from acting because the EU has occupied the field, and has exclusive implied powers.[158] Even where such powers are not present, the duty of loyal co-operation, embodied in Article 4(3) TEU, will often restrain Member States in ways which are not dissimilar to the effects of exclusive competence.[159]

One therefore wonders whether this area of EU external relations law could not be pacified by a legal-basis formula which reflects the difficulty of drawing the line. Such a formula could, for example, provide that an act with a clear environmental purpose and component, but which also has effects on trade, is based on Article 192(1) TFEU, and on Article 207 TFEU only 'to the extent that the measures provided for have effects on trade which are more than incidental, and are direct and immediate'.

The Treaty of Lisbon

The Treaty of Lisbon substantially amended the Treaty provisions on the common commercial policy, both in terms of substance and of decision-making mechanisms (see Article 207 TFEU).[160] It followed the more timid attempts of the Treaties of Amsterdam and Nice to expand the common commercial policy to include trade in services and the commercial aspects of intellectual property rights—in other words to match the EU's trade policy with the subject matter of the WTO agreements. The Treaty of Lisbon completes this process. It further introduces new competences for foreign direct investment, and confirms, as stated above, the exclusive character of the competences conferred on the EU in the area of the common commercial policy (Article 3(1)(e) TFEU). The decision-making mechanism is subjected to a Copernican revolution: whereas the former Treaty versions did not provide for any legislative role for the European Parliament, the common commercial policy

[157] *Commission v. European Parliament and Council* (n 140 above) para 12 of the Opinion. The Advocate General also referred to (current) Art 193 TFEU, which allows Member States to adopt more stringent measures of environmental protection than those provided by Community acts.

[158] See Ch 3.

[159] See Ch 7.

[160] See also M Krajewski, 'External Trade Law and the Constitution Treaty: Towards a Federal and More Democratic Common Commercial Policy?' (2005) 42 CML Rev 91; P-C Müller-Graff, 'The Common Commercial Policy enhanced by the Reform Treaty of Lisbon?' in A Dashwood and M Maresceau, *Law and Practice of EU External Relations* (CUP, 2008) 188.

is now subject to the ordinary legislative procedure, with full involvement of the Parliament. The analysis below focuses on the substantive amendments.[161]

It is also worth pointing out that the new Article 3 TEU, which sets out the EU's overall objectives, speaks in paragraph 5 about relations with the wider world, in which the Union 'shall contribute to ... free and fair trade'. Those concepts are not further defined, and it is in particular unclear what is meant by fair trade. In trade policy circles that notion has traditionally been used as a reference to certain trade protection instruments such as anti-dumping and anti-subsidy.[162] If that is the intended meaning of fair trade, the TEU would be emphasizing a rather protectionist dimension of commercial policy. It is, however, difficult to see any particular reasons for such an arguably retrograde step. The reference to fair trade is more naturally read as an instruction to take account of the interests of developing countries in the international trading system, because the reference is juxtaposed to 'the sustainable development of the earth', 'solidarity and mutual respect among peoples', and 'eradication of poverty and protection of human rights, in particular the rights of the child'. A veiled reference to protectionism seems very much out of kilter with those lofty ideals. No further reference to fair trade is made in the more detailed provisions on external action in Article 21 TEU. Paragraph 2 contains a more detailed list of objectives, which includes under letter (e) 'the integration of all countries into the world economy, including through the progressive abolition of restrictions on international trade'.

Trade in services and the commercial aspects of intellectual property

Article 207(1) TFEU makes reference to 'the conclusion of tariff and trade agreements relating to trade in goods and services, and the commercial aspects of intellectual property'. The concepts of 'services' and 'the commercial aspects of intellectual property' are not further defined, but it is clear from the context of the various Treaty amendments (Amsterdam, Nice, the Constitution for Europe, and Lisbon) that they refer to trade in services as defined in GATS and trade-related aspects of intellectual property rights as regulated in TRIPs. As regards GATS, this is confirmed by *Opinion 1/08*, which concerned agreements modifying the Schedules of Specific Commitments of the Community and its Member States under GATS, following the accession of new Member States to the EU. The Opinion is of limited relevance, as it was delivered on the last day before the Treaty of Lisbon entered into force, and therefore focused on the complex provisions of (then) Article 133 EC, as amended by the Nice Treaty. However, the Nice version of Article 133 EC already extended the common commercial policy, in paragraph 5, to 'the negotiation and conclusion of agreements in the fields of trade in services and the

[161] See further Ch 10. [162] On those policies see Ch 10.

commercial aspects of intellectual property'—Treaty language which is very similar to that of current Article 207(1) TFEU. The Court simply established that, next to services supplied under mode 1 of GATS, the Community was now also competent to conclude, under the common commercial policy, international agreements relating to trade in services supplied under modes 2 to 4.[163]

The common commercial policy, post-Lisbon, therefore matches the three pillars of the WTO: agreements on trade in goods (including GATT 1994), GATS, and TRIPs. It would therefore appear that all WTO matters are within the EU's exclusive competence. There is one exception, however. Article 207(5) TFEU provides that 'the negotiation and conclusion of international agreements in the field of transport shall be subject to Title VI of Part Three and to Article 218'. Title VI of Part Three concerns the common transport policy, an area of shared competence (Article 4(2)(g) TFEU). This means that WTO negotiations and agreements concerning transport services are not within the EU's exclusive competence (except in so far as the EU's implied powers in this field are exclusive in nature—see the next chapter). In *Opinion 1/08* the Court clarified, in relation to the similar provision in (then) Article 133(6), third subparagraph, EC, that the scope of that provision was not limited to agreements which were exclusively or predominantly concerned with transport, but extended to horizontal agreements (such as the modifications of the GATS Schedules in issue in the Opinion).[164]

It is clear, moreover, that the WTO may, in future, become involved in areas of policy-making, such as competition policy, which are not within the scope of the common commercial policy.

Article 207(1) TFEU refers only to the conclusion of agreements regarding services and the commercial aspects of intellectual property. There can be little doubt, however, that the EU is also capable of adopting internal 'autonomous' measures in these matters. As the Court stated in *Opinion 1/78*, the enumeration in what is now Article 207(1) is not exhaustive.[165] In *Opinion 1/75* the Court rightly emphasized that a commercial policy is made up by the combination and interaction of internal and external measures, without priority being taken by one over the others.[166] There is no reason to abandon those principles.

There may of course be questions about the precise delimitation of the concepts of trade in services, and the commercial aspects of intellectual property, in particular with respect to negotiations outside the framework of the WTO or for the adoption of EU legislation. In the light of the antecedents of these Treaty provisions, GATS and TRIPs are surely a guide for the interpretation of Article 207(1) TFEU. That may not prevent difficult questions from arising, in particular as regards the concept of 'commercial aspects of intellectual property'. As described above, the TRIPs Agreement effectively constitutes an attempt at worldwide harmonization

[163] *Opinion 1/08 re GATS Schedules* [2009] ECR I-11129, para 119.
[164] Ibid, paras 155–173. [165] N 21 above. [166] N 11 above.

of intellectual property laws. The dividing line between 'commercial aspects' and pure harmonization is therefore hard to draw.

This may be one reason for the final paragraph of Article 207 TFEU, which sets out limitations to the EU's competences under the common commercial policy. Article 207(6) TFEU provides:

> The exercise of the competences conferred by this Article in the field of the common commercial policy shall not affect the delimitation of competences between the Union and the Member States, and shall not lead to harmonization of legislative or regulatory provisions of the Member States insofar as the Treaties exclude such harmonization.

The second part of this provision is easier to interpret than the first. There is now a series of provisions in the TFEU which, in a number of areas of EU policy-making, expressly exclude harmonization of the laws and regulations of the Member States.[167] EU legislation and agreements under the common commercial policy cannot lead to harmonization of the laws and regulations of the Member States in areas such as education, culture, and health. These areas are relevant for GATS, but it is not easy to see in what way GATS commitments, which are in the nature of providing market access and national treatment, could lead to harmonization of the laws of the Member States. The fact that the Member States may need to ensure market access for certain health services, or national treatment (non-discrimination) for educational services, is not equivalent to legislative or regulatory harmonization.

The first part of Article 217(6) TFEU is more enigmatic. The exercise of competences under the common commercial policy shall not affect the delimitation of competences between the EU and the Member States. This is similar, but by no means identical, to the opening phrase of former Article 133(6), first subparagraph, EC, which provided: 'An agreement may not be concluded by the Council if it includes provisions which would go beyond the Community's internal powers'. In a pending case, regarding Vietnam's accession to the WTO, Kokott AG offered a detailed analysis of Article 133(6), first subparagraph. Its meaning and purpose, in her opinion, was, very generally, to put the Community's internal and external powers on a parallel footing and to prevent the Community from entering into external commitments to which it would be unable to give effect internally for want of sufficient powers. She applied that principle to certain elements of the WTO agreements. One of them concerned the EU's GATS commitments, which included restrictions on access to market for mode 3 (commercial presence) hospital services, which themselves included approval requirements in the framework of national health-care systems and in some cases also an economic needs test. She contrasted those commitments with the provisions of (then) Article 152(5) EC, which provided that Community action

[167] Art 19(2) TFEU (incentive measures anti-discrimination policies); Art 79(4) TFEU (integration of immigrants); Art 84 TFEU (crime prevention); Art 153(2) TFEU (social policy co-operation); Arts 165(4) and 166(4) TFEU (education and vocational training); Art 167(5) TFEU (culture); Art 168(5) TFEU (health); Art 173(2) TFEU (industry); Art 189(2) TFEU (space policy); Art 195(2) TFEU (tourism); Art 196(2) TFEU (civil protection); Article 197(2) TFEU (administrative co-operation).

in the field of public health should fully respect the responsibilities of the Member States for the organization and delivery of health services and medical care.[168] She concluded from this that the Community had no internal power within the meaning of Article 133(6) in relation, at least, to some of the market-access rules applying to hospital services. The same conclusion was reached for Article 61 TRIPs, which obliges WTO members to provide for criminal procedures and penalties for certain cases of counterfeiting or copyright piracy, and which refers to imprisonment and/or monetary fines. As Community law stood, the requirements of this provision went beyond the Community's internal powers.[169]

The present version of Article 207(6) TFEU does not refer to the notion of parallelism between external and internal powers. It applies to any commercial policy acts, legislative or conventional, and their exercise cannot affect the delimitation of competences generally.[170] It therefore remains to be seen whether the approach of Kokott AG, which at the time of writing the Court had not yet endorsed or rejected, can be extended to the new provision. In terms, the opening phrase of Article 207(6) TFEU appears to do no more than confirm the principle of conferral, set out in Article 5 TEU.

The last point to be mentioned here in relation to the new version of Article 207 TFEU is that paragraph 4 contains an exception to qualified majority decision-making. Unanimity is required for certain categories of agreements. They include, first of all, agreements in the fields of trade in services and the commercial aspects of intellectual property, as well as foreign direct investment, where such agreements include provisions for which unanimity is required for the adoption of internal rules. This provision appears to operate a dichotomy between internal and international action. The presumption is that the internal rules referred to are based on provisions in the Treaties, other than Article 207 TFEU, and require unanimity. The logic is that such unanimity is then extended to international action, thus preventing what might be seen as circumvention of the 'internal' unanimity requirement through external action subject to qualified majority voting. This subparagraph appears to confuse trade policy powers with implied powers. The circumstances to which it refers are such that under the doctrine of implied powers the Treaty provision giving 'internal' powers to the EU would have to be the legal basis for external action. The provision suggests that that is no longer the case, without clarifying its relationship with the doctrine of implied powers.

Unanimity is also required for agreements in the field of trade in cultural and audiovisual services, where these agreements risk prejudicing the Union's cultural and linguistic diversity; and for agreements in the field of trade in social, education, and health services, where these agreements risk seriously disturbing the national

[168] See at present Art 168(7) TFEU.

[169] Case C–13/07 *Commission v. Council*, Opinion of 26 March 2009, not yet reported, paras 142–156.

[170] *Contra* Krajewski (n 160 above), who at 115–18 argues that the phrase should be understood as limiting the internal, legislative competence of the EU and not its external, treaty-making competence.

organization of such services and prejudicing the responsibility of Member States to deliver them. These provisions may have been inspired by concerns over the negative effects of globalization on national institutions and governance structures, and the reluctance of Member States to lose control over the conclusion of international agreements which might interfere with such institutions and structures.

Foreign direct investment

From the entry into force of the Treaty of Lisbon, the common commercial policy extends to 'foreign direct investment' (Article 207(1) TFEU), and aims at the progressive abolition of restrictions on such investment (Article 206 TFEU). Given the exclusive nature of the commercial policy competence, this constitutes one of the most important expansions of the EU's competences in the whole of the Lisbon Treaty.[171]

The origins of this new provision lie, as is the case for most of the Lisbon Treaty, in the ill-fated Constitution for Europe. The proceedings of the Convention which drafted the Constitution do not shed much light on the purpose or scope of the new powers.[172] It is clear, though, that, for quite some time, the EU's external economic policies have included investment-related issues. The original plans for the Uruguay Round had a strong focus on investment, but the Round only produced the Agreement on Trade-Related Investment Measures (TRIMs) as a specific investment instrument. The EU was then involved in the (also ill-fated) OECD negotiations on a Multilateral Agreement on Investment. Bilateral agreements concluded by the EU often include provisions on establishment or investment.[173]

As a matter of fact, the common commercial policy has included some investment matters for a number of years now—since the Treaty of Nice expanded it to trade in services. GATS mode 3 involves, as will be recalled, the supply of services through commercial presence (Article 1(2)(c)), which means any type of business or professional establishment (Article XXVIII(d)). GATS includes commitments as regards both market access and national treatment for mode 3, so effectively covers certain forms of investment in the services sector. Where a WTO member enters into full commitments under mode 3, it is required to provide access to its market for foreign services companies and to ensure non-discrimination (national treatment) of such companies. This extension to what is effectively investment flows

[171] See generally J Ceyssens, 'Towards a Common Foreign Investment Policy? Foreign Investment in the European Constitution' (2005) 32 LIEI 259; A Radu, 'Foreign Investors in the EU—Which "Best Treatment"? Interactions Between Bilateral Investment Treaties and EU Law' (2008) 14 ELJ 237; L Mola, 'Which Role for the EU in the Development of International Investment Law?', Society of International Law Working Paper No 26/08; T Eilmansberger, 'Bilateral Investment Treaties and EU Law' (2009) 46 CML Rev 383; M Bungenberg, 'Going Global? The EU Common Commercial Policy After Lisbon' in C Hermann and JP Terhechte (eds) (2010) 1 *European Yearbook of International Economic Law* 135–51.

[172] Ceyssens (n 171 above) 273. [173] Ibid, 265–8.

from the broad conception of international trade in services. As services are intangible, the goal of trade liberalization of necessity requires a focus, not just on the products themselves, but also on the persons or companies supplying them. To some extent, this justifies the difference in treatment in WTO law between investment issues in the services sector—included in GATS and in the common commercial policy—and those in the goods sector—limited to TRIMs. However, as globalization progresses, trade and investment matters are increasingly entwined, and newer forms of protectionism are often investment-related.[174] From that perspective, the inclusion of foreign direct investment in the common commercial policy makes a lot of sense. From an international perspective, on the other hand, trade and investment have also to some extent developed as parallel universes. There is no broad-based multilateral agreement on investment. Instead, States increasingly conclude and apply bilateral investment treaties (BITs), which typically include many forms of investment and of investment protection, and provide for investor-State arbitration, which stands in stark contrast to inter-State trade dispute settlement. The Commission reports that EU Member States have concluded close to 1,200 BITs with non-member countries.[175] It is thus clear that a common policy on investment cannot be produced overnight, and that a lot of work and time will be required to transform Member State policies into an EU policy. It is also clear that the question of the scope of the EU's new powers is vital.

Articles 206 and 207 TFEU speak of 'foreign direct investment'. The term 'foreign' no doubt refers to investments from the EU into third countries, and to investments by third-country nationals or companies in the EU. This conforms to the logic of the common commercial policy, which regulates both imports and exports. The term 'direct investment', on the other hand, is not a new concept in EU law. Article 64 TFEU, part of the chapter on capital and payments, employs it. As is well known, the Treaty provides in Article 63 for the free movement of capital and payments between Member States, and between Member States and third countries. This is without prejudice, however, to existing restrictions 'in respect of the movement of capital to or from third countries involving direct investment—including in real estate' (Article 64(1) TFEU). The EU legislator can also adopt measures on capital movement involving direct investment (Article 64(2) TFEU). The Court of Justice has interpreted the concept of direct investment to mean 'investments of any kind undertaken by natural or legal persons and which serve to establish or maintain lasting and direct links between the persons providing the capital and the undertakings to which that capital is made available in order to carry out an economic activity'.[176] That definition is based on an older capital

[174] Cf P Eeckhout, 'The Scales of Trade—Reflections on the Growth and Functions of the WTO Adjudicative Branch' (2010) 13 JIEL 4.

[175] Communication from the Commission, *Towards a comprehensive European international investment policy*, COM(2010)343 final, at 4.

[176] See e.g. Case C–446/04 *Test Claimants in the FII Group Litigation* [2006] ECR I–11753, para 181.

movement directive,[177] which in turn corresponds to widely accepted definitions of the IMF and the OECD.[178] The Court distinguishes between direct investment and portfolio investment: the former includes 'investments in the form of participation in an undertaking through the holding of shares which confers the possibility of effectively participating in its management and control', whereas the latter involves 'investments in the form of the acquisition of shares on the capital market solely with the intention of making a financial investment without any intention to influence the management and control of the undertaking'.[179]

The distinction is clearly transposable to the notion of foreign direct investment in Article 207(1) TFEU. It is important for the purpose of determining to what extent the new commercial policy competence covers forms of investment protected under standard BITs. The latter, indeed, often extend to portfolio investment in the sense of short-term financial participation in undertakings, as well as the mere enjoyment of movable and immovable property, intellectual property rights, and monetary claims under contracts. In its recent Communication the Commission also distinguishes between direct investment and portfolio investment.[180] Therefore, without it being necessary at this stage to offer a complete definition of the notion of foreign direct investment, it is clear that it does not encompass all forms of investment which are covered by standard BITs concluded by Member States. Thus, for these BITs to be fully substituted by EU investment agreements, there needs to be a further legal basis in the Treaties. Chapter 4 explores the extent to which the TFEU provisions on the internal market provide further treaty-making powers, which may complement Article 207.

A further question is what types of measures affecting foreign direct investment come within the new powers. There is no need to produce a typology or definition of such measures. Standard BITs contain a number of basic norms, and the EU's policy will no doubt build on those BITs and also attempt to employ those norms.[181] They include: most-favoured-nation and national treatment; fair and equitable treatment; full security and protection; and protection from unlawful expropriation.[182] In the literature it has been argued that a distinction needs to be made between investment liberalization (market access), covered by the new competence, and the standards of protection listed above, which all concern the post-investment phase, and would not be included.[183] That argument is not convincing. It is clear that, for the purpose of making investment decisions, economic actors are

[177] Directive 88/361 for the implementation of Article 67 of the Treaty [1988] OJ L178/5.

[178] See further Commission Communication (n 175 above) footnote 4, and Ceyssens (n 171 above) 274.

[179] See lastly Case C–171/08 *Commission v. Portugal*, judgment of 8 July 2010, para 49, with further references.

[180] Commission Communication (n 175 above) 3. See also Ceyssens (n 171 above) 274–5; Eilmansberger (n 171 above) 394; Bungenberg (n 171 above) 147; J-C Piris, *The Lisbon Treaty—A Legal and Political Analysis* (CUP, 2010) 282.

[181] The Commission Communication (n 175 above) also emphasizes continuity, at 5–6.

[182] Ibid, 8.

[183] Krajewski (n 160 above) 112–14.

not only concerned about access to the relevant market, but are equally interested in legal stability post-investment. Moreover, GATS mode 3, which is within the scope of Article 207 TFEU, already extends to post-investment protection: commitments are made providing for both market access and national treatment of foreign service suppliers with a commercial presence in the EU. The EU clearly could not pursue a meaningful and effective policy on foreign direct investment if it were unable to negotiate on standards of post-investment protection.[184] In this respect, it makes little sense to distinguish between the various norms referred to above. In so far as the relevant investments are covered by the notion of 'foreign direct investment', there is little justification for limiting EU competence, for example, to providing for national treatment, and not fair and equitable treatment, or full security and protection. The international practice, which is as we have seen a relevant consideration for determining the scope of the common commercial policy, supports such a broad approach.

However, there is one possible limitation which is worth exploring a little further. Standard BITs often offer protection from expropriation, and it has been contended that the effect of Article 345 TFEU is to exclude EU competence to conclude investment agreements offering such protection. Article 345 provides that the Treaties shall in no way prejudice the rules in Member States governing the system of property ownership. On its face this provision may seem restrictive, but the Court of Justice has rarely, if ever, accepted arguments based on this provision, although such arguments are frequently put forward. In *Ospelt*, for example, a case concerning free movement of capital and Austrian legislation on a prior authorization procedure for the acquisition of agricultural and forestry plots, the Court recalled that the systems of ownership remained subject to the fundamental rules of Community law, including those of non-discrimination, freedom of establishment, and free movement of capital.[185] It is true that that principle is not as such applicable to the issue before us, which is one of EU competence, and not of compatibility of Member State legislation with fundamental rules in the EU Treaties. However, also where the EU's legislative activity is involved, the Court has not been willing to construe Article 345 as a strict limitation. *Spain v. Council* concerned a challenge to a regulation concerning the creation of a supplementary protection certificate for medicinal products (effectively providing for the extension of patent protection for pharmaceutical products to take account of time lost for the purpose of obtaining an authorization to put the products on the market).[186] Spain argued that the Community had no power to regulate substantive patent law, and could harmonize only those aspects relating to the exercise of industrial property

[184] Ceyssens (n 171 above) 277; Eilmansberger (n 171 above) 395.

[185] Case C–452/01 *Ospelt v. Schlössle Weissenberg Familienstiftung* [2003] ECR I–9743, para 24, with reference to Case 182/83 *Fearon* [1984] ECR 3677, para 7 and Case C–302/97 *Konle* [1999] ECR I–3099, para 38.

[186] Regulation 1768/92 concerning the creation of a supplementary protection certificate for medicinal products [1992] OJ L182/1.

rights which were capable of having an effect upon the achievement of the general objectives laid down in the Treaty. Such action could not take the form of a new industrial property right. The Court replied that (current) Article 345 TFEU did not reserve a power to regulate substantive patent law to the national legislature, to the exclusion of any Community action in the matter.[187] The analysis of Jacobs AG was a little more extensive. Referring to past case law, he was of the opinion that the Court had made it clear that the argument of exclusive national competence for matters covered by (current) Article 345 TFEU was not correct, and he saw no reason why that conclusion would not also be valid for the exercise of Community competence.[188]

Furthermore, in so far as provisions in investment treaties protect from unlawful expropriation by providing for adequate compensation, they are in conformity with general principles of EU law. The right to property is such a general principle and is protected by Article 17 of the EU Charter of Fundamental Rights. Certain types of interference with this right may require compensation, and the Court has also recognized, in a case where Community law required the destruction of infected fish on a fish farm, that the Community could consider, in the context of its broad discretion in the field of agricultural policy, that full or partial compensation was appropriate for owners of farms on which animals had been slaughtered and destroyed.[189] If compensation can be provided for within the context of the EU's agricultural policy, it is difficult to see on what grounds investment agreements concluded by the EU would be precluded from doing so.

To conclude, the EU's new competence extends to all the forms of protection which are current in modern international investment law, but not to all forms of investment. As mentioned above, Chapter 4 will explore whether other Treaty provisions complement the common commercial policy competences.

It is in any event clear that at least a number of matters traditionally regulated in BITs concluded by Member States are now within the EU's exclusive competence under Article 207 TFEU. This raises questions about the validity and fate of the close to 1,200 BITs which Member States have concluded prior to the entry into force of the Lisbon Treaty. At the time of writing, the Commission had made a proposal for a regulation establishing transitional arrangements for bilateral investment agreements between Member States and third countries. In the explanatory memorandum the Commission admits that the extent to which those existing agreements are incompatible with EU law can be the subject of discussions. However, to avoid any legal uncertainty, the Commission considers that a system for authorizing the maintenance in force of those agreements should be set up.[190] This

[187] Case C–350/92 *Spain v. Council* [1995] ECR I–1985, paras 13–22.

[188] Ibid, Opinion Jacobs AG, para 28.

[189] Joined Cases C–20 and 64/00 *Booker Aquaculture v. The Scottish Ministers* [2003] ECR I–7411, para 85.

[190] Commission proposal for a Regulation establishing transitional arrangements for bilateral investment agreements between Member States and third countries, COM(2010)344 final, at 3.

calls for some further comments. Clearly, under international law the validity of the existing agreements cannot be affected by EU law. The Lisbon Treaty cannot have the effect of modifying treaties between Member States and third countries, without the latter's consent. It is, moreover, doubtful that, even under EU law, the existing agreements became invalid on 1 December 2009, since, at the time of their adoption, there was no exclusive EU competence. Be that as it may, it is indeed preferable to provide for legal certainty.

Furthermore, the proposed regulation would enable the Commission also to authorize Member States to amend an existing agreement, or even to conclude a new one. The details of the proposed scheme need not concern us here. The principle is clearly in conformity with Article 2(1) TFEU, which provides that Member States may act in areas of exclusive EU competence 'only if so empowered by the Union'.

Conclusions

On the basis of the EEC Treaty provisions on a common commercial policy, the Court of Justice has been able to construct a firm doctrine of exclusive Community competence, not limited to the internal sphere of adopting 'autonomous' acts but extending to the conclusion of agreements with third countries. The growth of international trade, the expansion of GATT, in terms of both membership and subject matter, the creation of the WTO with its beyond-trade agenda, and the proliferation of regional trade agreements, which was first championed by the Community but is now a general phenomenon, have all contributed to making trade policy the hard core of the EU's external action. The Community's exclusive competence in trade matters thrust the Community onto the international scene, as an ineluctable partner for all countries wishing to trade with Europe. The EEC Treaty provisions on a common commercial policy were thus the very constitutional origin of EU external relations, and they were constitutionalized through the Court's interpretation, which interjected the notions of competence, exclusivity, and authorization,[191] thereby creating a Community territory in the realm of international relations.

As was pointed out, the Court created such territory with respect for national competence, through an approach which was both principled and pragmatic.[192] It left room for national legislation and measures, and for Member States' membership of the WTO, by using various legal devices, such as disconnecting financing, introducing the concept of authorization, adopting broad interpretations of exceptions contained in EC legislation, and limiting the scope of the Treaty concept of commercial policy in comparison with international developments and conceptions. At the same time, the Court's emphasis on exclusivity required some measure

[191] See further Ch 10.

[192] Tridimas and Eeckhout (n 10 above).

of Community involvement in all trade-related matters, effectively rendering the Community institutions the locus of decision-making on international trade.

The most notable and noted development has been the Court's refusal to allow the notion of commercial policy to expand so as to cover the entire WTO agenda. A majority of commentators took the view that *Opinion 1/94* was less bold than the Court's previous rulings.[193] This author does not agree. At most, the Court could have gone further as regards services, by adopting the internal-market logic of treating both goods and services as traded products, and by recognizing that both forms of trade require a unified external policy so as to avoid deflections of trade and distortions of competition. To decide, however, that the entire TRIPs agreement came within exclusive Community competence would have signified that any regulatory matter could, simply by using the trade label in an international negotiation, be transferred to EU legal territory. The halt which the Court called to the coextensive character of the common commercial policy and international trade policy was justified from a constitutional perspective, given the strong (exclusive) traits of EU competence. Managing to attach a trade label to an international negotiation or bringing a subject of economic (or even non-economic) regulation within the sphere of the WTO is not going to be sufficient to decree a transfer of powers from the national to the EU level.

In calling this halt the Court recognized the limits of the concepts contained in the original EEC Treaty, and opened up a space for constitutional development through express amendment. In other matters, too, there are examples of such judicial behaviour.[194] Constitutional amendment has indeed been taking place, and the Treaty of Lisbon actually confirmed the way in which institutional practice has moved away from the complex mixity which *Opinion 1/94* seemed to inaugurate.[195] The new Article 207 TFEU may seem to introduce a significant expansion of the commercial policy concept, but in effect it does little more than confirm that, at least as regards WTO matters and negotiations, competence, not in a legal but in a material sense, already lies with the EU institutions. They are the locus of decision-making, and the debate about national competence is really one about modalities of decision-making (unanimity or qualified majority), token sovereignty, and political carve-outs.

In the complex and, at heart, artificial exercise of delineating trade and non-trade policies the Court has managed to develop a convincing and balanced approach, both as regards trade-and-environment and trade-and-foreign policy. In this area, too, the Treaty of Lisbon may be able to pacify, at least as regards

[193] E.g. Kaddous (n 6 above).

[194] See, as regards accession to the ECHR, *Opinion 2/94* [1996] ECR I–1759, discussed in Ch 3, and A Arnull, 'Left to Its Own Devices? Opinion 2/94 and the Protection of Fundamental Rights in the European Union' in A Dashwood and C Hillion (eds), *The General Law of EC External Relations* (Sweet & Maxwell, 2000) 67; as regards standing in an action for annulment by private parties see Case C–50/00P *UPA v. Council* [2002] ECR I–6677.

[195] On mixity see Ch 7.

trade-and-environment policy, by harmonizing both legislative procedure across different legal bases in the TFEU and the procedure for negotiating and concluding international agreements. The distinction between exclusive and shared powers will remain, necessitating knowledge of the scope of the common commercial policy so as to determine what in any event needs to be decided at EU level; but whether, for example, a particular agreement is a trade or an environmental agreement may not matter much once the EU has decided to sign and conclude it. Overall, the Court has not taken sides in the battle between the institutions, and their scholastic positions. The Court focuses on both the aims and the content of a measure or an agreement. It is true that a measure or agreement which has trade clearly as its object is not removed from the scope of the common commercial policy by reasons of the non-commercial objectives which it pursues. However, that preponderance of the content of the measure or agreement is compensated by the emphasis on the need for it to have direct and immediate effects on trade.

The Treaty of Lisbon has, significantly, expanded the common commercial policy to foreign direct investment. It seems clear, however, that that notion does not cover all forms of investment regulated in modern BITs. The WTO competence saga may be followed by a second series, the investment competence saga. Here, too, it may perhaps be predicted that full and exclusive EU competence will follow rather than precede the development of the actual policy and the building-up of EU institutional competence that goes with it.

If, however, the case law on the common commercial policy has been of great constitutional significance for the EU's external action, no less great a role was cast for the doctrine of implied powers, to which the next chapter turns.

3

The doctrine of implied powers

Introduction

In the original EEC Treaty there were not many provisions which expressly referred to external action by the Community. There were provisions on the common commercial policy, discussed in the previous chapter of this book, which mentioned the conclusion of international agreements on commercial policy. Other references to external relations were confined to the last part of the Treaty, containing 'General and Final Provisions'. There one found Article 228 (now, with amendments, Article 218 TFEU), on the procedure for concluding international agreements 'where this Treaty provides for' such agreements. Article 229 EEC instructed the Commission to maintain 'all appropriate relations' with the United Nations, its specialized agencies, GATT, and other international organizations; Article 230 EEC provided that the Community was to establish all appropriate forms of co-operation with the Council of Europe; and Article 231 EEC spoke of establishing close co-operation with the Organization for Economic Co-operation and Development (OECD), the details of which were to be determined by common accord.[1]

It is clear that none of those final provisions conferred any substantive powers—in the sense of defining certain policy areas—to act under international law. There was one, last provision which did confer a more broadly-defined external competence: Article 238 (now Article 217 TFEU) on association agreements, according to which the Community could conclude with one or more States or international organizations agreements establishing an association involving reciprocal rights and obligations, common action, and special procedures. That provision was soon and often to be used; its scope and meaning are analysed in Chapter 4.

The question then arose of whether the external powers of the EEC were confined to developing a common commercial policy, concluding association agreements, and establishing co-operation with international organizations, or whether the EEC could act externally and conclude international agreements in other areas too. Whether, in other words, the Treaty contained implied external powers. The case law of the Court of Justice on these implied powers is of great constitutional

[1] Those provisions are now all subsumed in Art 220(1) TFEU.

significance,[2] and this chapter is devoted to its analysis. It takes the reader through the entire body of the case law, offering an extensive account and close scrutiny. The Treaty of Lisbon has attempted to codify this case law, and we will need to study the relevant provisions. In the last section the chapter offers some concluding reflections, and makes the link to Chapter 4, where this book looks at the main policy areas in the current TFEU which are relevant from an external relations perspective.

The *AETR* case: implied versus conferred powers?

The original EEC Treaty did not contain any provisions analogous to Article 101 EAEC Treaty, which was negotiated at the same time.[3] According to that provision, the EAEC could, 'within the limits of its powers and jurisdiction, enter into obligations by concluding agreements or contracts with a third State, an international organization or a national of a third State'. This article established a clear parallelism between internal and external powers. As no comparable provision was inserted into the EEC Treaty, it was not illogical to assume that the drafters of that Treaty were circumspect about creating general parallelism in the case of the much broader transfer of powers from the Member States to the EEC.

In 1970, the Commission brought the *AETR* case, named after the European Agreement concerning the work of crews of vehicles engaged in international road transport.[4] This agreement was first signed in 1962 under the auspices of the

[2] JHH Weiler, *The Constitution of Europe* (CUP, 1999) 189; for general analyses see R Kovar, 'Les compétences implicites: jurisprudence de la Cour et pratique communautaire' in P Demaret (ed), *Relations extérieures de la Communauté européenne et marché intérieur: aspects juridiques et fonctionnels* (Story Scientia, 1988) 15; I Macleod, ID Hendry, and S Hyett, *The External Relations of the European Communities* (OUP, 1996) 47–55; C Kaddous, *Le droit des relations extérieures dans la jurisprudence de la Cour de justice des Communautés européennes* (Helbing & Lichtenhahn, 1998) 240–55; C Denys, *Impliciete bevoegdheden in de Europese Economische Gemeenschap* (Maklu, 1990); A Dashwood and J Helikoski, 'The Classic Authorities Revisited' in A Dashwood and C Hillion (eds), *The General Law of EC External Relations* (Sweet & Maxwell, 2000) 3–19; D O'Keeffe, 'Exclusive, Concurrent and Shared Competence' in ibid, 179–99; J-V Louis, 'La compétence de la CE de conclure des accords internationaux' in J-V Louis and M Dony (eds), *Commentaire J Megret—Relations extérieures* (Etudes européennes, 2005) 59–71; P Koutrakos, *EU International Relations Law* (Hart Publishing, 2006) ch 3; R Holdgaard, *External Relations Law of the European Community—Legal Reasoning and Legal Discourses* (Wolters Kluwer, 2008) ch 4 and 97–119; G De Baere, *Constitutional Principles of EU External Relations* (OUP, 2008) 16–29 and 43–58; P Mengozzi, 'The EC External Competences: From the *ERTA* Case to the Opinion in the Lugano Convention' in M Poiares Maduro and L Azoulai, *The Past and Future of EU Law—The Classics of EU Law Revisited on the 50th Anniversary of the Rome Treaty* (Hart Publishing, 2010) 213; P Eeckhout, 'Bold Constitutionalism and Beyond' in ibid, 218; C Hillion, '*ERTA*, *ECHR* and *Open Skies*: Laying the Grounds of the EU System of External Relations' in ibid, 224; R Post, 'Constructing the European Policy: *ERTA* and the *Open Skies* Judgments' in ibid, 234; R Schütze, *From Dual to Cooperative Federalism—The Changing Structure of European Law* (OUP, 2009) ch 6.

[3] PJG Kapteyn and P VerLoren van Themaat, *Introduction to the Law of the European Communities* (3rd edn, by LW Gormley, Kluwer Law International, 1998) 1257.

[4] Case 22/70 *Commission v. Council* [1971] ECR 263.

UN Economic Commission for Europe by five of the six EEC Member States and a number of other European States. It did not, however, enter into force because there was not a sufficient number of ratifications. Negotiations for a revision of the agreement resumed in 1967, and at the same time substantively similar work was undertaken at Community level, resulting in Council Regulation 543/69 on the harmonization of certain social legislation relating to road transport.[5] The Council then discussed the attitude to be taken by the Member States in the AETR negotiations. It decided that those negotiations would continue to be conducted by the Member States, and thus did not agree with the Commission's proposal that the Community should negotiate instead of the Member States. The Council also agreed on a common position in the negotiations. The Commission then brought an action for the annulment of 'the Council proceedings'.

The Court's judgment has a complex structure, in that the examination of the Community's external powers is located in a section on the 'initial question', even before the analysis of the admissibility of the action. Indeed, the Council argued that the action for annulment was inadmissible, on the ground that the proceedings in question were not an act subject to review under (current) Article 263 TFEU. In order to decide this point, the Court was required to determine which authority was empowered to negotiate and conclude the AETR. The legal effect of the proceedings differed according to whether they were regarded as constituting the exercise of powers conferred on the Community (in which case one could properly speak of a Council act) or as acknowledging a co-ordination by the Member States of the exercise of powers which remained vested in them (in which case there simply was no Council act).[6]

The Commission argued that the Treaty provisions on a common transport policy, and (current) Article 91 TFEU in particular, applied to external relations just as much as to domestic measures, notwithstanding the absence of an express reference to that effect. The full effect of this provision would be jeopardized if the powers which it conferred, particularly that of laying down 'any appropriate provisions', within the meaning of (current) subparagraph (1)(d) of the Article, did not extend to the conclusion of agreements with third countries. Even if the Community's power did not originally embrace the whole sphere of transport, it would tend to become general and exclusive as and where the common policy in this field came to be implemented. The Council, by contrast, contended that since the Community only had such powers as had been conferred on it, authority to enter into agreements could not be assumed in the absence of an express provision. Article 91 related only to measures internal to the Community and could not be interpreted as authorizing the conclusion of international agreements. And even if it were otherwise, such authority could not be general and exclusive, but, at the most, concurrent with that of the Member States.[7]

[5] [1969] OJ Spec Ed (I) 170.
[6] *Commission v. Council* (n 4 above) paras 2–5.
[7] Ibid, paras 6–11.

Dutheillet de Lamothe AG agreed with the Council. He was of the opinion that recognizing external powers in the field of transport would involve the Court in a discretionary construction of the law—a judicial interpretation far exceeding the bounds which the Court had so far set regarding its power to interpret the Treaty. He referred to the opening sentence of (then) Article 228 EEC, on the procedure for negotiating and concluding international agreements, which spoke of 'where this Treaty provides for the conclusion of agreements'.[8] He did not accept the wide interpretation of that provision advocated by the Commission. In his view, recognition of the Community's authority in this case would concede by implication that the Community authorities exercised, in addition to the powers expressly conferred upon them by the Treaty, those implied powers whereby the US Supreme Court supplemented the powers of the federal bodies in relation to those of the confederated States. The Advocate General, for his part, considered that Community powers should be regarded as 'conferred powers', thereby contrasting that notion with the concept of implied powers.[9]

The constitutional import of the case was thus clearly identified by the time the Court delivered its ruling. The Court's reasoning on the issue of competence consisted of two parts. In the first part, the Court examined the question of principle.[10] It started by referring to (then) Article 210 EEC, which provided that 'the Community shall have legal personality'.[11] This provision, placed at the head of the Treaty's 'General and Final Provisions', meant that in its external relations the Community enjoyed the capacity to establish contractual links with third countries over the whole field of objectives defined in Part One of the Treaty. To determine in a particular case the Community's authority to enter into international agreements, the Court continued, regard had to be had to the whole scheme of the Treaty no less than to its substantive provisions. Such authority arose not only from an express conferment by the Treaty—as was the case with the provisions on tariff and trade agreements and on association agreements—but could equally flow from other provisions of the Treaty and from measures adopted, within the framework of those provisions, by the Community institutions. The Court then made this more specific: each time the Community, with a view to implementing a common policy envisaged by the Treaty, adopted provisions laying down common rules, whatever form these might take, the Member States no longer had the right, acting individually or collectively, to undertake obligations with third countries which affected those rules. As and when such common rules came into being, the Community alone was in a position to assume and carry out contractual obligations towards third countries affecting the whole sphere of application of the Community legal system. The conclusion was that, with regard to implementation of the provisions of the Treaty, the system of internal Community measures could not be separated from that of external relations.

[8] That phrase is omitted in (current) Art 218 TFEU.

[9] Ibid, 289–93. [10] Ibid, paras 13–19. [11] See now Art 47 TEU.

In the second part of its reasoning the Court applied these principles to the issues at hand.[12] It referred to Article 3(f) EEC, which mentioned a common policy in the sphere of transport as one of the Community's objectives, and to (current) Article 4(3) TEU, which defines the principle of Member State loyalty. If those provisions were read together, it followed that to the extent to which Community rules were promulgated for the attainment of the objectives of the Treaty, the Member States could not, outside the framework of the Community institutions, assume obligations which might affect those rules or alter their scope. The Court then analysed the Treaty provisions on transport, pointing out that under those provisions the Council could lay down 'any other appropriate provisions'. As regards the scope of the common transport policy, the Court referred to (current) Article 91(1)(a) TFEU, which speaks of 'international transport to or from the territory of a Member State or passing across the territory of one or more Member States'. This provision was equally concerned with transport from or to third countries, as regards that part of the journey which took place on Community territory. The provision thus assumed that the powers of the Community extended to relationships arising from international law, and hence involved the need for agreements with third countries. The Court then looked at Regulation 543/69, whose bringing into force necessarily vested in the Community power to enter into agreements with third countries relating to the subject matter governed by that regulation, as was expressly recognized by Article 3 of the regulation.[13] Since the subject matter of the AETR fell within the scope of the regulation, the Community had been empowered to negotiate and conclude the agreement since the entry into force of the regulation. These Community powers excluded the possibility of concurrent powers on the part of Member States, since any steps taken outside the framework of the Community institutions would be incompatible with the unity of the common market and the uniform application of Community law.

Thus, much as in its first major ruling on the Community's competences under the common commercial policy,[14] the Court not only confirmed external competence but also characterized it as being exclusive. However, and again much as with early decisions on the scope of the common commercial policy, the reader must be urged to read the full judgment. The Court, after having thus resolved the 'initial question' with which it was confronted, decided that the Commission's action was admissible, since the Council proceedings constituted an act having legal effects. On the substance, however, the Court rejected the Commission's claim for annulment of the proceedings. Essentially, the Court considered that the AETR negotiations were a mere continuation of the earlier negotiations, which in 1962 had resulted in an agreement which could not be ratified. At that time, power to conclude this

[12] Ibid, paras 20–31.

[13] Art 3 provided: 'The Community shall enter into any negotiations with third countries which may prove necessary for the purpose of implementing this regulation'.

[14] *Opinion 1/75 re Understanding on a Local Cost Standard* [1975] ECR 1355; see Ch 2.

agreement was still vested in the Member States, because the common transport policy was not yet sufficiently developed and Regulation 543/69 had not yet been adopted. To have suggested to the third countries involved that there was a new distribution of powers might have jeopardized the successful outcome of the negotiations. The Court thus accepted that it was appropriate for the Member States to carry on negotiating, and that the Community's interests were safeguarded through the common position which the Council had adopted and which the Member States would defend in the negotiations.[15]

The Court was thus both principled and pragmatic. On the issues of principle, it is questionable whether the Advocate General's stark contrast between conferred and implied powers was convincing. One of the main themes of this chapter is that it is useful and appropriate to distinguish between the Community's external competences in substantive terms, i.e. in terms of pursuing an external policy in a particular domain, and the Community's power to conclude international agreements in areas where the Treaty does not expressly provide for such agreements as an instrument (substantive and instrumental external powers or competences). If one makes that distinction, and applies it to an analysis of the *AETR* judgment, it will be seen that the Court was not guilty of creating, through judicial interpretation, a significant expansion of the Community's competences. In substantive terms, the Court was very careful and no doubt correct to point out that the common transport policy extended to transport from or to third countries, as regards the part of the journey which took place on Community territory.[16] Also, the actual subject matter of the AETR agreement—working conditions of crews of vehicles engaged in road transport—clearly came within the Community's law-making powers, as was confirmed by the adoption of Regulation 543/69. Where the *AETR* judgment was innovative was in its recognition of the power to conclude an international agreement in the absence of an express recognition of such power. Yet here again the analysis was not without foundation in the text of the Treaty. (Current) Article 91 TFEU allows the Council to adopt 'any other appropriate provisions', and (current) Article 218 TFEU recognizes that the Community may conclude international agreements. In fact, if the Court had sought to go the other way, it could only have based itself on a strict interpretation of the principle of conferred powers, and it would have had to disregard both the fact that the subject matter of the AETR agreement came within Community competence, and the fact that the Treaty provisions on a common transport policy were imprecise in terms of defining the legal instruments which could be employed. It is doubtful whether such a strict interpretation of the principle of conferred powers would have been justified, also because, at the time, this principle was nowhere precisely defined in the EEC Treaty. Subsequently, the Treaty of Maastricht inserted Article 5 EC into the Treaty,

[15] *Commission v. Council* (n 4 above) paras 81–91.

[16] Dashwood and Helikoski (n 2 above) 8 refer to the *effet utile* of the Treaty provisions on transport policy.

whose first sentence provided that 'the Community shall act within the limits of the powers conferred upon it by this Treaty and of the objectives assigned to it therein'.[17] Here the juxtaposition of powers and objectives chimes rather well with the Court's analysis in the *AETR* judgment, where it emphasized the objective of establishing a common transport policy.

As regards the exclusive nature of the Community's competence, it is clear from the judgment that this was only a consequence of the adoption of Regulation 543/69, which covered the same subject matter as the AETR agreement. If there had been no such regulation, the Court would no doubt have confirmed concurrent competence. Indeed, that was its ultimate conclusion, based on the fact that the regulation was not yet in force at the time of the adoption of the first version of the AETR agreement.

The crucial language on exclusive competence was that the Member States had no right to enter into international commitments which might affect or alter the scope of 'internal' Community rules. In all likelihood the Court's concern was that, in the absence of exclusive competence, the Member States might, advertently or inadvertently, conclude international agreements whose provisions would conflict with Community law. Member States would then be facing conflicting obligations. From a strictly legal perspective, the Community law reply to such conflicts could be to confirm the primacy of Community rules, to which the Member States would have to give precedence in their internal legal orders, and to leave possible problems at international level for the Member States themselves to resolve. Apparently, however, the Court was of the opinion that the prevention of such conflicts was preferable to later resolution. Also, from a transfer-of-competences perspective it made sense to characterize the Community's competences as exclusive once Community rules in a particular area had been adopted; exclusive in terms of both internal and international law-making. In this respect, the *AETR* judgment has its parallels in the Court's case law on the effect of Community legislation (through what is often referred to as occupying the field, or pre-emption) on the powers of the Member States to adopt internal legislation.[18]

The parallelism approach of *Opinion 1/76*

Some years later the Court handed down a new judgment on implied powers, this time on a reference from a court in the Netherlands. *Kramer* concerned the North-East Atlantic Fisheries Convention, an international agreement aimed at ensuring the conservation of fish stocks in the North-East Atlantic Ocean.[19] All the Member States

[17] See now Art 5(2) TEU.

[18] See K Lenaerts, 'Les répercussions des compétences de la Communauté européenne sur les compétences externes des Etats membres et la question de "preemption"' in Demaret (n 2 above) 447–72.

[19] Joined Cases 3, 4, and 6/76 *Kramer* [1976] ECR 1279.

except Italy and Luxemburg were parties to that agreement. Pursuant to a decision which had been taken within the framework of this convention, the Netherlands' authorities took measures to restrict catches of sole and plaice. A number of fishermen were prosecuted for failing to observe those restrictions, and in their defence they claimed that the Netherlands no longer had the power to participate in the operation of the convention because that power belonged exclusively to the Community.

The judgment was comparable to *AETR*. The Court recalled the general principles identified in that case, and then examined the Community's competence to act in the field of fish conservation measures. It referred to the Treaty provisions on the Common Agricultural Policy; to Council Regulations 2141/70 and 2142/70, respectively laying down a common structural policy for the fishing industry and on the common organization of the market in fishery products;[20] and to Article 102 of the Act of Accession,[21] which instructed the Council to 'determine conditions for fishing with a view to ensuring protection of the fishing grounds and conservation of the biological resources of the sea'. The Court considered that it followed from those provisions taken as a whole that the Community had at its disposal, on the internal level, the power to take any measures for the conservation of the biological resources of the sea. It further followed from those provisions, and from the very nature of things, that the rule-making authority of the Community *ratione materiae* also extended—in so far as the Member States had similar authority under public international law—to fishing on the high seas. The only way to ensure the conservation of the biological resources of the sea both effectively and equitably was through a system of rules binding on all the States concerned, including non-member countries. In these circumstances it followed from the very duties and powers which Community law had established and assigned to the institutions of the Community on the internal level that the Community had authority to enter into international commitments for the conservation of the resources of the sea.[22]

Such power did not, however, mean that the Netherlands no longer had the authority to adopt conservation measures. The Court pointed out that at the time of the facts the Community had not yet fully exercised its functions in the matter. The Member States could thus continue to act, provided they did not hinder the Community in carrying out its tasks. They were also under a duty, together with the Community institutions, to use, when the Community decided to start implementing its duties, all political and legal means at their disposal in order to ensure the participation of the Community in the Convention and in other similar agreements.[23]

The Court's judgment needs to be seen in the light of its later case law on the Community's powers as regards fish conservation. Indeed, in the 1981 *Commission v. United Kingdom* case the Court examined the effect of the expiry, on 1 January

[20] [1970] OJ Spec Ed III 703 and 707.
[21] The Act was on the accession of Denmark, Ireland, and the UK.
[22] *Kramer* (n 19 above) paras 21–33. [23] Ibid, paras 34–45.

1979, of the transitional period of Article 102 of the Act of Accession. It held that, since then, the power to adopt, as part of the common fisheries policy, measures relating to the conservation of the resources of the sea had 'belonged fully and definitively to the Community'. Member States were therefore no longer entitled to exercise any power of their own in the matter of conservation measures in the waters under their jurisdiction.[24] In other words, the Community's competence had become exclusive, as is now confirmed by Article 3(1)(d) TFEU.

The *Kramer* judgment was comparable to *AETR* in the sense that the power to conclude international agreements in the field in question was based, not only on the relevant Treaty provisions (including the Act of Accession, which has Treaty status), but also on Community legislation. Again one can distinguish between substantive competence and power to conclude agreements. As regards substantive external competence, the Court carefully analysed the relevant provisions of Community law to conclude that such competence extended to fishing on the high seas, and was not limited to fishing in the Member States' territorial waters. As regards power to conclude agreements, the Court then rightly indicated that the only way to ensure conservation was through an international system, involving also non-member countries. Indeed it is difficult to see how fish conservation could ever work in the absence of multilateral treaties and conventions, and in that sense the Community's substantive competence to ensure conservation effectively required that it should also have the power to take part in such international law-making.

The further question, whether there was also an implied power to conclude agreements in the absence of internal Community legislation covering the same subject matter, was considered by the Court in *Opinion 1/76*.[25] That Opinion concerned a draft Agreement establishing a European laying-up fund for inland waterway vessels. The agreement had been negotiated between the Commission, acting on behalf of the Community, and Switzerland, with the participation of six Member States which were parties to certain conventions on navigation of the Rhine and the Moselle. The objective of the agreement was to introduce a system intended to eliminate the disturbances arising from the surplus transport capacity for goods by inland waterways in the Rhine and Moselle basins and by all the Netherlands and German inland waterways linked to the Rhine basin. The system consisted of formulating an arrangement for the temporary laying-up of capacity in return for financial compensation. A fund was to be responsible for compensation and was to be financed by contributions imposed on all vessels using the inland waterways which were to be subject to the system. The Commission requested the Court's Opinion on the compatibility of the draft agreement with the Treaty because the system envisaged involved a delegation of powers of decision, and of judicial powers, to independent bodies. The Commission also asked for clarification of the Community's competence to conclude the agreement.

[24] Case 804/79 *Commission v. United Kingdom* [1981] ECR 1045, paras 17–18.

[25] *Opinion 1/76 re Inland Waterways* [1977] ECR 741.

The Court started its analysis by pointing out that the object of the draft agreement was to rationalize the economic situation of the inland waterway transport industry in a geographical region in which transport by inland waterway was of special importance within the whole network of international transport. Such a system was doubtless an important factor in the common transport policy, the establishment of which was included in the activities of the Community laid down in (then) Article 3 of the Treaty. In order to implement this policy, (current) Article 91 TFEU instructed the Council to lay down common rules applicable to international transport to or from the territory of one or more Member States. This article also supplied, as regards the Community, the necessary legal basis to establish the system concerned. In the case of the draft Agreement, however, it was impossible fully to attain the objective pursued by means of the establishment of common rules pursuant to Article 91, because of the traditional participation of vessels from a third State, Switzerland, in navigation by the principal waterways in question, which were subject to the system of freedom of navigation established by international agreements of long standing. It had thus been necessary to bring Switzerland into the scheme in question by means of an international agreement with this third State.[26]

The Court then conceded that the power to conclude such an agreement was not expressly laid down in the Treaty. However, it recalled that it had already had occasion to state, most recently in *Kramer*,[27] that authority to enter into international commitments could not only arise from an express attribution by the Treaty, but could equally flow implicitly from its provisions. The Court had concluded, *inter alia*, that whenever Community law had created for the institutions of the Community powers within its internal system for the purpose of attaining a specific objective, the Community had authority to enter into the international commitments necessary for the attainment of that objective even in the absence of an express provision in that connection. This was particularly so in all cases in which internal power had already been used in order to adopt measures which came within the attainment of common policies. It was, however, not limited to that eventuality. Although the internal Community measures were adopted only when the international agreement was concluded and made enforceable, as was envisaged in the case in question by the proposal for a regulation to be submitted to the Council by the Commission, the power to bind the Community vis-à-vis third countries nevertheless flowed by implication from the provisions of the Treaty creating the internal power and in so far as the participation of the Community in the international agreement was, as here, necessary for the attainment of one of the objectives of the Community.[28]

Opinion 1/76 confirmed that there is no requirement of prior internal Community legislation for the exercise of external competence. In later cases and analyses of the Opinion, reference has occasionally been made to the Court's statement on

[26] Ibid, paras 1–2. [27] *Kramer* (n 19 above). [28] *Opinion 1/76* (n 25 above) paras 3–4.

internal Community measures only being adopted when the international agreement is concluded and made enforceable. One should see that statement in its context. When the Commission requested the Court's Opinion, it had already prepared a proposal for a Council regulation which would, at the same time, conclude the agreement, and implement it through the adoption of internal rules. That is currently no longer the practice of the EU institutions: agreements are concluded by way of Council decision, and any implementing legislation which may be required is adopted by way of a separate act.[29] Whether any implementing legislation is necessary depends on the aims and provisions of the agreement in question, and such legislation is no precondition for the exercise of external competence, which is directly based on the Treaty provisions.

There is a second element in the Court's reasoning which attracted further discussion. The Court twice spoke of the Community's participation in the agreement being 'necessary' for the attainment of the Treaty's objectives. As will be seen, the Commission would rely on this term for the purpose of arguing that the Community had exclusive competence to conclude the WTO Agreement.[30] There will be further scope for discussing the meaning of that term below.

A third point of debate on the meaning of the Opinion is whether it established exclusive Community competence to conclude the draft agreement. Again, this will be further discussed when analysing *Opinion 1/94*, but some comments must none the less be made at this stage. The Court's reasoning as set out above made no reference to exclusive competence. However, the Court did look in the Opinion at what it called 'a special problem' arising because the draft agreement provided for the participation as contracting parties, not only of the Community and Switzerland, but also of six Member States (out of nine). Those Member States were parties to two older international conventions, which they undertook to modify in implementation of the draft agreement. The Court considered that this particular undertaking, given in view of the second paragraph of (current) Article 351 TFEU,[31] explained and justified the participation of those six States, which had to be considered as being solely for this purpose and not as necessary for the attainment of other features of the system. The Court also pointed out that, except for this special undertaking, the legal effects of the agreement with regard to the Member States resulted, in accordance with (current) Article 216(2) TFEU, exclusively from the conclusion by the Community. In those circumstances, the participation of the six Member States was not such as to encroach on the external

[29] See Ch 6.

[30] See the section on *Opinion 1/94*.

[31] Art 351 concerns international agreements concluded by Member States before membership. The second paragraph provides: 'To the extent that such agreements are not compatible with the Treaties, the Member State or States concerned shall take all appropriate steps to eliminate the incompatibilities established. Member States shall, where necessary, assist each other to this end and shall, where appropriate, adopt a common attitude'. See further Ch 9.

power of the Community. There was therefore no occasion to conclude that this aspect of the draft agreement was incompatible with the Treaty.[32]

Clearly, the Court was of the opinion that a particular justification was required for the participation as contracting parties of six Member States. Does that mean that, in principle, the Court regarded the Community's competence to conclude the draft agreement as exclusive? Such a reading of the Opinion is not persuasive.[33] First, the Court did not use any language referring to exclusive Community powers. It looked at the issue of participation by Member States as a 'special problem', which it addressed after having established the principle of Community competence. Secondly, in the *AETR* case the Court had clearly established that exclusive implied powers resulted from internal legislation, which could be affected or whose scope could be altered by the agreement. In the absence of such legislation, the Court had regarded the Community's power to conclude agreements in the sphere of transport as concurrent with the powers of the Member States. If the Court had sought to modify that principle in *Opinion 1/76*, one would have expected it to be clearer on this point. Thirdly, the Court has always regarded the Community's competence to develop a common transport policy as concurrent with the competence of the Member States.[34] It is difficult to see how, if internal legislative competence in transport matters is not exclusive, the Member States could have lost the power to conclude international agreements in this area.

There is a better reading of this passage in *Opinion 1/76*. That reading concentrates on the exercise of Community competence rather than on the nature of that competence, exclusive or concurrent, as a matter of principle. What the Court may have observed in *Opinion 1/76* is that, once the decision to exercise Community competence by way of concluding an international agreement is taken, participation by the Member States as contracting parties is permissible only if some parts or provisions of the agreement are not covered by Community competence at all.[35] That does not mean that the Community's competence is exclusive, for if the Community decides not to exercise it, the Member States retain their full powers. In Chapter 7 this will be further explored. Recent case law in any event shows that the EU need not exercise all its shared competences when concluding a mixed agreement, but is capable of exercising only part of its competences, thereby leaving other matters to the Member States.[36]

[32] *Opinion 1/76* (n 25 above) paras 6–7.

[33] Cf Dashwood and Helikoski (n 2 above) 13–14; J Helikoski, *Mixed Agreements as a Technique for Organizing the International Relations of the European Community and its Member States* (Kluwer Law International, 2001) 43–4.

[34] Dashwood and Helikoski (n 2 above) 13. See now Art 4(2)(g) TFEU.

[35] CWA Timmermans, 'Division of External Powers between Community and Member States in the Field of Harmonization of National Law—A Case Study' in CWA Timmermans and ELM Völker (eds), *Division of Powers between the European Communities and their Member States in the Field of External Relations* (Kluwer, 1981) 20.

[36] See e.g. Case C–459/03 *Commission v. Ireland (Mox Plant)* [2006] ECR I–4635.

Opinion 1/76 was generally regarded as establishing parallelism between the Community's internal and external powers.[37] That view may be correct, provided one bears in mind the distinction between substantive competence and the power to conclude agreements. Again, in the Opinion, the Court did not broaden the competence of the Community in transport matters in substantive terms. The object of the agreement, i.e. rationalizing the inland waterway transport sector as operating in the Rhine and Moselle basins, clearly came within the Community's powers in matters of transport. What the Court recognized was simply the power of the Community to achieve such rationalization through an international agreement rather than through the mere adoption of internal legislation.

The clarity of *Opinion 2/91*

The Court had the opportunity to connect and further clarify the various principles of external competence in an Opinion on a draft convention which had been negotiated in the International Labour Organization (ILO). The EU is not a member of the ILO, but has observer status. Apparently that creates a number of problems when conventions are negotiated in the ILO concerning matters covered by EU law. The institutions and the Member States have tried to find some *modus vivendi* which should enable the EU's position, where relevant, to be voiced and defended. A dispute arose, however, over the respective roles of the EU and the Member States in the adoption and implementation of Convention No 170 concerning safety in the use of chemicals at work. Following the adoption of that convention by the ILO Conference, the Commission wrote to the Council stating its view that the Member States were under an obligation to inform the Director-General of the International Labour Office that the competent authorities, within the meaning of Article 19(5)(c) of the ILO Constitution,[38] were in this case the Community institutions. Several Member States indicated their refusal to accept that the Community had exclusive competence to conclude the convention. The Commission then sought the Opinion of the Court of Justice, particularly as regards the Community's competence to conclude the convention and the consequences which this would have for the Member States.[39]

[37] J Groux, 'Le parallèlisme des compétences internes et externes de la Communauté économique européenne' (1978) 14 CDE 1; Dashwood and Helikoski (n 2 above) 12.

[38] Art 19(5)(c) provides: 'Members shall inform the Director-General of the International Labour Office of the measures taken in accordance with this article to bring the Convention before the said competent authority or authorities, with particulars of the authority or authorities regarded as competent, and of the action taken by them.'

[39] *Opinion 2/91 re ILO Convention No 170* [1993] ECR I-1061.

This was again a case in which the questions of principle were more important than any specific practical outcome. Indeed, the German and Netherlands governments contended that the request was inadmissible, because the Community could not itself conclude the agreement, as it was not a member of the ILO; they were referring to the rule that only ILO members can ratify ILO conventions.[40] The Court brushed this objection aside, by stating that the request for an Opinion did not concern the Community's capacity, on the international plane, to enter into an ILO convention, but related to the scope of the competence of the Community and the Member States within the area covered by Convention No 170. It was not for the Court to assess any obstacles which the Community could encounter in the exercise of its competence. In any event, its external competence could, if necessary, be exercised through the medium of the Member States acting jointly in the Community's interest.[41]

The most useful dimension of *Opinion 2/91* is that the Court started its analysis by setting out the principles of external competence.[42] It reasoned as follows. It first pointed out that, as it had stated in *Opinion 1/76*,[43] authority to enter into international commitments could not only arise from an express attribution by the Treaty, but could also flow implicitly from its provisions. In the Opinion the Court had concluded, in particular, that whenever Community law created for the institutions of the Community powers within its internal system for the purpose of attaining a specific objective, the Community had authority to enter into the international commitments necessary for the attainment of that objective even in the absence of an express provision in that connection. In *Kramer*[44] the Court had already pointed out that such authority could flow by implication from other measures adopted by the Community institutions within the framework of the Treaty provisions or the acts of accession.[45]

Having thus recalled the principles of express and implied powers to 'enter into international commitments', the Court turned to the nature of the Community's external competence, exclusive or concurrent. It stated that the exclusive nature of the Community's competence had been recognized with respect to (current) Article 207 TFEU (*Opinion 1/75*[46]) and to Article 102 of the Act of Accession (*Commission v. United Kingdom*[47]). It followed from that line of authority that the existence of such competence arising from a Treaty provision excluded any competence on the part of Member States which was concurrent with that of the Community, in the Community sphere and in the international sphere.[48] The Court thus recalled that exclusive competence which is based on the Treaty covers both internal law-making and the conclusion of international agreements.

[40] See Art 19(5)(d) ILO Constitution.
[41] *Opinion 2/91* (n 39 above) paras 1–6.
[42] Dashwood and Helikoski (n 2 above) 15.
[43] *Opinion 1/76* (n 25 above).
[44] *Kramer* (n 19 above).
[45] *Opinion 2/91* (n 39 above) para 7.
[46] *Opinion 1/75* (n 14 above).
[47] *Commission v. United Kingdom* (n 24 above).
[48] *Opinion 2/91* (n 39 above) para 8.

The Court then turned to exclusive implied powers. It stated that the exclusive or non-exclusive nature of the Community's competence did not flow solely from the provisions of the Treaty but could also depend on the scope of the measures which had been adopted by the Community institutions for the application of those provisions and which were of such a kind as to deprive the Member States of an area of competence which they were able to exercise previously on a transitional basis. As the Court had stated in the *AETR* case,[49] where Community rules had been promulgated for the attainment of the objectives of the Treaty, the Member States could not, outside the framework of the Community institutions, assume obligations which might affect those rules or alter their scope. Contrary to the contentions of a number of governments, the authority of the decision in that case could not be restricted to instances where the Community had adopted Community rules within the framework of a common policy (the argument by these governments was that the *AETR* principle was limited to what were nominally 'common policies' according to the EEC Treaty, such as the common transport policy). In all the areas corresponding to the objectives of the Treaty, the Court continued, (current) Article 4(3) TFEU required Member States to facilitate the achievement of the Community's tasks and to abstain from any measure which could jeopardize the attainment of the objectives of the Treaty. The Community's tasks and the objectives of the Treaty would also be compromised if Member States were able to enter into international commitments containing rules capable of affecting rules already adopted in areas falling outside common policies or of altering their scope.[50]

The Court thus recalled the scope of exclusive implied powers as well as their rationale, which is based on the principle of Member State loyalty. Much of the remainder of the Opinion was devoted to determining whether, and, if so, to what extent, there was Community legislation which could be affected, or whose scope could be altered, by Convention No 170. It is here too that the Opinion was helpful and clarified the law. But before conducting that examination the Court stated a final principle of external competence: an agreement could be concluded in an area where competence was shared between the Community and the Member States. In such a case, negotiation and implementation of the agreement required joint action by the Community and the Member States.[51]

The Court then applied the above principles. It recalled that Convention No 170 concerned safety in the use of chemicals at work and that its essential objective, according to its preamble, was to prevent or reduce the incidence of chemically induced illnesses and injuries at work by ensuring that all chemicals were evaluated to determine their hazards, by providing employers and workers with the information necessary for their protection, and, finally, by establishing principles for

[49] *Commission v. Council* (n 4 above).
[50] *Opinion 2/91* (n 39 above) paras 9–11.
[51] Ibid, para 12.

protective programmes. The field covered by Convention No 170 thus fell within the 'social provisions' of the EEC Treaty. Under Article 118a EEC,[52] Member States were required to pay particular attention to encouraging improvements, especially in the working environment, as regards the health and safety of workers, and to set as their objective the harmonization of conditions in this area. In order to help achieve this objective, the Council had the power to adopt minimum requirements by means of directives. It followed from Article 118a(3) that the provisions adopted pursuant to that article were not to prevent any Member State from maintaining or introducing more stringent measures for the protection of working conditions compatible with the Treaty. The Community thus enjoyed an internal legislative competence in the area of social policy. Consequently, Convention No 170, whose subject matter coincided, moreover, with that of several directives adopted under Article 118a, fell within the Community's area of competence.[53]

It may be noted that the Court again had no difficulty whatsoever in confirming that, in an area where the Community has the power to adopt internal legislation, it also has the power to conclude international agreements. This was so, notwithstanding the fact that, at the time, Community competence for the health and safety of workers was defined in subsidiary terms. Article 118a EEC referred to the Member States (not the Community) encouraging improvements in health and safety, instructed the Council 'to help achieve the objective' through the adoption of directives, and left intact the power of Member States to adopt more stringent provisions. Yet this subsidiary character of Community competence was not an obstacle to the recognition of treaty-making power.

The Court then examined whether Community competence was exclusive. It pointed out that the provisions of Convention No 170 were not of such a kind as to affect rules adopted pursuant to Article 118a. If, on the one hand, the Community decided to adopt rules which were less stringent than those set out in an ILO convention, Member States could, in accordance with Article 118a(3), adopt more stringent measures or apply for that purpose the relevant ILO convention. If, on the other hand, the Community decided to adopt more stringent measures, there was nothing to prevent the full application of Community law by the Member States under Article 19(8) of the ILO Constitution, which allowed Members to adopt more stringent measures than those provided for in conventions or recommendations adopted by that organization.[54]

The Court was faced here with a rather unique situation, in which, notwithstanding the fact that the international agreement covered the same subject matter as Community legislation, there was no exclusive competence, because both the agreement and the Community legislation allowed for the adoption of more stringent provisions. The tenor of the Court's reasoning is that, in the light of that

[52] The provisions of Art 118a EEC are now part, with amendments, of Art 153 TFEU.
[53] *Opinion 2/91* (n 39 above) paras 14–17.
[54] Ibid, para 18.

state of affairs, conflicts between the provisions of the convention and those of the Community directives were excluded. One should not, however, deduce from this reasoning that actual conflicts between Community norms and the provisions of an international agreement are required to vest exclusive competence in the EU.[55] The question of competence in principle arises even before an agreement is negotiated, for one needs to know which authority has power to negotiate. The precise provisions resulting from the negotiation are still unknown at that point, so it will be impossible to establish whether or not there is conflict. The rationale is rather that, where the agreement covers the same subject matter as EU legislation, the EU needs to negotiate so as to avoid conflict, or, alternatively, so as to be persuaded that new rules need to be adopted at international level which may require the amendment of existing EU legislation. In the case of Convention No 170, however, no such rationale was present, because of the character of minimum rules of both the Community directives and the provisions of the Convention.

In its submissions in *Opinion 2/91* the Commission had argued that it was sometimes difficult to determine whether a specific measure was more favourable to workers than another, and that Member States might be tempted, in order not to be in breach of an ILO convention, not to adopt provisions better suited to the social and technological conditions specific to the Community. The Court did not accept that argument. It stated that such difficulties, which might arise for the legislative function of the Community, could not constitute the basis for exclusive Community competence.[56]

However, the Court then went on to look at a number of directives, concerning classification, packaging, and labelling of dangerous substances and preparations,[57] which had been adopted pursuant to (current) Articles 114 and 115 TFEU. The Court compared the provisions of those directives with the provisions of Convention No 170. It concluded that, while there was no contradiction between the provisions of the convention and those of the directives, it nevertheless had to be accepted that Part III of the convention was concerned with an area which was already covered to a large extent by Community rules progressively adopted since 1967 with a view to achieving an ever greater degree of harmonization. In those circumstances, it had to be considered that the commitments arising from Part III of the convention were of such a kind as to affect the Community rules laid down in those directives and that consequently Member States could not undertake such commitments outside the framework of the Community institutions.[58]

In the penultimate section of the Opinion on the question of competence, the Court looked at the provisions of the convention on implementation. It held that, in so far as it had been established that the substantive provisions of the convention

[55] See the section below on the *Open Skies* cases.

[56] *Opinion 2/91* (n 39 above) paras 19–20.

[57] Council Directive 67/548 [1967] OJ Spec Ed 234 and Directive 88/379 [1988] OJ L187/14.

[58] *Opinion 2/91* (n 39 above) paras 22–26.

came within the Community's sphere of competence, the Community was also competent to undertake commitments for putting those provisions into effect. It was no obstacle that such implementation required consultation of representative organizations of employers and workers. The Court admitted that co-operation between both sides of industry was a matter falling predominantly within the competence of the Member States, yet it was not entirely withdrawn from the Community's competence: under Article 118b EEC the Commission was required to endeavour to develop the dialogue between management and labour at European level.[59] As regards, further, the implementation of the convention in terms of supervision, again it was no problem that the competent authorities supervising the use of hazardous chemicals were authorities at the level of the Member States: just as, for internal purposes, the Community could provide, in an area covered by Community rules, that national authorities were to be given certain supervisory powers, it could also, for external purposes, undertake commitments designed to ensure compliance with substantive provisions which fell within its competence and implied the attribution of certain supervisory powers to national authorities.[60]

Lastly, the Court accepted that the substantive scope of the convention lay outside the scope of the association scheme for overseas countries and territories (see Articles 198 to 204 TFEU), and that consequently it was for the Member States which were responsible for the international relations of those territories and which represented them in that regard to conclude the convention.[61] The Court's overall conclusion was that Convention No 170 came within the joint competence of the Member States and the Community.[62]

The meanderings of *Opinion 1/94*

Chapter 2 looked extensively at the GATT Uruguay Round negotiations, resulting in the WTO Agreement, and at *Opinion 1/94* in so far as that Opinion analysed Community competence under then Article 113 EC (now, with amendments, Article 207 TFEU).[63] The reader is referred to those pages for the background to the Opinion. Again the purpose of the Commission's request was to establish exclusive Community competence. The Commission did not confine its arguments to the common commercial policy, even if the relevant Treaty provisions offered the most credible basis for the Commission's claim. It also submitted, in a subsidiary argument, that implied powers under other Treaty provisions fully covered the various

[59] The current provisions of the TFEU on such dialogue are much more advanced, see Arts 154 and 155 TFEU.

[60] *Opinion 2/91* (n 39 above) paras 27–34.

[61] Ibid, para 35.

[62] Ibid, para 39.

[63] *Opinion 1/94 re WTO Agreement* [1994] ECR I-5267.

WTO agreements and that those powers were exclusive of those of the Member States. With respect, that argument had little if any basis in the Court's previous case law, and the Commission's lawyers must have been aware of this. The Court did not accept the argument, and the result, in this author's view, is an Opinion which, in an attempt to defuse arguments which were difficult to understand, does not contribute much to clarifying the law on implied powers.

As the Court accepted that the WTO agreements on trade in goods came within the Community's exclusive competence to develop a common commercial policy, there was no need to consider implied powers in that regard. The Court's analysis concentrated on trade in services (GATS) and intellectual property rights (TRIPs).[64] In the meantime, of course, the legal position has been modified by the Nice and Lisbon Treaties, in the sense that trade in services and the commercial aspects of intellectual property now also come within the scope of the common commercial policy.

GATS

As regards GATS, the Commission's first of three arguments was that there was no area or specific provision in GATS in respect of which the Community did not have corresponding powers to adopt measures at internal level; powers as set out in the Treaty chapters on the right of establishment, freedom to provide services, and transport. In the Commission's view, exclusive external competence flowed from those internal powers.[65]

In its reply, the Court first referred to transport, and recalled the *AETR* judgment;[66] it accepted that there was external competence but rejected the claim of exclusivity. The Court stated that it was only in so far as common rules had been established at internal level that the external competence of the Community became exclusive. However, not all transport matters were already covered by common rules. The Court also rejected the Commission's argument that the Member States' continuing freedom to conduct an external transport policy would inevitably lead to distortions in the flow of services and would progressively undermine the internal market. It observed that there was nothing in the Treaty which prevented the institutions from arranging concerted action in relation to non-member countries or from prescribing the approach to be taken by the Member States in their external dealings.[67]

[64] See also N Neuwahl, 'The WTO Opinion and Implied External Powers of the Community—A Hidden Agenda?' in A Dashwood and C Hillion (eds), *The General Law of EC External Relations* (Sweet & Maxwell, 2000) 139–51.

[65] *Opinion 1/94* (n 63 above) para 74.

[66] *Commission v. Council* (n 4 above).

[67] *Opinion 1/94* (n 63 above) paras 76–79.

The Court then turned to services other than transport. It pointed out that, unlike the chapter on transport, the chapters on the right of establishment and on freedom to provide services did not contain any provision expressly extending the competence of the Community to 'relationships arising from international law'. As had rightly been observed by the Council and most of the Member States which had submitted observations, the sole objective of those chapters was to secure the right of establishment and freedom to provide services for nationals of Member States. They contained no provisions on the problem of the first establishment of nationals of non-member countries and the rules governing their access to self-employed activities. One could not therefore infer from those chapters that the Community had exclusive competence to conclude an agreement with non-member countries to liberalize first establishment and access to service markets, other than those which were the subject of cross-border supplies within the meaning of GATS, which were covered by Article 113 EEC.[68]

This is one of the most significant paragraphs of *Opinion 1/94* and, unfortunately, it contains one turn of phrase which is deceptive. The Court refers to, and puts between quotation marks, 'relationships arising from international law',[69] which may be seen as hinting at the conclusion of international agreements. It is a quotation taken from paragraph 27 of the *AETR* judgment, where this turn of phrase concluded the Court's analysis of the substantive scope of 'external' Community competence: the part where the Court considered that the Treaty rules on the common transport policy extended to international transport to or from third countries, in so far as the transport takes place on Community territory. Similarly, here in *Opinion 1/94* the Court was not so much concerned with the power to conclude international agreements as with the question whether the Treaty chapters on right of establishment and freedom to provide services have a substantive external dimension. Did those chapters extend to first establishment, in the Community, by nationals of non-member countries?[70] Did they cover access by nationals of non-member countries to service markets and to self-employed activities within the EU? For that is the substantive scope of GATS. As the Court rightly pointed out, however, that is not the scope of the relevant Treaty provisions, which concern the internal market, and extend only to nationals of Member States. It was therefore impossible to base an exclusive external competence on those provisions. Essentially, the Court observed that, as regards services and establishment, the Treaty did not provide for an external dimension (with the exception of cross-border supplies of services), in contrast with goods, where the external dimension comes within the common commercial policy.

[68] Ibid, para 81.

[69] In the French version this is '*des relations relevant du droit international*', which could also be translated as 'relationships subject to international law'.

[70] See on that question Y Loussouarn, 'Le droit d'établissement des sociétés' (1990) 26 RTDE 229.

The reference to 'relationships arising from international law' is deceptive because the Court was addressing competence in general here, arguably encompassing internal law-making just as much as the conclusion of international agreements. Much as the Community could not claim exclusive competence to conclude agreements on first establishment and access to services markets, it could not claim exclusive competence to regulate those issues by way of Community directives and regulations. The Court did not expressly mention that, perhaps because it was not in issue, but it must be the correct reading to avoid an unworkable dichotomy between the Community's 'internal' and 'external' powers. Does that mean that the Community did not have any competence whatsoever to regulate the external dimension of the internal market in services? As we will see below, that is not the case, since there was some measure of Community competence, but clearly not exclusive in character.

The Commission's second implied powers argument in relation to GATS was based on a particular reading of *Opinion 1/76*.[71] The Commission argued that the Community's exclusive external competence was not confined to cases in which use had already been made of internal powers, but that, whenever Community law had conferred on the institutions internal powers for the purposes of attaining specific objectives, the international competence of the Community implicitly flowed from those provisions. It was enough that the Community's participation in the international agreement was necessary for the attainment of a Community objective. To show such necessity in the case of GATS (and TRIPs), the Commission put forward both internal and external reasons. At internal level, the coherence of the internal market would be impaired without such participation. At external level, the Community could not allow itself to remain inactive on the international stage: the need for the conclusion of the WTO Agreement was not in dispute.[72]

Rightly, the Court did not accept that reasoning, but its reply was not persuasive. It pointed out that the agreement in issue in *Opinion 1/76* was different from GATS, because in the case of the former it was impossible to achieve the objective of rationalization of the inland waterways sector in the Rhine and Moselle basins by the establishment of autonomous common rules, in the light of the traditional participation of vessels from Switzerland in navigation on those waterways. It was therefore necessary to bring Switzerland into the scheme. The Court also referred to its case law on the conservation of fish resources (see above), in which it had pointed out that restrictions of fishing on the high seas could hardly be effective in the absence of agreements. It was therefore understandable, the Court concluded, that external powers could be exercised, and thus become exclusive, without any internal legislation having first been adopted. That was not the situation in the sphere of services: attainment of freedom of establishment and freedom to provide services for nationals of the Member States was not inextricably linked to the

[71] *Opinion 1/76* (n 25 above). [72] *Opinion 1/94* (n 63 above) paras 82–83.

treatment to be afforded in the Community to nationals of non-member countries or in non-member countries to nationals of Member States of the Community.[73]

That reasoning raises various questions.[74] First, it is not clear why the Court felt compelled to examine an argument for exclusive competence when it had not yet established competence, as such, to begin with. Indeed, in the preceding part of the Opinion the Court stated that the Treaty provisions on right of establishment and freedom to provide services did not cover the subject matter of GATS. Secondly, it is also not clear why the Court referred to its fisheries case law, as there the relevant primary law provisions were interpreted as establishing exclusive Community competence. Thirdly, and most problematically, the Court appeared to agree with the Commission's analysis that *Opinion 1/76* was a case of exclusive competence. Above it was argued that such a reading is unconvincing, and the Court did not here clarify the basis for exclusivity. One understands, of course, that the inland waterways agreement was indispensable if the Community decided to rationalize the transport sector concerned. But that did not make Community competence exclusive. One fails to see on what grounds such rationalization, as an element of transport policy, would have been within the Community's exclusive powers when all other transport matters were not. Surely, as a matter of law the Community could have decided not to act in this regard, and to leave the relevant Member States to deal with the issues of excess capacity. It is also not clear what the Court meant when it considered that 'it is understandable . . . that external powers may be exercised, and thus become exclusive, without any legislation having first been adopted'. Taken literally, the Court is addressing here the consequences of the exercise of external powers (they thus become exclusive), but that was not in issue. The question was whether, *a priori*, before its exercise either internally or externally, the Community's competence to conclude GATS was exclusive. A couple of paragraphs further down in the Opinion,[75] the Court restated the idea in the following terms: 'Save where internal powers can only be effectively exercised at the same time as external powers . . . , internal competence can give rise to exclusive external competence only if it is exercised'. But how can there be exclusive 'external' competence where the 'internal' competence is not exclusive? In an area where the competences of the EU and the Member States are generally shared (let us take environmental protection as an example), what could be the justification for considering that, if the EU's competence can only be exercised usefully through the conclusion of an international agreement, the competence to conclude such an agreement becomes exclusive? Suppose there is the policy aim of protecting the tropical rainforests. The EU on its own is clearly unable to provide

[73] Ibid, paras 85–86.

[74] Cf R Schütze, 'Federalism and Foreign Affairs: Mixity as a (Inter)national Phenomenon' in C Hillion and P Koutrakos (eds), *Mixed Agreements Revisited—The EU and its Member States in the World* (Hart Publishing, 2010) 78–9.

[75] *Opinion 1/94* (n 63 above) para 89.

for such protection through the mere adoption of internal legislation. But on what grounds should that be a justification for exclusive EU competence to conclude an international agreement on the subject? Surely, in the event that the EU does not act, the Member States retain the power to conclude such an agreement, as they retain power over environmental protection generally, in the absence of EU action. Of course, once the EU has acted in a particular field, the Member States to some degree lose power.[76] But, again, that was not in issue in *Opinion 1/94*.

The Commission's third argument as regards implied powers was that (current) Articles 114 and 352 TFEU formed the basis for exclusive external competence, an argument if anything more difficult to understand than the two previous ones. The Court's reply to that argument clarified the extent of the Community's external powers in matters covered by GATS, and perhaps this part of the Court's reasoning should have preceded the rebuttal of the Commission's claim. As regards (current) Article 114 TFEU, the Court pointed out, it was undeniable that, where harmonizing powers had been exercised, the harmonization measures thus adopted could limit, or even remove, the freedom of the Member States to negotiate with non-member countries. However, an internal power which had not been exercised in a specific field could not confer exclusive external competence in that field on the Community. (Current) Article 352 TFEU, on the other hand, could not in itself vest exclusive competence in the Community at international level. Save where internal powers could only be effectively exercised at the same time as external powers (see comments above), internal competence could give rise to exclusive external competence only if it was exercised, and this applied *a fortiori* to Article 352.[77]

After having thus effectively restated the *AETR* principle, the Court further considered the extent of the Community's powers in matters covered by GATS. Whereas earlier in the Opinion the Court appeared to suggest that the Treaty chapters on services and establishment in no way extended to the treatment of non-nationals, it now qualified that approach. The Court stated that, although the only objective expressly mentioned in those chapters was the attainment of the freedoms in question for nationals of the Member States, it did not follow that the Community institutions were prohibited from using the powers conferred on them in that field in order to specify the treatment which was to be accorded to nationals of non-member countries. It then pointed to, and discussed, numerous Community acts which contained provisions to that effect, and found that very different objectives could be pursued by the incorporation of external provisions. The Court effectively accepted such practice, and concluded its description thereof by stating that, whenever the Community had included in its internal legislative acts provisions relating to the treatment of nationals of non-member countries or expressly conferred on its institutions powers to negotiate with non-member countries, it acquired exclusive competence in the spheres covered by those acts. The same

[76] See Ch 7 for recent case law illustrating this.

[77] *Opinion 1/94* (n 63 above) paras 87–89.

applied in any event, the Court continued, even in the absence of any express provision authorizing its institutions to negotiate with non-member countries, where the Community had achieved complete harmonization of the rules governing access to a self-employed activity, because the common rules thus adopted could be affected within the meaning of the *AETR* judgment if the Member States retained freedom to negotiate with non-member countries. That was not the case in all services sectors, however, as the Commission had acknowledged. It followed that competence to conclude GATS was shared between the Community and the Member States.[78]

The Court was surely right in accepting that EU harmonization measures in the areas of establishment and services may have an external dimension. It does not make much sense to harmonize, for example, the legislation of the Member States concerning banking activities in the internal market without at the same time defining, at least to some extent, the treatment of non-EU banks seeking to establish themselves in the EU.[79] The Court therefore acknowledged that the EU's substantive competence as regards establishment and services extends to the treatment of nationals of non-member countries, in so far as this is connected with internal market harmonization.[80] It essentially left it to the EU legislature to decide to what extent provisions to that effect are required. What is noteworthy is that, in this context, the Court also accepted that legislative provisions conferring on the EU external negotiating powers give rise to exclusive external competence. The EU legislature may, in other words, withdraw the competence to conclude international agreements from the Member States either by way of substantive regulation of a particular subject matter, or simply by stating that henceforth it will be for the EU to negotiate internationally.

Similarly, it is logical that once the rules on access to a particular self-employed activity are fully harmonized at EU level, the Member States have lost their freedom to conclude international agreements on access to that activity by nationals of non-member States.

TRIPs

As regards exclusive implied powers to conclude the TRIPs Agreement, the Commission relied on the same types of arguments, i.e. the existence of internal legislative acts which could be affected in the meaning of *AETR*; the need to participate in the conclusion in order to achieve one of the objectives of the Treaty; and (current)

[78] Ibid, paras 90–98.

[79] For a description of the external dimension of the internal market in financial services at the time of the Opinion, see P Eeckhout, *The European Internal Market and International Trade—A Legal Analysis* (OUP, 1994) ch 2.

[80] A Dashwood, 'The Attribution of External Competence' in Dashwood and Hillion (n 2 above) 130.

Articles 114 and 352 TFEU. The Court was able to brush those arguments aside in a couple of paragraphs. First, it regarded the reference to *Opinion 1/76* as being just as disputable here as in the case of GATS, because unification or harmonization of intellectual property rights in the Community did not have to be accompanied by agreements with non-member countries in order to be effective. Secondly, (current) Articles 114 and 352 could not in themselves confer exclusive competence. Thirdly, harmonization within the Community in certain areas covered by TRIPs was only partial, and in other areas there was no harmonization whatsoever. Trade marks were an example of partial harmonization, whereas protection of undisclosed technical information, industrial designs, and patents were subjects where there was no harmonization. The *AETR* principle therefore did not apply to the whole of TRIPs.[81]

The Court could have concluded its analysis there, but it chose to highlight the reverse of the coin as well.[82] Some Member States had argued that the TRIPs provisions on effective protection of intellectual property rights fell within national competence. The Court, however, pointed out that, if that argument was to be understood as meaning that all those matters were within some sort of domain reserved to the Member States, it could not be accepted. The Community was certainly competent to harmonize national rules on those matters, in so far as, in the words of (current) Article 115 TFEU, they 'directly affect the establishment or functioning of the internal market'. But the fact remained that the Community institutions had not yet exercised their powers in the field of the 'enforcement of intellectual property rights', with the exception of Regulation 3842/86 laying down measures to prohibit the release for free circulation of counterfeit goods.[83] The Court thus recalled its settled case law that there are no *a priori* areas of exclusive Member State competence. Much as the Court is unwilling to confirm exclusive EU powers other than in certain well-defined areas, it also rejects claims for exclusive national competence.

In the literature, *Opinion 1/94* was characterized as embodying greater reluctance by the Court to confirm external competence, compared to earlier case law. It was regarded as signalling a new phase of judicial retrenchment.[84] As regards implied powers, however, it is doubtful whether that perception was justified. The Court left *AETR* and *Opinion 1/76* fully intact. It even accepted the claim, not obvious, that *Opinion 1/76* established exclusive competence. The Court also identified the novel principle that legislative acts may bring about exclusive external competence when they provide for the conclusion of international agreements. It applied the *AETR* principle in much the same way as in its previous case law; the

[81] *Opinion 1/94* (n 63 above) paras 99–103.

[82] Ibid, para 104.

[83] [1986] OJ L357/1.

[84] J de la Rochère, 'L'ère des compétences partagées' (1995) 390 RMCUE 466; JHJ Bourgeois, 'The EC in the WTO and Advisory Opinion 1/94: An Echternach Procession' (1995) 32 CML Rev 780; M Hilf, 'The ECJ's Opinion 1/94 on the WTO—No Surprise, but Wise?' (1995) 6 EJIL 254 and 258.

pre-emption argument only extends to the precise and specific subject matter of the internal legislation. In fact, the Commission could have been successful with its implied-powers argument only if the Court had significantly expanded the scope of the relevant principles, or had accepted a new principle, such as a notion of political necessity which would determine exclusive external competence. If the Court had agreed with the Commission, certain external powers would have been exclusive where the corresponding internal competences were not.

As a matter of fact, the next ruling in which the Court addressed implied powers, *Opinion 2/94* on accession to the European Convention on Human Rights (ECHR), displayed far greater judicial restraint to confirm external powers.[85]

The limits of *Opinion 2/94*

The question of the scope and nature of the EU's powers in the area of the protection of human rights is central to European constitutionalism. As the EU grows into an ever more full-blooded polity, with a correspondingly rich legal system, it gets involved in an increasing number of policy areas which may affect basic rights and entitlements of citizens and non-citizens, such as immigration, asylum, non-discrimination, and criminal law. Such involvement requires a more intensified human rights discourse. The constitutional basis for the development of such a discourse has long been precarious, but was then confirmed and gradually strengthened through successive Treaty amendments. The present picture is one of a multiplicity of sources for human rights protection in the EU.

As is well known, the Court of Justice was compelled to 'discover' the protection of fundamental rights in the Community legal order through the construction of general principles of Community law, which included such rights. Those human rights in the form of general principles of Community law were derived from the constitutional traditions of the Member States, and from international human rights instruments to which the Member States are parties, in particular the ECHR. At the Maastricht intergovernmental conference the Member States, as masters of the Treaties, confirmed the jurisprudence in (then) Article 6(2) TEU. In 2000, a special Convention elaborated a Charter of Fundamental Rights of the European Union, and the Treaty of Lisbon incorporates the Charter by conferring on it the same legal status as the Treaties (see Article 6(1) TEU). Most importantly, for the purpose of this section, Article 6(2) TEU now provides that the EU 'shall accede to the European Convention for the Protection of Human Rights and Fundamental Freedoms'; however, this accession 'shall not affect the Union's competences as defined in the Treaties'.

[85] The Court essentially repeated the implied powers reasoning of *Opinion 1/94* in *Opinion 2/92 re Third Revised Decision of the OECD on national treatment* [1995] ECR I-521.

Human rights are not only ever more central to the EU's internal constitutional development, they are equally vital for the EU's external action. A mere cursory glance at the Treaties confirms the importance of human rights for external policies. According to Article 3(5) TEU, the objectives of the EU in its relations with the wider world include 'the protection of human rights'. This is elaborated upon in Article 21 TEU, paragraph 1 of which provides that the EU's action on the international scene will seek to advance 'democracy, the rule of law, the universality and indivisibility of human rights and fundamental freedoms, respect for human dignity, the principles of equality and solidarity'. Article 21(2)(b) confirms that EU external policies must aim to 'consolidate and support democracy, the rule of law, human rights and the principles of international law'. Given the number of troublespots in this world from the perspective of democracy and the protection of human rights, Articles 3 and 21 clearly set a broad and important agenda for the EU's external action. The EU has, for some time now, pursued an external human rights policy. Agreements with non-member countries are now as a rule predicated on respect for democracy, the rule of law, and human rights, and there are also autonomous external policies which are oriented towards human rights protection, for example in the area of trade preferences.

Since World War II, the protection of human rights has been the subject of intense international law-making.[86] It would seem natural that the EU should also be able to participate in such law-making, first of all with a view to ensuring that its policies comply with internationally agreed standards, and perhaps also so as to be able to bring its own experience of the protection of human rights to an international negotiating table. Prior to the entry into force of the Lisbon Treaty, however, there were no provisions in the Treaties which expressly conferred competence to conclude human rights treaties. In that context, further issues were posed by the absence of the EU from the system of the ECHR. In practice, the EU institutions needed to respect the provisions of the ECHR, because those provisions constituted general principles of EC law which the Court would uphold, but the lack of formal participation in the ECHR system meant that the European Court of Human Rights (ECtHR) had no jurisdiction over acts of the EU institutions.[87]

There has been a long and intense debate, in both political and legal terms, about the merits and drawbacks of full EC (or EU) participation in the ECHR system. This is not the place to engage with all aspects of that debate. In the course of 1994, however, the Council of Ministers decided to request the Opinion of the Court of Justice on the compatibility of EC accession to the ECHR with the EC Treaty. Technically, this was a request on an envisaged international agreement, notwithstanding the fact that no negotiations on the subject had taken place or were being

[86] H Steiner, P Alston, and R Goodman, *International Human Rights in Context—Law, Politics, Morals* (3rd edn, OUP, 2007).

[87] See, however, *Bosphorus Hava Yollari Turizm ve Ticaret Anonim Şirketi v. Ireland* [GC], no. 45036/98, ECHR 2005-VI.

conducted in the Council of Europe. There was even no consensus among the Member States on the question of principle as to whether such negotiations, and a resulting accession, were desirable. The Court none the less admitted the request, or at least one part of it, and took the opportunity to develop a judicial definition of the Community's powers in the field of human rights, including the power to conclude human rights treaties. It is from that angle that we analyse *Opinion 2/94* here.[88]

The Council had requested the Court's Opinion, both as regards (a) competence under the EC Treaty to join the ECHR, and (b) the compatibility of accession with substantive provisions and principles of Community law, in particular the exclusive jurisdiction of the Court of Justice and the autonomy of the Community legal order. The Court admitted only the first part of the request.[89] It considered that it was in the interests of the Community institutions and of the States concerned, including non-member countries, to have the question of competence clarified from the outset of negotiations, and even before the main points of the agreement were negotiated. The only condition was that the purpose of the envisaged agreement be known, and there was no doubt that that was the case as regards accession to the ECHR: the general purpose and subject matter of the ECHR and the institutional significance of accession were perfectly well known.[90] The second part of the request was not, however, admissible. In order fully to answer the question whether accession would be compatible with the rules of the Treaty, in particular with (current) Articles 19(1) TEU and 344 TFEU relating to the jurisdiction of the Court, the Court had to have sufficient information regarding the arrangements by which the Community envisaged submitting to the judicial control machinery established by the ECHR.[91]

The Court's reasoning on competence was as follows. It first referred to the principle of conferral (see current Article 5(1) and (2) TEU), which provided that the Community was to act within the limits of the powers conferred upon it by the Treaty and of the objectives assigned to it therein. It followed from that provision that the Community had only those powers which had been conferred upon it. That principle of conferred powers had to be respected in both the internal action and the international action of the Community. The Community acted ordinarily on the basis of specific powers which were not necessarily the express consequence of specific provisions of the Treaty but could also be implied from them. Thus, in the field of international relations it was settled case law that the competence of the

[88] *Opinion 2/94 re Accession to the ECHR* [1996] ECR I–1759. See also, *inter alia*, JHH Weiler and S Fries, 'A Human Rights Policy for the European Community and Union: The Question of Competences' in P Alston (ed), *The EU and Human Rights* (OUP, 1999) 147; A Arnull, 'Left To Its Own Devices? Opinion 2/94 and the Protection of Fundamental Rights in the European Union' in A Dashwood and C Hillion (eds), *The General Law of EC External Relations* (Sweet & Maxwell, 2000) 61–78.

[89] See also Ch 8.

[90] *Opinion 2/94* (n 88 above) paras 10–12.

[91] Ibid, para 20.

Community to enter into international commitments not only flowed from express provisions of the Treaty but could also be implied from those provisions. The Court then referred, more specifically, to the principle that, whenever Community law had created for the institutions of the Community powers within its internal system for the purpose of attaining a specific objective, the Community was empowered to enter into the international commitments necessary for attainment of that objective even in the absence of an express provision to that effect.[92]

After having thus identified the issue as one of external implied powers, the Court turned to the subject of human rights. It first pointed out that no Treaty provision conferred on the Community institutions any general power to enact rules on human rights or to conclude international conventions in this field. The Court then stated that, in the absence of express or implied powers, it was necessary to consider whether (current) Article 352 TFEU could constitute a legal basis for accession. That provision the Court characterized as designed to fill the gap where no specific provisions of the Treaty conferred on the Community institutions express or implied powers to act, if such powers appeared none the less to be necessary to enable the Community to carry out its functions with a view to attaining one of the objectives laid down by the Treaty. However, Article 352 could not serve as a basis for widening the scope of Community powers beyond the general framework created by the provisions of the Treaty as a whole and, in particular, by those that defined the tasks and the activities of the Community. On any view, Article 352 could not be used as a basis for the adoption of provisions whose effect would, in substance, be to amend the Treaty without following the procedure which it provided for that purpose.[93]

In the last part of the Opinion, the Court examined accession in the light of the scope of Article 352. It recalled the importance of respect for human rights, as emphasized in various declarations and provisions of the Treaties (see above). It further recalled that it was well settled that fundamental rights formed an integral part of the general principles of law whose observance the Court ensured. Respect for human rights was therefore a condition of the lawfulness of Community acts. However, the Court finally held, accession to the ECHR would entail a substantial change in the Community system for the protection of human rights in that it would entail the entry of the Community into a distinct international institutional system as well as integration of all the provisions of the ECHR into the Community legal order. Such a modification of the system for the protection of human rights in the Community, with equally fundamental institutional implications for the Community and for the Member States, would be of constitutional significance and would therefore be such as to go beyond the scope of Article 352. It could be brought about only by way of Treaty amendment. Therefore, as Community law stood, the Community had no competence to accede to the ECHR.[94]

[92] Ibid, paras 23–26. [93] Ibid, paras 27–30. [94] Ibid, paras 32–36.

The Court's reasoning in *Opinion 2/94* was not straightforward, and it is difficult to deduce broader principles from the ruling, in particular as regards general EU competence to conclude human rights treaties. One issue is the relationship between the implied powers doctrine and Article 352 TFEU. A possible reading is that the Court wrong-foots the student of the Opinion, by first reciting the implied powers principles, and then swiftly turning to Article 352, 'in the absence of express or implied powers'. That seems to suggest that Article 352 is not itself part of the implied powers doctrine, and that the Court needs to analyse it because the Treaty does not elsewhere contain express or implied powers in the human rights field. In itself that approach is unobjectionable, if it were not for the lack of any real analysis of whether other provisions of the Treaty conferred implied powers in this field. The Court simply asserted that 'no Treaty provision confers on the Community institutions any general power to enact rules on human rights or to conclude international conventions in this field'. It is true, of course, that there are no specific provisions to that effect. But if respect for human rights is a condition of the lawfulness of Community acts, as the Court confirms further down in the Opinion, could it not then be argued that the institutions have the duty, and therefore the power, in all the areas in which they might exercise conferred competences, to ensure that their acts do not violate fundamental rights? One could call this a functional human rights competence.[95] It is surely arguable that the EU is capable of binding itself, within the limits of the powers conferred upon it, to an international human rights instrument, so as to ensure that its legislation and executive acts comply with internationally agreed human rights standards. The Court, however, did not examine any such arguments in the section of its Opinion on implied powers.

Nor did it analyse competence in the sphere of protection of human rights when scrutinizing the scope of Article 352. The function of that provision is to fill the gap where no specific Treaty provisions confer express or implied powers, and such powers none the less appear necessary to enable the EU to carry out its functions with a view to attaining one of the objectives laid down by the Treaties. But the Court did not discuss whether human rights powers came within that category. It jumped to the point that Article 352 could not be used for the adoption of provisions whose effect would in substance be to amend the Treaty.[96]

That brings us to what was effectively the core of the Court's argument. Accession to the ECHR was in substance Treaty amendment. If one accepts that, it is obvious that no Treaty provision could confer the power to do so by way of conclusion of an international agreement; amendment had to take place through the proper procedure in the Treaty. In fact the Court could have taken this principle

[95] P Eeckhout, 'The EU Charter of Fundamental Rights and the Federal Question' (2002) 39 CML Rev 984.

[96] Cf Arnull (n 88 above) 71–2, where he argues that it would be a mistake to conclude that (current) Art 352 TFEU is completely devoid of potential in the field of human rights.

as its starting point, and could have avoided speaking about implied powers and Article 352 altogether.

As regards the constitutional significance of accession to the ECHR, requiring Treaty amendment, the Court pointed to the 'substantial change in the present Community system for the protection of human rights'. That substantial change included 'the entry of the Community into a distinct international institutional system' (obviously a reference to the jurisdiction of the ECtHR) as well as the 'integration of all the provisions of the Convention into the Community legal order'. Such a modification of the system had 'equally fundamental institutional implications for the Community and for the Member States'. The Court, however, did not clarify those implications. At the level of the institutions the most fundamental implication was obvious: accession to the ECHR would in effect mean that aggrieved citizens could complain to the ECtHR that their rights were violated by an act of an EU institution. It is not obvious at all, however, what the fundamental implications would be for the Member States. Nor is it obvious that the integration of all the Convention provisions into the EU legal order would be of a such a fundamental character. At the time of the Opinion, the Court had, for a number of years already, been applying the ECHR in the guise of general principles of EC law, and it is doubtful whether actual incorporation of the ECHR would of necessity lead to a stricter application of its provisions. The above dissection therefore reveals one single decisive argument against accession to the ECHR: the implications of external review, mainly by the ECtHR, for the institutions, including the Court itself.

The issue of accession to the ECHR is not as such the object of this section. The Lisbon Treaty now provides for such accession, which at the time of writing is in the process of negotiation. But does the EU have broader powers in the human rights field? Is it capable of concluding other international agreements for the protection of human rights? That is an implied powers question, and the answer to that question cannot be derived from *Opinion 2/94*. Whilst that Opinion showed that the Court was not favourably disposed towards recognizing broad competence in the field of human rights, its reasoning in the Opinion was too succinct to enable firm conclusions to be drawn. One should hope that the opportunity may come for the Court to engage with the argument for a functional human rights power, as discussed above. That there must be some measure of competence to conclude human rights treaties follows, in the current state of EU law, simply from the *AETR* principle. An example are the non-discrimination directives,[97] which would clearly be affected, in an *AETR* sense, if a new international anti-discrimination instrument were negotiated.

[97] Directive 2000/43 implementing the principle of equal treatment between persons irrespective of racial or ethnic origin [2000] OJ L180/22 and Directive 2000/78 establishing a general framework for equal treatment in employment and occupation [2000] OJ L303/16.

The *Open Skies* cases

A further development in the implied-powers doctrine consisted of a series of parallel judgments concerning Community and national competence to conclude air transport agreements. The Commission had been proposing the development of a common external air transport policy since the start of the 1990s, in parallel with the completion and liberalization of the internal air transport market.[98] The proposal had its merits, because the internal market cannot be genuinely completed and cannot function without distortion of competition as long as individual Member States continue to determine external traffic rights by concluding bilateral aviation agreements with non-member countries. Such agreements typically reserved external traffic rights for domestic carriers, i.e. carriers majority owned or controlled by a Member State's own nationals, whereas competition in the internal market between carriers was free. There was in effect a common regime for internal trade in transport services, and a fractured regime involving discrimination between air carriers for external trade.

The Commission's proposals none the less met with resistance in the Council. At some point the Council agreed that the Commission could start negotiations with, *inter alia*, the United States on air transport issues, but not negotiations covering exchange of traffic rights.[99] The United States in particular had developed the policy of concluding so-called 'open skies' agreements with individual Member States. It was generally regarded to have benefited in those negotiations from its stronger negotiating power.

In the proceedings for *Opinion 1/94* the Commission argued that external transport services came within the common commercial policy as defined in (then) Article 113 EC.[100] If the Court had agreed with that argument, Community competence to conclude air transport agreements would have been exclusive, and the Member States would have been compelled to relinquish power to the Community. The Court was not impressed, however, and pointed to its case law on implied powers in the transport sector, i.e. *AETR* and *Opinion 1/76*: international agreements in transport matters came within the Treaty provisions on a common transport policy. Implicitly, therefore, but not expressly, the Court confirmed that the power to conclude external transport agreements was shared, and not exclusive.

The Commission none the less did not abandon its efforts to bring about an external air transport policy. As its powers of political persuasion proved insufficient, it decided to bring proceedings against a large number of Member States, on the grounds that the 'open skies' agreements with the United States violated Community law. The Commission argued that those agreements were in breach of the principle of exclusive external competence, and that the clauses on ownership and

[98] See Eeckhout (n 79 above) ch 3.
[99] Case C–466/98 *Commission v. United Kingdom* [2002] ECR I–9427, Opinion of Tizzano AG, para 12.
[100] *Opinion 1/94* (n 63 above) paras 48–52; see Ch 2.

control of airlines in those agreements were contrary to (current) Article 49 TFEU, on the right of establishment.[101]

As regards external competence, the Commission advanced two arguments. It contended that there was an external competence within the meaning of *Opinion 1/76*, and that such competence was exclusive in nature. It further claimed that there was exclusive competence by virtue of the *AETR* principle: the internal Community legislation on air transport was affected by commitments to exchange traffic rights and to open up access for third-country carriers to the intra-Community market.

Opinion 1/76-type competence

The first Commission argument was particularly interesting. The Commission referred to the Court's statements in *Opinion 1/94*, to the effect that *Opinion 1/76* concerned exclusive competence in cases where an international agreement was required for the effective exercise of internal competence; and that external powers could be exercised, and thus become exclusive, without any internal legislation having first been adopted. The Commission claimed that in the field of air transport purely internal measures would hardly be effective, given the international nature of the activities carried on and the impossibility of separating the internal and external markets both economically and legally. The discrimination, the distortions of competition, and the disturbance of the Community market resulting from the bilateral open skies agreements proved that the aims of the common air transport policy could not be attained without the conclusion of an agreement between the Community and the United States.[102]

With this argument the Commission effectively invited the Court to make more sense of its statements in *Opinion 1/94* regarding the meaning of *Opinion 1/76*. Tizzano AG took up the gauntlet and mounted an impressive clarification of the judicial pronouncements in issue.[103] He recalled the Court's statements in *Opinion 1/76*, and compared them to the logic underlying (current) Article 352 TFEU, which in a sense, he observed, the Court had transposed to the sphere of the Community's external action. He then stressed that the conclusions drawn by the Commission from this case law stemmed from a mistaken belief that in

[101] *Commission v. United Kingdom* (n 99 above); in this case the Commission did not make the claim of exclusive competence); Case C–467/98 *Commission v. Denmark* [2002] ECR I–9519; Case C–468/98 *Commission v. Sweden* [2002] ECR I–9575; Case C–469/98 *Commission v. Finland* [2002] ECR I–9627; Case C–471/98 *Commission v. Belgium* [2002] ECR I–9681; Case C–472/98 *Commission v. Luxembourg* [2002] ECR I–9741; Case C–475/98 *Commission v. Austria* [2002] ECR I–9797; Case C–476/98 *Commission v. Germany* [2002] ECR I–9855; Case C–523/04 *Commission v. Netherlands* [2007] ECR I–3267.

[102] *Commission v. Germany* (n 101 above) paras 71–74.

[103] *Commission v. United Kingdom* (n 99 above) paras 46–59 of the Opinion (there was one Opinion for all the cases).

affirming the Community's competence in the situations referred to in *Opinion 1/76*, the Court also held this competence to be automatically exclusive. It was in his view apparent that all the Court had actually affirmed was that the 'necessity' for an agreement could enable the Community to affirm its external competence, but that it would always be the specific recognition of such 'necessity', i.e. the actual exercise of that competence, which would render it exclusive. The subsequent case law (*Opinions 2/91* and *1/94*) corroborated such a reading, but it was above all confirmed by the problems which the Commission's argument raised when one considered how and by whom the assessment should be carried out as to the 'necessity' of an agreement. That could only be done in accordance with the proper Treaty procedures. There could be no recognition of the 'necessity' for an agreement unless there had been a specific assessment by the competent institutions and the procedures prescribed had been followed. It could be debated, possibly even before the Court, whether in a specific case the assessment of the 'necessity' for an agreement was properly carried out (or omitted), but there could certainly be no escaping the fact that the institutions empowered to carry out the assessment and the procedures to be followed were those in the Treaty. Otherwise, there was a risk of introducing elements of uncertainty, even arbitrariness, into the division of powers between Community and Member States, and of distorting the procedures and the inter-institutional balances established by the Treaty. Applying those principles to the cases at hand, Tizzano AG pointed out that the Council had consistently rejected the need for an air transport agreement with the United States covering traffic rights. Of course, one could take the view that the Council's assessment was unlawful. But in that case the relevant Council decision should be challenged or an action for failure to act should be brought. In the absence of any steps of that nature, the Council's decisions had to be presumed lawful. In any event, their validity could not be challenged indirectly and by means of inappropriate procedures (such as enforcement proceedings against Member States).

The Advocate General's approach was broadly in line with the reading of *Opinion 1/76* suggested above, in that he recognized that this ruling did not establish an *a priori* exclusive competence of the kind which exists in matters of commercial policy and conservation of fish resources, or in cases where the EU has previously exercised internal competence by the adoption of internal rules which are liable to be affected by the provisions of an international agreement (*AETR*). It is only the exercise of competence which creates its exclusive character. Again one must repeat that the notion of exclusivity is hardly relevant in such cases, since in the disputes on competence one is invariably dealing with the question whether there is exclusivity prior to exercise. If the Community had already exercised its competences by concluding an air transport agreement with the United States, the cases under consideration could only have been of a radically different character: namely whether any agreements concluded by the Member States complied with the EC agreement with the United States.

The reading of the Advocate General thus effectively emasculated the exclusive nature of the *Opinion 1/76*-type external competence, and rightly so. Here, exclusive competence only becomes nascent at the moment of its exercise. It is then a stillborn concept, for the notion of power or competence logically precedes its exercise, or the acts adopted under it.

The Court, however, made no effort to clarify its statements linking necessity and exclusivity with the exercise of external competence. Instead, it distinguished the *Open Skies* cases from *Opinion 1/76*. The Court first recalled its various statements, reiterating that the hypothesis in *Opinion 1/76* was that internal competence could be effectively exercised only at the same time as the external competence, the conclusion of the international agreement thus being necessary in order to attain objectives of the Treaty that could not be attained by establishing autonomous rules. That was not the case as regards external air transport. The Court pointed out that the institutions could arrange concerted action in relation to the United States or prescribe the approach to be taken by the Member States in their external dealings, so as to mitigate any discrimination or distortions of competition. It had therefore not been established that, by reason of such discrimination or distortions of competition, the aims of the Treaty in the area of transport could not be achieved by establishing autonomous rules. The Court then drew attention to the fact that the Council had considered it unnecessary for the Community to exercise external competence by negotiating an agreement with the United States covering traffic rights.[104] It concluded that its findings could not be called into question by the fact that the measures adopted by the Council in relation to the internal market in air transport contained a number of provisions concerning nationals of non-member countries. Contrary to what the Commission maintained, the relatively limited character of those provisions precluded inferring from them that the realization of the freedom to provide services in the field of air transport in favour of nationals of the Member States was inextricably linked to the treatment to be accorded in the Community to nationals of non-member countries, or in non-member countries to nationals of the Member States. The Community could therefore not validly claim that there was an exclusive external competence, within the meaning of *Opinion 1/76*, to conclude an air transport agreement with the United States.[105]

If the Court did not, in contrast with the Advocate General, clarify *Opinion 1/76*-type exclusive implied powers, it would none the less seem that the scope for such powers is much restricted. One has difficulty imagining cases where internal competence could not be exercised without concluding an international agreement within the strict parameters set by the Court. It is even doubtful whether the agreement in issue in *Opinion 1/76* came within those parameters.

[104] The Commission did receive a mandate to negotiate with the US, and it is clear from the judgments that it disputed the restricted scope of that mandate. It is also obvious, however, that the Council never agreed to the inclusion of negotiations on traffic rights in that original mandate.

[105] *Commission v. Germany* (n 101 above) paras 80–90.

In that case the Court stated that limiting inland waterway capacity in the Rhine and Moselle basins required an agreement with Switzerland, because of traditional navigation of Swiss vessels, which were subject to the system of freedom of navigation established by international agreements of long standing. But could not the Council, here too, have arranged for concerted action towards Switzerland in the internal legislation, and could it not have prescribed the approach to be taken by the Member States in their external dealings with Switzerland on this issue?

By way of conclusion on this point, it may be repeated that *Opinion 1/76* is better looked at as a case which did not establish exclusive external competence, but simply confirmed general parallelism between internal and external powers.

AETR-type competence

In the air transport cases the Court also looked at *AETR*-type external competence. Again Tizzano AG offered a comprehensive and persuasive analysis. It is not necessary to describe his entire argument, in particular as the Commission alleged that the agreements concluded by the Member States affected a series of common rules, requiring detailed scrutiny. Instead it may be sufficient to highlight some of the general points which the Advocate General made, and to look at just a couple of applications.

Tizzano AG first recalled previous judicial statements on the matter. He concluded from them that, in principle, in matters covered by common rules, the Member States could not under any circumstances conclude international agreements, even if these were entirely consistent with the common rules, since any steps taken outside the framework of the Community institutions would be incompatible with the unity of the common market and the uniform application of Community law. Further consequences should, however, be inferred from the case law. First, Member States could not conclude international agreements, in matters covered by common rules, even if the texts of the agreements reproduced the common rules *verbatim* or incorporated them by reference. The conclusion of such agreements could also prejudice the uniform application of Community law. The 'reception' of common rules into the agreements would be no guarantee that the rules would then in fact be uniformly applied, and that any amendments which might be adopted internally would be fully and promptly transposed into the agreements. Further, any such 'reception' would have the effect of distorting the nature and legal regime of the common rules, and entail a real and serious risk that they would be removed from review by the Court under the Treaty. Secondly, the Member States could not undertake international obligations in matters governed by common rules even in order to eliminate conflicts between those rules and agreements concluded by them before the rules were adopted. Not even the requirement to ensure the full and correct application of Community law could justify unilateral action by Member States; that requirement was in principle to be fulfilled by the Community itself.[106]

The Advocate General also considered that, between the situations of agreements which were in clear conflict with common rules, and agreements which covered the same subject matter as that governed by common rules, there was a considerable area. As an example he mentioned agreements which concerned aspects which were contiguous, so to speak, to those governed by common rules, or agreements which, while they concerned a matter which was to a large extent covered by common rules, related, however, to aspects not, or not yet, regulated by those rules.[107]

Tizzano AG further stressed that in order to establish that the common rules were 'affected' it was not enough to cite general effects of an economic nature which the agreements could have on the functioning of the internal market; what was required instead was to specify in detail the aspects of the Community legislation which could be prejudiced by the agreements.[108]

The Advocate General then proceeded to apply those principles, and the manner in which he did this perfectly illustrates the *AETR* doctrine. One example is the Commission's claim that the agreements with the United States affected Regulation 2407/92 on licensing of air carriers[109] and Regulation 2408/92 on access for Community air carriers to intra-Community air routes.[110] According to the Commission, those regulations laid down exhaustively the conditions for access to intra-Community routes, with regard to all air carriers, and the disputed agreements effectively permitted US carriers not satisfying the requirements of Regulation 2407/92 also to operate on intra-Community routes. Tizzano AG replied, however, that the Commission had misread the regulations. They only secured access to intra-Community routes for Community air carriers, and did not concern third-country carriers. The disputed agreements and the regulations therefore applied to different situations.[111]

A second, contrasting, example concerned Regulation 2409/92 on fares and rates for air services.[112] That regulation explicitly restricted to Community carriers the right to introduce lower fares than the ones existing for identical products within the Community. The Advocate General considered that it thereby indirectly but unequivocally excluded that right for non-Community carriers, who were thus prohibited from introducing such fares. He then established that the disputed agreements did amend the pricing rules contained in earlier bilateral agreements, and therefore infringed exclusive Community competence. It was irrelevant that some of the disputed agreements effected only minor amendments, and that some of the amendments were in fact intended to preserve the application of the

[106] *Commission v. United Kingdom* (n 99 above) paras 71–74, Opinion of Tizzano AG.
[107] Ibid, para 75. [108] Ibid, para 77. [109] [1992] OJ L240/1. [110] [1992] OJ L240/8.
[111] *Commission v. United Kingdom* (n 99 above) paras 81–84, Opinion of Tizzano AG.
[112] [1992] OJ L240/15.

regulation. The Member States should have allowed the Community to negotiate on these matters, and, if that proved impossible, they should have acted within the framework of the Community institutions by seeking authorization to negotiate the necessary amendments, in concert and in close co-operation with those institutions.[113]

The Court essentially followed the approach of its Advocate General. It first examined whether the *AETR* reasoning actually applied to air transport, in the light of the wording of (then) Article 80(2) EC, which merely enabled the Council to 'decide whether, to what extent and by what procedure appropriate provisions may be laid down for... air transport'.[114] The Court none the less considered that, if the Member States were free to enter into international commitments affecting the common rules adopted on the basis of Article 80(2), that would jeopardize the attainment of the objective pursued by those rules and would thus prevent the Community from fulfilling its task in the defence of the common interest. The *AETR* findings thus applied.[115]

The Court then recalled all its previous pronouncements on *AETR*-type exclusive competence. Those paragraphs in the judgments usefully collated the various ways in which international agreements may affect common rules, thereby giving rise to exclusive Community competence.

Exclusive competence arose, the Court stated, where the international commitments fell within the scope of the common rules, or in any event within an area which was already largely covered by such rules. In the latter case, the Member States could not enter into international commitments outside the framework of the Community institutions, even if there was no contradiction between those commitments and the common rules. Thus it was that, whenever the Community had included in its internal legislative acts provisions relating to the treatment of nationals of non-member countries or expressly conferred on its institutions powers to negotiate with non-member countries, it acquired an exclusive external competence in the spheres covered by those acts. The same applied, even in the absence of any express provision authorizing its institutions to negotiate with non-member countries, where the Community had achieved complete harmonization in a given area, because the common rules thus adopted could be affected within the meaning of the *AETR* judgment if the Member States retained freedom to negotiate with non-member countries. On the other hand, any distortions in the flow of services in the internal market which might arise from bilateral 'open skies' agreements concluded by Member States with non-member countries did not in themselves affect the common rules adopted in that area and were thus not capable of establishing an external competence of the Community. There was nothing in the Treaty to prevent the institutions arranging, in the common rules laid down by

[113] *Commission v. United Kingdom* (n 99 above) paras 89–97.
[114] Now Art 100(2) TFEU, with amendments.
[115] *Commission v. Germany* (n 101 above) paras 104–106.

them, concerted action in relation to non-member countries or to prevent them from prescribing the approach to be taken by the Member States in their external dealings.[116]

The Court's application of those principles to the cases at hand followed Tizzano AG's Opinion. The Court established that there was exclusive Community competence as regards the setting of fares and rates by non-Community carriers (Regulation 2409/92[117]), as regards computerized reservation systems (CRS) used by such carriers in the Community (Regulation 2299/89 on a code of conduct for computerized reservation systems[118]), and as regards the allocation of slots at Community airports (Regulation 95/93[119]). To the extent that Member States had included provisions on these matters in the disputed agreements, they had violated the *AETR* principle. The Court characterized those violations as a breach of the combined provisions of (current) Article 4(3) TEU, embodying the principle of loyalty, and the regulations in issue.

The consolidation of *Opinion 1/03*

The last major development in the case law on implied powers is the Court's Opinion on competence to conclude the new Lugano Convention on jurisdiction and the recognition and enforcement of judgments in civil and commercial matters.[120] The original Lugano Convention was a convention between the EFTA States and the EU Member States,[121] and ran in parallel with the 1968 Brussels Convention on jurisdiction and the enforcement of judgments in civil and commercial matters, which was based on (then) Article 293 EC.[122] The entry into force of the Treaty of Amsterdam created new Community powers in the field of judicial co-operation in civil matters, in Articles 61(1) and 65 EC.[123] Those powers were, *inter alia*, used to turn the Brussels Convention into Regulation 44/2001.[124] As the regulation involved a revision of the Brussels Convention, it was considered necessary to renegotiate the Lugano Convention. In the course of that process the question arose of whether the new Lugano Convention fell entirely within the exclusive competence of the Community, or within the shared competence of the Community and the Member States. The Council decided to refer that question to the Court of Justice, requesting an Opinion pursuant to (current) Article 218(11) TFEU.

116 Ibid, paras 108–112. 117 N 112 above. 118 [1989] OJ L220/1.

119 [1993] OJ L14/1.

120 *Opinion 1/03 re Lugano Convention* [2006] ECR I–1145. The Convention is published at [2009] OJ L147/5; the Court examined a draft of the Convention.

121 [1988] OJ L319/9.

122 [1978] OJ L304/34.

123 Now, with amendments, Arts 67 and 81 TFEU.

124 Regulation 44/2001 on jurisdiction and the recognition and enforcement of judgments in civil and commercial matters [2001] OJ L12/1.

Both Regulation 44/2001 and the Lugano Convention are complex legal instruments with many detailed and technical provisions. A full analysis is therefore outside the scope of this examination. Suffice it to say that the regulation contains a set of rules on the jurisdiction of courts hearing civil and commercial matters, and aims to resolve conflicts between different rules of jurisdiction in the various legal systems of the Member States. It further contains rules on recognition and enforcement of judgments between Member States. The essential question was whether the draft Lugano Convention, which basically aimed to extend the system of the regulation to a number of EFTA countries, came within the Community's exclusive *AETR*-type implied powers, by virtue of its proximity to Regulation 44/2001.

The Court started its analysis by looking at competence to conclude international agreements in general terms, and by so doing sought to consolidate its implied-powers case law.[125] It recalled *AETR* and *Opinion 1/76*, and pointed out that the principle established in the former judgment was the one relevant to the case at hand. The Court then referred to *Opinion 2/91*, where it had stated that the *AETR* principle also applies where rules have been adopted in areas falling outside common policies and, in particular, in areas where there are harmonizing measures.[126] Next, the Court mentioned how in *Opinion 1/94* and in the *Open Skies* judgments it had set out three situations in which it recognized exclusive competence: (a) where the international commitments fell within the scope of common rules, or in any event within an area which was already largely covered by such rules; (b) whenever the Community had included in its internal legislative acts provisions relating to the treatment of nationals of non-member countries or expressly conferred on its institutions powers to negotiate with non-member countries; and (c) where the Community had achieved complete harmonization in a given area. Noting that those three situations had given rise to much debate, the Court, however, emphasized that they were only examples, formulated in the light of the particular contexts with which the Court was concerned. It recalled that, ruling in much more general terms, it had found there to be exclusive competence where the conclusion of an agreement by the Member States was incompatible with the unity of the common market and the uniform application of Community law; or where, given the nature of the existing Community provisions, any agreement in that area would necessarily affect the Community rules within the meaning of *AETR*. On the other hand, there was no exclusive competence in the minimum standards situation of *Opinion 2/91*, or where the alleged distortions in the flow of services, referred to in the *Open Skies* cases, could arise.

The Court subsequently recalled the principle of conferred powers. Any competence, especially where it was exclusive and not expressly conferred by the Treaty,

[125] *Opinion 1/03* (n 120 above) paras 114–133.

[126] *Opinion 2/91* (n 39 above) para 11.

had to have its basis in conclusions drawn from a specific analysis of the relationship between the agreement envisaged and the Community law in force and from which it was clear that the conclusion of such an agreement was capable of affecting the Community rules.

Continuing its reasoning, the Court further explored the test of 'an area which is already covered to a large extent by Community rules'.[127] It stated that it was not necessary for the areas covered by the agreement and the Community legislation to coincide fully. The assessment had to be based not only on the scope of the rules in question but also on their nature and content. It was also necessary to take into account not only the current state of Community law but also its future development, in so far as that was foreseeable at the time of the analysis. In short, the Court concluded, it was essential to ensure a uniform and consistent application of the Community rules and the proper functioning of the system which they established in order to preserve the full effectiveness of Community law.

In its general analysis the Court, lastly, considered three further points. First, any initiative seeking to avoid contradictions between Community law and the agreement envisaged did not remove the obligation to determine, prior to the conclusion of the agreement, whether it was capable of affecting the Community rules. The Court gave the example of a so-called 'disconnection clause' (present in the draft Lugano Convention), providing that the agreement did not affect the application by the Member States of the relevant provisions of Community law.[128] Such a clause did not constitute a guarantee that the Community rules were not affected; on the contrary, it could provide an indication that those rules were affected. Such a mechanism seeking to prevent any conflict in the enforcement of the agreement was not in itself a decisive factor in resolving the question of whether the Community had exclusive competence; the answer to that question had to be established before the agreement was concluded.

Secondly, the legal basis for the Community rules, and more particularly the condition relating to the proper functioning of the internal market laid down in (then) Article 65 EC,[129] were, in themselves, irrelevant in determining whether an agreement affected Community rules: legal basis was determined by the principal component, whereas the rule which could possibly be affected might be merely an ancillary component of the legislation. The purpose of Community exclusive competence was primarily to preserve the effectiveness of Community law and the proper functioning of the systems established by its rules.

Thirdly, where an international agreement contained provisions which presumed a harmonization of legislative or regulatory measures of the Member States in an area for which the Treaty excluded such harmonization, the Community did not

[127] Ibid, paras 25–26.

[128] On disconnection clauses, see M Cremona, 'Disconnection Clauses in EU Law and Practice' in Hillion and Koutrakos (n 74 above) 160.

[129] Now, with amendments, Art 81 TFEU.

have the necessary competence to conclude the agreement: those limits concerned the very existence of external competence and not whether it was exclusive.

The Court then concluded its general analysis. It followed from all the foregoing that a comprehensive and detailed analysis had to be carried out to determine whether the Community had the competence to conclude an international agreement and whether that competence was exclusive. In doing so, account had to be taken not only of the area covered by the Community rules and by the provisions of the agreement envisaged, in so far as the latter were known, but also of the nature and content of those rules and provisions, to ensure that the agreement was not capable of undermining the uniform and consistent application of the Community rules and the proper functioning of the system which they established.

The Court then proceeded to make a detailed analysis of the revised Lugano Convention, and of the Community's competence to conclude it. A full account of that analysis is outside the scope of this chapter. In essence, the Court emphasized that the rules on jurisdiction in Regulation 44/2001 formed a unified and coherent system resolving conflicts between different rules of jurisdiction, which applied also to relations between a Member State and a non-member country.[130] Given that system, any international agreement also establishing a unified system of rules on conflicts of jurisdiction such as that established by the regulation was capable of affecting those rules of jurisdiction.[131] The new Lugano Convention, although aiming to ensure consistency with the regulation, could lead to a different selection of the appropriate forum than would result from the regulation.[132] As regards the envisaged disconnection clause, the Court recalled what it had previously stated about disconnection clauses, and added that a disconnection clause in an international agreement of private international law had a particular nature and was different from a classical disconnection clause. Here, the purpose was not to ensure that Regulation 44/2001 was applied each time that that was possible, but rather to regulate in a consistent manner the relationship between the regulation and the convention. There were, moreover, exceptions to the disconnection clause.[133]

As regards the rules on the recognition and enforcement of judgments, the Court considered that they were not autonomous, and distinct from the rules on jurisdiction, but were closely linked.[134] The Court again found that Regulation 44/2001 established a unified and coherent system. It was demonstrated that the Community rules on the recognition and enforcement of judgments were indissociable from those on the jurisdiction of courts, with which they formed a unified and coherent system. The new Lugano Convention would affect the uniform and consistent application of the Community rules as regards both the jurisdiction of courts and the recognition and enforcement of judgments and the proper functioning of the unified system established by those rules.[135]

[130] *Opinion 1/03* (n 120 above) paras 141–144. [131] Ibid, para 151.
[132] Ibid, para 153. [133] Ibid, paras 154–158. [134] Ibid, para 164.
[135] Ibid, paras 168 and 172.

The Court concluded that the new Lugano Convention came within the Community's exclusive competence.

The Court's overall emphasis in *Opinion 1/03* was thus on safeguarding the uniformity and effectiveness of Community law. This led to an open and general conception of the *AETR* principle. The Court pointed out that the particular situations which it identified in *Opinion 1/94* and the *Open Skies* cases were only examples. This open-ended approach further informed the passage where the Court confirmed that it was not necessary for the areas covered by the international agreement and the Community legislation to coincide fully; and that it was necessary to take into account not only the current state of Community law in the area in question but also its future development, in so far as foreseeable at the time of the analysis. A further instance confirming the open-ended conception of *AETR* was the Court's assessment of disconnection clauses. The Court considered that such a clause did not constitute a guarantee that the Community rules were not affected but, on the contrary, could provide an indication that those rules *were* affected.

The Court's identification of the basic rationale for *AETR*-type exclusive competence is to be welcomed, but it is not obvious that this identification makes the task of applying the doctrine any easier. The specific analysis in *Opinion 1/03* illustrates, as did previous *AETR* cases, that a host of complex issues may arise. The references to ensuring the uniform and consistent application of Community rules and the proper functioning of the system which they establish work well for the system of conflict of law rules which was set up by Regulation 44/2001. But in other areas of Community law there may be less of a 'system' of rules, making the basic rationale for *AETR* more difficult to apply.

The codification by the Lisbon Treaty

The principles resulting from the above case law are now reflected in two provisions of the TFEU. Article 216(1) provides:

> The Union may conclude an agreement with one or more third countries or international organizations where the Treaties so provide or where the conclusion of an agreement is necessary in order to achieve, within the framework of the Union's policies, one of the objectives referred to in the Treaties, or is provided for in a legally binding act of the Union or is likely to affect common rules or alter their scope.

This provision addresses express and implied competences to conclude international agreements in general, and does not distinguish between exclusive and shared competences. Article 3(2) TFEU, on the other hand, focuses on exclusive competence:

> The Union shall also have exclusive competence for the conclusion of an international agreement when its conclusion is provided for in a legislative act of the Union or is necessary to enable the Union to exercise its internal competence, or insofar as its conclusion may affect common rules or alter their scope.

The formulation and interaction of those two provisions is somewhat puzzling. There are only limited differences in wording, yet those differences may appear important, since Article 3(2) concerns exclusive competence, and Article 216(1) addresses, one assumes, both shared and exclusive competence. The differences are that, for there to be exclusive competence, (a) there must be a legislative act providing for the conclusion of the agreement, and not just a legally binding act; and (b) the agreement must be necessary to enable the Union to exercise its internal competence, and not just to achieve a Union objective. The difference in wording as regards agreements affecting common rules or altering their scope appears insignificant, if not contradictory: for there to be exclusive competence it is sufficient that the agreement 'may' affect common rules or alter their scope, whereas for competence, generally, the agreement must be 'likely' to do so.[136]

However, one should not focus excessively on the precise wording of these provisions. They were copied from the Constitution for Europe, and it is clear that the drafters of the Constitution intended to codify (in summary form) the principles emanating from the case law which this chapter analyses.[137] Accordingly, one may assume that the Court will keep a certain freedom as regards developing its implied-powers case law. Indeed, it has already done so prior to the entry into force of the Lisbon Treaty, as *Opinion 1/03* post-dated the text of the Constitution for Europe, and attempted to develop a coherent and comprehensive approach towards, in particular, exclusive implied powers, an approach which is not wholly reflected in the TFEU provisions.

Conclusions

It may be useful at this stage of this book's analysis to offer some further reflections on the doctrine of implied powers, as elaborated in the above case law. It is in particular important to identify with precision the rules and principles which the Court established.[138]

As suggested, there is a basic distinction between two different dimensions of the external power question, which provides a key to a better understanding of the case law. That distinction is between (a) the material scope—the reach in terms of subject matter—of powers conferred upon the Community in specific policy fields, *both* as regards internal law-making *and* the conclusion of international agreements; and (b) what, as far as external relations are concerned, may be called the core

[136] The French, German, Dutch, Italian, and Spanish versions do not show a distinction between 'may' and 'is likely'.

[137] Final report of Working Group VII on External Action, CONV 459/02 at 4 and 15–6. See also M Cremona, 'The Draft Constitutional Treaty: External Relations and External Action' (2003) 40 CML Rev 1351.

[138] Compare with Dashwood and Helikoski (n 2 above) 18–19.

implied-powers question, i.e. does the EU have capacity to conclude international agreements in areas within its competence where the Treaties do not mention such capacity?

The latter, core question was clearly the most vital one for the Court to answer.[139] The EEC Treaty had conferred broad internal legislative powers in matters pertaining to the common market, transport, agriculture, and competition. It had, however, been much meaner with express powers to conclude international agreements, limiting those essentially to commercial policy and association agreements. Article 228 EEC appeared to confirm that the Community's treaty-making powers were limited to those instances by laying down provisions on procedure which were to apply 'where this Treaty provides for the conclusion of agreements'. None the less, the Court replied to this core implied-powers question with a resounding yes. It set the tone in *AETR* by emphasizing the Community's legal personality, which it construed as including *international* legal personality, and which it saw as overriding the absence of express Treaty language, in specific areas, on the conclusion of international agreements. In matters of transport it was sufficient that the Treaty authorized the Council to adopt 'appropriate provisions'. *Opinion 1/76* was also concerned with transport, but the language in both *AETR* and that Opinion was general, and suggested that the Community could act by way of entering into international commitments in all its areas of activity. After the first substantial amendment of the EEC Treaty through the Single European Act, involving a first expansion of the Community's competences, the Court even accepted treaty-making capacity in an area—health and safety of workers—where the powers conferred upon the Community were rather weak. Article 118a EEC instructed the *Member States* to pay particular attention to encouraging improvements as regards the health and safety of workers, and to set as their objective the harmonization of conditions in this area. The Council's task was only to help achieve that objective by adopting, by means of directives, *minimum* requirements for *gradual* implementation, which could not prevent any Member State from maintaining or introducing more stringent measures. None the less, the Court confirmed in *Opinion 2/91* that in this area, too, there was treaty-making power.

Obviously, there must be some limit to the EU's implied treaty-making capacity. In certain areas, such as culture and public health, the Treaty excludes harmonization of laws,[140] and it seems incontrovertible that this exclusion cannot be circumvented by concluding an international agreement which would in effect amount to such harmonization. But even in such areas the conclusion of international agreements on matters which do come within the EU's competence, for example cultural subsidies, should be possible in the light of the case law.

What is the broader meaning and import of this core implied power? The Court of Justice appears to have realized and valued the growing significance of

[139] For a different approach, see Schütze (n 2 above) 297–302.

[140] See Arts 167(5) and 168(5) TFEU.

international law-making.[141] By affirming general treaty-making power it asserted the Community's international capacity and laid the foundations for an effective international legal personality. It may be noted, in that regard, that such legal personality ultimately depends on the willingness of other international actors to contract, and cannot be unilaterally decreed. Yet, clearly, no such willingness could have been forthcoming if the Court had erected a constitutional barrier to the conclusion of treaties. The Court's broad affirmation no doubt contributed to the actual development of the Community's involvement and formal participation in international law-making, and to the gradual acceptance of the Community as an international actor. Today one may forget all too easily that such acceptance did not come automatically; witness the refusal of Soviet-dominated communist countries to recognize the Community.[142] And even today, there continues to be a particular form of international action which poses a lot of problems, namely membership of international organizations.[143]

When one compares the EU with other organizations between States, the implied-powers case law confirmed the general political character of the EU—its function to establish a European polity which transcends the format of traditional international organizations. Indeed, this case law, and the international action which it set in motion and enabled, is one of the hallmarks of such transcendence. Which other international organizations have capacity to conclude international agreements, in diverse policy areas, which bind not only their institutions but also their Member States? From that perspective, the implied-powers doctrine is rightly regarded as a core component of European constitutionalism.

Beyond this core of the implied-powers doctrine, there is a second, and different, dimension to the above case law. The Court may have unreservedly supported the claim to treaty-making power, but that support should not be identified with judicial laxness concerning the material scope of EU competences. In the *AETR* case Dutheillet de Lamothe AG contrasted implied powers with conferred powers. The latter principle, of conferred and limited powers, is at the very heart of EU constitutional law.[144] But the case law on implied powers does not in any way abandon it. In all of the above rulings the Court takes great care to define and circumscribe the material scope of EU competences, the subject area in which the EU may act, with reserve and precision.[145] It does not accept broad expansion of EU competences in material terms. *AETR* and *Opinion 1/76* concerned agreements regulating matters clearly within Community competence, i.e. social legislation relating to road

[141] Cf M Cremona, 'External Relations and External Competence: The Emergence of an Integrated Policy' in P Craig and G de Búrca, *The Evolution of EU Law* (OUP, 1999) 147–8.

[142] See J Maslen, 'European Community–CMEA: institutional relations' in M Maresceau (ed), *The Political and Legal Framework of Trade Relations between the European Community and Eastern Europe* (Martinus Nijhoff, 1989) 85–92. [143] See Ch 7.

[144] A Dashwood, 'The Limits of European Community Powers' (1996) 21 ELR 113.

[145] Cf A Dashwood, 'The Attribution of External Relations Competence' in Dashwood and Hillion (n 2 above) 128.

transport and inland waterway capacity in the Rhine and Moselle basins. The ILO Convention in issue in *Opinion 2/91* clearly concerned the health and safety of workers; indeed internal EC legislation had already been adopted as regards the use of chemicals. In *Opinion 1/94* the Court rejected the Commission's expansionist claim that the Treaty chapters on the right of establishment and freedom to provide services were a basis for regulating external trade in services. It did not exclude the possibility that internal market harmonization could extend to the treatment of non-nationals, but refused a sweeping extension of Community competence from the internal market in services to external trade. In *Opinion 2/94* the Court denied the Community general powers in the human rights field, notwithstanding the requirement of respect for human rights as a general principle of EC law.

This dimension of the implied-powers case law is in line with jurisprudence on 'internal' competence. There, too, the Court is careful, or at least has become careful, to uphold the limits to powers conferred upon the Community.[146] At the same time, the implied-powers case law also displays a degree of respect for the division of powers (or institutional balance) between the various political institutions, as well as between the legislature and the judiciary. Even if powers are limited, there is some latitude for the institutions vested with the authority to exercise such powers. Thus, in *Opinion 1/94* the Court accepted that there is exclusive treaty-making power where internal legislative acts confer powers to negotiate. In the air transport cases the Court also regarded it as vital that the Council had not decided that an agreement on traffic rights with the United States was necessary. Within the boundaries set by the Treaty, the EU legislature may to some extent determine the scope of external competence. In particular the recognition that the legislature may legislate on external competence is remarkable from a constitutional perspective. *Kompetenz-Kompetenz* does not seem to be limited to the Member States as *Herren der Verträge* (Masters of the Treaties). In fact, the masters of the Treaties themselves established such *Kompetenz-Kompetenz* for the Council in the Amsterdam and Nice amendments to Article 133 EC.[147] There is obviously some tension between the idea of limited powers and respect for the political discretion of the legislature, yet there need not be contradiction. Where the Treaties confer powers on the EU to act, it is natural that the institutions which have been given authority to exercise those powers are the first interpreters of the scope of such powers. There must, of course, be judicial review, but some degree of deference to the legislature seems appropriate. As regards *Kompetenz-Kompetenz* it is also worth piercing the institutional veil. Where the Court recognizes that the Council may, for example, confer exclusive negotiating authority by providing for negotiations in EU legislation, it is doubtless aware of the Council's function of representing the Member States, masters of the Treaties.

[146] See in particular Case C–376/98 *Germany v. European Parliament and Council* [2000] ECR I–8419 (the *Tobacco Advertising Directive* case).

[147] See Ch 2.

A third dimension of the implied-powers case law is the notion of exclusive competence. As can be seen, enormous institutional battles have been fought over the reach of exclusivity. Instead of simply concentrating on whether the EU has competence to conclude an agreement, the case law's real focus has been on exclusive competence. The cause is the antagonism between the Commission and the Council which, in the domain of international negotiations and the conclusion of international agreements, epitomizes the struggle between supranationalism and intergovernmentalism; perhaps more so than in any other domain of EU action. The Commission has consistently, over three or four decades, perceived the Council as the bodyguard of national competence, greatly reluctant to recognize and exercise external competence. The Council, i.e. the Member State governments, saw the Commission as purely intent on increasing its own, supranational powers, for it is the Commission which negotiated international agreements, and the negotiator holds many cards.[148] If proof there need be of this antagonism, it is to be found in the EU Treaty's provisions on CFSP, which do not provide for any significant Commission role.

It is understandable that the Court was drawn into the battle, for it has the ultimate authority to interpret the scope and meaning of the Treaties. One none the less wonders whether all the judicial energy spent on defining exclusive implied powers has had much effect on actual practice. As is discussed in Chapter 7, that practice is founded on the notion of mixity. Whenever there is doubt as to the scope of EU competences, international agreements are concluded as mixed agreements, requiring signature and conclusion by the EU and by each Member State. If the case law on exclusive implied powers has led to any actual expansion of the EU's involvement with the negotiation and conclusion of international agreements, it is barely visible.

A proper understanding of the case law is none the less indispensable. It may be helpful to look at the doctrine of exclusive implied powers (or *AETR*) as located somewhere between pure conflict pre-emption and *a priori* Treaty-based exclusive competence, such as in matters of commercial policy and conservation of fish resources. As emphasized by Tizzano AG in the air transport cases, and recognized by the Court, there need not be conflict between the provisions of an international agreement and internal EU legislation for the *AETR* principle to operate. There are many more positions, and as the Court emphasized in *Opinion 1/03*, it is important to bear in mind the overall rationale for exclusive implied powers, rather than the specific instances analysed in the case law.

The rationale for exclusive implied powers can perhaps be reformulated as follows. Particularly in the domain of action under international law, one cannot leave possible conflicts or frictions between provisions of EU law and, effectively, provisions of national law (albeit in the form of an international agreement concluded

[148] See Ch 6. It may be noted that, under the new provisions of Art 218 TFEU, the Commission is no longer the sole negotiator.

by a Member State) to resolution once the respective provisions have been enacted. The resolution itself would be straightforward: EU law prevails over national law, under any circumstances. But Member States may find themselves faced with conflicting commitments. Further, one should not separate the internal, in the sense of EU legislation, from the external, conclusion of international agreements. Where the EU legislates, the Member States effectively lose autonomous powers, including as regards treaty-making. A separation of the internal and the external would risk undermining the uniform interpretation of EU law. It would also affect the proper role and function of the EU institutions which have legislated on a particular matter. It would affect review by the Court of Justice. Lastly, it would undermine the autonomy of the EU legal order.

The case law is generally convincing, except for the characterization of *Opinion 1/76* as a case involving exclusive competence. One may refer here to the comments above. *Opinion 1/76* is simply better understood as establishing general parallelism, by emphasizing that implied external powers are Treaty-based and therefore not confined to areas where the EU has already legislated.[149] The notion that, in certain cases, exclusivity arises out of the necessity of concluding an international agreement so as to achieve the Treaty's objectives disregards the general distinction between exclusive and shared powers. It is only in areas where powers are shared that the question of exclusive implied external powers arises, for where Community powers are *a priori* exclusive there can be no debate. In such areas of shared competence, one fails to see on what basis treaty-making should, in contrast with the power to make legislation, be exclusive on grounds of necessity. Exclusive implied powers are best confined to the *AETR* doctrine.

The Court has rejected general effects on the internal market as a criterion for exclusive implied powers. The risk of distortion of competition, for example in the air transport market, even if central to the idea of an internal market,[150] is no basis for exclusive treaty-making power. Here the Court does not adopt its well-known teleological and contextual methods of interpretation of the Treaty. The internal market, vital as it has been for the development of the EU and of EU law, is not such a strong imperative as to establish exclusive external competence, other than through the common commercial policy. Instead of a broad economically-oriented, teleological, and contextual approach to implied powers, the Court has preferred a more doctrinal, constitutional, and institutional approach, which focuses on the autonomy and protection of the EU legal order. Again, this confirms the central function of implied powers in European constitutionalism.

To sum up, the ultimate conclusion from the analysis and the above reflections is that the Court established genuine parallelism between 'internal' and 'external' powers. It established such parallelism by giving the EU the authority to conclude

[149] Cf D McGoldrick, *International Relations Law of the European Union* (Longman, 1997) 61.
[150] *Tobacco Advertising Directive* case (n 146 above).

international agreements in all areas where powers have been conferred on it. It confirmed such parallelism by adopting a consistent approach towards the material scope of EU powers, whether exercised through the adoption of legislation or the conclusion of an international agreement. Even exclusive implied powers are nothing more than an extension, to the field of treaty-making, of the doctrine of legislative pre-emption.

On this basis, it is now possible to discuss in the next chapter the main domains in which the EU may act on the international scene, pursuant to the TFEU.

4

Express and implied competences under the TFEU

Introduction: external competences after Lisbon

The case law of the Court of Justice on the scope and nature of the common commercial policy and on the implied powers doctrine, discussed and analysed in the preceding chapters, offers a solid foundation for understanding the EU's external competences. With the entry into force of the Lisbon Treaty, those competences are currently divided in two general categories. On the one hand, the TEU forms the basis for the Common Foreign and Security Policy (CFSP). The competence to conduct that policy is not defined in the Treaties. Article 2(4) TFEU simply provides that the EU has competence to define and implement the CFSP, without characterizing such competence as exclusive, shared, or of a co-ordinating, supportive, or supplementary nature. CFSP competences and objectives, and their legal relationship to other forms of EU external action, are studied in the next chapter. The TFEU, on the other hand, characterizes all other competences according to the above categories. Those competences are constitutionalized, one could say, in the sense that they are governed by constitutional-type provisions on the nature of the relevant competences and their effect on Member States' competences. No such constitutionalization has taken place as regards the CFSP.

The aim of this chapter is to look further at the EU's external competences under the TFEU, building on the two previous chapters, which have sketched some of the main developments as regards the EC's external competences, particularly through case law. As the title indicates, the focus is on both express and implied competences. It is also, following the approach in the previous chapter, on external competences in a substantive sense—what kind of external policies is the EU capable of pursuing?—and on its ability to conclude international agreements.

Given that the Lisbon Treaty attempted to codify both competences in general, and external competences in particular, it may be useful to start with a short analysis of the relevant provisions.

Article 2(1) TFEU provides that, when the Treaties confer on the EU exclusive competence in a specific area, only the Union may legislate and adopt legally binding acts, the Member States being able to do so themselves only if so empowered by the Union or for the implementation of acts of the Union. The areas of exclusive competence are defined in Article 3(1):

(a) customs union;
(b) the establishing of the competition rules necessary for the functioning of the internal market;
(c) monetary policy for the Member States whose currency is the euro;
(d) the conservation of marine biological resources under the common fisheries policy;
(e) common commercial policy.

Areas (a), (d), and (e) have in the past been identified as areas of exclusive competence by the Court of Justice, as the preceding chapters set out. In those areas the conclusion of international agreements is part and parcel of the EU's policies. Exclusive competence as regards monetary policy for the euro-group is in the very nature of that policy, which may also of course lead to the conclusion of international agreements (see below). The area of competition policy is mainly an 'internal' competence, although again the conclusion of international agreements is not excluded.[1] In all of those areas only the Union may legislate and adopt legally binding acts, the latter concept clearly extending to treaties, conventions, and agreements under international law.

Article 2(2) TFEU provides that, when the Treaties confer on the EU a shared competence in a specific area, the EU and the Member States may legislate and adopt legally binding acts in that area. It further provides that, under shared competence, the Member States shall exercise their competence to the extent that the EU has not exercised its competence, or to the extent that the EU has decided to cease exercising its competence. The principal areas in which shared competence applies are listed in Article 4(2) as including the internal market; social policy; economic, social, and territorial cohesion; agriculture and fisheries (excluding the conservation of marine biological resources); environment; consumer protection; transport; trans-European networks; energy; area of freedom, security, and justice; and some public health matters. Again this clearly includes a number of areas (such as environment, transport, and area of freedom, security, and justice) in which the conclusion of international agreements is part and parcel of the EU's policies. In a couple of further fields of EU policy-making, i.e. research, technological development, and space on the one hand, and development co-operation and humanitarian aid on the other, Article 4(3) and (4) TFEU provide that the exercise of EU competence shall not result in Member States being prevented from exercising theirs. This principle is further analysed below, in the section on development co-operation.

[1] See e.g. Decision 98/386 concerning the conclusion of the Agreement between the European Communities and the Government of the United States of America on the application of positive comity principles in the enforcement of their competition laws [1998] OJ L173/26, based on (current) Art 103 TFEU.

Article 5 TFEU speaks about the co-ordination of economic, employment, and social policies at EU level. Article 6 TFEU, lastly, provides for EU action to support, co-ordinate, or supplement the actions of the Member States in the areas of protection and improvement of human health; industry; culture; tourism; education, vocational training, youth, and sport; civil protection; and administrative co-operation. There may be some measure of external policy in some of those areas, as well.

Is the EU, under the provisions of the TFEU, capable of concluding international agreements in all of those competence areas? Under Article 216(1) TFEU the EU may, first of all, conclude an agreement with one or more third countries or international organizations 'where the Treaties so provide'. These are the express external powers. It may be useful to provide a short overview of the TFEU provisions which refer to the conclusion of international agreements:

- Article 79(3) refers to agreements with third countries on the re-admission of illegal immigrants, within the context of immigration policy;
- Article 186 provides for agreements on co-operation in research and technological development;
- Article 191(4) speaks of international agreements in the area of environmental policy;
- Article 207 refers to agreements in the context of the common commercial policy;[2]
- Article 209(2) provides for agreements in the area of development co-operation;
- Article 212(2) concerns agreements for economic, financial, and technical co-operation with third countries;
- Article 214(4) provides for agreements on humanitarian aid;
- Article 217 concerns association agreements;
- Article 219(1) and (3) govern the conclusion of agreements in the sphere of monetary union.

With respect to education and sport (Article 165(3)), vocational training (Article 166(3)), culture (Article 167(3)), and public health (Article 168(3)), the TFEU merely provides that the Union and the Member States shall foster co-operation with third countries and the competent international organizations. As regards trans-European networks, Article 171(3) states that the Union may decide to co-operate with third countries. These provisions do not expressly mention the conclusion of international agreements, but there seems little doubt that international co-operation may require the conclusion of international agreements. There would in any event seem to be an implied power for that purpose.

Indeed, Article 216(1) provides that the Union may also conclude an agreement 'where the conclusion of an agreement is necessary in order to achieve, within the framework of the Union's policies, one of the objectives referred to in the Treaties,

[2] See Ch 2.

or is provided for in a legally binding act of the Union or is likely to affect common rules or alter their scope'. For the purpose of the analysis in this chapter, the first basis for treaty-making listed in this provision is the most significant. It effectively confirms the broad parallelism between internal and external powers,[3] as identified in the case law of the Court of Justice, analysed in Chapter 3. All that is required is that the conclusion of an agreement is necessary to achieve one of the objectives of the Treaties, and can be located within the framework of the EU's policies. This can simply be seen as a confirmation, in the sphere of the conclusion of international agreements, of the principle of conferred competences as set out in Article 5(2) TEU. In other words, there is nothing specific to the assessment of whether or not the conclusion of an international agreement is within the EU's competences: that assessment needs to be made for all EU acts, on the basis of the same basic principles. It is true that Article 216(1) TFEU requires that the agreement be 'necessary'. However, as analysed by Tizzano AG in his Opinion in the *Open Skies* cases, the decision on such necessity is to be taken by the competent EU institutions, in accordance with the proper Treaty procedures.[4] For the conclusion of international agreements, the Council is the main decision-maker pursuant to the provisions of Article 218 TFEU.[5] Review by the Court should be confined to issues of substantive competence, again in accordance with the principles that govern competence review as regards internal acts.

This means that the conclusion of international agreements cannot be excluded in any of the competence areas set out above, be they exclusive, shared, or supportive, co-ordinating, or complementary.

Lastly, Article 3(2) TFEU determines when the EU has exclusive competence for the conclusion of an international agreement in an area which is not as such within exclusive competence. That provision, which is in fact very similar to Article 216(1) TFEU, codifies the Court's case law on exclusive implied powers, and is analysed in Chapter 3.

This analysis of the main principles sets the scene for a more intense examination of external competence in the main areas of EU policy-making under the TFEU. We have already looked at commercial policy, and will hereafter consider association agreements, development co-operation, the internal market, environmental protection, social policy, EMU, and the Area of Freedom, Security, and Justice (AFSJ). In a number of those areas there is Court case law on external competence; in others there are no specific judicial statements as yet, but the principles governing external competence none the less enable us to make some observations. It must be stressed that the object of this chapter is not to provide a comprehensive overview of actual

[3] See Convention for the Future of Europe, Final report of Working Group VII on External Action, CONV 459/02, at 4.

[4] Case C-466/98 *Commission v. United Kingdom* [2002] ECR I-9427, Opinion of Tizzano AG, paras 46–59.

[5] See further Ch 6.

external practice.[6] That is beyond the scope of this book, and references to practice are by way of illustration rather than anything else. The emphasis is on the relevant principles.

Association agreements

Article 217 TFEU provides:

> The Union may conclude with one or more third countries or international organisations agreements establishing an association involving reciprocal rights and obligations, common action and special procedures.

The text is not a model of clear drafting. As noted by Stein, it highlights the structural components but resonates in silence on the substance.[7] Virtually any international agreement would involve reciprocal rights and obligations, and many agreements involve common action and special procedures. The concept of association itself is not defined. One possible reading is that, as the drafters of the EEC Treaty only mentioned the conclusion of agreements in matters of commercial policy and association, they envisaged that the EEC's international action was limited to trade agreements and general agreements with countries wishing to 'associate' themselves with the newborn organization. They seem to have been looking to provide a Treaty basis for agreements creating closer links with certain countries, and indeed international organizations, but the provision has never been used for agreements with the latter.[8]

(Current) Article 217 TFEU was immediately used to conclude association agreements with Greece, which was later to become a Member State,[9] and Turkey, which continues to aspire to membership.[10] Both of those agreements made explicit reference to the prospect of future membership, and that became a feature of many association agreements. There are, however, other agreements concluded on the basis of (current) Article 217 which never embodied prospective membership, expressly or by implication.[11] The provision was, for example, also used to

[6] For surveys of types of agreements concluded by the Community see M Maresceau, 'Bilateral Agreements Concluded by the European Community', Hague Academy of International Law (2004) 309 *Recueil des cours* part II; S Peers, 'EC Frameworks of International Relations: Co-operation, Partnership and Association' in A Dashwood and C Hillion (eds), *The General Law of EC External Relations* (Sweet & Maxwell, 2000) 160–76; K Lenaerts and E De Smijter, 'The European Community's Treaty-Making Competence' (1996) 16 YEL 20; for an earlier attempt at classification see C Flaesch-Mougin, *Les accords externes de la Communauté économique européenne—Essai d'une typologie* (Editions de l'ULB, 1979).

[7] E Stein, 'External Relations of the European Community: Structure and Process' in *Collected Courses of the Academy of European Law (1990)—Community Law*, Vol I, Book 1 (Martinus Nijhoff, 1991) 151.

[8] For an overview of the practice, see Maresceau (n 6 above) 314–422; D Hanf and P Dengler, 'Les accords d'association' in J-V Louis and M Dony (eds), *Commentaire J Megret—Relations extérieures* (Etudes européennes, 2005) 293.

[9] [1974] OJ Spec Ed 2nd Series, PEI, 4.

[10] [1964] JO 217.

[11] E.g. with Southern Mediterranean States: see Peers (n 6 above) 162.

manage the EEC's approach to relations with colonies of the Member States gaining independence, relations which developed into the broad partnership with ACP countries under the Lomé and Cotonou conventions.[12] It may further be noted that nearly all association agreements were concluded as mixed agreements, even if the Treaty provided for unanimity within the Council, thereby enabling all Member States to have a decisive voice and right of veto. Much as in other areas, the Commission argued for pure Community agreements, but was unable to persuade the Council.[13]

It took until 1987 before the Court of Justice was given an opportunity to clarify the scope of EC competence to conclude association agreements. *Demirel v. Stadt Schwäbisch Gmünd*[14] concerned Mrs Demirel, a Turkish national, who in 1984 came to Germany under a tourist visa, in order to join her husband who lived there. She remained in the country after the expiry of her visa, and was threatened with expulsion. Before the *Verwaltungsgericht* (Administrative Court) Stuttgart she sought to rely on provisions of the association agreement with Turkey, a mixed agreement. The court referred questions on the interpretation and effect of those provisions to the Court of Justice for a preliminary ruling. In those proceedings, the German and UK governments argued that the Court had no jurisdiction to reply to the questions, because the provisions in issue, on free movement of workers, had to be regarded as coming within the competence of the Member States, and not that of the Community.

Darmon AG emphasized the fact that the agreement aimed to 'establish ever closer bonds between the Turkish people and the peoples brought together in the European Economic Community', and created the prospect of accession. Those factors alone were in his opinion enough to classify the agreement as an act in the meaning of (current) Article 267 TFEU on preliminary rulings. When such a convention looked towards a further accession, he argued, the Community had of necessity to hold the most extensive powers to conclude agreements with non-member countries in order to cover all the fields of activity contemplated by the Treaty. There was no need to have recourse to the implied powers doctrine, as there was the express basis in (current) Article 217 TFEU, and the power which it conferred had to be exercised in keeping with the goal pursued and the interests of the Community, and was not to be construed restrictively. He none the less confined that analysis to agreements concluded with a view to accession, pointing out that there were agreements which had been based on (current) Article 217 TFEU which had aroused discussion as to their true nature. However, since one of the aims of an agreement concluded with a view to accession was the approximation of the economic and legal systems—and indeed political ones—in order to achieve 'full acceptance' by the associate country of the obligations arising out of

[12] For the Cotonou Agreement see [2000] OJ L317/3.

[13] Stein (n 7 above) 151.

[14] Case 12/86 *Demirel v. Stadt Schwäbisch Gmünd* [1987] ECR 3719.

the Treaty, it was necessary that all the subjects which were *a priori* to be covered by such acceptance be set out by the agreement in a Community perspective and that it be possible to interpret them with a view to their uniform application. That of course included the fundamental freedoms required for the establishment of the common market.[15]

The Court's analysis was much shorter. It followed the Advocate General's approach, but did not mention the dimension of prospective accession, and ruled on the scope of (current) Article 217 TFEU in general terms. The Court held that, since the agreement in question was an association agreement creating special, privileged links with a non-member country which was required, at least to a certain extent, to take part in the Community system, (current) Article 217 TFEU necessarily empowered the Community to guarantee commitments towards non-member countries in all the fields covered by the Treaty. Since freedom of movement for workers was one of the fields covered by that Treaty, it followed that commitments regarding free movement fell within the powers conferred by (current) Article 217. Thus the question of whether the Court had jurisdiction to rule on the interpretation of a provision in a mixed agreement containing a commitment which only the Member States could enter into in the sphere of their own powers did not arise.[16]

The Court's analysis offered only limited clarification of the concept of an association, by (a) referring to the creation of special, privileged links, and (b) requiring the associated country, at least to a certain extent, to take part in the Community system. The first dimension is self-explanatory, but the second is more ambiguous. Surely the Court did not have in mind genuine participation by the associated country in the work of the Community (now the EU) and its institutions. No association agreement provides for such participation.[17] The reference to participation in the Community system is in all likelihood to be interpreted in material terms. The system of the Treaty must in some policy areas, for example the internal market, or competition policy, be in some measure extended to the associated country.[18] Whether all agreements effectively adopted on the basis of (current) Article 217 comply with those criteria is not entirely free from doubt, but the tone of the *Demirel* ruling does not suggest strict scrutiny by the Court.

The most remarkable aspect of the judgment is that, particularly at the time of the case, it established broader external competence than under any other Treaty provisions. One should not be deceived by the Court's reference to free movement of workers, and its extension to Turkey. The Court's ruling effectively established that, in an association agreement, the Community could contract on matters of immigration. Turkey was, and is, a third country, and therefore provisions on the

[15] Ibid, Opinion of Darmon AG, para 14.

[16] Ibid, para 9. On this question of jurisdiction, see generally Ch 7.

[17] The EEA Agreement goes furthest because of its ambitious objective of extending the internal market, and even that agreement only establishes pre-legislative consultation: see Arts 97–104 ([1994] OJ L1/3).

[18] Lenaerts and De Smijter (n 6 above) 17.

treatment of Turkish workers in the EU are effectively provisions on the immigration and employment of third-country nationals. There was clearly at the time no basis in the EEC Treaty for an EEC immigration policy, but the Court none the less accepted that in the context of an association the Community could regulate immigration. It is therefore only in the context of association that one sees the full and complete external dimension of EU policies. For associations which prepare for accession, such broad EU competence is appropriate, but whether that is also the case for other associations may be more doubtful. However, with the gradual expansion of EU external powers such questions are increasingly irrelevant; immigration, for example, is currently expressly within EU competence (see below).

If the Court's judgment was among the most expansive in terms of competence, it did not much change the practice of concluding association agreements in mixed form. Often the official justification for mixity was that the agreement also established a political dialogue, which was outside Community competence.[19]

Association agreements have continued to be a preferred instrument for preparing non-member countries for accession.[20] They are also used for establishing privileged links, across a broad spectrum of EU policies.[21]

Development co-operation and other co-operation policies

Development co-operation prior to the TEU

The EU is a major global actor in the sphere of development co-operation. It works in tandem with the Member States, and together they make up the largest international donor.[22] The development of policies in this domain came naturally, in the first stages as a by-product of the EEC's other external policies, i.e. commercial policy and association. The association formula was quickly used to create a framework for relations with the African, Caribbean and Pacific (ACP) countries, in the Yaoundé and subsequently Lomé Conventions (see above). Those relations are predicated on the notion of development. The commercial policy sphere witnessed a shift of emphasis in the 1970s, away from a strict non-discrimination approach (MFN), and towards the idea that preferential terms of trade are necessary for developing countries.

[19] Cf ibid, 24.

[20] E.g. the Europe Agreements: see M Maresceau and E Montaguti, 'The Relations between the European Union and Central and Eastern Europe: A Legal Appraisal' (1995) 32 CML Rev 1327.

[21] Cotonou Agreement (n 12 above) and agreements with Mediterranean countries: see C Flaesch-Mougin, 'Differentiation and Association within the Pan-Euro-Mediterranean Area' in M Maresceau and E Lannon (eds), *The EU's Enlargement and Mediterranean Strategies—A Comparative Analysis* (Palgrave, 2001) 63–96.

[22] According to the Commission the EU and its Member States provide over half of all international official development assistance, see <http://ec.europa.eu/development/how/monterrey_en.cfm>.

The use of the association formula for EEC–ACP relations was never challenged, particularly as the Conventions were concluded as mixed agreements. However, as seen in Chapter 2, there has been a strong debate on whether EEC competence in matters of commercial policy extended to trade agreements or trade measures with a strong development component. In *Opinion 1/78* the Court confirmed that such competence covered commodities agreements which regulated rather than liberalized trade agreements drafted in the framework of UNCTAD and were thus specifically geared towards aiding the development of producer countries. It none the less allowed the financing of such agreements, and the buffer-stock systems which they set up, to be supplied by the Member States rather than the Community, in which case mixity was required.[23] What, from a constitutional perspective, seemed like making small allowance for pragmatism by recognizing Member States' involvement,[24] became, as will be shown, an important factor in the EU's development co-operation policies, where financing is obviously crucial. After *Opinion 1/78* the Court confirmed the broad approach towards the notion of commercial policy in the *GSP* case.[25] Unilateral trade preferences for developing countries also came within the scope of the common commercial policy.

If association agreements and trade policy offered vehicles for a Community development co-operation policy, their limitations were obvious. It is impossible to conclude association agreements with all developing countries, and the notion of development is much broader than the notion of trade, however generously defined. Community efforts turned, for example, towards humanitarian aid, where only (current) Article 352 TFEU could be used as a legal basis, and even then under a broad reading of doubtful constitutionality.[26] The same Treaty provision had to be employed in concluding co-operation agreements with non-member countries outside the Yaoundé and Lomé framework.[27]

The precarious constitutional foundations of the Community's development co-operation policy prior to the TEU are evident to the close reader of two Court judgments dating from 1993 and 1994.[28] In *Parliament v. Council and Commission* (the *Bangladesh* case) the Parliament challenged decisions on emergency aid for Bangladesh, claiming that they infringed its prerogatives in budgetary matters.[29] The decision of principle had been taken by the 'Member States meeting in the Council'. The Court pointed out that such decisions, which were not acts of a Community institution, could not be challenged in an action for annulment. It none the less

[23] *Opinion 1/78 re International Agreement on Natural Rubber* [1979] ECR 2871.

[24] T Tridimas and P Eeckhout, 'The External Competence of the Community and the Case-Law of the Court of Justice: Principle versus Pragmatism' (1994) 14 YEL 143.

[25] Case 45/86 *Commission v. Council* [1987] ECR 1493.

[26] Cf JHH Weiler, *The Constitution of Europe* (CUP, 1999) 54, footnote 117.

[27] Peers (n 6 above) 163.

[28] For analysis see A Ward, 'Community Development Aid and the Evolution of the Inter-institutional Law of the European Union' in Dashwood and Hillion (n 6 above) 42–7.

[29] Joined Cases C–181 and 248/91 *Parliament v. Council and Commission* [1993] ECR I–3685.

examined whether, having regard to its content and all the circumstances in which it was adopted, the act in question was not in reality a decision of the Council. If that had been the case, the Court would have had jurisdiction. However, one of the factors which led the Court to the conclusion that *in casu* there was no Council act was that the Community did not have exclusive competence in the field of humanitarian aid, and that consequently the Member States were not precluded from exercising their competence in that regard collectively in the Council or outside it.[30] The Court followed the Opinion of Jacobs AG, according to whom 'it [was] common ground that in the field of humanitarian aid the competence of the Community is not exclusive but concurrent with that of the Member States'.[31] Neither the Advocate General nor the Court, however, identified the legal basis in the Treaty for a Community humanitarian aid policy, and might have found themselves in some difficulty if they had opted to do so. In the end, the Court had no problems with allowing the Member States collectively to finance emergency aid, taking decisions when meeting in the Council, but not as Council, and entrusting co-ordination to the Commission, and yet acting outside the framework of the Treaty and of the budget.

In *Parliament v. Council* (the *Lomé IV* case) the Parliament again challenged its lack of involvement with the financial side of development co-operation policies.[32] The financial provisions of the Yaoundé and Lomé Conventions were traditionally implemented by means of a European Development Fund (EDF), set up for each convention by an internal agreement of the Member States. The EDF never formed part of the Community budget, despite pressure from the Parliament, the Commission, and the Court of Auditors.[33] Indeed, at the time of writing the EDF continues to be separate from that budget.[34] In the *Lomé IV* case the Parliament argued that the Financial Regulation of Lomé IV was adopted on the wrong legal basis, because the expenditure concerning the development aid provided for by the Convention was Community expenditure. The procedure of (then) Article 209 EC should have been used.[35]

Much of the argument in the case focused on external competence. The Court held that the Community's competence in the field of development co-operation was not exclusive, and that the Member States were accordingly entitled to enter into commitments themselves vis-à-vis non-Member States, either collectively or individually, or even jointly with the Community. The Court then interpreted the Convention in order to identify the parties which had entered into commitments. It established that, in accordance with the essentially bilateral character of the

[30] Ibid, paras 14–16.

[31] Ibid, Opinion of Jacobs AG, para 25.

[32] Case C–316/91 *Parliament v. Council* [1994] ECR I–625.

[33] Ibid, Opinion of Jacobs AG, paras 13–14.

[34] See Council Regulation 215/2008 on the Financial Regulation applicable to the 10th European Development Fund [2008] OJ L78/1.

[35] Now, with amendments, Art 322 TFEU.

co-operation, the obligation to grant 'the Community's financial assistance' fell on the Community and its Member States, considered together. As for the question of whether it was for the Community or for its Member States to perform that obligation, the Court again noted the non-exclusive nature of Community competence, so that the Member States were entitled collectively to exercise their competence in that field with a view to bearing the financial assistance to be granted to the ACP States. It followed that the competence to implement the Community's financial assistance was shared by the Community and its Member States and that it was for them to choose the source and methods of financing. The choice had been for the expenditure to be assumed directly by the Member States and distributed by a Fund which they had set up by mutual agreement, with the administration of which the Community institutions were associated. Consequently, the expenditure was not Community expenditure and the action failed.[36]

The Court's statements on the non-exclusive character of Community competence in the area of development co-operation could hardly be criticized. However, the conclusions it drew from those statements for the system of financing of EC-ACP development co-operation were less straightforward. Apparently, in budgetary matters one does not need to draw a clear line between the Member States and the EU. Once it had established that competences were shared, the Court accepted that the system of financing could be of a hybrid character, for that is what the EDF amounts to. It is financed from the budgets of the Member States, but operates under a financial regulation adopted by the Council, and involving the Commission, the European Investment Bank, the European Parliament, and the Court of Auditors.[37] Yet it remains outside the Community budget. In this case, as in *Opinion 1/78* and the *Bangladesh* case, the Court left great discretion to the Member States and the Community institutions as regards the systems of financing.

The EC Treaty provisions on development co-operation and *Portugal v. Council*

In the *Lomé IV* case both the Advocate General and the Court referred to (then) new EC Treaty provisions on development co-operation, inserted by the TEU. Indeed, the case was decided after the entry into force of the TEU, but the facts pre-dated it. Those provisions confirmed the non-exclusive nature of EC competence. In fact, the terms used in Article 130u(1) EC referred to the 'complementary' character of Community powers, rather than to the notion of shared competence.

The EC Treaty provisions on development co-operation were worded differently from the current TFEU provisions.[38] Article 130u(1) provided, next to confirming the complementary character of EC competence, that policy in this sphere had to foster:

[36] Ibid, paras 24–39. [37] Financial Regulation (n 34 above).
[38] Arts 130u–130y EC, later renumbered as Arts 177–181 EC.

— the sustainable economic and social development of the developing countries, and more particularly the most disadvantaged among them;
— the smooth and gradual integration of the developing countries into the world economy;
— the campaign against poverty in the developing countries.

Article 130u(2) provided that 'Community policy in this area shall contribute to the general objective of developing and consolidating democracy and the rule of law, and to that of respecting human rights and fundamental freedoms'. It put development co-operation squarely in the context of human rights, broadly defined. Article 130u(3) required that the Community and the Member States comply with the commitments and take account of the objectives they had approved in the context of the United Nations and other competent international organizations.

Questions as to the scope and nature of the Community's competence under the above provisions were raised before the Court of Justice, in a Portuguese action against the conclusion of a Co-operation Agreement between the EC and India (a pure Community agreement).[39] The agreement was based on the Treaty provisions on commercial policy and those on development co-operation. Portugal's challenge was broad. It considered that those Treaty provisions did not confer on the Community the necessary powers to conclude the Agreement as regards, first, the provision therein relating to human rights and, secondly, the provisions relating to various specific fields of co-operation (energy, tourism, and culture; drug abuse control; intellectual property; and commercial policy). Portugal further considered that recourse should also have been had to (current) Article 352 TFEU and to participation of all the Member States in the conclusion of the agreement.

La Pergola AG started his analysis by looking at the origins of the newly established Treaty provisions on development co-operation. He identified three types of development co-operation agreements since the first Yaoundé Convention. In the first-generation agreements the main focus was on Community aid; the second-generation agreements were basically geared to economic co-operation; and the third-generation agreements took into account the social structure of the developing countries as well as commercial relations.[40] The Advocate General then turned to the EC Treaty provisions, regarding it as clear from Article 130u(1) EC that the objectives of Community development co-operation reflected a complex vision of development, the product of interaction between its economic, social, and political aspects.[41] He described Community competence as equal and complementary to that of the Member States. He did not, however, agree with the claim that

[39] Case C–268/94 *Portugal v. Council* [1996] ECR I–6177. For the agreement see Council Decision concerning the conclusion of the Co-operation Agreement between the European Community and the Republic of India on Partnership and Development [1994] OJ L223/23. For academic comment see S Peers, 'Fragmentation or Evasion in the Community's Development Policy? The Impact of Portugal v. Council' in Dashwood and Hillion (n 6 above) 100–12.

[40] *Portugal v. Council* (above), Opinion of La Pergola AG, para 9.

[41] Ibid, para 13.

Community competence was subordinate to that of the Member States. The Treaty provisions on co-ordination and consultation referred to both national and Community policy, and Article 130w EC, on the adoption of measures by the Council, implied that the Community was empowered to conduct its own development co-operation policy.[42] There was no room for applying (current) Article 352 TFEU, because the Treaty specifically provided for a development co-operation policy.[43]

Those observations were useful, particularly as the Court itself did not engage in such general analysis. The Advocate General then turned to the human rights clause in Article 1(1) of the EC–India Agreement, which provided:

> Respect for human rights and democratic principles is the basis for the co-operation between the Contracting Parties and for the provisions of this Agreement, and it constitutes an essential element of the Agreement.

He first pointed out that the case law of the Court, as embodied in (then) Article 6(2) TEU, made respect for human rights an objective that must inform Union action as a whole. The Treaty interdependence of human rights and development co-operation did not mark a new departure in Community action: La Pergola AG traced and described various political resolutions and statements linking the two. He considered that the inclusion of the human rights clause in issue was specifically intended to adjust co-operation policy in line with respect for human rights. It was also designed to allow the Community to exercise the right to terminate the agreement, in accordance with Article 60 of the Vienna Convention on the Law of Treaties (VCLT), where the non-Member State failed to respect human rights within its own legal system.[44] The Advocate General went even further. The whole of Community action in this area illustrated the importance attaching to respect for human rights in development aid policy. If that was properly taken into account, the democracy clause had to be deemed necessary if development co-operation policy was to be lawfully pursued, and it would be a failure to adopt a clause of that type that would compromise the legality of Community action.[45]

The Court's approach was similar. It pointed out that the Treaty required the Community to take account of the objective of respect for human rights when it adopted measures in the field of development co-operation. The mere fact that Article 1(1) of the agreement provided that such respect 'constitutes an essential element' of the agreement did not justify the conclusion that that provision went beyond the objective of Article 130u(2) EC. The very wording of that article demonstrated the importance to be attached to respect for human rights and democratic principles, so that, among other things, development co-operation policy had to be adapted to the requirements of respect for those rights and principles. With regard to the argument that the characterization of respect for human rights as an essential element of co-operation presupposed specific means of action, it

[42] Ibid, paras 14–17. [43] Ibid, para 20.
[44] See Ch 6. [45] *Portugal v. Council* (n 39 above) paras 25–29.

first had to be stated that to adapt co-operation policy to respect for human rights necessarily entailed establishing a certain connection between those matters whereby one of them was made subordinate to the other. In that regard, it had to be borne in mind that a provision such as Article 1(1) could be an important factor for the exercise of the right to have a development co-operation agreement suspended or terminated where the non-member country violated human rights. Furthermore, the heading of Article 1 ('Basis and objectives') and the wording of the first paragraph provided confirmation that the question of respect for human rights and democratic principles was not a specific field of co-operation provided for by the agreement.[46]

The Portuguese claims were not confined to human rights. The applicant also contested provisions of the agreement concerning specific co-operation matters, as going beyond the combined Treaty provisions on commercial policy and development co-operation. Here the Court started its analysis at a general level. The Portuguese arguments, the Court stated, raised the question of the extent to which an agreement concluded on the basis of the Treaty provisions on development co-operation could lay down provisions on specific matters without there being any need to have recourse to other legal bases, or indeed to participation of the Member States in the conclusion of the agreement. The Court described the Community's competence as not exclusive but complementary to that of the Member States. In order to qualify as a development co-operation agreement, the agreement had to pursue the objectives in Article 130u EC. Article 130u(1) in particular made it clear that those were broad objectives in the sense that it had to be possible for the measures required for their pursuit to concern a variety of specific matters. That was so in particular in the case of an agreement establishing the framework of such co-operation. That being so, to require a development co-operation agreement to be based on another provision as well as on Article 130w and, possibly, also to be concluded by the Member States whenever it touched on a specific matter would in practice amount to rendering devoid of substance the competence and procedure described in Article 130w. It therefore had to be held that the fact that a development co-operation agreement contained clauses concerning various specific matters could not alter the characterization of the agreement, which had to be determined having regard to its essential object and not in terms of individual clauses, provided that those clauses did not impose such extensive obligations concerning the specific matters referred to that those obligations in fact constituted objectives distinct from those of development co-operation.[47]

The Court then tested the EC–India Agreement against those requirements, first in general, and then in specific areas identified by Portugal (see above). At a general level the Court was satisfied that the provisions of the agreement on

[46] Ibid, paras 23–28. [47] Ibid, paras 35–39.

specific matters established the framework of co-operation, and were limited to determining the areas for co-operation and to specifying certain of its aspects and various actions to which special importance was attached. By contrast, those provisions contained nothing that prescribed in concrete terms the manner in which co-operation in each specific area envisaged was to be implemented.[48] The Court also made it clear that the mere inclusion of provisions for co-operation in a specific field did not necessarily imply a general power such as to lay down the basis of a competence to undertake any kind of co-operation action in that field. It did not, therefore, predetermine the allocation of spheres of competence between the Community and the Member States or the legal basis of Community acts for implementing co-operation in such a field.[49]

At the level of specific areas of co-operation, Portugal took objection to, *inter alia*, the provisions on drug abuse control, under which the Contracting Parties affirmed their resolve to increase the efficiency of policies and measures to counter the supply and distribution of narcotic and psychotropic substances as well as preventing and reducing drug abuse. The co-operation in this field comprised training, education, health promotion, and rehabilitation of addicts; measures to encourage alternative economic opportunities; assistance in the monitoring of precursors' trade, prevention, treatment, and reduction of drug abuse; and exchange of all relevant information, including that relating to money laundering.[50] The Portuguese government argued that those matters came within the TEU provisions on justice and home affairs, as then in force.

The Court first stated that drug abuse control could not, as such, be excluded from the measures necessary for the pursuit of the objectives referred to in Article 130u, since production of narcotics, drug abuse, and related activities could constitute serious impediments to economic and social development. It then had to be considered whether Article 19 of the agreement remained within limits which did not necessitate recourse to a competence and to a legal basis specific to the sphere of drug-abuse control. The Court noted that the text of Article 19(1) contained nothing more than a declaration of intent to co-operate in drug-abuse control. In addition, it stated that the contracting parties were to act in conformity with their respective competences. The substance of the co-operation, defined in Article 19(2), constituted measures falling within the sphere of the development co-operation objectives. Here the Court specifically focused on exchange of information: it was in fact only in so far as that exchange made a contribution that was intimately linked to the other measures provided for by Article 19 that it could be included among the actions falling within the field of development co-operation, and a restrictive interpretation was called for.[51]

As regards the agreement's provisions on energy, tourism, and culture, the Court simply considered that they only established the framework of co-operation, and

[48] Ibid, para 45. [49] Ibid, para 47. [50] Art 19 of the agreement (n 39 above).
[51] *Portugal v. Council* (n 39 above) paras 60–66.

laid down obligations to take action which did not constitute objectives distinct from those of development co-operation.[52]

On intellectual property the Court observed, first, that the improvement in the protection of intellectual property rights sought by Article 10 of the agreement contributed to the objective in Article 130u(1) EC of smoothly and gradually integrating the developing countries in the world economy, and, secondly, that Article 10 merely provided that the contracting parties undertook to ensure as far as their laws, regulations, and policies allowed that suitable and effective protection was provided for intellectual property rights, reinforcing this protection where necessary. The further obligation to facilitate access to the databases of intellectual property organizations had only a very limited scope and was ancillary in nature, even in relation to the substance of intellectual property protection. Again, therefore, the obligations in this field constituted objectives distinct from those of development co-operation.[53]

Two dimensions of the Court's ruling in *Portugal v. Council* are of general significance. First, there is the location and precise meaning of the objective to develop and consolidate democracy and the rule of law, and to respect human rights. Peers noted that the Court transformed respect for human rights as an objective of development policy into an obligation to make such policy subject to the protection of human rights.[54] La Pergola AG indeed ventured to state that respect for human rights could constitute a condition for the legality of Community measures, but the Court did not confirm this in so many words. It considered that 'development co-operation policy must be adapted to the requirement of respect for those rights and principles'.[55] It was therefore in any event clear that respect for human rights had to permeate the whole sphere of development co-operation, and had to be fully integrated into the Community's policy. There was, however, debate on whether human rights protection constituted an objective in its own right, or whether it was only a general condition for the Community's policy.[56] The debate was linked to the contested scope for Community action in the domain of human rights generally.[57] However, the Treaty of Lisbon substantially modified the relevant provisions, and made the protection of human rights a general objective of external action (see below).

The Court also drew attention to the function of the human rights clause in the EC–India Agreement of permitting suspension or termination of the agreement in

[52] Ibid, para 54.

[53] Ibid, paras 73–76. The Court also recalled at para 77 its statements in *Opinion 1/94* on the ancillary character, from a perspective of commercial policy, of provisions for the organization of purely consultative procedures or clauses calling on the other party to raise the level of protection of intellectual property; see Ch 2.

[54] Peers (n 6 above) 103.

[55] *Portugal v. Council* (n 39 above), Opinion of La Pergola AG, para 24.

[56] E.g. E Fierro, *The EU's Approach to Human Rights Conditionality in Practice* (Martinus Nijhoff, 2003) 263–6.

[57] See Ch 3.

the case of non-respect of that provision. Indeed, the clause did not appear to have any other function, and the agreement did not envisage specific measures for the promotion of human rights. As with much of the EU's involvement with human rights, the respect-and-control function was preferred over the active promotion of human rights.[58]

This brings us to the second dimension of *Portugal v. Council*. The Court visibly struggled with the tension between the ever broader and inclusive notion of development and the principle of limited Community powers. The agreement's provisions on drug abuse control are a good example. Drug abuse is clearly a major development issue in a number of developing countries, yet the Community had virtually no general powers under the EC Treaty to develop an effective drugs policy. As far as crime policy was concerned, the Third Pillar was potentially relevant, but not the First. The Court appeared to fear that, through development co-operation policies, the limits of Community powers could be circumvented.[59] Theoretically, indeed, this was conceivable. The Community might, for example, have concluded an agreement on drug abuse control with a developing country which was so detailed and specific that it necessitated the development of an internal Community policy on drugs. Imagine that such an agreement contained provisions on specific criminal penalties for narcotics trade and drug abuse in the contracting parties. Clearly, it would not have been within the Community's competence to conduct a development co-operation policy which would have the effect of binding the Community and the Member States as regards such criminal penalties. Furthermore, such an agreement would not only have aimed at development co-operation, as one may assume that the EU is developed.

Whether there is a genuine threat of such abuse of the Treaty provisions on development co-operation is doubtful, but the Court was none the less correct in drawing attention to the limits of the Community's powers.[60] The right balance is difficult to strike, though. One may read the judgment as proclaiming that development co-operation agreements may only, in specific areas, provide for a general framework for co-operation. Yet effective development co-operation cannot be achieved through the mere establishment of such a general framework. All kinds of specific measures and actions may be required. Even if the Court did not accept Portugal's claims, it may have been too restrictive in its analysis, putting up high constitutional hurdles for an effective Community development co-operation policy.

[58] P Alston and JHH Weiler, 'An "Ever Closer Union" in Need of a Human Rights Policy: The European Union and Human Rights' in P Alston (ed), *The EU and Human Rights* (OUP, 1999) 1, in particular 9–14.

[59] Cf M Cremona, 'External Relations and External Competence: The Emergence of an Integrated Policy' in P Craig and G de Búrca, *The Evolution of EU Law* (OUP, 1999) 161.

[60] See also Ch 3.

The *Small Arms and Light Weapons* case

The Court was clearly less restrictive in the *Small Arms and Light Weapons (SALW)* case.[61] In issue was a Council decision, adopted as a CFSP measure, on the basis of a CFSP Joint Action.[62] The latter concerned the EU's contribution to combating the destabilizing accumulation and spread of small arms and light weapons. The challenged decision aimed to implement the joint action, by providing for a financial contribution and technical assistance in order to set up the Light Weapons Unit within the ECOWAS Technical Secretariat,[63] and to convert a moratorium on small arms and light weapons into a Convention. The Commission's claim was that the decision, and the joint action on which it was based, were in breach of (then) Article 47 TEU, which policed the border between the TEU and the EC Treaty. The Commission contended that the decision impinged upon competences conferred upon the Community in the area of development co-operation. The Court's judgment is analysed more fully in the next chapter, as it is of great significance for understanding the nature of the EU's CFSP competences, and their relationship with other external competences. What follows highlights the Court's reasoning as regards the development co-operation aspects of the case.

The Court agreed with the Commission, in the sense that it found that the decision simultaneously pursued a foreign and security policy objective and an objective of development co-operation, without one being incidental to the other. This led the Court to annul the decision, for being in breach of (then) Article 47 TEU. Referring to *Portugal v. Council*, the Court recalled that the objectives pursued by Article 130u EC were broad in the sense that it had to be possible for the measures required for their pursuit to concern various specific measures. It pointed out that the relevant Treaty provisions referred, not only to the sustainable economic and social development of developing countries, their smooth and gradual integration into the world economy, and the campaign against poverty, but also to the development and consolidation of democracy and the rule of law, as well as to respect for human rights and fundamental freedoms, in compliance also with commitments in the context of the United Nations and other international organizations.[64] The Court also referred to the so-called European Consensus on development policy,[65] according to which there could be no sustainable development and eradication of poverty without peace and security, and the pursuit of the objectives of the Community's development policy necessarily proceeded via the promotion of democracy and respect for human rights. While the objectives of development co-operation policy therefore did not have to be limited to measures directly related

[61] Case C–91/05 *Commission v. Council* [2008] ECR I–3651.
[62] Joint Action 2002/589 [2002] OJ L191/1.
[63] ECOWAS stands for Economic Community of West African States.
[64] See also Case C–403/05 *European Parliament v. Commission* [2007] ECR I–9045, para 56.
[65] Joint Statement by the Council and the representatives of the governments of the Member States meeting within the Council, the European Parliament and the Commission [2006] OJ C46/1.

to the campaign against poverty, it was none the less necessary, if a measure was to fall within that policy, that it contributed to the pursuit of that policy's economic and social development objectives. The Court then went on to establish that it was apparent from a number of documents emanating from the EU institutions and from the European Council that certain measures aiming to prevent fragility in developing countries, including those adopted in order to combat the proliferation of small arms and light weapons, could contribute to the elimination or reduction of obstacles to the economic and social development of those countries.[66]

The Court then proceeded to examine the specific aims and contents of the decision in issue. It established that the CFSP joint action which the decision aimed to implement did not exclude the possibility that its objectives could be achieved by measures adopted by the Community on the basis of its competences in the field of development co-operation. Recital 1 in the preamble to the decision stated that the excessive and uncontrolled accumulation and spread of small arms and light weapons not only posed a threat to peace and security, but also reduced the prospects for sustainable development, particularly in West Africa. It could not be denied that the decision formed part of a general perspective of preserving peace and strengthening international security. None the less, it could not be inferred from the decision that in comparison with its objectives of preserving peace and strengthening international security its concern to eliminate or reduce obstacles to the development of the countries concerned was purely incidental. The decision had the specific goal of strengthening the capacities of a group of African developing countries to combat a phenomenon which constituted an obstacle to the sustainable development of those countries. The decision therefore pursued a number of objectives, falling within the CFSP and development co-operation respectively, without one of those objectives being incidental to the other. An analysis of the content of the decision could only confirm this finding, as it was only in the light of the aims they pursued that a financial contribution or technical assistance could be regarded as falling within the scope of the CFSP or of Community development co-operation policy.[67]

The *SALW* judgment concerned autonomous EU action, and not the conclusion of an international agreement. It is none the less significant for determining the scope of the EU's competence, since it confirmed that development co-operation policy may cover a broad spectrum of measures. It is further notable that the Court extensively drew on policy documents emanating from the EU institutions to confirm that the contested decision had a development co-operation objective. That is understandable, and appropriate, in the light of the nature of development co-operation, which has two essential components: it is a form of co-operation with developing countries, and it aims at furthering their development. The latter component calls for an essentially political assessment.

[66] *SALW* (n 61 above) paras 64–70. [67] Ibid, paras 92–108.

The judgment also confirms that the approach of aiming to identify the main or predominant purpose or component of a measure, which we have already studied in chapter 2 in the context of trade and environment issues, extends to development co-operation policies.

The Treaty of Lisbon amendments

The Treaty of Lisbon introduces some amendments to the provisions on development co-operation policy. As already noted in the introduction to this chapter, Article 4(4) TFEU lists development co-operation and humanitarian aid among the competences which the EU shares with the Member States. However, in contrast with other shared competences, the provision states that 'the exercise of that competence shall not result in Member States being prevented from exercising theirs'. Effectively, therefore, the competences of the EU and of the Member States in this field complement each other. The lack of pre-emptive effect on Member States competences is in the nature of development co-operation policies, which do not involve any law-making of the kind justifying such pre-emption. The complementary character of EU and Member States competences is confirmed by Article 209(2) TFEU. That provision enables the EU to conclude international agreements in matters of development co-operation, but adds that this is without prejudice to Member States' competence to negotiate in international bodies and to conclude agreements.

The Treaties also redefine the objectives of the EU's development co-operation policy. That policy is situated in the TFEU part on External Action by the EU, and the general objectives of such action are set out in the TEU. Article 21(1) TEU provides that the EU shall be guided by the principles which inspired its own creation, development, and enlargement, including democracy, the rule of law, the universality and indivisibility of human rights and fundamental freedoms, respect for human dignity, the principles of equality and solidarity, and respect for the principles of the UN Charter. Article 21(2)(d) TEU speaks about fostering 'the sustainable economic, social and environmental development of developing countries, with the primary aim of eradicating poverty'. Article 208(1) TFEU, which specifically concerns development co-operation, cross-refers to those general objectives, by providing that that policy shall be conducted within the framework of the principles and objectives of the EU's external action as a whole. It further emphasizes that the policy shall have as its primary objective the reduction and, in the long term, the eradication of poverty.

Compared to the preceding EC Treaty provisions, the Treaties are thus in their current version both more specific and general. The eradication of poverty is clearly the central objective of development co-operation, but the policy also needs to pursue all of the general objectives of EU external action, which are broadly formulated. The EU's competences in this area have therefore not been reduced, and the principles emanating from the Court's case law continue to be valid and applicable.

Other co-operation agreements

The Court's rather restrictive approach towards the Community's competence for development co-operation in *Portugal v. Council* may have been one of the causes of the insertion into the EC Treaty of further provisions on 'Economic, Financial and Technical Cooperation with Third Countries',[68] by the Treaty of Nice. (Current) Article 212(1) TFEU, further amended by the Treaty of Lisbon, provides:

> Without prejudice to the other provisions of this Treaty, and in particular Articles 208 to 211 [on development cooperation], the Union shall carry out economic, financial and technical co-operation measures, including assistance, in particular financial assistance, with third countries other than developing countries. Such measures shall be consistent with the development policy of the Union and shall be carried out within the framework of the principles and objectives of its external action. The Union's measures and those of the Member States shall complement and reinforce each other.

This article clearly complements the provisions on development co-operation, as was clarified by the Court in *EP v. Council*.[69] That case concerned a challenge to a Council decision providing for a Community guarantee to the European Investment Bank (EIB) against losses under loans and loan guarantees for projects outside the Community. Those projects involved both developing countries and other third countries. The Council had adopted the decision on the basis of (current) Article 212 TFEU, whereas the Parliament considered that it should have been based also on the Treaty provisions on development co-operation. The Court analysed the relationship between the respective Treaty provisions. In its literal sense the term 'third countries' used in (current) Article 212 TFEU was sufficiently wide to encompass both developing countries and other third countries. It could not, however, be implied from this, without restricting the scope of the provisions on development co-operation, that all economic, financial, and technical co-operation measures with developing countries could be undertaken on the sole basis of (current) Article 212 TFEU. The fact that the Treaty provisions on development co-operation only referred to the adoption of 'measures' did not mean that such co-operation could not extend to economic, financial, and technical co-operation, which constituted a typical form of development co-operation. The Court reached the conclusion that (current) Article 212 TFEU was not intended to constitute the legal basis for measures pursuing the objectives of development co-operation within the meaning of the Treaty.[70]

[68] See also B Martenczuk, 'Cooperation with Developing and Other Third Countries: Elements of a Community Foreign Policy' in S Griller and B Weidel (eds), *External Economic Relations and Foreign Policy in the European Union* (Springer, 2002) 399–410.

[69] Case C–155/07 *European Parliament v. Council* [2008] ECR I–8103.

[70] Ibid, paras 39–47.

The Court also pointed out that the concept of 'developing country' was not defined in the Treaty. It found that Community practice was based on an OECD classification, but emphasized that the concept had to be given an autonomous Community interpretation, also in view of the dynamic nature of the developing country category, in the sense that it was liable to evolve in response to events which were difficult to predict. However, in the case at hand there was no need for a definition, as it was common ground that a number of countries benefiting from the EIB projects which the Community guaranteed were capable of falling within that concept, whatever its precise definition.[71]

The Court concluded that the decision concerned both developing countries and other third countries, and that both components were inseparably linked. This required a dual legal basis.

The concepts of economic, technical, and financial co-operation are not defined in the Treaty, but should not present major difficulties of interpretation, in particular in the light of established practice. They can be contrasted with the law-making function of international agreements, where a particular policy is pursued through the establishment of binding rules destined to be integrated into domestic legal systems. A co-operation agreement in matters of intellectual property, for example, could not involve the harmonization of intellectual property law.

Environment

The Community and the EU have long been involved with environmental protection policies. It is of course in the nature of many environmental problems that they cross borders between States, and increasingly such problems are of a global character. Therefore, much as EU involvement is natural, EU policy cannot stop at the external border. Environmental policies are often developed in international concert, leading to multilateral environmental agreements. EU competence in matters of environmental protection would be severely limited if there was no capacity to participate in the negotiation and conclusion of such agreements.[72]

The Single European Act 1986 inserted environmental protection policy into the EEC Treaty, and from the start provided for external action. (Current) Article 191(4) TFEU provides:

> Within their respective spheres of competence, the Union and the Member States shall co-operate with third countries and with the competent international organizations. The arrangements for Union co-operation may be the subject of agreements between the Union and the third parties concerned.

[71] Ibid, paras 52–53.

[72] For a more in-depth analysis of external competence see JH Jans, *European Environmental Law* (2nd edn, Europa Law Publishing, 2000) ch 2.

The previous subparagraph shall be without prejudice to Member States' competence to negotiate in international bodies and to conclude agreements.

In Chapter 2 the relationship between trade policy and environmental policy was looked at from an external competence perspective. In *Greece v. Council* the Court accepted that a regulation laying down the maximum level of radioactive contamination for imported agricultural products came within the scope of the common commercial policy.[73] In *Opinion 2/00*, by contrast, the Court established that the Cartagena Protocol was essentially concerned with environmental protection, and not with trade.[74] In the *Energy Star Agreement* case the conclusion was that an agreement with the United States on the labelling of products as regards their energy-efficiency was predominantly concerned with trade.[75] In the *Rotterdam Convention* and *Chemicals Regulation* cases the Court decided that a convention and a regulation on trade in hazardous chemicals required, exceptionally, a dual legal basis in the Treaty provisions on commercial policy and on environmental policy.[76] In the *Shipments of Waste* case the Court concluded that the regulation in issue came within the EC's environmental competences.[77] The reader is referred to those pages for further analysis of the delimitation of commercial policy and environmental policy, which may well continue to pose problems, particularly in the light of the exclusive nature of EU competence in matters of trade and the shared character of powers in the field of environmental protection (see, for the latter, Article 4(2)(e) TFEU).

There can be no attempt here to define EU competence in matters of environmental protection in material terms. The TFEU sets a number of objectives for EU policy and refers to a number of principles which must guide EU action (the precautionary principle, the principle of preventive action, and the polluter-pays principle).[78] It provides for different methods of decision-making.[79] The ordinary legislative procedure is the rule, but in certain areas the Council decides unanimously. In many areas environmental policy is developed through general action programmes.[80] The Treaty also specifies that EU measures shall not prevent any Member States from maintaining or introducing more stringent provisions.[81] It is clear from those provisions, and from the practice, that EU competence in environmental matters is wide and inclusive, yet shared with the Member States.

There is a further issue which needs to be looked at. The text of the TFEU provisions may suggest that all external action in matters of environmental protection must

[73] Case C–62/88 *Greece v. Council* [1990] ECR I–1527.

[74] *Opinion 2/00 re Cartagena Protocol on Biosafety* [2001] ECR I–9713.

[75] Case C–281/01 *Commission v. Council* [2002] ECR I–12049.

[76] Case C–94/03 *Commission v. Council* [2006] ECR I–1 and Case C–178/03 *Commission v. EP and Council* [2006] ECR I–107.

[77] Case C–411/06 *Commission v. European Parliament and Council* [2009] ECR I–7585.

[78] See Art 191 TFEU.

[79] Art 192 TFEU.

[80] E.g. Decision 1600/2002 of the European Parliament and of the Council laying down the Sixth Community Environment Action Programme [2002] OJ L242/1.

[81] Art 193 TFEU.

be based on the express provision of Article 191(4) (see above). That is, however, not the case. In *Opinion 2/00*[82] the Court of Justice held that (current) Article 191 defines the objectives to be pursued in the context of environmental policy, while (current) Article 192 constitutes the legal basis for the adoption of environmental measures. The latter provision contains alternative modes of EU decision-making, depending on the subject matter of the measures, but it does not expressly refer to the conclusion of international agreements. The Court appeared to confine the use of (current) Article 191(4) to 'arrangements for Community co-operation' with third parties, and pointed out that the Protocol did not merely establish such arrangements but laid down precise rules on the environmental issues which it covered. Accordingly, (current) Article 192(1) TFEU was the appropriate legal basis for the conclusion of the Protocol, and not, as the Commission had argued, (current) Article 191(4).[83] It is not wholly clear from the Opinion why the Commission took this view. It may have been concerned about the possible application of (current) Article 193 TFEU, according to which 'the protective measures adopted pursuant to Article 192 shall not prevent any Member State from maintaining or introducing more stringent protective measures', something the Commission might seek to avoid in relation to the Cartagena Protocol. If that was indeed the Commission's concern, it would in any event seem questionable whether Article 193 TFEU constitutes sufficient authority for the Member States to adopt protective measures more stringent than those provided for by the Protocol. According to Article 216(2) TFEU, agreements concluded by the EU are binding on the EU institutions and on the Member States, and it is submitted that the question of whether more stringent measures are allowed is to be resolved on the basis of the proper construction of the Cartagena Protocol.[84]

Be that as it may, the Opinion clarified that the EU's external environmental powers are not confined to the arrangements referred to in Article 191(4), but extend to all areas of EU environmental law-making.[85] The Opinion thus recognized implied external powers, and its approach may be relevant for other policy areas where the TFEU contains similar provisions on international co-operation.

It may further be recalled that the Opinion established, for external competence, the principle that when an agreement has a twofold purpose or component, one should aim to determine the predominant purpose or component. Only if the agreement simultaneously pursues several objectives which are inseparably linked without one being secondary and indirect in relation to the other may the agreement be founded on the corresponding legal bases.[86] This principle will no doubt

[82] N 74 above.

[83] See also, as regards the respective scope of paras 1 and 2 of (current) Art 192, Case C–36/98 *Spain v. Council* [2001] ECR I–779.

[84] See also the *PFOS* case, analysed in Ch 7, which concerned the effects of the duty of co-operation on the competences of the Member States in the context of a mixed environmental agreement (Case C–246/07 *Commission v. Sweden*, judgment of 20 April 2010.

[85] Cf A Dashwood, Annotation Opinion 2/00 (2002) 39 CML Rev 368.

[86] *Opinion 2/00* (n 74 above) paras 22–24.

become increasingly important, as agreements pursue multiple aims, and as the founding treaties have become more express on matters of competence.

Lastly, as EU competence in environmental matters is shared with the Member States, there is scope for mixed agreements having both the EU and the Member States as contracting parties. For pure environmental agreements mixity will not often be legally required, in the light of the fact that EU competences are broadly formulated. Most international environmental protection agreements could be concluded by the EU acting alone. That is not, however, the practice, as is further explored in Chapter 7. It is clear from the *Mox Plant* judgment that the Court accepts that EU competences are only partially exercised, in the sense that the Council, when concluding an agreement with the Member States, may elect to what extent it is exercising the EU's external competences in matters of environmental protection.[87] To clarify this with a hypothetical example: if the EU concludes an agreement, together with the Member States, on both air and water pollution, it could decide to limit its participation to the provisions on air pollution, even if the TFEU would also enable it to participate in the agreement with respect to water pollution.

The internal market and transport

The four freedoms, internal market harmonization, and competition policy

EU policies to establish and complete a well-functioning internal market, which operates like a single national market, are central and foundational for much of the EU construct, even if the current EU clearly transcends the core economic functions of the original EEC. Internal market policy is of course primarily an 'internal' policy, and it may at first glance seem curious to consider opportunities for external action and for the conclusion of international agreements in this sphere. The issue none the less needs to be considered, because there are important questions about the scope of EU powers in internal market-related matters.

The first point to note is that the common commercial policy complements the internal market; indeed it is a component of the internal market. In the conception of the Treaties a common policy on external trade is vital for internal free movement, since the internal market covers all products, those originating in the EU and those which are imported.[88] The scope and nature of EU competence in external trade matters are extensively analysed in Chapter 2.

That does not, however, mean that all EU measures which affect imported products come within the scope of the common commercial policy. One classic

[87] Case C–459/03 *Commission v. Ireland* [2006] ECR I–4635. See further Ch 7.

[88] Arts 28–29 TFEU; see also Ch 10.

mechanism for having a well-functioning internal market is the harmonization of national product regulations, based on Article 114 TFEU. Such measures of harmonization, usually in the form of directives, govern all products on the internal market, including imported products. For example, the directive on toys lays down certain essential requirements for the safety, etc. of toys,[89] with which all toys traded on the internal market need to comply, be they produced in the EU or, for that matter, China. A directive on toys comes within the scope of internal market competence, even if it also applies to Chinese toys, whereas a regulation limiting imports of toys from China falls within the common commercial policy.[90] At the level of EU internal legislation the distinction between general harmonization and import or export measures may be rather straightforward, but when it comes to concluding international agreements on product regulations (or technical regulations and standards, to use the WTO concepts) the issue of competence is less obvious.[91] What is the legal basis in the Treaties for the adoption of such agreements?

In *Opinion 1/94* the Court briefly looked at the WTO Agreement on Technical Barriers to Trade (TBT) and the Agreement on Sanitary and Phytosanitary Measures (SPS). As regards the former, the Netherlands government argued that the joint participation of the Community and the Member States was justified, since the Member States had their own competence in relation to technical barriers to trade by reason of the optional nature of certain Community directives in that area, and because complete harmonization had not been achieved and was not envisaged. The Court most succinctly replied by stating that the provisions of the TBT Agreement were designed merely to ensure that technical regulations and standards and procedures for assessment of conformity with technical regulations and standards did not create unnecessary obstacles to trade (see the preamble and Articles 2.2 and 5.1.2. TBT). It thus followed that the agreement came within the ambit of the common commercial policy. As regards the SPS Agreement the Court similarly referred to the preamble, according to which the agreement was confined to 'the establishment of a multilateral framework of rules and disciplines to guide the development, adoption and enforcement of sanitary and phytosanitary measures in order to minimise their negative effects on trade'. Such an agreement could be concluded on the basis of (then) Article 113 EC alone (now, with amendments, Article 207 TFEU).[92]

The Court's approach was logical for agreements which are predominantly oriented towards avoiding the negative effects on trade of technical regulations and standards, and of sanitary and phytosanitary measures, and which do not themselves provide for harmonization of such regulations and measures. However, in

[89] Directive 88/378 on the approximation of the laws of the Member States concerning the safety of toys [1988] OJ L187/1.

[90] Regulation 260/2009 on the common rules for imports [2009] OJ L84/1.

[91] See for further analysis ELM Völker, *Barriers to External and Internal Community Trade* (Kluwer, 1993) ch 5.

[92] *Opinion 1/94 re WTO Agreement* [1994] ECR I-5267, paras 28–33.

the *Energy Star Agreement* case the Court appeared to go a little further.[93] There the Court considered that the predominant purpose of an agreement effectively extending the US Energy Star programme to the Community was of a commercial-policy rather than environmental-policy nature, even if the programme itself ultimately aimed at greater environmental protection. The Court focused on the immediate and direct impact on trade of common labelling rules, rather than on the longer-term and indirect objective of environmental protection. The judgment goes further than *Opinion 1/94*, because there was an element of material harmonization in the agreement. It would, however, be wrong to conclude that all international agreements laying down technical regulations, standards, or common labelling rules come within the scope of the common commercial policy. In some cases, no doubt, effective harmonization will be more predominant than international trade concerns. Such agreements will have to be concluded on the basis of the Treaty provision enabling such harmonization, the most general one being Article 114 TFEU.[94]

The above observations apply to the production of and trade in goods, and, since the entry into force of the Lisbon Treaty, also to trade in services. The latter is at present also within the scope of the common commercial policy, and the above principles regarding the delimitation of trade measures and measures of internal harmonization can be transposed to services. For example, an international agreement establishing certain accounting standards for the protection of investors may well be insufficiently trade-related to come within the scope of Article 207 TFEU. It should be possible to conclude such an agreement on the basis of the EU's implied external powers in the sphere of the internal market, if the provisions in the agreement contribute to removing obstacles in the internal market or distortions of competition.[95]

The Treaty provisions on establishment, by contrast, are limited to self-employed activities and establishment by companies between Member States, in the internal market. As the Court recalled in *Lasertec Gesellschaft für Stanzformen*, the chapter of the Treaty relating to freedom of establishment does not include any provision which extends the scope of its provisions to situations involving nationals of non-member countries who are established outside the EU.[96] As with goods and services, that does not exclude that the internal competences to harmonize national legislation be employed to conclude an international agreement which effectively involves such harmonization, for example an agreement co-ordinating Member States' laws concerning the taking-up and pursuit of activities as self-employed persons in the sense of Article 53(1) TFEU. Moreover, one should also note that

[93] *Commission v. Council* (n 75 above).

[94] It is noteworthy that in the *Energy Star Agreement* case the Court hinted at the fact that directives on eco-labelling should have been based on (current) Art 114 TFEU rather than Art 192 TFEU: ibid, para 46.

[95] Cf Case C–376/98 *Germany v. European Parliament and Council* [2000] ECR I–8419 (*Tobacco Advertising Directive* case).

[96] Case C–492/04 *Lasertec Gesellschaft für Stanzformen v. Finanzamt Emmendingen* [2007] ECR I–3775.

establishment by non-EU nationals or legal persons comes within the concept of trade in services where the economic activity involved consists of the provision of services. Indeed, the notion of 'services' under WTO law is broader than under the TFEU. GATS applies to commercial presence, which covers permanent establishment by non-domestic service providers.[97]

As regards workers, it is not clear whether prior to the Treaty of Amsterdam the Treaty's internal market provisions offered any firm basis for external action, particularly in so far as non-EU citizens were involved. As analysed above, in *Demirel* the Court had no difficulty in accepting that an association agreement could cover provisions on non-EU workers,[98] but outside the context of associations the scope of Community competence was uncertain. One could argue that the Community had competence as regards non-EU workers legally resident and employed in a Member State, on the ground that the treatment of such workers could affect the internal labour market, but as regards access by non-EU citizens to the labour market and the connected subject of immigration there was no basis in the Treaty for Community competence.[99] The Treaty of Amsterdam changed that by projecting an EU migration policy as part of the Area of Freedom, Security, and Justice (see below).

In the domain of capital and payments, by contrast, there is clear-cut external competence. The Treaty not only prohibits restrictions on the movement of capital and payments between Member States, but also between Member States and third countries, subject to those restrictions which existed on 31 December 1993 under either national law or EU law, which involve direct investment, establishment, the provision of financial services, or the admission of securities to capital markets (Articles 63 and 64(1) TFEU). It is therefore clear that, after that date, the Member States are no longer entitled to introduce additional restrictions; only the Council may do so under either Article 64(2) TFEU (again as regards direct investment, establishment, provision of financial services, or admission of securities to capital markets), Article 66 TFEU (safeguard measures), or Article 215 TFEU (economic and financial sanctions). Those combined provisions leave little scope for Member State action, notwithstanding the principle of shared competence in internal market matters. The EU's competence is wide, and extends to the conclusion of international agreements on capital or payment restrictions.

Internal market harmonization measures may themselves form the basis for the conclusion of international agreements (cf Article 216(1) TFEU). However, such agreements must remain within the scope of the Treaty's internal market provisions. The Court applied that principle in *European Parliament v. Council and Commission* on an agreement with the United States on passenger name records (PNRs)

[97] For further reflections see P Eeckhout, 'Constitutional Concepts for Free Trade in Services' in G de Búrca and J Scott, *The EU and the WTO—Legal and Constitutional Issues* (Hart Publishing, 2001) 221–3.

[98] N 14 above.

[99] Cf Joined Cases 281, 283 to 285, and 287/85 *Germany and Others v. Commission* [1987] ECR 3203, para 30.

(the *PNR* case).[100] The case involved challenges to a Commission decision on the adequate protection of personal data contained in the PNRs of air passengers transferred to the US Bureau of Customs and Border Protection;[101] and to a Council decision on the conclusion of an agreement with the United States on the processing and transfer of PNR data.[102] The Commission decision on adequacy had been adopted in implementation of Directive 95/46 on the protection of individuals with regard to the processing of personal data and on the free movement of such data.[103] Article 25 of the directive concerned the transfer of personal data to a third country, and required that the Commission adopt decisions on whether the third country concerned ensured an adequate level of protection. The Council decision to conclude the agreement with the United States was based on (current) Article 114 TFEU and on the directive. The Court annulled both the adequacy decision and the decision to conclude the agreement. It focused on Article 3(2) of the directive, which excluded from the directive's scope the processing of personal data in the course of an activity which fell outside the scope of Community law, such as activities provided for by Titles V and VI of the (then) TEU, and in any case processing operations concerning public security, defence, State security, and the activities of the State in areas of criminal law. The Court established that the United States would use the PNR data strictly for purposes of preventing and combating terrorism and related crimes; other serious crimes, including organized crime, that were transnational in nature; and flight from warrants or custody for those crimes. It followed that the transfer of PNR data constituted processing operations concerning public security and the activities of the State in areas of criminal law. It was irrelevant that the PNR data were initially collected by airlines in the course of an activity which fell within the scope of Community law. The data processing to be taken into account was that by the US authorities. The decision on adequacy was therefore outside the scope of the directive. Furthermore, (current) Article 114 TFEU, read in conjunction with Article 25 of the directive, could not justify Community competence to conclude the PNR Agreement with the United States: the Agreement related to the same transfer of data as the decision on adequacy and therefore to data-processing operations which were excluded from the scope of the directive.[104]

In the specific sectors of agriculture, fisheries, and transport the case law analysed in Chapters 2 and 3 identifies the basis for and scope of EU competence. In *Opinion 1/94* the Court clarified that agreements on trade in agricultural products come within the scope of the common commercial policy, even if they affect the Common Agricultural Policy (CAP) as strongly as does the WTO Agreement on Agriculture.[105] An agreement not concerned with trade, by contrast, would come

[100] Joined Cases C-317 and 318/04 *European Parliament v. Council and Commission (PNR)* [2006] ECR I-4721.

[101] [2004] OJ L235/11.

[102] [2004] OJ L183/83.

[103] [1995] OJ L281/31.

[104] *PNR* (n 100 above) paras 54–57 and 67–68.

[105] *Opinion 1/94* (n 92 above) paras 28–31.

within the scope of the EU's implied external powers provided by the Treaty provisions on agriculture, if it can be linked to the objectives of the CAP. Those provisions do not confer exclusive competence, but there is so much EU legislation that the *AETR* principle would often apply. In the sphere of conservation of fish resources, there is exclusive EU competence, flowing from the relevant provisions of primary law, as discussed in the introduction to this chapter.[106]

The EU's competition policy is a further dimension of the internal market. In this area, too, the EU no doubt has competence to conclude international agreements, for example regarding co-operation with non-EU competition authorities.[107]

Investment treaties

Chapter 2 analysed the scope of the EU's new powers, under the common commercial policy, in matters of foreign direct investment. That analysis was carried out in relation to the subject matter and forms of protection of standard bilateral investment treaties (BITs). The conclusion was reached that the new competences cover all forms of protection, but do not extend to all forms of investment: pure portfolio investment is not included, following the definition of 'direct investment' employed by the Court of Justice in the context of the Treaty provisions on capital movement.

In its Communication on a European international investment policy, the Commission claims that the Treaty provisions on capital and payments complement the EU's exclusive competence under the common commercial policy, and provide for an implied exclusive competence. The Commission's reasoning is as follows.[108] It points out that the articulation of investment policy should be consistent with the TFEU chapter on capital and payments, which provides that, in principle, all restrictions on payments and capital movements, including those involving direct as well as portfolio investments, both between Member States and between Member States and third countries, are prohibited. The Commission recognizes that that chapter does not expressly provide for the possibility to conclude international agreements on investment, including portfolio investment. However, with reference to Article 3(2) TFEU, the Commission claims that, to the extent that international agreements on investment affect the scope of the common rules set by the chapter on capital and payments, the exclusive EU competence to conclude agreements in this area would be implied. If the Commission's analysis were correct, one would have to conclude that substantially all forms of investment covered by BITs are now within the EU's exclusive competence.

[106] See Ch 3; for further analysis see I Macleod, ID Hendry, and S Hyett, *The External Relations of the European Communities* (OUP, 1996) ch 10.

[107] See e.g. the agreement with the US (n 101 above).

[108] Communication from the Commission, *Towards a comprehensive European international investment policy*, COM(2010)343 final, at 8.

There are, however, serious doubts as to whether the Commission's reasoning conforms to the law of EU external competence. Assuming that Article 3(2) TFEU merely codifies the principles governing exclusive implied powers, the starting-point of our analysis must be to identify the substantive competences for which the TFEU provides in the area of capital movement. Indeed, as seen in Chapter 3, the Court invariably takes great care to define the EU's substantive competences in implied-powers cases. It is only once those competences are defined, that the further question as to whether they are exclusive can be answered.

Article 63 TFEU establishes the rule of free capital movement, also between Member States and third countries. Article 64(2) TFEU confers on the EU competence to adopt measures, in accordance with the ordinary legislative procedure, 'on the movement of capital to or from third countries involving direct investment—including investment in real estate—establishment, the provision of financial services or the admission of securities to capital markets'. Although the reference to the ordinary legislative procedure suggests that this provision aims at the adoption of internal EU legislation, the law on implied powers has clarified that such a competence may be used for the conclusion of an international agreement. However, the scope of the competence conferred by Article 64(2) does not extend to all portfolio investments. Direct investment is the opposite of portfolio investment. Measures concerning the provision of financial services or the admission of securities to capital markets may affect portfolio investment, but clearly do not cover all aspects of such investment.

Article 66 TFEU enables the Council to take safeguard measures, where, in exceptional circumstances, movements of capital to or from third countries cause, or threaten to cause, serious difficulties for the operation of economic or monetary union. Such safeguard measures, if ever adopted, would of course extend to portfolio investment. But again this does not constitute a general competence to regulate portfolio investments from third countries in the Member States. It does not, for example, confer competence to guarantee fair and equitable treatment as regards portfolio investments.

The same reasoning can be applied to the EU's competences under Article 75 TFEU, which, as regards preventing and combating terrorism, permits regulations defining a framework for administrative measures with regard to capital movements and payments, such as the freezing of funds, financial assets, or economic gains belonging to, or owned or held by, natural or legal persons, groups, or non-State entities; and to competences under Article 215 TFEU, to adopt restrictive measures involving 'the reduction, in part or completely, of economic and financial relations with one or more third countries'. Again these measures may affect portfolio investments, but do not confer general competence to regulate.

It is therefore difficult to see on what basis the EU could claim a general competence to conclude international agreements on portfolio investment. It is even more difficult to establish a basis for exclusive competence. Article 4(2)(a) provides for shared competence in internal market matters. This is confirmed by Article

65(1) TFEU, which recognizes that the Member States may still adopt certain measures restricting capital movements, for example 'measures which are justified on grounds of public policy or public security'.

Of course, such shared competence does not exclude the operation of the *AETR* principle, according to which there is exclusive competence to the extent that internal legislation may be affected, or its scope altered. However, as Maduro AG noted in two cases involving investment treaties, the EU has so far not made use of the competences under Article 64(2) or 66 TFEU.[109] In other words, there is as yet no internal legislation which may be affected or whose scope may be altered by an investment agreement covering portfolio investment. Nor could it be argued that the *Opinion 1/76*-type exclusive implied powers extend to portfolio investment. To paraphrase the Court's statement in the *Open Skies* cases, there is as regards portfolio investment no internal competence which could be effectively exercised only at the same time as the external competence, the conclusion of the international agreement thus being necessary in order to attain objectives of the Treaty that could not be attained by establishing autonomous rules.[110]

The Commission appears to consider that, on the mere basis that the Treaty provides for free movement of capital and payments between Member States and third countries, exclusive EU competence to conclude agreements covering the making and protection of portfolio investments is implied. That is, with respect, a reasoning which is too broad. In fact, it is not clear on what Treaty basis the EU has shared competence to regulate all aspects of portfolio investment between the Member States and third countries, let alone exclusive competence.[111]

Transport

As regards transport, *Opinion 1/94* and the implied-powers case law supply the relevant principles, and the reader may be referred to the analysis in the previous chapters. One further judgment is worth referring to. In *Commission v. Council* the Court decided that agreements concluded in 2001 with Bulgaria and Hungary on the carriage of goods by road and the promotion of combined transport should have been based on (current) Article 91 TFEU. Instead, the Council had based its decision to conclude the agreements also on (current) Article 113 TFEU, on the harmonization of indirect taxes. It had done so because the agreements contained provisions of a fiscal nature. Article 8 of both agreements concerned, first,

[109] Case C-205/06 *Commission v. Austria* [2009] ECR I-1301 and Case C-249/06 *Commission v. Sweden* [2009] ECR I-1335, Opinion of Maduro AG, para 3.

[110] Case C-476/98 *Commission v. Germany (Open Skies)* [2002] ECR I-9855, paras 80–90.

[111] In *Opinion 2/92 re Third Revised Decision of the OECD on national treatment* [1995] ECR I-521 the Court only examined whether the Community had exclusive competence to conclude this investment protection decision, and did not analyse which Treaty provisions could form a legal basis for such conclusion.

the application of the principle of equal treatment in terms of road vehicle taxation and other fiscal charges and, secondly, the granting of exemptions from taxes levied on transport operations, fuel contained in tanks, lubricants, spare parts, and tools required in case of breakdown. The Court established that such provisions, in particular those relating to fiscal exemptions, served to harmonize the laws of the Member States concerning indirect taxes for the purpose of implementing the agreements. However, the aspect of the agreements which concerned the harmonization of fiscal laws was, in the light of their aim and their content, only secondary and indirect in nature compared with the transport policy objective which they pursued. The fiscal provisions were closely linked to the simplification of transit through Bulgaria and Hungary for the purpose of facilitating the carriage of goods between Greece and other Member States. Moreover, Article 2 of the agreements characterized the fiscal measures as 'supporting measures'. The transport element was therefore the predominant purpose or component, and the Council should have used (current) Article 91 TFEU alone as the legal basis for the contested decisions.[112]

Social policy

The development of an EU social policy is a difficult process, largely owing to political differences regarding the aims and reach of EU involvement in this area. The original EEC Treaty envisaged little more than close co-operation between the Member States (Article 118 EEC), and did not confer legislative competence. The Single European Act changed that, but only as regards the health and safety of workers (Article 118a EEC). At the Maastricht negotiations there was strong pressure to create a much more meaningful social policy, but the United Kingdom resisted such pressure, leading to the Agreement on Social Policy between eleven Member States. In Amsterdam the Member States agreed to make that agreement part of the Treaty, leading ultimately to the current TFEU title on Social Policy, Articles 151 to 161 TFEU.

Chapter 3 includes an analysis of *Opinion 2/91*,[113] where the Court examined competence to conclude an ILO Convention concerning safety in the use of chemicals at work. It had no difficulty in confirming that Article 118a EEC conferred competence to conclude international agreements, even if the Community's internal legislative competence in the field of the health and safety of workers was defined in rather subsidiary terms.[114]

On the basis of that ruling and the other implied-powers case law, there can be no doubt that the EU may conclude agreements in the sphere of social policy.

[112] Case C–211/01 *Commission v. Council* [2003] ECR I–8913, paras 46–50.

[113] *Opinion 2/91 re ILO Convention No 170* [1993] ECR I–1061.

[114] See Ch 3.

Article 153 TFEU defines the areas in which the EU shall support and complement the activities of the Member States, which it may do by adopting, by means of directives, minimum requirements for gradual implementation. Those areas include the health and safety of workers; working conditions; information and consultation of workers; integration of persons excluded from the labour market; and equality between men and women. Here the ordinary legislative procedure applies. In other areas the Council acts unanimously; they include social security and social protection of workers; protection of workers where their employment contract is terminated; representation and collective defence of the interests of workers and employers; and conditions of employment for third-country nationals legally residing in EU territory. In all those areas the EU may act under international law. The same no doubt goes for the competence conferred by Article 157(3) TFEU to adopt measures to ensure the application of the principle of equal opportunities and equal treatment for men and women in matters of employment and occupation, including the principle of equal pay for equal work or work of equal value. It may be added that such external competence is exclusive where there is EU legislation which could be affected by the provisions of an international agreement. However, as the Court found in *Opinion 2/91*, that principle does not operate where both the EU legislation and the international agreement only provide for minimum rules.

Whereas there is thus extensive external competence in the field of social policy, a major obstacle to the exercise of such competence is the fact that the EU is not a member of the ILO, and cannot as such participate in the conclusion of ILO Conventions.[115] The ILO Constitution admits only States as members (Article 1(2)) and does not provide for ratification of ILO Conventions by non-members. In the ILO, therefore, the EU needs to be represented by its Member States.[116]

Economic and Monetary Union

The Treaty on European Union laid down provisions for the establishment of an Economic and Monetary Union (EMU), which is at present in full operation (the so-called third phase), with a single currency, even if a number of Member States do not participate in that final phase. The distinguishing feature of EMU, as compared with other EU policies, is that there is a specific institutional framework, the European System of Central Banks (ESCB), which comprises the European Central Bank (ECB) and the national central banks.

The TFEU distinguishes between economic and monetary policy. The chapter on economic policy does not confer strong law-making powers on the EU. It mostly contains instructions for the Member States and the EU institutions, including prohibitions on overdraft facilities (Article 123 TFEU), on privileged access to

[115] See *Opinion 2/91* (n 113 above) and Ch 7.

[116] So much follows from the duty of co-operation: see Ch 7.

financial institutions (Article 124 TFEU), on bail-outs (Article 125 TFEU), and on excessive government deficits (Article 126 TFEU). Co-ordination of economic policies is to take place within the Council, which may issue recommendations setting out broad guidelines following conclusions reached by the European Council (Article 121(1) and (2) TFEU). The Council and the Commission have general monitoring and supervisory powers (see Articles 121(3) to (5) and 126 TFEU).

The Treaty chapter on economic policy does not provide for express external competences, nor is there much scope for the application of the implied-powers doctrine. The kind of powers conferred on the EU do not lend themselves to the conclusion of formal international agreements,[117] and there are no examples of agreements concluded on the basis of any of the relevant Treaty provisions. There is however clearly scope for EU involvement in informal international co-ordination of economic policies, such as takes place in various international fora (e.g. the G20).

The EU's monetary policy is carried out through the ESCB, whose primary objective is to maintain price stability, and which shall support the general economic policies in the Community (Article 127(1) TFEU). The basic tasks of monetary policy are: [118]

- to define and implement the monetary policy of the Union;
- to conduct foreign exchange operations consistent with the provisions of Article 219;
- to hold and manage the official foreign reserves of the Member States;
- to promote the smooth operation of payment systems.

The ESCB shall, moreover, contribute to the smooth conduct of policies pursued by the competent authorities relating to the prudential supervision of credit institutions and the stability of the financial system (Article 127(5) TFEU), and the Council may confer upon the ECB specific tasks concerning policies relating to the prudential supervision of credit institutions and other financial institutions with the exception of insurance undertakings (Article 127(6) TFEU). The ECB has the exclusive right to authorize the issue of banknotes (Article 128(1) TFEU). Further provisions on the powers of the ECB are laid down in the Statute of the ESCB, and the ECB may exercise those powers by adopting its own regulations, decisions, and recommendations and opinions (Article 132 TFEU).

It is obvious that the running of a single currency and of monetary union may require action under international law, including the conclusion of international agreements. The TFEU recognizes that in Article 219, which contains the relevant provisions. The first two paragraphs concern the exchange rate of the euro in relation to non-EU currencies:

[117] C Zilioli and M Selmayr, 'The External Relations of the Euro Area: Legal Aspects' (1999) 36 CML Rev 289.

[118] Art 127(2) TFEU.

1. By way of derogation from Article 218, the Council, either on a recommendation from the European Central Bank or on a recommendation from the Commission and after consulting the European Central Bank, in an endeavour to reach a consensus consistent with the objective of price stability, may conclude formal agreements on an exchange-rate system for the euro in relation to the currencies of third States. The Council shall act unanimously after consulting the European Parliament and in accordance with the procedure provided for in paragraph 3.

The Council may, either on a recommendation from the European Central Bank or on a recommendation from the Commission, and after consulting the European Central Bank, in an endeavour to reach a consensus consistent with the objective of price stability, adopt, adjust or abandon the central rates of the euro within the exchange-rate system. The President of the Council shall inform the European Parliament of the adoption, adjustment or abandonment of the euro central rates.

2. In the absence of an exchange-rate system in relation to one or more currencies of third States as referred to in paragraph 1, the Council, either on a recommendation from the Commission and after consulting the European Central Bank or on a recommendation from the European Central Bank, may formulate general orientations for exchange-rate policy in relation to these currencies. These general orientations shall be without prejudice to the primary objective of the ESCB to maintain price stability.

The Treaty thus permits EU participation in a formal exchange-rate system, such as that of Bretton Woods or as existed in the EU prior to EMU. Short of the establishment of such a system, the Council may also formulate general orientations for exchange-rate policy.

Article 219(3) TFEU confers general power to conclude agreements concerning monetary or foreign-exchange regime matters, and lays down the procedure to be followed for the negotiation and conclusion of such agreements:

3. By way of derogation from Article 218, where agreements concerning monetary or foreign exchange regime matters need to be negotiated by the Union with one or more third States or international organisations, the Council, on a recommendation from the Commission and after consulting the European Central Bank, shall decide the arrangements for the negotiation and for the conclusion of such agreements. These arrangements shall ensure that the Union expresses a single position. The Commission shall be fully associated with the negotiations.

Paragraph (4) of Article 219 concerns the scope for agreements concluded and negotiated by the Member States:

4. Without prejudice to Union competence and Union agreements as regards economic and monetary union, Member States may negotiate in international bodies and conclude international agreements.

As regards external representation, and the participation of the EU in international financial institutions, Article 138 TFEU provides:

1. In order to secure the euro's place in the international monetary system, the Council, on a proposal from the Commission, shall adopt a decision establishing common positions on matters of particular interest for economic and monetary union within the competent

international financial institutions and conferences. The Council shall act after consulting the European Central Bank.

2. The Council, on a proposal from the Commission, may adopt appropriate measures to ensure unified representation within the international financial institutions and conferences. The Council shall act after consulting the European Central Bank.

3. For the measures referred to in paragraphs 1 and 2, only members of the Council representing Member States whose currency is the euro shall take part in the vote.

A qualified majority of the said members shall be defined in accordance with Article 238(3)(a).

As can be seen, those Treaty provisions lay down a complete system for the conduct of external relations in monetary matters. The core provision is Article 219(3) TFEU, which generally allows for the conclusion of international agreements on 'monetary or foreign exchange regime matters'. As with other external competences of the EU, one needs to determine both the scope and the nature of those competences.

This section cannot offer an extensive analysis of the concept of monetary policy and of the internal and external powers conferred upon the EU in this field. There is, in any event, little or no practice as yet, and there is no case law on Article 219 TFEU. It may none the less be noted that the concept of 'monetary or foreign exchange regime matters' appears broad, and can be read as encompassing all aspects of EU monetary policy. Through the broad reference in Article 219(3) TFEU the Treaty thus appears to establish full parallelism between the EU's internal and external powers. In the literature it has none the less been suggested that the scope of Article 219(3) TFEU is more limited, and extends only to 'monetary regime' and 'foreign-exchange regime' matters. The former notion is said to be confined to situations in which the monetary regime of the euro is extended to a third country.[119] It is indeed true that the different language versions of Article 219(3) TFEU are inconclusive as to the precise meaning of the phrase 'monetary or foreign exchange regime matters', some of them indicating that all 'monetary questions' are covered, others providing that external competence concerns 'monetary regime' matters. However, the correct conclusion rather seems to be that little independent meaning is to be attributed to the use of the notion of 'regime'. There is in any event no indication in the Treaty that the term 'monetary regime' has the precise and limited meaning referred to above.

As regards the nature of EU competence in the sphere of monetary policy, the TFEU now confirms in Article 3(1)(c) that it is exclusive, for the Member States whose currency is the euro. Thus, the EU's external powers under Article 219 TFEU are also of an exclusive character, notwithstanding the reference in Article 219(4) TFEU to national competence, which in any event is 'without prejudice to Union competence'.[120]

[119] Zilioli and Selmayr (n 117 above) 299–301; see also J Dutheil de la Rochère, 'EMU: Constitutional Aspects and External Representation' (1999–2000) 19 YEL 441.

[120] *Contra* Zilioli and Selmayr (n 117 above) 297; Dutheil de la Rochère (n 119 above) 441–3.

This has important consequences for EU representation in certain international organizations, in particular the IMF. At present the EU as such cannot become a member of the IMF because the latter admits only States, but as in the case of the ILO the Member States are required to act in common, representing the EU, in all matters of exclusive EU competence.[121]

The conclusion is that Article 219 TFEU is the core provision concerning the conduct of external relations in the sphere of monetary policy. There may be some scope for the implied-powers doctrine, in so far as certain aspects of monetary policy are considered not to be covered by Article 219 TFEU. It is, however, more natural to read the Treaty as establishing full parallelism between internal and external powers, through a broad interpretation of the concept of 'monetary or foreign exchange regime matters' in Article 219 TFEU.

Area of freedom, security, and justice

Introduction

The Treaty on European Union created the so-called Second and Third Pillars of EU action, respectively in the areas of foreign and security policy, and justice and home affairs. The CFSP continues to be located in the TEU, and is subject to special provisions, also as regards the nature of EU competences in this area (see Chapter 5). Matters are different, however, as regards justice and home affairs, which have been rebranded as policies aimed at creating an Area of Freedom, Security and Justice (AFSJ). The Treaty of Amsterdam first moved some of the justice and home affairs policies into the EC Treaty, in a separate Title denominated 'Visas, Asylum, Immigration and Other Policies Related to the Free Movement of Persons'. The Treaty of Lisbon then made a further transfer, of policies concerning police and judicial co-operation in criminal matters, from the TEU to the TFEU. This means that, with limited exceptions and transitional arrangements, the AFSJ policies are now pursued making use of the standard legal instruments and law-making processes of EU law. It also means that the general principles of EU external competences extend to this area.

For a number of years now AFSJ has been one of the main areas of EU activity, leading to the adoption of a series of legislative acts.[122] Unavoidably, such activity also expands to the international level. It is not the purpose of this section to review the external policies which are under development in this area.[123] The section is confined to a succinct analysis of the external powers of the EU under the relevant Treaty provisions, which, as regards treaty-making, are mostly of an implied charac-

[121] Ibid, 444–5; J Lebullenger, 'La projection externe de la zone euro' (1998) 34 RTDE 468.
[122] See e.g. S Peers, *EU Justice and Home Affairs Law* (3rd edn, OUP, 2011).
[123] See ibid, passim.

ter: with the exception of readmission agreements (see below), there are no express provisions on the conclusion of international agreements or action in international organizations. This is somewhat surprising in the light of the nature of some of the policies covered, such as visas, asylum, and immigration, which are by definition directed towards non-EU citizens.

The section is divided into four parts, reflecting the diverse content of AFSJ policies. At the outset it may also be noted that not all Member States participate in those policies. As regulated in two protocols, the United Kingdom and Ireland do not participate in, and are not bound by, AFSJ acts, unless they opt in,[124] whereas Denmark does not participate at all.[125] This raises specific questions which are beyond the scope of this chapter.[126]

Border checks, asylum, and immigration

The measures set out in the TFEU provisions on border checks, asylum, and immigration are nearly all concerned with non-EU citizens. In that sense, one can say that they form an externally-oriented policy of the EU, even if it mostly consists of the adoption of internal legislation. In the current set-up of the Treaties, these policies are the counterpart of the common commercial policy, as they concern movement of persons into the EU, in contrast to goods. It is obvious, however, that the policies are not as comprehensive as the common commercial policy. For a start, there is clearly no exclusive competence as regards border checks (including visas), asylum, and immigration. This is an area of shared competence, as confirmed by Article 4(2)(j) TFEU. EU competence is limited to specific aspects, and in a number of areas only minimum standards are to be adopted.

As regards border checks, the EU's policy is aimed at (a) ensuring the absence of any controls on persons when crossing internal borders, (b) carrying out checks on persons and efficient monitoring of the crossing of external borders, and (c) the gradual introduction of an integrated management system for external borders (Article 77(1) TFEU). To achieve those objectives, the EU shall adopt measures concerning:[127]

(a) the common policy on visas and other short-stay residence permits;
(b) the checks to which persons crossing external borders are subject;

[124] Protocol No 21 on the position of the United Kingdom and Ireland in respect of the Area of Freedom, Security and Justice [2010] OJ C83/295.

[125] Protocol No 22 on the position of Denmark [2010] OJ C83/299.

[126] M Wilderspin and A-M Rouchaud, 'La compétence externe de la Communauté européenne en droit international privé' [2004] Revue Critique de Droit International Privé 1.

[127] Art 77(2) TFEU. Art 77(3) TFEU further enables the EU to adopt provisions on passports, identity cards, residence permits, or any other such document, for the purpose of enabling the free movement and residence rights of EU citizens under Art 20(2)(a) TFEU. Art 77(4) TFEU provides that the competence of the Member States concerning the geographical demarcation of their borders, in accordance with international law, is not affected.

(c) the conditions under which nationals of third countries shall have the freedom to travel within the Union for a short period;
(d) any measure necessary for the gradual establishment of an integrated management system for external borders;
(e) the absence of any controls on persons, whatever their nationality, when crossing internal borders.

For purposes of external competence, the powers in the field of visas are clearly the most significant ones. Indeed, the Community (now EU) has concluded a number of visa waiver and visa facilitation treaties.[128] It may further be noted that Protocol No 23 on external relations of the Member States with regard to the crossing of external borders provides that the measures adopted pursuant to Article 77(2)(b) 'shall be without prejudice to the competence of Member States to negotiate or conclude agreements with third countries as long as they respect Union law and other relevant international agreements'. It is not clear what this confirmation of shared competences adds to the general provisions on shared competence in Article 4(2)(j) TFEU.

Article 78 TFEU provides for a common policy on asylum, subsidiary protection, and temporary protection. That policy must be in accordance with the 1951 Geneva Convention and the 1967 Protocol relating to the status of refugees, and other relevant treaties. The EU may adopt measures concerning:[129]

(a) a uniform status of asylum for nationals of third countries, valid throughout the Union;
(b) a uniform status of subsidiary protection for nationals of third countries who, without obtaining European asylum, are in need of international protection;
(c) a common system of temporary protection for displaced persons in the event of a massive inflow;
(d) common procedures for the granting and withdrawing of uniform asylum or subsidiary protection status;
(e) criteria and mechanisms for determining which Member State is responsible for considering an application for asylum or subsidiary protection;
(f) standards concerning the conditions for the reception of applicants for asylum or subsidiary protection;
(g) partnership and co-operation with third countries for the purpose of managing inflows of people applying for asylum or subsidiary or temporary protection.

On the basis of this provision the EU is conducting a process of legislative harmonization through directives, which no doubt trigger *AETR*-type implied powers. It may further be noted that the Stockholm Programme—the most recent general

[128] See Peers (n 122 above) 288–93.
[129] Art 78(2) TFEU. Art 78(3) TFEU enables the EU to adopt provisional measures in the event that one or more Member States are confronted with an emergency situation characterized by a sudden inflow of nationals of third countries.

policy programme regarding AFSJ—envisages EU accession to the Geneva Convention.[130]

The policy area which lends itself most to the conclusion of international agreements is immigration. Indeed, from its early days the Community has been concluding agreements including provisions on the entry and residence of third-country nationals: many association agreements as well as certain co-operation agreements regulate certain forms of immigration from the other contracting parties.[131]

According to Article 79 TFEU the EU shall develop a common immigration policy aimed at ensuring, at all stages, the efficient management of migration flows, fair treatment of third-country nationals residing legally in Member States, and the prevention of, and enhanced measures to combat, illegal immigration and trafficking in human beings. To achieve this the EU may adopt measures concerning:[132]

(a) the conditions of entry and residence, and standards on the issue by Member States of long-term visas and residence permits, including those for the purpose of family reunification;
(b) the definition of the rights of third-country nationals residing legally in a Member State, including the conditions governing freedom of movement and of residence in other Member States;
(c) illegal immigration and unauthorized residence, including removal and repatriation of persons residing without authorization;
(d) combating trafficking in persons, in particular women and children.

In practice, much of the EU's immigration policy is aimed at combating illegal immigration. The TFEU enables the EU to conclude readmission agreements with third countries, under Article 79(3):

> The Union may conclude agreements with third countries for the readmission to their countries of origin or provenance of third-country nationals who do not or who no longer fulfil the conditions for entry, presence or residence in the territory of one of the Member States.

Eleven such readmission agreements have already been concluded.[133] Again, however, competence is shared with the Member States, which also continue to conclude such agreements.

Judicial co-operation in civil matters

The second type of policy for which the AFSJ title provides concerns judicial co-operation in civil matters. Article 81 TFEU provides that the EU shall develop judicial co-operation in civil matters having cross-border implications, based on the

130 See Peers (n 122 above) 306.
131 See the section on association agreements above, and case law in Chs 8 and 9.
132 Art 79(2) TFEU.
133 Peers (n 122 above) 586–9.

principle of mutual recognition of judgments and of decisions in extrajudicial cases. To achieve this, the EU may adopt measures, particularly when necessary for the proper functioning of the internal market, aimed at ensuring:[134]

(a) the mutual recognition and enforcement between Member States of judgments and of decisions in extrajudicial cases;
(b) the cross-border service of judicial and extrajudicial documents;
(c) the compatibility of the rules applicable in the Member States concerning conflict of laws and of jurisdiction;
(d) co-operation in the taking of evidence;
(e) effective access to justice;
(f) the elimination of obstacles to the proper functioning of civil proceedings, if necessary by promoting the compatibility of the rules on civil procedure applicable in the Member States;
(g) the development of alternative methods of dispute settlement;
(h) support for the training of the judiciary and judicial staff.

In practice, the most significant acts coming within the scope of this provision concern conflict of laws and of jurisdiction. Again EU competence is shared, and it is in any event limited to what is necessary for the proper functioning of the internal market. The implied powers doctrine applies, in particular the *AETR*-type exclusive competence. Whenever an EU act is likely to be affected by an international negotiation the EU has exclusive competence. In the area of conflict of laws such exclusive competence will often arise, in light of two centre-pieces of EU legislation: Regulation 44/2001 on jurisdiction and the recognition and enforcement of judgments in civil and commercial matters, which is the successor to the first Brussels Convention;[135] and Regulation 1347/2000 on jurisdiction and the recognition and enforcement of judgments in matrimonial matters and in matters of parental responsibility for children of both spouses, the successor to the second Brussels Convention.[136] As many conflict of laws conventions touch upon matters of jurisdiction and recognition of judgments, the *AETR* effect will often be triggered.

One example of this *AETR* effect is the Lugano Convention, which came within the EU's exclusive competence, as the Court decided in *Opinion 1/03*.[137] That Opinion was analysed in Chapter 3, and the reader may be referred to that analysis. It is clear that the Lugano Convention was to some extent a special case, in that the fact that it aimed to extend the whole system of Regulation 44/2001 to the EFTA countries brought the whole of the convention within exclusive competence. That will rarely be the case for other conflict of law conventions or treaties, where EU exclusive competence is limited to those provisions (mostly on jurisdiction and enforcement) which affect EU legislation. The EU has in fact recognized that it may not always be possible or appropriate for it to become a party

[134] Art 81(2) TFEU. [135] [2001] OJ L12/1. [136] [2000] OJ L160/19.
[137] *Opinion 1/03 re Lugano Convention* [2006] ECR I-1145.

to such conventions or treaties, and that it should in certain cases allow the Member States to act on its behalf. Two Council regulations authorize, on the one hand, the power to negotiate treaties relating to conflict of law matters,[138] and, on the other, maintenance and family law jurisdiction matters.[139] These regulations offer a concrete example of the scope which Article 2(1) TFEU provides for empowering the Member States to act in areas of exclusive competence.

Complex questions are likely to arise as regards the relationship between the relevant EU law provisions and those of international conventions, and there are likely to be many mixed agreements. In the literature it has been argued that in this field the various Member States often have diverging approaches, which may create problems for the definition of a common position, and which may give rise to so-called partial mixity (where not all the Member States are parties to a mixed agreement).[140]

Judicial co-operation in criminal matters

Judicial co-operation in criminal matters shall, according to Article 82(1) TFEU, be based on the principle of mutual recognition of judgments and judicial decisions and shall include the approximation of the laws and regulations of the Member States, in a number of areas. Those areas include matters of criminal procedure, concerning (a) mutual admissibility of evidence between Member States; (b) the rights of individuals in criminal procedure; (c) the rights of victims of crime; and (d) any other specific aspects of criminal procedure which the Council has identified. For such matters, directives may be adopted, establishing minimum rules.[141] There is also scope for substantive criminal law approximation, pursuant to Article 83 TFEU. Directives may establish minimum rules concerning the definition of criminal offences and sanctions in the areas of particularly serious crime with a cross-border dimension. Those areas include: terrorism, trafficking in human beings and sexual exploitation of women and children, illicit drug trafficking, illicit arms trafficking, money laundering, corruption, counterfeiting of means of payment, computer crime, and organized crime (Article 83(1) TFEU). Moreover, directives establishing minimum rules may also be adopted if the approximation of criminal laws and regulations of the Member States proves essential to ensure the effective implementation of an EU policy in an area which has been subject to harmonization measures (Article 83(2) TFEU).

[138] Regulation 662/2009 establishing a procedure for the negotiation and conclusion of agreements between Member States and third countries on particular matters concerning the law applicable to contractual and non-contractual obligations [2009] OJ L200/25.

[139] Regulation 664/2009 establishing a procedure for the negotiation and conclusion of agreements between Member States and third countries concerning jurisdiction, recognition and enforcement of judgments and decisions in matrimonial matters, matters of parental responsibility and matters relating to maintenance obligations, and the law applicable to matters relating to maintenance obligations [2009] OJ L200/46.

[140] Wilderspin and Rouchaud (n 126 above).

[141] Art 82(2) TFEU.

In all those areas there are implied powers to conclude international agreements, in so far as the provisions of such agreements come within the EU's substantive powers.[142] Prior to the entry into force of the Treaty of Lisbon, the EU negotiated and signed a number of agreements with third countries, the most prominent being the United States, on extradition and mutual legal assistance.[143] This was done under TEU Third Pillar provisions. One assumes that there continues to be competence, under the TFEU, to conclude such agreements, even if they cannot easily be tied to the provisions of Articles 82 and 83 TFEU.

Police co-operation

Lastly, the TFEU also provides for police co-operation (Articles 87 to 89 TFEU). Such co-operation mainly takes place through the operation of Europol. That organization has concluded treaties with third States or bodies, a practice which has been criticized as lacking legitimacy and accountability.[144] The basic Treaties do not provide for such treaty-making capacity, whose legal basis is the Council Decision establishing Europol.[145] It is not readily apparent from the Treaties that the EU has the competence to set up bodies or agencies with treaty-making capacity. The constitutionality of these arrangements is therefore doubtful.

Measures concerning police co-operation may also involve the collection, storage, processing, analysis, and exchange of relevant information (Article 87(2)(a) TFEU). Before the entry into force of the Treaty of Lisbon, the EU, for example, negotiated agreements with the United States and Australia on passenger name records,[146] and with the United States as regards access to financial information for anti-terrorist purposes. The original version of the latter agreement did not receive the consent of the European Parliament (post-Lisbon), and had to be renegotiated.[147] Again one assumes that the conclusion of such agreements comes within the EU's implied powers pursuant to the TFEU provisions on police co-operation.

Conclusions

The analysis in this chapter is of a diverse character, as each EU policy has its own specific characteristics. It none the less demonstrates the wide scope for external

[142] Cf V Mitsilegas, 'The External Dimension of EU Action in Criminal Matters' (2007) 12 EFA Rev 457.

[143] Agreement on extradition between the European Union and the United States [2003] OJ L181/27 and Agreement on mutual legal assistance between the European Union and the United States [2003] OJ L181/34.

[144] Peers (n 122 above) 943, with further references.

[145] [2009] OJ L121/37; see Art 23(2).

[146] Respectively [2008] OJ L213/47 and [2007] OJ L204/18. The agreement with the US was the successor to the PNR Agreement struck down in *European Parliament v. Council and Commission (PNR)* (n 100 above).

[147] For the first version, see [2010] OJ L8/11. For the renegotiated version, see [2010] OJ L195/5.

action, due to the growing importance of international law-making, which affects all significant policy areas. Also, a couple of general observations are worth making.

The analysis confirms the broad parallelism between internal and external powers. The case law examined in this chapter and in Chapter 3 generally recognizes that the EU may conclude international agreements in any area of policy-making coming within its competence. Perhaps the strongest confirmation of parallelism comes from *Opinion 2/00*, where the Court decided that the Cartagena Protocol had to be concluded on the basis of (current) Article 192(1) TFEU, notwithstanding the express reference in Article 191(4) TFEU to the conclusion of agreements. The Court apparently considered that one should first look at the Treaty provision conferring legislative competence in a particular area for the purpose of finding the correct legal basis for international action.

If one looks at the current TFEU, there is a broad basis for engaging in relations with third countries, covering many different areas, and for participating in multilateral negotiations and agreements. The EU is far beyond the period of preponderant external competence in trade matters. Development co-operation policies have gained equal weight; there is now a constitutional basis for co-operation, in all the spheres of EU competence, with any third country; agreements can be concluded on migration and movement of persons just as much as on imports and exports; conflict of laws conventions will increasingly require EU participation; there is broad competence in matters of environmental policy, social policy, and monetary policy.

That may raise the question of the appropriate legal basis in the Treaty for certain agreements. The principle that one should identify the predominant purpose or component is no doubt useful, in particular for delineating exclusive competences, such as in matters of commercial policy, and non-exclusive competences. The hope may none the less be expressed that it will be possible to move away from legal conflicts over the scope and nature of external competence, for the benefit of effective international action by the EU and its Member States. The Treaty of Lisbon may contribute to that, through its unified procedure for the conclusion of agreements (Article 218 TFEU; see Chapter 6) and its confirmation of parallel external powers.

5

Competence to conduct a Common Foreign and Security Policy

Introduction

The preceding chapters offer an account of the EU's competences and objectives as regards external action, under the TFEU. The emphasis there was on the first concept, competences, rather than the second, objectives. The original EEC Treaty was sparsely worded as regards the objectives of the Community's external policies, and external action was quickly turned into a legal battleground over the location of the border between the Community's and the Member States' competences, in particular as regards treaty-making. With the amendments made by the Maastricht Treaty came more EC Treaty language on the objectives of external action, in particular concerning development co-operation, yet lawyers continued to focus on issues of the nature and delimitation of competences.

The Maastricht Treaty created the European Union, founded, according to Article 1, on the European Communities, but supplementing them by the policies and forms of co-operation established by that Treaty: a Common Foreign and Security Policy (CFSP) and Justice and Home Affairs. The CFSP in particular was of course a purely external policy, supplementing, to borrow from the TEU again, the external Community policies. Yet its denomination did not suggest a mere supplementary role. Rather, it suggested broad coverage, as nearly any form of external action could be brought within the terms 'foreign and security policy'. This raised difficult questions of the interrelationship between EC external policies and the CFSP. Those questions arose against the broader canvas of constitutional confusion over the nature of the EU, and its three pillars.[1] The Treaty of Lisbon has modified this pillar structure, yet it may be helpful to make some general observations about the past debates. The EC pillar was said to be supranational, with much majority voting, and a strong role for supranational institutions such as the Commission, the European Parliament, and the

[1] JHH Weiler, 'Neither Unity Nor Three Pillars—The Trinity Structure of the Treaty on European Union' in J Monar, W Ungerer, and W Wessels (eds), *The Maastricht Treaty on European Union* (European Interuniversity Press, 1993) 49; DM Curtin and I Dekker, 'The EU as a "Layered" International Organization: Institutional Unity in Disguise' in P Craig and G de Búrca (eds), *The Evolution of EU Law* (OUP, 1999) 83; B de Witte, 'The Pillar Structure and the Nature of the European Union: Greek Temple or French Gothic Cathedral?' in T Heukels, N Blokker, and M Brus (eds), *The European Union after Amsterdam* (Kluwer Law International, 1998) 51.

Court of Justice. Constitutionalism was the hallmark of its legal order, with direct effect and supremacy as the operating systems of such constitutionalism.[2] The EC was governed by Community law, a 'new legal order'.[3] The second and third pillars, by contrast, were said to be intergovernmental in character, with unanimity as a rule and a much smaller role for the supranational institutions. Particularly as regards the CFSP, the Commission and the Parliament stood more or less at the sidelines, and the Court of Justice appeared to have no role whatsoever. *Community* law did not apply, and many commentators regarded the CFSP as a form of co-operation coming within the sphere of international law instead.[4] The latter view was not uncontested, however. Increasingly the EU was looked at as a single organization, and EU law as a distinct, unified legal discipline, even if not all Community law principles and concepts might as such apply to the second and third pillars.[5]

The Lisbon Treaty has confirmed this trend towards greater unity. The EC has been abolished, and there is now a single EU. It is still governed by two treaties, the TEU and the TFEU, but that is an accident of the EU's constitutional history, rather than a matter of conscious design. The one EU has legal personality (Article 47 TEU), putting to an end debates about whether the EU, as distinct from the EC, had such personality. In the sphere of external action, this quest for unity is particularly prevalent, as is shown by the fact that there is an overall set of objectives for such external action (Articles 3(5) and 21(2) TEU), and great emphasis on ensuring consistency between the different areas (e.g. Article 21(3) TEU). Whereas previous Treaty versions attempted to arrive at such consistency through mere constitutional command (see old Article 3 TEU), the Treaty of Lisbon built an institutional bridge across the various areas of external action: the High Representative of the Union for Foreign Affairs and Security Policy (hereafter High Representative), assisted by the European External Action Service (EEAS).

However, the fact that the EU is more unified, in particular as regards external action, does not mean that its competence to conduct a CFSP can simply be analysed along the same lines as its other external competences (see Chapter 4). The Treaty of Lisbon has largely conserved the CFSP's intergovernmental traits. Decision-making continues to be in the hands of the Council, deciding by unanimity, and the Commission, the European Parliament, and the Court of Justice still have very limited roles to play. In a sense, the CFSP continues to be a pillar of its own, even if the pillar image

[2] Cf JHH Weiler, *The Constitution of Europe* (CUP, 1999) 221.

[3] Case 26/62 *Van Gend en Loos v. Nederlandse Administratie der Belastingen* [1963] ECR 1.

[4] E Denza, *The Intergovernmental Pillars of the European Union* (OUP, 2002) 19; MR Eaton, 'Common Foreign and Security Policy' in D O'Keeffe and P Twomey, *Legal Issues of the Maastricht Treaty* (Chancery Law, 1994) 222; I McLeod, ID Hendry, and S Hyett, *The External Relations of the European Communities* (OUP, 1996) 412; M Koskenniemi, 'International Law Aspects of the Common Foreign and Security Policy' in M Koskenniemi (ed), *International Law Aspects of the European Union* (Kluwer Law International, 1998) 30.

[5] A von Bogdandy, 'The Legal Case for Unity: the European Union as a Single Organization with a Single Legal System' (1999) 36 CML Rev 887; I Pernice, 'Multilevel Constitutionalism and the Treaty of Amsterdam: European Constitution-Making Revisited?' (1999) 36 CML Rev 703; CWA Timmermans, 'The Constitutionalization of the European Union' (2002) 21 YEL 1.

has now become very awkward indeed, as only two pillars remain standing, which conjures up a picture of decay and ruin rather than design and construction. Be that as it may, the conservation of this intergovernmental pillar produces some important questions of EU competence to conduct a CFSP. Those questions first pertain to the nature of that competence. It is clear from Article 2(4) TFEU that the EU's CFSP competence is neither exclusive nor shared, but rather in an undefined category of its own.[6] The effects on national competence are therefore difficult to determine. But secondly, and more importantly, there are complex questions of scope, in particular in relation to other areas of external action. The decision that a particular measure, or the provisions of an international agreement, come within the scope of the CFSP means that the intergovernmental mechanisms of decision-making apply. The decision that such a measure or agreement pertains to other areas of external action, for example development co-operation, triggers supranational decision-making, involving the Commission and the Parliament, next to the Council. For internal action, it also determines the use of legal instruments such as directives and regulations, which are not available to the CFSP.

The focus of this chapter is therefore mostly on the scope of the CFSP, and its delimitation from other EU external policies. Although the Treaty of Lisbon introduces some important modifications in that respect, much of the analysis concerns the law as it has evolved under the previous versions of the TEU and of the EC Treaty. This evolutionary approach is arguably to be preferred, since the Lisbon Treaty innovations and modifications can only be understood and interpreted from an evolutionary perspective.

The structure of the analysis is as follows. The following section explores the Treaty language concerning the objectives of the CFSP, and the competences conferred upon the EU institutions to pursue those objectives, in contrast with other external competences. The chapter then further explores the delimitation of competences, on the basis of an analysis of the case law of the Court of Justice on (old) Article 47 TEU. That is followed by an attempt to interpret the new delimitation provision, (current) Article 40 TEU. From the issue of delimitation, the chapter moves to the concept of consistency between the various areas of external action.

CFSP objectives and competences

Scope

The TEU and TFEU, as amended by the Treaty of Lisbon, are extremely short as regards the scope and nature of the EU's competence to conduct a CFSP. The scope

[6] J-C Piris, *The Lisbon Treaty—A Legal and Political Analysis* (CUP, 2010) 77; S Griller, 'External Relations' in B de Witte (ed), *Ten Reflections on the Constitutional Treaty for Europe* (RSCAS, 2003) 141–2; G De Baere, *Constitutional Principles of EU External Relations* (OUP, 2008) 109–12.

of the EU's competence in CFSP matters is not particularly well-defined. Article 24(1) TEU provides:

> The Union's competence in matters of common foreign and security policy shall cover all areas of foreign policy and all questions relating to the Union's security, including the progressive framing of a common defence policy that might lead to a common defence.

As can be seen, there are two elements to this definition. On the one hand, the CFSP covers all areas of foreign policy; on the other, it extends to all questions relating to the EU's security. The former element is not further defined in the TFEU. The latter, by contrast, forms the object of an entire section, with the heading 'Provisions on the Common Security and Defence Policy' (hereafter, CSDP). According to Article 42(1) TEU, the CSDP shall provide the EU with an operational capacity drawing on civilian and military assets, which may be used on missions outside the EU for peace-keeping, conflict prevention and strengthening international security in accordance with the principles of the UN Charter. This is elaborated in Article 43(1) TEU, which provides that the tasks referred to in Article 42(1):

> Shall include joint disarmament operations, humanitarian and rescue tasks, military advice and assistance tasks, conflict prevention and peace-keeping tasks, tasks of combat forces in crisis management, including peace-making and post-conflict stabilization. All these tasks may contribute to the fight against terrorism, including by supporting third countries in combating terrorism in their territories.

Article 42(2) TEU further provides that the CSDP shall include the progressive framing of a common EU defence policy, which will lead to a common defence, when the European Council, acting unanimously, so decides.[7]

There is thus a great contrast between the relatively precise and detailed description of the scope and content of the security and defence element of the CFSP, and the totally undefined foreign policy element. The previous version of the TEU was different in this respect, in the sense that it set out a specific set of CFSP objectives,[8] which could be called in aid of determining the scope of 'all areas of foreign policy'. The Treaty of Lisbon has replaced these specific CFSP objectives with a set of overall objectives for EU external action. Article 21(2) TFEU provides:

[7] On the CDSP, see Piris (n 6 above) 265–79.

[8] See old Art 11(1) TEU:

The Union shall define and implement a common foreign and security policy covering all areas of foreign and security policy, the objectives of which shall be:

— to safeguard the common values, fundamental interests, independence and integrity of the Union in conformity with the principles of the United Nations Charter;
— to strengthen the security of the Union in all ways;
— to preserve peace and strengthen international security, in accordance with the principles of the United Nations Charter, as well as the principles of the Helsinki Final Act and the objectives of the Paris Charter, including those on external borders;
— to promote international co-operation;
— to develop and consolidate democracy and the rule of law, and respect for human rights and fundamental freedoms.

The Union shall define and pursue common policies and actions, and shall work for a high degree of cooperation in all fields of international relations, in order to:

(a) safeguard its values, fundamental interests, security, independence and integrity;
(b) consolidate and support democracy, the rule of law, human rights and the principles of international law;
(c) preserve peace, prevent conflicts and strengthen international security, in accordance with the purposes and principles of the United Nations Charter, with the principles of the Helsinki Final Act and with the aims of the Charter of Paris, including those relating to external borders;
(d) foster the sustainable economic, social and environmental development of developing countries, with the primary aim of eradicating poverty;
(e) encourage the integration of all countries into the world economy, including through the progressive abolition of restrictions on international trade;
(f) help develop international measures to preserve and improve the quality of the environment and the sustainable management of global natural resources, in order to ensure sustainable development;
(g) assist populations, countries and regions confronting natural or man-made disasters; and
(h) promote an international system based on stronger multilateral cooperation and good global governance.

In the literature it is often indicated that this means that the scope of the CFSP can no longer be determined by reference to the objectives pursued.[9] Such statements need to be qualified, however. Objectives (d) to (g) clearly refer to other areas of external action, i.e. development co-operation, trade, environmental protection, and humanitarian aid. Objective (c), on the other hand, concerning the preservation of peace, the prevention of conflicts, and the strengthening of international security, is clearly at the heart of the CFSP. Objectives (a), (b), and (h), lastly, are more of a cross-sectoral nature.

Those are the objectives and subject matter of the CFSP. In terms of powers to achieve those objectives, the TEU enumerates and defines a number of instruments. The CFSP mainly operates by way of decisions, which may concern either 'action to be undertaken by the Union' (previously called Joint Actions), or 'positions to be taken by the Union' (previously called Common Positions) (Article 25 TEU). As already mentioned, the adoption of legislative acts is excluded, but the EU may conclude international agreements concerning CFSP matters (Article 37 TEU). This enumeration of instruments does not assist much with the determination of the scope of the CFSP. Indeed it is useful to contrast the CFSP instruments with what would normally be regarded as instruments of a full-blown foreign policy. Keukeleire distinguishes diplomatic, military, and economic and financial

[9] C Herrmann, 'Much Ado about Pluto? The "Unity of the Legal Order of the European Union" Revisited' in M Cremona and B De Witte (eds), *EU Foreign Relations Law—Constitutional Fundamentals* (Hart Publishing, 2008) 47.

instruments.[10] Decisions on positions to be taken by the EU, and to some extent actions to be undertaken, come within the category of diplomatic instruments. The EU also has some military instruments. The use of economic and financial instruments for foreign policy purposes, however, appears to be largely a matter for external action under the TFEU, as that Treaty provides for a common commercial policy, a development co-operation policy, and other co-operation policies, and a common monetary policy for the Eurozone.[11]

It is likewise interesting to contrast the scope of the CFSP, as outlined in the TEU provisions, with the basic constitutional powers which would be required for a European foreign policy 'worthy of its name', in the approach of an eminent international relations scholar.[12] Those powers would need to extend to war and peace; raising armed forces; treaty-making; regulation of commerce (sanctions); external borders (immigration); cession or acquisition of territory. Again it is clear that the CFSP does not come anywhere near covering all that, but that a number of those powers are present within the TFEU. In that sense the notion 'all areas of foreign policy' is deceptive. Clearly, there are important areas of what in the practice of a state would be called foreign policy, which are not within the scope of the CFSP, but within that of external action under the TFEU. The delimitation between the CFSP competences and other EU external action competences is therefore crucial.

The objectives of the CFSP, as previously outlined in (old) Article 11(1) TEU,[13] and now part of the EU's overall external action objectives, also merit brief further comment.[14] Keukeleire pointed out that those objectives are in the nature of underlying policy principles rather than precise operational objectives. This led him to contrast the 'common' foreign and security policy with common policies under the (then) EC Treaty, which were much more precisely defined. The result was that the CFSP threatened to be squeezed between Community external competences and national competences.[15] Koskenniemi has been critical of the CFSP objectives, arguing that they were meaningless abstract principles, which laid down no substantive priorities for Union foreign policy. He has pointed out that, as always with open-ended standards, power was transferred from the legislators to the executive.[16] It is indeed possible to read the CFSP provisions as the continuation of executive dominance over foreign affairs, as it exists in at least a number of Member States. Such a reading may be

[10] S Keukeleire, *Het buitenlands beleid van de Europese Unie* (Kluwer, 1998) 34–8.

[11] For a 'full' concept of EU foreign policy, see S Keukeleire and J MacNaughtan, *The Foreign Policy of the European Union* (Palgrave Macmillan, 2008) ch 1.

[12] C Hill, 'The Capability-Expectations Gap, or Conceptualizing Europe's International Role' (1993) 31 JCMS 316.

[13] n 8 above.

[14] For a detailed analysis see R Wessel, *The European Union's Foreign and Security Policy—A Legal Institutional Perspective* (Kluwer Law International, 1999) 56–70.

[15] Keukeleire (n 10 above) 154.

[16] Koskenniemi (n 4 above) 28.

more interesting than the traditional approach of contrasting intergovernmentalism and supranationalism, and of explaining the intergovernmental character of the CFSP by national sovereignty concerns.

The objectives of EU external action do have a positive dimension as well. They project and constitutionalize, at least to some degree, certain core values of the EU. As such they may develop into a strong guiding force for EU external action.

Nature of the competences

Article 2(4) TFEU provides that the Union shall have competence, in accordance with the provisions of the TEU, to define and implement a common foreign and security policy, including the progressive framing of a defence policy. The nature of that competence is not clarified, in contrast with the preceding paragraphs of Article 2, which define exclusive and shared competences. It has always been clear of course that the CFSP is not an exclusive competence, but the concept of shared or concurrent competence has been applied to it.[17] The Treaty drafters nevertheless chose not to define CFSP competence as shared with the Member States. One reason for this may be that shared competences are described as having a pre-emptive effect. Article 2(2) TFEU provides, *inter alia*, that, in areas of shared competence, the Member States shall exercise their competence to the extent that the Union has not exercised its competence. The same provision also defines such competence as authorizing both the EU and the Member States to legislate and adopt legally binding acts. Article 24(1) TEU, however, excludes the adoption of legislative acts within the scope of the CFSP. In that sense, too, the CFSP is not a shared competence. It is not an area of general law-making, or normative action, where EU acts have a pre-emptive effect on national competence.

The above does not of course mean that Member States are not legally bound by decisions adopted under the CFSP. The CFSP does not present itself, through the Treaty language, as an *à la carte* form of co-operation, merely ad hoc and optional. Article 24(1) TFEU provides that the Union's competence *shall* cover *all* areas of foreign policy and *all* questions relating to the Union's security. Article 24(3) TEU instructs the Member States to support the policy *actively* and *unreservedly* in a spirit of loyalty and mutual solidarity, and to comply with the Union's action in this area. Decisions on operational action shall commit the Member States in the positions they adopt and in the conduct of their activity (Article 28(2) TEU). Member States shall also ensure that their national policies conform to the Union's positions (Article 29 TEU). They shall consult one another within the European Council and the Council on any matter of foreign and security policy of general interest in order to determine a common approach (Article 32 TEU). In international organizations and at international conferences the Member States shall co-ordinate

[17] E.g. R Gosalbo Bono, 'Some Reflections on the CFSP Legal Order' (2006) 43 CML Rev 364.

their action, and uphold the Union's positions (Article 34(1) TEU). Member States which are members of the UN Security Council will concert and keep the other Member States and the High Representative fully informed, and will, in the execution of their functions, defend the positions and interests of the Union, without prejudice to their responsibilities under the provisions of the UN Charter (Article 34(2) TEU).

Those provisions impose strong discipline as regards respect for, implementation of, and participation in, the CFSP by the Member States. As such the Treaty language ought to be sufficient for the construction of a meaningful CFSP. The actual policy, however, is often regarded as insufficient, unsatisfactory, and ineffective. Part of the reason may lie in the absence of enforcement mechanisms for the various duties and obligations which the TEU imposes. In contrast to the position under the TFEU, no EU institution or Member State can be brought before the Court of Justice for non-compliance. The supervision is merely political.

Delimitation of TEU and TFEU competences

Article 47 TEU, pre-Lisbon

The above discussion shows that the scope and nature of the EU's powers under the CFSP do not lend themselves to strict legal analysis, because of the open texture of the Treaty provisions and the lack of authoritative interpretation through case law. However, when it comes to the interaction between the CFSP and the EU's other external policies and powers one can hardly be satisfied with some general reflections. It matters a lot whether a decision is taken under the TEU or the TFEU: decision-making procedures are different, parliamentary and judicial scrutiny is different, and so are the legal effects of the decisions.

The paradox of the relationship between the CFSP and other EU external action—indeed, one could say the original sin of overall EU external action—is that the CFSP *supplements* the TFEU with a less integrated policy,[18] and yet is intended to cover *all areas* of foreign and security policy. But commercial policy, development co-operation policy, etc. are of course also forms of foreign policy. As Koskenniemi points out, everyone agrees that it is difficult to separate foreign policy from other aspects of policy and that the most credible conception of security is the comprehensive one.[19] This original sin of EU external action produces many effects. Within the supranational context of other EU policies it creates concerns about contamination by the CFSP. Those concerns have an obvious institutional dimension: as the Council is the central CFSP institution, with only limited roles for the

[18] Although it must be noted that the Treaty of Lisbon has deleted the notion, in (old) Art 1 TEU, of the CFSP supplementing other policies.

[19] Koskenniemi (n 4 above) 36.

Commission and the Parliament, the latter institutions do not like to see certain types of decisions effectively transferred to the second pillar.[20] Moreover, there has been concern that CFSP decisions, taken unanimously under intergovernmental procedures, could contain instructions for the other EU policies, and could be seen as hierarchically superior.[21] Those concerns were present at the inception of the pillar structure. Accordingly, the TEU contained a number of provisions which were aimed at avoiding undue interference with (then) EC policies. Article 2 TEU provided that one of the Union's objectives was 'to maintain in full the acquis communautaire and build on it with a view to considering to what extent the policies and forms of co-operation introduced by this Treaty may need to be revised with the aim of ensuring the effectiveness of the mechanisms and the institutions of the Community'. It thus appeared to foreshadow a gradual integration of the pillars. The central provision on the matter was (old) Article 47 TEU:

> Subject to the provisions amending the Treaty establishing the European Economic Community with a view to establishing the European Community ...and to these final provisions, nothing in this Treaty shall affect the Treaties establishing the European Communities or the subsequent Treaties and Acts modifying or supplementing them.

This provision was clearly intended to protect the acquis communautaire, and to prevent intergovernmental contamination of supranational decision-making. To vary the pillar image, Article 47 TEU aimed to compartmentalize the Community, on the one hand, and the CFSP (as well as Police and Judicial Co-operation in Criminal Matters (PJCCM)), on the other.

That was not, however, the entire Treaty picture, because the drafters also realized that, at least at a political level, the CFSP needed to be co-ordinated with external Community policies. Article 3, second paragraph, TEU provided that the Union had to ensure the consistency of its external activities as a whole in the context of its external relations, security, economic, and development policies.

In one particular area, that of economic and financial sanctions, the connection between CFSP and EC decisions was clarified in the EC Treaty itself. Article 301 EC provided:[22]

> Where it is provided, in a common position or in a joint action adopted according to the provisions of the Treaty on European Union relating to the common foreign and security policy, for an action by the Community to interrupt or reduce, in part or completely, economic relations with one or more third countries, the Council shall take the necessary urgent measures. The Council shall act by a qualified majority on a proposal from the Commission.

[20] See e.g. Commission, *Report on the Operation of the Treaty on European Union* (EC Commission, May 1995), as reported by G Edwards, 'Common Foreign and Security Policy' (1994) 14 YEL 545.

[21] CWA Timmermans, 'The Uneasy Relationship between the Communities and the Second Union Pillar: Back to the "Plan Fouchet"?' (1996/1) LIEI 61.

[22] See also Art 60 EC.

That provision illustrated the constitutional and institutional complexity of the interaction between the pillars. Common positions or joint actions on economic sanctions were adopted by the Council, acting unanimously, and did not require a Commission proposal or initiative. Nevertheless, the Commission then needed to make a proposal for an EC regulation, which the Council could adopt by qualified majority. The Council could not act without such a proposal. As long as the Council and the Commission co-operated and agreed, there were no problems, but there was nothing in the Treaties which regulated disagreement, other than the general provision on the obligation of inter-institutional co-operation in Article 3 TEU.[23]

The Court of Justice did not have jurisdiction over the Second Pillar, with the exception, however, of (old) Article 47 TEU. In the light of the concerns over the relationship between the pillars, it comes as no surprise that the Court was asked to decide when measures adopted under the (then) Second and Third Pillars 'affected', in the words of Article 47, the EC Treaty.[24] After a series of judgments which concerned the First and the Third Pillar,[25] the Court was finally asked to rule in a case involving the delimitation of CFSP and EC competences. *Small Arms and Light Weapons* (hereafter, *SALW*) concerned a Council decision implementing a joint action with a view to an EU contribution to ECOWAS in the framework of that organization's Moratorium on Small Arms and Light Weapons.[26] Although (old) Article 47 TEU has been substantially amended by the Treaty of Lisbon, the judgment continues to be important for delimiting CFSP competences from those in other areas of external action.

The facts can be summarized as follows. In 2002 the Council adopted a CFSP joint action on the EU's contribution to combating the destabilizing accumulation and spread of small arms and light weapons.[27] It provided, *inter alia*, for financial and technical assistance to programmes and projects which made a direct contribution to its objectives. Problems with the accumulation and spread of small arms and light weapons are of course particularly prevalent in certain African countries.

[23] On economic sanctions see further Ch 12.

[24] See also A Dashwood, 'Article 47 TEU and the relationship between first and second pillar competences' in A Dashwood and M Maresceau, *Law and Practice of EU External Relations* (CUP, 2008) 70; D Curtin, *Executive Power of the European Union—Law, Practices, and the Living Constitution* (OUP, 2009) 179–94.

[25] Case C–170/96 *Commission v. Council (Airport Transit Visas)* [1998] ECR I–2763; Case C–176/03 *Commission v. Council (Environmental Penalties)* [2005] ECR I–7879; and Case C–440/05 *Commission v. Council (Shipsource Pollution)* [2007] ECR I–9097.

[26] Case C–91/05 *Commission v. Council (SALW)* [2008] ECR I–3651. The decision is published in [2004] OJ L359/65. ECOWAS stands for Economic Community of West African States. For comment see also B Van Vooren, 'EU-EC External Competences after the Small Arms Judgment' (2009) 14 EFA Rev 7 and 'The Small Arms Judgment in an Age of Constitutional Turmoil' (2009) 14 EFA Rev 231; A Dashwood, 'The Law and Practice of CFSP Joint Actions', in M Cremona and B De Witte (n 9 above) 65–77; G De Baere, *Constitutional Principles of EU External Relations* (OUP, 2008) 283–94; C Hillion and R Wessel, 'Competence Distribution in EU External Relations after *Ecowas*: Clarification or Continued Fuzziness?' (2009) 46 CML Rev 551.

[27] Joint Action 2002/589/CFSP [2002] OJ L191/1.

It is therefore not surprising that the Cotonou Agreement, between the EC and its Member States and ACP countries, also referred to such problems. Article 11 of the Agreement, concerning 'Peace-building policies, conflict prevention and resolution', provided for activities addressing, *inter alia*, 'an excessive and uncontrolled spread, illegal trafficking and accumulation of small arms and light weapons' (see paragraph 3). On that basis, in 2004 the Commission had started to prepare a financing proposal in support of the efforts of ECOWAS to implement a UN moratorium on the import, export, and production of small arms. At the end of 2004, the Council adopted the contested decision, based on the joint action and on (then) Article 23(2) TEU.[28] The decision provided for a financial contribution and technical assistance to set up the Light Weapons Unit within the ECOWAS Technical Secretariat and to convert the UN moratorium into a convention on small arms and light weapons between the ECOWAS member States. The Commission, however, did not agree with the adoption of the Decision within the CFSP framework. It made a declaration, expressing its view that the joint action should not have been adopted and the project ought to have been financed from the Ninth European Development Fund under the Cotonou Agreement. It further claimed that the joint action fell within the shared competences on which Community development policy and the Cotonou Agreement were based, and that such shared competences were just as much protected by (old) Article 47 TEU as the areas of exclusive competence. The Commission subsequently brought an action for the annulment of the Decision, in which it also claimed that the Joined Action was inapplicable, because of its illegality, pursuant to (current) Article 277 TFEU.

Advocate General Mengozzi started his analysis concerning the application of (old) Article 47 TEU by setting out the arguments of the Commission and the Parliament, the Council, and the UK government. The Commission and the Parliament contended that Article 47 aimed to protect the Community's competences as against the activity of the EU based on the TEU by establishing a 'fixed' boundary between the respective competences. In order to delimit the competences of the EC and of the EU, recourse could not be had to the principle of pre-emption. Even if, in an area of shared competence, the Member States retained the competence to act by themselves, whether individually or collectively, to the extent that the Community had not yet exercised its competence, the same could not be said for the EU which, under (old) Article 47 TEU, had to respect the competences of the Community, whether exclusive or not, even if they had not been exercised. The Council, by contrast, submitted that (old) Article 47 aimed to maintain the balance of powers established by the Treaties and could not be interpreted as aiming to protect the competences of the Community to the detriment of those conferred upon the EU. (Old) Article 47 did not prevent the adoption of measures in the framework of the CFSP which used the same instruments as those used by the

[28] Council Decision 2004/833 [2004] OJ L359/65.

Community in the framework of development co-operation, where those measures did not aim to achieve the objectives of development co-operation but those arising from the CFSP. The United Kingdom, lastly, contended that two conditions had to be fulfilled for (old) Article 47 to be violated. First, the Community had to be competent to adopt a measure having the same purpose and the same content as the challenged measure. Secondly, the measure based on the TEU had to encroach on a competence conferred upon the Community by preventing or limiting the exercise of that competence. Such a pre-emptive effect was impossible in the area of development co-operation, where the Community had only concurrent competences.[29]

Analysing those submissions, Mengozzi AG effectively sided with the Commission and the Parliament. He pointed out that the function of (old) Article 47 TEU was to protect the competences which the EC Treaty conferred on the Community. This was not limited to exclusive EC competences, but extended to all the competences given to the Community, which deserved to be protected against any encroachment on the part of the EU. The nature of the EC competence and the distribution of competences between the EC and the Member States was immaterial for the purpose of applying (old) Article 47 TEU. The Advocate General was further of the opinion that the distribution of spheres of competence between the Community and the Member States had to be distinguished from the distribution of competence between the Community and the Second and Third Pillars. Whereas the Member States were in principle free to act in an area such as development co-operation, action of the EU within the framework of the Second and Third Pillars was in principle excluded because adequate competences were provided for by the EC Treaty, irrespective of the nature of those competences (exclusive, shared, or concurrent). Echoing a concept referred to in the first edition of this book,[30] the Advocate General stated that (old) Article 47 TEU aimed to keep watertight, so to speak, the primacy of Community action under the EC Treaty over actions undertaken under the TEU, so that if an action *could* be undertaken on the basis of the EC Treaty, it *must* be undertaken by virtue of that Treaty. It was a matter of protecting the Community's areas of activity, so that the EU had to refrain from interfering in those areas by using forms of co-operation less integrated than those provided for by the EC Treaty. In the final analysis, the CFSP covered 'all areas of foreign and security policy', with the exception of the forms of foreign policy which fell within the competence of the Community, such as the common commercial policy or the development co-operation policy, irrespective of the distribution of competences between the Member States and the Community. This approach appeared to be the only one which ensured the overall coherence of the provisions of the TEU.[31]

[29] *SALW* (n 26 above) Opinion of Mengozzi AG, paras 75–83.

[30] P Eeckhout, *External Relations of the European Union—Legal and Constitutional Foundations* (OUP, 2004) 126.

[31] *SALW* (n 26 above) Opinion of Mengozzi AG, paras 92–122.

As regards the substance of the action, the Advocate General did not, however, accept the Commission's submissions. He analysed the scope of the EC's competences in matters of development co-operation. He then considered that, where a measure was likely to fall within the scope of the aims of the CFSP and also to contribute to the social and economic aims of the Community development co-operation policy, it was necessary to seek the measure's main aim in order to secure a balance between the observance of (old) Article 47 TEU and of (old) Article 5 EC (on the principle of conferral). If an EU action pursued the main aim of preserving peace and strengthening international security (and *a fortiori* if that was the exclusive aim) while at the same time contributing indirectly to the social and economic development of developing countries, any encroachment on the Community's competences was precluded. On the other hand, if the two aims were indissociably linked, without one being secondary and indirect in relation to the other, priority had to be given to the Community legal basis because it seemed particularly difficult, if not impossible as the law stood, to contemplate recourse to a dual legal basis without breaching (old) Article 47 TEU.[32]

The Advocate General then established, on the basis of an analysis which need not be summarized here, that the purpose of the contested decision appeared to be mainly, if not exclusively, related to security. The objective of sustainable development appeared rather remote and, in any case, indirect and secondary by comparison with that of preserving the regional security of the Member States of ECOWAS. The content of the decision did not modify that finding, as a financial contribution and technical assistance were instruments which could equally be employed for CFSP and development co-operation purposes.[33] Accordingly, the Advocate General was of the opinion that the action had to be dismissed.

The Court basically followed the Opinion of the Advocate General as regards the interpretation of (old) Article 47 TEU, but not as regards the substance. Concerning the former, the Court considered it necessary to determine whether the provisions of the contested decision affected competences enjoyed by the Community under the EC Treaty, on the ground that they could have been adopted on the basis of the Treaty. (Old) Article 47 TEU aimed to maintain and build on the acquis communautaire. A measure having legal effects adopted under (old) Title V of the TEU affected the provisions of the EC Treaty within the meaning of (old) Article 47 TEU whenever it could have been adopted on the basis of the EC Treaty, it being unnecessary to examine whether the measure prevented or limited the exercise by the Community of its competences. If it was established that the provisions of a measure adopted under the TEU, on account of both their aim and their content, had as their main purpose the implementation of a policy conferred by the EC Treaty on the Community, and if they could properly have been adopted on the

[32] Ibid, paras 173–176.
[33] Ibid, paras 204–211.

basis of the EC Treaty, the Court had to find that those provisions infringed (old) Article 47 TEU. It was not relevant whether in an area such as development co-operation—which did not fall within the exclusive competence of the Community and in which, therefore, the Member States were not precluded from exercising, individually or collectively, their competences—such a measure could have been adopted by the Member States in the exercise of their competences. Moreover, the question of whether the provisions of such a measure fell within the competence of the Community related to the attribution and, thus, the very existence of that competence, and not its exclusive or shared nature. It was therefore necessary to determine whether the contested decision infringed (old) Article 47 TEU inasmuch as it could have been adopted on the basis of the provisions of the EC Treaty.[34]

The Court then recalled that the objectives of EC development co-operation policy were broad, and established, on the basis of a number of documents from the EU institutions, that certain measures aiming to prevent fragility in developing countries, including those adopted in order to combat the proliferation of small arms and light weapons, could contribute to the elimination or reduction of obstacles to the economic and social development of those countries. Nevertheless, a concrete measure aiming to combat such proliferation could be adopted by the Community under its development co-operation policy only if that measure, by virtue of its aims and its content, fell within the scope of the competences conferred upon the Community. That was not the case if such a measure, even if it contributed to the economic and social development of the developing country, had as its main purpose the implementation of the CFSP. The Court then referred to the principles emanating from its case law on the delimitation of legal bases in the EC Treaty. If examination of a measure revealed that it pursued a twofold aim or that it had a twofold component, and if one of those was identifiable as the main one, whereas the other was merely incidental, the measure had to be based on a single legal basis, namely that required by the main aim or component. It followed that measures combating the proliferation of small arms and light weapons did not fall within the competences of the Community in the field of development co-operation if, on account of their main aim or component, they were part of the pursuit of the CFSP. With regard to a measure which simultaneously pursued a number of objectives or which had several components, without one being incidental to the other, the Court had held that such a measure had to be founded, exceptionally, on the various corresponding legal bases. However, and this was a crucial finding by the Court, under (old) Article 47 TEU, such a solution was impossible with regard to the delimitation of EU and EC competences. Since (old) Article 47 precluded the Union from adopting, on the basis of the EU Treaty, a measure which could properly be adopted on the basis of the EC Treaty, the Union could not have recourse to a legal basis falling within the

[34] Ibid, paras 58–63 of the judgment.

CFSP in order to adopt provisions which also fell within a competence conferred by the EC Treaty on the Community.[35]

The Court then carried out an extensive analysis of the aims and content of the contested decision. As regards the aim, it first established that it could not be inferred from the joint action on which the decision was based that the implementation of the campaign against the proliferation of small arms and light weapons which the joint action set out would necessarily take the form of measures which pursued CFSP objectives, such as the preservation of peace and the strengthening of international security, rather than objectives of Community development policy. It therefore had to be examined whether the decision itself had to be regarded as a measure which pursued objectives falling within Community development co-operation policy. The Court established that it could not be denied that the decision formed part of a general perspective of preserving peace and strengthening international security. None the less, it could not be inferred from the decision that in comparison with its objectives of preserving peace and strengthening international security its concern to eliminate or reduce obstacles to the development of the countries concerned was purely incidental. The contested decision had the specific goal of strengthening the capacities of a group of African developing countries to combat a phenomenon which, according to the preamble to the decision, constituted an obstacle to the sustainable development of those countries. It followed that the decision pursued a number of objectives, falling within the CFSP and development co-operation policy respectively, without one of those objectives being incidental to the other.[36]

As regards the content of the decision, the Court agreed with the Advocate General that it was only in the light of the aims that they pursued that a financial contribution or technical assistance could be regarded as falling within the scope of the CFSP or of Community development co-operation policy. While there could be measures, such as the grant of political support for a moratorium or even the collection and destruction of weapons, which fell rather within action to preserve peace and strengthen international security or to promote international co-operation, being CFSP objectives, the decision to make funds available and to give technical assistance to a group of developing countries in order to draft a convention was capable of falling both under development co-operation policy and the CFSP.[37]

The Court concluded that the contested decision contained two components, neither of which could be considered to be incidental to the other, one falling within Community development co-operation policy and the other within the CFSP. This meant that (old) Article 47 TEU had been infringed and that the decision had to be annulled.[38]

The *SALW* judgment established three important principles. First, (old) Article 47 TEU protected all EC competences, be they exclusive or shared. If, having regard to the aim and content of an act, it could have been adopted under the EC

[35] Ibid, paras 64–77. [36] Ibid, paras 79–99. [37] Ibid, paras 100–105.
[38] Ibid, paras 108–110.

Treaty, it was impossible to adopt it under the TEU. Whether or not the Member States were capable of adopting the act, individually or collectively, because it came only within the shared competences of the EC, was irrelevant. This meant that the Member States could not act collectively under the CFSP in cases where they were entitled to act collectively, outside the EU framework. The CFSP could thus cover all areas of foreign and security policy, but where the EC Treaty conferred upon the Community competence for a specific form of foreign policy, such as commercial policy and development co-operation, those competences took precedence. They were, one could say, *lex specialis*. However, as *lex specialis* they were not to be interpreted narrowly, but rather on their own terms, in no way confined by the TEU provisions on the CFSP.

Secondly, the only qualification to this first principle was that, as in other areas of external action, the delimitation of the respective competences had to be done focusing on the main purpose or component of the measure in issue. This meant that the EU could adopt CFSP measures with an incidental effect on trade, development co-operation, or other EC matters. It also meant that there could be cases, like *SALW*, where there were two purposes or components, neither of which was incidental to the other.

In the latter cases, the third principle came into play: in contrast with other external competences, the Court as a matter of principle excluded recourse to a dual legal basis in such cases. (Old) Article 47 TEU simply precluded such a dual legal basis. The Court did not further elaborate on the reasons for this finding. Mengozzi AG drew attention in a footnote to the incompatibility of the decision-making processes under, respectively, the TEU and the EC Treaty.[39] Clearly, this rejection of a dual legal basis may make it more difficult to pursue a coherent EU external policy, since it precludes the use of all-encompassing legal instruments, having both foreign policy and other EU policy dimensions.

It remains to be seen whether, after the entry into force of the Treaty of Lisbon, those principles continue to be valid.

Article 40 TEU, post-Lisbon

The legal relationship between the CFSP and other forms of EU external action is substantially modified by the Treaty of Lisbon. (Current) Article 40 TEU, which replaces (old) Article 47 TEU, provides:

> The implementation of the common foreign and security policy shall not affect the application of the procedures and the extent of the powers of the institutions laid down by the Treaties for the exercise of the Union competences referred to in Articles 3 to 6 of the Treaty on the Functioning of the European Union.

[39] Ibid, Opinion of Mengozzi AG, footnote 76.

> Similarly, the implementation of the policies listed in those Articles shall not affect the application of the procedures and the extent of the powers of the institutions laid down by the Treaties for the exercise of the Union competences under this Chapter.

As can be seen, this provision not only protects EU competences under the TFEU (former EC competences), but also works the other way round, to protect CFSP competences. It therefore appears to introduce a more balanced approach to questions of delimitation. Furthermore, the new provision does not generally preclude that one Treaty affect the other, but refers, more specifically, to the application of the procedures and the extent of the powers of the institutions laid down by the Treaties for the exercise of the various EU competences.

The amendment of this provision is not the only significant modification. The current Treaties no longer contain provisions such as (old) Articles 1 to 3 TEU. (Old) Article 1 provided that the Union was founded on the Communities, *supplemented* by the policies and forms of cooperation (i.e. CFSP and PJCCM) established by the TEU. (Old) Article 2 TEU provided that one of the objectives of the EU was 'to maintain in full the acquis communautaire and build on it with a view to considering to what extent the policies and forms of co-operation introduced by this Treaty may need to be revised with the aim of ensuring the effectiveness of the mechanisms and the institutions of the Community'. (Old) Article 3 referred to the EU's single institutional framework which had to respect and build upon the acquis communautaire.

Also relevant, no doubt, are the attempts to create a more integrated legal framework for external action. The CFSP is no longer characterized by a set of objectives of its own, as referred to above; instead, Articles 3(5) and 21 TEU list and describe the EU's objectives for its external action as a whole. There is also an attempt to institutionalize this integrated framework by creating the double-hatted position of the High Representative, served by the External Action Service.

Against that revised Treaty background, what is one to make of the new Article 40 TEU? Which of the principles established by the Court in *SALW*, if any, continue to be valid?

It is clear that on the basis of Article 40 the Court can in future be asked to review, not just whether a CFSP act ought to have been adopted under other EU competences, provided for by the TFEU, but also whether an act adopted under the TFEU is in reality a CFSP act. That in itself does not, however, mean the withdrawal of the principle that a CFSP act which could have been adopted, in the light of its aim and content, under the (current) TFEU, violates (current) Article 40 TEU—i.e. the first principle emanating from *SALW*. If anything, (current) Article 40 TEU is more specific in that respect. The implementation of the CFSP may not affect the TFEU procedures and the powers of the institutions under the TFEU for the exercise of TFEU competences. The facts of *SALW* clearly come within those terms: as the contested decision also had an aim and component of development co-operation, for that purpose the relevant procedures under (current) Articles 208 to 211 TFEU should have been employed, involving all three EU political institutions, the Commission, the Parliament, and the Council, under the ordinary legislative procedure. It is difficult to see any basis for a more restrictive reading of (current) Article 40 TEU, for example along the lines suggested by the Council and the UK Government in *SALW*.

It is true of course that the new provision also protects the CFSP. On a first reading that may lead one to think that the CFSP is no longer purely supplementary, and that, as was mentioned, some kind of more 'balanced' approach is required for the delimitation of competences; an approach requiring, in some cases, that TFEU competences give way to the CFSP. There are, however, two difficulties with such an argument.

First, the scope of the CFSP continues to be as ill-defined as before. Indeed, some commentators point out that the absence of specific CFSP objectives in the TEU make it even more difficult to define that scope.[40] That is probably exaggerated, as it is clear that the CFSP continues to be focused on questions of peace and international security. Nevertheless, those aims are very broad—does not development aid or free trade also contribute to peace and international security?—and so is the reference in Article 24(1) TEU to 'all areas of foreign policy'—which again could easily be seen to encompass development co-operation and trade. Yet it is clear that one of the purposes of (new) Article 40 TEU is to safeguard the EU's competences in those specific matters, and the applicable decision-making procedures and involvement of the various institutions. Again, the better view is that the relationship between the CFSP and other competences is in the nature of *lex generalis* and *lex specialis*.[41] That means that an analysis of whether (current) Article 40 TEU is violated, because a CFSP act affects TFEU procedures and competences, will need to be conducted along the lines of *SALW*.

Secondly, the Court's approach in *SALW* effectively introduced a balanced delimitation, by applying the test of the main purpose or component. It so happened that in the case at hand the Court found two indissociably linked purposes and components, but the Court also expressly recognized that a CFSP act could, in principle, incidentally affect non-CFSP matters such as development co-operation.[42] Of course, that also means that a non-CFSP act, adopted under the TFEU, may incidentally affect the CFSP. It is not clear what methodology to applying (current) Article 40 TEU would constitute a more balanced approach.

In *SALW* the Court focused nearly exclusively on the aims of the contested decision, as its content—financial support and technical co-operation—could equally come within the scope of the CFSP as within that of development co-operation. There is of course an element of subjectivity, so to speak, in determining the aims

[40] Herrmann (n 9 above).

[41] See above, and also M Cremona, 'Defining competence in EU external relations: lessons from the Treaty reform process' in Dashwood and Maresceau (n 24 above) 46.

[42] *SALW* (n 26 above) paras 73–74.

of a measure. The institutions adopting the measure will often have considerable discretion in determining, and expressing, those aims. It is clear that the Court in *SALW* sought to reduce the scope for such discretion by analysing a whole series of political documents and statements, to support the conclusion that the decision had both development and CFSP aims. That approach carries the risk that, in practice, it will often have to be concluded that a measure has more than one aim, in particular after the entry into force of the Treaty of Lisbon. Since there is now a unified set of objectives for EU external action, the institutions will often, in their policy-making, refer to several objectives. Indeed, they are required to do so (see e.g. Article 205 TFEU). Such multiplicity of objectives will not make the task of delimiting the CFSP and other external competences any easier. Moreover, the objectives of the CFSP are so broadly defined—'preserve peace, prevent conflicts and strengthen international security' (Article 21(2)(c) TEU)—that many acts can be seen to pursue them.

Of course, there will be cases where it is not just the aim of the measure which matters, but also its content.[43] In that respect, the current version of the TEU introduces an interesting concept: it twice confirms that, within the framework of the CFSP, 'the adoption of legislative acts shall be excluded' (Articles 24(1) and 31(1) TEU). This is a puzzling provision. The concept of a legislative act is defined, in purely formal terms, in Article 289 TFEU. That provision distinguishes between the ordinary legislative procedure, and special legislative procedures. Articles 24(1) and 31(1) TEU could therefore simply be read as meaning that CFSP acts are not adopted under those procedures. However, such a reading suggests that these provisions are wholly superfluous: it is clear from Article 31 TEU, and other relevant TEU provisions, that CFSP acts (decisions) are taken by the European Council or the Council, acting alone. The CFSP is without doubt subject to specific procedures of its own, and there was therefore no need to indicate that legislative acts are excluded to confirm this. A more effective interpretation of the exclusion of legislative acts would need to focus on a substantive concept of legislative act. Such an interpretation would mean that general normative action is excluded within the framework of the CFSP. That exclusion is supported by the reference, in Articles 25 and 31 TEU, to 'decisions' as the legal instruments for the implementation of the CFSP. Pursuant to Article 288 TFEU, decisions stand in contrast to regulations and directives. The reason for the exclusion of legislative acts could be found in the EU's democratic principles (Articles 9 to 12 TEU), which provide that the functioning of the Union is founded on representative democracy (Article 10(1) TEU), and that the citizens are directly represented at Union level in the European Parliament (Article 10(2) TEU). Under the TFEU, virtually no general normative acts can be adopted without the involvement of the European Parliament, but CFSP decision-making excludes the Parliament,

[43] See further Herrmann (n 9 above) 40–3.

except for its mere consultation (Article 36 TEU). From that perspective, it would therefore make sense to prefer a substantive interpretation of the exclusion of legislative acts: one which precludes the European Council and the Council from using the CFSP for the purpose of normative action. That would equally make sense from a perspective of judicial review and scrutiny. CFSP acts are not within the jurisdiction of the Court of Justice (Article 275 TFEU), an exclusion which is less objectionable in a Union governed by the rule of law if the CFSP were interpreted as not permitting general normative action. In Chapter 11 the exclusion of legislative acts is further explored. At this point, suffice it to conclude that, pursuant to Article 40 TEU, the Court could be asked what that exclusion involves, since it is clear that legislative acts can be adopted under the TFEU, and since this is a question concerning the powers of the institutions and the procedures for exercising competences.

A final question concerning Article 40 TEU is whether a dual legal basis continues to be excluded, and whether therefore the third principle emanating from *SALW* remains in place. Can acts with a dual purpose or component, one within the scope of the CFSP, the other within that of a TFEU competence, ever be adopted on a dual legal basis? At least for one type of act, i.e. international agreements concluded by the EU, the provisions of the TFEU suggest that this is conceivable.[44] Article 218 TFEU contains procedural provisions on the conclusion of agreements, which apply to both CFSP agreements and to other agreements. Under Article 218(3), it is respectively the Commission or the High Representative which makes recommendations to the Council for the opening of negotiations; the High Representative has this power 'where the agreement envisaged relates exclusively or principally to the common foreign and security policy'. Furthermore, Article 218(6) TFEU sets out the procedure for concluding the agreement, and provides for the involvement of the European Parliament 'except where agreements relate exclusively to the common foreign and security policy'. Those provisions strongly suggest that an agreement may contain provisions coming within the scope of the CFSP as well as other provisions. Indeed, it would be rather nonsensical if, notwithstanding all the attempts to create a unified legal framework for EU external action, the EU would not be capable of concluding an agreement with a third country which contains elements of foreign policy as well as other forms of co-operation, or provisions on trade, or the environment, etc. If, none the less, the Court were to decide that Article 40 TEU does not permit a dual legal basis for the conclusion of an agreement, at least the agreement itself should continue to be unified, and the institutions could simply conclude it by way of two decisions, one concerning the CFSP elements, and the other for the other provisions.

[44] See also RA Wessel, 'Cross-Pillar Mixity: Combining Competences in the Conclusion of EU International Agreements' in C Hillion and P Koutrakos (eds), *Mixed Agreements Revisited—The EU and its Member States in the World* (Hart Publishing, 2010) 30.

However, also for autonomous EU acts, a case can be made for allowing a dual legal basis, in the TEU and the TFEU, where an act has a twofold purpose or component. Unfortunately, the Court did not, in *SALW*, clarify why a dual legal basis is excluded, other than by referring to (old) Article 47 TEU. As was mentioned, Mengozzi AG was more specific, and considered that the respective CFSP and EC procedures were incompatible. There is indeed long-standing case law of the Court of Justice on when different procedures for decision-making can and cannot be combined, and on when an act can or cannot be adopted on a dual legal basis in the light of these differences. In the 1991 *Titanium Dioxide* case the Court had established that it was not possible to combine the so-called co-operation procedure (the predecessor to the current ordinary legislative procedure, but not yet involving full co-decision by the Parliament) with a procedure requiring unanimity in the Council, because that would divest the co-operation procedure (involving a qualified majority in the Council) of its substance.[45] However, more recent case law has become substantially more liberal in this respect. In *International Fund for Ireland* the Court considered that (old) Articles 159 and 308 EC should have formed the legal basis of the act in issue, notwithstanding the fact that the former article provided for the co-decision procedure and the latter for unanimity.[46] Similarly, in *Kadi and Al Barakaat* the Court accepted the combined application of (old) Articles 60, 301, and 308 EC, notwithstanding the fact that the first two articles provided for decision-making by qualified majority, without involving the Parliament, whereas Article 308 EC provided for unanimity and consultation of the Parliament.[47] In the light of this more liberal case law, the question can at least be raised of whether there are genuinely huge obstacles to an act being based on, say, both the CFSP provisions in the TEU, and Article 209 TFEU on development co-operation, which provides for the ordinary legislative procedure. As in *International Fund for Ireland*, that procedure would simply need to be combined with unanimity in the Council.

If, however, a dual legal basis continues to be excluded, how should the institutions proceed in the case of an act with a dual purpose or component (like the decision on small arms and light weapons)? Which procedure ought to be followed? It must be emphasized that the Court did not state in *SALW* that the EC procedure was to be preferred. It simply annulled the CFSP act, without indicating how the institutions should have proceeded. Now that Article 40 TEU also protects the CFSP method of decision-making, it is difficult to contend that the TFEU procedures should take precedence over those of the CFSP. The only solution appears to be for the act to be split in two: one with a main or predominant CFSP purpose

[45] Case C–300/89 *Commission v. Council (Titanium Dioxide)* [1991] ECR I–2867, para 18.

[46] Case C–166/07 *European Parliament v. Council (International Fund for Ireland)* [2009] ECR I–7135, para 69.

[47] Joined Cases C–402 and 415/05P *Kadi and Al Barakaat v. Council and Commission* [2008] ECR I–6351, paras 235–236. For further analysis of the issue of dual legal basis, see RH Lauwaars and RH van Ooik, 'De problematiek van de dubbele rechtsgrondslagen in het Europese recht' (2010) 58 SEW 293.

or component; the other with a main or predominant TFEU purpose of component. How that should work in the case of an act with a single content and a dual purpose, such as the financial support and technical co-operation of the *SALW* decision, remains a mystery.

It may finally be noted that specific cross-pillar issues arise in the area of sanctions, or what the Treaties now call 'restrictive measures' (Article 215 TFEU). Those issues are best examined separately, in Chapter 12. The reader is, however, referred to that analysis for the purpose of completing the picture of the interaction between CFSP and TFEU competences.

Consistency

Ever since the inception of the pillar structure, there has been a need for strong language, like that used in (old) Article 3 TEU, one of the first provisions of that Treaty, indicating the drafters' concern that that structure may obstruct coherent and consistent external action.[48] After the amendments by the Treaty of Lisbon, consistency as regards external action no longer occupies such a prominent position in the TEU. However, the concept has by no means been abandoned. Article 21(3), second sentence, TEU provides:

> The Union shall ensure consistency between the different areas of its external action and between these and its other policies. The Council and the Commission, assisted by the High Representative of the Union for Foreign Affairs and Security Policy, shall ensure that consistency and shall cooperate to that effect.

At one level the emphasis on consistency is what could be expected in the light of the broad scope of EU external action. Globalization has led to the ever-growing importance and sophistication of external policies, thereby inevitably involving a variety of institutional actors; and in individual States, too, there are mechanisms and procedures for ensuring consistency so as to overcome policy fragmentation and inconsistencies. Nevertheless, within States consistency would rarely be raised to the constitutional level, as has been the case in the EU. The fact that consistency is such a high-level concern is no doubt related to the pillar structure itself, and the tension between intergovernmentalism and supranationalism, particularly at institutional level. The CFSP, to recall the main relevant features again, is dominated by the Council acting unanimously. Under the TFEU, the Commission and the Parliament occupy a much more central role. Unavoidably, the pillar structure created inter-institutional tension in the conduct of EU external relations. From an institutional perspective it matters a lot whether a particular policy is located in the TFEU or is pursued as a CFSP matter. As we have seen, it is difficult to delimit competences between the pillars, because

[48] See e.g. C Hillion, 'Tous pour un, un pour tous! Coherence in the External Relations of the European Union' in M Cremona (ed), *Developments in EU External Relations Law* (OUP, 2008) 10.

the issues are complex and the overall set-up inherently paradoxical, and because the Court has but limited jurisdiction. One could therefore say that the constitutional emphasis on consistency is something of a subterfuge, an attempt to cover up inter-institutional strife, to throw a constitutional blanket on the struggles between the Council and the Commission, not to mention the Parliament.

The inter-institutional dimension of the consistency requirement could be seen in the text of (old) Article 3, second paragraph, TEU, where the Council and the Commission were made responsible for ensuring consistency and an obligation of co-operation was imposed on them. However, the Treaty did not spell out any specific consequences of that obligation. It did not, in particular, resolve the issue of hierarchy between the pillars. As the CFSP covered all areas of foreign and security policy, thus projecting an EU role in general international politics, it was in the nature of things that certain CFSP decisions set policies with ramifications for EC external action. The question therefore arose of whether CFSP decisions could contain legally binding instructions for EC action. Nuttall reported that this question crystallized in 1994, on the occasion of deciding upon common positions concerning Rwanda and Ukraine.[49] The Council had in mind combining action under both the First and Second Pillars, but the Commission strongly objected to the fact that this combined approach was exclusively defined under the CFSP. The Council legal service took the view that it had not been the intention to exclude matters of EC competence from the CFSP provisions, but admitted that the Commission could not be obliged to act by a decision taken under those provisions, which would impair its autonomy under the EC Treaty. The Commission legal service contested the view that CFSP provisions could apply to EC matters, and denied that the Commission could be reduced to a body for implementing CFSP policy. In its view, common positions were addressed to the Member States and not the Commission. The dilemma was partially resolved when in March 1995 the Council noted an operational guide (*mode d'emploi*) on common positions.[50] This *mode d'emploi* provided that common positions committed the Union as a whole, and respected the consistency of the Union's external activities in accordance with (old) Article 3 TEU; they could thus refer to the Union's external activities as a whole, but had to preserve the powers specific to each institution, including the Commission's power of initiative.[51]

The Commission's position was understandable, and appeared correct in so far as CFSP decisions attempted to interfere with the Commission's right of initiative under the EC Treaty. If, however, consistency is to be meaningful, some degree of political superiority of the CFSP over other external policies seems unavoidable. It is doubtful whether such superiority risks undermining the supranational character of (now) TFEU decision-making. In the absence of the CFSP, international politics would not

[49] S Nuttall, *European Foreign Policy* (OUP, 2000) 263–4.

[50] The *mode d'emploi* was not published. See for a description R Wessel, 'The Inside Looking Out: Consistency and Delimitation in EU External Relations' (2000) 37 CML Rev 1154–5.

[51] See also Timmermans (n 21 above) 63–4.

disappear, and Member State governments, present in the Council, would also decide on certain external policies from a broader political perspective. For example, one could hardly imagine potential negotiations on trade with Iran not being affected by high international politics. The benefit of the CFSP is that it makes that dimension visible, and subject to a formal process of deliberation. Once such deliberation has taken place, the Member States are bound by its conclusions, including when they act within the TFEU framework. That may actually be helpful, rather than detrimental, for effective EU decision-making. Of course there is the tension between unanimous CFSP decision-making and the TFEU ordinary legislative procedure. But it may be something of an illusion to think that, in the absence of a CFSP with the more onerous unanimity requirement, TFEU decision-making on sensitive external policies would be less fractured and more effective. From that perspective it makes little sense to focus too closely on the question of whether CFSP decisions can impose legally binding obligations on the institutions, acting under the TFEU.[52]

The Treaty of Lisbon attempted to find further institutional answers to the consistency conundrum by introducing the double-hatted position of High Representative of the Union for Foreign Affairs and Security Policy. According to Article 18(2) TEU, the High Representative on the one hand conducts the Union's CFSP. Pursuant to Article 18(4) TEU, the High Representative shall also be one of the Vice-Presidents of the Commission, 'responsible within the Commission for responsibilities incumbent on it in external relations and for co-ordinating other aspects of the Union's external action'. The High Representative is expressly mandated to 'ensure the consistency of the Union's external action' (Article 18(4) TEU), though, as we have seen, Article 21(3) TEU also instructs the Commission and the Council, 'assisted by the High Representative', to ensure consistency. The High Representative is in turn assisted by the European External Action Service (EEAS), which at the time of writing is in the process of being set up. The EEAS comprises officials from the Council's General Secretariat and from the Commission, as well as staff seconded from national diplomatic services of the Member States (Article 27(3) TEU). Again, this shows an attempt at institutional integration. It confirms the fact that the consistency concept is mainly aimed at avoiding inter-institutional tension.

Whether these institutional reforms will achieve that goal remains to be seen. The institutional integration is by no means complete, since important areas of external action such as trade and development co-operation continue to be managed by specific Commissioners and Commission departments, and not by the High Representative and the EEAS. Moreover, the High Representative has not been given any legal tools to overcome inter-institutional strife. EU competences for the CFSP and for other areas of external action still have to be delimited. The roles of the Commission and the Parliament in the conduct of the CFSP remain restricted. The High Representative, so it seems, can only use political tools to produce a better consensus among the institutions.

[52] A negative reply is given by Wessel (n 50 above) 1156, as regards the pre-Lisbon legal position.

Conclusions

Several general conclusions can be drawn from this chapter's analysis of the EU's CFSP competences.

The sphere of action of the CFSP is defined in the broadest terms, as encompassing all areas of foreign and security policy. Whereas before Lisbon the CFSP was governed by its own set of objectives, that is no longer the case, which has made the task of defining the scope of this policy even more difficult than before. A lot of different activities are undertaken within the framework of this policy, but increasingly it appears that its specificity is concentrated in security and defence matters, where the TEU clarifies the kind of activities which the EU is destined to undertake. Another important strand of the CFSP is the policy on sanctions ('restrictive measures'), analysed in Chapter 12.

If the CFSP were to exist in isolation, its broad definition, indeed its lack of real definition, would not necessarily raise many issues. However, the CFSP is constitutionally juxtaposed to other EU external policies, by virtue of Article 40 TEU. The Court polices the boundaries between the CFSP and competences and policies under the TFEU. Its judgment in *SALW* continues to be relevant, even if Article 40 TEU looks both ways, in contrast to (old) Article 47 TEU. Thus, the CFSP may not trespass on TFEU external action territory. As the latter continues to expand, the CFSP may indeed shrink to security and defence policy. Its vocation to cover all areas of foreign and security policy is thus much qualified: there should be a footnote to the Treaty stating that this provision applies only in so far as there is no other EU external competence.

The way in which the Court policed the borders between the EC Treaty and the TEU also confirmed that there is a unified concept of EU law, and the Treaty of Lisbon has sealed that development. The TEU and the TFEU are organically linked, and competences therefore have to be allocated. A development co-operation measure, for example, cannot be taken under the CFSP. The institutional provisions of the Lisbon Treaty wholly confirm this unified concept, by creating the position of the High Representative and the EEAS. It is to be hoped that this will lead to the better co-ordination and greater effectiveness of external policies. There will, however, still be scope for institutional turf battles. The High Representative may unify the external action administration, but decision-making procedures remain different (e.g. unanimity in CFSP matters) and so does the role of the various institutions.

This chapter concludes the analysis of the legal and constitutional foundations of the EU's external competences and objectives. One must again draw attention to the broad overall scope of such competences. There appear to be virtually no significant areas of international law-making in which the EU cannot participate.

Part II

International Foundations: Treaties and International Law

6

The life cycle of international agreements

Introduction

This chapter examines the procedure for the EU's negotiation, conclusion, and termination of an international agreement.[1] At face value this may seem like a terse and self-referential legal subject. It will become clear, however, that there are important constitutional and institutional issues beneath the procedural surface. The scope and depth of the EU's treaty-making practice are such that it has become a central instrument of law-making, often of a general normative or legislative character. Policy areas such as trade, development co-operation, and environmental protection are obvious examples of areas of EU activity where much law-making effectively takes place by way of participation in international negotiations. Examining the role of the various EU institutions (and of the Member States) in the negotiation and conclusion of international agreements therefore implies identifying important constitutional functions.

Those functions can be approached from two perspectives. First, there is the perspective of institutional balance.[2] Each of the EU's political institutions—the Commission, the Council, including the High Representative for Foreign Affairs and Security Policy and the European Parliament—has a particular role to play in the process of entering into international commitments. The definition of that role is an important factor in the overall balance of political power as distributed among those institutions. Secondly, and more fundamentally, there is the perspective of democracy and legitimacy. The EU often struggles with questions about the legitimacy and democratic character of its action. In one sense, the EU's participation in international law-making is even more remote from the citizen than

[1] See also I Macleod, ID Hendry, and S Hyett, *The External Relations of the European Communities* (OUP, 1996) 75–105; M Maresceau, 'Bilateral Agreements Concluded by the European Community' (2004) 309 *Recueil des Cours* 212; A De Walsche, 'La procédure de conclusion des accords internationaux' in J-V Louis and M Dony (eds), *Commentaire J Megret—Relations extérieures* (Etudes européennes, 2005) ch 6; G De Baere, *Constitutional Principles of EU External Relations* (OUP, 2008) 77–92.

[2] See e.g. B De Witte, 'Institutional Principles: A Special Category of General Principles of Law' in U Bernitz and J Nergelius (eds), *General Principles of European Community Law* (Kluwer Law International, 2000) 150–2.

is the creation of 'internal' legislation. There is a stronger role for the executive, as opposed to representatives of the people, which is a general feature of States' participation in international law-making. Indeed, as analysed below, even though the European Parliament needs to give its consent to certain types of international agreements, that does not always imply a strong role for the Parliament in the actual negotiation of international commitments. There are thus, in this area, significant issues of legitimacy and democracy which receive remarkably little attention in either public debate or academic literature.[3]

This chapter does not aim to present a definitive analysis of such issues. It aims to describe the law and practice as regards the different phases in the life of an international agreement: negotiation, signature, conclusion, implementation, suspension, and termination. The relevant provisions are contained in Article 218 TFEU, the successor to Article 300 EC, which was much amended and expanded in the course of time, from two to seven, and now eleven paragraphs, thus reflecting the intense treaty-making activity of the EU and the resulting problems and practices, some of which were addressed through Treaty amendments. Article 218 TFEU is not, however, the only provision on the conclusion of agreements. First, Article 218(1) TFEU refers to Article 207 TFEU for the negotiation and conclusion of agreements concerning the common commercial policy. The analysis of those provisions, which are generally in line with the overall procedure, is integrated with the general analysis. Secondly, agreements on an exchange-rate system, or on monetary or foreign exchange regime matters are subject to special procedures described in Article 219(1) and (3) TFEU, and are separately analysed below. Furthermore, since the Treaty of Amsterdam the EU has also been capable of concluding international agreements concerning the (then) Second and Third Pillars. (Old) Article 24 TEU contained the relevant provisions, but those have now been incorporated in Article 218 TFEU.[4] Therefore, in contrast to other acts of law-making in, respectively, CFSP matters and other EU policies, there is a unified procedure. In substance, though, the involvement of the various institutions in the conclusion of agreements concerning CFSP matters is as intergovernmental as for internal acts (see in that respect Chapter 11): the Council acts unanimously, and the agreement is (presumably, as we will see) negotiated by the High Representative.

This chapter does not examine the role of the Court of Justice in the process of negotiation and conclusion. Under Article 218(6) TFEU the Court can be asked to

[3] But see D Thym, 'Parliamentary Involvement in European International Relations' in M Cremona and B De Witte (eds), *EU Foreign Relations Law—Constitutional Fundamentals* (Hart Publishing, 2008) 201; R Passos, 'Mixed Agreements from the Perspective of the European Parliament' in in C Hillion and P Koutrakos (eds), *Mixed Agreements Revisited—The EU and its Member States in the World* (Hart Publishing, 2010) 272–86.

[4] On agreements based on (old) Art 24 TEU, see R Wessel, 'The EU as a party to international agreements: shared competences, mixed responsibilities' in A Dashwood and M Maresceau, *Law and Practice of EU External Relations* (CUP, 2008) 152.

deliver an Opinion on the compatibility of an envisaged agreement with the Treaty, but that procedure is analysed in Chapter 8.

At the outset a point of legal terminology is also worth noting. Articles 218 and 219 TFEU consistently refer to 'agreements', but that term needs to be broadly interpreted as encompassing all forms of international contractual obligations entered into, be they in the form of a treaty, convention, agreement, memorandum of understanding, or any other instrument. So much follows both from the case law of the Court of Justice, which recognizes the EU's general capacity to enter into international commitments and consistently identified Article 300 EC (current Article 218 TFEU) as the Treaty provision containing the relevant procedural rules,[5] and from established institutional practice.[6]

Negotiations

Article 218 TFEU

Under (old) Article 300 EC the Commission had the prerogative of proposal, reflecting its general right of initiative. However, as Article 218 TFEU encompasses agreements on both CFSP matters and other EU policy matters, the right of initiative is split between the Commission and the High Representative. Article 218(3) and (4) TFEU provide:

> 3. The Commission, or the High Representative of the Union for Foreign Affairs and Security Policy where the agreement envisaged relates exclusively or principally to the common foreign and security policy, shall submit recommendations to the Council, which shall adopt a decision authorising the opening of negotiations and, depending on the subject of the agreement envisaged, nominating the Union negotiator or the head of the Union's negotiating team.
>
> 4. The Council may address directives to the negotiator and designate a special committee in consultation with which the negotiations must be conducted.

In practice, it is fair to say that the initiative to start a particular negotiation may come from various corners and that, depending on the type of negotiation, there may be a period of reflection prior to the decision to open negotiations. Often such reflection is accompanied by discussion papers which the Commission produces—and presumably, in the future, the High Representative and the EEAS.[7] The European Council is also actively involved in determining the general direction of policies in the field of external relations.

[5] *Opinion 1/75 re Local Cost Standard* [1975] ECR 1355, 1360.

[6] The VCLT also operates a holistic approach to the concept of a treaty: see Art 2(1)(a).

[7] E.g. Communication from the Commission to the European Parliament and the Council—EU relations with the Islamic Republic of Iran, COM(2001)71 final.

The division of labour as regards CFSP and non-CFSP matters between the High Representative and the Commission appears to reflect the methodology which the Court of Justice has developed for delimiting different legal bases in the Treaties: that of the main or principal purpose of component of the measure.[8]

In contrast with (old) Article 300 EC, the current provisions do not indicate the Commission as the negotiator. Instead, they do not even identify the Union's negotiator, but simply leave it to the Council to nominate the negotiator or the head of the negotiating team 'depending on the subject of the agreement envisaged'. Notwithstanding such indeterminate language, it is clear from the other provisions of Article 218, as well as from the general division of powers between the institutions and the principle of institutional balance, that the choice for the negotiator is between the Commission and the High Representative. In fact, a coherent interpretation of Article 218, reflecting the division of powers, suggests that the Council ought to nominate the negotiator in accordance with the principle expressed in the opening lines of Article 218(3): the Commission should be the negotiator, except where the agreement envisaged relates exclusively or principally to the CFSP. A textual argument in support of that conception is that Article 17 TEU confers on the Commission the power to 'ensure the Union's external representation', with the exception of the CFSP and other cases provided for in the Treaties. The negotiation of international agreements is arguably a form of external representation. Moreover, there is clearly a need for the Commission, which ensures the application of the Treaties and of EU legislation (again with the exception of the CFSP), to be the negotiator for agreements covering matters of internal policy-making under the TFEU. The negotiated agreement will need to fit into the broader framework of EU law, and the Commission has the institutional capacity and memory to ensure this. The better reading of Article 218(3) TFEU is thus that the Commission continues to negotiate international agreements, except those which relate exclusively or principally to the CFSP.

Article 207(3) TFEU contains the following provisions regarding the negotiation of agreements coming within the scope of the common commercial policy:

> Where agreements with one or more third countries or international organisations need to be negotiated and concluded, Article 218 shall apply, subject to the special provisions of this Article.
>
> The Commission shall make recommendations to the Council, which shall authorise it to open the necessary negotiations. The Council and the Commission shall be responsible for ensuring that the agreements negotiated are compatible with internal Union policies and rules.
>
> The Commission shall conduct these negotiations in consultation with a special committee appointed by the Council to assist the Commission in this task and within the framework of such directives as the Council may issue to it. The Commission shall report regularly to the special committee and to the European Parliament on the progress of negotiations.

[8] See Chs 4 and 5.

Here it is clear that the Commission is the sole negotiator. It is also noteworthy that the Commission needs to report, not only to the special committee, but also to the Parliament. Such a provision is lacking in Article 218(3) TFEU. The reason for this may be that agreements negotiated pursuant to Article 218 do not of necessity require the consent of the Parliament. As is argued below, the situation is different for trade agreements.

Questions may arise as to the nomination of the negotiator of an agreement concerning both trade and non-trade matters, in particular if the latter concern the CFSP. Article 207(3) TFEU appears to imply that, as soon as part of a negotiation concerns trade, the Commission must be the negotiator for that part.

The 'recommendations' which the Commission or the High Representative make to the Council for the purpose of a decision to open a negotiation are not published. The Council may then authorize the negotiator to proceed; the 'shall' in Article 218(3) TFEU does not of course imply an obligation for the Council to agree with the recommendations.[9] The Council takes that decision by qualified majority or unanimity, depending on the type or content of the agreement, under the same rules as apply to the conclusion of agreements (see below).

The negotiator conducts negotiations in accordance with directives which the Council may issue to it. The term 'directives' here does not have the same meaning as in Article 288 TFEU, which defines directive as a legislative instrument. In the context of international negotiations, the Council's directives are not addressed to the Member States, but to the negotiator.[10] Nor are they published, as this would permit the other party to the negotiations to have knowledge of the negotiator's precise brief too easily. The content of the directives is none the less often reported in the press, and the practice appears to be for the directives to be rather general in character. That does not mean that the negotiator has a free hand. Through the 'special committees', consisting of national government representatives, the Council machinery keeps a close eye on how the negotiations are evolving. The negotiator is therefore often a double negotiator: both with the other party to the negotiations and with Member States' representatives or the Council itself.

Notwithstanding such supervision by the Council, the negotiation of international agreements has in the past been a significant Commission prerogative. The Commission is generally in a position to try to find a common denominator of the, often varying, interests of the Member States. Moreover, in some cases the Commission could be quite deft in the use of its authority to negotiate. Two examples, both from the Uruguay Round negotiations leading to the establishment of the WTO, illustrate this.

The first example is the so-called Blair House agreement. Faced with the fact that the Uruguay Round could be successful only if an agreement could be reached with the United States on agriculture, the Commission entered into unofficial

[9] Macleod, Hendry, and Hyett (n 1 above) 87.

[10] Ibid, 89. In other language versions the terminology differs.

negotiations with the United States, resulting, in 1992, in the above outline agreement on the basic principles of the future WTO Agreement on Agriculture, which was the breakthrough which the Round needed. The Commission did this largely on its own, and some Member States, with France in the lead, immediately reacted, stating that they could not accept the outcome of the negotiations. However, by the time the Round was concluded (end of 1993) the resistance had melted away, and all Member States accepted the Agreement on Agriculture as part of the overall WTO package.[11]

The second example concerns bananas, and is more technical. Following the adoption of the common market organization on bananas in 1993[12] a number of Latin American countries brought complaints against the Community under GATT. The Commission reacted by requesting the Council's authorization to open negotiations with the complainant countries on compensation. In March 1994, one month before the final conclusion of the Uruguay Round, the Commission reached a 'framework agreement' with those countries. However, the Commission was aware that the agreement, on its own, would not muster a qualified majority in the Council, and could therefore not as such be concluded by the Community. It then decided to make the agreement part of the Community's tariff commitments in the Uruguay Round, without first seeking the Council's approval, and sent a letter to that effect to the GATT Secretariat. When in April 1994 the WTO Agreement was due to be signed, in Marrakesh, it contained that framework agreement as part of the Community's tariff schedule, and for obvious political reasons none of the Member States was in a position not to sign the WTO Agreement, merely for the sake of trade in bananas. Some Member State delegations fiercely protested against this course of events, and Germany brought two cases against the framework agreement before the Court of Justice. The first was a request for an Opinion under (then) Article 300(6) EC, which Germany made in July 1994, several months before the WTO Agreement entered into force. It argued, *inter alia*, that the Council had not given the Commission authority to negotiate the framework agreement, or at least that the Commission had gone beyond the Council's instructions. The Court, however, did not examine that claim, as it did not manage to deliver its Opinion before 1 January 1995, when the WTO Agreement, of which the framework agreement formed part, had already entered into force. The request for an Opinion had thus become devoid of purpose, as the Court's Opinion can examine only an envisaged agreement.[13] In its second challenge, an action for the annulment of the Council's decision to conclude the WTO Agreement in so far as it contained the banana framework agreement, Germany no longer argued that the Commission had failed to respect its negotiating mandate.[14]

[11] P Van den Bossche, 'The European Community and the Uruguay Round Agreements' in JH Jackson and AO Sykes (eds), *Implementing the Uruguay Round* (OUP, 1997) 62–6.

[12] Council Regulation 404/93 on the common organization of the market in bananas [1993] OJ L47/2.

[13] *Opinion 3/94 re Framework Agreement on Bananas* [1995] ECR I–4577; see Ch 8.

[14] Case C–122/95 *Germany v. Council* [1996] ECR I–973.

It is thus not clear at this stage whether observance of the Council's negotiating directives is subject to judicial review. In principle, any act producing legal effects can be challenged on grounds of violation of the Treaty in an action for annulment, with the exception of CFSP acts (see Chapter 11). In so far as the negotiator adopts such an act in the framework of an international negotiation, it would seem possible to argue a violation of the provisions of Article 218(3) TFEU. The case is unlikely to arise, however, as the negotiator's actions are subject to political review by the Council. If the latter is unhappy with the outcome of a negotiation, it may simply refuse to conclude the agreement. Where it does conclude the agreement, it obviously agrees with the negotiator's approach, and a challenge to particular conduct in the course of negotiations would then in any event be unable to affect the outcome, namely conclusion of the agreement, as this is a separate Council act.

The phase of negotiating an international agreement is often concluded by the initialling of the text.[15] This is the act whereby the negotiators authenticate the text resulting from the negotiations. As this forms part of the negotiation, the Commission has authority to undertake such initialling.

It is remarkable that the European Parliament is nowhere mentioned in Article 218(3) TFEU, and thus has no formal say in either the decision to launch an international negotiation, the directives issued to the negotiator, or the supervision of the negotiator's conduct of the negotiations. Article 218(10) merely provides that the Parliament shall be immediately and fully informed at all stages of the procedure for concluding agreements, which of course includes the negotiation phase. After the entry into force of the Lisbon Treaty, the Parliament has already been demanding a closer involvement in the negotiation of international agreements, threatening not to give its consent if its opinions are not taken into consideration. This was successful in the case of an agreement with the United States on the exchange of financial information for anti-terrorist purposes.[16]

Furthermore, the Parliament and the Commission have, during the course of 2010, concluded an inter-institutional agreement, pursuant to Article 295 TFEU, which contains provisions on the Parliament's involvement in international negotiations conducted by the Commission. Annex 3 to that agreement provides that the Commission shall inform Parliament about its intention to propose the start of negotiations; it shall present the draft negotiating directives to the Parliament; it shall take due account of Parliament's comments throughout the negotiations and shall regularly and promptly inform it about the conduct of the negotiations; and in the case of agreements requiring the Parliament's consent it shall provide to the Parliament all relevant information that it also provides to the Council (or the

[15] Macleod, Hendry, and Hyett (n 1 above) 90–1.

[16] For the first version of the agreement see [2010] OJ L8/11. For the renegotiated version see [2010] OJ L195/5.

special committee appointed by the Council). At paragraph 25 of the agreement it is provided that, at international conferences, the Commission shall facilitate the inclusion of a delegation of Members of the European Parliament.[17]

The Council immediately expressed its dismay with these arrangements, which it claimed undermined the institutional balance and the limits on the powers of the institutions (see Article 13(2) TEU). It further threatened to bring actions before the EU Courts against specific applications of these provisions.[18] Whether such actions are likely to be successful remains to be seen. Institutional balance is indeed an important principle, but there are competing principles, such as that of representative democracy (Article 10 TEU), which surely justify the further involvement of the Parliament in international negotiations.

Article 219 TFEU

In the monetary field the procedure for the conclusion of international agreements is different, or at least potentially different, since the Treaty leaves it to the Council to decide on the appropriate arrangements. Article 219(3) TFEU provides, *inter alia*, that:

> ... the Council, acting on a recommendation from the Commission and after consulting the European Central Bank, shall decide the arrangements for the negotiation and conclusion of... agreements. These arrangements shall ensure that the Union expresses a single position. The Commission shall be fully associated with the negotiations.

The Treaty therefore does not identify the negotiator of agreements based on Article 219(1) or (3) TFEU, presumably because there may be cases in which the ECB would, bearing in mind its expertise, be the natural negotiator, or at least would need to be involved in the process of negotiation.[19]

Signature and conclusion

Article 218 TFEU

Concepts

Under international treaty law, as codified in the Vienna Convention on the Law of Treaties (VCLT), there are various alternative modes of expressing consent to

[17] Framework Agreement on Relations between the European Parliament and the European Commission [2010] OJ L304/47.

[18] See Council Document 15018/10 of 18 October 2010, at 3.

[19] See further C Zilioli and M Selmayr, 'The External Relations of the Euro Area: Legal Aspects' (1999) 36 CML Rev 302.

be bound by a treaty.[20] They include signature, exchange of instruments, ratification, acceptance, approval, and accession, the choice between them depending on the treaty in question. Those modalities all concern action on the international plane. It is important to distinguish between such international action and a State's internal legal act enabling that State to engage in such international action.[21] A State's constitution would typically contain a number of rules which have to be followed when undertaking international commitments. Similarly, Article 218(5) to (8) TFEU lay down the EU's internal decision-making procedure for concluding international agreements. It is only by following that procedure that the EU can lawfully—under EU law—express its consent to be bound. Article 218(5) and (6) TFEU indicate that the Council adopts the decisions to sign the agreement; if necessary, to apply it provisionally; and to conclude the agreement. The provision must be read as applying to all forms of expressing consent at international level. Conclusion by the Council is thus a generic term for Council decisions on undertaking international commitments. The suggested sequence of signature and conclusion need not always be present. Again this depends on what the agreement itself provides for. The prevailing practice as regards significant treaties or agreements is that, through their signature, the representatives of the contracting parties agree to submit the agreement for domestic approval. In such cases, signature does not express the final consent to be bound, but it creates the obligation not to defeat the object and purpose of the agreement.[22] There are, however, numerous agreements which are concluded upon signature, in which case the Council has to take a decision on conclusion prior to signature.

Signature may be accompanied by a decision on provisional application before entry into force. This provision was inserted by the Amsterdam Treaty. It reflects Article 25 VCLT, according to which a treaty may provide for such provisional application or the negotiating States may agree to it. The EU regularly makes use of that opportunity in the case of mixed agreements, which require ratification by all Member States, often a time-consuming exercise.[23]

Council decision-making

After some initial hesitation, the Council developed the practice of concluding international agreements by way of decision. Such decisions typically consist of a preamble, identifying, *inter alia*, the legal basis in the Treaty for the conclusion of the agreement, and a couple of articles expressing conclusion or approval as well as indicating the person (usually the President of the Council) who is instructed to

[20] See Arts 11–17 VCLT.

[21] JHJ Bourgeois, 'The European Court of Justice and the WTO: Problems and Challenges' in JHH Weiler, *The EU, the WTO and the NAFTA* (OUP, 2000) 77.

[22] Art 18 VCLT. For an application of that obligation see Case T–115/94 *Opel Austria v. Council* [1997] ECR II–39, paras 90–95; see further Ch 9.

[23] A Rosas, 'The European Union and Mixed Agreements' in A Dashwood and C Hillion (eds), *The General Law of EC External Relations* (Sweet & Maxwell, 2000) 208.

notify the other contracting party or parties of EU conclusion.[24] The decision may of course contain further provisions, for example as regards EU representation in bodies or organs set up by the contracting parties.[25]

It follows from Article 218(8) TFEU that, as a rule, the Council concludes agreements acting by a qualified majority on a proposal from the negotiator. However, unanimity is required in four cases.

First, when the agreement covers a field for which unanimity is required for the adoption of an act of the Union. If, for example, an agreement is concluded on matters of indirect taxation coming within Article 113 TFEU, the Council is required to act unanimously since that provision provides for unanimous decision-making. Effectively, therefore, Article 218(8) confirms the doctrines of implied powers and parallelism between internal and external powers, as it recognizes that Treaty provisions conferring internal legislative competence may form the basis for the conclusion of an international agreement.[26] It may be noted that this unanimity requirement will nearly always apply to agreements covering CFSP matters, as qualified majority voting on CFSP decisions is exceptional (see Chapter 11).

Secondly, unanimity is also required for association agreements referred to in Article 217 TFEU. Thirdly, and likewise, it is required for agreements referred to in Article 212 TFEU (concerning economic, financial, and technical co-operation with third countries) with the States which are candidates for accession. The idea here is no doubt that such agreements are very significant, and therefore require every Member State's agreement.

Fourthly, unanimity is required for the agreement on EU accession to the ECHR. Moreover, the decision concluding that agreement shall enter into force after it has been approved by the Member States in accordance with their constitutional requirements. Clearly, the Treaty drafters considered that such accession is of great constitutional significance.

There is a fifth case to be added. Pursuant to Article 207(4) TFEU, certain trade agreements also require unanimity (see further Chapter 2).

Role of the European Parliament

The Parliament's involvement with the conclusion of agreements has been growing. Article 218(6) TFEU contains the relevant provisions:

> Except where agreements relate exclusively to the common foreign and security policy, the Council shall adopt the decision concluding the agreement:

[24] See e.g. Council Decision 2002/245 on the conclusion of an agreement on co-operation and customs union between the European Economic Community and the Republic of San Marino and of the Protocol thereto following the enlargement which took effect on 1 January 1995 [2002] OJ L84/41.

[25] See e.g. Decision 2002/309 of the Council, and of the Commission as regards the Agreement on Scientific and Technological Cooperation, on the conclusion of seven Agreements with the Swiss Confederation [2002] OJ L114/1.

[26] See Ch 3.

(a) after obtaining the consent of the European Parliament in the following cases:
    (i) association agreements;
    (ii) agreement on Union accession to the European Convention for the Protection of Human Rights and Fundamental Freedoms;
    (iii) agreements establishing a specific institutional framework by organising cooperation procedures;
    (iv) agreements with important budgetary implications for the Union;
    (v) agreements covering fields to which either the ordinary legislative procedure applies, or the special legislative procedure where consent by the European Parliament is required.

The European Parliament and the Council may, in an urgent situation, agree upon a time-limit for consent.

(b) after consulting the European Parliament in other cases. The European Parliament shall deliver its opinion within a time-limit which the Council may set depending on the urgency of the matter. In the absence of an opinion within that time-limit, the Council may act.

This provision greatly expands the number of cases in which the Council will need to seek the Parliament's consent, because it creates a parallelism with the ordinary legislative procedure, which is the default procedure for internal law-making, and refers equally to any special legislative procedure which requires the Parliament's consent. The previous version, (old) Article 300(3) EC, required such consent (or assent as it was called) only for agreements amending acts adopted under the (then) co-decision procedure. There was no compelling logic for limiting the assent requirement to such cases, as one does not see on what grounds the Parliament should be less involved in the conclusion of agreements laying down, for the first time, rules which in the internal decision-making process require its consent, as opposed to amendment of existing provisions. In this context one should also bear in mind that international agreements concluded by the EU may have direct effect (see Chapter 9), and that the provisions of a directly effective agreement may thus have effects similar to those of legislative acts. It was therefore incongruous that the EC Treaty did not require Parliamentary assent for all acts adopted in a field where the co-decision procedure applied. That incongruity has now been removed.

The requirement of Parliamentary consent for matters covered by the ordinary legislative procedure extends to trade agreements. This follows from the combined provisions of Article 207 and 218 TFEU. Article 207(3) TFEU provides that: 'Where agreements... need to be negotiated and concluded, Article 218 shall apply, subject to the special provisions of this Article'. It is true that the Parliament is not mentioned in these 'special provisions' of Article 207. However, the ordinary legislative procedure now governs EU decision-making in trade matters, and it would be wholly incongruous to construe Article 207 as implying the exclusion of the Parliament from the conclusion of international agreements in this field. The better interpretation is for the provisions of Article 218(6) concerning the role of the Parliament as regards the conclusion of an agreement to be read into Article 207. In practice, the consent requirement for trade agreements is probably the most significant increase in the Parliament's powers regarding the EU's treaty-making.

Parliament's consent must also be obtained for further types of agreement. The first category, association agreements, is easy to define, at least in formal terms: it encompasses all agreements concluded on the basis of Article 217 TFEU. The second category, accession to the ECHR, is equally straightforward. However, the third type of agreement, namely those establishing a specific institutional framework by organizing co-operation procedures, is more difficult to determine. Its scope is ill-defined, as a great many international agreements contain some type of institutional framework,[27] and as it is not clear what is meant by 'organizing cooperation procedures'.

The fourth category, agreements with important budgetary implications for the EU, is based on the rationale that the Parliament occupies a central institutional position in budgetary matters,[28] and that therefore agreements entailing considerable expenditure have to receive the Parliament's assent. Again the terms are open to varying interpretations, and it is very much a matter of judgment as to what constitutes an 'important' effect on the budget. The Parliament has sought further clarification of the provision by challenging a Council decision not to ask for its assent to the conclusion of a fisheries agreement with Mauritania.[29] The agreement was concluded for a period of five years from 1 August 1996, and entailed financial compensation in exchange for fishing rights amounting to ECU 266.8 million (distributed over those five years). The Court made the following analysis. It first rejected the Council's argument that the agreement's expenditure should be set against the overall budget of the (then) Community. It pointed out that appropriations allocated to external operations of the Community traditionally accounted for a marginal fraction of the Community budget (barely exceeding five per cent in 1996 and 1997). A comparison between the annual financial cost of an agreement and the overall Community budget therefore scarcely appeared significant, and to apply such a criterion might render the relevant Treaty wording wholly ineffective. The Court then examined the three criteria proposed by the Parliament. The first referred to the fact that expenditure was spread over several years, and the Court agreed that relatively modest annual expenditure could, over a number of years, represent a significant budgetary outlay. It did not, however, accept the criterion of the relative share of the agreement's expenditure in relation to expenditure of the same kind under the budget heading concerned, because budget headings varied considerably in importance so that the relative share could be large even though the expenditure in question was small. Nor did it accept the criterion of the rate of increase in expenditure under the agreement in relation to the financial section of

[27] J Sack, 'The European Community's Membership of International Organizations' (1995) 32 CML Rev 1238; Macleod, Hendry, and Hyett (n 1 above) 102; PJG Kapteyn and P VerLoren van Themaat, *Introduction to the Law of the European Communities* (3rd edn, by LW Gormley, Kluwer Law International, 1998) 1267–8.

[28] See Arts 313–316 TFEU.

[29] Case C–189/97 *European Parliament v. Council* [1999] ECR I–4741.

the previous agreement. That rate could be high, whilst the amounts involved could be small. The Court then returned to the criterion of comparison of the expenditure under an agreement with the overall amount of appropriations designed to finance the Community's external operations, which offered an appropriate means of assessing the financial importance which the agreement actually had for the Community. Further, where a sectoral agreement was involved, as in this case, that criterion could in appropriate cases, and without excluding the possibility of taking other factors into account, be complemented by a comparison between the expenditure entailed by the agreement and the whole of the budgetary appropriations for the sector in question, taking the internal and external aspects together. However, since the sectors varied substantially in terms of their budgetary importance, that examination could not result in the financial implications of an agreement being found to be important where they did not represent a significant share of the appropriations designed to finance the Community's external relations. The Court then applied those criteria to the facts of the case. It pointed out that the five-year period of the agreement with Mauritania was not particularly lengthy, and that the financial compensation provided for, whilst exceeding five per cent of expenditure on fisheries, represented barely more than one per cent of the whole of the payment appropriations allocated for external operations of the Community. This could scarcely be described as important. Lastly, the Court rejected the Parliament's argument that an analogy be drawn with the powers of national parliaments when approving international agreements with financial implications.[30]

The judgment is convincing and useful, and goes some way towards clarifying the term 'important'. None the less, it may not lay to rest differences of opinion between the Council and the Parliament, due to the great imprecision of the Treaty terms, and the Court may have gone about as far as it could in attempting to remedy this. There appear to be two further avenues for greater clarification. The first is to bring a string of further cases before the Court, which is hardly attractive. The second is for the Commission, the Council, and the Parliament to agree on a number of further guiding principles and benchmarks in an inter-institutional agreement.

The Parliament has used its power of consent in a number of cases so as to achieve modifications in agreements, in particular in cases involving human rights.[31]

Commission powers

A last issue concerning the rules on the conclusion of international agreements is whether the Commission has autonomous powers to conclude certain agreements. The question was raised in the past because of the enigmatic opening phrase of (old) Article 300(2) EC: 'Subject to the powers vested in the Commission in this

[30] Ibid, paras 26–34.

[31] See for an overview K Lenaerts and P Van Nuffel, *Constitutional Law of the European Union* (R Bray (ed and trans), Sweet & Maxwell, 1999) 659–60.

field, the signing', etc. It was not impossible to interpret that phrase as recognizing such autonomous powers, but there was no clear indication, in either Article 300 or any other Treaty provision, what those powers might have covered or what the limits of those powers might have been.

In 1991 the Commission made use of what it regarded as its power to conclude certain types of agreements by signing an agreement with the United States in the field of competition law. The aim of the agreement was to promote co-operation and co-ordination, and to lessen the possibility or impact of differences between the parties in the application of their competition laws. The Commission had consulted the Member States, but had not obtained a mandate from the Council and had refused to take account of objections of principle against its powers to conclude the agreement. Thereupon, France challenged the Commission's decision to conclude the agreement before the Court of Justice.[32] In its defence the Commission argued that the agreement constituted an administrative agreement which it was competent to conclude, and that failure to perform the agreement would not result in an international liability claim but merely in termination. The Court did not agree with that analysis. It pointed out that it was the Community alone, having legal personality, which had the capacity to bind itself by concluding international agreements, and that the agreement in question was no doubt binding on the Community and could give rise to liability at international level. The Court also examined the Commission's claim that it had power to conclude what it called international administrative agreements. To that effect, the Commission had built a complex argument based on the French wording of (old) Article 300(2) EC and on the analogy with Article 101 of the EAEC Treaty. Essentially, the Commission took the view that it could derive its powers from sources other than the Treaties, such as the practices followed by the institutions, and that under the EC Treaty it had the same powers to conclude agreements as under Article 101 EAEC.[33] The Court was unimpressed. It referred, *inter alia*, to (current) Article 13(2) TEU, according to which each institution shall act within the limits of the powers conferred upon it in the Treaties. It also pointed out that a mere practice could not override the Treaty provisions. It regarded the analogy with the EAEC Treaty as inappropriate. Lastly, it rejected the argument that the agreement with the United States could be concluded in the light of the Commission's specific powers in the field of competition: that internal power was not such as to alter the allocation of powers between the Community institutions with regard to the conclusion of international agreements. The Court thus

[32] Case C-327/91 *France v. Commission* [1994] ECR I-3641.

[33] Under Art 101 EAEC agreements or contracts whose implementation does not require action by the Council and which can be effected within the limits of the relevant budget are negotiated and concluded solely by the Commission.

upheld the plea of lack of competence, and annulled the act whereby the Commission had concluded the agreement.[34]

From a constitutional perspective, the Court's denial of Commission competence to conclude the agreement with the United States was convincing. A vague and ill-defined provision such as that of the opening sentence of (old) Article 300(2) EC could hardly form the basis for an important law-making power, which the conclusion of international agreements constitutes, particularly as the remainder of the provision was clear in its attribution of competence to the Council. The judgment showed that parallelism between external and internal competences is not necessarily reflected in the balance of powers of the institutions.[35]

Article 219 TFEU

Article 219(3) TFEU, the general provision on the conclusion of agreements concerning monetary or foreign exchange regime matters, simply provides that 'the Council, acting on a recommendation from the Commission and after consulting the European Central Bank, shall decide the arrangements for the negotiation and for the conclusion of such agreements'. The provision does not mention the European Parliament, but it is no doubt in the Council's power to provide for consultation (or even the consent) of the Parliament. The Treaty is more precise as regards formal agreements on an exchange-rate system for the euro in relation to currencies of third States. Article 219(1) TFEU provides that the Council acts either on a recommendation from the European Central Bank (ECB) or on a recommendation from the Commission and after consulting the ECB, and also needs to consult the European Parliament. The role of the ECB is justified on account of its expertise and function in monetary policy-making. In the light of the potential economic importance of international agreements on an exchange-rate system, one wonders whether the consent of the Parliament should not be required.

In the literature it has been suggested that the ECB has autonomous powers to conclude international agreements.[36] This argument derived from the conception that the ECB is an independent international legal person, distinct from the EU. However, it did not find support in the case law of the Court of Justice. In the light of that case law,[37] which characterized the ECB as a Community institution, there was no basis for accepting that the ECB had the power to conclude international agreements on monetary matters. It is only in the small world of banking operations that the ECB is recognized as an international legal person with certain powers,

[34] *France v. Commission* (n 32 above) paras 19–43. In Case C–233/02 *France v. Commission* [2004] ECR I–2759 the Court established that a set of guidelines agreed between the Commission and US authorities were not legally binding and therefore did not violate the Council's prerogative to conclude international agreements.

[35] M Cremona, 'External Relations and External Competence: The Emergence of an Integrated Policy' in P Craig and G de Búrca, *The Evolution of EU Law* (OUP, 1999) 150.

[36] Zilioli and Selmayr (n 19 above) 290–335.

[37] Case C–11/00 *Commission v. ECB* [2003] ECR I–7147.

stemming from the merely operational tasks it is entrusted with.[38] The post-Lisbon TEU now confirms that the ECB forms part of the EU's institutional framework in much the same way as any of the other institutions (see Article 13 TEU).

Implementation, amendment, and adoption of EU positions

Once concluded, an international agreement needs to be implemented and applied. This raises the question of the effects, in EU law, of an international agreement concluded by the EU. In that respect, Article 216(2) TFEU merely provides that agreements are binding on the institutions of the Union and on Member States. As the question of the legal effects of an agreement raises complex issues, it is dealt with separately in Chapter 9.

However, Article 218 TFEU contains a few further provisions on decision-making related to implementing, applying, and amending an agreement. First, Article 218(9) addresses decision-making as regards 'the positions to be adopted on the Union's behalf in a body set up by an agreement, when that body is called upon to adopt acts having legal effect, with the exception of acts supplementing or amending the institutional framework of the agreement'.[39] That provision was inserted by the Amsterdam Treaty. Originally, it related only to association agreements, but the Treaty of Nice broadened this to any agreement. EU decision-making on such positions follows the same procedure as that for the conclusion of an agreement, the Council acting on a proposal from the Commission or the High Representative. However, the Parliament is not involved by way of consultation or consent. The justification for that is said to be the frequency with which such positions may be called for, which would mean that parliamentary involvement would impair effective EU participation in these bodies.[40]

Secondly, on the subject of modification of an agreement, Article 218(7) TFEU provides: 'the Council may, by derogation from paragraphs 5, 6 and 9, authorize the negotiator to approve on the Union's behalf modifications to the agreement where it provides for them to be adopted by a simplified procedure or by a body set up by the agreement. The Council may attach specific conditions to such authorization'.

[38] CW Herrmann, 'Monetary Sovereignty over the Euro and External Relations of the Euro Area: Competences, Procedures and Practice' (2002) 7 EFA Rev 9.

[39] See J Helikoski, 'Adoption of Positions under Mixed Agreements (Implementation)' in C Hillion and P Koutrakos (eds), *Mixed Agreements Revisited—The EU and its Member States in the World* (Hart Publishing, 2010) 138.

[40] A Dashwood, 'External Relations Provisions of the Amsterdam Treaty' in D O'Keeffe and P Twomey (eds), *Legal Issues of the Amsterdam Treaty* (Hart Publishing, 1999) 207. On the legal effects in Community law of decisions adopted by bodies set up under an agreement, see Ch 9. In Case C–370/07 *Commission v. Council* [2009] ECR I–8917 the Court decided that a Council decision establishing the positions to be adopted on behalf of the Community in a body established by an international convention has to identify its legal basis in the Treaties.

In the absence of such an authorization one would expect the standard procedure for the conclusion of an agreement to extend to its modification. That follows from the fact that the legal consequences of conclusion and modification are the same: the EU enters into specific international commitments.

Suspension and termination

The original EEC Treaty did not contain provisions on how to suspend or terminate an international agreement. That lacuna was partly filled by the Amsterdam Treaty amendments. There is now some Treaty language concerning the suspension of an international agreement, no doubt as the result of a couple of cases of threatened or applied suspension which created problems (see below). There are, however, no provisions on terminating an agreement: here again one would expect the same procedure to apply as that governing the conclusion of the agreement.

Article 218(9) TFEU in essence provides that a decision to suspend the application of an agreement follows the procedure for conclusion, only without the Parliament's involvement. The Parliament's lack of real powers here is more noteworthy than with respect to decisions by bodies set up under an agreement. This is an area where the Parliament is often quite vocal, because the (threatened) suspension of an international agreement is a highly political act in external relations. The refusal to involve the Parliament more fully signals a reluctance by the Treaty drafters to enable it to interfere with questions of general foreign policy.[41]

The provisions on suspension must be seen against the backdrop of the EU's policy on suspending international agreements, particularly in the case of human rights violations. After having fared somewhat badly with the suspension of a co-operation agreement with Yugoslavia at the time of the war in and between the various Republics of the former Yugoslavia, because the agreement did not contain a suspension clause,[42] the institutions developed the practice of including suspension provisions in agreements with third countries. It must also be noted that suspension and termination raise delicate questions in the case of mixed agreements (see Chapter 7).

Conclusions

The procedure for concluding international agreements has been substantially modified in the course of time, on the whole in the direction of greater involvement of the European Parliament. As such, the modifications correspond to the gradual expansion of the Parliament's role in the internal legislative process. It is of course true that a stronger parliamentary role is no panacea for the issues of

[41] See also Ch 11.
[42] See Case C–162/96 *Racke v. Hauptzollamt Mainz* [1998] ECR I–3655, analysed in Ch 9.

democracy and legitimacy afflicting the EU in the conduct of its external relations. Formal democratic processes are no guarantee of effective democracy. Even in the absence of a formal role, the Parliament may be able to influence the process of decision-making through the authority of its positions, as has to some extent been the case in the area of trade policy.[43] Such informal input is, however, no substitute for constitutional guarantees of involvement. Formal parliamentary scrutiny at European level may not be sufficient, but is certainly indispensable in order to attain higher levels of legitimacy and accountability.

One can distinguish three types of argument against greater involvement by the Parliament in the process of negotiating and concluding international agreements. Such involvement may be too cumbersome and time-consuming and thus obstruct effective international decision-making. The open parliamentary process is ill-suited to an international negotiation, which may require a measure of secrecy more conducive to striking deals. And certain agreements are so technical as to resist involvement by non-experts. None of those arguments is convincing. It is clear that parliamentary input is not required for each and every agreement, and the relevant constitutional rules should be aimed at defining those agreements which raise issues necessitating parliamentary scrutiny. The secrecy and effectiveness arguments do not recognize the important law-making function of many international agreements. For the negotiation of such agreements, the search for greater effectiveness cannot justify the absence of public debate to which secrecy gives rise.

The current provisions of Article 218 TFEU go a long way towards recognizing the role of the Parliament. Further improvements are none the less conceivable.

At present, the Parliament's formal role is limited to the phase of the conclusion of an agreement, where the Parliament is either consulted or needs to give its consent. Conclusion of course takes place when the negotiations are finished, and even if the requirement of parliamentary scrutiny may allow the Parliament to influence the negotiations, in particular where its consent is needed, there is scope for a formal role in the decision to open negotiations and in the negotiations themselves.

The non-participation of the Parliament in decisions to suspend an international agreement and in the establishment of positions to be adopted in a body set up under an agreement (with the exception of institutional-type decisions) is difficult to justify. Decisions on suspension are nearly always highly charged political acts, and the fact that the Parliament may be more vocal in this area does not warrant its exclusion from the decision-making process. As regards decisions by bodies set up under an agreement, often such decisions have a significant law-making function,[44] meriting parliamentary involvement as much as the conclusion of agreements in

[43] Macleod, Hendry, and Hyett (n 1 above) 98–100.

[44] E.g. decisions of the EC–Turkey Association Council; see Ch 9 for case law regarding such decisions.

areas where the legislative procedure applies. The Parliament also continues to be excluded from participation in the negotiation and conclusion of agreements on CFSP matters. That is clearly untenable. The EU is developing its defence capacity, it is setting up military operations, it is concluding international agreements regarding such operations, and no parliamentary organ is formally involved in the process.

7

Mixed external action and membership of international organizations

Introduction

Previous chapters discussed the EU's external competence and treaty-making powers. The analysis revealed that the Treaties enable the EU institutions to undertake external action in many different areas of policy-making, often broadly defined. The Treaties provide for an impressive array of legal foundations for external action. The dimensions of the actual practice based on those foundations are equally impressive. However, notwithstanding those firm and broad foundations, that practice is generally characterized by what has come to be denoted as mixity: more often than not, international agreements are concluded by the EU and its Member States, acting jointly, rather than the EU simply acting on its own. It is difficult to quantify this phenomenon, as there are so many different types of conventional international law-making, but all observers agree that mixity is a hallmark of the EU's external relations.[1] 'Pure' EU agreements are more exceptional than one would expect in the light of the legal foundations.

The *prima facie* legal justification for a mixed agreement is that parts of the agreement do not come within the EU's competence, and that conclusion of the

[1] E.g. I Macleod, ID Hendry, and S Hyett, *The External Relations of the European Communities* (OUP, 1996) 142; D McGoldrick, *International Relations Law of the European Union* (Longman, 1997) 78; C Kaddous, *Le droit des relations extérieures dans la jurisprudence de la Cour de justice des Communautés européennes* (Helbing & Lichtenhahn, 1998) 263; PJG Kapteyn and P VerLoren van Themaat, *Introduction to the Law of the European Communities* (3rd edn, by LW Gormley, Kluwer Law International, 1998) 1263; M Cremona, 'External Relations and External Competence: The Emergence of an Integrated Policy' in P Craig and G de Búrca (eds), *The Evolution of EU Law* (OUP, 1999) 154; K Lenaerts and P Van Nuffel, *Constitutional Law of the European Union* (R Bray (ed and trans), Sweet & Maxwell, 1999) 648; J Heliskoski, *Mixed Agreements as a Technique for Organizing the International Relations of the European Community and its Member States* (Kluwer Law International, 2001) 3 and Appendix 1 (list of mixed agreements); M Dony, 'Les accords mixtes' in J-V Louis and M Dony (eds), *Commentaire J Megret—Relations extérieures* (Etudes européennes, 2005) ch 6; P Koutrakos, *EU International Relations Law* (Hart Publishing, 2006) ch 4; E Neframi, *Les accords mixtes de la Communauté européenne: aspects communautaires et internationaux* (Bruylant, 2007); R Holdgaard, *External Relations Law of the European Community—Legal Reasoning and Legal Discourses* (Wolters Kluwer, 2008) ch 8; G De Baere, *Constitutional Principles of EU External Relations* (OUP, 2008) ch 7; C Hillion and P Koutrakos (eds), *Mixed Agreements Revisited—The EU and its Member States in the world* (Hart Publishing, 2010).

agreement therefore requires joint action by the EU and its Member States, the latter complementing, as it were, the otherwise insufficient powers of the EU.

This chapter aims to analyse the law and practice of mixed external action. It does not, however, merely concentrate on the conclusion of international agreements. It also addresses EU membership of international organizations. In principle this could be dealt with separately, as such membership presents a number of political and legal problems of its own, and as there is no logical link with mixity: the EU could, in theory, become a member of an international organization without any of its Member States also being a member. In practice, however, there are virtually no examples of sole EU membership. The EU's participation in the work of other international organizations is thus also governed by mixity, and the problems to which the latter gives rise in this context are similar to those created by mixed agreements—as well as often being more acute. Further, both the conclusion of mixed agreements and mixed membership of international organizations are governed by the same overarching legal principle identified by the Court of Justice, namely the duty of co-operation between the Member States and the EU institutions.

The structure of this chapter is as follows. It first provides a general and concise overview of the practice and its causes, as regards both mixed agreements and membership of international organizations. It then analyses the case law on the duty of co-operation between the EU and the Member States, and attempts to spell out the foundations and possible impact of that overarching principle. The chapter subsequently turns to a number of the problems and legal issues to which mixity gives rise.

Cause and practice of mixed agreements

Competence

The legal justification for mixity is that an agreement cannot be concluded by the EU alone, because its competences do not cover the entire agreement. Several authors have attempted to draw up a classification or typology of mixed agreements, centred on the scope and nature of the EU's competences.[2] However, the practice of mixity does not readily lend itself to such attempts.[3] The interaction between the diverse external powers of the EU and the multitude and variety of international conventions, treaties, and agreements is such that classification may have the effect, either of over-simplifying the phenomenon, or of rendering it even

[2] See for such a classification A Rosas, 'The European Union and Mixed Agreements' in A Dashwood and C Hillion (eds), *The General Law of EC External Relations* (Sweet & Maxwell, 2000) 203–7.

[3] NA Neuwahl, 'Joint Participation in International Treaties and the Exercise of Power by the EEC and its Member States: Mixed Agreements' (1991) 28 CML Rev 717.

less accessible. Moreover, such interaction does not take place in a theoretical legal sphere, but rather in the day-to-day politics of the EU. It is therefore preferable to look at the practice on its own merits, and not to base oneself on a preconceived typology.[4]

Notwithstanding that approach, it is necessary at the outset to recapitulate a few basic principles of external competence. A first distinction is between exclusive and non-exclusive competences. The former are limited to the customs union; competition rules necessary for the functioning of the internal market; monetary policy for the Member States whose currency is the euro; the conservation of marine biological resources; the common commercial policy; and certain implied powers (see Article 3 TFEU). Whenever the provisions of an international agreement are fully covered by any of those exclusive EU competences only the EU is entitled to conclude the agreement. In practice, such exclusive competence is limited to commercial policy and fisheries, as there are very few examples of international agreements which fall wholly within the Community's exclusive implied powers, or within any of the other express exclusive competences. As regards non-exclusive EU powers it is appropriate to distinguish between the shared competences listed in Article 4 TFEU, and the co-ordinating, supporting, and supplementing competences set out in Articles 5 and 6 TFEU. In the case of shared competences, the Member States retain the competence to conclude an agreement for as long as the EU has not made use of its own competence, and thus has not 'occupied the field'. Examples of such powers are transport, and environmental and agricultural policy.

In the literature on external competence and mixed agreements, such non-exclusive treaty-making competences are often termed 'potential' or 'virtual'.[5] It is indicative that this terminology is used only to denote external powers, and not for the EU's internal legislative competence. The terms are confusing, as the EU's non-exclusive external competences are, in legal terms, every bit as real as (and in many cases co-extensive with) its internal competences. It is in the nature of competences that they enable public action, and the competence question logically precedes its exercise. Potentiality is thus the very hallmark of all competences. However, it is not without reason that non-exclusive external competences have been characterized as potential or virtual. The terminology is in effect a reflection of the fact that, often, a mixed agreement is concluded where it is legally possible for the EU to conclude the agreement on its own, without the participation of the Member States, by making use of these 'potential' or 'virtual' competences. It has been noted that at the political level in the EU there is a tendency to consider that, unless an agreement falls wholly within the exclusive competence of the EU, mixity is required.[6]

[4] But see, for a valiant attempt at classification, M Maresceau, 'A Typology of Mixed Bilateral Agreements' in Hillion and Koutrakos (n 1 above) 11.

[5] CD Ehlermann, 'Mixed Agreements—A List of Problems' in D O'Keeffe and HG Schermers (eds), *Mixed Agreements* (Kluwer, 1983) 6.

[6] Rosas (n 2 above) 206.

Practice and case law

The following short survey of the practice is written from a historical perspective, and attempts to make reference to the different kinds of mixed agreements as well as to the intervening statements (which are rather limited) made by the Court of Justice.

The practice of negotiating and concluding mixed agreements has existed since the early days of the Community, and thus pre-dates the case law of the Court of Justice on external competence.[7] Mixity none the less soon came before the Court. As early as the *AETR* case,[8] the Court was confronted with a situation where the Member States were required to engage in further negotiation of the European Road Transport Agreement, on the basis of a common position reached in the Council, constituting the exercise of Community competence in the field of transport. In *Kramer* the Court similarly pointed out that, as long as the Community had not fully exercised its functions in the matter of the conservation of fish resources, as was the case at the time, the Member States were under a duty, together with the Community institutions, to use all political and legal means at their disposal in order to ensure participation of the Community in the North-East Atlantic Fisheries Convention.[9] Both judgments were in that respect a first expression and reflection of the need for the Community and its Member States to co-operate in the conduct of external relations.

The Court's first serious attempt to grapple with issues of mixity was *Opinion 1/76*.[10] As discussed in Chapter 3, the Court in this case confirmed and developed the doctrine of implied powers in relation to transport policy. The Court did more than that, however. Chapter 3 discussed the Court's apparent need to find a justification for the participation, as contracting parties to the draft agreement, of six of the then nine Member States. It was submitted that this need was not explained by a finding of exclusive Community competence. In the Opinion, the Court did not suggest exclusivity, nor did it at any other time accept that the Community or the EU has exclusive competence over transport. EU competence in matters of transport is shared with Member State competence. None the less, the Court felt compelled to address the 'special problem' arising from the participation by six Member States. It pointed out that those six States were parties to two earlier conventions, which would need to be amended, as provided for by Article 3 of the draft agreement. The undertaking to carry out such amendment explained and justified the participation by those Member States, which had to be considered 'as being solely for this purpose and not as necessary for the attainment of other features of

[7] See e.g. the association agreements with Greece ([1974] OJ Spec Ed 2nd Series, PE 1, 4) and with Turkey ([1964] JO 217).

[8] Case 22/70 *Commission v. Council* [1971] ECR 263; see Ch 3.

[9] Joined Cases 3, 4, and 6/76 *Kramer* [1976] ECR 1279, paras 34–35; see again Ch 3.

[10] *Opinion 1/76 re draft Agreement establishing a European laying-up fund for inland waterway vessels* [1977] ECR 741.

the system'.[11] The Court moreover considered that, under Article 4 of the agreement, enforceability extended to the territories of all the Member States, and that, except for this special undertaking, the legal effects of the agreement resulted, in accordance with (current) Article 216(2) TFEU, exclusively from the conclusion by the Community.[12] In those circumstances, the Court decided that the participation of the six Member States was not such as to encroach on the external power of the Community.[13] By contrast, the Court did consider that the participation of those six States in the negotiations had led to results beyond their objective, as defined above. To summarize the Court's analysis, it pointed out that the part played by the Community institutions in the bodies and organs which the agreement set up was extremely limited, and that the provisions of the agreement called into question the power of the institutions, and altered in a manner inconsistent with the Treaty the relationships between Member States within the context of the Community. The agreement constituted both a surrender of the independence of action of the Community in its external relations and a change in the internal constitution of the Community. As a result, the Court's Opinion on the compatibility of these aspects with the Treaty was negative. It expressly mentioned that the possibility that the agreement might constitute the model for future arrangements in other fields had confirmed it in its critical attitude: the repetition of such procedures was in fact likely progressively to undo the work of the Community irreversibly.[14]

Opinion 1/76 thus constituted an attempt by the Court to carry out a significant review of a particular manifestation of mixity. Cremona observed that the Court had seen that the danger of mixed agreements (and their attraction for Member States) lay in their tendency to over-emphasize, at the expense of the Community, the participation of the Member States as traditional international legal persons.[15] In any event, the most convincing reading of this section of *Opinion 1/76* is that, where an agreement comes entirely within the Community's (now the EU's) shared competences, such as those for developing a common transport policy, as was the case here, mixity requires a specific justification and is not simply optional.[16] There is considerable logic in such an approach. As mentioned above, shared competences are as real as exclusive ones. The difference between them is only that the EU may decide not to exercise its shared competence and leave it to the Member States to act. Thus, in an area of shared competence, such as transport or environmental

[11] Ibid, para 7.

[12] Art 216(2) TFEU provides that agreements concluded by the EU are binding on the institutions and on the Member States: see Ch 9.

[13] *Opinion 1/76* (n 10 above) para 7.

[14] Ibid, paras 8–14.

[15] M Cremona, 'The Doctrine of Exclusivity and the Position of Mixed Agreements in the External Relations of the European Community' (1982) 12 OJLS 414.

[16] CWA Timmermans, 'Division of External Powers between Community and Member States in the Field of Harmonization of National Law—A Case Study' in CWA Timmermans and ELM Völker (eds), *Division of Powers between the European Communities and their Member States in the Field of External Relations* (Kluwer, 1981) 20.

protection, the EU may decide not to participate in an international negotiation or not to conclude a particular agreement. However, where the EU does become a party, and the agreement comes entirely within its competence, it is difficult to see the justification for mixity. The EU then decides to exercise its competence for only one part of the agreement, as it were, and not to exercise it for another. Yet, particularly where all the Member States become parties themselves, as is the standard approach, there is no mistaking that the agreement will establish common rules for the entire EU. In that case, mixity, with all its associated difficulties (as discussed below), could, at least in some cases, be considered to violate Article 4(3) TEU: by participating in the agreement the Member States may be making it more difficult and cumbersome for the EU to achieve its objectives.

After *Opinion 1/76* the Court did not have, or take, many more opportunities to scrutinize the use of mixity as such. In *Ruling 1/78*, an EAEC Treaty case which is also looked at below, it was undisputed that certain provisions of the convention at issue did not come within the powers of the EAEC, and the Court simply recognized that the convention concerned in part the jurisdiction of the Member States and in part that of the Community.[17] Then came *Opinion 1/78*, on the (at the time) important question of competence for the conclusion of international commodity agreements in the framework of UNCTAD. The Court's decision in that case, despite affirming the wide scope of the Treaty provisions on a common commercial policy, appeared much more accommodating towards mixity. As discussed in Chapter 2, the Court considered that, if the Member States were to finance the buffer stock which was to be the central element of the International Agreement on Natural Rubber, their participation in the agreement was necessary, and the agreement thus had to be mixed. It also pointed out that, in any event, mixity was required in so far as certain Member States represented 'dependent territories' not belonging to the Community, whilst stressing that the Member States in question could on this basis participate only in their capacity as representatives of these territories.[18] The latter illustrates that mixity may have many different causes.

Opinion 1/78 was criticized for accepting Member State participation too easily, and for not ruling that, as the agreement came within the Community's exclusive trade policy competence, the Community ought to have ensured financing of the buffer stock.[19] The Opinion led to one of the first major institutional settlements in favour of mixity. In 1981 the Council adopted the so-called 'PROBA 20' arrangement, a compromise 'intended to improve the Community's external image and to

[17] *Ruling 1/78 re Convention on the Physical Protection of Nuclear Materials, Facilities and Transports* [1978] ECR 2151, para 31.

[18] *Opinion 1/78 re International Agreement on Natural Rubber* [1979] ECR 2871, paras 52–62. As regards overseas countries and territories, see also *Opinion 2/91 re Convention No 170 of the ILO* [1993] ECR I-1061, para 35.

[19] JHH Weiler, 'The External Legal Relations of Non-Unitary Actors: Mixity and the Federal Principle' in O'Keeffe and Schermers (n 5 above) 72, idem in *The Constitution of Europe* (CUP, 1999) 174; Kapteyn and VerLoren van Themaat (n 1 above) 1281; Cremona (n 15 above) 418–19.

strengthen its internal cohesion and solidarity'.[20] It was based on the understanding that all legal and institutional considerations regarding the respective competences of the Community and the Member States were to be set aside, and that instead the Community and the Member States would participate jointly in all the commodities agreements concerned, and that such participation would involve a joint delegation expressing the joint position with a single voice.[21] That approach was indeed followed for these types of agreements.[22]

In the 1970s and early 1980s the Community participated, together with the Member States, in negotiations leading to the UN Convention on the Law of the Sea (UNCLOS), one of the most wide-ranging and complex mixed agreements ever to be concluded by the Community.[23] The latter's participation was necessary in the light of its exclusive competence in matters of the conservation of fish resources. In contrast with most mixed negotiations, the Community and its Member States did not in this case manage to assume an overall common position. Indeed, Simmonds reports a comment according to which the only issue on which the group was united was advocating the right of the Community to become a party to the Convention, and characterizes the comment as harsh, but not unjust.[24] Community signature and participation were not readily accepted by non-member countries, and there was in particular a lack of understanding of, and fear for, the consequences of Community participation if not all the Member States were to become parties. Other delicate problems concerned the consequences for third States of the progressive expansion of the Community's treaty-making powers; membership of Convention institutions and voting rights; responsibility for breach of obligations; and participation in the dispute-settlement procedures.[25] In the end, Community signature and participation were permitted, subject, however, to fairly stringent conditions, laid down in Annex IX to the Convention. The annex enables an international organization to join the Convention, provided a majority of its Member States are joining as well. It also spells out that the organization's participation is limited to matters coming within its competence, and that it does not have rights and obligations beyond those matters. Article 4(5) expressly provides that the participation of an international organization 'shall in no case confer any rights under this Convention on member States of the organization which are not States Parties to this Convention'.

[20] The text was never officially published, but can be found in ELM Völker and J Steenbergen, *Leading Cases and Materials on the External Relations Law of the EC* (Kluwer, 1985) 48. For comments see Ehlermann (n 5 above) 8–9; J Groux, 'Mixed Negotiations' in O'Keeffe and Schermers (n 5 above) 96; KR Simmonds, 'The European Community and the New Law of the Sea' (1989/VI) 218 Hague Recueil 39–40; J Sack, 'The European Community's Membership of International Organizations' (1995) 32 CML Rev 1253.

[21] Ehlermann (n 5 above).

[22] See e.g. Council Decision 96/704 concerning the provisional application of the International Natural Rubber Agreement 1995 by the Community [1996] OJ L324/1.

[23] See Simmonds (n 20 above); M Ederer, *Die Europäische Wirtschaftsgemeinschaft und die Seerechtskonvention der Vereinten Nationen von 1982* (Verlag V. Florentz, 1988).

[24] Ibid, 115. [25] Ibid, 108–9.

UNCLOS is, to some extent, a model for mixity as regards other multilateral instruments in the areas of transport, environmental protection, and fisheries. As a rule, the EU participates in such instruments together with the Member States, and the requirement of submitting a declaration of competences is not unusual.

The 1970s and 1980s were also the period of development and expansion of the Community's relationships with the ACP countries, through the successive Lomé Conventions (later replaced by the Cotonou Convention). Those conventions were all mixed agreements, as they were wide-ranging instruments for North–South co-operation, drawing extensively upon the Member States' resources. One important feature of the Lomé Conventions was that they generally took care to indicate whether the obligations they created were binding on the Community, on its Member States, or on both.[26]

Whereas mixity is clearly justified for these conventions, there can be more doubts as regards some of the association agreements concluded on the basis of (current) Article 217 TFEU, where mixity is again the rule. The Court's ruling in *Demirel* clarified that the Community's powers under this provision were extensive, in the sense that it enabled the Community to undertake commitments in all the areas covered by the Treaty.[27] It would therefore not require much creative effort or loss of subject matter to design association agreements in such a way that they may be concluded as pure EU agreements. Often the only justification for mixity has been that such agreements also provided for a political dialogue, which was beyond the EC's competence.[28] Similar considerations apply to partnership agreements and to certain types of bilateral agreement in the trade and investment domain.

In the 1980s and 1990s, the most complex mixed negotiation was the GATT Uruguay Round, leading to the establishment of the WTO. In practice, however, the negotiations themselves did not give rise to particular problems of mixity, as the Community's preponderant role was recognized and accepted by the Member States.[29] It was only towards the end of the negotiations that the issue of mixity was raised, engendering the great legal battle of *Opinion 1/94*.[30] As regards the political sensitivity of the Member States' role in the creation of this new organization, one may again refer to the signing episode at the Marrakesh Ministerial Conference.[31] The Court's Opinion was extensively discussed in Chapters 2 and 3, and its statements on the duty of co-operation are examined below. There

[26] See the case law discussed in Ch 4.

[27] Case 12/86 *Demirel v. Stadt Schwäbisch Gmünd* [1987] ECR 3719; see Ch 4.

[28] See e.g. Europe Agreements establishing an association between the European Communities and their Member States, of the one part, and the Republic of Hungary, of the other part [1993] OJ L347/2, Arts 2–5. It remains to be seen what the approach will be after Lisbon, given the express treaty-making powers also in the area of the CFSP.

[29] P Van den Bossche, 'The European Community and the Uruguay Round Agreements' in JH Jackson and AO Sykes (eds), *Implementing the Uruguay Round* (OUP, 1997) 53–9.

[30] *Opinion 1/94 re WTO Agreement* [1994] ECR I-5267.

[31] See Ch 2.

is, however, one aspect of the Opinion to which attention may be drawn here. The Commission's request for an Opinion was to some extent ambiguous on an issue which was crucial from the perspective of the law on mixity. The overall tenor of the Commission's submissions was to establish that the Community's competence over all matters covered by the WTO Agreement was exclusive,[32] yet there was some suggestion, particularly in the formulation of the actual questions, that the Commission was also inquiring into the scope of the Community's non-exclusive competences. The Court, however, did not read the Commission's request in such a way and, prompted by submissions of the Council, ruled that the Opinion was concerned only with the question of exclusive competence.[33] As a result, the Opinion did not systematically analyse whether the Community's shared competences in the areas of services and intellectual property covered the WTO Agreement. The Court did not pass the threshold of exclusivity, and declined to rule on whether mixity is permitted in the case of the exercise of shared ('potential' or 'virtual') competences. That approach was markedly different from the intense scrutiny of mixity in *Opinion 1/76*. It is particularly in this regard, and arguably only in this regard, that *Opinion 1/94* can be said to be more conservative and deferential towards the Member States' international action than some earlier rulings.[34]

This survey may be concluded by referring to more recent practice as regards bilateral trade and co-operation agreements. Here it appears that the Court's judgment in *Portugal v. Council*, on the Co-operation Agreement with India,[35] has stimulated recourse to pure Community agreements. As Rosas reported, it became the practice of the Community to conclude fairly comprehensive agreements, providing for co-operation in many different areas, on its own.[36]

Causes

It is useful to explore somewhat the causes and reasons for the persistent recourse to mixity. In this respect, the analysis by Ehlermann, even if it dates from the early 1980s, continues to stand out.[37] As he indicated, there appeared to be few, if

[32] N Neuwahl, 'The WTO Opinion and Implied External Powers of the Community—A Hidden Agenda?' in Dashwood and Hillion (n 2 above) 141.

[33] See *Opinion 1/94* (n 30 above) 5282–3. CWA Timmermans, 'Organising Joint Participation of EC and Member States' in Dashwood and Hillion (n 2 above) 240.

[34] E.g. J de la Rochère, 'L'ère des compétences partagées' (1995) 390 RMCUE 446; JHJ Bourgeois, 'The EC in the WTO and Advisory Opinion 1/94: An Echternach Procession' (1995) 32 CML Rev 780; M Hilf, 'The ECJ's Opinion 1/94 on the WTO—No Surprise, but Wise?' (1995) 6 EJIL 254 and 258.

[35] Case C–268/94 *Portugal v. Council* [1996] ECR I–6177; see Ch 4.

[36] Rosas (n 2 above) 218.

[37] Ehlermann (n 5 above) 4–9. The author was at the time Director-General of the Commission's Legal Service. See also JHJ Bourgeois, 'Mixed Agreements: A New Approach?' in JHJ Bourgeois, J-L Dewost, and M-A Gaiffe (eds), *La Communauté européenne et les accords mixtes—Quelles Perspectives?* (Interuniversity Press, 1997) 83–6; Helikoski (n 1 above) 9–21.

any, 'external' reasons for recourse to mixity: it was not the case in practice that non-member countries insisted on mixity. Mixity was therefore almost exclusively the outcome of decision-making processes internal to the Community. Ehlermann pointed out that mixity could often be avoided if the Council wanted to avoid it, either by limiting the subject matter of an agreement to the Community's existing powers, or by adopting a broader interpretation of those powers. In particular, certain mixed agreements could be avoided if the Council was willing to make use of 'virtual', non-exclusive powers, but it was most reluctant to do so. One of the reasons for that attitude was purely political: 'Member States wish to continue to appear as contracting parties in order to remain visible and identifiable actors on the international scene'.[38] The European Commission often acquiesced in the use of mixity to avoid inter-institutional tension. In any event it could only challenge mixity before the Court of Justice, and recourse to the Court was considered to be an instrument of coercion in a struggle for power. Acceptance of mixity could also be a means of achieving acceptance of Community participation, even in the case of agreements where the part covered by Community competence was small. Further, the mixed agreement formula avoided the necessity of agreeing on the exact delimitation of Community and Member States' powers, a subject of obvious complexity—unless of course non-member countries insisted on such delimitation. Ehlermann summed up his analysis by concluding that 'the attempt to reach exclusive Community participation usually means tension and inter-institutional struggle while the mixed agreement formula is considered as implying mutual understanding, accommodation and peace-making'.[39] There is one further and obvious reason for mixity which Rosas noted:[40] mixed agreements to which all the Member States are parties inevitably require unanimity, since all the Member States need to conclude and ratify the agreement in accordance with domestic constitutional requirements, whereas pure EU agreements may be concluded by the Council with qualified majority voting, depending on the subject matter.[41] As an example of an area where such considerations no doubt play an important role one may refer to negotiations on trade in services in the WTO. *Opinion 1/94*,[42] by deciding that GATS came within the joint competence of the Community and its Member States, enabled each Member State government to insist upon agreeing with the detail of any GATS negotiation. The complex revision of Article 133 EC in the Treaty of Nice confirmed the importance of the voting issue in these areas, and the latest version of the commercial policy provisions continues to provide for unanimity in certain cases (Article 207(4) TFEU).[43]

[38] Ehlermann (n 5 above) 6.

[39] Ibid, 9.

[40] Rosas (n 2 above) 202; the author was at the time Director for External Relations in the Commission's Legal Service.

[41] Art 218(8) TFEU; see Ch 6.

[42] N 30 above.

[43] See Ch 2.

Membership of international organizations

Membership and non-membership

There are no Treaty provisions generally regulating possible EU membership of an international organization.[44] The Treaty of Lisbon has, however, introduced, in the TFEU provisions on external action, a Title VI on the Union's relations with international organizations and third countries and Union delegations. In substance, the relevant provisions are not much different from preceding EC Treaty articles. Article 220 TFEU provides that the EU 'shall establish all appropriate forms of co-operation with the organs of the United Nations and its specialized agencies, the Council of Europe, the Organization for Security and Cooperation in Europe and the Organization for Economic Cooperation and Development'. It further provides that the EU 'shall also maintain such relations as are appropriate with other international organizations', and that the High Representative for Foreign Affairs and Security Policy 'shall be instructed to implement this Article'. Article 221 provides that 'Union delegations in third countries and at international organizations shall represent the Union'; and that 'Union delegations shall be placed under the authority of the High Representative' and 'shall act in close co-operation with Member States' diplomatic and consular missions'. EU membership of an international organization is not expressly envisaged in those Treaty provisions.[45] The Treaties are none the less not an obstacle to EU accession to an international organization. There is agreement that the EU may exercise its competences, in the external sphere, through accession to an organization which deals with matters coming within those competences.[46] External competences are not limited to concluding international agreements, but extend to joining international organizations and participating in their work.[47] Implicitly, that is confirmed by *Opinion 1/94*, where the Court acknowledged EU competence for the creation of the WTO.[48]

In practice, however, EU membership of international organizations stands in sharp contrast to its treaty-making activity. Whereas the latter is fully fledged and

[44] General literature includes: Sack (n 20 above); R Frid, *The Relations between the EC and International Organizations—Legal Theory and Practice* (Kluwer, 1995); E Denza, 'The Community as a Member of International Organizations' in N Emiliou and D O'Keeffe, *The EU and World Trade Law after the GATT Uruguay Round* (John Wiley & Sons, 1996); Macleod, Hendry, and Hyett (n 1 above) ch 7; I Govaere, J Capiau, and A Vermeersch, 'In-Between Seats: The Participation of the European Union in International Organizations' (2004) 9 EFA Rev 155; C Flaesch-Mougin, 'Les relations avec les organisations internationales et la participation à celles-ci' in Louis and Dony (n 1 above) 337; F Hoffmeister, 'Outsider or Frontrunner? Recent Developments under International and European Law on the Status of the European Union in International Organizations and Treaty Bodies' (2007) 44 CML Rev 41.

[45] A number of other Treaty provisions speak of co-operation with international organizations in specific areas, e.g. Art 191(4) TFEU.

[46] *Opinion 1/76* (n 10 above) para 5.

[47] See for a fuller analysis Frid (n 44 above) 119–32 and 345–59.

[48] N 30 above.

largely corresponds to the EU's competences, even if agreements may be mixed, full EU membership of international organizations is much more limited. Following Sack's approach,[49] one can distinguish between accession to an international organization as such, i.e. an organization with an independent existence and a genuine membership structure, and participation in an international treaty on a specific subject which creates some sort of organizational structure. This section concentrates on the former category; as regards the latter, it is difficult to draw the dividing line with mixed agreements generally, since treaty-making, particularly at multilateral level, is increasingly accompanied by the creation of various institutions and bodies. At the level of international organizations as such, EU accession has been confined to the FAO, the EBRD, the WTO, the Codex Alimentarius Commission, and the Hague Conference on Private International Law.[50] The EU is not a member of the United Nations or of any of the major UN organizations, except for the FAO. It is not, for example, a member of the ILO, in spite of its significant competences and legislative activity in the field of social policy. It is not a member of the IMO, even if it has extensive competences in maritime matters. It is not a member of the IMF or the World Bank. Nor is it a member of the Council of Europe. These are all international organizations dealing, at least from time to time, with matters within the province of the EU.

If the Treaties are not an obstacle, what then are the causes of the EU's apparent incapacity to join international organizations? Some of those causes are similar to those for recourse to mixed agreements. The Member States are reluctant to abandon their role in international organizations by promoting the EU's entry, let alone by ceding their place to the EU, essentially for reasons of sovereignty.[51] In contrast to mixed agreements, however, there are also significant difficulties at international level. The most basic of these is that, traditionally, and in particular within the UN system, international organizations permit accession only by States. Whenever that is the case, EU accession requires modification of the organization's constitutional rules, and it may be difficult to persuade third countries, members of the organization, that such modification is in their interest or is appropriate. Such modification is not simply a threshold issue. When the EU joins, its Member States continue to be members, and this mixed membership gives rise to complex issues of participation in the organization's decision-making processes. A central issue concerns voting rights. How many votes will accrue to the EU? How does one allocate voting rights? Should this be on an alternative basis, or can the EU add its vote to those of the Member States? Other members of the organization would find the latter difficult to accept. Yet if the former approach is taken one needs to define in which cases the EU, and in which cases its Member States, have the right to vote. Third countries are also concerned about questions of responsibility, and may wonder

[49] Sack (n 20 above) 1238–9.

[50] For a more detailed overview see Hoffmeister (n 44 above).

[51] Sack (n 20 above) 1233.

whether the EU can require its Member States to keep to the commitments it has entered into. Also, there may be concern that EU participation would lead to the formation of 'blocks' within an organization.[52]

The apprehensive approach towards EU membership, particularly within the UN system, is well illustrated by an opinion of the UN legal office on the occasion of Community accession to the FAO. As regards the alternative exercise of membership rights, which was the solution adopted in the FAO for organizing participation by the Community and its Member States (see below), the opinion took the view that this should remain confined to the FAO and should not be used to justify attempts to encroach on the principle of 'one state one vote' contained in Article 18 of the UN Charter. A change in the Charter on this critical issue was considered to have no realistic probability of success, and the FAO solution was not to be invoked in the future as a precedent in the UN context.[53] It is doubtful, however, whether this approach is persuasive. Where an international organization takes decisions on matters coming within the EU's exclusive competences, the Member States are in any event required to adopt a common position and will form a block. Whether the expression of such a common position takes place by way of Member State voting, or by way of an EU vote, should not in any way alter the outcome of the process.

The types of difficulties to which the lack of EU membership of an international organization may give rise are exemplified by the relationship between the EU and the ILO.[54] The EU has but observer status in that organization, which has as its main task the negotiation and adoption of international labour conventions. The issue of Community participation in the negotiation of such conventions first arose as regards Convention No 153 on working hours and rest periods in transport (1977 to 1979). It proved impossible to find an arrangement then for such participation on account of the fears of employers and workers with regard to their own position in the tripartite ILO approach towards rule-making. Documents drawn up by the Governing Body of the International Labour Office in 1981 and 1989 proposed that the Member States could authorize the Commission to propose amendments on their behalf, that the authority responsible for implementation might be the EC Council, and that ratification could be done through an appropriate statement by the Community, provided that prior notification from all the Member States confirmed that this constituted ratification by them. The documents also referred to issues of liability. The problem of Community competence again arose in connection with Convention No 162 concerning safety in the use of asbestos (1983 to 1986), an area covered by four EC directives. As the Community could not take part in the Conference in 1986, the Council, after some skirmishes with the Commission, adopted a decision

[52] Ibid, 1235–7.

[53] FAO Doc CL 100/9-Sup. 1, at 2–3, cited by FL Kirgis, *International Organizations in their Legal Setting* (2nd edn, West Publishing Company, 1993) 166.

[54] The following description is taken from *Opinion 2/91* (n 18 above) 1066–8.

on Community participation in areas of exclusive Community competence. The decision imposed full compliance with the tripartite consultation procedure required by the ILO. It also stipulated that the Community replies to the ILO questionnaire (the instrument for consultation of both sides of industry) had to be adopted by the Council following a proposal from the Commission. In the Conference, the Commission would speak on behalf of the Community and act in close consultation with the Member States. The delegates of the Member States would retain their right to speak during the plenary session of the Conference. In 1988 then, several Member States contested the Community's exclusive competence as regards Convention No 170. There were again discussions between the Commission and the Council, the latter agreeing to re-examine its 1986 decision and to supplement it with provisions covering cases of joint competence. However, when, following the adoption of the Convention, the Commission wrote to the Council stating its view that the Member States should notify the ILO that the Community institutions were the competent authorities for the implementation of the Convention, several Member States indicated their refusal to accept that the Community had exclusive competence. The Commission then requested *Opinion 2/91*, asking for clarification of the competence question. The German government contested the admissibility of the request, arguing that the Community was in any event incapable of concluding an ILO Convention, as it was not a member of the ILO. The Court rejected that argument, pointing out that the request did not concern the Community's capacity on the international plane, but only the question of Community competence, and that it was not for the Court to assess any obstacles which the Community might encounter in the exercise of its competence. In any event, Community competence could be exercised through the medium of the Member States acting jointly in the Community's interest.[55] Further in the Opinion, after having concluded that Convention No 170 came within the joint competence of the Community and its Member States, the Court referred to the duty of co-operation, which is analysed below. The Opinion did not, however, resolve the differences between the Member States and the Commission. As Sack reported in 1995, the Member States refused to make national ratifications of the conventions subject to a previous Council decision, and the whole ratification process of ILO conventions was blocked.[56] The position appears not to have changed since then.[57]

The International Maritime Organization (IMO) is another example of an organization of which the EU is not a member, notwithstanding its extensive competences and legislation in maritime matters which are within the IMO's remit.[58]

[55] Ibid, paras 1–5. [56] Sack (n 20 above) 1239.

[57] See Denza (n 44 above) 10–11. In 1994 the Commission adopted a proposal for a Council Decision on the exercise of the Community's external competence at international labour conferences in cases falling within the joint competence of the Community and its Member States (COM(94)2 final). The Council did not act upon this proposal, which was withdrawn on 9 June 2000.

[58] See further J Wouters, S de Jong, A Marx, and P De Man, *Study for the Assessment of the EU's Role in International Maritime Organizations*, April 2009, available at <http://ec.europa.eu/maritimeaffairs/studies/eu_role_international_organisations_en.pdf>.

The IMO Convention does not at present allow an international organization to join, but all the EU Member States are IMO members. The EU, however, is incapable of itself participating in the work of the IMO, and cannot conclude maritime conventions elaborated within that organization. Recent Court of Justice case law illustrates the problems that this may create.

In *Intertanko* the Court was confronted with a challenge to a directive on ship-source pollution, based in part on a breach of Marpol 73/78.[59] The latter is a convention on marine pollution which all the Member States have concluded, but not the EU. The Court decided that this IMO convention was not binding on the Community, and refused to accept the analogy with the case of GATT 1947: in the 1971 *International Fruit Company* judgment the Court had found that the Community was bound by GATT, even if it had never formally concluded it, because it had effectively succeeded in the rights and obligations of the Member States in international trade.[60] In *Intertanko* the Court stated that the Community had not assumed, under the EC Treaty, the powers previously exercised by the Member States in the field to which Marpol 73/78 applied. In the absence of a full transfer of the powers previously exercised by the Member States to the Community, the latter could not, simply because all those States were parties to Marpol 73/78, be bound by the rules set out therein, which it had not itself approved.[61] This meant that the challenged directive could not be reviewed in the light of Marpol 73/78. The Court did not, however, deny all significance to the convention: in view of the customary international law principle of good faith, and of (current) Article 4(3) TFEU, it was incumbent upon the Court to interpret the provisions of the directive taking account of Marpol 73/78.[62] The ruling shows how unsatisfactory it is for the EU not to be an IMO member, and to be incapable of concluding its conventions. The result is that the Member States may be faced with conflicting obligations.

Similar problems occurred in *Commune de Mesquer v. Total*.[63] The case arose from the *Erika* tanker accident in 1999, off the coast of Brittany. The *Commune de Mesquer* (municipality of Mesquer), which was a victim of the extensive oil pollution resulting from the sinking of the *Erika*, tried to obtain damages from Total France and Total International, the owners of the oil and charterers of the *Erika*. Two IMO conventions were relevant to the *Commune*'s claims: the so-called Liability Convention and the Fund Convention.[64] Again the Community was not a party to

[59] Case C–308/06 *Intertanko and Others* [2008] ECR I–4057.

[60] Joined Cases 21 to 24/72 *International Fruit Company v. Produktschap voor Groenten en Fruit* [1972] ECR 1219; see further Ch 9.

[61] *Intertanko and Others* (n 59 above) paras 48–49.

[62] Ibid, para 52.

[63] Case C–188/07 *Commune de Mesquer v. Total France* [2008] ECR I–4501.

[64] Respectively the International Convention on Civil Liability for Oil Pollution Damage adopted at Brussels on 29 November 1969, as amended by the Protocol signed in London on 27 November 1992 [2004] OJ L78/32 and the International Convention on the Establishment of an International Fund for Compensation for Oil Pollution Damage adopted at Brussels on 18 December 1971, as amended by the Protocol signed in London on 27 November 1992 [2004] OJ L78/40.

those conventions, but they had been concluded by most Member States. However, the questions for a preliminary ruling referred to the Court of Justice concerned Directive 75/442 on waste,[65] and the polluter-pays principle which it embodied. One of the important issues to be decided was the relationship between the provisions of that directive, and those of the two conventions, which had the effect of limiting liability. The Court effectively decided that the directive offered some scope for French law to comply with the conventions, but that this scope was not unlimited. Again the Court did not accept that the conventions were binding on the Community, since it had not acceded to them, and could not be regarded as having taken the place of its Member States, if only because not all of them were parties to those conventions.[66] It may further be noted that reference was made to a 2004 Council decision[67] which authorized the Member States to conclude a 2003 Protocol to the Fund Convention, 'in the interest of the Community'.[68] Article 4 of that decision provides that Member States must, at the earliest opportunity, use their best endeavours to ensure that the relevant international instruments are amended in order to allow the Community to become a Contracting Party.

There is a third case concerning the IMO. In *Commission v. Greece* the question arose of whether Greece was entitled to submit a proposal to the IMO, on its own behalf and not that of the Community, in an area covered by Community law.[69] The Court found that the Community's competence over the relevant matters was exclusive, pursuant to the principles identified in the *AETR* case law.[70] It established that the Greek proposal initiated a procedure which could lead to the adoption by the IMO of new rules, and that such adoption would have an effect on the relevant provisions of Community law. The Court therefore found a breach of Article 4(3) TEU and the TFEU provisions on a common transport policy.[71] The breach was not excused by the fact that the Community was not a member of the IMO. Lack of membership did not prevent the Community's competence from being in fact exercised, in particular through the Member States acting jointly in the Community's interest.[72]

The duty of co-operation thus governs action by the Member States in international organizations of which the EU is not a member, in so far as that organization

[65] [1975] OJ L194/39, as amended by Commission Decision 96/350 [1996] OJ L135/32.

[66] *Commune de Mesquer* (n 63 above) para 85.

[67] Decision 2004/246 authorizing the Member States to sign, ratify or accede to, in the interest of the European Community, the Protocol of 2003 to the International Convention on the Establishment of an International Fund for Compensation for Oil Pollution Damage, 1992, and authorizing Austria and Luxemburg, in the interest of the European Community, to accede to the underlying instruments [2004] OJ L78/22.

[68] Ibid, Art 1.

[69] Case C–45/07 *Commission v. Greece* [2009] ECR I–701. See also M Cremona, 'Extending the Reach of the AETR Principle' (2009) 34 ELR 754.

[70] See Ch 3.

[71] *Commission v. Greece* (n 69 above) paras 21–22.

[72] Ibid, para 31.

deals with matters coming within EU competence or governed by EU law. It may be noted that the EEC Treaty used to contain a more ambitious provision, Article 116, which provided that the Member States were required, in respect of all matters of particular interest to the common market, to proceed within the framework of international organizations of an economic character only by common action. The TEU deleted that provision, for reasons which are unclear.[73] It is true that Article 34(1) TEU, in the title on the CFSP, provides that the 'Member States shall coordinate their action in international organizations and at international conferences'. However, that provision cannot extend to EU action outside the sphere of the CFSP, in the light of Article 40 TEU.[74] In the sphere of monetary policy Article 138(1) TFEU provides that 'In order to secure the euro's place in the international monetary system, the Council, on a proposal from the Commission, shall adopt a decision establishing common positions on matters of particular interest for economic and monetary union within the competent international financial institutions and conferences', after consulting the ECB. Article 138(2) TFEU allows the Council 'to adopt appropriate measures to ensure unified representation within the international financial institutions and conferences'.

If non-membership may create difficulties, so may membership. It is useful briefly to describe the organization of and experience with EU membership of the FAO and of the WTO.

The negotiations for Community accession to the FAO took four years,[75] and were successfully concluded in 1991.[76] As the FAO Constitution permitted accession only by States, its provisions had to be amended. Article II, as modified, permits admission of regional economic integration organizations, constituted by States a majority of which are members of the FAO, and benefiting from a transfer of competence over a range of matters within the purview of the FAO. The regional economic integration organization has to submit a declaration of competence, and Member States of the organization are presumed to retain competence over all other matters. Subsequent changes in the distribution of competence need to be notified. Membership rights are exercised on an alternative basis, depending on where competence lies. The organization which joins the FAO shall have a number of votes equal to the number of its Member States which are entitled to vote, but voting rights can only be exercised by either the organization or its Member

[73] The deletion is deplored by C Kaddous, *Le droit des relations extérieures dans la jurisprudence de la Cour de justice des Communautés européennes* (Helbing & Lichtenhahn, 1998) 187–8.

[74] See Ch 5.

[75] Sack (n 20 above) 1237.

[76] See also A Tavares de Pinho, 'L'admission de la Communauté économique européenne comme membre de l'Organisation des Nations Unies pour l'alimentation et l'agriculture' (1993) 370 RMCUE 656; R Frid, 'The European Economic Community A Member of a Specialized Agency of the United Nations' (1993) 4 EJIL 239; J Schwob, 'L'amendement à l'acte constitutif de la FAO visant à permettre l'admission en qualité de membre d'organisations d'intégration économique régionale de la Communauté économique européenne' (1993) 29 RTDE 1; Frid (n 44 above) ch 5.

States. In accordance with those provisions, the Community submitted a declaration of competence. Moreover, the General Rules of the FAO were also modified in order to create more precision in the handling of joint membership. Rule XLI provides that any member of the FAO may request information regarding the division of competence in respect of any specific question. It also requires the member organization and its Member States to indicate, before any FAO meeting, where competence lies in respect of any specific question to be considered and which, as between the member organization and its Member States, shall have the right to vote in respect of each particular agenda item. Where an agenda item covers matters of mixed competence, both the member organization and its Member States may participate in the discussion, but the meeting, in arriving at its decisions, shall take into account only the intervention of the party which has the right to vote.[77]

Those provisions have been described as a straitjacket,[78] and it is easy to see that, when applied strictly, they risk becoming a source of constant tension, particularly within the EU, where decisions on competence and voting rights need to be taken constantly due to the numerous FAO meetings. It is also obvious that such complex rules require some form of agreed decision-making process within the EU. The Commission and the Council therefore concluded an arrangement, in 1991, providing for co-ordination meetings at various levels, for mechanisms ensuring an adequate flow of information, for rules on interventions and voting at FAO meetings, and for rules on participation in drafting committees. Some of the provisions of that arrangement are further examined below, in the section on the duty of co-operation. At this stage it is sufficient to indicate that, at least in the view of the Commission, EU participation in the work of the FAO did not work well, due to the constant haggling over issues of competence and voting rights.[79] This led the Commission to involve the Court of Justice, in a case brought against the Council for its alleged failure to apply the arrangement correctly (see below). Perceptions will of course differ, and the Commission may simply be unhappy with the limits on its proper role in FAO activities. Yet given the legal complexities of the division of competences between the EU and its Member States in their external relations and the constant tension between supranationalism and intergovernmentalism in the European integration process as a whole, a system whereby competences need to be defined and allocated for every item on the agenda of every meeting of an international organization is no doubt an ideal recipe for malfunctioning.

The case of the WTO can in some sense be contrasted with that of the FAO. The antecedents are very different, because the Community was already a *de facto* member of GATT (itself a *de facto* international organization), owing to its extensive

[77] This provision appears to require that other FAO members have special powers so as to participate in a discussion with both a member organization and its Member States but to take into account only the intervention of the party with the right to vote.

[78] Sack (n 20 above) 1243.

[79] Ibid, 1245–6.

and exclusive competences in matters of tariffs and trade. The Community was one of the main players in the Uruguay Round, which led to the establishment of the WTO. The Uruguay Round negotiations were conducted by the Commission, and the Council of Ministers was the central organ for deciding the EC common position. It was therefore only natural for the Community to become a founding member of the WTO, and the question was rather what type of role would be available for the individual Member States. Article XIV of the WTO Agreement simply provides that the agreement is open for acceptance by contracting parties to GATT 1947 and the European Communities. There is no requirement for a declaration of competence, and there are only a few basic provisions on voting: Article IX provides that each WTO member has one vote; that the EC has a number of votes equal to the number of its Member States which are members of the WTO; and, in a footnote, that the number of votes of the EC and its Member States shall in no case exceed the number of the Member States. The latter provision suggests alternating the exercise of voting rights, but as the WTO is an organization where voting almost never takes place, the issue is largely theoretical. There appears to be nothing else in WTO law regulating membership by the EU and its Member States. Nor is there much more at internal EU level. After the conclusion of the Uruguay Round negotiations, but before the Court issued *Opinion 1/94*, the Council, the Commission, and the Member States did manage to agree on a 'code of conduct' for future negotiations on services. That code, which is quoted in the factual part of *Opinion 1/94*,[80] provided that the Commission should continue to negotiate on behalf of the Community and the Member States; that it should fully inform the Member States; that it should express positions reached on all issues according to the relevant decision-making procedures (with a footnote expressing disagreement between the Commission and the Council about what that means); that it should ensure that representatives of Member States were in a position to attend all substantive meetings and negotiations; and that it should promptly circulate all notes. The code also provided that the Council resolved to review regularly the progress of negotiations, and that it would consider the formulation of negotiating objectives and reserved the right to give the Commission appropriate directives. Then came the Court's Opinion, in which it emphasized the duty of co-operation, without, however, further spelling out the consequences of that duty (see below). The Commission, the Council, and the Member States subsequently entered into negotiations on a general code of conduct for the Community's and the Member States' participation in the operation of the WTO, but that negotiation was never concluded, as it became part of the 1996 Inter-Governmental Conference (IGC) leading to the Amsterdam Treaty, which only managed to achieve a limited modification of then Article 133 EC, on commercial policy (current Article 207 TFEU).[81] As a result, more than

[80] *Opinion 1/94* (n 30 above) 5365.
[81] See Ch 2.

fifteen years into the operation of the WTO there is still no general document on EU and Member States' participation. None the less, there appear to be few serious problems, as the practice of acting in common and allowing the EU to be the central player in the system is continued. Even at the level of dispute settlement, when a third country brings a complaint against an EU Member State, it is the legal service of the Commission which takes up the defence.[82] There are no doubt a number of factors which explained the success of this joint membership. Perhaps the most important one is that the legal, economic, and diplomatic expertise in trade issues is generally located in the EU institutions, particularly the Commission. With the Lisbon changes to the EU's competence in commercial policy matters (see Chapter 2), the legal position now fully matches the facts on the ground, in the sense that there is exclusive EU competence for all WTO matters, with the sole exception of transport.

International organizations, the autonomy of the Community legal order, and the exclusive jurisdiction of the Court of Justice

A separate point which deserves to be discussed with respect to the EU's relationship with international organizations is case law, which emphasizes that EU participation in agreements setting up their own institutions must not affect the autonomy of the EU legal order.[83]

Opinion 1/76 was the first case in which the Court identified that principle.[84] It concerned the European laying-up fund for inland waterway vessels, to be established by the Community, some of its Member States, and Switzerland. The legal system contained in the draft agreement provided for the grant of certain powers to the Fund Tribunal, composed of six judges from the Court of Justice and one judge from Switzerland. The Tribunal was to have the power to give preliminary rulings concerning not only the validity and interpretation of decisions adopted by the organs of the Fund but also the interpretation of the agreement itself. The Court pointed out that once the agreement was concluded, it would itself have jurisdiction to interpret its provisions. It examined the hypothesis that the jurisdiction of the Tribunal and of the Court would be parallel so that it would be for the national court of a Member State to refer the matter to one or other of the two legal organs. The Court drew attention to the risk of conflicts of jurisdiction. It recognized that the need to establish judicial remedies and legal procedures which

[82] See e.g. *EC—Measures Affecting Asbestos and Asbestos-Containing Products* (WT/DS/135), a case brought by Canada against French legislation. See further Helikoski (n 1 above) 178–93.

[83] See also I Govaere, 'Beware of the Trojan Horse: Dispute Settlement in (Mixed) Agreements and the Autonomy of the EU Legal Order' in Hillion and Koutrakos (n 1 above) 187; R Holdgaard, *External Relations Law of the European Community—Legal Reasoning and Legal Discourses* (Wolters Kluwer, 2008) 79–88.

[84] N 10 above.

would guarantee the observance of the law could justify the principle underlying the system adopted. None the less, a difficulty would arise because the six members of the Court required to sit on the Fund Tribunal could be prejudicing their position as regards questions which could come before the Court after having been brought before the Tribunal, and vice versa. The arrangement could conflict with the obligation on the judges to give a completely impartial ruling on contentious questions when they came before the Court. In extreme cases the Court could find it impossible to assemble a quorum. For those reasons, the Fund Tribunal could be established only on condition that judges belonging to the Court of Justice were not called upon to serve on it.[85]

The Court had similar objections to the first version of the EEA Agreement. That agreement was an ambitious attempt to extend the policies, principles, and rules of the internal market to the EFTA countries without requiring them to become members of the Community.[86] In the original negotiation every effort had been made to ensure that the extension of the internal market was complete, and that the internal market would function in exactly the same way in the whole of the EEA. To achieve this, the first version of the EEA Agreement copied EEC Treaty provisions as much as possible, and provided, *inter alia*, for extension of the case law of the Court of Justice, as well as for the creation of an EEA Court, composed of judges from the Court of Justice and from the EFTA countries, and with jurisdiction to interpret the agreement. In *Opinion 1/91* the Court emphasized the remaining differences between the objectives of the (then) EEC Treaty and those of the agreement, notwithstanding the negotiators' attempt to create as much homogeneity as possible.[87] It then examined the jurisdiction of the EEA Court, and objected to two aspects.

First, the EEA Court would, when interpreting the term 'Contracting Party' in the agreement, have to rule on the respective competences of the Community and the Member States as regards the matters governed by the provisions of the agreement. It followed that the jurisdiction conferred on the EEA Court was likely adversely to affect the allocation of responsibilities defined in the Treaties and, hence, the autonomy of the Community legal order, respect for which had to be assured by the Court of Justice pursuant to (current) Article 19(1) TEU. This exclusive jurisdiction was confirmed by (current) Article 344 TFEU, pursuant to which the Member States undertook not to submit a dispute concerning the interpretation or application of the Treaties to any method of settlement other than those provided for in the Treaties.[88]

As a second point the Court examined the effect of the case law of the EEA Court on the interpretation of Community law. Echoing *Opinion 1/76*, the Court

[85] Ibid, paras 17–22.
[86] Agreement on the European Economic Area [1994] OJ L1/3.
[87] *Opinion 1/91 re Agreement on the European Economic Area* [1991] ECR I-6079; see also Ch 8.
[88] Ibid, paras 31–35.

recalled that it would have jurisdiction to interpret the EEA Agreement. It pointed out that where an international agreement provided for its own system of courts, including a court with jurisdiction to settle disputes between the Contracting Parties, and, as a result, to interpret its provisions, the decisions of that court would be binding on the Community institutions, including the Court of Justice. An international agreement providing for such a system of courts was in principle compatible with Community law. The Community's competence in the field of international relations and its capacity to conclude international agreements necessarily entailed the power to submit to the decisions of a court which was created or designated by such an agreement as regards the interpretation and application of its provisions. The problem was, however, that the EEA Agreement took over an essential part of the rules which governed economic and trading relations within the Community and which constituted, for the most part, fundamental provisions of the Community legal order. The Court then referred to the agreement's provisions on homogeneity and uniformity, and came to the conclusion that in so far as it conditioned the future interpretation of the Community rules on free movement and competition, the machinery of courts provided for in the agreement conflicted with (current) Article 344 TFEU and, more generally, with the very foundations of the Community.[89]

Moreover, the fact that judges from the Court of Justice were to sit on the EEA Court accentuated the general problems arising from the court system which the draft agreement purported to set up. Those judges would have to apply and interpret the same provisions (in the EC Treaty and in the EEA Agreement) but using different approaches, methods, and concepts in order to take account of the nature of each treaty and of its particular objectives. In those circumstances, it would be very difficult, if not impossible, for those judges, when sitting in the Court of Justice, to tackle questions with completely open minds where they had taken part in determining those questions as members of the EEA Court.[90]

After the Court's negative Opinion the agreement was renegotiated as regards the system of judicial supervision. The most significant modification was the replacement of the EEA Court with an EFTA Court, composed only of judges from the EFTA countries and with more limited jurisdiction. The Court then issued a positive Opinion.[91]

The principle of the autonomy of the EU legal order was also discussed in the context of *Opinion 2/94*, on the issue of accession to the ECHR.[92] The Council had requested the Court's Opinion on the question of Community competence to join the ECHR, and on the question of whether accession would be compatible with the EC Treaty, and in particular (current) Articles 19(1) TEU and 344 TFEU.

[89] *Opinion 1/91* (n 87 above) paras 37–46.
[90] Ibid, paras 47–52.
[91] *Opinion 1/92 re Agreement on the European Economic Area* [1992] ECR I-2821.
[92] *Opinion 2/94 re Accession to the ECHR* [1996] ECR I-1759; see also Ch 3.

However, the Court declined to reply to that question because it did not have sufficient information regarding the arrangements by which the Community envisaged submitting to the judicial control machinery established by the ECHR.[93]

In *Opinion 1/00*, regarding the proposed agreement on the establishment of a European Common Aviation Area (ECAA), the Court again examined whether there were any threats to the autonomy of the Community legal order.[94] The agreement was modelled after the EEA Agreement. The Court recalled, and applied, the principles resulting from its previous case law. Where an agreement clearly separated the Community from the other contracting parties from an institutional point of view, and did not affect either the exercise by the Community and its institutions of their powers by changing the nature of those powers, or the interpretation of Community law, the autonomy of the Community legal order could be considered to be secure.[95] After an extensive examination of the ECAA Agreement's provisions, the Court concluded that those requirements were met.

The above case law on the autonomy of the EU legal order is, notwithstanding its importance, of limited scope. It is confined to agreements extending EU policies to neighbouring countries, where there is a risk of confusion as to the origin, nature, and methods of interpretation of duplicated legal provisions. Different issues may, however, arise in connection with systems of international dispute settlement which are more independent from the EU.

This is shown by the *Mox Plant* case.[96] Ireland had objected to a UK project to build a Mox plant (involving the recycling of plutonium) at Sellafied, on the coast of the Irish Sea. Ireland was concerned about the environmental and nuclear safety risks which the plant presented. Dissatisfied with the UK response, it brought proceedings under UNCLOS, claiming that the Mox plant project breached various provisions of UNCLOS, mainly concerning marine and environmental pollution. Those proceedings were instituted before an UNCLOS arbitral tribunal. Ireland also submitted a request for provisional measures to the International Tribunal for the Law of the Sea (ITLOS), in which it requested that the United Kingdom immediately suspend the authorization for the operation of the Mox plant.

It is worth noting at this point that, in substitution of the dispute-settlement mechanisms provided for by UNCLOS itself, Article 282 of UNCLOS allows disputes to be submitted to a system of dispute settlement provided for in a general, regional, or bilateral agreement:

> If the States Parties which are parties to a dispute concerning the interpretation or application of this Convention have agreed, through a general, regional or bilateral agreement or otherwise, that such dispute shall, at the request of any party to the dispute, be submitted to a

[93] Ibid, para 20.

[94] *Opinion 1/00 re the ECAA Agreement* [2002] ECR I–3493.

[95] Ibid, para 6.

[96] Case C–459/03 *Commission v. Ireland (Mox Plant)* [2006] ECR I–4635. For the background, see also R Churchill and J Scott, 'The Mox Plant Litigation: The First Half-Life' (2004) 53 ICLQ 643.

procedure that entails a binding decision, that procedure shall apply in lieu of the procedures provided for in this part, unless the parties to the dispute otherwise agree.

Both before ITLOS and the arbitral tribunal the United Kingdom raised an objection of lack of jurisdiction, contending that certain aspects of Ireland's complaints fell within the scope of Community law and that the Court of Justice therefore had exclusive jurisdiction. ITLOS rejected that objection, and declared that it had *prima facie* jurisdiction. The arbitral tribunal, by contrast, was more careful, suspended its proceedings, and asked to be more extensively informed as to the implications of Community law with regard to the dispute.[97]

In the meantime, the Commission had been informed of the proceedings brought by Ireland. It took the view that they constituted a breach of (current) Articles 4(3) TEU (duty of sincere co-operation) and 344 TFEU (exclusive jurisdiction of the Court of Justice).[98] Ireland disagreed, and the Commission brought the case before the Court of Justice. There were three heads of complaint. First, Ireland had failed to respect the exclusive jurisdiction of the Court of Justice. Secondly, the submission by Ireland of instruments of Community law for interpretation and application by the UNCLOS arbitral tribunal amounted to a breach of (current) Article 344 TFEU. Thirdly, Ireland had violated (current) Article 4(3) TEU, first, by instituting proceedings on the basis of UNCLOS provisions falling within the competence of the Community, and secondly, by bringing those proceedings unilaterally without first having informed and consulted the competent Community institutions.

The Court broadly followed the Opinion of Maduro AG, accepting most of the Commission's complaints. Maduro AG highlighted the point that the Court's jurisdictional monopoly, pursuant to (current) Article 344 TFEU, was a means of preserving the autonomy of the Community legal order. It served to ensure that Member States did not incur legal obligations under public international law which could conflict with their obligations under Community law. Member States were under a duty of loyalty to the judicial system created by the Treaties.[99] One assumes that the Advocate General referred to the risk of an international tribunal imposing obligations on a Member State in breach of Community law.

As regards the first head of complaint—breach of (current) Article 344 TFEU—the Court started by pointing out that UNCLOS was concluded by the Community and its Member States on the basis of shared competence. It then recalled the principle that mixed agreements have the same legal status as pure Community agreements, as regards provisions which are within Community competence. It also recalled that, in ensuring respect for commitments arising from an agreement concluded by the Community institutions, the Member States fulfilled, within the Community system, an obligation in relation to the Community, which had assumed responsibility for the due performance of that agreement. These principles

[97] For a fuller account of the reasoning of the tribunal, see paras 42–46 of the judgment.

[98] The Commission also referred to Arts 192 and 193 EA, which are not further discussed here.

[99] *Mox Plant* (n 96 above) paras 9–10.

led the Court to examine the scope of Community competence in relation to the provisions of UNCLOS (in Part XII on Protection and Preservation of the Marine Environment) which were in issue in the international proceedings brought by Ireland. The Court identified (current) Article 192(1) TFEU as the appropriate legal basis for the conclusion of international agreements on protection of the environment. It admitted that the Community's external competence with regard to protection of the environment was shared with the Member States. However, the question of whether a provision of a mixed agreement came within the Community's competence was one which related to the attribution, and thus the very existence of that competence, and not to its exclusive or shared nature. Thus, the Community could enter into environmental agreements even if the specific matters covered were not, or were only very partially, the subject of rules at Community level, which, by reason of that fact, were not likely to be affected in the sense of the *AETR* case law.[100]

The Court then proceeded to examine whether and to what extent the Community, by becoming a party to UNCLOS, elected to exercise its external competences in matters of environmental protection. In other words, the Court did not assume that the Community had necessarily made use of the full scope of those competences in relation to the UNCLOS provisions on environmental protection. Instead, it focused on the Council decision concluding UNCLOS, which was based on the Treaty provisions on environmental protection, and which stated that the Community became a party 'within the limits of its competence'. The Court subsequently turned to the Declaration of Community competence made at the time of the Community's acceptance of UNCLOS, as clarifying the scope of the Community's participation. Ultimately, the analysis turned on a fairly ambiguous sentence in the Declaration, providing that 'When Community rules exist but are not affected, in particular in cases of Community provisions establishing only minimum standards, the Member States have competence, without prejudice to the competence of the Community to act in this field'. Ireland read this provision as meaning that the Member States retained competence, other than in areas of exclusive competence pursuant to the *AETR* case law. However, the Court opted for a different construction. It established that, within the specific context of the Convention, a finding that there had been a transfer to the Community of areas of shared competence was contingent on the existence of Community rules within the areas covered by the Convention provisions in issue, irrespective of what could otherwise be the scope and nature of those rules. In this regard, the Court considered an appendix to the Declaration of Community competence, listing various EC law measures—a useful reference basis, even if it was not exhaustive.[101]

The Court then proceeded to a more specific analysis. It found that the matters covered by the provisions of the Convention relied on by Ireland before the UNCLOS arbitral tribunal were very largely regulated by Community measures,

[100] Ibid, paras 83–95. [101] Ibid, paras 96–109.

several of which were expressly mentioned in the appendix to the competence declaration. The detail of that analysis need not concern us here. The Court concluded that the Convention provisions on the prevention of marine pollution relied on by Ireland, which clearly covered a significant part of the Mox plant dispute, came within the scope of Community competence which the Community had elected to exercise by becoming a party to the Convention. Thus, those provisions formed part of the Community legal order, and the Court had jurisdiction to deal with disputes relating to the interpretation and application of those provisions and to assess a Member State's compliance with them.[102]

The next question to answer was whether the Court's jurisdiction was exclusive. The Court recalled that an international agreement could not affect the allocation of responsibilities defined in the Treaties and, consequently, the autonomy of the Community legal system, compliance with which the Court ensured under (current) Article 19(1) TEU. (Current) Article 344 TFEU confirmed that exclusive jurisdiction. The Court then pointed out that Article 282 of UNCLOS (referred to above) precisely made it possible to avoid such a breach of the Court's exclusive jurisdiction. It followed from that provision that the system for the resolution of disputes set out in the EC Treaty, in principle had to take precedence over UNCLOS' own system. Moreover, as the UNCLOS dispute was between two Member States with regard to an alleged failure to comply with Community law obligations resulting from the relevant provisions of the Convention, it was clearly covered by one of the methods of dispute settlement established by the EC Treaty, namely the procedure set out in Article 259 TFEU (Member State versus Member State).[103]

To conclude its analysis on the first head of complaint, the Court rejected the Irish objection that the dispute also concerned certain UK obligations connected with terrorism. It was sufficient that a significant part of the dispute related to the interpretation and application of Community law. Nor did the Court accept that the UNCLOS arbitration proceedings offered certain advantages compared to an action before the Court. Even if that was demonstrated, it could not in any event justify a Member State in avoiding its Treaty obligations.[104] The Court therefore upheld the first head of complaint.

It is possible to deal more briefly with the second head of complaint, where the Commission claimed that Ireland submitted instruments of Community law for interpretation and application by the arbitral tribunal, amounting also to a breach of Article 344 TFEU. The Court established that it was common ground that in its statement of claim and in its written submissions Ireland had invoked a number of Community measures. It was also common ground that this had been done pursuant to Article 293(1) UNCLOS, which provides that an arbitral tribunal is to 'apply this Convention and other rules of international law not incompatible with this Convention'. It thus appeared that Ireland had submitted instruments

[102] Ibid, paras 110–121. [103] Ibid, paras 122–128. [104] Ibid, paras 134–137.

of Community law to the arbitral tribunal for the purposes of their interpretation and application in the context of proceedings seeking a declaration that the United Kingdom had breached the provisions of those instruments. This was at variance with the obligation on Member States to respect the exclusive nature of the Court's jurisdiction to resolve disputes concerning the interpretation and application of provisions of Community law, in particular by having recourse to the procedure in (current) Article 259 TFEU for the purpose of obtaining a declaration that another Member State had breached its obligations. There was thus, also in this respect, a breach of (current) Article 344 TFEU. The Court concluded by pointing out that, in those circumstances, the institution and pursuit of proceedings before the arbitral tribunal involved a manifest risk that the jurisdictional order laid down in the Treaties and, consequently, the autonomy of the Community legal system could be adversely affected. Any formal assurances by Ireland to the contrary did not remove that risk.[105]

Under the third head of complaint the Commission claimed that Ireland was in breach of (current) Article 4(3) TEU in two respects: first, by instituting proceedings under the Convention on the basis of provisions falling within Community competence; and secondly, by bringing those proceedings unilaterally without first having informed and consulted the competent Community institutions. On the first point, the Court simply held that (current) Article 344 TFEU must be understood as a specific expression of Member States' more general duty of loyalty resulting from (current) Article 4(3) TEU. In that sense, this Commission claim had the same subject matter as the first head of complaint, analysed above. On the second point, the Court emphasized again that the Member States and the Community institutions had an obligation of close co-operation in fulfilling the commitments undertaken by them under joint competence when they concluded a mixed agreement. That was in particular the position in the case of a dispute which, as here, related essentially to undertakings from a mixed agreement that related to an area, namely the protection and preservation of the marine environment, in which the respective areas of competence of the Community and the Member States were liable to be closely interrelated. The act of submitting a dispute of this nature to a judicial forum such as the arbitral tribunal involved the risk that a judicial forum other than the Court would rule on the scope of obligations imposed on the Member States pursuant to Community law. In those circumstances, the obligation of close co-operation within the framework of a mixed agreement involved, on the part of Ireland, a duty to inform and consult the competent Community institutions prior to instituting dispute-settlement proceedings. As Ireland had not done so, the Court found a breach of (current) Article 4(3) TEU.

This important judgment calls for a number of comments. Its significance lies, first, in the fact that the Court has now unequivocally confirmed that the EU

[105] Ibid, paras 146–157.

institutions, when concluding a mixed agreement in an area of shared competence, can decide to what extent the EU elects to exercise such shared competence. In other words, there is no requirement for the EU to make full use of the competences which have been conferred on it, for example in matters of environmental protection. To use a hypothetical example, the EU could opt to participate in a multilateral environmental agreement in so far as it includes provisions on marine pollution, but not to conclude that agreement's provisions on air pollution—notwithstanding the fact that the latter provisions also come within its competence. That part of the agreement would therefore be concluded by the Member States. In practice, however, the EU institutions rarely manage to take such clear decisions when concluding an agreement. As in *Mox Plant*, one will therefore in most cases need to look at other factors and elements. Here, the Court scrutinized the Community's declaration of competence, as well as the extent to which there was Community legislation in matters covered by the relevant UNCLOS provisions. The Court clearly opted for a wide interpretation of that declaration, precisely in the light of the existing legislation. The extent to which the EU has legislated internally is therefore a strong indicator of the extent to which it has exercised external competence. This is not to be confused with *AETR*-type exclusive implied powers. The presence of such powers is the object of a precise legal analysis of the relationship between the relevant international obligations and internal EU legislation. In the absence of such exclusive powers, by contrast, the analysis in areas of shared competence is broader and more general. It is, as it were, presumed that the EU also elected to exercise its shared external competences where a mixed agreement includes provisions on matters for which there is some degree of internal EU policy. The *PFOS* judgment, analysed below, follows the same trend.[106]

This approach has merit. However, it is not the end of the story for issues such as those which arose in *Mox Plant*. The Court found that many, if not most, of the UNCLOS obligations on which Ireland sought to rely before the arbitral tribunal had effectively been entered into by the Community, as an exercise of its environmental competences, and not therefore by the Member States. What then is the nature of those obligations for the Member States? Do the relevant UNCLOS provisions on marine pollution create obligations between EU Member States under international law, or are the Member States bound by those provisions only as a matter of EU law? The Court did not analyse those questions. It focused on the EU law nature of the relevant provisions, and then jumped to the breach of its exclusive jurisdiction: clearly Member States cannot take a dispute on EU law between them to an international tribunal. Yet, awkward questions remain as to whether EU law and international law will always be congruent. As further analysed below,[107] the presumption under international law is that a mixed agreement

[106] Case C-246/07 *Commission v. Sweden (PFOS)*, judgment of 20 April 2010.

[107] See the subsection on responsibility, below.

creates joint liability for the EU and its Member States. It is certainly arguable that, from an international law perspective, the EU Member States also created independent obligations between them when concluding UNCLOS, including in matters of marine pollution. It is equally arguable that other UNCLOS contracting parties could claim that an EU Member State violates the relevant UNCLOS provisions. What, then, does that mean for the position of the Member States in UNCLOS dispute settlement? Could, for example, Spain, if it were affected by marine pollution caused by Morocco, bring an UNCLOS claim against that non-Member State? Obviously, such a claim would not violate the exclusive jurisdiction of the Court of Justice, since the dispute could not be brought before that Court. However, it could still be contended that, as a matter of EU law, Spain would not be entitled to bring such a claim, as the relevant provisions are within the competences which the EU elected to exercise when concluding UNCLOS. The argument would be that only the EU can decide to start an UNCLOS dispute on such matters. Whether an UNCLOS arbitral tribunal seised of such a dispute brought unilaterally by a Member State would be as willing as the *Mox Plant* tribunal to defer to EU law, remains to be seen. Its jurisdiction over such a dispute would not of course be limited by Article 282 UNCLOS, as the Court of Justice would clearly not have jurisdiction. And what if Morocco started an UNCLOS dispute against Spain, on matters of marine pollution? Surely Spain could not contend that there is no case to argue, on the mere ground that the EU entered into the relevant UNCLOS obligations, not Spain. Under international law, that cannot be the effect of the Community's declaration of competence. Again, as will be further analysed, there is joint liability of the EU and its Member States. At most, it would seem, Spain ought to involve the EU institutions in the dispute.

In *Mox Plant* the Court's finding was greatly assisted by Article 282 UNCLOS, which gave way to the EU's regional dispute-settlement system. Other important mixed agreements do not contain such a provision. For example, Article 23(1) of the WTO's Dispute Settlement Understanding (DSU) provides that, when seeking redress of a violation of WTO obligations, WTO members 'shall have recourse to, and abide by, the rules and procedures of this Understanding'. In other words, they cannot settle their disputes elsewhere. What if (even though that is in practice most unlikely) two EU Member States brought their dispute to the WTO? Under EU law, that would constitute a clear violation of Article 344 TFEU. Under WTO law, however, the reverse would seem to be the case: if two members brought a dispute on WTO law before the Court of Justice, and not before a WTO panel, there would seem to be a violation of Article 23(1) DSU. The Court's *Mox Plant* decision does not engage much with such questions of potential conflict.

It is in any event clear that the Court's exclusive jurisdiction is a limited principle, in the sense that, as regards mixed agreements, it can only extend to disputes where the Court indeed has jurisdiction pursuant to the TFEU. That does not include disputes with non-Member States.

The autonomy of the EU legal order is clearly not threatened by accession to an independent international organization with a dispute-settlement system of its own, such as the WTO. The Court is particularly minded to safeguard its own autonomy in the interpretation of EU law, but at the same time recognizes that it may need to submit to the rulings of a dispute-settlement organism of an agreement or organization which the EU has respectively signed or joined. Provided such an organism does not rule on pure questions of EU law, such as the division of powers between the EU and its Member States, the powers of the institutions, or provisions of the founding Treaties or of EU legislation, there can be no objections to such submission, which is an inherent feature of participation in international law-making.

The duty of co-operation

Establishing the principle

The above survey of the practice as regards mixed agreements and mixed membership of international organizations reveals some of the problems and difficulties to which mixity gives rise. It may enable the reader better to appreciate the importance of the overarching legal principle governing mixity, namely the duty of co-operation. This section analyses the case law of the Court of Justice on the meaning of that principle, looks for its foundations, examines its legal consequences, and seeks to advance the debate on the forms and modalities of the principle's application.[108]

The first judicial statements on the duty of co-operation were made in *Ruling 1/78*, an EAEC case.[109] In contrast with the EEC Treaty, the EAEC Treaty expressly provided for parallelism between the EAEC's internal and external powers (Article 101). It also mentions mixed agreements in Article 102. Pursuant to Article 103 the Member States are required to communicate to the Commission all draft agreements or contracts relating to matters within the purview of the Treaty. The Commission may then object, in which case the Member State may ask for a ruling by the Court of Justice. *Ruling 1/78* was made upon a request by the Belgian government, as regards competence to conclude the Convention on the Physical Protection of Nuclear Materials, Facilities and Transports. There is no need to examine the complex issues of competence, as analysed by the Court. Suffice it to say that the Court concluded that the Community could not be excluded from participation in the convention. In other words, the convention was to become a mixed agreement. The Court did not stop there, however. It drew attention to Article 192 EAEC, which is identical to current

[108] See also C Hillion, 'Mixity and Coherence in EU External Relations: The Significance of the "Duty of Cooperation"' in Hillion and Koutrakos (n 1 above) 87.

[109] N 17 above.

Article 4(3) TEU, formulating the principle of Member States' loyalty. The Court considered that there could be no doubt that unilateral action by the Member States, even if it were collective and concerted action, would have the effect of calling into question certain of the essential functions of the Community and of affecting detrimentally its independent action in external relations. It followed that the draft convention could be implemented as regards the Community only by means of a close association between the institutions of the Community and the Member States both in the process of negotiation and conclusion and in the fulfilment of the obligations entered into. The Court then reiterated the scope for concluding mixed agreements under the provisions of the EAEC Treaty. It added that it was not necessary to set out and determine, as regards other parties to the convention, the division of powers in this respect between the Community and the Member States, particularly as this could change in the course of time. It was sufficient, in the Court's opinion, to state to the other contracting parties that the matter gave rise to a division of powers within the Community, it being understood that the exact nature of that division was a domestic question in which third parties had no need to intervene. Lastly, as regards implementation of the convention, the same principles as governed the division of powers with regard to negotiation and conclusion applied: once the convention had entered into force, its application would entail close co-operation between the Community institutions and the Member States. The former would act within the scope of the Community competences, on the basis of the Treaty and the provisions of the convention. The Member States would have to adopt implementing provisions, each in its own territory, for matters not covered by Community competence. The Court concluded its analysis by stating that here 'there is to be found once more the necessity for harmony between international action by the Community and the distribution of jurisdiction and powers within the Community which the Court of Justice had occasion to emphasize in its case law originating with the [*AETR* judgment]'.[110]

There are a few points to be noted here. First, the fact that the case concerned the EAEC Treaty and not the EEC Treaty appears to be of limited relevance. The Court itself made the link between the two Communities by referring to the principle of loyalty and to the *AETR* judgment, and in later decisions under the EC Treaty it referred back to *Ruling 1/78*. Secondly, the principle of loyalty appears to be at the basis, to some extent at least, of the duty of co-operation as spelled out in the ruling. Thirdly, shared competence requires 'close association' in the process of negotiating, concluding, *and* implementing the mixed agreement. Implementing measures follow the division of competence; in other words the conclusion of a mixed agreement does not permit the EU (or, for that matter, the Member States) to adopt implementing measures in areas which do not come within their competence. Fourthly, the comment on there being no need to clarify the division of powers is

[110] Ibid, paras 33–36.

rather peculiar, as for third countries such clarification may well be a precondition for negotiating a mixed agreement.[111] Fifthly, the Court was particularly concerned with achieving 'harmony' between internal and external action.

In *Opinion 2/91*, on ILO Convention No 170, the Court again had occasion to address the duty of co-operation. As discussed above,[112] the Court concluded in that case that the convention came within the joint competence of the Community and its Member States. The Court referred to its comments in *Ruling 1/78* on a close association between the Community institutions and the Member States both in the process of negotiation and conclusion and in the fulfilment of obligations entered into. This duty of co-operation also had to apply in the context of the EEC Treaty since it resulted from the requirement of unity in the international representation of the Community. The Court pointed out that in the case of the ILO, co-operation was all the more necessary in view of the fact that the Community could not, as international law stood, itself conclude an ILO convention and had to do so through the medium of the Member States. It was therefore necessary for the Community institutions and the Member States to take all the measures necessary to ensure such co-operation both in the procedure of submission to the competent authority and ratification of Convention No 170 and in the implementation of commitments resulting from that Convention.[113]

These statements constituted a useful recapitulation of the duty of co-operation. A new element was that this duty resulted from the requirement of unity in the international representation of the Community. By contrast, there was no mention of (current) Article 4(3) TEU. Nor did the Court expand much on how co-operation could be achieved; it merely demanded 'all the measures necessary', without attempting to define the content of such measures. Subsequent events demonstrated that the Opinion did not resolve the issues concerning EU involvement in the work of the ILO (see previous section).

Then came *Opinion 1/94* on the WTO Agreement, where the Court again, in the final part of the Opinion, turned to the duty of co-operation. At the hearing, the Commission had drawn the Court's attention to the problems which would arise, as regards the administration of the agreements, if there was shared competence. The Member States would undoubtedly seek to express their views individually on matters falling within their competence whenever no consensus was found. Interminable discussions would ensue to determine whether a given matter fell within the competence of the Community, so that the Community mechanisms laid down by the relevant provisions of the Treaty would apply, or whether it was within the competence of the Member States, in which case the consensus rule would operate. The Community's unity of action vis-à-vis the rest of the world would thus

[111] PM Olson, 'Mixity from the Outside: the Perspective of a Treaty Partner' in Hillion and Koutrakos (n 1 above) 335–7.

[112] See Ch 3 and previous section.

[113] *Opinion 2/91* (n 18 above) paras 36–38.

be undermined and its negotiating power greatly weakened. The Court replied by stating that these concerns were legitimate, but that problems of co-operation could not modify the answer to the question of competence. It then recalled its statements on the duty of co-operation in *Ruling 1/78* and *Opinion 2/91*. It concluded by pointing out that the duty of co-operation was all the more imperative in the case of the substantive trade agreements annexed to the WTO Agreement, which were inextricably interlinked, and in view of the cross-retaliation measures established by the Dispute Settlement Understanding.[114] Here the Court appeared to assume that the EU and its Member States would each on their own participate in dispute settlement, but that is not what in effect happened. Again, however, the Court did not try to spell out in what way flesh could be put on the bones of the duty of co-operation.

The Court made more significant and detailed statements on the duty of co-operation in *Commission v. Council* on participation in the FAO.[115] The general organization of joint membership by the EU and its Member States is described above. The Commission, however, became increasingly unhappy with Member States' reluctance to recognize and support the Community's role, particularly in cases of mixed competence. In practice, the provisions of the internal 'arrangement' which had been negotiated between the Commission and the Council proved crucial. It is therefore useful to elaborate a little on those provisions. Section 1.11 of the arrangement provides that the Commission, in preparation for FAO meetings, communicates to the Member States its proposals concerning the exercise of responsibilities and interventions on a particular issue. Section 1.12 provides that, if no agreement is reached between the Commission and the Member States on those proposals, the question shall be settled in accordance with the rules and procedures of the Treaty and in accordance with agreed practice. If no agreement is reached on that basis the question is submitted to the Committee of Permanent Representatives of the Member States (Coreper). Section 1.13 states that decisions referred to in section 1.12 are without prejudice to the respective competences of the Community and its Member States. Section 2 lays down the rules on interventions and voting. Section 2.1 provides that where an item on the agenda concerns an area of exclusive Community competence, the Commission is to take the floor and vote. Section 2.2 provides that where an item on the agenda concerns an area of national competence, the Member States take the floor and vote. Section 2.3 deals with cases of shared competence, and provides that in such cases the aim will be to achieve a common position by consensus. If that is achieved, the Presidency of the Council shall express the common position when the thrust of the issue lies in an area outside the exclusive competence of the Community, the Member States and the Commission may

[114] *Opinion 1/94* (n 30 above) paras 106–109.

[115] Case C–25/94 *Commission v. Council* [1996] ECR I–1469. See also J Helikoski, 'Internal Struggle for International Presence: The Exercise of Voting Rights Within the FAO' in Dashwood and Hillion (n 2 above) 79–99.

speak to support or supplement, and the Member States will vote. When the thrust of the issue lies in an area within the exclusive competence of the Community, the Commission shall express the common position, Member States may speak so as to support or supplement, and the Commission will vote. Lastly, section 2.4 provides that, if a common position cannot be reached, the Member States are free to intervene and vote.[116]

The case brought by the Commission concerned the negotiation and adoption, in the framework of the FAO, of an agreement to promote compliance with international conservation and management measures by vessels fishing on the high seas. The details of the negotiation and contents of that agreement need not concern us here. Suffice it to say that there was disagreement on the division of competence, in particular as regards provisions on registration and flagging of fishing vessels. Throughout the negotiation, the Commission considered that the thrust of the agreement came within the Community's exclusive competence in the area of fisheries, so that it should have the right to vote under section 2.3 of the arrangement, whereas the Member States considered that they should have the right to vote. When, towards the end of the FAO negotiation, Coreper confirmed the latter position, the Commission brought the issue before the Council, which, two days before the agreement was finally adopted by the FAO, decided that indeed the Member States should vote. The Commission then challenged that Council decision before the Court.

It is worth noting that the dispute between the Commission and the Member States was confined to the issue of voting rights. Throughout the negotiation of the agreement, the Community and its Member States formulated and defended a common position, and there was no disagreement as to the substance of the negotiations. On that basis, Jacobs AG considered that the action was inadmissible, as in his opinion there was no genuine dispute between the parties.[117] The Court took a different approach, however. It admitted the action, and, as it was generally acknowledged that there was shared competence, set out to examine whether the agreement concerned an issue whose main thrust lay in an area of exclusive Community competence (see section 2.3 of the arrangement). Its conclusion was that it did, and the Court then turned to the duty of co-operation, recalling its statements in *Ruling 1/78*, and *Opinions 2/91* and *1/94*. Then comes a vital paragraph, where the Court stated that section 2.3 of the arrangement between the Commission and the Council represented fulfilment of that duty of co-operation between the Community and its Member States within the FAO. It was clear, moreover, from the terms of the arrangement that the two institutions intended to enter into a binding commitment towards each other; and the Council had not contested its effect at any moment in the proceedings. Consequently, by giving the right to vote to the

[116] See the description in the Opinion of Jacobs AG in *Commission v. Council* (n 115 above) paras 12–13.

[117] Ibid, para 59.

Member States the Council had acted in breach of section 2.3 of the arrangement which it was required to observe, and its decision had to be annulled.[118]

This judgment constituted a major advance in the law on the duty of co-operation, but equally gave rise to many questions. The Court recognized that it was possible, even informally, to conclude some form of inter-institutional agreement, materializing and codifying the duty of co-operation in cases of mixed external action, and that such an agreement is binding on the institutions. Such recognition was not wholly without precedent, as in other areas too the Court has been giving effect to such agreements. The Community budget is an example.[119] The difference with other inter-institutional agreements, however, is that the FAO Arrangement concerned co-operation between the Community and its Member States, whereas other instances concerned only inter-institutional co-operation. It is noteworthy that the Court recognized the arrangement, notwithstanding the fact that it was agreed between the Commission and the Council, and that the Member States did not formally agree to it in their individual capacity. The Court thus appeared to accept that the Council could represent the Member States in this regard, possibly on the grounds that the duty of co-operation is an EU law principle.[120]

A further question is whether, if it is possible to codify the duty of co-operation by adopting a binding inter-institutional agreement, there is not also some form of obligation for the institutions to conclude such an agreement, at least as regards mixed membership in important international organizations, such as the WTO, or for Member States' participation in the work of organizations of which the EU cannot become a member, despite its competences in the matter, such as the ILO.

Recent case law

Since the FAO case there has been a series of judgments which have further clarified the scope and effects of the duty of co-operation.[121] They show the important constraints which that duty creates for Member States. They also clarify that this case law is firmly based on what is now Article 4(3) TEU (former Article 10 EC, as amended).

In 2005, the Court was asked to identify the consequences of a Community decision to start a multilateral negotiation, for the treaty-making powers of the Member States. At the end of 1992, the Council had adopted a decision authorizing the Commission to start negotiations for a multilateral agreement on transport

[118] Ibid, paras 40–51 of the judgment.

[119] See for an overview J Monar, 'Interinstitutional Agreements: the Phenomenon and its New Dynamics after Maastricht' (1994) 31 CML Rev 693. See now Art 295 TFEU.

[120] Timmermans (n 33 above) 244.

[121] See also M Cremona, 'Defending the Community Interest: the Duties of Co-operation and Compliance' in M Cremona and B De Witte (eds), *EU Foreign Relations Law—Constitutional Fundamentals* (Hart Publishing, 2008) 147–52.

by inland waterway with a number of Central and East European countries (most of which later joined the EU). Such transport was at that point regulated in bilateral agreements between those countries and EU Member States. Notwithstanding the Commission's mandate to negotiate, Luxemburg and Germany continued to negotiate, ratify, and implement bilateral agreements with some of those countries. The Commission objected to this, and brought proceedings against those Member States before the Court.[122] It claimed that there was a breach of *AETR*-type implied powers, but as in the *Open Skies* judgments the Court did not accept that the existing Community legislation governed the position of non-Community carriers.[123] However, the Commission also claimed that the continued bilateral actions by Luxemburg and Germany violated (current) Article 4(3) TEU. That claim met with success.

The reasoning in both judgments is very similar. The Court started by referring to the provision in (current) Article 4(3) TEU which requires the Member States to facilitate the achievement of the Community's (now Union's) tasks and to abstain from any measure which could jeopardize the attainment of the objectives of the Treaty. It then recalled that this duty of genuine co-operation was of general application and did not depend either on whether the Community competence concerned was exclusive or on any right of the Member States to enter into obligations towards non-member countries. The Court then referred to an older judgment in the sphere of fisheries,[124] in which it had held that the Member States were subject to special duties of action and abstention in a situation in which the Commission had submitted to the Council proposals which, although they had not been adopted by the Council, represented the point of departure for concerted Community action. The Court then applied this principle to the circumstances of the cases: the adoption of a decision authorizing the Commission to negotiate a multilateral agreement marked the start of a concerted Community action at international level and required, for that purpose, if not a duty of abstention on the part of the Member States, at the very least a duty of close co-operation between the latter and the Community institutions in order to facilitate the achievement of the Community tasks and to ensure the coherence and consistency of the action and its international representation.[125] In *Commission v. Germany* the Court added that the adoption of the Council decision instructing the Commission to negotiate led to a substantial change in the legal framework in which Germany was concluding bilateral agreements, and required closer co-operation and concerted action with the Commission before those agreements could be ratified and implemented.[126]

[122] Case C–519/03 *Commission v. Luxemburg* [2005] ECR I–3067 and Case C–433/03 *Commission v. Germany* [2005] ECR I–6985.

[123] See Ch 3.

[124] Case 804/79 *Commission v United Kingdom* [1981] ECR I–1045, para 28.

[125] *Commission v. Luxemburg* (n 122 above) paras 57–60; *Commission v. Germany* (n 122 above) paras 63–66.

[126] Ibid, para 67.

The Court also gave short shrift to Luxemburg and German counter-arguments. In the Luxemburg case it established that that Member State had negotiated, concluded, ratified, and implemented the contested bilateral agreements without co-operating or consulting with the Commission.[127] The argument that negotiations with the (then) Czech and Slovak Republic were opened before the Council took its decision was irrelevant, given that the contested agreements were all signed and ratified after that date.[128] Germany, by contrast, had consulted the Commission, but only before the Council decision was adopted—and it had afterwards proceeded with ratification and implementation without co-operating or consulting with the Commission.[129] Furthermore, in both judgments the Court highlighted that consultation with the Commission was all the more necessary because the Council and the Commission had agreed a set of rules of conduct in a gentleman's agreement, providing for close co-ordination between the Commission and the Member States.[130] Although those rules concerned the actual conduct of the multilateral negotiations by the Community, the Court considered as relevant a provision such as: 'the representatives of the Member States must take no action which is likely to handicap the Commission in its work'. Lastly, the Court considered that Luxemburg and German undertakings to terminate and denounce the bilateral agreements once the Community had succeeded in concluding a multilateral agreement did not establish compliance with the duty of loyal co-operation: as it was to take place after the negotiation and conclusion of that agreement, it would have had no practical effect since it would not have facilitated the multilateral negotiations conducted by the Commission.[131]

As can be seen, the Court's analysis in the two judgments did not engage with the question of whether, on the facts, the actions by Luxemburg and Germany interfered with the Community negotiations for a multilateral agreement. It is worth noting that those negotiations never led to an agreement, presumably because for a number of the countries concerned they were overtaken by the accession process. The Court's approach was very principled, however: unilateral treaty-making action by a Member State coinciding with an EU negotiation cannot be tolerated, unless that Member State consults and co-operates with the EU, and in particular with the Commission. The negative consequences of such unilateral action are not spelled out in the judgments. It is in the Opinion of Tizzano AG that we find some further clarification. He took the view that even the mere ratification of a bilateral agreement in a field in which the Community was preparing to negotiate was likely to limit, if not undermine, the common action which the institutions were

[127] *Commission v. Luxemburg* (n 122 above) para 61.
[128] Ibid, para 63.
[129] *Commission v. Germany* (n 122 above) para 68.
[130] *Commission v. Luxemburg* (n 122 above) para 62; *Commission v. Germany* (n 122 above) para 68.
[131] *Commission v. Luxemburg* (n 122 above) para 65; *Commission v. Germany* (n 122 above) para 72.

preparing to take. It prevented them from presenting themselves as the architects of a common position, unless it was at the same time guaranteed that the agreement concluded by the Member State in question was in accordance with the common interest and followed the line desired and decided by the Community bodies. Still less then could it be guaranteed that the rules laid down in the Member State's agreement would exactly reflect the terms that the Community intended to lay down in the common agreement. He considered that ratification in such circumstances constituted *per se* a measure 'which could jeopardise the attainment of the objectives of [the] Treaty'.[132]

The Advocate General also did not accept that Germany could act so as to avoid a legal vacuum. That concern could not justify non-observance of the duty of co-operation. Member States always had to act in a way that was consonant with that duty. If Germany had complied with it, the Commission would have been in a position to set out the Community's reasons appropriately and in good time and to provide information needed to ensure that the Member State's unilateral initiative would have proceeded in accordance with, or at least without prejudice to, Community requirements. The Commission could, for example, have sought amendments designed to ensure that the rules contained in the bilateral agreements were essentially in line with the provisions that the Commission intended to include in the Community agreement.[133]

What these judgments show is that, also in areas of shared competence, where the Member States retain competence as long as the EU has not acted, there are important obligations with which they need to comply. The Court did not establish that Luxemburg and Germany had acted in breach of the Community's exclusive competences. Instead, it found that the duty of co-operation precluded those Member States from further exercising their competences, once the Council had instructed the Commission to negotiate the multilateral agreement, other than in close co-operation and consultation with the Commission. The effect, however, is similar to a case of exclusive competence. Member States may still be permitted to negotiate, but only if this fits with the EU policy.

Also, as in the FAO case, the Court again sought support in a kind of inter-institutional agreement, i.e. the gentleman's agreement concluded between the Commission and the Council which was annexed to the Council decision opening the negotiations. It did so even if the provisions of that agreement did not directly address the question of bilateral action by the Member States. It shows that the Court prefers to identify some sort of legislative basis for clarifying the scope and effects of the duty of co-operation.

The Court returned to the duty of co-operation in the context of the exercise of shared competences in the so-called *PFOS* judgment.[134] Where in *Commission*

[132] Ibid, Opinion of Tizzano AG, paras 82–84.
[133] Ibid, paras 85–88 and 94–95.
[134] *Commission v. Sweden (PFOS)* (n 106 above).

v. Luxemburg and *Commission v. Germany* the negotiation, conclusion, ratification, and implementation of bilateral agreements was in issue, *PFOS* concerned the mere making of a proposal for the nomination of a new substance under a mixed agreement. The case concerned the Stockholm Convention on Persistent Organic Pollutants (POPs), concluded by the Community and the Member States.[135] That convention aims to regulate such pollutants, which are toxic, resist degradation, bioaccumulate, and whose negative effects are cross-border. It must also be noted that there was an internal Community regulation on POPs, adopted around the same time as the convention was concluded.[136] Neither the convention nor the regulation listed PFOS (perfluoroctane sulfonates). Under the Stockholm Convention, the procedure for listing new substances is, in general outline, as follows. Parties to the convention can nominate such a substance, triggering a technical review leading to a recommendation on the possible addition of the substance. The decision on inclusion is reached by the Conference of the Parties, either by consensus, or by a three-quarters majority. However, any party can refuse to be bound by the amendment, and has a period of one year in which to make that decision.

When, in 2004, the Commission sought authorization from the Council to submit a certain number of chemicals, Sweden proposed to the Council's Working Party on International Environmental Issues to add PFOS to the list. The Working Party did not immediately accept this, and instead appeared to defer to prior Commission work on internal control measures for PFOS. In July 2005, Sweden was dissatisfied with the lack of progress at Community level, and unilaterally submitted, in its name and on its own behalf, a proposal to list PFOS in Annex A to the Stockholm Convention. The Commission took the view that this had the consequence of splitting the international representation of the Community and of compromising the unity so far achieved in the framework of the Convention. It considered that this constituted a breach of (current) Article 4(3) TEU, and brought an action against Sweden before the Court.

Maduro AG started his analysis by pointing out that there was no infringement of exclusive Community competence. He referred to the relevant Treaty provisions on environmental protection (current Articles 191 to 193 TFEU), under which the distribution of competences was biased towards action: neither Member States nor the Community could block the other from pursuing a higher level of environmental protection. The Community regulatory framework therefore had to be understood as introducing minimum standards, and as it did not cover PFOS, the Community could not have acquired exclusive competence.[137]

As regards infringement of (current) Article 4(3) TEU, the Advocate General distinguished two questions: (a) whether Sweden could propose to add PFOS to

[135] See Council Decision 2006/507 concerning the conclusion, on behalf of the European Community, of the Stockholm Convention on Persistent Organic Pollutants [2006] OJ L209/1.

[136] Regulation 850/2004 on persistent organic pollutants and amending Directive 79/117 [2004] OJ L158/7.

[137] *Commission v. Sweden (PFOS)* (n 106 above) Opinion of Maduro AG, paras 28–30.

the convention, and (b) whether such a proposal could be made while the Community decision-making process was ongoing. On the first question, the Advocate General rejected the Commission's claim that the Member States can never act individually in the context of a mixed agreement involving shared competences. The test, in his view, should be whether the exercise of shared competence by the Member State was liable seriously to compromise the exercise of a Community competence. Sweden's proposal did not have that effect. It neither forced the Community to be subject to rules that it did not want, nor did it affect its ability to propose rules that it did want. Maduro AG did not accept that difficulties alluded to by the Commission—that the Community had to act to avoid being bound by the addition of PFOS, and that such an addition would trigger demands for compensation from developing countries—were excessive. Those difficulties had to be balanced against the legitimate rights of Member States; in this case Sweden's right adequately to protect its environment and the health of its citizens.[138]

On the second question the Advocate General took a different line. He considered that Sweden's action risked undermining the Community decision-making process. Where such a process was triggered, the Member State had to engage fully and in good faith in it. This implied a duty to co-operate with the decision-making process, and a duty to refrain from taking individual action, at least for a reasonable period of time, until a conclusion to that process had been reached. Sweden had failed to discharge those duties entirely. The Swedish objection that the abstention from making a unilateral proposal would have delayed matters for at least one more year could not meet with approval. The Community decision-making process was slow, and Member States had to acknowledge that results could not be achieved as promptly as when they acted individually. A degree of prudence had to be exercised with regard to Member States using their external competences to interfere with the internal balance of power of the Community decision-making process. In that sense there had been a breach of (current) Article 4(3) TFEU.[139]

The Court's reasoning was different. It started by rejecting Sweden's contention that the duty of co-operation was limited in scope when what were involved were areas of shared competence: the duty of co-operation was of general application and did not depend either on whether the Community competence was exclusive or on any right of the Member States to enter into obligations towards non-member countries. The Court then found that the Commission did not claim exclusive Community competence, and it was therefore assumed that competence was shared. It subsequently recalled the principles concerning the duty of co-operation established in previous cases, including *Commission v. Luxemburg* and *Commission v. Germany* on the effects of a Council decision to start multilateral negotiations. The Court stated that it was settled ground that, at the time when Sweden made the proposal for the listing of PFOS, the Council had not adopted any formal decision as regards a proposal to list substances in the annex to the Stockholm Convention.

[138] Ibid, paras 35–45. [139] Ibid, paras 46–58.

However, the Court had to examine whether, as the Commission maintained, there was at the time a Community strategy, which was not to propose the listing of PFOS immediately, *inter alia*, for economic reasons (i.e. possible demands for compensation by developing countries). In that regard, it was not indispensable that a common position take a specific form, provided that the content of that position could be established to the requisite legal standard.[140]

The Court then analysed, in considerable detail, the state of the Community decision-making process as regards PFOS at the time when Sweden made the proposal, and thereafter. The Court concluded from that analysis that there was, in 2005, a common strategy not to propose, at that time, to list PFOS in the annex to the Stockholm Convention. The institutions considered it preferable to take into account all the relevant factors, including economic factors. It followed that, in unilaterally proposing the addition of PFOS, Sweden had dissociated itself from a concerted common strategy within the Council.[141]

The Court did not stop there. It then analysed in what way Sweden's unilateral proposal had consequences for the EU in the framework of the Stockholm Convention. The Court drew attention to the provisions of that convention which determine (a) that a regional economic integration organization such as the EU cannot exercise its right to vote if any of its Member States exercises their right, and vice versa; and (b) that such an organization and its Member States are not entitled to exercise rights under the convention concurrently. A proposal by a Member State could therefore give rise to a situation where either the EU voted against that proposal, thus depriving the Member State of the possibility of defending its proposal, or the Member State voted, thereby depriving the EU of its right to vote. As regards the possibility for the EU to opt out of an amendment, triggered by a Member State proposal voted on by the Member States, the Court considered that that possibility could be precluded as a result of the rule that the EU and its Member States cannot exercise their rights concurrently. The Court acknowledged that the scope of that rule was uncertain (at the hearing there were different interpretations of the rule). However, even supposing that the EU could still notify a declaration of non-acceptance of an amendment proposed and voted for by several Member States, such a situation could give rise to legal uncertainty for the Member States, the Secretariat of the Stockholm Convention, and for other parties to the convention. And irrespective of those considerations, it was common ground that the objective of a listing proposal was the adoption of an international legal rule which would be binding on the parties to the convention. The EU could thus be bound by the resulting amendment.[142]

Finally, the Court did not accept the analogy with a national measure, more stringent than a minimum EU measure and therefore permitted by (current) Article 193 TFEU.

[140] Ibid, paras 70–77 of the judgment.
[141] Ibid, paras 78–91.
[142] Ibid, paras 92–101.

The difference was that the EU could be bound by an amendment to an annex to the Stockholm Convention, whereas it was not bound by such a national measure.[143]

The Court concluded its analysis by reiterating that the Member States were subject to special duties of action and abstention in a situation in which the Commission had submitted to the Council proposals which, although they had not been adopted, represented the point of departure for concerted Community action. That was especially true in a situation such as that in the case at issue, which was characterized by a unilateral proposal which dissociated the Member State in question from a concerted common strategy within the Council and was submitted within an institutional and procedural framework such as that of the Stockholm Convention. Such a situation was likely to compromise the principle of unity in the international representation of the EU and its Member States and weaken their negotiating power with regard to other parties to the convention.[144]

This important judgment calls for several comments. At first reading it would seem that, even in an area of shared competence, the duty of co-operation precludes unilateral external action by the Member States. The effects are almost identical to those of exclusive EU competences. Has the Court then not effectively expanded the territory of exclusive competence, beyond what are now express Treaty terms in Article 3 TFEU? Is it not ignoring one of the most fundamental constitutional EU principles, that of conferred powers (Article 5 TEU)? The answer to those questions must be nuanced. The judgment needs to be read in the light of the specific set of facts and circumstances of the case. Clearly, the EU had to a large extent occupied the field as regards POPs. It had concluded the Stockholm Convention (as well as other international instruments), albeit together with the Member States. And it had adopted an internal regulation on POPs, designed to give effect to the relevant international instruments. The Court assumed that competences were shared, as the Commission did not argue for exclusive competence, but clearly the EU had already exercised its shared competences in the sphere of POPs when Sweden made its unilateral proposal. There is some analogy here with *Commission v. Luxemburg* and *Commission v. Germany*, discussed above, where the Council had decided to exercise the EU's shared external competences in the sphere of transport, even if that exercise had not yet resulted in an international agreement. There is perhaps even more of an analogy with *Mox Plant*, analysed in a previous section.[145] In that case the Court also emphasized the extent to which the EU had adopted internal acts to combat marine pollution, leading to a finding that UNCLOS provisions on such pollution came within the scope of EU competences which the Council had decided to exercise when concluding UNCLOS. In cases where there are significant EU policies and legislation, the duty of co-operation must mean something, and it is not unjustifiable for it to produce effects akin to cases of exclusive competence.

[143] Ibid, para 102. [144] Ibid, paras 103–104. [145] N 96 above.

In fact one may raise the question of whether *PFOS* should not have been analysed within the paradigm of *AETR*-type exclusive implied powers. It is of course correct, as the Advocate General emphasized, that the EU's competences in the field of environmental protection are shared, and that the Member States are always entitled to adopt more stringent measures (Article 193 TFEU). It is also correct that when Sweden presented its proposal, PFOS was not regulated at EU level. However, there was an internal regulation on POPs, and Sweden's claim was that PFOS was also such a POP, which should be regulated. As the Court accepted, there was nothing in EU law to prevent Sweden from adopting domestic legislation on PFOS, as Article 193 TFEU expressly allows that. Such legislation would not have affected the POP Regulation. However, the Swedish proposal to the Stockholm Convention could have implications for that regulation, as again the Court identified. Unless the EU managed to opt out of an eventual Stockholm Convention amendment, the POP Regulation would ultimately have required updating so as to include PFOS. Does that not mean that the Swedish proposal put in motion an international process (negotiation) which could 'affect or alter the scope' of the POP Regulation (to use the terms of *AETR* and of Article 3(2) TFEU)?

Be that as it may, the Court opted to analyse the lawfulness of Sweden's action under the duty of co-operation. The principle that Member States need to abide by concerted EU action, from the moment such action was started, is difficult to contest. It is less clear though that the discussions in the Council Working Party and between Sweden and the Commission deserved the epitheton of concerted action, at the time when Sweden made its unilateral proposal. Moreover, there is a paradox here. If Sweden had never mentioned PFOS in Brussels, and had gone straight to the Stockholm Convention, it would have been more difficult to identify a concerted EU action on listing PFOS. Yet from the perspective of co-operation between the Member States and the EU, such a course of action would clearly have been worse.

The Court was on much more solid ground when analysing the effects of the Swedish proposal for the EU's participation in the Stockholm Convention. There were indeed awkward questions about the exercise of voting rights and of the right not to accept an amendment. What these questions show is that, once a mixed agreement has been concluded under shared competences, it is difficult to tolerate unilateral action by a Member State. The EU and its institutions need to be involved. It remains possible, of course, for the EU to decide that the Member States can act, for example by voting on a matter within their competences—the FAO Arrangement, discussed above, provides for that. But unilateral action is likely to interfere with the EU's policy, and to constitute a breach of the duty of co-operation.

These are sound principles. What is so far missing in the case law, though, is an analysis of countervailing principles of EU law. The duty of co-operation is not the sole relevant principle. There can be tension with other principles, such as the principle of conferred competences. In the *PFOS* case, it could have been argued (perhaps it was) that the precautionary principle required swift action on PFOS. Under that principle, Sweden should be entitled to push for such swift action. The analysis of such countervailing principles could perhaps lead to a slightly more balanced application of the duty of co-operation. It works in both directions, of course: the EU institutions are also subject to it.

The above case law on the duty of co-operation and the Community's experience with work in international organizations suggest that the principle's effectiveness is limited if it is not fleshed out. There is an obvious case for creating some EU Treaty language on this crucial principle for mixed external action. There is also an obvious case for basic legal texts on how to conduct co-operation in the framework of international organizations.

This section can be concluded by addressing the question as to the basis in EU law of the duty of co-operation itself, a question which has received some attention in the literature.[146] Timmermans took the view that the duty of co-operation is more specific than the general principle of loyalty,[147] but that does not stand in the way of identifying the principle of loyalty as its foundation. He also drew attention to the Court's references to 'the requirement of unity in the international representation of the Community'. In a sense, that requirement of unity and the principle of loyalty can be seen as the twin foundations of the duty of co-operation. By insisting on unity, loyalty, and co-operation the Court expresses a particular conception of mixed external action, a conception which does not consist of simple recognition of split competences, possibly resulting in independent action by the EU and its Member States, but rather one where competences are truly shared or joint, necessitating a common approach maintaining unity.

Further issues

Having thus elaborated on the duty of co-operation, this chapter can now address some of the major problems and legal issues to which mixity gives rise, as the application of the duty of co-operation may contribute towards the resolution of at least some of them. The following analysis is structured according to the various stages of the life of a mixed agreement.

Negotiation

There are no established rules on how to negotiate a mixed agreement. In principle, a mixed negotiation could be divided into an EU and a Member States part, with different negotiators for each part. In practice, however, most mixed agreements are

[146] Helikoski (n 1 above) 95–6; Timmermans (n 33 above) 241; Hillion (n 108 above) 88–92.
[147] Ibid.

negotiated under the EU method, albeit with a more preponderant role for Member States' representatives.[148] Much, however, will depend on the type of agreement and the type of negotiation. The duty of co-operation in any event requires 'close association' between the EU institutions and the Member States.

A reflection of those issues at the level of substance is whether a mixed negotiation always needs to be conducted on the basis of a common position, or whether it is sufficient that there is such a position for the EU part of the agreement.[149] Under a strict division-of-competences approach it would appear sufficient that there is a single negotiating stance for the EU part of the agreement. If, however, the above reading of the Court's case law on the duty of co-operation is correct, that duty would require that a common approach is maintained at all times. Experience teaches that it is difficult to distinguish and separate the EU and non-EU parts of an agreement anyway, in the light of the nature of EU competences and their linkages with national competences, and because a negotiation may float in different directions.[150]

In connection with mixed negotiations it is worth noting that the EU and its Member States are often a cumbersome partner to negotiate with, particularly, but not only, in a bilateral context.[151] For third countries it often appears that the real negotiation takes place within the EU. Once a common position is reached, all flexibility is lost, and the other negotiating partner essentially needs to accept or reject the outcome. Mixed negotiations also offer temptations to Member States governments to extract particular concessions, as agreement by all Member States is necessary.[152]

Clarification of the division of powers

Third countries participating in a mixed negotiation may ask for clarification of the division of powers between the EU and its Member States, as happened with regard to UNCLOS.[153] Such clarification may also be a precondition for joining an international organization, as in the case of the FAO (see above). The EU practice is for these clarifications to be fairly concise and basic, and that approach is no doubt appropriate bearing in mind the complexities involved in defining the exact scope

148 Macleod, Hendry, and Hyett (n 1 above) 151–3; Helikoski (n 1 above) 78–80.

149 Macleod, Hendry, and Hyett (n 1 above) 149–50.

150 See for a good illustration the internal Community debate on competence in the context of the *FAO* case, as described by Jacobs AG (n 115 above) paras 15–22.

151 Cf C Franklin, 'Norway' in XL Xenopoulos (ed), *FIDE—External Relations of the EU and the Member States: Competence, Mixed Agreements, International Responsibility and Effects of International Law* (Theopress Nicosia, 2006) 165.

152 That was the case in negotiations on trade with South Africa, where Italy and Greece sought concessions on ouzo and grappa: see A Rosas, 'The Future of Mixity' in Hillion and Koutrakos (n 1 above) 368–70.

153 Rosas (n 2 above) 204.

and nature of the EU's competences, and the evolving character of EU competence, both through amendments to the Treaties and the adoption of EU legislation creating an *AETR* effect.

In *Ruling 1/78* the Court stated that in a mixed negotiation there was no need to set out and determine, as regards other parties, the division of powers, which is an internal question.[154] That observation is somewhat curious, as surely third countries are not in any way bound by the Court's decisions, and may simply require clarification before allowing the negotiation to go ahead. The statement may in fact originate in a desire to stress the need for joint action in cases of mixity, and to move away from looking at a mixed negotiation through the prism of division of competence.[155]

The request for a clarification of the division of powers may in part be inspired by an understanding that the EU and its Member States, when concluding a mixed agreement, enter into the agreement and bind themselves only in so far as they are respectively competent to do so. Third countries may be concerned to have precise knowledge of the competences issue, so as to be clear about whether it is the EU or the Member States which may be held to account for possible violations.[156] It is doubtful, however, whether there is such a link between competence and responsibility. That issue is analysed below.

Clarification of competence may also be required in the day-to-day practice of an international organization, such as the FAO. Here experience suggests that the EU should do its utmost to avoid such a requirement being imposed on it.[157] In a case concerning the EAEC's accession to the Nuclear Safety Convention the Court considered an action for annulment which the Commission had brought against the Council's accession decision, in so far as that decision included a declaration of competences which the Commission considered incorrect.[158] Such a declaration was required pursuant to Article 30(4)(iii) of the convention. The Court clarified that the Council, when it approved accession to an international convention without any reservation, had to respect the conditions for accession laid down by that convention, since an accession decision which did not comply with those

[154] N 17 above; see previous section.

[155] In his Opinion in Case C-29/99 *Commission v. Council* [2002] ECR I-11221, paras 112–113, Jacobs AG pointed out that in the context of *Ruling 1/78* 'the Commission had asked the Court to state that the usual practice for mixed agreements should be followed, namely that the internal division of powers between the Community and the Member States was not to be defined as far as third parties were concerned', and that 'The Court's statement ...must therefore be read as a mere endorsement of the practice of the Communities of avoiding as far as possible at the negotiating stage the indication to third parties of the internal division of powers between the Community and its Member States. In view of the considerable legal and political difficulties of drafting declarations of competence that practice is indeed to be endorsed, since it allows the Communities and their Member States to focus on more important matters such as the substantive provisions of the agreement'.

[156] Kapteyn and VerLoren van Themaat (n 1 above) 1263.

[157] Sack (n 20 above) 1243–7.

[158] *Commission v. Council* (n 155 above).

conditions would be in breach of the Community's obligations from the moment it entered into force. In the case at hand, Article 30(4)(iii) of the convention had, in the interest of the other contracting parties, to be interpreted to mean that the declaration of competences under that provision had to be complete. It followed that the Council was, under Community law, required to attach a complete declaration of competences to its decision approving accession to the convention.[159] The Court subsequently made a careful examination of the scope of the EAEC's competences in relation to the convention, and annulled the incomplete Council declaration. The judgment, whose principles can no doubt be transposed to EU law, emphasizes the importance of full respect for the EU's competences when making a declaration.[160]

Ratification and conclusion

Most international agreements of some significance do not merely require signing by the contracting parties for their entry into force, but also a further act of municipal endorsement in accordance with a State's constitutional provisions on participation in international law-making. In the case of pure EU agreements, the procedure is fairly straightforward, in particular where the European Parliament's consent is not required.[161] Mixed agreements, however, need to be concluded and ratified by each Member State. Depending on the subject matter of the agreement, procedures within a Member State may be complex and time-consuming, particularly in federal countries in which the component entities have a role to play in the endorsement of the agreement.[162] Some international agreements are of such political importance that these difficulties are easily overcome. The WTO Agreement, for example, was ratified and concluded by the Community institutions and by the Member States in the period between 15 November 1994, when the Court delivered *Opinion 1/94*, and 1 January 1995, when the agreement entered into force. Such swiftness is, however, exceptional. It is a recurring problem of mixed agreements that their entry into force is delayed because some Member States do not manage to ratify.[163] In a fast-evolving international constellation this may undermine the effectiveness of the EU's external action. Rosas reports the extreme case of the agreement on customs union and co-operation with San Marino, where after eight years the agreement had not yet entered into force for lack of ratification

159 Ibid, paras 67–71.

160 On the consequences under international law of a declaration of competences see Macleod, Hendry, and Hyett (n 1 above) 161–2.

161 See Art 218 TFEU, further analysed in Ch 6.

162 See e.g., with respect to ratification of the WTO Agreement, P Eeckhout, 'Belgium' in Jackson and Sykes (n 29 above) 108–10; and M Hilf, 'Negotiating and Implementing the Uruguay Round: The Role of EC Member States—The Case of Germany' in ibid, 125–132.

163 See also J Czuczai, 'Mixity in Practice: Some Problems and Their (Real or Possible) Solution' in Hillion and Koutrakos (n 1 above) 241–5.

by some Member States.[164] It has to be noted that the EU's practice is that the Council will conclude a mixed agreement only once all the Member States have ratified.[165] That is no doubt a safe practice, as otherwise problems of so-called partial mixity may be created (see below).

The EU developed two methods for handling these temporal problems. The first, for agreements containing a trade dimension, is to conclude an interim agreement on trade, which is a pure EU agreement and which can enter into force by way of a simple Council decision.[166] The second method is to provide for provisional application of the agreement at the time of signature, as permitted and regulated by Article 25 VCLT. Since the Amsterdam Treaty, (current) Article 218(5) TFEU also expressly provides for that opportunity. It is obvious, however, that those methods cannot fully replace the definitive entry into force of the entire agreement.

The question thus arises of whether a Member State which does not manage to ratify a particular mixed agreement is in breach of the duty of co-operation. There are arguments for and against such a view. On the one hand, it could be argued that, once a Member State has signed the agreement, it has already expressed its willingness to enter into the agreement together with the EU and the other Member States, and therefore should not hold back on ratification. The reply to that argument from a domestic constitutional perspective would be that municipal procedures deserve to be taken seriously as they constitute the exercise of sovereign national powers, not transferred to the EU. In practice, therefore, much will depend on the reasons for delay. There have been cases where the need for ratification at Member State level became a tool for extracting last-minute commercial concessions from a third country.[167] Such cases may well constitute misuse of national powers, in violation of the duty of co-operation.

Representation and voting

Once a mixed agreement has been concluded, or the EU has joined an international organization, questions of representation and voting rights arise. As the duty of co-operation requires a 'close association' between the EU institutions and the Member States, one would expect a common representation in the bodies set up under a mixed agreement or in an international organization. As to voting rights, the difficulties associated with the allocation of such rights have already

[164] Rosas (n 2 above) 208.

[165] Art 102 EAEC expressly provides for such an approach as regards mixed agreements concluded under that Treaty. See, however, Helikoski (n 1 above) 93, pointing to derogations from this practice; and F Hoffmeister, 'Curse or Blessing? Mixed Agreements in the Recent Practice of the European Union and its Member States' in Hillion and Koutrakos (n 1 above) 256.

[166] E.g. Europe Agreements with Central and East European countries, see M Maresceau, 'On Association, Partnership, Pre-Accession and Accession' in M Maresceau (ed), *Enlarging the European Union* (Longman, 1997) 7.

[167] Agreement with South Africa (n 152 above).

been considered above, in connection with the EU's membership of the FAO. In that organization the alternative exercise of voting rights appears to be the greatest obstacle to an effective joint participation.

The *FAO* judgment pointed the way towards organizing the representation of the EU and its Member States. An inter-institutional agreement can regulate this, and is binding on the institutions because it constitutes implementation of the duty of co-operation.

Implementation, interpretation, and effect

In *Ruling 1/78* the Court of Justice clearly stated that the implementation of a mixed agreement follows the division of powers between the Community and the Member States.[168] Thus, the EU can only implement the provisions of the agreement in the areas of its proper competence, and provisions not coming within the EU's competence can only be implemented by the Member States. Mixed agreements do not therefore entail an expansion of EU competence, even in relation to the particular agreement in question.

That approach is confirmed by a judgment in an enforcement action for failure to fulfil Treaty obligations between the Commission and Ireland.[169] Under Article 5 of Protocol 28 of the EEA Agreement, a mixed agreement, the Contracting Parties undertook to obtain their adherence before 1 January 1995 to the Berne Convention for the Protection of Literary and Artistic Works. The Commission brought an action for Ireland's failure to do so. The Court, referring to its judgment in *Demirel*,[170] held that mixed agreements had the same status in Community law as pure Community agreements, in so far as they contained provisions coming within Community competence. As a consequence, the Member States, in ensuring respect for commitments arising from an agreement concluded by the Community, fulfilled an obligation in relation to the Community, which had assumed responsibility for the due performance of the agreement. The Court then stated that, as the provisions of the Berne Convention covered an area which came in large measure within the scope of Community competence, the requirement of adherence to it came within the Community framework. Accordingly, the Commission was competent to assess compliance with that requirement, subject to review by the Court.[171] Ireland was thus found to have failed to fulfil its obligations under the Treaty.

The Commission can therefore monitor compliance by the Member States with a mixed agreement only if that agreement comes within EU competence. The

[168] *Ruling 1/78* (n 17 above) para 36.
[169] Case C–13/00 *Commission v. Ireland* [2001] ECR I–2943.
[170] N 27 above.
[171] *Commission v. Ireland* (n 169 above) paras 14–20.

judgment also illustrates, however, that such competence may extend to provisions of a mixed agreement which require the Member States to act in a particular way. It is not the case that the EU part of a mixed agreement cannot impose any obligations on the Member States. On the contrary, that part may contain obligations for, or require particular action by, the Member States. It is a general feature of EU law that the implementation of EU acts often needs to take place at national level. There is thus a distinction between competence and legal effects of an agreement.

There is also apparently a distinction between EU competence and the jurisdiction of the Court of Justice to interpret the provisions of a mixed agreement. It is established case law that pure EU agreements are acts of the EU institutions, and that, as such, the Court has jurisdiction to interpret their provisions in the preliminary rulings procedure (Article 267 TFEU).[172] It is logical that that approach is extended to mixed agreements, if they come within EU competence. The Court, however, has gone further in a couple of judgments on the TRIPs Agreement in the context of the WTO. In *Hermès* and *Christian Dior* the Court interpreted Article 50 of TRIPs, a provision on the judicial enforcement of intellectual property rights, in cases involving domestic law on trade marks and patents.[173] The Court's approach was based on the fact that the same provision also governed EC law intellectual property rights, such as the Community trade mark, and that a uniform interpretation was therefore required. It also based its decision on the fact that the WTO Agreement was concluded by the Community and ratified by the Member States without any allocation between them of their respective obligations towards the other contracting parties. In other words, the Community and Member States' parts of the agreement were not expressly identified. Arguably, therefore, if there were a mixed agreement which makes such distinctions, the Court's interpretative jurisdiction would in any event be limited to the EU part, as only that part would be an act of the EU institutions. This case law is further analysed in Chapter 8.

A final important question is to what extent EU law governs the type of legal effect a mixed agreement may have in the EU's and the Member States' legal orders. For pure EU agreements the Court may or may not recognize the direct effect of the agreement, a concept which is hugely significant for day-to-day legal practice. Again this is a subject which will be looked at in Chapter 8, as well as in Chapter 9. Suffice it to say that, as regards mixed agreements, the Court confines its decisions on direct effect to the part of the agreement which comes within EU competence.[174] For other parts of the agreement, the question of the internal legal effect of the agreement is governed by the law of the Member State in which the agreement is relied upon. That approach is not without dangers from a perspective of legal clarity and certainty. It presupposes that the respective competences can be clearly

[172] See Ch 8.

[173] Cases C–53/96 *Hermès v. FHT* [1998] ECR I–3603 and C–392/98 *Parfums Christian Dior v. Tuk Consultancy* [2000] ECR I–11307.

[174] Ibid.

delineated, which is obviously not a foregone conclusion. In many cases, the competence question will need to be clarified before a domestic court would be able to decide on the effect of the provision in question. There is also a possibility that a domestic court could decide on direct effect, whereas the Court of Justice may have jurisdiction to lay down a uniform interpretation of that provision, as its jurisdiction is broader than the provisions of WTO law covered by Community competence. So much follows from *Christian Dior*, where the Court adopted an interpretation but left the question of direct effect for the referring court to decide.[175]

International responsibility

Mixed agreements may raise delicate questions concerning the respective international responsibilities of the Community and of the Member States.[176] Intuitively, one may be inclined to allocate responsibility according to the division of competences between the EU and its Member States.[177] Each could be held responsible only within the scope of its competences. There is, however, little support for that approach in either the case law or the literature, in particular in cases where the division of powers was not clarified at the time of the negotiation and conclusion of the agreement. The prevailing view is thus that, where no declaration of competences was made and the agreement contains no indication of which obligations were entered into by which party (EU or Member States), there is joint responsibility. In such cases the EU and its Member States are jointly liable for the performance of the agreement.[178] In *Parliament v. Council*, regarding Lomé IV, Jacobs AG stated that under a mixed agreement the Community and the Member States were jointly liable unless the provisions of the agreement point to the opposite conclusion.[179]

[175] See Ch 8 for further analysis.

[176] See also M Björklund, 'Responsibility in the EC for Mixed Agreements—Should Non-Member Countries Care?' (2001) 70 Nord J Int L 373; PJ Kuijper and E Paasivirta, 'Further Exploring International Responsibility: The European Community and the ILC's Project on Responsibility of International Organizations' (2004) 1 IOLR 111; P Eeckhout, 'The EU and its Member States in the WTO—Issues of Responsibility' in L Bartels and F Ortino (eds), *Regional Trade Agreements and the WTO Legal System* (OUP, 2006) 449; F Hoffmeister, 'The Contribution of EU Practice to International Law' in M Cremona (ed), *Developments in EU External Relations Law* (OUP, 2008) 64–9; PJ Kuijper, 'International Responsibility for EU Mixed Agreements' in Hillion and Koutrakos (n 1 above) 208; P Eeckhout, 'General Report' in Xenopoulos (n 151 above) 209–303; M Cremona, 'Community Report' in ibid, 341–8.

[177] This approach is advocated by C Kaddous, *Le droit des relations extérieures dans la jurisprudence de la Cour de justice des Communautés européennes* (Helbing & Lichtenhahn, 1998) 173–4.

[178] E Stein, 'External Relations of the European Community: Structure and Process' in *Collected Courses of the Academy of European Law (1990)—Community Law*, Vol I, Book 1 (Martinus Nijhoff, 1991) 162; G Gaja, 'The European Community's Rights and Obligations under Mixed Agreements' in O'Keeffe and Schermers (n 5 above) 135; C Tomuschat, 'The International Responsibility of the European Union' in E Cannizzaro (ed), *The European Union as an Actor in International Relations* (Kluwer Law International, 2002) 185.

[179] Case C–316/91 *Parliament v. Council* [1994] ECR I–625, para 69.

In *Hermès*, which concerned the WTO Agreement, the Court referred to the fact that the agreement was concluded by the Community and ratified by its Member States without any allocation between them of their respective obligations towards the other contracting parties.[180]

There is, however, minority academic opinion,[181] as well as the Opinion of Mischo AG in *Commission v. Ireland*, who took the view that recourse to the formula of a mixed agreement announced to non-member countries that that agreement did not fall wholly within Community competence and that, consequently, the Community was, *a priori*, only assuming responsibility for those parts falling within its competence.[182] The Commission elaborated on this in the observations it submitted to the ILC, which is currently in the process of drawing up draft articles on the responsibility of international organizations.[183] The central provision of the draft articles, as they currently stand, is Article 2, which provides in paragraph 2 that:

> There is an internationally wrongful act of an international organization when conduct consisting of an action or omission:
> (a) Is attributable to the international organization under international law; and
> (b) Constitutes a breach of an international obligation of that international organization.

In the Commission's view, the question of what it calls 'apportionment' of obligations between the international organization and its members needs to be distinguished from the question of attribution of conduct. The former question needs to be answered first, and it is 'entirely determined by the rules of the organization'.[184] The difficulty with that position is that it forces the EU's treaty partners to have expertise on complex matters of EU external competence, leading to the possibility that they may fear that such matters could be an obstacle to invoking the responsibility of the EU or its Member States under a mixed agreement.[185] Moreover, there are contexts in which the Commission is most eager to argue that the EU has full international responsibility under a mixed agreement: that is the case in the WTO, where the EU invariably acts as a respondent in dispute settlement, even when Member State measures are in issue.[186]

The ILC's work remains to be finalized, and the draft articles will no doubt contain a number of provisions which are relevant to the EU's and the Member States' responsibility under a mixed agreement. That being said, the starting-point, in this author's view, must be the question of attribution of conduct. That

[180] *Hermès* (n 173 above) para 24; see also the Opinion of Tesauro AG, paras 14 and 20, and *Dior* (n 173 above) para 33.

[181] J. Groux and P. Manin, *The European Communities in the International Order* (Brussels, 1984) 143.

[182] N 169 above, para 30 of the Opinion.

[183] See ILC, Report of the Sixty-first session (2009), UN Doc A/64/10.

[184] ILC, Second Report on Responsibility of International Organizations, UN Doc A/CN.4/545, at 13–14; see further Kuijper and Paasivirta (n 176 above) 116–23.

[185] Cf Olson (n 15 above) 343–4.

[186] Eeckhout (n 176 above) 451–6.

question is different from the division of competences between the EU and the Member States. The latter may easily adopt measures which are in breach of international obligations contracted by the EU under a mixed agreement. A clear example is tax discrimination of products imported from third countries. Such discrimination may result from national legislation, but the applicable international law rule, Article III:2 GATT 1994, which is part of WTO law, comes within the EU's exclusive competence, as it concerns trade in goods.[187] In those cases where the mixed agreement itself does not distinguish between an EU and a Member States part, the other contracting parties appear to have every right to focus on the question of attribution of conduct under international law, rather than the internal division of competences between the EU and its Member States.

Partial mixity

Many of the above problems and questions become even thornier in cases of partial mixity, where not all the Member States are parties alongside the EU. A clarification of the division of powers becomes more important, arrangements for representation may become more difficult, and there are likely to be more significant issues of implementation, interpretation, legal effect, and international responsibility. As Article 216(2) TFEU provides that agreements concluded by the EU are binding on the institutions *and* on the Member States, a Member State which does not participate in the conclusion of a mixed agreement risks none the less being bound by its provisions. A partially mixed agreement should therefore clarify the commitments entered into by the EU, and indicate the limits of the EU's participation, or the division of responsibility between the EU and the Member States.

Conclusions

Weiler has defended mixity on the ground that it offers an alternative to a centralist and unitarist model of external relations, avoiding a multiplicity of external relations and a weakening of the strength inherent in united action.[188] There are indeed no doubt certain advantages to mixed external action, but this chapter demonstrates that they can hardly be outweighed by the disadvantages. In many cases, mixity is an unnecessary burden, making the EU a more cumbersome and inflexible international actor, difficult to negotiate with, and slow to ratify agreements. Third

[187] See Ch 2.

[188] JHH Weiler, *The Constitution of Europe* (CUP, 1999) 184–6. See also Cremona (n 121 above) 1126, where she defends the flexibility which mixed agreements offer.

countries risk being confused as regards the division of competences between the EU and the Member States; indeed actors within the EU run the same risk. Third countries may also be uncertain as to which party, the EU or the Member States, can be held responsible for failure to implement the agreement. As regards decision-making within the Council, mixity implies unanimity, whereas many pure EU agreements can be concluded by qualified majority. Within the EU legal order, mixity gives rise to highly complex questions concerning jurisdiction to interpret and legal effects (further explored in Chapter 8). By contrast, from a legal perspective there seem to be few, if any, advantages to a mixed agreement. Pure EU agreements are also fully binding on the Member States and, where directly effective, prevail over national law.

Mixity is therefore best avoided, even if it will never be eradicated as long as the EU is based on the principle of conferred powers. Nevertheless, there may be increasing opportunities for avoiding mixity, in particular after the entry into force of the Treaty of Lisbon. At present, many cases of mixity are justified on the basis of the inclusion in an agreement of provisions on a political dialogue. With the development of the CFSP, and with the abolition of the pillar structure, it should become possible to conclude agreements with both a TFEU and CFSP dimension. The establishment of a political dialogue will no longer be such as to justify the participation by Member States. The Treaty of Nice also broadened the Treaty provisions on co-operation with third countries, offering further opportunities for avoiding mixity.

The Court should also become more proactive in cases involving mixity. It should in particular enforce the principle that, when the EU decides to exercise its competences by concluding an international agreement, it cannot at will do so only partially. Where an agreement falls wholly within the EU's non-exclusive external competences, and the EU concludes the agreement, there is no legal justification for mixity. The requirement of unity in the international representation of the EU demands pure EU agreements in such cases.

As regards EU membership of international organizations, there is still a long road to travel before such membership will reflect the EU's competences. The reasons for this are as much located in resistance by international organizations themselves and by third countries, as in traditional concerns over sovereignty in the Member States. The EU's international legal personality is fully recognized at the international level as far as the conclusion of international agreements is concerned, but much less so with respect to membership of international organizations.

It is true that EU law offers remedies for non-membership, but those are only second-best alternatives. There are strong legal rules centred on the duty of co-operation, but the practice shows that such remedies cannot replace full membership. Even where there is such membership, mixity may present problems. The duty of co-operation is an abstract principle which requires embodiment. The case law has shown the way forward, through the rule that inter-institutional agreements on representation in an international organization are binding and can be enforced. However, the practice also shows that a lot may depend on other factors, in particular the location of relevant expertise: there is no general inter-institutional agreement on representation in the WTO, yet the organization of EU and Member States membership appears to raise few problems, and the EU is genuinely able to exercise its competences.

8

The courts and international agreements

Introduction

International agreements are an important instrument of law-making by the European Union. Where States or, as in this case, international organizations act under international law there are, of necessity, two legal dimensions to their action.

First, of course, their legal acts produce effects under international law itself. That is particularly the case where an international agreement is concluded. Such an agreement is binding, and questions of interpretation or effect may at some stage be submitted to an international judicial organ. As regards the EU's participation in treaty-making, the most obvious example is the WTO Agreement, under which dispute panels and the Appellate Body decide whether a member has violated provisions of the covered agreements. Other agreements may also include some form of dispute-settlement system, involving some type of international judicial action.[1] The EU's position and role before international jurisdictions do not in principle differ from those of a State acting under international law, and do not require particular attention in this book.[2]

Secondly, however, international agreements may also produce effects in the internal legal order of the State or organization concluding such agreements. As law-making through international action continues to become more common, it will come as no surprise that international agreements are used in argument before domestic courts. Such use raises at least two kinds of questions. First, does the domestic court have jurisdiction to consider the agreement? Secondly, on the assumption that the reply to the first question is positive, what are the precise legal effects of the agreement in the domestic legal order? It is to those two questions that this chapter and the next respectively turn.

This chapter examines the position of international agreements under the main heads of jurisdiction of the EU's courts:[3] in the first place the Court of

[1] MA Gaudissart, J-V Louis, and L Van den Hende, 'Les clauses de règlement des différends dans les accords internationaux conclus par les communautés européennes' in *Arbitration and European Law* (Bruylant, 1997) 141–81.

[2] See Ch 7 for a few comments on dispute settlement in the WTO.

[3] See also P Koutrakos, *EU International Relations Law* (Hart Publishing, 2006) ch 5.

Justice and the General Court (the former Court of First Instance (CFI)), but also, in particular as regards questions of interpretation or validity of EU law, courts at the level of the Member States. The types of jurisdiction looked at are the following. First, before an agreement is concluded it may form the subject of a request for an Opinion by the Court of Justice as to its compatibility with the Treaties (Article 218(11) TFEU). Secondly, once an agreement is concluded and has entered into force, the interpretation of its provisions may form the subject of a question for a preliminary ruling by the Court of Justice (Article 267 TFEU). Thirdly, an agreement may be relied upon to challenge the legality (or validity) of an act of an institution, in a direct action for annulment (Article 263 TFEU), or again in a question for a preliminary ruling. Fourthly, a party may invoke breach of the provisions of an international agreement in the context of a claim concerning the EU's non-contractual liability (Articles 268 and 340 TFEU). Fifthly, the Commission (or a Member State) may rely upon an agreement concluded by the EU in an enforcement action against a Member State (Article 258 TFEU). Those are the main types of jurisdiction, but the chapter does not end there. It goes on to consider some issues of interpretative approach as regards provisions of international agreements.

Chapter 9 will then analyse the legal effects of international law, including international agreements, in EU law. It is important, however, to bear the interconnections between the two chapters in mind. The separate treatment of jurisdiction and effects is merely an analytical tool, and in reality the two are indissociably linked. For example, the interpretation of the provisions of an international agreement by the Court of Justice in a preliminary ruling case cannot be separated from the legal effects which that agreement produces, for the act of interpreting does not take place in a legal vacuum but will rather serve a particular legal purpose. It is none the less appropriate first to discuss issues of jurisdiction, as a prior understanding of the forms of action in which international agreements may become relevant is indispensable for a proper analysis of the effects of such agreements. Too often, as will be seen, the question of the 'direct effect' of international law is approached without full consideration of important jurisdictional issues, leading to confusion as to what direct effect does and does not entail.

Requests for an Opinion

Article 218(11) TFEU provides that a Member State, the European Parliament, the Council, or the Commission may obtain the Opinion of the Court of Justice on whether an envisaged agreement is compatible with the provisions of the Treaties. Where the Opinion is adverse, the agreement may not enter into force unless it is amended or the Treaties are revised. The *ratio* of the latter provision is of course that, where an agreement is incompatible with the Treaties, following the procedure for amendment may cure any such incompatibility. The provision thereby implicitly confirms that the Court's Opinions are binding on the institutions, which is not immediately apparent from the ordinary meaning of the term 'opinion'.[4]

Originally, the procedure was not available to the European Parliament, in spite of its important role in the conclusion of some types of international agreements, but the Treaty of Nice rectified this lacuna. Private parties are incapable of requesting an Opinion, which is understandable from the perspective that they are not directly involved in the negotiation of agreements. Also, private requests for an Opinion could interfere with the actual negotiation process.[5]

As early as its first Opinion the Court identified the general purpose of the procedure. *Opinion 1/75* concerned a draft 'Understanding on a Local Cost Standard', drawn up within the OECD.[6] The Commission asked whether the Community had competence to conclude this Understanding, and whether its competence was exclusive. In a section on the admissibility of the request, the Court stated that the compatibility of an agreement with the provisions of the Treaty had to be assessed in the light of all the rules of the Treaty, i.e. both those rules which determined the extent of the powers of the institutions and the substantive rules. This followed from the purpose of the Opinion procedure, which was to forestall complications which would result from legal disputes concerning the compatibility with the then EEC Treaty of international agreements binding upon the Community. In fact, the Court continued, a possible decision of the Court to the effect that such an agreement was, by reason either of its content or of the procedure adopted for its conclusion, incompatible with the provisions of the Treaty, could not fail to provoke serious difficulties, not only in a Community context but also in that of international relations, and might give rise to adverse consequences for all interested parties, including third countries. For the purpose of avoiding such complications, the Treaty had recourse to the exceptional procedure of a prior reference to the Court, which therefore had to be open for all questions capable of submission for judicial consideration, either by the Court or possibly by national courts, in so far as such questions gave rise to doubt as to either the substantive or formal validity of the agreement with regard to the Treaty. The Court then pointed out that the

[4] See, *inter alia*, V Christianos, 'La compétence consultative de la Cour de justice à la lumière du Traité sur l'Union européenne' (1994) 374 RMCUE 37; C Kaddous, *Le droit des relations extérieures dans la jurisprudence de la Cour de justice des Communautés européennes* (Helbing & Lichtenhahn, 1998) 112–25; R Plender, 'The European Court's Pre-Emptive Jurisdiction: Opinions under Article 300(6) EC' in D O'Keeffe and A Bavasso (eds), *Judicial Review in European Union Law—Liber Amicorum in Honour of Lord Slynn of Hadley* (Kluwer Law International, 2000) i, 203–20; G Gattinara, 'La compétence consultative de la Cour de justice après les avis 1/00 et 2/00' (2003) RMCUE 687; A De Walsche, 'Le contrôle juridictionnel des accords internationaux' in J-V Louis and M Dony (eds), *Commentaire J Megret—Relations extérieures* (Etudes européennes, 2005) 141–55.

[5] Plender (n 4 above) 219 none the less pleads for allowing private parties who are directly and individually concerned to seise the Court. It is not, however, easy to see which type of international agreement would be of direct and individual concern.

[6] *Opinion 1/75 re Local Cost Standard* [1975] ECR 1355; see Ch 2.

question of whether the conclusion of a given agreement was within the power of the Community and whether such power had been exercised in conformity with the provisions of the Treaty was, in principle, a question which could be submitted to the Court, either directly, under what are now Articles 258 and 263 TFEU, or in accordance with the preliminary rulings procedure. It therefore had to be admitted that the matter could be referred to the Court in a request for an Opinion.[7]

This is a clear ruling on the rationale and scope of Opinions. The complications to which the Court alludes are not difficult to understand. Once an agreement is concluded under international law, a contracting party cannot invoke the unlawfulness of that agreement under its municipal law, except under the restrictive conditions of Article 46 of the Vienna Convention on the Law of Treaties (VCLT).[8] Where the act of concluding an agreement is annulled for violation of municipal law, the contracting party is faced with the awkward position of continuing to be bound under international law. It is then, one presumes, obliged to terminate or renegotiate the agreement, a position clearly to be avoided. An Opinion may thus, in case of doubts, clarify (in)compatibility and thereby prevent such difficulties. By taking this approach in *Opinion 1/75* the Court also decided that it indeed has jurisdiction to rule on the legality, under EU law, of the conclusion of an international agreement (see also below on actions for annulment and questions of validity).

In *Opinion 1/75* the Court also clarified that the term 'agreement' in (current) Article 218(11) TFEU has to be broadly interpreted as including 'any undertaking entered into by entities subject to international law which has binding force, whatever its legal designation'.[9] Such a broad interpretation corresponds to the general purpose of the Opinion procedure: the above complications may arise in connection with any type of international law commitment.[10]

It follows from the general purpose of the procedure that an Opinion is appropriate only where an agreement is 'envisaged', and is not yet concluded. In subsequent cases, the Court looked at the two outer boundaries of the notion of an envisaged agreement. Which are the conditions for there to be an agreement which

[7] Ibid, 1360–1. On competence and legal basis, see also *Opinion 2/00 re Cartagena Protocol on Biosafety* [2001] ECR I-9713, paras 1–19.

[8] Art 46 provides:

> 1. A State may not invoke the fact that its consent to be bound by a treaty has been expressed in violation of a provision of its internal law regarding competence to conclude treaties as invalidating its consent unless that violation was manifest and concerned a rule of its internal law of fundamental importance.
>
> 2. A violation is manifest if it would be objectively evident to any State conducting itself in the matter in accordance with normal practice and in good faith.

[9] *Opinion 1/75* (n 6 above) 1360. See also *Opinion 1/08 re GATS Schedules* [2009] ECR I-11129, paras 96–105, where the Court decided that, next to compensatory adjustments to those schedules, modifications and withdrawals also constituted agreements with the other WTO members.

[10] See further Plender (n 4 above) 207, where he argues that the word 'agreement' is wide enough to embrace undertakings expressed by the casting of votes in international organizations.

is genuinely envisaged, so that the Court does not look into a mere flight of fancy of an institution or a Member State? And at what point is the agreement no longer merely envisaged, but rather definitive, such that the procedure may no longer serve its purpose?

The first question came up in *Opinion 2/94*. That case concerned EC accession to the ECHR, which has been a contentious issue for decades. For a long time there was no consensus among Member States that such accession was required or appropriate for strengthening Community fundamental rights protection. None the less, in late 1993 the Belgian Presidency again put the issue on the agenda of the Council, and managed to persuade the Council to request the Court's Opinion on (a) whether there was competence under the EC Treaty to join the ECHR, and (b) whether accession would be compatible with the Treaty. The Council could decide to make such a request by simple majority. Before the Court, the governments of Ireland, the United Kingdom, Denmark, and Sweden submitted that the request was inadmissible, or at any rate premature. In their view, an agreement could not be said to be envisaged where the Council had not even adopted a decision in principle to open negotiations. In its reply, the Court recalled the general purpose of the procedure. It then indicated that no negotiations had been commenced, nor had the precise terms of accession been determined. In order to assess the extent to which this affected the admissibility of the request, the Court felt it was necessary to distinguish the purposes of the request. As regards the question of Community competence, the Court held that it was in the interests of the Community institutions and of the States concerned, including non-member countries, to have that question clarified from the outset of negotiations and even before the main points of the agreement were negotiated. The only condition was that the purpose of the envisaged agreement be known before negotiations were commenced. That was clearly the case as regards Community accession to the ECHR, as the general purpose and subject matter of the ECHR and the institutional significance of accession for the Community were perfectly well known. The fact that the negotiations had not been commenced did not stand in the way of admissibility. As regards substantive compatibility of the accession agreement with the Treaty, however, matters were different. Here the Court needed sufficient information regarding the arrangements by which the Community would envisage submitting to the judicial control machinery established by the ECHR. As no such information was available the Court was not in a position to give its Opinion on this aspect.[11]

It is doubtful whether the Court's reasoning is entirely convincing. Much as the purpose of the envisaged agreement was clear, so were the general institutional consequences of accession: the Community would be bound by the provisions of the ECHR, as authoritatively interpreted by the European Court of Human

[11] *Opinion 2/94 re Accession to the ECHR* [1996] ECR I–1759, paras 1–22.

Rights (ECtHR). But this leads us into questions of substance which cannot be further considered here.

Two other cases concern the point at which the agreement is no longer 'envisaged', but has become binding. In *Opinion 1/94*, concerning the WTO Agreement, the Spanish government argued that the request was inadmissible because the agreement had already been signed, entailing an obligation on the part of the signatories to submit it for the approval of their respective authorities. The Court brushed this objection aside, pointing out that it may be called upon to state its Opinion at any time before the Community's consent to be bound by an agreement is finally expressed (thereby referring to the conclusion of the agreement by the Council). Unless and until that consent is given, the agreement remains an envisaged agreement.[12]

Whilst the Court delivered *Opinion 1/94* in time for the Council to be able to conclude, and for the Member States to be able to ratify, the WTO Agreement before 1 January 1995,[13] it did not manage to do the same with respect to *Opinion 3/94*, on bananas. At some point in the unfolding bananas saga, only a couple of weeks before the signing of the WTO Agreement, the Commission negotiated a 'framework agreement' on imports of bananas with a number of Latin American countries, and then made the substance of that agreement part of the Community's GATT tariff schedules, which are in turn an integral part of the WTO Agreement. Disagreeing with that course of action, Germany requested the Court's Opinion on the compatibility of the framework agreement, as incorporated in the WTO Agreement, with the EC Treaty. It made the request in July 1994, three months after the signature of the WTO Agreement. The Court managed to produce its Opinion only in December 1995, one year after the Council concluded the WTO Agreement.

In the light of that state of affairs, the Court addressed the question of whether, for it to be able to deliver an Opinion, it is sufficient that the agreement be envisaged when the request is lodged, or whether it must still be so when the Court delivers the Opinion. The Court considered the text and purpose of (current) Article 218(11) TFEU. At the textual level, the Court drew attention to the fact that, where the Court's Opinion was adverse, the agreement could enter into force only in accordance with the procedure for amendment of the Treaties. It would therefore be contrary to the internal logic of the relevant Treaty provision to accept that it was appropriate for the Court to rule on the compatibility of an agreement which had already been concluded, since a negative Opinion would not have the prescribed legal effect. The purpose of the procedure confirmed this: the preventive intent of an Opinion could no longer be achieved if the Court ruled on an agreement which had already been concluded. Nor was the Court convinced

[12] *Opinion 1/94 re WTO Agreement* [1994] ECR I-5267, paras 10–12.

[13] Council Decision 94/800 concerning the conclusion on behalf of the European Community, as regards matters within its competence, of the agreements reached in the Uruguay Round multilateral negotiations (1986–1994) [1994] OJ L336/1.

that considerations of judicial protection altered that conclusion. Requests for an Opinion did not aim to protect the interests and rights of the Member State or the institution which had made the request. In any event, that State or institution could bring an action for annulment of the Council's decision to conclude the agreement and could in that context apply for interim relief. The Court's conclusion was that the request for an Opinion had become devoid of purpose, and that there was accordingly no need to respond.[14]

The Court's reasoning was surely correct, but it did not in any way address what should be the conduct of the various institutions or Member States, when a request for an Opinion is made and the Court may not be able to deal with it before the agreement is concluded.[15] Is the Council required to await the Court's Opinion before concluding the agreement? If so, does it then not risk becoming the hostage of actors which are opposed to the agreement and which make a request for dilatory purposes? Should not the Court be more proactive in ensuring that Opinions are delivered before the agreement is concluded, particularly in those cases where there is urgency? Questions and problems of this kind can only be resolved through a concerted effort by all the actors involved, which, unfortunately, was lacking in the case of *Opinion 3/94*. A similar problem arose in the passenger name records (PNR) case, where the Parliament initially requested the Court's Opinion on a draft PNR agreement with the United States. When the Council concluded the agreement, the Parliament withdrew its Opinion, and instead brought an action for annulment, which was successful.[16] The Council was then obliged to renegotiate the PNR agreement, which proved to be a difficult exercise.[17]

A major part of the Court's Opinions concerns questions of external competence, rather than questions of substantive compatibility.[18] By assuming this type of jurisdiction, the Court significantly contributed to shaping the legal principles governing the EU's external action. There can be little doubt that there would have been fewer opportunities to do so had the procedure not existed. It is reasonable conjecture to assume that the Commission, for example, would have found it much harder to question, in law, the scope and the nature of the Community's various external powers if it had been obliged to proceed by way of actions for the annulment of Council

[14] *Opinion 3/94 re Framework Agreement on Bananas* [1995] ECR I–4577.

[15] See also Plender (n 4 above) 213–15; I Macleod, ID Hendry, and S Hyett, *The External Relations of the European Communities* (OUP, 1996) 113.

[16] Joined Cases C–317 and 318/04 *European Parliament v. Council (PNR)* [2006] ECR I–4721, paras 39 and 45.

[17] Council Decision 2007/551 on the signing, on behalf of the European Union, of an Agreement between the EU and the United States of America on the processing and transfer of Passenger Name Record (PNR) data by air carriers to the United States Department of Homeland Security (DHS) [2007] OJ L204/16.

For analysis and critical comment see V Papakonstantinou and P De Hert, 'The PNR Agreement and Transatlantic anti-terrorism Cooperation: No firm human rights framework on either side of the Atlantic' 46 (2009) CML Rev 907.

[18] See A Dashwood, Annotation Opinion 2/00 (2002) 39 CML Rev 366 for a list of competence issues. See also the two latest Opinions: *Opinion 1/03 re Lugano Convention* [2006] ECR I–1145, para 112 and *Opinion 1/08* (n 9 above) paras 109–110.

decisions whereby agreements were concluded. Such actions challenge definitive agreements, and give rise to the political and legal complications referred to above. The Opinion procedure has in effect amounted to some type of coalition between the Commission and the Court for strengthening the legal dimension of the EU's external relations, as is also clear from previous chapters. The Court's eagerness to rule on questions of competence in Opinions is illustrated by *Opinion 2/91*, concerning ILO Convention No 170. There the objection was that no Community agreement was envisaged, since the EC was not a member of the ILO and since only members could ratify ILO conventions. The Court replied that the request for an Opinion did not concern the Community's capacity on the international plane but related to the scope of the Community's competence under Community law.[19] It is doubtful, however, whether this approach is still in line with the general purpose of the procedure, which is to avoid complications arising from challenges to the lawfulness of a concluded agreement: the ILO Convention could never be an EU agreement.[20]

The Commission and the Court have certainly not always agreed on the precise outcome, but they have together injected a strong dose of legality into the EU's external policies. How strong the effects of that dose on the EU's practice have been is open to debate.

It may finally be noted that requests for an Opinion may apparently concern any agreement which the EU plans to conclude, including an agreement concerning CFSP matters. This seems to be an exception to the exclusion of the Court's jurisdiction over CFSP matters in Article 275 TFEU.

Preliminary rulings on questions of interpretation

General issues

The procedure of Article 218(11) TFEU is confined to envisaged agreements. Once concluded, an agreement may form the object of a reference under Article 267 TFEU. Such a reference may concern the validity of the agreement, in which case the issues are similar to those arising in the context of actions for annulment. The next section examines such challenges to the lawfulness of an agreement. However, most references for a preliminary ruling involving an international agreement concluded by the EU are concerned with the interpretation of such an agreement. It is obvious that the reference to the Court of Justice, by a court or tribunal in a Member State, of questions of interpretation of an agreement is useful only if (a) the Court has jurisdiction to interpret and (b) the referring court may or must give

[19] *Opinion 2/91 re ILO Convention No 170* [1993] ECR I–1061, paras 1–5.

[20] See also *Opinion 2/92 re Third Revised Decision of the OECD on national treatment* [1995] ECR I–521, paras 9–14 and *Opinion 2/00* (n 7 above) paras 1–9, both as regards the issue of legal basis, where again the Court adopted a broad approach towards its jurisdiction. Plender (n 4 above) 212 defends the approach.

effect to the provisions of the agreement in the case before it. The effects of an agreement are analysed in the following chapter. This section examines the Court's jurisdiction to interpret.[21] As will be shown, the Court readily accepted that it has such jurisdiction, and even extended it to acts adopted under an agreement. The most difficult issue concerns mixed agreements: what is the scope of the Court's jurisdiction over provisions in an agreement concluded by both the EU and its Member States?

The first reference which came to the Court as regards an agreement was in *Haegeman*. The Haegeman company imported wines from Greece into Belgium. At the time Greece was not yet a Member State, but was linked to the Community through an association agreement (the Athens Agreement). Haegeman had to pay a countervailing charge on the wines it imported, and claimed that the charge was not in conformity with the association agreement. The Tribunal de Première Instance (First Instance Tribunal) of Brussels referred a question of interpretation of the agreement's provisions (as well as a question of validity of a regulation, in the light of the agreement) to the Court of Justice. The Court did not agree with Haegeman's submissions, but it did accept jurisdiction. It referred to the first paragraph of Article 177 EEC (current Article 267 TFEU), according to which 'the Court shall have jurisdiction to give preliminary rulings concerning... the interpretation of acts of the institutions of the Community'. As the Athens Agreement was concluded by the Council it was, in so far as concerned the Community, an act of one of the institutions. The Court added that the provisions of the agreement, from the coming into force thereof, formed an integral part of Community law. Thus, within the framework of Community law, the Court had jurisdiction to give preliminary rulings concerning the interpretation of the agreement.[22]

Since *Haegeman* there have been many more cases in which provisions of agreements concluded by the Community came up for interpretation, and the Court has never hesitated to reply to them (with qualifications, however, in the case of mixed agreements: see below). None the less, the assumption of jurisdiction has been criticized. Hartley has argued that there is a distinction between an agreement and the decision of conclusion, and that the Court has jurisdiction to interpret the latter, which is properly an act of an institution, but not the former, which is an act of the EU as a whole, and not of an institution of the EU.[23] That argument is not persuasive. It is artificial not to regard an international agreement as an act of the institutions of the EU, simply on the grounds that it is not unilateral. Article 267 TFEU does not restrict the notion of an act of an institution to unilateral acts. It is true that the agreement as such is to be distinguished from the act of conclusion, but the former is as much an act of the institutions (together with the other contracting parties) as the latter. The Court has generally, and correctly, adopted a

[21] See also Kaddous (n 4 above) 70–86.

[22] Case 181/73 *Haegeman v. Belgium* [1974] ECR 449, paras 2–6.

[23] TC Hartley, *The Foundations of European Community Law* (4th edn, OUP, 1998) 263.

broad interpretation of its jurisdiction to interpret EU law in the setting of the preliminary rulings procedure.[24] Its jurisdiction effectively extends to interpreting all rules of EU law. By not assuming jurisdiction over the interpretation of agreements concluded by the EU the Court would have introduced an awkward dichotomy between 'internal' and 'external' EU law. It would have established an inappropriate judicial *non liquet* as regards the EU's international action.[25]

The broad approach to jurisdiction was confirmed in cases concerning decisions of bodies set up under an agreement. *Sevince* concerned decisions of the Association Council set up to implement the Ankara Agreement[26] establishing an association between the EEC and Turkey (a mixed agreement). The Association Council comprises, on the one hand, members of the governments of the Member States, of the Council, and of the Commission and, on the other hand, members of the Turkish government. It has the power, acting unanimously, to take decisions in order to obtain the objectives laid down by the agreement. As regards the free movement of workers, the Association Council had adopted two decisions containing provisions on access to employment in the Member States. Sevince was a Turkish national residing in the Netherlands who relied on those decisions against the refusal of a residence permit. The Court recalled the principle that the provisions of an agreement concluded by the Community form an integral part of the Community legal system as from the entry into force of that agreement. It then referred to a previous decision in which it had held that, since they were directly connected with the agreement to which they gave effect, the decisions of an Association Council, in the same way as the agreement itself, formed an integral part, as from their entry into force, of the Community legal system.[27] Therefore, since the Court had jurisdiction to give preliminary rulings on the agreement, in so far as it was an act adopted by one of the institutions of the Community, it also had jurisdiction to give rulings on the interpretation of the decisions adopted by the authority established by the agreement and entrusted with responsibility for its implementation. That finding, the Court continued, was reinforced by the fact that the function of the preliminary rulings procedure was to ensure the uniform application throughout the Community of all provisions forming part of the Community legal system and to ensure that the interpretation thereof did not vary according to the interpretation accorded to them by the various Member States.[28]

The Court's reasoning in this case followed the logic of *Haegeman* and of the Court's general approach towards its preliminary rulings jurisdiction. Perhaps the

[24] D Anderson and M Demetriou, *References to the European Court* (2nd edn, Sweet & Maxwell, 2002) 58.

[25] Cf I Cheyne, 'International Instruments as a Source of Community Law' in A Dashwood and C Hillion (eds), *The General Law of EC External Relations* (Sweet & Maxwell, 2000) 257–8; Kaddous (n 4 above) 72.

[26] [1964] JO 217.

[27] Case 30/88 *Greece v. Commission* [1989] ECR 3711, para 13.

[28] Case C–192/89 *Sevince* [1990] ECR I–3461, paras 8–11.

most remarkable aspect of the decision is that it concerned a mixed agreement, and that the Court made no effort to examine whether the decisions of the Association Council, on which the Member States are also represented as such, came within the scope of the Community's powers or of those of the Member States. Those decisions concerned access to employment. The Court had, however, previously decided, in *Demirel*, that the provisions of the Ankara Agreement on movement of workers came within the Community's powers,[29] and it may therefore have assumed that those powers extended to the decisions in issue.

Deutsche Shell extended interpretative jurisdiction to non-binding recommendations made under an agreement. The case concerned a 'resolution' adopted by the Joint Committee set up under the 1987 Convention on a Common Transit Procedure between the EEC and the EFTA countries. The Court examined whether a non-mandatory measure, adopted on the basis of an agreement concluded by the Community, formed part of the Community legal order. Recalling *Sevince*, the Court found that the recommendation was directly linked to the convention and concerned its implementation. The recommendation therefore formed part of Community law. In line with other case law, the fact that the measure had no binding effect did not preclude the Court from ruling on its interpretation. Although the recommendations of the Joint Committee could not confer upon individuals rights which they could enforce before national courts, the latter were nevertheless obliged to take them into consideration in order to resolve disputes submitted to them, especially when they were of relevance in interpreting the provisions of the convention.[30]

That decision is perfectly in line with previous judgments. It also illustrates that interpretation may not only be sought in order to identify enforceable rights for a private party: provisions of an agreement or acts adopted under an agreement may produce other types of effect. In Chapter 9 these effects are explored further.

Mixed agreements—first developments

The most complex questions concerning the Court's jurisdiction to interpret provisions of an agreement arise as regards mixed agreements.[31] In principle, a mixed agreement does not wholly come within the EU's competence. One of the difficulties, however, is that the division of competence between the

[29] Case 12/86 *Demirel v. Stadt Schwäbisch Gmünd* [1987] ECR 3719.

[30] Case C–188/91 *Deutsche Shell v. Hauptzollamt Hamburg-Harburg* [1993] ECR I–363, paras 14–18. See also Case C–162/97 *Nilsson and Others* [1998] ECR I–7477, para 49.

[31] See Ch 7; P Koutrakos, 'The Interpretation of Mixed Agreements under the Preliminary Reference Procedure' (2002) 7 EFA Rev 25 and 'Interpretation of Mixed Agreements' in C Hillion and P Koutrakos (eds), *Mixed Agreements Revisited—The EU and its Member States in the World* (Hart Publishing, 2010) 116–23; A Dashwood, 'Preliminary Rulings on the Interpretation of Mixed Agreements' in O'Keeffe and Bavasso (eds) (n 4 above) 167–75.

EU and the Member States may not be clarified in either the agreement or the decision to conclude it. That is precisely one of the advantages of mixed agreements, as it avoids the often complex, disputed, and therefore tortuous delineation of powers. None the less, intuitively at least, it would seem logical to assume that the Court's interpretative jurisdiction is limited to the provisions of a mixed agreement which are covered by EU competence.[32] Is the Court to determine then, in each reference involving a mixed agreement, whether the provisions forming the object of questions of interpretation come within EU competence?

The foundational *Haegeman* judgment itself concerned a mixed agreement, but the Court did not consider the issue.[33] In *Demirel*, a case concerning the provisions on movement of workers in the Ankara Agreement, the German government argued that those provisions did not come within Community competence, and that the Court therefore did not have jurisdiction. The Court, however, disagreed with the German competence analysis, and stated that the question of whether it had jurisdiction to rule on the interpretation of a provision in a mixed agreement containing a commitment which only the Member States could enter into in the sphere of their own powers did not arise.[34] It is indicative, though, that the Court mentioned the issue as a question rather than simply confirming that its interpretative jurisdiction was coextensive with Community competence.

For a long time the Court managed to steer clear of the jurisdiction question. As indicated, *Sevince* also concerned a mixed agreement, but the Court did not mention that aspect.[35] In the later *Kus* case, which also dealt with the decisions of the EC–Turkey Association Council on movement of workers, the German government attempted to persuade the Court to reverse *Sevince*, by arguing, *inter alia*, that the decisions of the Association Council dealt with matters coming within the competence of the Member States and thus were not acts of a Community institution. The Court, however, saw no reason to depart from *Sevince*, and did not give a material reply to the German arguments on competence.[36]

[32] E.g. HG Schermers, 'The Internal Effect of Community Treaty-making' in HG Schermers and D O'Keeffe (eds), *Essays in European Law and Integration* (Kluwer, 1982) 174–5; E Stein, 'External Relations of the European Community: Structure and Process' in *Collected Courses of the Academy of European Law (1990)—Community Law*, Vol I, Book 1 (Martinus Nijhoff, 1991) 165; L Hancher, 'Constitutionalism, the Community Court and International Law' [1994] NYIL 284; CWA Timmermans, 'The Implementation of the Uruguay Round by the EC' in JHJ Bourgeois, F Berrod, and E Gippini Fournier (eds), *The Uruguay Round Results—A European Lawyers' Perspective* (European Interuniversity Press, 1995) 507; Macleod, Hendry, and Hyett (n 15 above) 157.

[33] *Haegeman* (n 22 above).

[34] *Demirel* (n 29 above) paras 6–12.

[35] *Sevince* (n 28 above).

[36] Case C–237/91 *Kus v. Landeshaupstadt Wiesbaden* [1992] ECR I–6781, para 9; Darmon AG referred to *Demirel*: see paras 17–18 of his Opinion.

Mixed agreements—case law on TRIPs

The jurisdiction question came squarely before the Court in *Hermès*, which concerned provisions of the TRIPs Agreement.[37] TRIPs is a broad agreement on intellectual property protection which is part of the package of trade agreements managed by the WTO (and is legally part of the overall WTO Agreement). The question of the Court's jurisdiction over trade agreements coming under the WTO umbrella is of great significance, essentially for two reasons. First, those agreements cover a wide range of areas and contain many significant provisions for the conduct of international trade and for international economic relations. Depending on the effects which courts are willing to give to the agreements, those provisions could be regularly used in court proceedings. Secondly, as is well known (and will be analysed in the next chapter), the Court denies the provisions of the WTO Agreement direct effect in EU law. The lack of direct effect seriously restrains the scope for application of the WTO Agreement at the instance, for example, of private parties to a dispute before a national court. It is here that the jurisdiction point becomes significant. In so far as the Court of Justice were to decline jurisdiction to interpret parts of the WTO Agreement, national courts might be inclined to plot their own course on the effects of the agreement, rather than follow the Court's ruling on the lack of direct effect. They could, for instance, decide that certain provisions of WTO law do have direct effect in domestic law.

The case of the WTO Agreement is also significant because it illustrates the difficulties associated with taking the EU's competence as the criterion for the Court's jurisdiction. The WTO Agreement covers areas where Community and national competence used to be particularly entangled, as was demonstrated by the complexity of *Opinion 1/94*.[38] If competence is the criterion for jurisdiction, the latter will be the hostage of the complexity of the former. However, as regards the specific case of TRIPs and WTO law, the Treaty of Lisbon appears to have removed the complexity of mixed competence. As analysed in Chapter 2, the common commercial policy now extends to 'the conclusion of tariff and trade agreements relating to trade in goods and services, and the commercial aspects of intellectual property' (Article 207(1) TFEU). Subject to confirmation by the Court, this means that GATS and TRIPs come within the EU's exclusive competence (with the exception of transport). Logically, it follows that the provisions of those agreements come within the Court's preliminary rulings jurisdiction. The case law analysed below is therefore outdated, and no longer of direct relevance. Nevertheless, the principles which the Court developed in the TRIPs cases may be relevant for other mixed agreements (such as UNCLOS). Their study therefore continues to be useful.

The facts of *Hermès* were as follows. Article 50 TRIPs concerns the ordering of provisional measures by judicial authorities to prevent certain infringements of

[37] Case C–53/96 *Hermès International v. FHT* [1998] ECR I–3603.

[38] *Opinion 1/94* (n 12 above); see Chs 2 and 3.

intellectual property rights. In the course of 1995, Hermès took the view that the company FHT Marketing Choice BV was marketing copies of its ties. Issues arose which turned on the interpretation of Article 50 TRIPs, and the President of the District Court referred a question concerning that provision to the Court of Justice. The Netherlands, French, and UK governments argued before the Court that it had no jurisdiction to reply to the question. In support, they referred to paragraph 104 of *Opinion 1/94*,[39] in which the Court held that the provisions of TRIPs on measures to secure effective protection of intellectual property rights fell essentially within the competence of the Member States, and not that of the Community. Thus, Article 50 TRIPs did not fall within the scope of application of Community law and the Court had no jurisdiction to interpret that provision.[40] The Commission, by contrast, argued that there was no necessarily absolute parallelism between the Community's competence to conclude agreements and the Court's interpretative jurisdiction. A mixed agreement was a single agreement whose interpretation and application had to be uniform, and the WTO agreements formed a whole that required interpretation based on the same criteria, avoiding the risk of diverging interpretations by the Court and the national courts on questions of major importance, such as direct effect.[41]

In a long and powerfully argued Opinion, Tesauro AG proposed that the Court should reply to the question of interpretation. In essence, the Advocate General considered that the principle that the Court had jurisdiction to interpret only the provisions that come within the Community's competence was only superficially clear and simple, but in fact proved to be fraught with problems. Provisions of one and the same agreement could be interconnected, and a given 'national' interpretation could affect the application of 'Community' provisions and/or the functioning of the system as a whole. The requirement of uniformity in interpretation and application could therefore quite properly be regarded as fundamental. The Advocate General also drew attention to the international responsibility of the Community, which extended to all of the WTO agreements. In his view, this meant that the Court of Justice had jurisdiction to ensure uniformity in interpretation and application throughout the Community and to protect the Community's interest in not being obliged to assume responsibility for infringements committed by one or more Member States. As a third point, the Advocate General referred to the duty of co-operation and the requirement of unity in the international representation of the Community, which extended to the negotiation, conclusion, and implementation of the commitments entered into. From that perspective it had to be recognized that the absence of centralized interpretation could completely undo the results achieved by the obligation to co-operate in the negotiation and conclusion of the provisions in question: the possibility could not be ruled out that, on the very

[39] Ibid; see Chs 2 and 3.

[40] *Hermès International* (n 37 above) paras 22–33.

[41] Ibid, Opinion of Tesauro AG, para 17.

points on which a consensus had been reached, the national courts might suddenly produce fifteen different interpretations (the then number of Member States), making an absolute nonsense of co-operation when it came to applying the provisions in question. Thus, interpretation by the Court could represent its contribution to the fulfilment of the duty of co-operation between institutions and Member States. Lastly, the Advocate General made a comment of a more general nature. Although the Community legal system was characterized by the simultaneous application of provisions of various origins—international, Community, and national—it nevertheless sought to function and to represent itself to the outside world as a unified system. That was, in the Advocate General's view, the inherent nature of the system which, while guaranteeing the maintenance of the realities of States and of individual interests of all kinds, also sought to achieve a unified *modus operandi*. Its steadfast adherence to that aim was lent considerable weight by the judicial review mechanism which was defined in the Treaty and relied on the simultaneous support of the Community court and the national courts.[42]

The Court largely followed the approach which Tesauro AG had advocated. It started its analysis by pointing out that the WTO Agreement was concluded by the Community and ratified by its Member States without any allocation between them of their respective obligations towards the other contracting parties. Equally, the Court continued, without there being any need to determine the extent of the obligations assumed by the Community in concluding the agreement, it had to be noted that at the time of signature of the WTO Agreement Council Regulation 40/94 on the Community trade mark had been in force.[43] The Court then identified the legal relationship between that regulation and Article 50 TRIPs. Article 99 of the regulation concerned 'provisional, including protective, measures'. The Court admitted that the measures there envisaged and the relevant procedural rules were those provided for by the domestic law of the Member State concerned for the purposes of the national trade mark. However, since the Community was a party to TRIPs and since that agreement applied to the Community trade mark, the courts referred to in Article 99 of the regulation, when called upon to apply national rules with a view to ordering provisional measures for the protection of rights arising under a Community trade mark, were required to do so, as far as possible, in the light of the wording and purpose of Article 50 TRIPs. It followed, the Court continued, that it had, in any event, jurisdiction to interpret that provision. It was immaterial that the dispute in the main proceedings concerned Benelux trade marks. First, it was solely for the national court to assess the need for a preliminary ruling and, where the question referred to it concerned a provision which it had jurisdiction to interpret, the Court of Justice was in principle bound to give a ruling. Secondly, where a provision could apply both to situations falling within the scope of national law and to situations falling within the scope of Community law, it was clearly in the Community's interest that, in order to forestall future differences

[42] Ibid, paras 20–21. [43] [1994] OJ L11/1.

of interpretation, that provision should be interpreted uniformly, whatever the circumstances in which it was to apply. The Court therefore had jurisdiction.[44]

The Court's reasoning appeared to consist of three parts. First, by referring to the absence of any allocation of obligations between the Community and its Member States, the Court suggested that, from an international law point of view, the Community was bound by all the provisions of the WTO Agreement. This is a significant point. If the international responsibility of the EU could be invoked in connection with any provision of a mixed agreement, should this not be reflected in the scope of the Court's jurisdiction? Does it not mean that the entire agreement forms part of the body of EU law which the Court may be called upon to interpret on a reference from a national court? However, the Court did not develop this point, and it is therefore difficult to measure the precise implication of this observation.

The second part of the Court's reasoning concerned the effect of Regulation 40/94. The Court considered that, as Article 99 of that regulation concerned provisional measures in respect of Community (now EU) trade marks, Article 50 TRIPs could affect the interpretation of that regulation. It was of no relevance here that Article 99 was to be applied by national courts, under national procedural rules. Therefore, the Court in any event had jurisdiction to interpret Article 50 TRIPs.

The third part of the Court's reasoning was a reply to the objection that the *Hermès* case did not concern a Community trade mark, but rather a Benelux trade mark, not covered by Regulation 40/94. Here the Court referred to some general principles concerning its jurisdiction under the preliminary rulings procedure. It is indeed solely for the national court to assess the need for a preliminary ruling, and, where it has jurisdiction, the Court is in principle bound to reply. Further, even though in the *Hermès* case Article 50 TRIPs applied to a situation falling within the scope of national rather than Community law, its interpretation by the Court could forestall future differences of interpretation. The idea seems to be that if the Court were to decline jurisdiction, national courts might develop their own interpretation of Article 50 TRIPs, which at a later stage might conflict with the interpretation given by the Court in, for example, a case concerning the Community trade mark.

The *Hermès* judgment appeared decisive as regards the Court's jurisdiction to interpret Article 50 TRIPs, no matter which intellectual property right, harmonized at EU level or not, was in issue. The Court none the less saw fit to add a layer of complexity in *Parfums Christian Dior*.[45] That case—in fact two joined references from Dutch courts—also concerned Article 50 TRIPs. One of the references was made by the Dutch Supreme Court (Hoge Raad) in a case involving wrongful copying of an industrial design, a type of intellectual property right for which

[44] *Hermès International* (n 37 above) paras 24–33.

[45] Joined Cases C–300 and 392/98 *Parfums Christian Dior v. Tuk Consultancy* [2000] ECR I–11307.

there was no Community harmonization at the material time, in contrast with trade marks. The Supreme Court therefore asked whether the scope of the *Hermès* judgment, relating to the jurisdiction of the Court of Justice to interpret Article 50 TRIPs, was restricted solely to situations covered by trade mark law.

The Court answered by making a distinction between (a) trade marks where, as regards provisional measures covered by Article 50 TRIPs, there was Community legislation as far as the Community trade mark was concerned, but not as regards national trade marks; and (b) industrial designs, for which there was no Community legislation at all at the material time. The distinction is not immediately apparent in the section of the judgment dealing with the Court's jurisdiction, but it appears more clearly in the section on the legal effect (direct or not) of Article 50. In the section on jurisdiction the Court first held that, as TRIPs was concluded by the Community and its Member States under joint competence, the Court had jurisdiction to define the obligations which the Community had assumed and, for that purpose, to interpret TRIPs. It then distinguished two situations, whilst referring to *Hermès*. First, the Court had jurisdiction to interpret Article 50 TRIPs in cases involving provisional measures for the protection of rights arising under Community legislation falling within the scope of TRIPs; in other words intellectual property rights harmonized by Community law. Secondly, where a provision such as Article 50 could apply both to situations falling within the scope of national law and to situations falling within that of Community law, as was the case in the field of trade marks, the Court had jurisdiction to interpret it in order to forestall future differences of interpretation. The Court then built on that rule, by referring to the obligation of close co-operation in fulfilling the commitments undertaken under joint competence, an obligation to which Tesauro AG referred in *Hermès*,[46] but which the Court itself did not mention in that judgment. Since Article 50 constituted a procedural provision which should be applied in the same way in every situation falling within its scope and was capable of applying both to situations covered by national law and to situations covered by Community law, the obligation of close co-operation required the judicial bodies of the Member States and the Community, for practical and legal reasons, to give it a uniform interpretation. The Court then stated that it alone, acting in co-operation with the courts and tribunals of the Member States, was in a position to ensure such uniform interpretation. The jurisdiction of the Court to interpret Article 50 TRIPs was thus not restricted solely to situations covered by trade mark law.[47]

It is not easy to see why the Court introduced the duty of co-operation in this judgment, not having mentioned it in *Hermès*.[48] Furthermore, in the next section of the judgment, on the direct effect of TRIPs, the Court distinguished between the field of trade marks, where the Community had already legislated, and industrial designs, where that was not yet the case. As regards the former, the case law regarding the effects in Community law of the WTO Agreement applied: the provisions

[46] See also Ch 7. [47] *Dior* (n 45 above) paras 33–39. [48] Koutrakos (n 31 above) 38.

of TRIPs did not have direct effect, but the judicial authorities of the Member States were required by virtue of Community law, when called upon to apply national rules with a view to ordering provisional measures for the protection of rights falling within such a field, to do so as far as possible in the light of the wording and purpose of Article 50 TRIPs. In other words, the duty of consistent interpretation applied,[49] even where, for example, national trade mark law was concerned, and provisional measures were taken, on which there was no Community legislation. On the other hand, however, in a field in respect of which the Community had not yet legislated and which consequently fell within the competence of the Member States (such as *in casu* industrial designs), the protection of intellectual property rights, and measures adopted for that purpose by the judicial authorities, did not fall within the scope of Community law. Accordingly, Community law neither required nor forbade that the legal order of a Member State should accord to individuals the right to rely directly on Article 50 TRIPs or that it should oblige the courts to apply that rule of their own motion.[50] In other words, the question of the legal effect of Article 50 was then left to national law, and the relevant Community law principles did not apply.

In *Schieving-Nijstad*, *Heidelberger Bauchemie*, and *Anheuser-Busch*,[51] the Court confirmed its jurisdiction to interpret the TRIPs Agreement in the context of trade mark disputes. In *Merck Genéricos* it confirmed and applied its ruling in *Dior*, to the effect that in areas of TRIPs where there is as yet no EU legislation, the legal effect of TRIPs is a question of national, and not EU law. The case concerned Article 33 TRIPs, which provides for a minimum term of patent protection of twenty years. It had been referred by the Portuguese Supreme Court of Justice (Supremo Tribunal de Justiça), which asked the questions (a) whether the Court of Justice had jurisdiction to interpret that provision, and (b) whether private parties could rely on it. The referring court also pointed out that, in accordance with the principles of Portuguese law governing the interpretation of international agreements, Article 33 TRIPs had direct effect. The Court of Justice restated the *Dior* principle that, when the field was one in which the Community had not yet legislated and which consequently fell within the competence of the Member States, the protection of intellectual property rights and measures taken for that purpose by the judicial authorities did not fall within the scope of Community law, so that the latter neither required nor forbade the legal order of a Member State to accord to individuals the right to rely directly on a rule laid down in the TRIPs Agreement or to oblige the courts to apply that rule of their own motion.[52] In order to see whether that principle applied, it was necessary to examine the matter of

[49] See Ch 9. [50] *Dior* (n 45 above) paras 46–48.

[51] Case C–88/99 *Schieving-Nijstad v. Groeneveld* [2001] ECR I–5851, para 3; Case C–49/02 *Heidelberger Bauchemie* [2004] ECR I–6129, para 20; and Case C–245/02 *Anheuser-Busch v. Budějovický Budvar, národní podnik* [2004] ECR I–10989, para 42.

[52] Case C–431/05 *Merck Genéricos—Produtos Farmacêuticos v. Merck & Co* [2007] ECR I–7001, para 34.

the sharing of competence between the Community and its Member States. That question called for a uniform reply that the Court alone was capable of supplying, and there was therefore some Community interest in considering the Court as having jurisdiction to interpret Article 33 TRIPs in order to ascertain whether it was contrary to Community law for that provision to be given direct effect.[53] The Court then established that there was, at the time, no Community patent legislation: the fact was that the Community had not yet exercised its powers in the sphere of patents or that, at the very least, at internal level, that exercise had not been of sufficient importance to lead to the conclusion that, as matters stood, that sphere fell within the scope of Community law.[54] It was therefore not contrary to Community law for the Portuguese courts to recognize the direct effect of this TRIPs provision.

How should one assess this case law? In *Schieving-Nijstad* Jacobs AG commented that it was not easy to understand why Community law governed the effect of Article 50 TRIPs not only where a Community trade mark was involved but also in situations concerning national trade marks.[55] In *Merck Genéricos* Colomer AG launched a more sweeping critique. The Advocate General considered that successive developments in the case law had constructed a long and winding path, whose complex route demanded certain adjustments in order to help its confused users find their way.[56] However, he did more than suggesting such adjustments, arguing more radically that the Court should accept unlimited jurisdiction over TRIPs. He emphasized the international law dimension of the WTO Agreement, which had virtually become a 'constitutional' framework for world trade. Joint conclusion of the agreement by the Community and its Member States required co-operation between them, also in the process of implementing WTO law. The best way of guaranteeing observance of international agreements and of achieving the necessary harmony in the interpretation of mixed agreements was to ensure that they were interpreted uniformly. This did not imply a transfer to the Community of legislative powers. But to deny the Court of Justice jurisdiction to examine the WTO Agreement until legislation had been adopted in respect of specific matters was as illogical as prohibiting a national court from interpreting a framework law until the authorities to whom the legislative power had been delegated had exercised it. Legal certainty required a change of course.[57]

The critique is persuasive. It may, however, have lost its relevance, at least for the case of the WTO Agreement, including TRIPs. Indeed, as mentioned, the EU's exclusive competence now extends, pursuant to Article 207(1) TFEU, to 'the commercial aspects of intellectual property'. That surely means that the whole of TRIPs comes within the scope of EU law. Whether or not there is EU legislation on a

[53] Ibid, paras 36–38. [54] Ibid, para 46.

[55] *Schieving-Nijstad* (n 51 above) para 40 of the Opinion.

[56] *Merck Genéricos* (n 52 above) para 33 of the Opinion.

[57] Ibid, paras 55–60.

particular intellectual property right can no longer be relevant for delineating the Court's jurisdiction. Nor would it seem possible to maintain the principle, in those areas where the EU has not yet legislated, that it is for national law to determine the legal effects of TRIPs. Surely, the Court's jurisdiction and its authority to determine the legal effects of an agreement can only be limited in areas of shared competence. It is true that the WTO Agreement continues to be a mixed agreement under international law: the EU and its Member States are all contracting parties, as no efforts have been undertaken to make the Member States withdraw from the WTO. This may have relevance for issues of international responsibility. But as the Treaties now provide for exclusive competence in all WTO matters (except transport), the Court's jurisdiction, which is a question of EU law, not international law, must be construed as complete.

Mixed agreements—other case law

The problems and questions of jurisdiction concerning the TRIPs Agreement have not been replicated in recent case law concerning other mixed agreements. In the judgments analysed below, the Court accepted jurisdiction to interpret, often without even referring to the mixed nature of the agreement in issue.

That was the case, for example, in *Syndicat professionnel coordination des pêcheurs de l'étang de Berre et de la région*. The reference concerned the Barcelona Convention for the Protection of the Mediterranean Sea against Pollution, and in particular one of its Protocols (as amended). The Convention and Protocols were concluded by the Community as mixed agreements, but that feature was not even mentioned in the judgment. The Court simply interpreted and applied the Protocols.[58] A few months later, the Court did consider its jurisdiction to apply the Barcelona Convention in a parallel enforcement action brought by the Commission against France, discussed in the relevant section below.[59]

A couple of cases concerned the agreement with Switzerland on free movement of persons. In *Zentralsbetriebsrat der Landeskrankenhäuser Tirols* there is only an Opinion of Colomer AG, as the main proceedings were indefinitely suspended before the Court could issue its judgment.[60] The case concerned the interpretation of Article 9 of Annex I to the agreement, which concerns equal treatment in matters of employment. The Advocate General (echoing *Demirel*[61]) simply stated that that provision laid down a commitment in a Community field, from which it followed that, because the provision related to the free movement of workers, the Court had jurisdiction to carry out an interpretation.[62] In *Stamm and Hauser*, a case

[58] Case C–213/03 *Syndicat professionnel coordination des pêcheurs de l'étang de Berre et de la région v. EDF* [2004] ECR I–7357.

[59] Case C–239/03 *Commission v. France* [2004] ECR I–9325.

[60] Case C–339/05 *Zentralbetriebsrat der Landeskrankenhäuser Tirols v. Land Tirol* [2006] ECR I–7097.

[61] N 29 above. [62] *Zentralbetriebsrat* (n 60 above) para 30.

concerning the agreement's equal treatment provisions regarding self-employed persons, the Court did not even examine its jurisdiction, and simply interpreted the agreement.[63]

The EU is also a party, together with the Member States, to the Montreal Convention for the Unification of Certain Rules for International Carriage by Air, which, *inter alia*, regulates the liability of carriers for damage incurred by passengers. There is EU legislation aimed at implementing that convention, as well as laying down certain supplementary provisions.[64] *Walz* concerned a preliminary reference concerning Article 22(2) of the Montreal Convention, on certain limitations to liability, and the Court simply stated that, since the provisions of the convention had been an integral part of the EU legal order from the date on which the convention entered into force, it had jurisdiction to give a preliminary ruling concerning its interpretation.[65]

Review of legality

Under Article 263 TFEU the General Court and the Court of Justice have jurisdiction to review the legality of acts adopted by the EU institutions. Such so-called direct actions for annulment, which are available to natural and legal persons only under the restrictive conditions of Article 263 TFEU, fourth paragraph, are complemented by the opportunity for national courts to refer questions of validity of acts of the institutions to the Court of Justice under the preliminary rulings procedure. This is a different procedure, but as regards the grounds for review questions of validity are treated in an identical way to review of legality in a direct action.[66] In Article 263 the Treaty lists those grounds as including lack of competence, infringement of an essential procedural requirement, infringement of the Treaty or of any rule of law relating to its application, or misuse of powers.

Agreements concluded by the EU may be relevant for cases involving review of legality in two contrasting ways. The conclusion of the agreement itself may be subject to review, and, conversely, an 'internal' act of an institution may be reviewed on grounds of violation of an EU agreement. This section looks at those types of review in turn.

[63] Case C–13/08 *Erich Stamm and Anneliese Hauser* [2008] ECR I–11087.

[64] Regulation 2027/97 on air carrier liability in respect of the carriage of passengers and their baggage by air [1997] OJ L285/1, as amended by Regulation 889/2002 [2002] OJ L140/2.

[65] Case C–63/09 *Axel Walz v. Clickair,* judgment of 6 May 2010, para 20. See also, regarding the same convention, Case C–173/07 *Emirates Airlines* [2008] ECR I–5237, para 44 and Case C–549/07 *Wallentin-Hermann v. Alitalia* [2008] ECR I–11061, para 28 (the questions of interpretation in those cases did not concern the Montreal Convention as such). See further the Opinion of Sharpston AG of 15 July 2010 in Case C–240/09 *Lesoochranárske zoskupenie VLK v. Ministerstvo životného prostredia Slovenskej republiky*, not yet reported.

[66] M Brealey and M Hoskins, *Remedies in EC Law* (2nd edn, Sweet & Maxwell, 1998) 228.

Review of an agreement

As analysed above, in *Opinion 1/75* the Court identified the rationale of requests for an Opinion under (current) Article 218(11) TFEU as the prevention of complications which would result from legal disputes concerning the compatibility with the Treaty of international agreements binding upon the Community, thereby clarifying that, in principle, such agreements may be subject to review.[67] It took until 1994, however, before there was a first challenge to a concluded agreement.[68] *France v. Commission* concerned the Agreement between the Commission and the United States regarding the application of their competition laws.[69] France objected to the Commission having concluded this agreement on its own, without involving the Council, and argued that this was contrary to the provisions of (current) Article 218 TFEU.[70] As France had challenged the agreement as such, the Commission raised the question of whether the action should have been directed at the Commission decision whereby it authorized its Vice-President to sign the agreement, rather than at the agreement itself.

Tesauro AG was unimpressed by the Commission's arguments. He referred to *Opinion 1/75* and to *Haegeman*[71] as authority for the view that an international agreement is as much an act of the institutions as is the decision to conclude it. He further considered that the question was merely one of form, and that, under the Community legal system—which made provision for judicial review, without exception, of all the acts and practices of the institutions, of individuals, and of the Member States, which affected the system itself—it was not reasonably possible to exclude review of the legality of the procedure for concluding an agreement with a non-member country. The possibility of doing so on the basis of a complaint expressly directed at the agreement as such, or at the act connected therewith, or else at an implied act, struck the Advocate General as a secondary and wholly irrelevant matter.[72]

The Court was equally unimpressed, but developed a slightly different reasoning. It recalled that for an action for annulment to be admissible the contested act had to be an act of an institution which produced legal effect. It then found that, as was apparent from its actual wording, the agreement in issue was intended to produce legal effects, and that, consequently, the act whereby the Commission sought to conclude the agreement had to be susceptible to an action for

[67] *Opinion 1/75* (n 6 above). The Court expressly mentioned Art 173 EEC (now Art 263 TFEU) in its judgment. For a general analysis see Kaddous (n 4 above) 40–61.

[68] Case 165/87 *Commission v. Council* [1988] ECR 5545 concerned a challenge to the Council decision concluding the International Convention on the Harmonized Commodity Description and Coding System, on the ground of incorrect legal basis. The Court dismissed the application.

[69] Case C-327/91 *France v. Commission* [1994] ECR I-3641.

[70] See Ch 6.

[71] N 22 above.

[72] *France v. Commission* (n 69 above) Opinion of Tesauro AG, paras 9–11.

annulment. The Court stressed that the exercise of powers delegated to the Community institutions in international matters could not escape judicial review. It concluded that France's action had to be understood as being directed against the act whereby the Commission sought to conclude the agreement, and that the action was admissible.[73]

The Court is right in principle to exercise review of acts through which the EU concludes an agreement.[74] If agreements, on the grounds of their international law character, were outside the Court's jurisdiction, it would be impossible to uphold the rule of law in a significant segment of EU policy- and law-making. As to the specific reasoning, the Advocate General's approach is more convincing. If, in the context of questions for a preliminary ruling, the agreement itself is an act of the institutions, as the Court decided in *Haegeman*, one cannot see why that should not also be the case as regards actions for annulment. The slight artificiality of having to (re)direct the action against the decision of conclusion of the agreement is then avoided. Moreover, there may be cases where the alleged illegality arises, not so much from the procedure followed for the conclusion of the agreement (as was the case in *Commission v. France*), but from substantive provisions of the agreement itself. That such provisions, too, are subject to review was borne out by the subsequent *Germany v. Council* case on the Framework Agreement on bananas.[75] In that case the applicant and the Court maintained the *France v. Commission* approach of understanding the action as being directed against the decision to conclude the agreement. That decision concerned the conclusion of the entire WTO Agreement, as the Framework Agreement on bananas formed part of the Community's tariff schedule for bananas. The Court found that the Framework Agreement, by creating an unjustified difference in treatment between various categories of importers of bananas, violated the general principle of non-discrimination. Accordingly, it annulled the Council decision to conclude the WTO Agreement 'to the extent that the Council thereby approved the conclusion of the Framework Agreement on Bananas...in so far as that Framework Agreement exempts Category B operators from the export-licence system for which it provides'. The judgment shows that partial annulment of an agreement (formally the act concluding the agreement) is possible, much as such partial annulment is possible with respect to any other act subject to judicial review.[76] It thereby raises the question of the legal effects of annulment. Those effects are identical to the effects of annulment of 'internal' acts: the act is null and void *ab initio*, and the institutions concerned are required to take the necessary measures to comply with the judgment of the Court (Article 266 TFEU). Under international law, however, the agreement remains valid unless the EU is able to

[73] Ibid, paras 13–17 of the judgment.
[74] *Contra* Kaddous (n 4 above).
[75] Case C-122/95 *Germany v. Council* [1998] ECR I-973.
[76] Brealey and Hoskins (n 6 above) 329.

argue invalid consent under the law of treaties.[77] Clearly, the Court of Justice has no jurisdiction to annul the agreement itself as an act of international law.[78] In practice, therefore, an agreement affected by an annulment verdict by the Court will have to be renegotiated or terminated; if not, the EU will find itself in a position of conflicting EU law and international law obligations.[79]

Alternatively, the Court may limit the effects of annulment. That is what it did in *Parliament v. Council*, a case involving a challenge to Council decisions on the conclusion of a government procurement agreement with the United States and on the extension of the benefits of a Community directive to the United States.[80] The Court annulled the decisions on the ground that they were adopted on the wrong legal basis, but decided to grant the Council's request to limit the effects of annulment. It observed that if the decisions were simply annulled, this would be liable adversely to affect the exercise of rights arising under them. Account also had to be taken of the fact that the agreement had already expired. In those circumstances there were important reasons of legal certainty, comparable to those which arose where certain regulations were annulled, which warranted the Court's exercising the power conferred upon it by (current) Article 264, second paragraph, TFEU by indicating the effects of the decisions which had to be conserved. In the specific circumstances, all the effects had to be conserved.[81]

In *Germany v. Council* the Council also argued that the action was inadmissible because the Framework Agreement represented only one of the many agreements reached in the Uruguay Round and that its annulment would compromise the delicate balance of the reciprocal commitments and concessions negotiated in that context. The Court, however, brushed aside this objection on the ground that the Council had not given any specific indication of how annulment would render inoperative such other reciprocal commitments and concessions.[82] The Court thus showed that it is not easily impressed by arguments derived from the special nature of international relations and agreements so as to resist annulment of acts concluding agreements.

France v. Commission and *Germany v. Council* also exemplify on what grounds the act of concluding an international agreement may be challenged. Those grounds

[77] See Art 46 VCLT, cited in n 8, and Art 46(2) of the Vienna Convention on the Law of Treaties Between States and International Organizations or Between International Organizations (1986) (VCLTIO), which provides: 'An international organization may not invoke the fact that its consent to be bound by a treaty has been expressed in violation of the rules of the organization regarding competence to conclude treaties as invalidating its consent unless that violation was manifest and concerned a rule of fundamental importance'.

[78] Cf K Lenaerts and E de Smijter, 'The European Union as an Actor under International Law' (1999/2000) 19 YEL 102.

[79] For further discussion see Macleod, Hendry, and Hyett (n 15 above) 130–1.

[80] Case C–360/93 *Parliament v. Council* [1996] ECR I–1195.

[81] Ibid, paras 32–36. Art 264, second para, TFEU provides: 'However, the Court shall, if it considers this necessary, state which of the effects of the act which it has declared void shall be considered as definitive'. The pre-Lisbon version, Art 231 EC, textually confined this competence to regulations, but was interpreted as extending to other acts. See also *European Parliament v. Council (PNR)* (n 16 above) paras 71–74.

[82] *Germany v. Council* (n 75 above) paras 43–45.

are in practice (if not in theory) limited to the Treaties, with the provisions on competence and procedure for the conclusion of agreements as the most likely basis for challenge,[83] and to general principles of EU law, such as non-discrimination, proportionality, and fundamental rights. As EU legislation (regulations, directives, etc.) itself needs to conform to agreements binding on the EU, it cannot form the basis for challenging the legality of an agreement.

As a last point, two more recent decisions of the CFI are noteworthy. In *Polyelectrolyte Producers Group* the applicant sought essentially the annulment, not of an international agreement concluded by the EU, but of a decision of the EEA Joint Committee. Such decisions are binding on the Contracting Parties, and the Committee takes them by agreement between the EU and the EFTA States. The Court established that the action was inadmissible, however. It recalled that it had jurisdiction only in actions brought against Community institutions and organs established by the Treaties. Consequently, it had no jurisdiction to adjudicate on the decision of the Joint Committee, since the latter was not a Community institution or organ. The Court then examined whether it had jurisdiction to review the Community's position towards the EEA Joint Committee's decision. The Commission's proposal for that position could not be challenged, because it was a mere preparatory act. The Council decision adopting the Community's position, on the other hand, was not of direct and individual concern to the applicant, who therefore did not meet the requirements of then Article 230, fourth paragraph, EC. The Court also noted that the Council decision could not be assimilated to an international agreement as understood in *France v. Commission*.[84]

The Court's analysis is persuasive, but it should not be understood as excluding review of the legality of acts adopted by international institutions in whose work the EU participates. That participation must be subject to judicial review just as much as the conclusion of international agreements. The rule of law requires that all acts of the institutions are reviewable.[85] The EU's position leading to an act of an international institution must therefore in principle be open to challenge.

The second case goes by the enticing name of *Commune de Champagne*. It was brought by a Swiss commune which goes by the name Champagne, and by winegrowers in that commune. They challenged the Council's decision to conclude an agreement with Switzerland on trade in agricultural products. One of the effects of that agreement was to exclude the use of the name 'champagne', both in the EU and in Switzerland, for white non-sparkling wines produced in Swiss Champagne. The CFI distinguished, ingeniously, between the effects of the agreement in the

[83] In the *PNR* case (n 16 above) the Court, for example, struck down an agreement with the US on passenger name records because (current) Art 114 TFEU did not justify Community competence to conclude the agreement.

[84] Case T–376/04 *Polyelectrolyte Producers Group v. Council and Commission* [2005] ECR II–3007, paras 29–36.

[85] See e.g. Case 294/83 *Les Verts v. Parliament* [1986] ECR 1339 and Joined Cases C–402 and 415/05P *Kadi and Al Barakaat v. Council and Commission* [2008] ECR I–6351.

Community and in Switzerland. As regards the former, the agreement did not modify the legal position of the applicants, because Community legislation applicable at the time of the conclusion of the agreement already reserved the name champagne for French sparkling wines from that region. As regards the effects of the agreement in Switzerland, however, the Court also dismissed the action as inadmissible, in essence because the Council decision concluding the agreement could not produce legal effects outside Community territory. The Court pointed out that the principle of sovereign equality enshrined in Article 2(1) of the United Nations Charter meant that it was, as a rule, a matter for each State to legislate in its own territory and, accordingly, that generally a State could unilaterally impose binding rules only in its own territory. Similarly, under (then) Article 299 EC the EC Treaty applied only to the territory of the Member States. It followed that an act of an institution adopted pursuant to the Treaty, as a unilateral act of the Community, could not create rights and obligations outside the territory thus defined. It therefore had to be held that the contested decision did not bring about a change in the applicants' legal position in Switzerland, such position being governed only by that State in the exercise of its sovereign power. The Court also pointed out that, allowing the action as admissible would mean that the Community court would rule on the legality, in the light of Community law, of rights conferred on a non-Member State, or obligations assumed by it, under an international agreement to which it had subscribed freely and at its absolute discretion in the course of conducting its external relations. Such a review was clearly outside the jurisdiction of the CFI as defined by the Treaty.[86]

Though perhaps at first glance convincing, the point is debatable. An international agreement is a joint act of the contracting parties. In purely hypothetical terms, it is not inconceivable to think of cases where the effects of an agreement in the territory of the other contracting party ought to be open to challenge before the EU courts. Imagine an agreement containing a human rights clause (as is now customary in the EU's bilateral agreements), but with a derogation which allows the other contracting party to commit acts of torture. As the EU is founded on respect for fundamental rights,[87] surely that would be a provision to which the EU institutions could not lawfully agree under the Treaties. It would shake the very foundations of the EU, even if it is technically correct that the hypothetical acts of torture would be committed in the exercise of the other party's sovereign power.

Review on grounds of violation of an agreement

'Internal' acts of the EU institutions may themselves be in conflict with provisions of an international agreement binding on the EU.[88] The question then arises of

[86] Case T–212/02 *Commune de Champagne and Others v. Council and Commission* [2007] ECR II–2017, paras 89–91 and 94.

[87] *Kadi and Al Barakaat* (n 85 above).

[88] See also Kaddous (n 4 above) 62–9.

whether the violation of an agreement can be invoked to challenge the legality or validity of such acts. That question is of far greater practical significance than the issues discussed in the previous subsection. In the light of the scale of both the EU's internal legislative activity and its participation in international treaty-making, and of the increasing interconnectedness of those two dimensions of EU action, there is much scope for argument that provisions of EU legislation may not conform to the EU's international commitments.

It is thus no surprise that the issue came before the Court fairly early. In the 1972 *International Fruit Company* case an importer of apples questioned, before a court in the Netherlands, the validity of a number of Community regulations restricting such imports, arguing that the regulations violated Article XI GATT.[89] The court referred the case to the Court of Justice, its first question being whether the validity of measures adopted by the institutions of the Community also referred, within the meaning of (current) Article 267 TFEU, to their validity under international law. The Court of Justice decided that, before the compatibility of a Community measure with a provision of international law could affect the validity of that measure, the Community first of all had to be bound by that provision.[90] That condition is rather obvious, but in the case of GATT it posed some problems, because the Community had never formally signed or joined GATT. The Court none the less found, for reasons which need not be explored here,[91] that the Community was bound by the provisions of GATT. However, the Court also introduced a second condition. It stated that, before invalidity could be relied upon before a national court, the provision of international law also had to be capable of conferring rights on citizens of the Community which they could invoke before the courts.[92] The Court did not indicate on what grounds it introduced this second condition, but it clearly followed the Opinion of Mayras AG. The Advocate General argued that, before regulations could be held invalid under the provisions of the law of an international agreement, which was outside the legal system of the Community, the applicants had to be able to rely on rights deriving from those provisions. In other words, he continued, those provisions had to have a *direct effect* within the Community.[93] The Advocate General referred to the principle of direct effect as it had been established by the Court's case law. He pointed out that it was applied in the relationship between Community law and national law, and considered that it also had to be applied in the relations between international law and Community law.[94] The Advocate General thus equated the conferral of rights on individuals with direct effect, but it may be noted that the Court itself did not refer to the concept of direct effect in its judgment. In all other respects the reasoning of the Advocate General and the Court were similar, as they respectively concluded, on the same

[89] Joined Cases 21 to 24/72 *International Fruit Company v. Produktschap voor Groenten en Fruit* [1972] ECR 1219.

[90] Ibid, para 7. [91] See Ch 9. [92] *International Fruit Company* (n 89 above) para 8.

[93] Ibid, 1234, emphasis in the original. [94] Ibid, 1234–5.

grounds, that GATT was not directly applicable in the Community legal system and did not confer rights on individuals. Ever since, *International Fruit Company* has been commented upon, and has been much criticized, as the judgment which denied the provisions of GATT direct effect.

There will be opportunity in the next chapter to analyse the concept of direct effect, its relationship with the notion of conferring rights on individuals, and the lack of direct effect of GATT and WTO law. What is of interest for the present discussion is that *International Fruit Company* concerned a reference for a preliminary ruling on the validity of Community acts, and not a direct action for annulment. Moreover, the Court appeared to have established a link between the condition that an agreement confer rights on private parties and the type of action: that condition must be fulfilled 'before invalidity can be relied upon before a national court'.[95] Some commentators therefore took the view that the rights (or direct effect) condition did not apply to direct actions for annulment.[96] They reasoned that direct effect, as a principle, could only be relevant in cases before national courts where Community law was relied upon, and that the Court had never spoken of direct effect as a condition for relying on certain provisions of Community law in direct actions for annulment. Their opinion appeared vindicated by the *Nakajima* judgment.[97] That case involved a challenge to an anti-dumping regulation in which the applicant relied, *inter alia*, on the then GATT Anti-Dumping Code. The Council replied that the code, like GATT, did not confer rights on individuals and that its provisions were not directly applicable within the Community. The Court considered this irrelevant. It pointed out that Nakajima was not relying on the direct effect of the code. The applicant was in fact questioning, in an incidental manner under (current) Article 277 TFEU, the applicability of the basic anti-dumping regulation by invoking one of the grounds for review of legality referred to in (current) Article 263 TFEU, namely that of infringement of the Treaty or of any rule of law relating to its application.[98] At the time it was reasonable to read the judgment as authority for the view that direct effect or applicability, or the conferring of rights was not a

[95] Ibid, para 8.

[96] M Maresceau, 'The GATT in the Case Law of the European Court of Justice' in M Hilf, FG Jacobs, and E-U Petersmann, *The European Community and GATT* (Kluwer, 1986) 114–18; PJG Kapteyn, 'Quelques réflexions sur les effets des accords internationaux liant la Communauté dans l'ordre juridique communautaire' in Pérez González *et al* (eds), *Hacia un nuevo orden internacional y Europeo—Estudios en homenaje al Professor Don Manual Diez de Velasco* (Tecnos, 1993) 1014–15; Hancher (n 32 above) 280.

[97] Case C–69/89 *Nakajima v. Council* [1991] ECR I–2069. See also Case 70/87 *Fediol v. Commission* [1989] ECR 1781.

[98] *Nakajima* (n 97 above) paras 27–28. The reference to (then) Art 241 EC complicates matters a little, but is not difficult to understand. Nakajima was in fact arguing that a provision of the basic anti-dumping regulation, which had been crucial to the determination of dumping in the specific regulation it was challenging, was contrary to the Anti-Dumping Code. Under Art 241 any party could, in proceedings in which a regulation is at issue, plead the grounds specified in the second paragraph of Art 230 in order to invoke the inapplicability of that regulation. Arguably, this element had no bearing on the Court's ruling that Nakajima could effectively rely on the Anti-Dumping Code in a direct action for annulment. Current Article 277 TFEU refers to acts of general application rather than regulations.

precondition for relying on an agreement concluded by the Community in a direct action for annulment.[99] That suggested that there was a dichotomy between validity questions under the preliminary rulings procedure and legality review in an action for annulment.

The Court's judgment in Germany's challenge to the 1993 EC banana regime, however, showed this to be an erroneous reading of *Nakajima*.[100] Germany brought an action for the annulment of Council Regulation 404/93 on the common organization of the market in bananas,[101] arguing, *inter alia*, that the regulation violated a number of GATT provisions. Not only was this a direct action for annulment; it had been brought by a Member State, not by a private party, and it was therefore not unreasonable to assume that the condition of the agreement conferring rights on private parties would not apply. The assumption proved incorrect, however. The Court, following the Opinion of Gulmann AG, recalled the reasons for its earlier, settled case law that GATT did not confer rights—reasons which will be further explored in the next chapter. It then held that the relevant features of GATT also precluded the Court from taking provisions of GATT into consideration to assess the lawfulness of a regulation in an action for annulment brought by a Member State. The Court made an exception, however, thereby at the same time explaining its ruling in *Nakajima*, for cases in which the Community was intending to implement a particular GATT obligation or in which the Community act expressly referred to GATT.[102] Again, that exception to the lack of direct effect of GATT is analysed in the next chapter. For the purposes of the present discussion, however, the ruling in the *Bananas* case clarified that there is no dichotomy between preliminary rulings cases on validity and direct actions for annulment, nor between the position of private parties and that of Member States. Whether or not an international agreement can be relied upon in order to challenge the legality or validity of an internal EU act depends on the direct effect of the agreement, and it does not matter (a) whether the agreement is relied upon in a direct action for annulment; (b) whether that action was brought by a private party, an EU institution, or a Member State; or (c) whether the agreement is relied upon before a national court to question the validity of an EU act.

From the perspective of a coherent approach towards the review of the legality of EU acts this is eminently defensible.[103] Where the Court determines on which grounds an EU act may be illegal, it should indeed not matter under which

[99] See e.g. the German government's arguments in the *Bananas* case (n 100 below), Opinion of Gulmann AG, para 125; J Vanhamme, *Volkenrechtelijke beginselen in het Europees recht* (Europa Law Publishing, 2001) 192.

[100] Case C–280/93 *Germany v. Council* [1994] ECR I–4973.

[101] [1993] OJ L47/1.

[102] *Germany v. Council* (n 100 above) paras 105–111.

[103] Cf M Waelbroeck, 'Effect of GATT within the Legal Order of the EEC' (1974) 8 JWTL 622. See also the Opinion of Maduro AG in Joined Cases C–120 and 121/06 P *FIAMM and Fedon* [2008] ECR I–6513.

procedure the question of legality is posed or by which type of party. There are differences between, on the one hand, EU institutions and Member States, and, on the other, private parties, as regards standing before the Courts in actions for annulment (see Article 263, fourth paragraph, TFEU). However, once standing is granted it is hardly defensible to argue that, on the substance of what may be fully identical claims, the Court should rule differently according to the identity of the claimant.

The Court's approach is also coherent with the notion of direct effect. Without pre-empting the discussion in the next chapter, the issue of the direct effect of agreements concluded by the EU concerns the relationship between the international legal order and the EU legal order. Applied to challenges to the legality/validity of EU acts, it concerns the question of whether that relationship is such that the provisions of international law may form a basis for judicially enforceable illegality. Forms of action or identities of plaintiffs are and should be irrelevant in that respect.

The judgment in *Germany v. Council* was none the less much criticized,[104] in particular as at the time, before the establishment of the WTO, the Community was not a formal GATT Contracting Party, in contrast to its Member States. The judgment effectively meant that Germany, as a GATT Contracting Party, was obliged to apply provisions of Community law on imports of bananas—provisions which GATT and later on WTO dispute settlement established to be in breach of the General Agreement—without being able to challenge the legality of those provisions, on that basis, before the Community Court.

Once the WTO Agreement had entered into force, the Court extended the above approach to that agreement, even if it advanced partially different reasons for not permitting review on the basis of a violation of WTO law provisions, compared to the previous case law on GATT. In *Portugal v. Council*, again a case brought by a Member State, the Court decided that the WTO agreements are not in principle among the rules in the light of which the Court is to review the legality of measures adopted by the Community institutions.[105] It may be noted that here the Court did not speak of either direct effect or conferring rights, but simply denied WTO law the capacity to serve as a basis for the legality review of Community acts. The Court then completed the circle in *Parfums Christian Dior*, in which it was asked whether Article 50(6) TRIPs has direct effect. It stated that, for the same reasons as those which it mentioned in *Portugal v. Council*, the provisions of TRIPs, an annex to the WTO Agreement, were not such as to create rights upon which individuals could rely directly before the courts by virtue of Community law.[106]

[104] MJ Hahn and G Schuster, 'Le droit des Etats membres de se prévaloir en justice d'un accord liant la Communauté' (1995) 99 RGDIP 367; U Everling, 'Will Europe Slip on Bananas? The Bananas Judgment of the Court of Justice and National Courts' (1996) 33 CML Rev 421; Kaddous (n 4 above) 68–9.

[105] Case C–149/96 *Portugal v. Council* [1999] ECR I–8395, para 47.

[106] *Dior* (n 45 above) para 44.

In *International Fruit Company* the Court had started its case law on GATT by denying that the provisions of GATT created rights for individuals; in *Parfums Christian Dior* it completed its case law on the effects of the WTO Agreement by denying that the provisions of WTO law created such rights.[107]

It is reasonable to conclude, on the basis of the above case law, that direct effect is required if an agreement is to form the basis for review of the legality or validity of EU acts.

However, the Court complicated the picture in its judgment on the Netherlands' challenge to the directive on the protection of biotechnological inventions.[108] One of the claims was that the directive violated both TRIPs and the Agreement on Technical Barriers to Trade (TBT, one of the WTO agreements), as well as the European Patent Convention and the Convention on Biological Diversity. A particular feature of the case was that Article 1(2) of the directive provided that it was without prejudice to the obligations of the Member States pursuant to international agreements, and in particular TRIPs and the Convention on Biological Diversity. As regards the European Patent Convention the Court pointed out that, as the Community was not a party to that agreement, the lawfulness of a Community instrument did not depend on conformity with it (thus applying the first condition of *International Fruit Company*). As regards TRIPs and TBT the Court first referred to *Portugal v. Council*, thus initially declining review. However, it then complicated matters in two different ways.

First, as regards the Convention on Biological Diversity the Court stated that the sort of exclusion from judicial review applicable to WTO law could not be extended to the Convention, which, unlike the WTO Agreement, was not strictly based on reciprocal and mutually advantageous arrangements. It then, curiously, held that, even if, as the Council had maintained, the Convention contained provisions which did not have direct effect, in the sense that they did not create rights which individuals could rely on directly before the courts, that fact did not preclude review by the courts of compliance with the obligations incumbent on the Community as a party to that agreement.[109] This paragraph is difficult to understand in the light of previous case law which, at least as regards GATT and the WTO Agreement, appeared to treat direct effect, the creation of rights, and inclusion in grounds of review as synonymous from the perspective of review of legality or validity. As the Court has it here, an agreement may, notwithstanding its incapacity to create rights, be included in the grounds for review of an EU act. Whether that approach is convincing remains to be seen.

The second complication is that the Court then stated that, in any event, the plea based on the violation of those four agreements had to be understood as being

[107] See also Ch 9.

[108] Directive 98/44 of the European Parliament and the Council [1998] OJ L213/13; Case C–377/98 *Netherlands v. European Parliament and Council* [2001] ECR I–7079.

[109] Ibid, paras 52–54. On the last point the Court referred to Case C–162/96 *Racke* [1998] ECR I–3655; see Ch 9.

directed, not so much at a direct breach by the Community of its international obligations, as at an obligation imposed on the Member States by the directive to breach their own obligations under international law, while the directive itself claimed not to affect those obligations.[110] The Court accordingly proceeded to examine the alleged violations of those agreements, but found none.

The reasoning of the Court as to the basis for exercising this type of review, despite the lack of direct effect of WTO law and the fact that the EU is not bound by the European Patent Convention, is elliptical and leaves many questions unanswered. First, it is not clear whether the directive's provision to the effect that it is without prejudice to the obligations of Member States pursuant to international agreements is a decisive factor for the exercise of review. If it is, then it is difficult to understand: the directive could then, if it indeed violated such agreements, be annulled for breach of its own provisions. If it is not, then it is unclear how much legal weight it carries. Secondly, particularly as regards the European Patent Convention, the judgment appears to imply that EU legislation may not violate agreements to which only the Member States are party. That would be an important novel principle of Community law, which should hardly be introduced in the stealth-like fashion of this judgment.[111] Thirdly, the Court did not clarify whether this type of reasoning was specific to directives, which are, in contrast with regulations, addressed to the Member States, and require transposition in national law. Fourthly, neither did the Court clarify whether this type of review was available to all types of applicants, or whether only Member States which are themselves bound by the agreement allegedly violated could initiate it.

One possible reading of the judgment is indeed that the Court felt embarrassed by the incapacity of the Member States to seek judicial review on grounds of violation of certain agreements, particularly mixed agreements, to which they are themselves as much committed as is the EU, because the Court generally refuses such review. In other words, *Netherlands v. European Parliament and Council* may be an escape route for *Germany v. Council* and *Portugal v. Council*. Further case law is in any event needed in order to shed more light on the current state of the law.

Lastly, the meaning and implications of an international agreement may be clarified in international litigation. Indeed, such litigation may even concern the EU legislation or acts whose legality is challenged before the EU courts. Does that affect the conditions under which the agreement can be relied upon? The question has in particular arisen as regards WTO law, which lacks direct effect, and is examined in greater depth in Chapter 9. The reader is referred to that analysis, but the short answer to the question is that the EU Courts do not consider that WTO dispute decisions are capable of disturbing the finding that WTO law does not have direct effect.

[110] *Netherlands* (n 108 above) para 55.
[111] On agreements concluded by the Member States, see also Ch 9.

Non-contractual liability

By virtue of Articles 268 and 340, second paragraph, TFEU the General Court and, on appeal, the Court of Justice have jurisdiction in disputes relating to the non-contractual liability of the EU. The Treaty provisions oblige the EU to make good, in accordance with the general principles common to the laws of the Member States, any damage caused by its institutions or by its servants in the performance of their duties. At first sight this type of action may seem an unlikely setting for any significant role for international agreements concluded by the EU. However, from the early stages the Court of Justice recognized that the EU may incur non-contractual liability for certain types of wrongful normative action.[112] In *Bergaderm* the Court re-examined the relevant principles. EU law confers a right to reparation where three conditions are met: the rule of law infringed must be intended to confer rights on individuals; the breach must be sufficiently serious; and there must be a direct causal link between the breach of the obligation resting on the State and the damage sustained by the injured parties. As to the second condition, the decisive test for finding that a breach of EU law is sufficiently serious is whether the EU institution concerned manifestly and gravely disregarded the limits on its discretion. The general or individual nature of a measure taken by an institution is not a decisive criterion for identifying the limits of the discretion enjoyed by the institution in question.[113]

International agreements may be relevant to the application of those principles.[114] In particular, breach of the provisions of an agreement binding on the EU may in principle form the basis for a claim in damages. However, in accordance with *Bergaderm* the provisions in question must be intended to confer rights. As all of the cases so far in which an action in damages was brought on the basis of violation of an agreement concerned WTO law, no claims have been successful.[115]

In *FIAMM and Fedon* the Court of Justice confirmed the principles and justification regarding the extension of the case law on the lack of direct effect of WTO law to damages actions. The Court recalled that to accept that the Community courts had the direct responsibility for ensuring that Community law complied with the WTO rules would effectively deprive the Community's legislative or executive organs of the scope for manoeuvre enjoyed by their counterparts

[112] See A Arnull, 'Liability for Legislative Acts under Article 215(2) EC' in T Heukels and A McDonnell, *The Action for Damages in Community Law* (Kluwer Law International, 1997) 129.

[113] Case C-352/98P *Laboratoires Pharmaceutiques Bergaderm v. Goupil* [2000] ECR I-5291.

[114] See also Kaddous (n 4 above) 108–12.

[115] Case T-18/99 *Cordis v. Commission* [2001] ECR II-913; Case T-30/99 *Bocchi Food Trade International v. Commission* [2001] ECR II-943; Case T-52/99 *T Port v. Commission* [2001] ECR II-981; Case T-2/99 *T Port v. Council* [2001] ECR II-2093; Case T-3/99 *Bananatrading v. Council* [2001] ECR II-2123; Case T-174/00 *Biret International v. Council* [2002] ECR II-17; Case T-210/00 *Etablissements Biret v. Council* [2002] ECR II-47; Case T-19/01 *Chiquita v. Commission* [2005] ECR II-315; *FIAMM and Fedon* (n 103 above).

in the Community's trading partners. It found that there was no reason to draw a distinction according to whether the legality of the Community action was to be reviewed in annulment proceedings or for the purpose of deciding an action for compensation. The prospect of actions for damages was liable to hinder exercise of the powers of the legislative authority whenever it had occasion to adopt, in the public interest, legislative measures which could adversely affect the interests of individuals. Further, any determination by the Community courts that a Community measure was unlawful, even when not made in the exercise of their jurisdiction to annul measures, was inherently liable to have repercussions on the conduct required of the institution that adopted the measure in question. Just like annulment judgments and preliminary rulings on invalidity, a judgment delivered in an action for compensation in which it was found that a measure was unlawful had the legal effect of requiring the competent Community institutions to take the necessary measures to remedy that illegality.[116]

The Court therefore sees no good reason for distinguishing between annulment and compensation actions. It has been argued that the award of compensation is a softer type of remedy than annulment, because it would allow the institutions to maintain the EU act which is unlawful under WTO law, and thereby to keep the room for manoeuvre which the Court considers so important.[117] On the other hand, those who are the victims of such unlawfulness would be protected by the award of compensation. Such an approach would strike some sort of balance between political room for manoeuvre and the rights or expectations of traders. The Court, however, opts for consistency between the remedies of annulment and compensation. Indeed, given that the requirement for compensation is, generally, that there must be a sufficiently serious breach of a rule intended to confer rights on private parties, it would be awkward to find that WTO law does not confer such rights for the purpose of annulment, but that it does for the purpose of actions for damages.

The next chapter will further analyse the relevant concepts of direct effect and the creation of rights.

In theory, the conclusion of an international agreement may itself be an act causing damage to a private party. It is, however, difficult to envisage a realistic scenario in which the relevant conditions would be met, and there are as yet no relevant cases.

Enforcement actions

Under Article 258 TFEU the Commission may, after having issued a reasoned opinion, bring a Member State before the Court of Justice where it considers that that

[116] Ibid, paras 119–124; see also Opinion of Maduro AG, paras 49–50.
[117] A Thies, Case Note on *FIAMM and Fedon* (2006) 43 CML Rev 1145.

Member State has failed to fulfil an obligation under the Treaties. This power of the Commission enables it to exercise its important function of guardian of the Treaties, defined in Article 17(1) TEU as the duty to ensure that the provisions of the Treaties and the measures taken by the institutions pursuant thereto are applied. In principle, it is also open to a Member State to bring another Member State before the Court of Justice on the same ground (Article 259 TFEU), but in practice the Member States refrain from doing so, other than in exceptional cases.

As Article 216(2) TFEU provides that agreements concluded by the EU are binding on the institutions of the EU and on Member States, the TFEU contains a clear obligation for the Member States to respect such agreements in all their provisions.[118] Much as the Member States need to comply with the provisions of the founding Treaties and of EU legislation, they are required to act in conformity with EU agreements. There can therefore be no doubt that the Commission may bring an enforcement action against any Member State which fails to act in accordance with that rule, and in the first couple of cases involving pure Community agreements which the Court dealt with, it did not even bother to express the principle, but confined itself to examining whether the alleged non-compliance had taken place.[119] In *Commission v. Germany* on the International Dairy Arrangement, where there was some debate as to whether the Commission should have awaited the opinion of the (then) Article 113 Committee (the Council's committee dealing with trade), the Court simply confirmed the Commission's autonomous power to bring enforcement actions. It stated that the Commission was responsible for ensuring the application of the Treaty and, accordingly, compliance with international agreements concluded by the Community which were binding both on the Community institutions and the Member States. For the Commission to succeed in that task, it could not be hindered in the exercise of its power to bring proceedings before the Court, and the initiation of such proceedings could not depend on the outcome of consultations within the Article 113 Committee. *A fortiori* it could not hinge on whether a consensus between the Member States had first been found to exist within the Committee with regard to the interpretation of the Community's commitments under international agreements.[120]

Those statements are no doubt correct in principle, and would not be remarkable were it not for the type of agreement which was in issue in *Commission v. Germany*: the International Dairy Arrangement was an agreement concluded at the end of the GATT Tokyo Round, and although a separate agreement, it was clearly part of the GATT family of agreements. It would therefore appear that there is no requirement of direct effect or creation of rights, or any other form of

[118] See in general Kaddous (n 4 above) 34–40.

[119] See e.g. Joined Cases 194 and 241/85 *Commission v. Greece* [1988] ECR 1037; Case C–228/91 *Commission v. Italy* [1993] ECR I–2701.

[120] Case C–61/94 *Commission v. Germany* [1996] ECR I–3989, para 15. See also *Opinion 1/91 re EEA Agreement* [1991] ECR I–6079, para 38.

requirement, for an agreement to qualify as the basis for an enforcement action.[121] The position of the Member State in question is not enviable: in 1994 it found itself unable to challenge the legality of the Community banana regulation on grounds of violation of GATT,[122] and in 1996 it had to defend itself (unsuccessfully) for failing correctly to implement a GATT agreement.

The sole issue with respect to enforcement actions based on non-respect of an agreement binding on the EU concerns mixed agreements. Much as in the case of jurisdiction to interpret a mixed agreement (see above), various alternative approaches could be envisaged. The question first came up in *Commission v. Ireland*, concerning Ireland's failure to adhere to the Berne Convention for the Protection of Literary and Artistic Works (Paris Act).[123] The obligation for Member States to join that convention is laid down in a protocol to the EEA Agreement, which is a mixed agreement. Before the Court, Ireland accepted its failure to fulfil its obligations, but the United Kingdom, which had intervened, argued that the Court had no jurisdiction to hear the dispute as the Paris Act of the Berne Convention did not fall wholly within the Community's competence. The Court rejected that argument as inadmissible, because an intervener has no standing to raise a plea of inadmissibility not raised by the defendant, but none the less examined its jurisdiction of its own motion. The Court stated that it was necessary to examine whether the obligations devolving on Ireland came within the scope of Community law. It referred to previous case law according to which mixed agreements had the same status in Community law as pure Community agreements, in so far as they contained provisions coming within Community competence. As a consequence, the Member States, in ensuring respect for commitments arising from an agreement concluded by the Community institutions, fulfilled, within the Community system, an obligation in relation to the Community, which had assumed responsibility for the due performance of the agreement. The Court then applied those principles to the case at hand, and considered that there could be no doubt that the provisions of the Berne Convention covered an area which came in large measure within the scope of Community competence. First, the protection of literary and artistic works was to a very great extent governed by Community legislation. Secondly, the Court previously had occasion to rule, in the *Phil Collins* case,[124] that copyright and related rights fell within the scope of application of the Treaty. The Berne Convention thus created rights and obligations in areas covered by Community law, and there was therefore a Community interest in ensuring that all Contracting Parties to the EEA Agreement adhered to that convention.[125]

[121] See also Opinion of Maduro AG in *FIAMM and Fedon* (n 103 above) para 40.
[122] *Germany v. Council* (n 100 above).
[123] Case C–13/00 *Commission v. Ireland* [2002] ECR I–2943; see also Ch 7.
[124] Joined Cases C–92 and 326/92 *Phil Collins and Others* [1993] ECR I–5145, para 28.
[125] *Commission v. Ireland* (n 123 above) paras 14–20.

The Court's approach to determining Community competence over the Berne Convention was looser than its reasoning in *Opinion 1/94* on TRIPs.[126] The Court did not establish that there was Community competence for the whole of the convention. Also, the reference to *Phil Collins* is not convincing, as that case was not concerned with the Community's law-making competence; it concerned the scope of application of the EC Treaty with a view to applying the principle of non-discrimination on grounds of nationality embodied in (current) Article 18 TFEU, which is a different question. The Court's analysis is none the less essentially correct, for it was sufficient that there was some degree of Community competence in relation to the Berne Convention for the duty to join that Convention to be considered a Community law obligation.[127]

This approach was confirmed in *Commission v. France (Étang de Berre)*.[128] This case was the enforcement action counterpart to the preliminary rulings case *Syndicat professionnel coordination des pêcheurs de l'étang de Berre et de la région*, discussed above.[129] In issue was France's compliance with the Barcelona Convention and its Protocol—a mixed agreement. The complaint was that, by allowing Electricité de France (EDF) to discharge fresh water into the Étang de Berre, a large saltwater marsh at the Mediterranean, France violated the convention's anti-pollution provisions. The Court recalled the principles concerning its jurisdiction to interpret and apply mixed agreements. It then established that the convention and the protocol without doubt covered a field which fell in large measure within Community competence. Environmental protection was in very large measure regulated by Community legislation, including with regard to the protection of waters against pollution. Since the convention and protocol thus created rights and obligations in a field covered in large measure by Community legislation, there was a Community interest in compliance by both the Community and its Member States with the commitments entered into under those instruments. The fact that discharges of fresh water and alluvia into the marine environment had not yet been the subject of Community legislation was not capable of calling that finding into question.[130]

It is lastly worth comparing this case law on mixed agreements with the Court's jurisdiction to interpret provisions of a mixed agreement in a reference for a preliminary ruling (see above). In its case law on such jurisdiction the Court makes little or no reference to Community or EU competence, and arguably adopts a broader approach. It is questionable whether that approach should be extended to enforcement actions. The Court may have jurisdiction to interpret Article 50 TRIPs in cases concerning national trade mark law or national law on the protection of industrial designs, but that does not imply that the implementation and application

[126] *Opinion 1/94* (n 12 above); see Ch 3.

[127] See the comments by Mischo AG on the indivisibility of the Berne Convention: as States cannot adhere to the Berne Convention in part, Community law could only require adherence to the Convention as a whole (*Commission v. Ireland* (n 123 above) paras 47–48 Opinion).

[128] N 59 above.

[129] N 58 above.

[130] *Commission v. France (Étang de Berre)* (n 59 above) paras 27–30.

of this provision in such cases is a Community law obligation for the Member States which could be sanctioned with an enforcement action.

Methods of interpretation

Introduction

It is clear from the above analysis that the EU courts may find occasion to interpret and apply provisions of international agreements binding on the EU in different contexts. Such agreements form part of EU law, and as such come within the courts' jurisdiction. They are none the less different from other segments of the EU legal order in that they are also part of international law. Thus, the courts, when interpreting provisions in an agreement, are interpreting what is essentially an act of international law. Indeed, it would be wrong to conclude from the fact that agreements form part of the EU legal order that they are automatically and fully assimilated to 'internal' EU law, in particular as regards methods of interpretation. The agreement, despite being integrated in the EU legal order, remains an act of international law. When concluding the agreement with the EU, the other contracting parties do not of course intend to have EU law methods of interpretation extended to the agreement, unless expressly indicated. For them, the agreement is simply an act under international law, to be interpreted in accordance with recognized methods of interpretation of international treaties and agreements, and where the EU courts are to interpret those agreements they should follow those methods if they wish the EU law effects of the agreements to correspond with their substance, as governed by and interpreted under international law.

The above already suggests that there may be differences in the methods of interpreting, respectively, EU law and international law. It is clear that, at face value, i.e. at the level of general expressions of methods of interpretation, there are variations, at least in emphasis. The international law rules of treaty interpretation are embodied in Articles 31 and 32 VCLT, which is recognized as codifying customary law.[131] The basic principle of those provisions is that a 'treaty shall be interpreted in good faith in accordance with the ordinary meaning to be given to the terms of the treaty in their context and in the light of its object and purpose' (Article 31(1)), and both international practice[132] and commentaries[133] emphasize the central position

[131] See WTO Appellate Body, *United States—Standards for Reformulated and Conventional Gasoline*, WT/DS2/AB/R, adopted 20 May 1996, with further references. On the relationship between the EC (now EU) and the second Vienna Convention see P Manin, 'The European Communities and the Vienna Convention on the Law of Treaties between States and International Organizations or between International Organizations' (1987) 24 CML Rev 457.

[132] Cf D McRae, 'The WTO in International Law: Tradition Continued or New Frontier?' (2000) 3 JIEL 35.

[133] E.g. R Jennings and A Watts (eds), *Oppenheim's International Law* (9th edn, Longman, 1992) 1271; I Brownlie, *Principles of Public International Law* (6th edn, OUP, 2003) 602; P-M Dupuy, *Droit international public* (6th edn, Dalloz, 2002) 309.

of the ordinary meaning of terms in an agreement as the most reliable expression of the intentions of the contracting parties. In EU law, by contrast, there is a greater tendency to stress the objectives pursued by the act or provision in question, in particular (but not exclusively) as regards essential provisions of the founding treaties. This is the so-called teleological method of interpretation, and even if its importance is sometimes exaggerated, it is indisputable that it plays a significant role in the case law of the EU Courts. An example is Article 34 TFEU, which prohibits quantitative restrictions on imports 'and all measures having equivalent effect'. An interpretation of that provision which regards the ordinary meaning of its terms as crucial would take as a starting point whether a particular measure has effects equivalent to a quota. There is, however, virtually no trace of such an interpretation in the case law of the Court of Justice. Instead, the Court almost immediately adopted a broad definition of 'measures having equivalent effect', as encompassing all measures liable to hinder, directly or indirectly, actually or potentially, intra-Community trade,[134] on the ground that the fundamental objective of building an internal market required such a broad approach. It suffices to consult any overview of the case law to be quickly apprised of the plethora of state measures which, under EU law, are considered to have an effect equivalent to a quota.

The different methods of interpretation need not of themselves lead to difficulties. The EU courts are perfectly capable of applying the correct method, depending on the act before them. The issue is none the less worth exploring further, because of the tendency to include provisions in international agreements concluded by the EU which are materially similar or even identical to provisions of EU law.[135] That tendency, which is not confined to technical issues but largely manifests itself in connection with basic principles of free movement of goods and persons, puts the respective methods of interpretation in the spotlight. To take the above example of measures having equivalent effect, how should one interpret a provision in an agreement between the EU and a third country prohibiting quantitative restrictions and measures having equivalent effect? Should one completely disregard the 'internal' EU law interpretation of that notion, or are there grounds for extending that interpretation to the agreement? Which, if any, may be those grounds? Those are taxing questions with which the EU courts have had to deal, and this section explores the courts' case law which has attempted to answer them.[136] Such an exploration is useful, from the perspective of putting some flesh on the bones of both the Courts' jurisdiction over international agreements, and the legal effects of agreements (see the next chapter). It is also useful from the perspective of exemplifying and illustrating at least some of the contents of the EU's wide-ranging treaty-making practice, and its potential relevance for daily legal life. The analysis first focuses on the early case law of the Court of Justice. It separately analyses the

[134] Case 8/74 *Procureur du Roi v. Dassonville* [1974] ECR 837.
[135] In some cases the origin of the provision may lie further back, e.g. in GATT.
[136] See also Kaddous (n 4 above) 325–46.

approach towards the EEA Agreement, which is the strongest attempt to extend EU law principles to relations with third countries. And it concludes by looking at the most recent case law, concerned with the free movement of persons rather than goods.

Early case law

In the 1979 *Bouhelier* case the Court was asked whether agreements with Greece, Spain, and Austria (all third countries at the time) prohibited certain types of export licence or certificate required under French legislation.[137] The case followed an earlier judgment by the Court in which it had held that the legislation, in so far as it applied in the context of intra-Community trade, contravened EEC Treaty provisions on the free movement of goods.[138] For various reasons the agreements in question did not apply, but the Court had already emphasized that the agreements had to be considered on their own terms. Capotorti AG considered that the agreements, as instruments of commercial policy, had their own objectives, and that this obviously implied that even when they were similar in content to certain provisions of the Treaty they were not necessarily identical in meaning. The important consideration, he stated, was the context of each agreement, which had to be interpreted without regard to that of the Community Treaty.[139]

That is, however, easier said than done when the agreement and the Treaty are identical or very similar in wording, and the Treaty provision in question has been interpreted in a particular way. In three 1982 cases the Court was invited to extend interpretations of Treaty provisions on the free movement of goods to trade with third countries with which the Community had concluded agreements. The first case was *Polydor*, where the issue was whether the internal market doctrine of the exhaustion of intellectual property rights also applied to trade with Portugal, by virtue of the free trade agreement with that country, which contained provisions materially identical to (current) Articles 34 and 36 TFEU.[140] The Court contrasted the objectives of that agreement—to establish a free-trade area in accordance with the relevant GATT provisions—with those of the Treaty concerning the common market—which was to unite national markets into a single market having the characteristics of a domestic market. It followed that, in the context of the agreement, restrictions on trade in goods could be considered to be justified on the ground of the protection of industrial and commercial property in a situation in which

[137] Case 225/78 *Bouhelier* [1979] ECR 3151.

[138] Case 53/76 *Procureur de la République v. Bouhelier* [1977] ECR 197.

[139] *Bouhelier* (n 137 above) 3164.

[140] Case 270/80 *Polydor v. Harlequin Record Shops* [1982] ECR 329. Under the exhaustion of rights doctrine, intellectual property rights may not be relied upon so as to restrict imports into a Member State where the product was placed on the market of another Member State by the proprietor of the right or with its consent.

their justification would not be possible within the Community. Such a distinction was all the more necessary, the Court concluded, because the instruments which the Community had at its disposal in order to achieve the uniform application of Community law and the progressive abolition of legislative disparities within the common market had no equivalent in the context of the relations between the Community and Portugal. The principle of exhaustion of rights could therefore not be extended to trade with Portugal.[141]

While in *Polydor* the Court firmly established the principle that provisions in an agreement identical to provisions of 'internal' Community law should not as a matter of course be interpreted in the same way, a few months later it also made clear that there may be cases in which such identical interpretation is indeed called for. *Pabst & Richarz* concerned the Association Agreement with Greece, Article 53(1) of which prohibited tax discrimination in terms similar to those of (current) Article 110 TFEU. In issue was a German system of tax relief for spirits which Pabst & Richarz claimed to be discriminatory towards imports. The Court first established that (current) Article 110 TFEU applied, as far as imports from other Member States were concerned. It then pointed to the similar wording of Article 53(1) of the agreement, and stated that that provision fulfilled, within the framework of the Association Agreement with Greece, the same function as that of (current) Article 110: it formed part of a group of provisions the purpose of which was to prepare for the entry of Greece into the Community by the establishment of a customs union, by the harmonization of agricultural policies, by the introduction of free movement for workers, and by other measures for the gradual adjustment to requirements of Community law. The Court concluded that it followed from the wording of Article 53(1) and from the objective and nature of the association agreement that it also precluded the tax relief in question, in so far as imports from Greece were discriminated against.[142]

Then came the Court's judgment in *Kupferberg*,[143] which again concerned the free-trade agreement with Portugal, not as regards the prohibition of quantitative restrictions and measures having equivalent effect, but as regards the prohibition of tax discrimination. Article 21, first paragraph, of the agreement stated, in terms which were comparable but clearly not identical to (current) Article 110 TFEU, that the contracting parties were to 'refrain from any measure or practice of an internal fiscal nature establishing, whether directly or indirectly, discrimination between the products of one Contracting Party and like products originating in the territory of the other Contracting Party'. Like *Pabst & Richarz* the case concerned a German system of tax on spirits and spirituous products. Here the Court replied that, although Article 21 and (current) Article 110 TFEU had the same object inasmuch as they were aimed at the elimination of tax discrimination, both provisions, which were moreover worded differently, had to be considered and interpreted in their

[141] Ibid, paras 10–22.

[142] Case 17/81 *Pabst & Richarz v. Hauptzollamt Oldenburg* [1982] ECR 1331, paras 25–28.

[143] Case 104/81 *Hauptzollamt Mainz v. Kupferberg* [1982] ECR 3641.

own context. The Court then referred to its statements in *Polydor* on the different objectives of the Treaty and the agreement. It followed that the interpretations given to (current) Article 110 TFEU could not be applied by way of simple analogy to the free-trade agreement. Article 21 had to be interpreted according to its terms and in the light of the objective which it pursued in the system of free trade.[144] The Court subsequently proceeded to examine the tax in issue in the light of those findings, adopting a narrow interpretation of the 'like products' concept, and holding that there was no tax discrimination where there was no like product on the market in the Member State in question.

On the basis of those three judgments it looked as though the nature of the agreement—whether it established an association preparing for accession, or whether it merely established free trade—was decisive as regards the extension of interpretations of 'internal' Community law to the provisions of an agreement. With respect to trade in goods, the Association Agreement with Greece and the free-trade agreement with Portugal were treated differently, notwithstanding similar wording, on the sole basis of the difference in objectives. The former was interpreted in accordance with case law on the common market, while the latter was not. However, a further string of cases from the beginning of the 1990s made clear that no such generalization was possible.

In *Legros and Others* the Court analysed the system of '*octroi de mer*' (dock dues) applicable to imports into Réunion, a French overseas department to which the free movement of goods in the EU extends (see Article 227(2) EEC, since amended). The Court had little problem establishing that the dock dues were effectively a charge having equivalent effect to customs duties, contrary to (current) Articles 28 and 30 TFEU in so far as imports from other Member States were concerned. It then examined whether those dues were also in breach of Article 6 of the free-trade agreement with Sweden, which equally prohibited charges having equivalent effect. France argued that the *Polydor* principle applied, and that the Treaty interpretation should not be extended to the agreement with Sweden. This time, however, the Court considered such an extension appropriate. It described the purpose of the free-trade agreement in the same terms as it had used in *Polydor*, referring to the objective of establishing a free-trade area in accordance with Article XXIV(8) GATT. It followed that, in the context of the objective of eliminating obstacles to trade, the elimination of customs duties was of prime importance, as was the elimination of charges having equivalent effect, which, according to the Court's case law, were closely linked to customs charges *stricto sensu*. The Court concluded that the agreement would have been deprived of much of its effectiveness if the term 'charge having equivalent effect' contained in Article 6 were to be interpreted as having a more limited scope than the same term appearing in the EC Treaty.[145]

144 Ibid, paras 28–31.

145 Case C-163/90 *Administration des douanes et droits indirects v. Legros and Others* [1992] ECR I-4625.

It thus became clear that it is not ruled out that provisions in a 'mere' free-trade agreement, identical or very similar in wording to provisions of the Treaty, are also identically interpreted. This was confirmed in two further cases. *Commission v. Italy* concerned Italian systematic health inspections on imports of fish as well as a prohibition of imports of certain kinds of fish. The Court found that the Italian measures were contrary to the provisions of (current) Articles 34 and 36 TFEU, and then examined whether they were also, in that they applied to imports of fish from Norway, in violation of the free-trade agreement with Norway. The Court established that Articles 15 and 20 of that agreement contained rules identical to those of (current) Articles 34 and 36 TFEU. It then simply stated that there were no grounds, in the case before it, for interpreting those rules differently from those articles of the Treaty. It accordingly extended the interpretation of the Treaty to the agreement, including the application of the principle of proportionality.[146]

Eurim-Pharm concerned parallel imports of pharmaceutical products from Austria into Germany. The German authorities required that Eurim-Pharm produce certain documents concerning the product (a medicine called Adalat R), notwithstanding the fact that the marketing of the product had previously been authorized in Germany, that the authorities were therefore in possession of those documents, and that there was no doubt that the Adalat R imported by Eurim-Pharm was genuine and identical to the Adalat R already on the market. The *De Peijper* case had clarified that, in intra-Community trade, the parallel importer of medicines is not required to produce such documents.[147] As regards imports from Austria, Eurim-Pharm relied on Articles 13 and 20 of the free-trade agreement with that country, which substantially reproduced (current) Articles 34 and 36 TFEU, arguing in favour of an extension of the *De Peijper* case law to trade with Austria. However, the UK and Italian governments and the Commission argued against such an extension, on the ground that the agreement made no provision either for harmonization of legislation or for administrative co-operation in the pharmaceutical sector. The Court did not accept that objection. It stated that, even on the assumption that its case law on (current) Articles 34 and 36 TFEU could not be applied to the interpretation of Articles 13 and 20 of the agreement, it was sufficient to note that, since the German health authority already possessed all the necessary information about the medicine and there was no dispute that the imported medicine and the authorized medicine were identical, the authority had no need to secure co-operation of any kind from the Austrian authorities. In those circumstances, the Court concluded, to hold that Articles 13 and 20 of the agreement did not preclude rules of the kind at issue in the case would have deprived those articles of much of their effectiveness.[148]

[146] Case C-228/91 *Commission v. Italy* [1993] ECR I-2701.
[147] Case 104/75 *De Peijper* [1976] ECR 613.
[148] Case C-207/91 *Eurim-Pharm v. Bundesgesundheitsamt* [1993] ECR I-3723.

In the *Eurim-Pharm* case Tesauro AG also made some interesting general statements concerning the issue of extension of interpretation. He referred to the *Polydor* and *Kupferberg* judgments, according to which the interpretation of provisions in the EEC Treaty could not be applied by way of simple analogy to the corresponding provisions of a free-trade agreement. However, he continued, whilst that statement of principle was perfectly acceptable in itself, it had to be seen in its proper perspective and was certainly not intended to encourage or justify in general terms divergent interpretations of the Treaty and the corresponding rules in free-trade agreements to which the Community was a party. The ruling in question really constituted, in his view, no more than the application of a general principle of legal interpretation, which was also taken up in the VCLT, whereby a rule was to be interpreted having regard to the most general context in which it appeared. He concluded that, whilst it was true in principle that an interpretation given by the Court in the context of the EEC Treaty was not automatically applicable in the context of an agreement with a non-member country, it was equally true that, when faced with provisions drafted in substantially identical terms and laying down rules of fundamental importance in the context either of the EEC Treaty or of a free-trade agreement, it was still necessary to determine the specific reasons which could lead to a divergent interpretation. That, in the Advocate General's view, was the more correct reading of the *Polydor* judgment, confirmed by *Legros and Others*.[149]

A few months later, in *Metalsa*, the Court itself re-stated the relevant principles.[150] The case concerned the question of whether the Court's ruling in *Drexl* could be extended to imports from Austria.[151] In that case the Court had held that national legislation which penalized offences concerning the payment of value added tax on importation more severely than those concerning the payment of value added tax on domestic sales of goods was incompatible with (current) Article 110 TFEU, in so far as that difference was disproportionate to the dissimilarity between the two categories of offences. As Article 18 of the free-trade agreement with Austria also prohibited tax discrimination, the question was whether the same interpretation should prevail. The Court started its analysis by pointing out that, although the wording of Article 18 differed from that of the first paragraph of (current) Article 110 TFEU, the object of both provisions was to prohibit all direct or indirect fiscal discrimination against products of the other Contracting Party, in the first case, and of Member States, in the other. It then referred to the case law analysed above, drawing attention to the fact that in some cases it had considered an extension of interpretation appropriate, while in others it had not. The Court continued that it was clear from the case law that the extension of the interpretation of a provision in the Treaty to a comparable, similarly or even identically worded provision of an agreement concluded by the Community with a non-member country depended, *inter alia*, on the aim pursued by each provision in its particular context and that

[149] Ibid, Opinion of Tesauro AG, paras 15–17.

[150] Case C–312/91 *Metalsa* [1993] ECR I–3751.

[151] Case 299/86 *Drexl* [1988] ECR 1213.

a comparison between the objectives and context of the agreement and those of the Treaty was of considerable importance in that regard. The Court subsequently referred to the VCLT: an international treaty must not be interpreted solely by reference to the terms in which it is worded but also in the light of its objectives; Article 31 VCLT stipulated in that respect that a treaty was to be interpreted in good faith in accordance with the ordinary meaning to be given to its terms in their context and in the light of its object and purpose.[152]

Applying those principles, the Court found that the *Drexl* interpretation had been based on the far-reaching objective of establishing a single market, an objective which the free-trade agreement with Austria did not pursue. Accordingly, the interpretation could not be extended. Article 18, first paragraph, of the agreement was limited to prohibiting discrimination resulting from any measure or practice which had a direct or indirect effect on the calculation, applicability, and methods of collection of taxes on products of the other Contracting Party, but did not require that there be any comparison between the penalties imposed by Member States for tax offences occurring on importation of goods from Austria and those imposed for tax offences arising on domestic transactions or on imports from other Member States.[153]

The EEA Agreement

Metalsa was not the first case in which the Court expressly referred to the VCLT in support of its reasoning as regards the interpretation of agreements. A couple of years earlier the Community had concluded the Agreement on the European Economic Area (EEA), a most ambitious attempt to extend the policies, principles, and rules of the internal market to the European Free Trade Area (EFTA) countries without requiring them to become members of the EU.[154] In the original negotiation every effort had been made to ensure that the extension of the internal market was complete, and that the internal market would function in exactly the same way in the whole of the EEA. To achieve this the first version of the EEA Agreement copied EEC Treaty provisions as much as possible, and provided, *inter alia*, for extension of the case law of the Court of Justice, as well as for the creation of an EEA Court, composed of judges from the Court of Justice and from the EFTA countries, competent to interpret the agreement. However, in the light of the ambition and novelty of the agreement, the Commission first requested the Opinion of the Court of Justice on the compatibility of the EEA Agreement with the Treaty, in particular with regard to the system of judicial supervision.[155] The Court issued a negative Opinion, in which it emphasized the remaining differences between the

[152] *Metalsa* (n 150 above) paras 9–12. [153] Ibid, paras 15–20.
[154] [1994] OJ L1/3. [155] *Opinion 1/91 re EEA Agreement* [1991] ECR I-6079.

objectives of the EEC Treaty and those of the EEA Agreement, notwithstanding the strenuous attempts to create as much homogeneity as possible between those two international agreements. The Opinion is a landmark in the case law on the autonomy and fundamental characteristics of the EU legal order.[156] It need not be fully analysed here, but in the context of the present survey it is necessary to describe what the Court said regarding extension of interpretation.

The Court started its analysis by comparing the aims and context of the agreement with those of Community law. It again recalled the principle that identical wording does not necessarily mean identical interpretation, because under Article 31 VCLT an international treaty was to be interpreted not only on the basis of its wording, but also in the light of its objectives. The Court then compared those objectives, observing that the agreement was concerned with the application of rules on free trade and competition in economic and commercial relations between the Contracting Parties while, as far as the Community was concerned, those rules on free trade and competition had developed and formed part of the Community legal order, the objectives of which went beyond that of the agreement. The treaty aimed to achieve economic integration leading to the establishment of an internal market and economic and monetary union. Article 1 of the Single European Act 1986 made it clear, moreover, that the objective of all the Community treaties was to contribute together to making concrete progress towards European unity. It followed that the EEC Treaty provisions on free movement and competition, far from being an end in themselves, were only means for attaining those objectives. The Court also considered that the context in which those objectives were situated differed: the EEA Agreement merely created rights and obligations between the contracting parties, and involved no transfer of sovereign rights to the intergovernmental institutions which it set up, whereas the EEC Treaty constituted the constitutional charter of a Community based on the rule of law and established a new legal order, including transfer of sovereign rights, primacy, and direct effect. The Court concluded that homogeneity of the rules of law throughout the EEA was not secured by the fact that the provisions of Community law and those of the corresponding provisions of the agreement were identical in their content or wording.[157]

After the Court's negative Opinion the agreement was renegotiated as regards the system of judicial supervision. The most significant modification was the replacement of the EEA Court with an EFTA Court, composed only of judges from the EFTA countries and with more limited jurisdiction. The Court then issued a positive Opinion which need not be further discussed here.[158] The revised and definitive version of the EEA Agreement continues to aim at as much homogeneity as possible, notwithstanding the Court's scepticism. To that effect it, *inter alia*, contains a provision on interpretation (Article 6):

[156] See Ch 7. [157] *Opinion 1/91* (n 155 above) paras 13–22.
[158] *Opinion 1/92 re EEA Agreement* [1992] ECR I-2821.

> Without prejudice to future developments of case-law, the provisions of this Agreement, in so far as they are identical in substance to corresponding rules of the [EEC Treaty and the ECSC Treaty] and to acts adopted in application of these two Treaties, shall, in their implementation and application, be interpreted in conformity with the relevant rulings of the Court of Justice of the [EC] given prior to the date of signature of the agreement.

The reason for the limitation to prior case law is that the EFTA countries did not wish to commit themselves to future, unforeseeable developments in the case law of the EU courts on which they are not represented.

The EEA Agreement has lost much of its practical significance by reason of the accessions of Austria, Finland, and Sweden, and is now confined to trade and economic relations with Norway, Iceland, and Liechtenstein. There is none the less a significant amount of EU courts' case law which interprets the agreement. Despite the Court of Justice's emphasis on the differences in objectives, nearly all of the case law readily accepts that Community law interpretations of provisions in the Treaty or in legislation are to be extended to the whole of the EEA, thereby applying Article 6 of the agreement.[159]

An interesting application is *Opel Austria*.[160] In that case the CFI examined the issue of identical interpretation. The case concerned the legality of a Council regulation withdrawing tariff concessions for imports of certain types of car gearboxes from Austria. The regulation had been adopted just a few days before the EEA Agreement entered into force, but the CFI none the less decided, on grounds which will be discussed in the next chapter, to examine its compatibility with that agreement. Opel Austria argued that the regulation was in breach of Article 10 EEA, which prohibits customs duties and charges having equivalent effect. The Council contended, however, that this provision should not be interpreted in the same way as the corresponding provisions of the EC Treaty, because there were major differences between the EC Treaty and the EEA Agreement. The CFI did not accept that argument. It carried out an extensive examination of the objectives and content of the EEA Agreement, emphasizing the high degree of integration aimed at, with objectives exceeding those of a mere free-trade agreement, and with strong mechanisms to ensure homogeneity. The Court did not consider *Opinion 1/91* particularly relevant: in that case the Court of Justice was considering the judicial system contemplated by the EEA Agreement for the purpose of ascertaining whether that system might jeopardize the autonomy of the Community legal order in pursuing its own objectives; and not a specific case in which it was necessary to determine whether a provision of the EEA Agreement identical in substance to a provision of Community law had to be interpreted in conformity with the rulings of the Court of Justice and the CFI. The conclusion was that Article 6 EEA, on extension of interpretation, fully

[159] E.g. Case C–355/96 *Silhouette International Schmied v. Hartlauer Handelsgesellschaft* [1998] ECR I–4799.

[160] Case T–115/94 *Opel Austria v. Council* [1997] ECR II–39.

applied, and that Article 10 EEA had to be interpreted in the same way as (current) Articles 28 and 30 TFEU.[161]

The CFI's reasoning is convincing. The differences in objectives on which the Court based its analysis in *Opinion 1/91* were no doubt relevant to the general issue of the autonomy of the Community legal order and of its judicial system. They are, however, much less relevant to the interpretation of specific provisions, and in the light of Article 6 EEA, as well as other provisions emphasizing homogeneity, there would have to be strong reasons for not extending EU law interpretations.

Recent case law

All of the case law discussed so far concerns trade in goods.[162] There are, however, also judgments relating to the movement or treatment of persons under provisions of an agreement which are similar or identical to Treaty provisions on the free movement of persons. There is a long line of cases on the association agreement with Turkey, but most of those are less relevant because they turn on the interpretation of specific provisions of decisions adopted by the Association Council, provisions which do not copy 'internal' EU law provisions. One decision is worth mentioning, though. In *Bozkurt* the Court was asked whether a Turkish international lorry driver employed by a Netherlands company was a worker for the purpose of applying the association agreement and its implementing decisions. Mr Bozkurt relied on the Court's judgment in *Lopes da Veiga*, which concerned the free movement of workers within the Community.[163] The Court accepted the extension on the basis that Article 12 of the agreement provided that the Contracting Parties agreed to be guided by (current) Articles 45 to 47 TFEU for the purpose of progressively securing freedom of movement for workers between them. As the relevant decision of the Association Council was aimed at going one stage further in that respect, the Court considered it essential to transpose, so far as was possible, the principles enshrined in those Treaty provisions to Turkish workers who enjoyed the rights conferred by the decision.[164]

In 2001, the Court decided five cases on the interpretation and effect of provisions on free movement of persons in the Europe Agreements with Central and East European countries. The judgments again illustrate the nuanced approach taken by the Court, pursuant to which the reply to the question of extension of interpretation depends on the objectives of the agreements, the wording of the provisions in their context, and the facts of cases.

[161] Ibid, paras 103–111.

[162] See also Joined Cases C–114 and 115/95 *Texaco and Olieselskabet Danmark* [1997] ECR I–4263, paras 27–33.

[163] Case 9/88 *Lopes da Veiga v. Staatssecretaris van Justitie* [1989] ECR 2989.

[164] Case C–434/93 *Bozkurt* [1995] ECR I–1475, paras 15–20.

In three judgments of the same date the Court refused to extend the interpretation of (current) Article 49 TFEU on the right of establishment to similarly worded provisions in the Europe Agreements with the Czech Republic, Bulgaria, and Poland. The three cases concerned nationals of those countries who had fraudulently obtained leave to enter the United Kingdom, and subsequently claimed the right to establish themselves there. The Court referred to the difference in objectives: the Europe Agreements were designed simply to create an appropriate framework for gradual integration into the Community, with a view to possible accession, whereas the purpose of the Treaty was to create an internal market. It also referred to the wording of the Europe Agreements, which each contained a further provision clarifying that the rights of entry and residence conferred as corollaries of the right of establishment were not absolute privileges, inasmuch as their exercise could, where appropriate, be limited by the rules of the host Member State concerning entry, stay, and establishment of nationals of the countries concerned.[165]

In two other cases, by contrast, the Court considered an extension of interpretation appropriate. *Jany and Others* concerned Polish and Czech prostitutes active in the Netherlands. One of the questions was whether their activity came within the scope of the concept of 'economic activities as self-employed persons' to which freedom of establishment under the relevant Europe Agreements extended. The Court referred to the similar concept of 'activities as self-employed persons' included in (current) Article 49 TFEU. It again described the objective of the Europe Agreements, but concluded that there was nothing in the context or purpose of the Europe Agreements to suggest that the parties intended to give the expression 'economic activities as self-employed persons' any meaning other than its ordinary meaning of economic activities carried on by a person outside any relationship of subordination with regard to the conditions of work or remuneration and under his own responsibility. Consequently, there was in this respect no difference in meaning between (current) Article 49 TFEU and the relevant provisions of the Europe Agreements.[166]

The Court adopted a similar approach in *Pokrzeptowicz-Meyer*. That case concerned Article 37(1) of the Europe Agreement with Poland, which prohibited discrimination based on nationality as regards workers of Polish nationality legally employed in the territory of a Member State. Mrs Pokrzeptowicz-Meyer, a Polish-language assistant at the University of Bielefeld, objected to her fixed-term contract, and argued for the extension of the Court's ruling in *Spotti* to the above non-discrimination provision. In *Spotti* the Court had decided that the provisions

[165] Case C–235/99 *The Queen v. Secretary of State for the Home Department, ex parte Kondova* [2001] ECR I–6427, paras 51–55; Case C–257/99 *The Queen v. Secretary of State for the Home Department, ex parte Barkoci and Malik* [2001] ECR I–6557, paras 51–55; and Case C–63/99 *The Queen v. Secretary of State for the Home Department, ex parte Gloszczuk and Gloszczuk* [2001] ECR I–6369, paras 47–52.

[166] Case C–268/99 *Aldona Malgorzata Jany and Others v. Staatssecretaris van Justitie* [2001] ECR I–8615, paras 32–38.

on fixed-term contracts for foreign-language teachers violated (current) Article 45(2) TFEU and could therefore not be applied to nationals of other Member States.[167] The Court agreed. It followed from a comparison of the aims and context of the Europe Agreement with those of the EC Treaty that there was no ground for giving Article 37(1) a meaning different from that of (current) Article 45(2) TFEU as found in *Spotti*. In particular, it followed from the wording of Article 37(1) as well as from its aims that the prohibition of any kind of discrimination against Polish workers based on their nationality applied just as much to direct discrimination as to indirect discrimination which might affect their conditions of employment.[168]

The analysis in these judgments is convincing, except perhaps for the treatment of the objectives of the Europe Agreements in the *Kondova* group of cases. As the Europe Agreements prepared for accession to the EU it is difficult to envisage agreements whose objectives came closer to those of the founding Treaties.[169] Surely this must be a strong argument for an extension of interpretation as regards similarly or identically worded provisions. However, it was not so much the difference in objectives that was crucial, as the fact that the Europe Agreements expressly subjected the exercise of the right of establishment to compliance with the provisions in Member States on entry and residence. That is not the case with the EC Treaty (now TFEU). It was thus the difference in overall wording which justified the difference in interpretation.

Reliance Industries is a further case worth noting. It involved challenges to EU anti-dumping and anti-subsidy decisions. The CFI first established that the relevant EU legislation had to be interpreted in the light of the WTO Anti-Dumping and Anti-Subsidy Agreements. It then referred to Article 31 VCLT, but added that the rule of interpretation set out in that provision corresponded to the rule applied by the Community judicature when called upon to interpret a provision of Community law. Thus, the Court of Justice had repeatedly held that, in interpreting a provision of Community law, it was necessary to consider its wording, its context, and its aims.[170] That statement is, with respect, rather misleading. As analysed in the introduction to this section, there are substantial differences between the interpretative methods which the EU Courts employ for questions of, respectively, EU law and international law. It is true that those differences are greater where the EU law questions concern fundamental provisions of the founding treaties, and are perhaps less obvious where EU legislation is interpreted. However, there remains a sharp contrast, at least with WTO law. In *Reliance Industries* the Court went on to consider the aims of certain provisions of the Anti-Dumping and Anti-Subsidy Agreements.

[167] Case C–272/92 *Spotti* [1993] ECR I–5185.

[168] Case C–162/00 *Land Nordrhein-Westfalen v. Beata Pokrzeptowicz-Meyer* [2002] ECR I–1049, paras 31–42.

[169] Cf Opinion of Maduro AG in Case C–327/02 *Panayotova and Others v. Minister voor Vreemdelingenzaken en Integratie* [2004] ECR I–11055, paras 24–26.

[170] Case T–45/06 *Reliance Industries v. Council and Commission* [2008] ECR II–2399, paras 100–101.

That is a heuristic device which is hardly ever employed by the WTO dispute-settlement organs, in particular the Appellate Body.[171]

Grimme concerned the Agreement on the free movement of persons with Switzerland. The Court noted that that agreement was signed after the rejection by the Swiss Confederation of the EEA Agreement. The Swiss Confederation, by its refusal, did not subscribe to the project of an economically integrated entity with a single market, based on common rules between its members, but chose the route of bilateral arrangements in specific areas. Therefore, the Swiss Confederation did not join the internal market of the Community, the aim of which is the removal of all obstacles to create an area of total freedom of movement analogous to that provided by a national market. In that context, the interpretation given to the provisions of Community law concerning the internal market could not be automatically applied by analogy to the interpretation of the agreement, unless there were express provisions to that effect laid down in the agreement itself.[172]

The last case to note is *Camar*, oddly enough involving a question of interpretation, in 2010, of the First Yaoundé Convention with the ACP States, which dates from 1963 and was replaced by the Second Yaoundé Convention as far back as 1969.[173] The question arose in proceedings before the Tribunale di Firenze (District Court, Florence), in which the claimants sought to reopen, effectively, earlier Italian proceedings in which the Corte Suprema di Cassazione (Court of Cassation) had refused to make a reference to the European Court of Justice. The argument was that this constituted a violation of (current) Article 267 TFEU. It was for the purpose of assessing that argument that the Florence court referred questions on the compatibility of a 1964 Italian consumption tax on bananas with the First Yaoundé Convention. The case clearly had a longer shelf life than the bananas in issue, which were imported, taxed, and hopefully consumed many decades ago.

Article 14 of the convention provided that the contracting parties had to refrain 'from any internal fiscal measure or practice that directly or indirectly leads to discrimination between its own products and like products originating in the territory of the other Contracting Parties'. The Court examined whether that provision had to be interpreted along the lines of the case law on (current) Article 110 TFEU on tax discrimination. It considered that Article 14 was analogous to the first paragraph of Article 110 TFEU, concerning similar products, but that it did not extend to the prohibition of indirect protection in the second paragraph of the Treaty provision. As Italy did not produce bananas at the time, and as other fruit could not be considered like or similar, the consumption tax had not violated the convention. The Court stressed the difference in underlying objectives of the Treaty and convention

171 McRae (n 132 above).

172 Case C-351/08 *Grimme v. Deutsche Angestellten-Krankenkasse* [2009] ECR I-10777, paras 27-29.

173 Case C-102/09 *Camar v. Presidenza del Consiglio dei Ministri*, judgment of 29 April 2010.

provisions on tax discrimination. The Treaty aimed to guarantee complete fiscal neutrality, in the context of establishing an internal market. Those objectives were absent from the First Yaoundé Convention.[174]

Assessment

The case law on the extension of interpretation of 'internal' Community law provisions to similarly or identically worded provisions in agreements binding on the Community is, on the whole, careful and convincing.[175] The Court has avoided easy generalizations, in the direction of either automatic transposition or automatic refusal. It has correctly based the interpretation of provisions in agreements on the relevant rules of customary international law. One can none the less make a few small observations, by way of footnotes to the case law.

The very starting point of similarly or identically worded provisions has some distortive effects, in particular where there are previous interpretations of 'internal' Community law which appear relevant. Notwithstanding the principle that each agreement should be interpreted on its own terms, the issue then really becomes one of extending or not extending such interpretations. That may not always be to the benefit of an independent interpretation of the agreement. One can, for example, argue that the Court's interpretation of the prohibition of tax discrimination in the *Kupferberg*[176] and *Metalsa*[177] cases is insufficiently considered and sophisticated; one can also argue that the application of the principle of proportionality to the free-trade agreement with Norway (*Commission v. Italy*[178]) finds little basis in the actual agreement. To some extent, therefore, the issue of extension of interpretation may be a red herring leading away from the real questions of interpretation.

As a second point, the Court's emphasis on differences in objectives between the founding Treaties and agreements concluded by the EU is arguably too strong. There is no denying such differences. However, on occasion the Court has exaggerated them; *Opinion 1/91* and the *Kondova* line of cases are instances of such exaggeration. It is also questionable whether under international law the objectives of an agreement are as vital for determining their meaning as is the case in the Court's judgments. The irony of the Court's case law is that the teleological method is often used in order to deny the extension of teleological interpretations of 'internal' Community law.

A last footnote is that the Court's characterization of free-trade agreements appears to play down the significance of such agreements, particularly in the setting of GATT or the WTO. Agreements establishing a free-trade area are advanced and demanding agreements, going beyond standard GATT disciplines. It is questionable whether the Court's interpretation of those agreements has always corresponded to

[174] Ibid, paras 32–34. [175] *Contra* Kaddous (n 4 above) 346.
[176] N 143 above. [177] N 150 above. [178] N 146 above.

their importance. The case law on tax discrimination, in particular,[179] does not take into account the GATT origin of the prohibition in question (which is binding on all GATT Contracting Parties or, at present, WTO Members, and is not confined to free-trade areas). It would be worth examining whether that case law is in conformity with the interpretation of Article III(2) GATT, the source and foundation of all prohibitions of tax discrimination, including that in Article 110 TFEU, as developed in GATT and WTO dispute settlement. Such an examination, however, is beyond the scope of the present analysis.[180]

Conclusions

This chapter examined a variety of issues concerning the courts' jurisdiction over international agreements concluded by the EU. This concluding section offers some further reflections concerning two important problems: jurisdiction to interpret mixed agreements,[181] and the position of the Member States as regards compliance with EU agreements.

The Court, having steered clear of the question of its jurisdiction to interpret provisions in a mixed agreement, was forced in *Hermès* and *Parfums Christian Dior* to address that question as regards Article 50 TRIPs. It clearly adopted a broad approach towards its own jurisdiction, but the judgments are disappointing in that they fail to clarify the general rules or principles which apply. The Court has mentioned the fact that the WTO Agreement (like most other mixed agreements) was concluded without an express allocation and division of competence between the Community and its Member States, suggesting that the EU's international law obligations may cover the entire agreement. It has not, however, clarified the relevance of that factor for determining its jurisdiction. In *Hermès* it based its reasoning on the existence of Regulation 40/94 on the EU trade mark, whose provisions on provisional measures are subject to Article 50 TRIPs. That, together with the principle that it is for national courts to decide which questions to refer to the Court, was sufficient to establish jurisdiction, even if the case was concerned with a national trade mark not governed by the regulation. What the Court did not discuss, however, in either *Hermès* or *Parfums Christian Dior*, is the issue of EU competence: under the principles of EU law governing implied powers one could have expected the Court to state that, as Article 50 TRIPs affects a piece of EU legislation, the *AETR* principle applies, and there is exclusive EU competence (even if Article 50 also governs national intellectual property law).[182] That would clearly have been sufficient to

[179] *Kupferberg* (n 143 above) and *Metalsa* (n 150 above).

[180] Cf M Slotboom, 'The Elimination of Discriminatory Internal Taxes in EC and WTO Law' (2001) 4 JIEL 557.

[181] See also JHJ Bourgeois, 'The European Court of Justice and the WTO: Problems and Challenges' in JHH Weiler, *The EU, the WTO and the NAFTA* (OUP, 2000) 85–88.

[182] See Ch 3.

establish jurisdiction. In *Hermès*, however, the Court contrasts its reasoning with that of the Member States which had argued for competence as the criterion for jurisdiction. We are left in the dark as to the relevance of the competence aspect. In *Parfums Christian Dior*, then, the Court bases the extension of its jurisdiction to cases concerning intellectual property rights—which are not subject to any harmonization whatsoever—on the duty of co-operation between the EU institutions and the Member States, which extends to fulfilling the commitments entered into, and thus to judicial interpretation. It is not, however, clear why the Court did not refer to that duty in *Hermès*, declining the invitation by Tesauro AG. We thus appear to be left with four different reasons for broad jurisdiction: the scope of the EU's obligations, the relationship with harmonized EU law, the approach towards references by national courts, and the duty of co-operation. As argued by Koutrakos, our understanding of the mechanisms of the interpretation and application of mixity would be greatly enhanced by a clearer reasoning.[183]

It is submitted that the underlying principle which should govern the Court's jurisdiction over mixed agreements is whether the provisions in issue come within the scope of EU law. There are a number of different manifestations of that principle.

First, where the agreement itself, or the act of concluding it, clarifies which commitments are entered into by the EU and which are not, only the relevant provisions come within the scope of EU law. There is then clearly a part of the agreement which comes within the Court's jurisdiction, because it is an EU act, and another part which is an act of the Member States which the Court cannot interpret. Such agreements are rare, however.

Secondly, provisions of an agreement which affect other provisions of EU law, in particular EU legislation, also come within the scope of EU law and should be subject to the Court's jurisdiction. The case of Article 50 TRIPs, which affected the EU trade mark regulation, is an example. This is not a question of EU competence, even if owing to the *AETR* principle there is exclusive EU competence where the provision of an agreement affects an EU act. A special case of this second alternative is where the Court is asked to interpret a provision which affects an EU act, but the reference to the Court is made in a case where the provision affects national law, and not EU law. *Hermès* and *Parfums Christian Dior* were such instances. Here the Court has jurisdiction in principle, because the provision comes within the scope of EU law, but the case itself is *prima facie* not concerned with EU law. There may be doubts here as to whether it is appropriate for the Court to accept jurisdiction where the case itself does not appear to concern EU law.[184] However, the third alternative would govern such cases, and justify the Court's jurisdiction.

[183] Koutrakos (n 31 above) 52; see also J Helikoski, *Mixed Agreements as a Technique for Organizing the International Relations of the European Community and its Member States* (Kluwer Law International, 2001) 59–61.

[184] See further Case C–306/99 *BIAO v. Finanzamt für Grossunternehmen in Hamburg* [2003] ECR I–1, Opinion of Jacobs AG, paras 40–70.

This third alternative takes EU competence as a criterion for the Court's jurisdiction. What if the Court is asked to interpret a provision in a mixed agreement, where the agreement does not distinguish between an EU and a non-EU part, and the provision does not affect any EU acts? Should the Court decline jurisdiction on the ground that the provision does not come within the scope of EU law? The answer must be negative, it is submitted, where the provision comes within EU competence. It is such competence which was exercised at the occasion of the conclusion of the agreement. The provisions of a mixed agreement therefore come within the scope of EU law in so far as they come within EU competence. One may connect this principle to the international law dimension. Where the EU concludes an agreement it commits itself under international law within the areas of its competence. It should therefore ensure that the relevant provisions are applied and enforced, also in relation to the Member States and national law. To take an example, let us assume that Article III:2 GATT, on national treatment of imports in matters of taxation, does not affect any EU acts. Article III:2 none the less comes within the EU's exclusive competence pursuant to Article 133 EC.[185] It follows that the Court has jurisdiction to interpret this provision in cases involving national taxation.

Is such jurisdiction limited to areas of exclusive EU competence? Arguably, it is not. As analysed in previous chapters, non-exclusive external competences are as genuine and real as those which are exclusive. By definition, such competences have been exercised where an agreement has been concluded. They are at that stage certainly no longer 'potential' or 'virtual'.[186] The EU has committed itself to ensuring good-faith performance of the agreement. It cannot, under EU law, act beyond the limits of its powers, but within those limits it is required to ensure correct implementation. The relevant provisions of the agreement therefore come within the scope of EU law.

Those should be the relevant criteria for determining the Court's jurisdiction. They should also be applied to the question of whether EU law determines the legal effects of the provisions of a mixed agreement. Again, the reply to that question should depend on whether the provisions come within the scope of EU law. The Court should therefore not have ruled in *Schieving-Nijstad* that national law governed the legal effect of Article 50 TRIPs in so far as industrial designs were concerned, on which there was no EU legislation at the time. The distinction between jurisdiction to interpret and authority to determine legal effects is not convincing. The question of the legal effects of the provisions of an international agreement is closely connected to those provisions' interpretation, indeed one could say that it is itself a specific question of interpretation concerning the agreement.

A second issue deserving some further comments concerns the position of the Member States, in particular where they seek to ensure that the EU fulfils

[185] See Ch 2. [186] See Ch 7.

its international obligations. The current constellation is not satisfactory. Where an agreement does not have direct effect, neither a private party nor a Member State government is capable of relying on the agreement in cases involving judicial review of EU acts. It was argued above that, in principle, this equal treatment of all parties is correct. The judgment in *Netherlands v. Council* suggests that there may be certain ways in which a Member State can none the less base a claim on non-respect of an agreement which lacks direct effect. The reasoning in that judgment is not particularly clear, however.

Given the special position of the Member States in the EU construction and its legal system there are certainly arguments in favour of enabling the Member States to challenge non-respect of the EU's international obligations. However, actions for annulment are not necessarily an appropriate remedy. It must be borne in mind that annulment operates *ex tunc*, and is therefore a radical type of remedy. A different type of remedy may be more suitable. Unfortunately, the Treaty does not provide for an action for a declaration. Such a type of action would allow a Member State to seek a declaration by the Court of Justice that the EU has failed to fulfil an international obligation. It would be more akin to an enforcement action brought by the Commission against a Member State. In the absence of such an action for a declaration, it may be worth examining whether a Member State could make use of Article 265 TFEU, the action for failure to act. Could such an action be brought, not against the EU's failure to act as such, but against its failure to act in accordance with its international obligations? In any event, it would seem desirable to continue the search for ways to enable the Member States to engage in judicial action against the EU's failure to respect its international obligations, even where the agreement does not have direct effect.

9

The legal effects of international law

Introduction

The effect of international law

This chapter explores the legal effects of various forms of international law, which broadly correspond to some of the main sources of international law. Article 38 of the ICJ Statute is usually the starting-point for an analysis of those sources. It refers to international conventions; to international custom and general principles of law; and to judicial decisions and teachings of the most highly qualified publicists. Not all of those sources are equally relevant for the EU's practice. Clearly, the EU (formerly the EC) is a very active treaty-maker, and the reader is already aware that agreements concluded by the EC (now the EU) may have all kinds of legal effects.[1] Much of this chapter is devoted to the study of those effects. However, the EU is not only confronted with international agreements it has itself concluded. Its Member States, sovereign entities, are also bound by treaties, conventions, and agreements, many of which do not have the EU as a contracting party. As the EU is an international organization (albeit *sui generis*), composed of its Member States, and not an independent sovereign, questions arise as to the legal effects of such agreements—for example the UN Charter. The EU is also increasingly confronted with international custom and general principles of law, and with international judicial decisions.

This is a subject which is at the centre of the law of the EU's external relations. It is one thing for the EU to be involved in international affairs and to give effect to such involvement by acting under international law. Such action creates important links and produces many types of legal effect in international law. What, however, are the legal effects of such action, not at the international level, where the relevant actors remain by and large States and international organizations, but within the internal legal order? What are the effects in EU law of an agreement concluded by the EU? What are the effects of a general rule of international law, or of provisions in an agreement binding on one or more Member States? Is international law, in doctrinal terms,

[1] It may again be noted that the terms 'convention', 'treaty', and 'agreement' are largely synonymous. EU law generally employs the term 'agreement' as a generic denominator; see also Ch 6.

separate from 'internal' EU law, or are there channels connecting one with the other? If so, which are those channels, and what is the effect of the international law rules flowing through them? May or must the EU's courts, including courts and tribunals at the level of Member States, apply such international law rules? What effect are they to give to such rules? Can private parties base their claims on rules of international law? In other words, may international law create rights for individuals?

The last set of questions creates an association with the concept of direct effect. The fact that provisions of EU law have direct effect in the legal orders of the Member States is one of the very hallmarks and defining features of the EU's constitution. When the Court in *Van Gend en Loos* decided that the EEC Treaty had set up a new legal order, whose subjects included not just States but also their citizens, it started a legal revolution.[2] That revolution effectively involved setting EU law apart from all other forms of international law. Even though the Court spoke of 'a new legal order of international law', it soon became clear that, particularly in the early stages, Community law was defining itself in opposition to, rather than in conformity with, the 'old' legal order of international law.[3] That may be less so at present, yet it remains indisputable that direct effect and supremacy continue to be the foundations of the EU legal order. Through those concepts EU law is the law of the land, taking precedence over any conflicting rules of national law. That is not merely the theory, but also very much the practice, as private parties have effective remedies for ensuring that EU law is correctly applied, so that they may benefit from any rights which EU law may confer on them. International law, by contrast, does not of itself have the characteristics of direct effect and supremacy. A State may, under its constitution, confer these features on international law, but it is not required by international law to do so. The latter only demands, in very general terms, that it is complied with. Precisely which effects international law may have in domestic or 'municipal' legal systems is a matter largely left to such a system's basic rules.

It is this ancestry of the concept of direct effect which renders the subject of this chapter so fascinating. Indeed, to some extent the EU legal order defined itself in opposition to international law, by the creation of direct effect. Ever since, EU law has been distinct from international law. Yet what, then, is the relationship between them? Like any other municipal legal order, EU law itself largely determines the effects of international law rules in its legal system. What are those effects? Is the EU legal order prepared to give direct effect to international law under the same conditions as those which apply to 'internal' EU law? Or is there unwillingness to do so, perhaps inspired by the birthgiving act of opposition? Is the EU willing to extend its own approach to transnational legal relations to rules of law created outside its own legal premisses? The question of the effects of international law in the EU legal order strikes at the heart of the EU's constitution.

[2] Case 26/62 *Van Gend en Loos v. Nederlandse Administratie der Belastingen* [1963] ECR 1.

[3] CWA Timmermans, 'The EU and Public International Law' (1999) 4 EFA Rev 181; see also D McGoldrick, *International Relations Law of the European Union* (Longman, 1997) 23–5.

The title of this chapter generally refers to the effects of international law. The choice is deliberate. In judicial and academic discussion it is customary to refer to the concept of direct effect as a shorthand for the issue of the relationship between international and EU law. However, shorthands have drawbacks.[4] A close reading of the case law leads one to conclude that international agreements and other forms of international law may produce many different types of legal effect, and an exaggerated use of the direct-effect notion may lead to some degree of myopia, resulting in failure to see the full picture. It is none the less the case that the question of direct effect occupies a central position in the case law, compelling us to examine it carefully, and to attempt to understand it.

Agreements are binding

Article 216(2) TFEU provides that agreements concluded by the EU are binding on the institutions of the Union and on Member States. This is first of all an expression of the vital international law principle of *pacta sunt servanda*. The provision's interest lies in the second part, where it indicates the actors which are bound: not just the EU institutions, but also the Member States. Through this indication the provision clarifies that it addresses the effects of agreements in EU law, and not their effects in international law. The Member States are not *prima facie* bound under international law by agreements concluded by the EU, unless those agreements are mixed and have the Member States as contracting parties together with the EU.[5]

The extension of the binding effect of EU agreements to the Member States need not surprise the observer. One should not make the mistake of thinking that, because the EU may only conclude agreements which come within its treaty-making competences, such agreements cannot contain provisions which require action by the Member States. On the contrary, this is a classic function of EU law, a staple feature of the basic Treaties, of EU legislation (directives are by definition addressed to the Member States), and indeed of agreements. To give just one example, in *Opinion 1/94* the Court of Justice had little or no difficulty in deciding that the WTO agreements on trade in goods (Annex 1A to the WTO Agreement, which includes GATT 1994) came within the Community's exclusive competence to carry on a common commercial policy.[6] Yet many of the GATT provisions have limited relevance for the EU as such, and are mostly targeted, in the

[4] Cf J Klabbers, 'International Law in Community Law: The Law and Politics of Direct Effect' (2002) 21 YEL 263.

[5] I Macleod, ID Hendry, and S Hyett, *The External Relations of the European Communities* (OUP, 1996) 125–8; R Schütze, 'Federalism and Foreign Affairs: Mixity as a (Inter)national Phenomenon' in C Hillion and P Koutrakos (eds), *Mixed Agreements Revisited—The EU and its Member States in the World* (Hart Publishing, 2010) 76; A De Walsche, 'La procédure de conclusion des accords internationaux' in J-V Louis and M Dony (eds), *Commentaire J Megret—Relations extérieures* (Etudes européennes, 2005) 106–9.

[6] *Opinion 1/94 re WTO Agreement* [1994] ECR I-5267; see Ch 2.

EU context, at the Member States. Article III:2 GATT, for example, prohibits discrimination against imported products in matters of taxation. As indirect taxation remains largely the province of the Member States, the provision primarily affects national tax laws and regulations.

Article 216(2) TFEU refers only to agreements concluded by the EU. It does not refer to other forms of international law, such as general rules of international law. The Court has none the less recognized the binding effect of such general rules, and has without reservation accepted that the EU is bound by international law. The Treaty of Lisbon confirms this fundamental openness towards and respect for international law. Article 3(5) TEU provides that the EU shall contribute 'to the strict observance and the development of international law, including respect for the principles of the United Nations Charter'.[7] Of course, the EU is not, and cannot become, a contracting party to the UN Charter as it is not a sovereign State. Prior to the entry into force of the Lisbon Treaty, the Court decided, in the famous *Kadi and Al Barakaat* decision,[8] that the Charter cannot have the effect of excluding the judicial review of a regulation on grounds of violation of fundamental rights. Whether Article 3(5) TEU will affect that finding, remains to be seen.

At any rate, as regards international agreements to which the EU itself is not a party, but which are binding on the Member States, there is the separate provision of Article 351 TFEU. That provision concerns the consequences of rights and obligations contracted by Member States before they became Members of the EU, and enables those Member States to continue to comply with some of their international obligations.

In that connection, in the case of one agreement, namely GATT in its original 1947 version, the Court of Justice accepted that the Community was bound by its provisions, notwithstanding the absence of formal signature, conclusion, or accession.[9] It is not clear whether, in practice, this principle is ever likely to be applied to other agreements concluded by the Member States.

Some would view Article 216(2) TFEU as establishing the full direct effect and supremacy, in EU law, of agreements concluded by the EU. In other words, the provision could be read as confirming a monist approach towards international law.[10] However, the EEC Treaty nowhere expressly introduced the concepts of direct effect and supremacy, and when the Court in *Van Gend en Loos* confirmed the direct effect of EU law, there was a fair amount of opposition from some founding

[7] This is repeated in Art 21(1) TEU.

[8] Joined Cases C–402 and 415/05P *Kadi and Al Barakaat v. Council and Commission* [2008] ECR I–6351.

[9] Joined Cases 21 to 24/72 *International Fruit Company v. Produktschap voor Groenten en Fruit* [1972] ECR 1219.

[10] On monism and dualism, see e.g. FG Jacobs, 'Introduction' in FG Jacobs and S Roberts (eds), *The Effect of Treaties in Domestic Law* (Sweet & Maxwell, 1987) xxiv–xxvi; JH Jackson, 'Status of Treaties in Domestic Legal Systems: A Policy Analysis' (1992) 86 AJIL 313; L Henkin, *International Law: Politics and Values* (Martinus Nijhoff, 1995) 64 *et seq*.

Member States.[11] From that perspective it is not convincing to consider that the Treaty drafters intended international agreements to have such effect. Once the Court had established direct effect and supremacy, through its act of interpreting the Treaty, it of course became arguable that that approach should be extended to international agreements. However, the Court did not, as we will see, take that course (or at least not completely). The Court's case law may be criticized, but to base such criticism on (current) Article 216(2) TFEU is not persuasive. The provision is limited to expressing the binding character of agreements concluded by the EU, and it does not describe the legal consequences or effects of this characteristic. Furthermore, full monism did not and does not reflect the legal traditions of the Member States as regards the relationship between international and domestic law.[12] If that had been otherwise, arguments based on (current) Article 216(2) TFEU would have been more convincing, since the provision could then have been read as an expression of those traditions. It is thus clear that the wording of the Treaty does not exhaust the legal effects of agreements concluded by the EU.

Transposition and implementation

In its case law on the effects of agreements the Court has consistently held that, as from the entry into force of the agreement, its provisions form an integral part of the EU legal system.[13] There is therefore no need for any particular act of transposition; it is sufficient that an agreement is concluded by the Council in accordance with the Article 218 TFEU procedure for it to produce full effect.[14] Of course, the type of effect which the agreement produces may differ, depending on the nature of the agreement and on its provisions, as analysed below.

The fact that no act of transposition is necessary is not to be confused with questions of implementation.[15] Whether the correct application of an agreement requires particular implementing measures again depends on the nature and provisions of the agreement. In *Kupferberg* the Court pointed out that the measures needed to implement the provisions of an agreement concluded by the Community were to be adopted, according to the state of Community law for the time being in the areas affected by the provisions of the agreement, either by the Community institutions or by the Member States.[16] In other words, the binding effect of

[11] *Van Gend en Loos* (n 2 above), observations of the Netherlands and Belgian governments, at 6.

[12] Cf Jacobs and Roberts (n 10 above).

[13] Case 181/73 *Haegeman v. Belgium* [1974] ECR 449, paras 2–6.

[14] Cf J Rideau, 'Les accords internationaux dans la jurisprudence de la Cour de justice des Communautés européennes' (1990) 94 RGDIP 308.

[15] Macleod, Hendry, and Hyett (n 5 above) 128.

[16] Case 104/81 *Hauptzollamt Mainz v. Kupferberg* [1982] ECR 3641, para 12. In para 13 the Court added that, in ensuring respect for commitments arising from an agreement concluded by the Community institutions, the Member States fulfilled an obligation not only in relation to the non-member country concerned but also and above all in relation to the Community which had assumed responsibility for the due performance of the agreement.

agreements is automatic and extends to the requirement of implementation, both as regards the EU as such (the EU institutions) and as regards the Member States. To take the above example of Article III:2 GATT: a Member State may be required by that provision to amend its tax legislation without there being any need for a separate EU act requiring such amendment. As regards the EU institutions, too, the provisions of an agreement are a sufficient legal basis for adopting acts of implementation or application.[17]

It is difficult, if not impossible, to generalize about questions of implementation and application, as each agreement is different and may thus require various types of action or inaction. This may, *inter alia*, involve: no action at all, either because EU or national law already complies with the agreement, or because the agreement imposes a requirement of refraining from certain action; the adoption of general implementing legislation, which is needed so as to adjust either EU or national law to the EU's international commitments; taking certain forms of administrative or executive action; or the incurring of certain expenditure. In the light of this variety it is not possible to point to any consistent implementation practice. There have been cases, however, where no implementing legislation was adopted even where at least for reasons of transparency such legislation was desirable.[18]

Judicial application—direct and indirect effects

As a rule, the EU and its Member States faithfully implement and apply EU agreements, and they abide by the general rules of international law. However, a rule will only exercise the strongest legal force when it is capable of being applied by the judiciary. Where that is the case, and where there is a judicial system offering effective remedies, a rule may be regarded as legally perfect from the point of view of its application or enforcement. In the context of EU agreements, parties to litigation before the EU courts (which include national courts when dealing with questions of EU law) may seek to enforce agreements or general rules of international law where that is in their interest. It is at this point that the direct effect doctrine comes into play. Under what conditions may parties to litigation, in particular but not exclusively private parties, rely on such provisions or rules of international law? That question is vital, not because of any misguided overrating of judicial applications as opposed to other forms of implementing or applying international law. Indeed it is clear that most provisions of agreements will never come before the courts, and none the less need to be applied. However, the type of effect courts are willing to give to particular rules is bound to have a significant impact on the attitude towards those rules, and action taken by institutional actors such as the EU's

[17] See, as an example, Case 30/88 *Greece v. Commission* [1989] ECR 3711, paras 10–17.

[18] Cf P Eeckhout, 'The Domestic Legal Status of the WTO Agreement: Interconnecting Legal Systems' (1997) 34 CML Rev 25.

political institutions and legislatures and public authorities at national level. Where, for example, it is clear that a provision has direct effect, so that it confers rights on individuals which they may enforce in court, a public authority will endeavour to avoid court action by applying those provisions in accordance with the courts' interpretation. If this sounds abstract, it becomes much less so when one looks, for example, at the case law of the Court of Justice on the rights of Turkish workers in the EU.[19] It is by no means certain that these people would have been in the same legal (and factual) position in matters of employment and social security in the absence of this case law.

There are forms of judicial application of EU agreements where, apparently, the binding effect as formulated in Article 216(2) TFEU is sufficient for the agreement to be fully applied; where, in other words, no further conditions, such as direct effect, are imposed. As discussed in the previous chapter, an agreement may form the basis for actions against Member States for failing to fulfil Treaty obligations (Article 258 TFEU): where a Member State violates an EU agreement, the Commission need only prove such violation. This is a particular type of action. Another form of judicial application, unrelated to any specific judicial action, is the principle of consistent interpretation, discussed in a separate section below. According to that principle 'internal' EU law has to be interpreted in the light of the EU's international commitments. Again there are no further conditions.

For other forms of judicial application, however, there are such further conditions, commonly denominated with the concept of direct effect. Chapter 8 described the direct effect requirement as applying in the context of the review of the legality or validity of EU acts (whether challenged before a domestic court—see Article 267 TFEU—or challenged directly before the EU Courts under Article 263 TFEU); in the context of the non-contractual liability of the EU (Articles 268 and 340 TFEU); and in the context of actions before national courts where a party relies on an agreement as against national law.

The concept of direct effect does not, however, exhaust all forms of judicial application where conditions are imposed for an agreement to be relied upon. In the context of its case law on the lack of direct effect of GATT and WTO law, the Court has allowed certain forms of application of such law, where the EU intended to implement a particular obligation or where an EU act expressly refers to such law. This may be called indirect effect, or the principle of implementation. Furthermore, there are suggestions in recent case law that there may be still other forms of judicial application.

Before examining all of this, and before exploring in particular direct effect as a condition for certain forms of judicial application of rules of international law, it is necessary to make a comment on the concept of direct effect as such. One of the problems of that concept is that its use is not limited to the forms of international law which we are discussing here, but was first developed in the setting of 'internal'

[19] See the cases cited in n 58 below.

EU law, and then transposed to international law. This extension should not conceal that we are dealing with different issues; nor should we fail to define, in a correct manner, the sources of law involved.[20] In 'internal' EU law the concept of direct effect is used in order to denote the relationship between EU law—provisions of the Treaties or of EU legislation—and national law. A provision of the Treaties which has direct effect needs to be applied and respected, even in the face of inconsistent national law. By contrast, as regards EU agreements and other forms of international law, the concept of direct effect is used in order to denote the relationship between international law and EU law. A provision of an EU agreement which has direct effect needs to be applied and respected, even in the face of inconsistent 'internal' EU law. Moreover, as EU law overrides national law, and as the provisions of an EU agreement are an integral part of EU law, such provisions also have direct effect in national law. There is thus an important distinction between 'internal' and 'external' direct effect, which arguably justifies some differences in the way in which the concept is handled and applied.

Structure of the chapter

The structure of this chapter is as follows. The next section aims to provide an analysis of the Court of Justice's approach towards the direct effect of agreements concluded by the EU.[21] The focus is on the essential principles, as well as on the lack of direct effect of WTO law and of UNCLOS. The chapter then turns to the principles of consistent interpretation and of implementation, which complete the picture as regards the effects of agreements concluded by the EU. It subsequently focuses on the arguably different question of the legal effects of international judicial decisions. It concludes the part on the legal effects of EU agreements with a general assessment of the case law.

The second part of the chapter is devoted to an analysis of the effects of general international law, in particular rules of customary international law.

The third part examines the effects of agreements binding on the Member States. It essentially studies three topics: under what conditions such agreements are binding in EU law; the *Kadi* litigation, concerning the effects of UN Charter law; and Article 351 TFEU on agreements which the Member States have concluded prior to accession.

[20] Cf Opinion of Maduro AG in Joined Cases C–120 and 121/06P *Fiamm and Fedon* [2008] ECR I–6513.

[21] See also P Koutrakos, *EU International Relations Law* (Hart Publishing, 2006) chs 6, 7, and 8; C Kaddous, *Le droit des relations extérieures dans la jurisprudence de la Cour de justice des Communautés européennes* (Helbing & Lichtenhahn, 1998) 353–80 and 'Effects of International Agreements in the EU Legal Order' in M Cremona and B De Witte (eds), *EU Foreign Relations Law—Constitutional Fundamentals* (Hart Publishing, 2008) 291; I Cheyne, 'Haegeman, Demirel and their Progeny' in A Dashwood and C Hillion (eds), *The General Law of EC External Relations* (Sweet & Maxwell, 2000) 20–41; Klabbers (n 4 above) 274–85; M Maresceau, 'Bilateral Agreements Concluded by the European Community' (2004) 309 *Recueil des Cours* 246.

Agreements concluded by the EU

A survey of the case law on direct effect

GATT and Yaoundé

The Court's exploration of the conditions for the direct effect of international agreements concluded by the (then) Community started with the judgment in *International Fruit Company*.[22] In issue was, on a reference by a Netherlands court, the validity of an EEC regulation restricting imports of apples. International Fruit Company argued that the regulation violated Article XI GATT. The Court, following the Opinion of Mayras AG, which in turn largely followed the position of the Commission, found that, for the incompatibility of a Community measure with a provision of international law to affect the validity of that measure, the Community first had to be bound by that provision.[23] Secondly, before invalidity could be relied upon before a national court, that provision of international law also had to be capable of conferring rights on citizens of the Community which they could invoke before the courts.[24] International Fruit Company's claim stumbled over the second condition. With a view to establishing whether that condition was fulfilled the Court examined what it called 'the spirit, the general scheme and the terms of the General Agreement'.[25] It considered that GATT, which according to its preamble was based on the principle of negotiations undertaken on the basis of 'reciprocal and mutually advantageous arrangements', was characterized by great flexibility, particularly as regards derogations, safeguard measures, and settlement of disputes. The Court analysed the relevant provisions, drawing attention to the importance of consultations between the Contracting Parties; to the various alternatives offered by Article XXIII GATT in case of disputes; and to Article XIX on safeguard measures. The conclusion was that Article XI GATT was not capable of conferring rights on citizens.[26] The Court itself did not expressly refer to the concept of direct effect, but the Opinion of Mayras AG spoke of conferring rights and direct effect as one and the same issue.[27] The Advocate General also distinguished the direct effect of international law from that of 'internal' Community law, and he considered the issue of direct effect to be a problem of interpretation requiring various judicial and technical processes, including: analysis of the provisions; examination of the context and general scheme of the treaty; the aim of the provision in question, having regard

[22] N 9 above.

[23] See above on the binding effect of the GATT of 1947.

[24] *International Fruit Company* (n 9 above) paras 7–8.

[25] Ibid, para 20. In the French version of the judgment the Court speaks of '*l'esprit, l'économie et les termes de l'Accord général*'. In the 1973 *Schlüter* judgment the same terms are expressed in English as 'the meaning, the structure, and the wording of the General Agreement': Case 9/73 *Schlüter v. Hauptzollamt Lörrach* [1973] ECR 1135, para 28.

[26] Ibid, paras 21–27.

[27] *International Fruit Company* (n 9 above) 1234.

to the overall objective of the measure; and circumstances in which the contracting parties had decided to apply the treaty.[28]

Four years later, in *Bresciani*, the Tribunale of Genoa asked the Court whether Article 2(1) of the Yaoundé Convention of 1963 had 'immediate' effect so as to confer on Community citizens an individual right, which the courts had to protect, not to pay to a Member State a charge having an effect equivalent to customs duties (which that article prohibited). The Yaoundé Conventions were the predecessors of the Lomé and Cotonou Conventions. They followed the association with overseas countries and territories provided for by the Fourth Part of the original EEC Treaty. This case did not concern the validity of a Community act, but the direct effect of the Convention, so as to set aside inconsistent national law. The Court stated that, simultaneously, regard had to be paid to the spirit, the general scheme, and the wording of the Convention and of the provision concerned. It recalled the roots of the Yaoundé Conventions, which were intended to maintain the association with former overseas countries and territories. It then analysed the Convention's provisions on charges having equivalent effect, pointing out that the Community had committed itself to abolishing those charges on a non-reciprocal basis. The Court considered that it was apparent from those provisions that the Convention was not concluded in order to ensure equality in obligations, but in order to promote the development of the associated States. This imbalance, which was inherent in the special nature of the Convention, did not prevent recognition by the Community that some of its provisions had direct effect. Under Article 2 the Community was automatically to proceed to the abolition of charges having equivalent effect, and as that provision referred to (then) Article 13 EEC the Community undertook precisely the same obligation to abolish such charges as, in the Treaty, the Member States assumed towards each other. Since the obligation was specific and not subject to any implied or express reservation, it was capable of conferring rights on citizens.[29]

The Court followed the Opinion of Trabucchi AG, who made some interesting general statements on the direct effect of international law. The Advocate General expressed scepticism as regards the extension of the 'internal' direct effect doctrine to international agreements, particularly with respect to agreements containing identical mutual obligations, based strictly on the criterion of reciprocity—not, he said, in making the direct applicability of its provisions dependent on the extent to which, in practice, they were observed by the third State concerned but in establishing whether the agreement was, in principle, capable of creating directly applicable provisions. He felt that in *International Fruit Company* the Court had rightly refrained from automatically applying to the relationship between Community law and international law the concepts and criteria which it had accepted in comparing Community law with national law, in view of the differences between

[28] Ibid, 1235.

[29] Case 87/75 *Bresciani v. Amministrazione Italiana delle Finanze* [1976] ECR 129, paras 16–26.

the Community and the international legal order. However, those considerations did not apply to the Yaoundé Conventions, which were 'the perfect continuation of the system which was originally laid down in the [EEC] Treaty'. The conventions were mainly concerned with privileges granted by the Community and its Member States to the associated countries in order to help their development. The alignment of individual rights with the obligations imposed on Member States by the conventions in question therefore appeared to be consistent with the nature and purpose of the conventions.[30]

The Court confirmed its ruling in *International Fruit Company* in *Schlüter*,[31] in *SIOT*,[32] and in *SPI and SAMI*.[33] *SIOT* was a case concerning Italian charges on the transit of goods, and it therefore differed from *International Fruit Company* in that it did not concern the validity of a Community act. Here the Court used the concept of direct effect, by stating that the GATT provision in question could not have direct effect for the reasons stated in *International Fruit Company*, and that therefore individuals could not rely on it in order to challenge the (national) charges in question.[34] It is also worth noting that Reischl AG agreed with the Court's analysis in *International Fruit Company*, by noting that GATT was flexible and that direct effect was connected with rigidity. He also pointed out that nearly all Member States rejected the direct effect of GATT in their internal legal order, that this was also the case for other GATT Contracting Parties, and that if the Community did recognize direct effect it would impair its negotiating power and its capacity to react to infringements by other parties.[35]

In *Razanatsimba* the Court turned to the first Lomé Convention, the successor of the Yaoundé Conventions, but as it considered the relevant provision inapplicable it did not expressly rule on direct effect. Reischl AG was of the opinion that the convention was capable of having direct effect. However, as the provision at issue contained an open-ended reservation, granting the participating States a wide discretionary power, it was impossible to consider its direct application.[36]

Early case law on free-trade and association agreements

In the 1980s the Court had the opportunity to clarify whether the free-trade agreement with Portugal (part of the group of free-trade agreements with the EFTA countries), as well as association agreements with Greece and Turkey, were directly effective.

In *Pabst & Richarz* the question was whether an importer of spirits could rely on the prohibition of tax discrimination in Article 53 of the association agreement

[30] Ibid, Opinion of Trabucchi AG, para 5.

[31] N 25 above.

[32] Case 266/81 *SIOT v. Ministero delle Finanze* [1983] ECR 731.

[33] Joined Cases 267 to 269/81 *Amministrazione delle Finanze dello Stato v. SPI and SAMI* [1983] ECR 801.

[34] *SIOT* (n 32 above) para 28.

[35] *SIOT* (n 32 above) 790–1.

[36] Case 65/77 *Razanatsimba* [1977] ECR 2229, Opinion of Reischl AG at 2243–4.

with Greece. The Court considered that that provision had to be interpreted in the same way as (current) Article 110 TFEU. It then simply established that Article 53 contained a clear and precise obligation which was not, in its implementation or effects, subject to the adoption of any subsequent measure, and that, accordingly, it had to be considered as directly applicable.[37] These are the classic direct effect conditions, to which the Court constantly refers when examining the direct effect of 'internal' EU law. The swiftness with which the Court concluded that there was direct effect appeared to indicate that association agreements are in principle capable of producing direct effect.

Around the same time the Court was confronted with provisions in the free-trade agreement with Portugal. In *Polydor*, where the question was whether the prohibition of measures having equivalent effect involved exhaustion of intellectual property rights, the Court said nothing about direct effect, since it did not in any event agree with the proposed interpretation.[38] However, a few months later, in *Kupferberg*, the Court addressed the issue, in connection with claims based on the prohibition of tax discrimination in the agreement with Portugal.[39] Rozès AG had argued against direct effect, on the basis that the reasoning of *International Fruit Company* should be extended to free-trade agreements based on reciprocity.[40] The Court did not follow her Opinion, and took the opportunity to elaborate on the direct effect of agreements concluded by the Community. To date, *Kupferberg* still contains the fullest general statement on the direct-effect question.

The Court first pointed to the binding effect of agreements, as expressed in (current) Article 216(2) TFEU. It then made a few statements on the implementation of agreements, as a responsibility of the Community institutions or of the Member States, depending on the circumstances (see previous section). However, the Court then emphasized the Community nature of provisions in an agreement concluded by the Community, from which it followed that their effect could not be allowed to vary according to whether their application was in practice the responsibility of the Community institutions or of the Member States and, in the latter case, according to the effects in the internal legal order of each Member State which the law of that State assigned to international agreements. It was therefore for the Court, within the framework of its jurisdiction in interpreting the provisions of agreements, to ensure their uniform application throughout the Community.[41] This is an important starting point: even if implementation of an EU agreement may be the responsibility of the Member States, EU law exclusively governs the legal effects which the agreement may produce, including its effects in national law.

The Court then described arguments by Member States which had submitted observations to the effect that the provisions of a free-trade agreement were not

[37] Case 17/81 *Pabst & Richarz v. Hauptzollamt Oldenburg* [1982] ECR 1331, paras 25–27.
[38] Case 270/80 *Polydor v. Harlequin Record Shops* [1982] ECR 329.
[39] N 16 above.
[40] Ibid, 3674. [41] Ibid, paras 11–14.

directly effective, in the light of the principle of reciprocity, the institutional framework for settling disputes, and safeguard clauses.[42] It did not, however, agree with those arguments.

It was true, the Court said, that the effects within the Community of provisions of an agreement could not be determined without taking account of the international origin of the provisions in question. In conformity with the principles of public international law, Community institutions which had power to negotiate and conclude an agreement with a non-member country were free to agree with that country what effect the provisions of the agreement were to have in the internal legal order of the contracting parties. Only if that question had not been settled by the agreement, the Court continued, did it fall for decision by the courts having jurisdiction in the matter, and in particular by the Court of Justice within the framework of its jurisdiction under the Treaty, in the same manner as any question of interpretation relating to the application of the agreement in the Community.[43] Those are two important principles. First, the agreement may itself determine its effects. That, however, is in practice the exception rather than the rule.[44] As States, under their constitutional rules, have different approaches towards the legal effects of agreements, and as they may have different attitudes towards international law, they tend rarely to agree on the precise legal effects of agreements in the municipal legal order, and to keep matters at the general level of the international law principle of *pacta sunt servanda*.[45] Secondly, if the agreement does not determine its legal effects, it is for the Court of Justice to do so, as a matter of interpretation of the agreement.

The Court then turned to the arguments which had been advanced against the direct effect of the agreement with Portugal. First, as regards reciprocity, the Court made the following statements. It referred to the international law principle of *bona fide* performance of every agreement, adding that, although each contracting party was responsible for executing fully the commitments which it had undertaken, it was nevertheless free to determine the legal means appropriate for attaining that end in its legal system, unless the agreement itself specified those means. Subject to that reservation, the fact that the courts of one of the parties considered that certain of the stipulations in the agreement were of direct application, whereas the courts of the other party did not recognize such direct application, was not in itself such as to constitute a lack of reciprocity in the implementation of the agreement.[46] In other words, direct effect does not in principle depend on whether the courts in the other contracting parties also recognize it. As we will see, however, there may none the less be cases where this is an important factor: in its case law on the lack of direct effect of WTO law the Court emphasizes reciprocity.

[42] Ibid, paras 15–16. [43] Ibid, para 17.

[44] D McGoldrick, *International Relations Law of the European Union* (Longman, 1997) 127. For such an exception see Case C–1/96 *R v. MAFF, ex parte Compassion in World Farming* [1998] ECR I–1251, para 35.

[45] Cf Henkin (n 10 above) 63. [46] *Kupferberg* (n 16 above) para 18.

Secondly, the Court examined the institutional framework of free-trade agreements, consisting of joint committees responsible for the administration of the agreements and for their proper implementation. It considered that the mere fact that the contracting parties had established a special institutional framework for consultations and negotiations *inter se* in relation to the implementation of the agreement was not in itself sufficient to exclude all judicial application: the fact that a court of one of the parties applied to a specific case before it a provision of the agreement involving an unconditional and precise obligation and therefore not requiring any prior intervention on the part of the joint committee did not adversely affect the powers which the agreement conferred on that committee.[47] This is classic direct-effect reasoning. Also as regards 'internal' Community law the Court has always taken the approach of considering the absence of certain implementing measures irrelevant if the provision in question is sufficiently clear, precise, and unconditional.[48]

Thirdly, as regards safeguard clauses the Court observed that they applied only in specific circumstances, and as a general rule after consideration within the joint committee in the presence of both parties. Apart from specific situations which could involve their application, the existence of such clauses, which did not affect the provisions prohibiting tax discrimination, was not sufficient in itself to affect the direct applicability which could attach to certain stipulations in the agreement.[49]

From all this, the Court concluded that neither the nature nor the structure of the agreement with Portugal prevented a trader from relying on its provisions before a court in the Community. However, that was not the end of the matter. It was still left for the Court to examine whether the provision in issue was unconditional and sufficiently precise to have direct effect, a question which had to be considered in the context of the agreement of which it formed part. In other words, it was necessary to analyse Article 21 of the agreement in the light of both the object and purpose of the agreement and of its context.[50]

The Court then described the purpose of the agreement (essentially to create a system of free trade), and stated that the function of Article 21 in that context was to prevent the liberalization of trade in goods from being rendered nugatory by fiscal practices of the contracting parties. From that it appeared that the provision imposed on the contracting parties an unconditional rule against discrimination in matters of taxation, which was dependent only on a finding that the products affected by a particular tax system were of like nature, and the limits of which were the direct consequence of the purpose of the agreement. As such, this provision could be applied by a court and thus produce direct effects throughout the Community. The overall conclusion was that the provision was directly applicable and capable of conferring upon individual traders rights which the courts had to protect.[51]

[47] Ibid, paras 19–20.
[48] e.g. Case 2/74 *Reyners v. Belgium* [1974] ECR 631, para 26.
[49] *Kupferberg* (n 16 above) para 21. [50] Ibid, paras 22–23. [51] Ibid, paras 24–27.

This second part of the judgment confirmed that the direct effect analysis indeed consists of two parts. The first part involves an examination of whether the nature and structure of the agreement, as such, prevent direct effect. It was appropriate for the Court to put this in the negative for, as we will see, the Court rarely considers this to be a problem. The second part concerns an examination of the specific provisions relied upon: whether those provisions, interpreted in the light of the objective of the agreement and of their context, are clear, precise, and unconditional; in other words the classic conditions for direct effect.

In *Kupferberg* the Court recognized the direct effect of free-trade agreements, thereby clarifying that such effect was not limited to association agreements. A few years later, in *Demirel*, the Court denied direct effect to certain provisions in the association agreement with Turkey.[52] The case concerned a Turkish national, Mrs Demirel, who, having joined her husband in Germany, claimed the right to remain there on the basis of the agreement. The Court made a careful examination of the objective and provisions of the agreement in the field of movement of workers. At the outset it stated, apparently summarizing *Kupferberg*, that a provision in an agreement concluded by the Community had to be regarded as directly applicable when, regard being had to its wording and the purpose and nature of the agreement itself, the provision contained a clear and precise obligation which was not subject, in its implementation or effects, to the adoption of any subsequent measure.[53] That was to become the standard statement concerning the direct effect of international agreements, to be repeated in nearly all the relevant case law. As can be seen, however, it does not put in much relief the distinction between the structure and nature of the agreement as such, and the conditions for the direct effect of specific provisions.

The Court then described the purpose and content of the association agreement. It noted that, in structure and content, the agreement was characterized by the fact that it set out the aims of the association and laid down guidelines for the attainment of those aims without itself establishing the detailed rules for doing so. In order to achieve the aims, the agreement conferred decision-making powers on the Association Council. As regards freedom of movement of workers, Article 12 provided that the contracting parties agreed to be guided by (current) Articles 45 to 47 TFEU for the purpose of progressively securing freedom of movement for workers. Article 36 of the Additional Protocol provided that freedom of movement was to be secured by progressive stages, and that the Association Council was to decide on the rules necessary to that end. The Court then pointed out that this provision gave the Association Council exclusive powers to lay down detailed rules for the progressive attainment of freedom of movement for workers in accordance with political and economic considerations; and that the only decision which the Association Council had adopted on the matter did not concern the sphere of

[52] Case 12/86 *Demirel v. Stadt Schwäbisch Gmünd* [1987] ECR 3719.

[53] Ibid, para 14.

family reunification. The Court therefore concluded that Article 12 of the agreement and Article 36 of the protocol essentially served to set out a programme and were not sufficiently precise and unconditional to be capable of governing directly the movement of workers. That conclusion was not affected by Article 7 of the agreement, which, in very general terms, provided that the contracting parties were to take all appropriate measures, whether general or particular, to ensure fulfilment of the obligations arising from the agreement and that they were to refrain from any measures liable to jeopardize the attainment of the objectives of the agreement: that provision imposed no more than a general obligation of co-operation and could not directly confer on individuals rights which were not already vested in them by other provisions of the agreement.[54] This was again a classic direct-effect analysis. The Court could in fact have been considerably shorter: there simply was, at the time, no provision in the association agreement which specifically provided for the rights of family reunification to which Mrs Demirel laid claim. The problem did not therefore reside in the structure and nature of the agreement as such, but in its specific content.

Further case law on bilateral agreements

In the subsequent case law on the direct effect of free-trade, co-operation, and association agreements the Court has never decided against direct effect on the basis of the structure and nature of the agreement as such. Nearly all questions of direct effect revolve around the clear, precise, and unconditional nature of the provisions in issue. What follows is a short overview of the most interesting cases and statements.

As regards the association agreement with Turkey, the Court had pointed out in *Demirel* that most of the agreement itself was programmatic, and that its implementation required decisions by the Association Council. In *Sevince* the question arose of whether such decisions could have direct effect.[55] The Court decided that the same conditions applied as those governing the agreement itself. It referred to the standard statement in *Demirel* (see above), and proceeded first to examine the terms of the provisions in question, which dealt with (a) the right of a Turkish worker, after a number of years' legal employment in a Member State, to enjoy free access to any paid employment of his choice; and (b) a prohibition on the introduction of new restrictions on the conditions of access to employment applicable to workers legally resident and employed. The Court found that those provisions were clear, precise, and unconditional, and that the finding that they were capable of having direct effect was confirmed

[54] Ibid, paras 15–25. *Demirel* is confirmed in Case T–367/03 *Yedaş Tarim ve Otomotiv Sanayi ve Ticaret Aş v. Council and Commission* [2006] ECR II–873, paras 39–44, itself confirmed on appeal in Case C–255/06P *Yedaş Tarim ve Otomotiv Sanayi ve Ticaret Aş v. Council and Commission* [2007] ECR I–94, paras 36–39.

[55] See, for a general analysis regarding decisions of international organizations, N Lavranos, *Legal Interaction between Decisions of International Organizations and European Law* (Europa Law Publishing, 2004) ch 3.

by the purpose and nature of the decisions of which they formed part and of the agreement to which they related. The fact that the decisions stated that the procedures for applying the rights conferred on Turkish workers were to be established under national rules was no obstacle for direct effect: those provisions merely clarified the obligation of the Member States to take such administrative measures as could be necessary for the implementation of the provisions in question, without empowering them to make conditional or restrict the application of the precise and unconditional rights which the decisions granted. Nor was non-publication of the decisions an obstacle, or the safeguard clauses, which applied only to specific situations.[56]

Sevince confirmed that there is no objection in principle to recognizing the direct effect of the association agreement with Turkey, including the decisions of the Association Council. In *Kziber* the Court extended this approach to the EEC–Morocco co-operation agreement. Miss Kziber claimed rights under Article 41(1) of the agreement, which provided for non-discriminatory treatment of workers of Moroccan nationality as well as members of their families in the field of social security. The Court followed the *Sevince* scheme of analysis, first referring to the standard statement on direct effect in *Demirel*, then examining the terms of the provision, and concluding its analysis by looking at the purpose and nature of the agreement. As regards the terms of Article 41(1) the Court considered that they were clear, precise, and unconditional. The fact that paragraphs (2) to (4) of the article laid down certain limits to that prohibition with reference to specific social security issues did not bar direct effect, as it did not divest the prohibition of discrimination of its unconditional character in respect of any other question which arose in the field of social security. With regard to the purpose and nature of the agreement the Court stated that those factors did not contradict direct effect. The object of the agreement was to promote overall co-operation between the contracting parties, in particular in the field of labour. The fact that the agreement was intended essentially to promote the economic development of Morocco, and that it confined itself to instituting co-operation without referring to Morocco's association with or future accession to the Community, did not prevent direct effect.[57]

Kziber was the first case in which the Court recognized the direct effect of provisions of a 'mere' co-operation agreement, in a sense the weakest type of bilateral agreement between the EU and a third country. It confirmed that, for such agreements, too, the structure and nature of the agreement are unlikely to form an obstacle to direct effect. In a number of subsequent cases the Court either proceeded to interpret provisions in agreements without even mentioning direct effect

[56] Case C–192/89 *Sevince* [1990] ECR I–3461, paras 14–26. See also the Opinion of Darmon AG for an extensive analysis of the nature of the agreement, comparing it with the association agreement with Greece. See further P Gilsdorf, 'Les organes institués par des accords communautaires: effets juridiques de leur décisions' (1992) 357 RMCUE 328.

[57] Case C–18/90 *Kziber* [1991] ECR I–199, paras 15–23.

or established such effect with little or no problem.[58] A few judgments are worth a short discussion.

[58] Case C–163/90 *Administration des Douanes et Droits Indirects v. Legros and Others* [1992] ECR I–4625 (assumes direct effect free-trade agreement with Sweden); Case C–237/91 *Kus v. Landeshauptstadt Wiesbaden* [1992] ECR I–6781, paras 27–31 (reiterates *Sevince*); Case C–207/91 *Eurim-Pharm v. Bundesgesundheitsamt* [1992] ECR I–3723 (assumes direct effect free-trade agreement with Austria); Case C–432/92 *Anastasiou and Others* [1994] ECR I–3087, paras 23–27 (direct effect association agreement with Cyprus); Case C–58/93 *Yousfi* [1994] ECR I–1353, paras 16–19 (reiterates *Kziber*); Case C–355/93 *Eroglu v. Land Baden-Württemberg* [1994] ECR I–5113, para 11 (reiterates *Sevince*); Case C–103/94 *Krid v. CNAVTS* [1995] ECR I–719, paras 21–24 (direct effect co-operation agreement with Algeria); Case C–434/93 *Bozkurt v. Staatssecretaris van Justitie* [1995] ECR I–1475 (EU–Turkey association); Case C–469/93 *Amministrazione delle Finanze dello Stato v. Chiquita Italia* [1995] ECR I–4533, paras 30–35 (direct effect of the Fourth Lomé Convention; reiterates *Bresciani*); Case C–126/95 *Hallouzi-Choho v. Bestuur van de Sociale Verzekeringsbank* [1996] ECR I–4807, paras 19–20 (reiterates *Kziber*); Case T–115/94 *Opel Austria v. Council* [1997] ECR II–39, paras 100–102 (CFI; direct effect of the EEA Agreement); Case C–171/95 *Tetik v. Land Berlin* [1997] ECR I–329 (EU–Turkey association); Case C–386/95 *Eker v. Land Baden-Württemberg* [1997] ECR I–2697 (EU–Turkey association); Case C–285/95 *Kol v. Land Berlin* [1997] ECR I–3069 (EU–Turkey association); Joined Cases C–114 and 115/95 *Texaco and Olieselskabet Danmark* [1997] ECR I–4263 (assumes direct effect free-trade agreement with Sweden); Case C–36/96 *Günaydin v. Freistaat Bayern* [1997] ECR I–5143 (EU–Turkey association); Case C–98/96 *Ertanir v. Land Hessen* [1997] ECR I–5179 (EU–Turkey association); Case C–113/97 *Babahenini v. Belgian State* [1998] ECR I–183, paras 17–18 (reiterates *Krid*); Case C–1/97 *Birden v. Bremen* [1998] ECR I–7747 (EU–Turkey association); Case C–416/96 *Eddline El-Yassini v. Secretary of State for the Home Department* [1999] ECR I–1209, paras 25–31 (reiterates *Kziber*); Case C–179/98 *Belgian State v. Mesbah* [1999] ECR I–7955 (EU–Morocco agreement); Case C–340/97 *Nazli v. Stadt Nurnberg* [2000] ECR I–957 (EU–Turkey association); Joined Cases C–102 and 211/98 *Kocak and Örs* [2000] ECR I–1287 (EU–Turkey association); Case C–171/01 *Wählergruppe 'Gemeinsam Zajedno/Birlikte Alternative und Grüne GewerkschafterInnen/UG', and Bundesminister für Wirtschaft und Arbeit and Others* [2003] ECR I–4301 (EU–Turkey association); Case C–467/02 *Inan Cetinkaya v. Land Baden-Württemberg* [2004] ECR I–10895 (EU–Turkey association); Case C–374/03 *Gaye Gürol v. Bezirksregierung Köln* [2005] ECR I–6199 (EU–Turkey association); Case C–373/03 *Ceyhun Aydinli v. Land Baden-Württemberg* [2005] ECR I–6181 (EU–Turkey association); Case C–383/03 *Ergül Dogan v. Sicherheisdirektion für das Bundesland Vorarlberg* [2005] ECR I–6237 (EU–Turkey association); Joined Cases C–23 to 25/04 *Sfakianakis AEVE v. Elliniko Dimossio* [2006] ECR I–1265 (Europe Agreement with Hungary); Case C–502/04 *Ergün Torun v. Stadt Augsburg* [2006] ECR I–1563 (EU-Turkey association); Case C–336/05 *Echouikh v. Secrétaire d'Etat aux Anciens Combattants* [2006] ECR I–5223 (reiterates *Kziber*); Case C–4/05 *Hasan Güzeli v. Oberbürgermeister der Stadt Aachen* [2006] ECR I–10279 (EU–Turkey association); Case C–97/05 *Mohamed Gattoussi v. Stadt Rüsselsheim* [2006] ECR I–11917 (Euro–Med Agreement with Tunisia; reiterates *El-Yassini*); Case C–325/05 *Ismail Derin v. Landkreis Darmstadt-Dieburg* [2007] ECR I–6495 (EU–Turkey association); Case C–276/06 *Mamate El Youssfi v. Office national des pensions* [2007] ECR I–2851 (reiterates *Kziber*); Case C–56/06 *Euro Tex Textilverwertung v. Hauptzollamt Duisburg* [2007] ECR I–4859 (Europe Agreement with Poland); Case C–16/05 *The Queen, on the application of Veli Tum and Mehmet Dari v. Secretary of State for the Home Department* [2007] ECR I–7415 (EU–Turkey association); Case C–349/06 *Murat Polat v. Stadt Rüsselsheim* [2007] ECR I–8167 (EU–Turkey association); Case C–294/06 *The Queen, on the application of Payir, Akyuz and Ozturk v. Secretary of State for the Home Department* [2008] ECR I–203 (EU–Turkey association); Case C–152/08 *Real Sociedad de Fútbol SAD and Nihat Kahveci v. Consejo Superior de Deportes and Real Federación Española de Fútbol* [2008] ECR I–6291 (EU–Turkey association); Case C–453/07 *Hakan Er v. Wetteranrkreis* [2008] ECR I–7299 (EU–Turkey association); Case C–337/07 *Ibrahim Altun v. Stadt Böblingen* [2008] ECR I–10323 (EU–Turkey association); Case C–13/08 *Erich Stamm and Anneliese Hauser* [2008] ECR I–11087 (agreement with Switzerland on free movement of persons); Case C–228/06 *Mehmet Soysal and Ibrahim Savatli v. Bundesrepublik Deutschland* [2009] ECR I–1031 (EU–Turkey association); Case C–242/06 *Minister voor Vreemdelingenzaken en Integratie v. Sahin* [2009] ECR I–8465; Case C–70/09 *Hengartner and Gasser v. Landesregierung Vorarlberg*, judgment of 15 July 2010 (agreement with Switzerland on free movement of persons); Case C–462/08 *Bekleyen v. Land Berlin*, judgment of 21 January 2010 (EU–Turkey association); Case C–14/09 *Genc v. Land Berlin*, judgment of 4 February 2010 (EU–Turkey association); Case C–300/09 *Staatssecretaris van Justitie v. Toprak and Oguz*, judgment of 9 December 2010 (EU–Turkey association); Case C–303/08 *Land Baden-Württemberg v. Bozkurt*, judgment of 22 December 2010 (EU–Turkey association).

Taflan-Met was a reference for a preliminary ruling on the direct effect of Decision 3/80 of the EU–Turkey Association Council. That decision set out to co-ordinate Member States' social security schemes with a view to enabling Turkish workers employed or formerly employed in the Community, members of their families, and their survivors to qualify for benefits in the traditional branches of social security. Its provisions referred for the most part to particular provisions of the well-known Regulation 1408/71 on social security,[59] and, less frequently, to Council Regulation 574/72 laying down the procedure for implementing Regulation 1408/71.[60] The Court compared Decision 3/80 with the two regulations, and came to the conclusion that the decision did not contain a large number of precise, detailed provisions, even though such were deemed indispensable for implementing Regulation 1408/71. The Court held that, by its nature, the decision was intended to be supplemented and implemented in the Community by a subsequent act of the Council. At the time, there was indeed a proposal for a Council regulation, but it had not yet been adopted. It followed that, even though some of its provisions were clear and precise, Decision 3/80 could not be applied as long as supplementary measures had not been adopted by the Council.[61]

A few years later, however, the Court in *Sürül* qualified that assessment by clarifying that some provisions of the decision could be directly effective. It pointed out that *Taflan-Met* was concerned with co-ordination rules regarding invalidity or survivors' pensions, and that the Court's reasoning there applied to all the provisions of the decision which required additional measures for their application in practice. However, that reasoning could not be transposed to the principle of equal treatment in the field of social security, embodied in Article 3(1) of the decision, which was the provision at issue in *Sürül*. That provision did not require further implementation, and the circumstances of the case (alleged discrimination in the grant of family allowances) were not such as to give rise to problems of a technical nature relating in particular to the aggregation of periods completed in different Member States, to non-overlapping of benefits paid by different competent institutions, or to determination of the applicable national legislation. The Court therefore proceeded to examine whether Article 3(1) was directly effective, examining its wording as well as the purpose and nature of the agreement. After a lengthy analysis, which merely reiterated previous case law, it found in favour of direct effect.[62]

The Court again looked at the association agreement with Turkey in *ex parte Savas*. The question in this case was whether Article 13 of the agreement and Article 41(1) of the additional protocol had direct effect. Article 13 provided that the contracting parties agreed to be guided by (current) Articles 49 to 52 and Article 54 TFEU for the purpose of abolishing restrictions on freedom of establishment

[59] Council Regulation 1408/71 on the application of social security schemes to employed persons and their families moving within the Community [1971] OJ Spec Ed (II), 461.

[60] [1972] OJ Spec Ed (I), 159.

[61] Case C–277/94 *Taflan-Met and Others* [1996] ECR I–4085, paras 23–38.

[62] Case C–262/96 *Sürül v. Bundesanstalt für Arbeit* [1999] ECR I–2685, paras 48–74.

between them. The Court considered that, like Article 12 on the free movement of workers (which it had held not to be directly effective in *Demirel*[63]), Article 13 did no more than lay down in general terms the principle of eliminating restrictions on freedom of establishment, and did not itself establish precise rules for the purpose of attaining that objective. Further, the Association Council had adopted no measures to implement freedom of establishment. Article 13 was therefore incapable of directly governing the legal situation of individuals and could not have direct effect. Article 41(1) of the protocol, by contrast, provided that the contracting parties were to refrain from introducing between themselves any new restrictions on the freedom of establishment and the freedom to provide services. The Court stated that the very wording showed that this provision laid down, clearly, precisely, and unconditionally, an unequivocal 'standstill' clause. It was thus capable of directly governing the legal position of individuals, and this conclusion was not invalidated by an examination of the purpose and subject matter of the agreement. In this respect the Court referred to previous case law on association agreements.[64]

In *Racke* the Court recognized the direct effect of the co-operation agreement with Yugoslavia,[65] but as the importance of the judgment lies in the effect it gives to rules of customary international law it is more convenient to discuss it in the section on general international law, below.

Further, in a string of recent judgments the Court, logically, acknowledged that provisions on freedom of establishment and non-discrimination against legally employed workers in association agreements with Poland, Bulgaria, the Czech Republic, and Slovakia (so-called Europe Agreements) had direct effect. The Court followed the classic pattern of analysis, first examining whether the wording of the provisions in question, in their context, was clear, precise, and unconditional, and then finding that the conclusion of direct effect was not invalidated by an examination of the purpose and nature of the agreement.[66] The same approach was adopted towards the Partnership Agreement with Russia, in *Simutenkov*, a case in which a Russian football player employed in Spain relied on the provision of that agreement concerning non-discrimination on grounds of nationality. The Court, after having found that that provision was clear, precise, and unconditional, indicated that the finding of direct effect was not gainsaid by the agreement's purpose

[63] N 52 above.

[64] Case C–37/98 *The Queen v. Secretary of State for the Home Department, ex parte Savas* [2000] ECR I–2927, paras 41–55.

[65] Case C–162/96 *Racke v. Hauptzollamt Mainz* [1998] ECR I–3655.

[66] Case C–235/99 *The Queen v. Secretary of State for the Home Department, ex parte Kondova* [2001] ECR I–6427, paras 30–39; Case C–257/99 *The Queen v. Secretary of State for the Home Department, ex parte Barkoci and Malik* [2001] ECR I–6557, paras 30–39; Case C–63/99 *The Queen v. Secretary of State for the Home Department, ex parte Gloszczuk and Gloszczuk* [2001] ECR I–6369, paras 29–38; Case C–268/99 *Aldona Malgorzata Jany and Others v. Staatssecretaris van Justitie* [2001] ECR I–8615, paras 26–28; Case C–162/00 *Land Nordrhein-Westfalen v. Beata Pokrzeptowicz-Meyer* [2002] ECR I–1049, paras 19–30; Case C–438/00 *Deutscher Handballbund eV v. Maros Kolpak* [2003] ECR I–4135; Case C–327/02 *Panayotova and Others v. Minister voor Vreemdelingenzaken en Integratie* [2004] ECR I–11055.

and nature. The fact that the agreement was limited to establishing a partnership, without providing for an association or a future accession, was no obstacle. It was clear from the Court's case law that when an agreement established co-operation between the parties, some of the provisions of that agreement could directly govern the legal position of individuals.[67]

GATT and WTO law

As a contrast with the previous section of this survey, it is necessary to return to the lack of direct effect of GATT and WTO law; for a long time, the GATT and WTO agreements have been the only ones which the Court of Justice has considered not to be capable of producing direct effect, in the light of the structure and nature of the agreements as a whole.[68] However, in 2008, the Court established that UNCLOS, too, does not have direct effect, as will be analysed in the following section.

As described above, in *International Fruit Company* the Court held that GATT 1947 did not confer rights on individuals.[69] In subsequent case law on the original

[67] Case C–265/03 *Igor Simutenkov v. Ministerio Educación y Cultura and Real Federación Española de Fútbol* [2005] ECR I–2579, paras 20–29.

[68] Literature on the subject includes Kaddous (n 22 above) 389–401; A Rosas, 'Annotation Case C–149/96, *Portugal v. Council*' (2000) 37 CML Rev 797; M Hilf and F Schorkopf, 'WTO und EG/ Rechtskonflikte vor den EuGH?' (2000) 35 Europarecht 74; GA Zonnekeyn, 'The Status of WTO Law in the Community Legal Order: Some Comments in the Light of the *Portuguese Textiles* Case' (2000) 25 ELR 293; A Desmedt, 'ECJ Restricts Effect of WTO Agreements in the EC Legal Order' (2000) 3 JIEL 191; S Griller, 'Judicial Enforceability of WTO Law in the European Union: Annotation to Case C–149/96, *Portugal v. Council*' (2000) 3 JIEL 441; F Berrod, 'La Cour de justice refuse l'invocabilité des accords OMC: essai de régulation de la mondialisation' (2000) 36 RTDE 419; I Cheyne, 'International Instruments as a Source of Community Law' in Dashwood and Hillion (n 22 above) 266–72; JHJ Bourgeois, 'The European Court of Justice and the WTO: Problems and Challenges' in JHH Weiler (ed), *The EU, the WTO and the NAFTA* (OUP, 2000) 104–21; S Peers, 'Fundamental Right or Political Whim? WTO Law and the European Court of Justice' in G de Búrca and J Scott (eds), *The EU and the WTO—Legal and Constitutional Issues* (Hart Publishing, 2001) 111–30; A von Bogdandy and T Makatsch, 'Collision, Co-existence or Co-operation? Prospects for the Relationship between WTO Law and European Union Law' in de Búrca and Scott (above) 143–50; N van den Broek, 'Legal Persuasion, Political Realism and Legitimacy: The European Court's Recent Treatment of the Effect of WTO Agreements in the EC Legal Order' (2001) 4 JIEL 411; J Vanhamme, *Volkenrechtelijke beginselen in het Europees recht* (Europa Law Publishing, 2001) 200–21; A von Bogdandy, 'Legal Equality, Legal Certainty and Subsidiarity in Transnational Economic Law—Decentralized Application of Art 81.3 EC and WTO Law: Why and Why Not' in A von Bogdandy, P Mavroidis, and Y Mény (eds), *European Integration and International Co-ordination—Studies in Transnational Economic Law in Honour of Claus-Dieter Ehlermann* (Kluwer Law International, 2002) 13; T Cottier, 'A Theory of Direct Effect in Global Law' in von Bogdandy, Mavroidis, and Mény (above) 99; J-V Louis, 'L'insertion des accords dans l'ordre juridique de la Communauté et des Etats membres' in J-V Louis and M Dony (eds), *Commentaire J Megret—Relations extérieures* (Etudes européennes, 2005) 122–37; PJ Kuijper and M Bronckers, 'WTO Law in the European Court of Justice' (2005) 42 CML Rev 1313; A Antoniadis, 'The *Chiquita* and *Van Parys* Judgments: Rules, Exceptions and the Law' (2005) 32 LIEI 461; A Laget-Annamayer, 'Le statut des accords OMC dans l'ordre juridique communautaire: en attendant la consécration de l'invocabilité' (2006) RTDE 249; C Tietje, 'The status of international law in the European legal order: the case of international treaties and non-binding international instruments' in J Wouters, A Nollkaemper, and E de Wet (eds), *The Europeanisation of International Law* (TMC Asser Press, 2008) 59–64; R Uerpmann-Wittzack, 'The Constitutional Role of International Law' in A von Bogdandy and J Bast, *Principles of European Constitutional Law* (2nd edn, Hart Publishing, 2010) 137–47.

[69] N 9 above.

GATT the Court maintained that approach, clarifying that the lack of direct effect prevented parties from relying on the provisions of GATT, both in cases of judicial review of Community acts and in cases involving national law.[70] In *Fediol*[71] and *Nakajima*,[72] however, the Court none the less proceeded to examine the legality of Community acts in the light of provisions of, respectively, GATT itself and the GATT Anti-Dumping Code. The Court considered that those cases did not raise issues of direct effect in an analysis which is discussed and examined under the heading 'The principle of implementation' below.

In *Germany v. Council*, a case concerning the legality of the 1993 banana regime, the Court recalled the features of GATT which stood in the way of direct effect, as identified in *International Fruit Company*. It then stated that those features, from which it had concluded that an individual could not invoke GATT in a court to challenge the lawfulness of a Community act, also precluded the Court from taking the provisions of GATT into consideration to assess the lawfulness of a regulation in an action for annulment brought by a Member State. The special features of GATT showed that the GATT rules were not unconditional and that an obligation to recognize them as rules of international law which were directly applicable in the domestic legal systems of the Contracting Parties could not be based on the spirit, general scheme, or terms of GATT. In the absence of such an obligation following from GATT itself, it was only if the Community intended to implement a particular obligation entered into within the framework of GATT, or if the Community act expressly referred to specific provisions of GATT, that the Court could review the lawfulness of the Community act in question from the point of view of the GATT rules (*Fediol* and *Nakajima*).[73] The judgment was especially noteworthy for extending the direct effect requirement (even if the Court did not refer to the concept of direct effect) to an action brought by a Member State.[74]

Shortly after the judgment in the *Bananas* case, the WTO Agreement entered into force.[75] The establishment of the WTO, as a successor to, but at the same time a significant expansion and upgrade of GATT 1947, clearly injected a much stronger legal element into the multilateral trade agreements.[76] Not only was the territory of such agreements expanded so as to include trade in services and the protection of intellectual property—the latter, of course, being an inherently rights-oriented subject—but GATT itself, some of whose provisions are indeed general and vague, employing complex and economically-oriented concepts, was given much more precision through a number of further agreements or 'understandings on interpretation'.[77] Two of those agreements subjected the important international

[70] See case law at nn 32–33 above and *Chiquita Italia* (n 58 above).

[71] Case 70/87 *Fediol v. Commission* [1989] ECR 1781.

[72] Case C–69/89 *Nakajima v. Council* [1991] ECR I–2069.

[73] Case C–280/93 *Germany v. Council* [1994] ECR I–4973, paras 103–112.

[74] See Ch 8.

[75] 1 January 1995.

[76] See e.g. J Scott, 'GATT and Community Law: Rethinking the "Regulatory Gap"' in J Shaw and G More (eds), *New Legal Dynamics of European Union* (Clarendon Press, 1995) 153.

[77] See the instruments in Annex 1A to the WTO Agreement.

trade sectors of agriculture, and textiles and clothing, to a process of liberalization which stood in stark contrast to the preceding lack of real disciplines (agriculture) or even organized protectionism (textiles and clothing).[78] The scope for exceptions, derogations, and safeguard measures under GATT was reduced by other agreements and understandings.[79] Most importantly, however, the WTO's institutional basis is much stronger than that of GATT 1947. That institutional basis includes an advanced, sophisticated, and in many respects judicialized system of dispute settlement.[80] In contrast to the previous panel system, which was dependent on political consensus within GATT both as regards the establishment of panels and as regards approval of panel reports, the present system has more compulsory elements. WTO members can ask for submission of a dispute to a panel as of right, and the consensus rule for the adoption of panel reports has been reversed: it is only in the (very unlikely) event of a negative consensus among the WTO members that a report is not adopted. Furthermore, the diplomatic elements in the dispute-settlement system and the approach towards GATT law as a more or less self-contained system have much diminished as a result of the introduction of an appeal system, on points of law, before a standing Appellate Body. There is no denying that the case law of that organ—which could as well be called the World Trade Court[81]—has contributed much to the legalization of international trade relations. It is probably fair to say that, as a result, WTO law imposes a stronger legal discipline than many other international agreements, including agreements which the Court of Justice recognized to be directly effective.

The establishment of the WTO triggered a great debate on the direct effect of WTO law, at political, judicial, and academic levels. The importance of the question could hardly be overestimated. In the light of the broad scope of WTO law, covering trade in goods, trade in services, and intellectual property law, and bearing in mind its many connections with EU law, the recognition of the direct effect of WTO law provisions would have opened up large avenues for claims based on WTO law, claims no doubt often directed at invalidating or setting aside either EU or national legislation. At a political level, the Council and the Commission clarified from the outset that they were opposed to the recognition of direct effect. Their position was reflected in two legal documents. First, the Schedule of Commitments of the Community and its Member States under GATS states in an introductory note that the rights and obligations arising from GATS, including the Schedule of Commitments, shall have no self-executing effect and thus confer no rights directly on individual natural persons or juridical persons. Secondly, the Council Decision concluding the WTO Agreement on behalf of the EC states, in its preamble, that by

[78] Agreement on Agriculture, and Agreement on Textiles and Clothing.

[79] See e.g. the understandings concerning waivers, balance-of-payments provisions, and the interpretation of Art XXIV GATT (regional integration), as well as the Agreement on Safeguards.

[80] See the Dispute Settlement Understanding (DSU).

[81] JHH Weiler, 'The Rule of Lawyers and the Ethos of Diplomats: Reflections on the Internal and External Legitimacy of WTO Dispute Settlement' (2001) 35 JWT 202.

its nature the agreement, including the annexes, is not susceptible to being directly invoked in Community or Member State courts.[82]

The academic debate on the question of the direct effect of WTO law cannot be summarized in just a few sentences; there will be opportunity in the assessment section below to discuss some of the main elements of that debate. At judicial level, Cosmas AG opened the discussion in *Affish* by arguing for a continuation of the line of argument in *International Fruit Company*. He considered that the WTO Agreement was still characterized by great flexibility, and he was not impressed by the modifications to the dispute-settlement system and to the conditions for taking safeguard measures.[83] He pointed to the preamble to Decision 94/800,[84] which, in the absence of a corresponding provision in the text of the decision itself, could not by itself preclude direct effect, but none the less confirmed the fact that the weighty reasons against direct effect as expressed in the case law had not ceased to apply.[85] The Court, however, did not consider those issues, as it decided that they were not within the terms of the reference by the national court.

Almost a year later, Tesauro AG delivered a powerful and thoroughly considered Opinion in *Hermès*,[86] both as regards the Court's jurisdiction to interpret the WTO Agreement[87] and as regards direct effect. The Advocate General first looked at the statement in the preamble to Decision 94/800, but was of the opinion, like Cosmas AG, that it did not bind the Court. In contrast to Cosmas AG, however, Tesauro AG did not accept that the *International Fruit Company* line of reasoning could as such be extended to the WTO Agreement. He first expressed some scepticism as regards that case law, taking the view that the characteristics of GATT were not very different from those of agreements which the Court recognized to be directly effective. He then looked at the modifications by the WTO Agreement, and considered that, as regards the flexibility which was at the basis of *International Fruit Company*, there were fundamental changes. The relationship between rules and exceptions as regards waivers and other exceptional measures had changed, and the dispute-settlement system had undergone a Copernican revolution through the reversal of the consensus requirement. The Advocate General was not impressed by the opportunity, still available to WTO members, of offering compensation instead of complying with a dispute ruling, pointing out that such compensation was a purely provisional

[82] Council Decision 94/800 concerning the conclusion on behalf of the European Community, as regards matters within its competence, of the agreements reached in the Uruguay Round multilateral negotiations (1986–1994) [1994] OJ L336/1.

[83] Cosmas AG referred, *inter alia*, to an influential analysis by CWA Timmermans, 'The Implementation of the Uruguay Round by the EC' in JHJ Bourgeois, F Berrod, and E Gippini Fournier (eds), *The Uruguay Round Results—A European Lawyers' Perspective* (European Interuniversity Press, 1995) 501.

[84] N 82 above.

[85] Case C–183/95 *Affish v. Rijksdienst Keuring Vee en Vlees* [1997] ECR I–4315, paras 112–128 of the Opinion.

[86] Case C–53/96 *Hermès v. FHT* [1998] ECR I–3603. In the meantime Elmer AG had also argued against direct effect, but his Opinion contained little reasoning: see Joined Cases C–364 and 365/95 *T Port v. Hauptzollamt Hamburg-Jonas* [1998] ECR I–1023, paras 27–31 of the Opinion.

[87] See Ch 8.

measure. His conclusion from all this was that the Court could not credibly maintain the *International Fruit Company* line of reasoning. He none the less left the door open for a continued denial of direct effect. He looked at the issue of reciprocity, pointing out that some other WTO members (notably the United States, Canada, and Japan) did not recognize direct effect, and that, in the absence of reciprocity in this respect, direct effect would place Community traders at a disadvantage compared with their foreign competitors. He then examined the Court's previous statements on reciprocity, particularly in *Kupferberg*.[88] The Advocate General effectively turned the Court's analysis there on its head: from the formulation that lack of reciprocity as regards direct effect did not in itself constitute lack of reciprocity as regards implementation of the agreement, he concluded that there might be cases where one did lead to the other. As regards the WTO Agreement, there could be no doubt that reciprocity was required, not only in the negotiation of the agreement but also in its performance, and the absence of recognition of direct effect by some other contracting parties could not but lead, at the very least, to an imbalance in the fulfilment of commitments. The Advocate General left it to the Court to undertake the, necessarily abstract, evaluation of whether the lack of reciprocity in terms of direct effect would actually lead to lack of reciprocity in implementation. He concluded by reiterating his opinion that the *International Fruit Company* line of reasoning was no longer convincing, and that, if the Court intended to leave to the 'political' institutions the interpretation and, more generally, the 'management' of the provisions at issue, it should opt for reciprocity.[89]

In *Hermès*, too, the Court managed to avoid deciding the issue, by considering that the case was simply one of consistent interpretation and not of direct effect. Again a year later the Court had to rule in *Portugal v. Council*, a case concerning the legality of a Council decision concluding agreements on trade in textile products with Pakistan and India. Portugal claimed that the decision constituted a breach of certain rules and fundamental principles of the WTO, in particular those of GATT 1994, the Agreement on Textiles and Clothing, and the Agreement on Import Licensing Procedures.[90] Here the Court could no longer avoid the issue.

Saggio AG argued that Portugal should be entitled to rely on WTO law. He was perplexed as regards the *International Fruit Company* line of cases, in so far as the Court imposed the requirement of direct effect in actions concerning the legality or validity of Community acts. In his view, all agreements binding on the Community could form the basis for challenging Community acts, and such review could not be conditional upon direct effect.[91] He was not impressed by arguments based on reciprocity, drawing attention to the means available under general international law for taking action against the failure of another contracting party to implement

[88] N 16 above.

[89] *Hermès* (n 86 above) Opinion of Tesauro AG, paras 28–35.

[90] Case C-149/96 *Portugal v. Council* [1999] ECR I-8395.

[91] See also Ch 8 and below.

an agreement. Nor did he consider the statement in the preamble to Council Decision 94/800 relevant: the Council did not have the authority to interfere with the operation of the Treaty provision (currently Article 216(2) TFEU), stating that agreements are binding or within the jurisdiction of the Court of Justice or of national courts.[92]

The Court, however, did not follow the Advocate General's Opinion as regards direct effect. It effectively maintained its existing case law, but based it on a different reasoning. The analysis consists of two parts. In the first part,[93] the Court started by referring to *Kupferberg*: contracting parties were free to agree what effect the provisions of an agreement were to have, but if the question was not settled by the agreement it was for the Court to decide, as with any question of interpretation; also, according to the general rules of international law there had to be *bona fide* performance of every agreement, but although each contracting party was responsible for executing fully the commitments which it had undertaken, it was nevertheless free to determine the legal means appropriate for attaining that end in its legal system, unless the agreement, interpreted in the light of its subject matter and purpose, itself specified those means. On that basis, the Court examined the WTO Agreement. It acknowledged the strengthening of the system of safeguards and the mechanism for resolving disputes, but nevertheless considered that the resulting system accorded considerable importance to negotiation between the parties. To demonstrate that, the Court turned to the dispute-settlement system, and in particular to the scope for compensation under the provisions of Article 22(1) and (2) DSU. It conceded that Article 22(1) showed a preference for full implementation of a recommendation to bring a measure into conformity with the WTO agreements in question, but pointed out that under Article 22(2), in the event of failure to implement, a member was required to enter into negotiations with a view to finding mutually acceptable compensation. Consequently, the Court continued, to require the judicial organs to refrain from applying the rules of domestic law which were inconsistent with the WTO agreements would have the consequence of depriving the legislative or executive organs of the contracting parties of the possibility afforded by this provision of entering into negotiated arrangements even on a temporary basis. It followed that the WTO agreements, interpreted in the light of their subject matter and purpose, did not determine the appropriate legal means of ensuring that they were applied in good faith in the legal order of the contracting parties.

At first glance this reasoning may seem conclusive. Yet the Court added a second part,[94] which can only be understood against the background of its previous case law on direct effect. Indeed, the Court readily recognizes the direct effect of other international agreements, even though most of them do not 'determine the appropriate legal means of ensuring that they are applied in good faith etc.' either. So there needed to be further reasons for denying WTO law direct effect.

[92] *Portugal v. Council* (n 90 above) Opinion of Saggio AG, paras 18–24.
[93] Ibid, paras 34–41 of the judgment. [94] Ibid, paras 42–49.

The Court opened this second part by indicating that it concerned, 'more particularly', the application of the WTO agreements in the Community legal order. It noted that the WTO was still founded, like GATT 1947, on the principle of negotiations with a view to 'entering into reciprocal and mutually advantageous arrangements' (see the preamble), and was thus distinguished, from the viewpoint of the Community, from agreements concluded between the Community and non-member countries which introduced a certain asymmetry of obligations or created special relations of integration with the Community, such as the agreement which the Court was required to interpret in *Kupferberg*. The Court added that it was common ground that some of the contracting parties, which were among the most important commercial partners of the Community, had concluded from the subject matter and purpose of the WTO agreements that they were not among the rules applicable by their judicial organs when reviewing the legality of their rules of domestic law. The Court then acknowledged its statements on reciprocity in *Kupferberg*, but considered that, in the case of the WTO agreements, based as they were on reciprocity, lack of reciprocity as regards judicial application could lead to a 'disuniform' application of the WTO rules. It added that to accept that the role of ensuring that Community law complied with those rules devolved directly on the Community judicature would deprive the legislative or executive organs of the Community of the scope for manoeuvre enjoyed by their counterparts in the Community's trading partners. The Court concluded that it followed from all those considerations that, having regard to their nature and structure, the WTO agreements were not in principle among the rules in the light of which the Court was to review the legality of measures adopted by the Community institutions. That interpretation, moreover, corresponded with the statement in the preamble to Council Decision 94/800. Finally, the Court maintained the *Fediol* and *Nakajima* exception: it was only where the Community intended to implement a particular obligation assumed in the context of the WTO, or where the Community measure referred expressly to the precise provisions of the WTO agreements, that it was for the Court to review the legality of the Community measure in the light of the WTO rules.

In *Portugal v. Council* the Court did not mention the concept of direct effect, but that was not illogical: neither did the Court do so in *International Fruit Company* or in *Germany v. Council*, also cases concerning the validity/legality of Community acts. As analysed above, under the case law on GATT 1947 the same reasons led to (a) the conclusion that GATT does not confer rights on citizens, (b) the exclusion of GATT from grounds of review of the legality/validity of Community acts, and (c) the lack of direct effect of GATT in proceedings before national courts involving challenges to national law. As regards WTO law, the Court takes the same approach. In *Dior* national courts expressly referred to the Court the question of whether Article 50(6) TRIPs had direct effect, and the Court simply replied by stating that, for the reasons set out in *Portugal v. Council*, the provisions of TRIPs, an annex to the WTO Agreement, were not such as to create rights upon which individuals could rely directly before the courts by virtue of Community law. In the next paragraph the Court called this 'the finding that the provisions of TRIPs do not have direct effect'.[95]

It may be added that the Court, in the light of the mixed character of the WTO Agreement, confined this lack of direct effect to fields in respect of which the Community has already legislated, as was the case with trade marks. On the other hand, stated the Court, in a field in respect of which the Community had not yet legislated and which consequently fell within the competence of the Member States, the protection of intellectual property rights, and measures adopted for that purpose by the judicial authorities (the subject matter of Article 50(6) TRIPs), did not fall within Community law. Accordingly, Community law neither required nor forbade that the legal order of a Member State should accord to individuals the right to rely directly on the provision in question or that it should oblige the courts to apply that provision of their own motion.[96] In other words, the lack of direct effect extended only to provisions coming within Community competence.

In later cases parties have argued that there is a distinction between cases involving WTO law in general, governed by the lack of direct effect, and cases where there is a WTO dispute-settlement decision which establishes a violation of WTO law. That potential distinction, which the Court rejected, is analysed in the section, below, on the effects of international litigation.

Other multilateral agreements

All of the above case law concerns either GATT and WTO law, or bilateral agreements with non-member countries aimed at developing a particular kind of general relationship with such countries (co-operation, free-trade, or association). There are fewer cases on the legal effects of multilateral agreements, other than GATT or the WTO Agreement. That case law is developing, however, and has thrown up a second ruling on the lack of direct effect of an important multilateral agreement, namely UNCLOS.

The EEA Agreement is a special type of multilateral agreement, in the sense that, in terms of substance, it is more akin to bilateral association agreements than to the other multilateral agreements discussed here. It is, in terms of *Portugal v. Council*,[97] an agreement creating 'special relations of integration' with the EU. In *Opel Austria*,[98] a case concerning the effect of the EEA Agreement even prior to its entry into force, the Court of First Instance (CFI) established that the agreement has direct effect. The judgment is analysed below, in the section on general international law. Ever since, the direct effect of the EEA Agreement has been beyond doubt, and the provisions of the agreement are frequently interpreted and applied in EU litigation.[99]

[95] Joined Cases C–300 and 392/98 *Parfums Christian Dior v. Tuk Consultancy* [2000] ECR I–11307, paras 41–45. See also Case C–89/99 *Schieving-Nijstad v. Groeneveld* [2001] ECR I–5851, paras 52–55.

[96] *Dior* (n 95 above) paras 46–48. See also Ch 8.

[97] N 90 above.

[98] Case T–115/94 *Opel Austria v. Council* [1997] ECR II–39.

[99] For a recent example see Case C–157/07 *Finanzamt für Körperschaften III in Berlin v. Krankenheim Ruhesitz am Wannsee-Seniorenheimstatt* [2008] ECR I–8061.

Ex parte Compassion in World Farming concerned a challenge to the validity of a directive on minimum standards of protection of calves,[100] in connection with the use of the so-called veal crate system. Compassion in World Farming argued that the directive was in breach of the European Convention for the Protection of Animals kept for Farming Purposes,[101] drawn up within the Council of Europe, and of the Recommendation concerning cattle adopted within the framework of that convention. The Court did not agree. It considered that it was clear from the actual wording of the convention that the contracting parties had considerable discretion in the choice of appropriate methods for implementing it. The concern expressed in the convention to make the contracting parties aware of the need to maintain rearing conditions which respected the well-being of animals in vital areas was not followed up by the definition of standards whose non-observance could affect the validity of the directive. The recommendation, on the other hand, provided expressly that it was not directly applicable in the national law of the contracting parties and that it was to be implemented according to the method that each party considers adequate. The Court further considered that a document of that kind did not contain legally binding obligations.[102]

In *Netherlands v. European Parliament and Council* the applicant argued that the Directive on the legal protection of biotechnological inventions[103] was in breach of, *inter alia*, the Convention on Biological Diversity.[104] The Court contrasted that convention with WTO law, and stated that the exclusion from grounds of review relating to WTO law could not be applied to the convention, which, unlike the WTO Agreement, was not strictly based on reciprocal and mutually advantageous arrangements. It then stated, without further explanation, that, even if the convention contained provisions which did not have direct effect, in the sense that they did not create rights which individuals could rely on directly before the courts, that fact did not preclude review by the courts of compliance with the obligations incumbent on the Community as a party to that agreement.[105] Thus, the Court appeared to disentangle direct effect from grounds of review of Community acts, but it did not further clarify that, as it subsequently turned its reasoning to a different type of argument: that the Netherlands' plea should be understood as being directed, not so much at a direct breach by the Community of its international obligations, as at an obligation imposed on the Member States by the directive not to breach their own obligations under international law.[106]

The next case concerned the Barcelona Convention for the Protection of the Mediterranean Sea against Pollution,[107] and its Protocol for the Protection of the

[100] Council Directive 91/629 [1991] OJ L340/28.
[101] Approved by Council Decision 78/923 [1978] OJ L323/12.
[102] *Compassion in World Farming* (n 45 above) paras 30–37.
[103] Directive 98/44 of the European Parliament and the Council [1998] OJ L213/13.
[104] Approved by Council Decision 93/626 [1993] OJ L309/1.
[105] Here the Court referred to *Racke* (n 65 above); see below on general international law.
[106] Case C–377/98 *Netherlands v. European Parliament and Council* [2001] ECR I–7079, paras 52–55.
[107] Approved by Council Decision 77/585 [1977] OJ L240/1.

Mediterranean Sea against Pollution from Land-based Sources.[108] *Syndicat professionnel coordination des pêcheurs de l'étang de Berre* involved French interlocutory proceedings for the shutting down of a hydroelectric power station, on the grounds that the station was responsible for the discharge of fresh water into the Etang de Berre, causing damage to the aquatic environment of that saltwater marsh. The Syndicat relied on the Protocol to the Barcelona Convention as prohibiting such environmental damage. The Court found that the relevant provisions of the protocol were clear, precise, and unconditional. That finding was supported by the purpose and nature of the protocol. That purpose was to prevent, abate, combat, and eliminate pollution of the Mediterranean Sea area caused by discharges from rivers, coastal establishments, or outfalls, or emanating from any other land-based sources. To that end, the protocol required the Contracting Parties to take 'all appropriate measures'. The system of prior authorization by the competent national authorities for the discharge of substances (in issue in the case) contributed to the elimination by Member States of pollution from land-based sources in the area covered by the protocol. Recognition of the direct effect of the provision in question could only serve the purpose of the protocol, and reflect the nature of the instrument, which was intended, *inter alia*, to prevent pollution resulting from the failure of public authorities to act. The relevant provisions of the protocol therefore had direct effect, so that any interested party was entitled to rely on those provisions before the national courts.[109]

In *IATA*, too, the Court applied a multilateral agreement. The case involved a challenge to a regulation on compensation for stranded air passengers.[110] On a reference from the English High Court, the Court of Justice examined the validity of that regulation in the light of the Montreal Convention for the Unification of Certain Rules for International Carriage by Air.[111] The Court was extremely succinct on the point of whether the parties could rely on the Montreal Convention. It described how the convention was concluded by the Community, and referred to the Treaty provision on the binding effect of international agreements, as well as to the *Haegeman* principle that agreements are an integral part of the Community (now EU) legal order. The Court then noted that the relevant provisions of the convention were among the rules in the light of which the Court reviewed the legality of acts of the institutions since, first, neither the nature nor the broad logic of the convention precluded this and, secondly, those provisions appeared, as regards their content, to be unconditional and sufficiently precise.[112] No further analysis

[108] Approved by Council Decision 83/101 [1983] OJ L67/1; amendments approved by Council Decision 1999/801 [1999] OJ L322/18.

[109] Case C–213/03 *Syndicat professionnel coordination des pêcheurs de l'étang de Berre v. EDF* [2004] ECR I–7357. See also the parallel Case C–239/03 *Commission v. France* [2004] ECR I–9325, discussed in Ch 7.

[110] Regulation 261/2004 establishing common rules on compensation and assistance to passengers in the event of denied boarding and cancellation or long delay of flights [2004] OJ L46/1.

[111] Approved by Council Decision 2001/539 [2001] OJ L194/38.

[112] Case C–344/04 *The Queen on the application of International Air Transport Association and European Low Fares Airline Association v. Department for Transport* [2006] ECR I–403, paras 35–39.

was offered in either the judgment or the Advocate General's Opinion, though it must be added that the Court did not establish a violation of the convention and found the challenged regulation to be valid.

At this point it seemed that there was as much of a presumption in favour of the direct effect of multilateral agreements as there was for bilateral agreements—with the lone exception of GATT and WTO law. However, *Intertanko* substantially modified that outlook.[113]

The *Intertanko* case concerned UNCLOS, the importance of which as a multilateral agreement hardly requires emphasis. Indeed it is often referred to as the constitution of the law of the sea, in part because many of its provisions codify customary international law. Multilateral agreements of such breadth and significance are not often concluded by the EU.

The claimants comprised a group of organizations within the maritime shipping industry representing most of that industry. They were opposed to provisions on liability (including criminal liability) in Directive 2005/35 on ship-source pollution and on the introduction of penalties for infringements.[114] The international norms in issue are primarily laid down in Marpol 73/78.[115] This is a convention to which all the Member States are parties, but not the EU. The claimants argued that the (then) Community nevertheless had to respect the provisions of Marpol 73/78. This aspect of *Intertanko* is examined in the section entitled 'Agreements binding on the Member States', below. However, the claimants also contended that some of the Marpol 73/78 standards were binding as a result of certain provisions of UNCLOS, which limit the jurisdiction and powers of the Contracting Parties in non-territorial sea areas to implementing international rules and standards. In addition, other UNCLOS provisions, such as those concerning the right of innocent passage, were invoked. That right is part of customary international law, codified in UNCLOS.

UNCLOS is a mixed agreement. The EC and the Member States made a declaration of competences at the time of concluding UNCLOS, but the internal division of competences played virtually no role in *Intertanko*. That was different in the Court's other significant judgment on UNCLOS, *Commission v. Ireland (Mox Plant)*. There the Court held that a Member State could not bring proceedings under UNCLOS against another Member State before an arbitral tribunal, in so far as those proceedings related to matters coming within EC competence.[116]

The Opinion of Kokott AG offered a careful analysis of the many issues involved. She started her examination of whether the claimants could rely on UNCLOS,

[113] Case C–308/06 *The Queen on the application of Intertanko and Others v. Secretary of State for Transport* [2008] ECR I–4057.

[114] [2005] OJ L255/11. The Directive is complemented by Council Framework Decision 2005/667 [2005] OJ L255/165. In Case C–440/05 *Commission v. Council* [2005] ECR I–9097 the Framework Decision was annulled because it violated (then) Art 47 TEU.

[115] International Convention for the Prevention of Pollution from Ships, signed in London on 2 November 1973, as supplemented by the Protocol of 17 February 1978.

[116] Case C–459/03 *Commission v. Ireland (Mox Plant)* [2006] ECR I–4635; see Ch 7.

by pointing out that the Court had effectively applied UNCLOS even before that convention entered into force, when in *Poulsen and Diva Navigation* it applied rules of customary international law which UNCLOS codifies. That case involved individuals relying on the Convention.[117] The Court had since applied UNCLOS in a couple of other cases, too.[118] However, it had not as yet examined the 'nature and broad logic' of UNCLOS—an exercise in which the Advocate General subsequently engaged. She did not consider the principle of reciprocity relevant. It did not matter that other Contracting Parties did not give effect to the provisions of UNCLOS in their municipal law. The reciprocity argument was at odds with the nature of UNCLOS as a 'constitution of the sea'. UNCLOS promoted the peaceful use of the seas and oceans, and this reference was directed precisely at individuals involved in maritime transport. As regards dispute settlement, there was no exclusive competence for any particular UNCLOS institutions, but rather flexibility for the Contracting Parties in the choice of dispute-settlement schemes.[119] Such flexibility did not, however, extend to the substantive provisions of the Convention and was therefore not an argument against finding that individuals were entitled to rely on its provisions.

As can be seen, the above arguments in the Advocate General's discussion of the direct effect of UNCLOS were derived from WTO case law. For the Advocate General, UNCLOS was radically different from WTO law: it did not require reciprocity, was not flexible, and was intended to enable individuals to benefit from the peaceful use of the seas and oceans. It therefore 'constitutes the criterion for the legality of the actions of Community institutions'.[120]

The Court did not follow Kokott AG's Opinion. It examined whether the nature and broad logic of UNCLOS, as disclosed in particular by its aim, preamble, and terms, precluded examination of the validity of Community measures. After a short description of the main objective of UNCLOS, the Court stated that, for the marine areas covered, the convention sought to strike a fair balance between the interests of States as coastal States and the interests of States as flag States, which could conflict. Individuals, by contrast, were in principle not granted independent rights and freedoms by virtue of UNCLOS. This was so because individuals could enjoy freedom of navigation only if they established a close connection between their ship and a State which granted its nationality to the ship and became the ship's flag State. This connection was formed under a State's domestic law. The Court admitted that the wording of certain provisions of UNCLOS appeared to attach rights to ships. It did not, however, follow that those rights were thereby conferred

[117] Case C–268/90 *Poulsen and Diva Corp.* [1992] ECR I–6019; see the section entitled 'General international law', below.

[118] Case C–410/03 *Commission v. Italy* [2005] ECR I–3507 and Case C–111/05 *Aktiebolaget NN* [2007] ECR I–2697.

[119] See Art 280 UNCLOS.

[120] *Intertanko* (n 113 above) para 59 of the Opinion.

on the individuals linked to those ships, such as their owners, because a ship's international legal status was dependent on the flag State and not on the fact that it belonged to certain natural or legal persons.[121] It was also the flag State which had to take measures to ensure safety at sea and to protect the interests of other States. The fact that Part XI of UNCLOS involved natural and legal persons in the exploration, use, and exploitation of the sea-bed and ocean floor was irrelevant: the case did not concern the provisions of Part XI.

The conclusion was that UNCLOS did not establish rules intended to apply directly and immediately to individuals and to confer upon them rights or freedoms capable of being relied upon against States, irrespective of the attitude of the ship's flag State.[122] Thus, the nature and broad logic of the convention prevented the Court from being able to assess the validity of a Community measure in its light.

There is therefore a second case of an important multilateral agreement which lacks direct effect. It is noteworthy that, when examining the broad nature and purpose of an agreement (previously described as the spirit, scheme, and terms), the Court for the first time focused on whether the agreement conferred rights or freedoms. That test is to be applauded, but its negative outcome as regards UNCLOS is open to criticism—as will be discussed in the assessment section, below.

The principle of consistent interpretation

Direct effect is not the only type of effect which an agreement may produce. The Court has also confirmed the principle of consistent interpretation. In *Commission v. Germany* the Court referred to that principle in general terms. It reasoned that, when the wording of secondary Community legislation was open to more than one interpretation, preference had to be given as far as possible to the interpretation which rendered the provision consistent with the Treaty, and that, likewise, an implementing regulation had, if possible, to be given an interpretation consistent with the basic regulation. Similarly, the Court continued, the primacy of international agreements concluded by the Community over provisions of secondary Community legislation meant that such provisions had to be interpreted, as far as possible, in a manner that was consistent with those agreements.[123] This principle is logical and obvious. The coherence of a legal system requires that its various provisions are as much as possible interpreted in the light of each other, so as to avoid conflict between them, and consistent interpretation is a preferred judicial technique for such conflict prevention. As international agreements concluded by the EU form an integral part of the EU legal order, it is appropriate that EU legislation, which should comply with such agreements because the latter are binding on the EU institutions, be interpreted in conformity with them.

[121] Ibid, para 61 of the judgment. [122] Ibid, para 64.

[123] Case C–61/94 *Commission v. Germany* [1996] ECR I–3989, para 10.

The technique of consistent interpretation is not often applied for the simple reason that most agreements have direct effect, leading to their direct application and obviating the need for consistent interpretation. It is none the less a useful instrument, in particular as regards agreements which are not directly effective, i.e. GATT and the WTO agreements, and UNCLOS. The EU Courts rarely hesitate to make use of consistent interpretation for the purpose of applying GATT and WTO law.[124] Again that is logical, because consistent interpretation does not lead to a direct application of the provisions involved. The legal instrument that is applied is the piece of EU legislation in issue, which is simply interpreted in a particular way. Interesting examples of the application of the consistent interpretation technique involving GATT are the Court's judgments in *Werner* and *Leifer*. In those cases the question arose of whether Article 1 of Regulation 2603/69 establishing common rules for exports, which prohibited 'quantitative restrictions on exports', extended to national licensing requirements for exports of so-called dual-use goods. The Court gave an affirmative reply, and stated that its finding was supported by Article XI GATT, which could be considered to be relevant for the purposes of interpreting a Community instrument governing international trade. Article XI, headed 'General Elimination of Quantitative Restrictions', refers in its first paragraph to 'prohibitions or restrictions other than duties, taxes or other charges, whether made effective through quotas, import or export licences or other measures'.[125]

There is, however, one type of case involving WTO law in which the EU Courts appear to hesitate to apply the consistent interpretation principle: those cases in which reference is made, not just to provisions of WTO law, but also to WTO dispute decisions adopted against the EU. An example is *Ikea Wholesale*, a case in which it would have been obvious to interpret the EU anti-dumping regulation in the light of WTO dispute decisions, and yet the Court preferred an autonomous EU law interpretation.[126] We will return to the case in the section entitled 'The effects of international litigation', below.

It is also clear from the case law that the principle of consistent interpretation has general application, and that a party invoking the principle need not show that

[124] See e.g. Case 92/71 *Interfood v. Hauptzollamt Hamburg* [1972] ECR 231, para 6; Case C–79/89 *Brown Boveri* [1991] ECR I–1853, paras 15–19; Joined Cases T–163 and 165/94 *NTN Corporation and Koyo Seiko v. Council* [1995] ECR II–1381, para 65; *Commission v. Germany* (n 123 above); *Hermès* (n 86 above); Case C–245/02 *Anheuser-Busch Inc. v. Budějovický Budvar, národní podnik* [2004] ECR I–10989; Case C–306/05 *Sociedad General de Autores y Editores de España (SGAE) v. Rafael Hoteles SA* [2006] ECR I–11519; Case C–428/08 *Monsanto Technology v. Cefetra and Others*, judgment of 6 July 2010, paras 70–77. An awkward judgment was delivered in Case C–335/05 *Řízení Letového Provozu ČR, s p v. Bundesamt für Finanzen* [2007] ECR I–4307. The case involved a permissive clause in the 13th VAT directive, which, it was argued, had to be interpreted in the light of the most-favoured-nation provision in GATS (Art II). The Court, however, simply left it to each Member State to apply the permissive clause in accordance with GATS, without imposing a uniform interpretation.

[125] Case C–70/94 *Werner v. Germany* [1995] ECR I–3189, para 23 and Case C–83/94 *Leifer and Others* [1995] ECR I–3231, para 24.

[126] Case C–351/04 *Ikea Wholesale v. Commissioners of Customs & Excise* [2007] ECR I–7723; see also Case T–274/02 *Ritek Corp and Prodisc Technology Inc v. Council* [2006] ECR II–4305.

the Community legislation in issue was adopted with a view to implementing the international agreement influencing its interpretation. Nevertheless, in *SGAE v. Rafael Hoteles* the Court stated that Community legislation had to be interpreted consistently 'in particular where its provisions are intended specifically to give effect to an international agreement concluded by the Community'.[127]

Furthermore, a parallel may be drawn with the legal effects of directives. As is well known, directives lack so-called horizontal direct effect, in the sense that a directive cannot as such impose obligations on a private party.[128] As a result, there is pressure to apply the principle of consistent interpretation in cases between private parties involving an unimplemented directive. It is fair to say that, as a result, the Court has undertaken some creative interpretation so as to give effect to directives, stretching the language and meaning of the interpreted provisions.[129] One may wonder whether the Court would be willing to do the same as regards international agreements which are not directly effective, in particular the WTO agreements and UNCLOS.

The principle of implementation

Both in *Germany v. Council*, as regards the lack of direct effect of the GATT of 1947,[130] and in *Portugal v. Council*, concerning the lack of direct effect of the WTO Agreement,[131] the Court made an exception: it is only where the Community (now EU) intended to implement a particular obligation assumed in the context of the WTO or where the Community measure refers expressly to the provisions of the WTO agreements that it is for the Court to review the legality of the Community measure in the light of the WTO rules. That exception, which can be called the principle of implementation, is now established case law, and it is therefore necessary to examine its origins, rationale, and application.

Origins

The origins of this exception go back to the judgments in *Fediol*[132] and *Nakajima*.[133] In *Fediol* the EEC Seed Crushers' and Oil Processors' Federation challenged a Commission decision rejecting its complaint under what at the time was called the New Commercial Policy Instrument.[134] That instrument, which was

[127] N 124 above, para 35.

[128] Case 152/84 *Marshall v. Southampton and South-West Hampshire Area Health Authority (Teaching)* [1986] ECR 723, para 48.

[129] See e.g. Case C–106/89 *Marleasing* [1990] ECR I–4135.

[130] N 73 above. [131] N 90 above. [132] N 71 above. [133] N 72 above.

[134] Council Regulation 2641/84 on the strengthening of the common commercial policy against illicit practices [1984] OJ L252/1.

the predecessor to the current Trade Barriers Regulation,[135] allowed Community producers to lodge a complaint with the Commission regarding illicit commercial practices by third countries, so as to initiate an examination procedure which could ultimately result in the adoption of commercial policy measures (i.e. trade sanctions) against the country concerned. Fediol's complaint concerned practices by Argentina which, in its opinion, violated Articles III, IX, and XXIII GATT. The Commission, however, disagreed with that analysis and rejected the complaint. Before the Court the Commission maintained that, in view of the lack of direct effect of GATT, Fediol could not challenge the decision on grounds of wrong interpretation of the relevant GATT provisions. Van Gerven AG did not concur with the Commission's defence. He distinguished the lack of direct effect of GATT from cases where a Community act referred to GATT, as did, implicitly, the New Commercial Policy Instrument. He likened such cases to the private international law instrument of *renvoi* to provisions of foreign law. In a footnote, he made interesting general statements about this type of effect. Van Gerven AG was of the opinion that a provision (like those of GATT) which did not have direct effect per se could none the less be transformed within a particular legal order, by a rule of that legal order, into a rule having direct effect, that is to say a rule which could be invoked by individuals; for instance, GATT provisions which were incorporated in a Community regulation or to which a Community regulation referred and from which individuals could therefore to a greater or lesser extent derive rights pursuant to and within the limits of that regulation.[136]

The Court essentially followed that approach. It acknowledged the lack of direct effect of GATT, but considered that it could not be inferred from the case law that citizens could not rely on the provisions of GATT in order to obtain a ruling on whether conduct criticized in a complaint lodged under Regulation 2641/84 constituted an illicit commercial practice within the meaning of that regulation: the GATT provisions formed part of the rules of international law to which that regulation referred. As regards the flexibility of GATT, that did not prevent the Court from applying the rules of GATT with reference to a given case, in order to establish whether certain specific commercial practices should be considered incompatible with those rules, as the GATT provisions had an independent meaning which, for the purposes of their application in specific cases, was to be determined by way of interpretation. The fact that Article XXIII GATT provided a special procedure for the settlement of disputes did not preclude interpretation by the Court. Here the Court referred to its judgment in *Kupferberg*, where it had stated that the mere fact that the Contracting Parties had established a special institutional framework for consultations and negotiations *inter se* in relation to the implementation of

[135] Council Regulation 3286/94 laying down Community procedures in the field of the common commercial policy in order to ensure the exercise of the Community's rights under international trade rules, in particular those established under the auspices of the WTO [1994] OJ L349/71; see Ch 10.

[136] *Fediol* (n 71 above) Opinion of Van Gerven AG, paras 11–13, in particular n 8.

the agreement was not in itself sufficient to exclude all judicial application of the agreement. It followed that, since the regulation entitled the economic agents concerned to rely on the GATT provisions in the complaint they lodged with the Commission in order to establish the illicit nature of the commercial practices which they considered to have harmed them, those same economic agents were entitled to request the Court to exercise its powers of review over the legality of the Commission's decision applying those provisions.[137]

The judgment in *Fediol* was straightforward. There was a Community regulation which required the Commission to examine whether third-country commercial practices were illegal under international law, and judicial review of that examination would have been meaningless if the Court could not look at the provisions of GATT. In *Fediol* the Court did not find that the Commission had erroneously interpreted GATT, but even if it had, the result would only have been that the Commission's rejection of Fediol's complaint would have been annulled on grounds of wrong implementation of the regulation. That did not amount to giving direct effect to GATT, as it created no immediate GATT rights for private parties.

In *Nakajima* the applicant challenged a Council regulation imposing a definitive anti-dumping duty on imports of serial-impact dot-matrix printers originating in Japan. One of its claims was that the basic regulation on anti-dumping in force at the time was in breach of the GATT Anti-Dumping Code.[138] The Council objected that, like GATT, the Anti-Dumping Code lacked direct effect. Lenz AG did not agree with that objection, but it is not completely clear from the Opinion on which grounds he felt that review should be possible. In any event, he considered that there was no violation of the Code.[139] The Court took as its starting point that Nakajima was not relying on the direct effect of the provisions of the Code. Rather, it was questioning, in an incidental manner under (current) Article 277 TFEU, the applicability of the basic regulation by invoking one of the grounds for review of legality referred to in (current) Article 263 TFEU, namely that of infringement of the Treaty or of any rule of law relating to its application. The Court then noted that, like GATT, the Anti-Dumping Code was binding on the Community. It further noted that, according to the second and third recitals in the preamble to the basic anti-dumping regulation, it was adopted in accordance with existing international obligations, in particular those arising from Article VI GATT and from the Anti-Dumping Code. It followed that the basic regulation, which the applicant had called into question, was adopted in order to comply with the international obligations of the Community, which, as the Court had consistently held, was therefore under an obligation to ensure compliance with the GATT and its implementing measures.[140] The Court accordingly

[137] Ibid, paras 19–22 of the judgment.

[138] Council Regulation 2423/88 on protection against dumped or subsidized imports from countries not members of the EEC [1988] OJ L209/1.

[139] *Nakajima* (n 72 above) Opinion of Lenz AG, paras 52–57.

[140] Ibid, paras 28–32 of the judgment.

examined whether the basic regulation was in breach of the Code, but came to the conclusion that it was not.

The reasoning in *Nakajima* was more difficult to understand than that in *Fediol*. As stated in Chapter 8, it was reasonable at the time to read the judgment as establishing that the direct-effect requirement did not apply to direct actions for annulment. However, the judgment in *Germany v. Council* on the banana regulation proved that that reading was incorrect.[141] There the Court declined to examine alleged violations of GATT provisions on the same grounds as those which precluded direct effect. But it nevertheless maintained the *Fediol* and *Nakajima* case law, and for the first time stated the principle of implementation. The Court did not, however, clarify the scope or rationale of the principle. It followed the Opinion of Gulmann AG on this point. The Advocate General had analysed the statements in *Fediol* and *Nakajima*, considering it decisive that in both judgments the Court based its reasoning on the fact that due to references to the relevant GATT rules there were special reasons for undertaking a review as regards compliance with GATT. There was no doubt, in his view, that in the banana regulation the Community legislature did not refer to GATT in such a way that the agreement should be incorporated into the legal basis for the Court's review of legality.[142]

Rationale and further application

As was mentioned, the *Fediol* type of application of GATT or WTO law is relatively straightforward; it is also of limited scope, and currently probably applies only to the Trade Barriers Regulation.[143] However, the Court consistently expresses the principle in more general terms: where the Community intended to implement a particular obligation assumed in the context of the WTO or where a Community act expressly refers to WTO law, judicial review on grounds of violation of WTO law will be undertaken. At first sight, this exception to the lack of direct effect may seem self-defeating and not very useful: where WTO rules are implemented there will be much less need for judicial review based on those rules than in other cases, where *ex hypothesi* those rules were not taken into account or observed. It may, however, be possible to define a basis for the exception. The theoretical justification could be that, even if WTO law does not as such have direct effect, in those cases where it has been transformed and incorporated into EU law by the EU legislature it becomes part of EU law, in the sense—and to such an extent—that it can be relied upon in court proceedings concerning the legality or validity of EU acts. The act of implementing WTO law makes such law fit for full judicial application,

[141] N 73 above.

[142] Ibid, paras 147–150, Opinion of Gulmann AG. The banana regulation did not expressly refer to GATT, and clearly did not reflect any particular GATT provisions or obligations. It had none the less been adopted in full knowledge of the potential difficulties with GATT.

[143] N 135 above.

and the exception may therefore be called the principle of implementation. Such an approach clearly has a dualist element. In a sense the Court is saying that the EU institutions need to be consistent in their legislative and administrative action. If an international agreement binding on the EU does not as such have direct effect, the institutions are none the less required to observe its provisions in those areas where the agreement has been implemented. In so far as there is implementation, the agreement ceases to be a mere instrument of international law. After implementation the obligation to implement correctly and in good faith, which is an obligation of international law and of EU law (see Article 216(2) TFEU) obviates the need for direct effect. The EU institutions have then used and forfeited the international scope for manoeuvre which the agreement may have given them.

Why did the Court create this exception?[144] One possible reading is that the Court attempted to strike some balance between lack of direct effect and respect for the EU's international commitments. To put it differently, the principle of implementation may well reflect some type of compromise reached within the Court. If that is the case, the interpretation and application of the implementation principle risk not being guided by any particular underlying rationale, but will rather be the outcome of internal struggle—between monists and dualists, one might say. This may be all the more so as the formulation of the implementation principle is fairly cryptic, particularly as to its first limb: when does the EU 'intend' to implement a 'particular obligation'?

In any event, the case law has gradually reduced the scope for invoking the principle. It is regularly referred to in the field of anti-dumping, where part of its ancestry lay.[145] That is natural, given how meticulously EU anti-dumping legislation transposes the WTO Anti-Dumping Agreement, and given that the EU legislation was indisputably adopted so as to give effect to the particular obligations which WTO law imposes in this respect. However, it must be noted that even that case law is often unclear on whether the Courts apply the implementation principle, or simply the principle of consistent interpretation.[146] Moreover, there appear to be no instances in which the conclusion was reached that EU anti-dumping legislation violated the implementation principle. At most, individual anti-dumping decisions are considered to be contrary to the combined application of the EU legislation and the WTO Anti-Dumping Agreement.

There are not many other examples of a receptive approach to the implementation principle. In *Italy v. Council* the Italian government sought the annulment of a Council regulation concerning tariff quotas for imports of rice, which had

[144] Cf Cheyne (n 22 above) 33.

[145] Case C–69/89 *Nakajima v. Council* [1991] ECR I–2069, para 31; Case C–188/88 *NMB v. Commission* [1992] ECR I–1689, para 23; Case T–162/94 *NMB and Others v. Commission* [1996] ECR II–427, para 99; Case T–256/97 *BEUC v. Commission* [2000] ECR II–101; Case C–76/00P *Petrotub and Republica v. Council* [2003] ECR I–79, paras 53–58; Case T–45/06 *Reliance Industries v. Council* [2008] II–2399, paras 87–91.

[146] See eg *Petrotub and Republica* and *Reliance Industries* (n 145 above).

been adopted pursuant to agreements concluded between the EC and Australia and Thailand, subsequent to GATT Article XXIV(6) negotiations required by the accession of Austria, Finland, and Sweden. It was argued that the regulation was in breach of Article XXIV(6) and of paragraphs 5 *et seq*. of the Understanding on the Interpretation of Article XXIV. The Council relied on the lack of direct effect of GATT, but the Court referred to the principle of implementation, and held that by adopting the regulation pursuant to agreements concluded with non-member countries following negotiations conducted on the basis of Article XXIV(6) GATT, the Community sought to implement a particular obligation entered into within the framework of GATT.[147]

In one further case the Opinion of Ruiz-Jarabo Colomer AG again contained an interesting application of the implementation principle. *Kloosterboer Rotterdam* concerned a challenge by a Dutch customs agent to a Commission regulation concerning the establishment of the import price of frozen chicken fillets, for the purpose of applying additional customs duties. Kloosterboer Rotterdam argued that the regulation did not comply with the basic Council regulation on the common organization of the market in poultry. The latter regulation had been amended in 1995 so as to implement Article 5(1)(b) of the WTO Agreement on Agriculture which provides for the establishment of the relevant import prices on the basis of cif prices. The Council regulation therefore also referred to cif prices, but the Commission implementing regulation contained exceptions to that rule. Ruiz-Jarabo Colomer AG considered that this called for the application of the implementation principle. He pointed out that the Council regulation had been amended with a view to implementing the Agreement on Agriculture, particularly as to its provisions on additional duties—that emerged from the preamble to the amending regulation. The amendments also charged the Commission with adopting implementing rules, particularly as regards the application of Article 5 of the Agreement on Agriculture. The Commission had thus been instructed by the Council to adopt implementing rules complying with the relevant WTO provisions, but had failed to do so, as the Agreement on Agriculture only permitted the use of cif prices. The Advocate General found confirmation of this interpretation of the relevant provisions of WTO law in the Appellate Body's report in *EC—Measures affecting the importation of certain poultry products*.[148] That case dealt with exactly the same issue, and the Advocate General relied on it without reservation, considering that this was a clear case for applying the implementation principle. The Court, however, did not mention the implementation principle, and looked only at the relationship between the basic and the implementing regulation.[149]

[147] Case C–352/96 *Italy v. Council* [1998] ECR I–6937, para 20. See also the Opinion of Mischo AG at paras 21–22.

[148] WT/DS69/AB/R, adopted 23 July 1998.

[149] Case C–317/99 *Kloosterboer Rotterdam* [2001] ECR I–9863, Opinion of Ruiz-Jarabo Colomer AG, paras 28–38, and paras 23–36 of the judgment.

There are no other cases, outside the field of anti-dumping, in which the application of the implementation principle was accepted. Parties have attempted to rely on the principle, in particular in cases which are part of the EU's attempts to implement WTO dispute decisions finding violations in the twin sagas of the EU's import regime for bananas, and its legislation prohibiting beef treated with hormones. In judgments on actions for damages based on the violation of WTO law in the context of the EU's banana import regime, the CFI declined to apply the implementation principle. The actions challenged a 1998 Commission regulation, adopted in implementation of the amendments to the EC's banana import regime which the Council of Ministers introduced, also in 1998, subsequent to the EC's defeat in the WTO. The fullest expression of the rejection of the implementation principle can be found in *Chiquita v. Commission*.[150] The Court stated that, as an exception to the principle that individuals may not rely directly on WTO provisions before the Community judicature, the rule arising from *Nakajima* had to be interpreted restrictively. It noted that, outside the context of anti-dumping disputes, the EU Courts had declined to apply the *Nakajima* case law. The Court described the particular relationship between EU anti-dumping legislation and the WTO Anti-Dumping Agreement, and considered that, for *Nakajima* to apply, the challenged measure had specifically to transpose prescriptions arising from the WTO Agreement into Community law. In the case of bananas, neither the Community provisions the legality of which was challenged nor the provisions of the WTO Agreement allegedly infringed supported the conclusion that there was an intention to implement a particular obligation assumed in the context of the WTO, for the purposes of *Nakajima*. The relevant provisions of GATT and GATS laid down principles and obligations which were general in character, and clearly different from the detailed prescriptions of the Anti-Dumping Agreement. Even if the applicant's argument could be interpreted as seeking to rely on an infringement of the Community's obligation to implement the recommendations and the rulings of the WTO's Dispute Settlement Body (DSB), it could not be accepted. The obligation to ensure the conformity of internal measures with international undertakings arising from the WTO Agreements was undoubtedly of a general character, which contrasted with the rules of the Anti-Dumping Agreement.[151]

This approach was broadly confirmed by the Court of Justice in the *Van Parys* judgment, issued one month after *Chiquita*, and also involving the banana regime. The Court found that, by undertaking after the adoption of the DSB decision on the EC banana regime to comply with the WTO rules, the Community did not

[150] Case T–19/01 *Chiquita v. Commission* [2005] ECR II–315. See also Case T–18/99 *Cordis Obst und Gemüse Grosshandel v. Commission* [2001] ECR II–913, para 59; Case T–30/99 *Bocchi Food Trade International v. Commission* [2001] ECR II–943, para 64; Case T–52/99 *T Port v. Commission* [2001] ECR II–981, para 59; Case C–307/99 *OGT Fruchthandelsgesellschaft v. Hauptzollamt Hamburg-St Annen* [2001] ECR I–3159; Joined Cases T–64 and 65/01 *Afrikanische Frucht-Compagnie v. Council and Commission* [2004] ECR II–521.

[151] *Chiquita v. Commission* (n 150 above) paras 114–127 and 156–161.

intend to assume a particular obligation in the context of the WTO, capable of justifying an exception to the impossibility of relying on WTO rules before the Community Courts and enabling the Community Courts to exercise judicial review of the relevant Community provisions in the light of those rules.[152] The Court supported that finding with an analysis of the WTO dispute-settlement system along the lines of that offered in *Portugal v. Council*.[153]

Those cases, together with others, put the spotlight on the question of whether WTO dispute decisions have any particular effect in EU law—a question further considered in the next section. But even leaving that question to one side, the above rulings clearly operated a very restrictive and even unpersuasive reading of the implementation principle. It is true that the challenged Commission regulation on imports of bananas did not in any way refer to WTO provisions or to the WTO dispute. However, it was adopted on the basis of the amended basic Council regulation, the amendments to which expressly referred to the Council's desire that the EU comply with its international commitments (including WTO law) and instructed the Commission to adopt implementing rules which would achieve that aim.[154] The Commission, however, did not manage to achieve that in 1998, as the modified regime was found wanting, too.[155] As to the 'particular obligations' which the EU intended to implement, again it is not difficult to identify those: the panel and Appellate Body reports, as confirmed by the DSB, instructed the EU to bring its laws and regulations into conformity, and identified the relevant WTO provisions. In fact, it is hard to envisage a more precise identification of relevant obligations than that resulting from WTO dispute settlement.

Lastly, even in the field of anti-dumping law, the scope for applying the implementation principle has been reduced by the Court of Justice's judgment in *Ikea Wholesale*.[156] The case involved a claim for reimbursement of anti-dumping duties on imports of bed linen from India and Pakistan, on the basis that the relevant regulation was invalid. Again, as with bananas, a breach of WTO law had been established in WTO dispute settlement.[157] The case was referred by the English High

[152] Case C–377/02 *Van Parys v. Belgisch Interventie- en Restitutiebureau* [2005] ECR I–1465, para 41. It may be noted that in this judgment the Court also decided that the (then) framework agreement with the Cartagena Agreement and its member countries, which contained a most-favoured-nation clause borrowed from GATT, did not have direct effect. This was confirmed, as regards the successor co-operation agreement, in Case C–160/09 *Katsivardis and Tsitsikas v. Ipourgos Ikonomikon*, judgment of 10 May 2010, paras 32–45.

[153] N 90 above.

[154] Council Regulation 1637/98 amending Regulation (EEC) No 404/93 on the common organization of the market in bananas [1998] OJ L210/28, para (2) of the preamble and Art 20(e) of the amended basic Regulation.

[155] WTO Arbitrators, *European Communities—Regime for the Importation, Sale and Distribution of Bananas—Recourse to Arbitration by the European Communities under Article 22.6 of the DSU*, WT/DS27/ARB, 9 April 1999 and WTO Panel Report, *European Communities—Regime for the Importation, Sale and Distribution of Bananas—Recourse to Article 21.5 by Ecuador*, WT/DS27/RW/ECU, 12 April 1999.

[156] N 126 above.

[157] WTO Appellate Body, *EC—Bed Linen*, WT/DS141/AB/R, adopted 12 March 2001.

Court, which asked the Court to determine whether the regulation was valid in the light of the Anti-Dumping Agreement, as subsequently interpreted by the recommendations and decisions of the DSB and also in the light of the basic regulation.

Before looking at how the Court replied to that question, one needs to mention that, in 2001, the Council adopted Regulation 1515/2001 on the measures that may be taken by the Community following a report adopted by the WTO DSB concerning anti-dumping and anti-subsidy matters.[158] That regulation enables the Council, whenever the DSB adopts a report concerning an EU measure, to repeal or amend the disputed measure or to adopt any other special measures (see Art 1(1)). The Council had used that power subsequent to the WTO bed linen reports, but had not provided in the relevant regulations for the reimbursement of sums already paid.

The Court relied on Regulation 1515/2001, and the use which had been made of it in the bed linen case, to reject the application of the implementation principle. The reasoning is very succinct. The Court described the relevant provisions of Regulation 1515/2001, and pointed out that the action taken under that regulation could not provide any basis for the reimbursement of duties paid. It followed that the challenged (original) anti-dumping regulation could not be reviewed in the light of the Anti-Dumping Agreement, as subsequently interpreted by the DSB's recommendations, since it was clear from the subsequent regulations that the Community, by excluding repayment of rights paid, did not in any way intend to give effect to specific obligations assumed in the context of the WTO.[159]

The effects of international litigation

As indicated in the introduction to this chapter, Article 38 of the ICJ's Statute refers to judicial decisions as a source of international law. It is clear of course that such decisions are of a different nature to the other sources: conventions, customs, and general principles of law. International courts and tribunals interpret and apply the norms of international law produced by those other sources. Moreover, they do not have inherent jurisdiction. Their authority to hear and decide cases is usually conferred by an international agreement, and requires the consent of States. As international law is fragmented, there is no complete and coherent system of jurisdiction and remedies. In some areas of international law litigation is rare. In others it is highly developed. Moreover, there is great diversity in the systems of dispute settlement, and the extent to which those systems are judicial in character.

Although Article 38 ICJ Statute mentions judicial decisions as a separate source of law, it makes more sense to discuss the legal effect of such decisions in EU law under the broader heading of agreements concluded by the EU. It is within the setting of such agreements that dispute-settlement systems have been created, which

[158] [2001] OJ L201/10. [159] *Ikea Wholesale* (n 126 above) paras 30–35.

may lead to judicial—or quasi-judicial—decisions, involving the EU. What is the effect of such decisions in EU law?[160] Is there any such effect, separate and different from the effect of the agreement which the international adjudicator applies? Is there an effect on how that agreement needs to be interpreted within the scope of EU law? Could the decision of the adjudicator perhaps even override the lack of direct effect of an agreement? These are increasingly significant questions, as the EU becomes ever more active on the international scene, and as international litigation proliferates.

The question of the effects in EU law of international litigation has so far mainly arisen in the context of the EU's WTO membership.[161] It is, however, by no means confined to WTO law. To give just one other example, once the EU has joined the ECHR (see Article 6(2) TEU), the answer to the question will determine what effect to give to judgments of the European Court of Human Rights (ECtHR).

In fact, the Court of Justice considered the question, in outline, in its first Opinion on the EEA Agreement.[162] In that Opinion the Court intensely scrutinized, and rejected, the judicial system which had been set up to interpret and apply the agreement.[163] The envisaged EEA Court was considered to be a threat to the autonomy of (then) EEC law, because notwithstanding the parallelism between the EEA Agreement and Community internal market law, the objectives of the agreement and of the Treaty were different. One of the Court's objections concerned the effect that the decisions of the envisaged EEA Court could have on the interpretation of Community law. The Court referred to the binding effect of agreements, which became an integral part of the Community legal order when they entered into force. Where an international agreement provided for its own system of courts, including a court with jurisdiction to settle disputes between the contracting parties to the agreement, and, as a result, to interpret its provisions, the decisions of that court would be binding on the Community institutions, including the Court of Justice. Those decisions would also be binding in the event that the Court was called upon to rule, by way of preliminary ruling or in a direct action, on the interpretation of the international agreement, in so far as that agreement was an integral part of the Community legal order. An international agreement providing for such a system of courts was in principle compatible with Community law. The Community's competence in the field of international relations and its capacity to conclude international agreements necessarily entailed the power to submit to

[160] See also Lavranos (n 56 above) ch 4.

[161] See also M Mendez, 'The impact of WTO rulings in the Community legal order' (2004) 29 ELR 517; A von Bogdandy, 'Legal Effects of World Trade Organization Decisions Within European Union Law: A Contribution to the Theory of the Legal Acts of International Organizations and the Action for Damages Under Article 288(2) EC' (2005) 39 JWT 45; M Bronckers, 'The Relationship of the EC Courts with Other International Tribunals: Non-Committal, Respectful or Submissive?' (2007) 44 CML Rev 601 and 'From "Direct Effect" to "Muted Dialogue"—Recent Developments in the European Courts' Case Law on the WTO and Beyond' (2008) 11 JIEL 885.

[162] *Opinion 1/91 re Agreement on the European Economic Area* [1991] ECR I-6079.

[163] See also Ch 7.

the decisions of a court which was created or designated by such an agreement as regards the interpretation and application of its provisions.[164]

These statements show that the Court is in principle receptive towards international judicial decisions. However, what the Court did not discuss in *Opinion 1/91* was whether the binding nature of an international judicial decision is dependent upon the direct effect of the international agreement within the setting of which the decision is made. If an agreement lacks direct effect, does that mean that judicial decisions reached under the agreement are also not binding? Neither did the Court analyse the requirements for a system of dispute settlement to be considered of a judicial character, or the extent to which a fully judicial system is required for the relevant decisions to be binding. It should also be borne in mind that, as analysed above in the section entitled 'Further case law on bilateral agreements', non-judicial decisions adopted under an agreement concluded by the EU may have direct effect, under the same conditions as those applying to the agreements as such.

Both of the above issues came up in case law on the WTO agreements. This author was one of the first to suggest a distinction between the lack of direct effect of WTO law, in general, and the binding effect of WTO dispute decisions. The argument was that the Court's reasons for the lack of direct effect of WTO law, such as the agreement's flexibility or the scope for negotiations, could not justify not giving effect to a final, binding dispute decision, which established that the Community (now EU) had violated WTO law. In cases where there was such a decision, the principle of *pacta sunt servanda* should trump the lack of direct effect.[165]

To cut a long story short, however, the EU Courts have not accepted this distinction. In part, their rejection of any self-standing effect of WTO dispute decisions is based on doubts about the judicial character of those decisions: the Courts emphasize the never-ending scope for negotiations in the WTO. What follows is a survey of the Courts' reasoning in the relevant case law, followed by some dissenting statements by Advocates General. As the reader is by now familiar with the issues and cases, the emphasis is on the arguments and not on the specific context of each case. The next section, which will generally assess the case law on direct effect, will offer a critique of the rulings on the effect of WTO dispute decisions.

Judicial developments took off with the *Biret* case, on non-contractual liability for failing to comply with WTO law and dispute rulings as regards legislation on beef treated with hormones. On appeal, the Court established that the CFI had made an error of law by not addressing the argument of the applicants that the legal effects of the DSB decision regarding hormones called into question the lack of direct effect of WTO law and provided grounds for a review by the Community courts of the legality of the relevant EC legislation.[166] The Court thus suggested that there was at least reason for a separate examination of the legal effects of WTO

[164] Ibid, paras 37–40. [165] Eeckhout (n 18 above) 51–5.

[166] Case C–93/02P *Biret International v. Council* [2003] ECR I–10497, para 57; see also Case C–94/02 *Etablissements Biret v. Council* [2003] ECR I–10565, para 60.

dispute decisions. Its statements were in the nature of obiter dicta, however, because on the facts the error of the CFI turned out to be irrelevant.

Where the Court appeared to leave the door open in *Biret*, it firmly closed it later on. In *Chiquita* the CFI made some statements on the nature of WTO dispute settlement. It considered that the DSU did not establish a mechanism for the judicial resolution of international disputes by means of decisions with binding effects comparable with those of a court decision in the internal legal systems of the Member States. To support this, it referred to the Court of Justice's analysis of the WTO dispute-settlement system in *Portugal v. Council*, and in particular the scope which that system offers for negotiated arrangements.[167] The CFI added that that analysis was not confined to cases where the reasonable period laid down by Article 21(3) DSU for implementing DSB recommendations or rulings had not yet expired. Even at the expiry of that period and after the introduction of measures under Article 22 DSU to offer compensation or suspend concessions, the DSU continued to reserve an important place for negotiation between the parties. In this respect, the Court referred to Articles 21(6) and 22(8) DSU, which in essence instruct the DSB to keep the implementation of its rulings under surveillance. It then established that, at the time, the WTO dispute was still pending and on the agenda of the DSB. The Community judicature could not therefore review the legality of the Community measures in question without depriving Article 21(6) DSU of its effectiveness, for as long as the question of implementing the recommendations or rulings of the DSB was not resolved.[168]

In *Van Parys* the Court of Justice confirmed this type of analysis of WTO dispute settlement. It had to be noted that even where there was a decision of the DSB holding that the measures adopted by a member were incompatible with the WTO rules, the WTO dispute-settlement system nevertheless accorded considerable importance to negotiation between the parties. It was true that, according to Articles 3(7) and 22(1) DSU, compensation and suspension of concessions were temporary measures available in the event that the recommendations and rulings of the DSB were not implemented within a reasonable period of time, the latter of those provisions showing a preference for full implementation of a recommendation to bring a measure into conformity with the WTO agreements in question. However, Article 22(8) provided that, if the member concerned failed to enforce those recommendations and decisions within a reasonable period, it was to enter into any negotiations with any party having invoked the dispute-settlement procedures with a view to agreeing compensation. If no satisfactory compensation was agreed, the complainant could request authorization from the DSB to suspend the application of concessions. Furthermore, Article 22(8) provided that the dispute remained on the agenda of the DSB, until it was resolved. Where there was no agreement as to the compatibility of the measures taken to comply with the

[167] N 90 above. [168] N 150 above, paras 162–166.

DSB's recommendations and decisions, Article 21(5) of the understanding provided that the dispute had to be decided 'through recourse to these dispute settlement procedures', including an attempt by the parties to reach a negotiated solution. In those circumstances, the Court concluded, to require courts to refrain from applying rules of domestic law which were inconsistent with the WTO agreements would have the consequence of depriving the legislative or executive organs of the contracting parties of the possibility, afforded by Article 22 DSU, of reaching a negotiated settlement, even on a temporary basis. The Court then described the negotiations, at WTO level, which had taken place between 1997 and 2001, leading to agreements with the United States and Ecuador. Such an outcome could be compromised if the Community courts were entitled to judicially review the lawfulness of the Community measures in question upon the expiry of the time limit granted by the DSB. The expiry of that limit did not imply that the Community had exhausted the possibilities under the DSU of finding a solution; judicial review could have the effect of undermining the Community's position in its attempt to reach a mutually acceptable solution to the dispute.[169]

In *Ikea Wholesale* the company relied mainly on the WTO bed linen ruling,[170] but the Court, as set out in the previous section, chose to ignore that ruling on the ground that the implementation principle did not apply.[171] Paradoxically, that worked to the advantage of Ikea Wholesale. The Court decided that the EU's basic anti-dumping regulation had been violated through the use of the so-called zeroing technique. In substance, therefore, it arrived at the same conclusion as the WTO Panel and Appellate Body, without, however, basing its finding on their reports. The advantage for Ikea Wholesale was that the challenged anti-dumping regulation was considered null and void *ab initio*, leading to a finding that the duties paid should be reimbursed. It is less clear that such a finding could have been reached if the Court had applied the WTO ruling, since such rulings are considered to be prospective.[172]

It may further be noted that in *Ikea Wholesale* there was an Opinion of Léger AG which was very negative about the effect of WTO dispute decisions. The Advocate General urged the Court not to accept such decisions as binding, claiming that to do so would constitute a threat to the autonomy of Community law.[173]

The last set of cases involved actions in damages of a peculiar kind. They were brought by companies whose exports to the United States were affected by the WTO-authorized trade sanctions ('suspension of concessions') in the bananas and hormones disputes. They claimed damages, contending that those sanctions resulted from the Community's failure to comply with WTO law and with the WTO dispute rulings, and that this failure constituted unlawful conduct as from the

[169] N 152 above, paras 42–51. [170] N 157 above. [171] N 126 above.

[172] For a further discussion of this principle, see P Eeckhout, 'Remedies and Compliance' in D Bethlehem, D McRae, R Neufeld, and I Van Damme (eds), *Oxford Handbook of International Trade Law* (OUP, 2009) 448–51; see also the preamble to Regulation 1515/2001 (n 158 above).

[173] N 126 above, paras 77–89 of the Opinion.

expiry of the reasonable period of time granted under WTO law to comply with the rulings. The CFI rejected the actions, and as regards the effect of WTO dispute rulings essentially repeated *Van Parys*.[174] Two of the judgments were appealed.

In the appeal in *FIAMM and Fedon* Maduro AG made an effort to review the overall case law on direct effect, and the lack thereof in the case of WTO law. Echoing some of the concepts and ideas discussed in the introduction to this chapter, he distinguished the direct effect of international agreements from the direct effect of (internal) Community law. The two concepts were assessed differently: the direct effect of international agreements was determined in accordance with the *Kupferberg* critera, discussed above, whereas Community law had the capacity to produce direct effect. The scope of the two concepts was also different: direct effect of an international agreement determined the ability to rely on it not only before a national court but also before a Community court, irrespective of the status of the applicant (individual or privileged applicant). This was justified, because as guardian of the Community legal order, the Court of Justice must, if a rule deriving from the international legal order was relied upon, define its effects in an all-embracing and uniform manner that was valid for the entire Community legal order. The direct effect requirement was necessary whatever the type of action and the status of the applicant, and whether the dispute had been brought before national courts or before the Community courts.[175]

The Advocate General then referred to the reasons for the inability to rely on WTO law, emphasizing the scope for negotiations, and the need to leave the Community institutions a margin of political freedom. However, the fact that WTO law could not be relied upon before a court did not mean that it did not form part of the Community legal system; it was merely a question of the provision's enforceability, and of the jurisdiction of the courts to take cognizance of it. It was only to the extent that the judicial application of WTO law could adversely affect the political freedom of the Community institutions within the WTO sphere that WTO law could not be effectively relied upon before the Court of Justice. This also explained the modifications to the principle that WTO law could not be relied upon. First, the principle of consistent interpretation left the institutions with the option of preferring the path of a negotiated solution, by adopting or retaining an act clearly contrary to WTO law. Secondly, an action by the Commission against a Member State, based on WTO law, would not involve a Community act that was contrary to WTO law. Thirdly, the implementation principle could also be justified, since it applied only where the Community institutions had voluntarily forgone their room for manoeuvre.[176]

As regards the ability of the appellants to rely on WTO dispute decisions, the Advocate General then examined whether it could also justify a modification to the principle that WTO law cannot be relied upon. The test was whether that ability

[174] N 152 above. [175] N 20 above, paras 24–31 of the Opinion. [176] Ibid, paras 32–37.

would affect neither the scope for negotiations, nor the reciprocity and balance in the application of the commitments undertaken. To perform that test required an examination of whether such political freedom continued to exist in the specific circumstances of the cases in point. The debate ultimately hinged on the binding force of the DSB decision: did the DSU require the rulings and recommendations of the DSB to be implemented in full? To answer this question the Advocate General recalled the analysis of the DSU which the Court made in *Van Parys*. He considered that the Community remained free to make the political choice to lay itself open initially to retaliatory measures, and an important place continued to be reserved at all events for negotiation between the parties to the dispute. Whether one viewed the perennial possibility of reaching a negotiated solution to the dispute as a freedom limited to the choice of the means of implementing DSB decisions or as the freedom to prefer an alternative to implementation of the decision, it still constituted freedom of choice. That freedom would be undermined, also by a ruling of unlawfulness in an action for damages. It was true that such a ruling would not lead formally to either the annulment or the invalidation of the legislation in issue, which thus remained an integral part of the legal order and theoretically applicable. The finding of unlawfulness nevertheless constituted *res judicata*, and the political organs of the Community could not allow such unlawfulness to persist, short of disregarding the principle of a Community based on the rule of law. Moreover, the prospect of the financial burden which successful actions in damages would entail would likewise force the political organs of the Community to eliminate the incompatible measure. The scope for political manoeuvre would thus undeniably be jeopardized.[177]

It may lastly be noted that the Advocate General did side with the appellants on a subsidiary claim which they had made, namely that they could rely on a principle of no-fault Community liability.[178]

The Court of Justice started its analysis in *FIAMM and Fedon* by referring to its established case law on WTO law. The focus here is on the additional points which the Court made. It had to be remembered, the Court emphasized, that the decisive factor was that the resolution of disputes concerning WTO law was based, in part, on negotiations between the contracting parties. Withdrawal of unlawful measures was admittedly the solution recommended by WTO law, but other solutions were also authorized. There was no reason to draw a distinction according to whether the legality of the Community action was to be reviewed in annulment proceedings or for the purpose of deciding an action for compensation. First, the prospect of actions for damages was liable to hinder exercise of the powers of the legislative authority. Second, any determination by the Community courts that a Community measure was unlawful was inherently liable to have repercussions on the conduct required of the institution that adopted the measure in question. The Court thus confirmed the analysis by Maduro AG of the effects of an unlawfulness ruling in an action for damages.[179]

177 Ibid, paras 42–50.
178 Ibid, paras 53–88.
179 Ibid, paras 122–124 of the judgment.

There was also no basis for the distinction between the 'direct effect' of the WTO rules imposing substantive obligations and the 'direct effect' of a decision of the DSB. A DSB decision, which had no object other than to rule on whether a WTO member's conduct was consistent with the obligations entered into, could not in principle be fundamentally distinguished from the substantive rules which conveyed such obligations. A recommendation or ruling of the DSB was no more capable than the substantive rules of conferring upon individuals a right to rely thereon before the Community courts for the purpose of having the legality of the conduct of the Community institutions reviewed. To support this finding the Court again referred to the general reasons for the lack of direct effect of WTO law (nature of the WTO agreements; reciprocity and flexibility; room for discretion and scope for negotiations). It further referred to Article 3(2) DSU, according to which recommendations and rulings of the DSB cannot add to or diminish the rights and obligations provided in the agreements concerned.[180] The Court also rejected the claim that the cases called for the application of a principle of no-fault liability.

As can be seen, the Court's rejection of any independent or binding effect of WTO dispute decisions is founded on two main considerations. The Court considers that the WTO dispute-settlement system continues to provide room for negotiations, even after the expiry of the reasonable period of time which the WTO grants for implementing dispute decisions. As pointed out by Maduro AG, this involves an assessment of the binding effect of WTO dispute decisions, and construes the latter as leaving perennial room for political manoeuvre. The second consideration is that the effect of WTO rulings in EU law is inextricably bound up with the lack of direct effect of WTO law in general. Dispute decisions cannot be relied upon, simply because WTO law as a whole cannot be relied upon.

It is clear that this second consideration can be relevant for other international agreements which lack direct effect. UNCLOS, for example, has its own system of dispute settlement, which may involve the International Tribunal for the Law of the Sea, or ad hoc arbitral tribunals. Would the Court be equally unwilling to recognize the binding effect of those tribunals' decisions?

Before moving on to a general assessment of the case law on the direct effect of agreements concluded by the EU, it is useful to point out that the above case law on WTO dispute decisions did not come about with the unanimous support of the Advocates General involved.

In *Biret* Alber AG made a strong plea in favour of recognizing the binding effect of WTO dispute settlement. He started his assessment with an analysis of the WTO dispute-settlement system, which reached radically different conclusions from those the Court arrived at. The Advocate General considered that, once a recommendation or ruling had been adopted, it had to be 'unconditionally' accepted (Article 17(4) DSU). The parties were no longer free to reach a settlement and could only

[180] Ibid, paras 125–131.

agree on the period of time within which to comply with the DSB ruling (Article 21(3)(b) DSU) or the terms of a mutually satisfactory solution (Article 22(8) DSU). Mutually agreed solutions had to be consistent with the WTO agreements (Article 3(5) DSU). The DSU also provided that 'prompt' compliance was 'essential' to ensure the effective resolution of disputes (Article 21(1) DSU). Compensation and suspension of concessions were 'temporary measures' (Article 22(1) DSU) and neither of them was preferred to full implementation of a recommendation to bring a measure into conformity (Article 22(1) DSU). The fact that the DSB kept implementation under surveillance meant that even where compensation had been paid or concessions had been suspended there was still a duty to comply with the DSB recommendations or rulings. It therefore had to be concluded that there was ultimately no alternative but to implement the recommendations or rulings of the DSB, which could not be circumvented by negotiation between the parties.[181]

The Advocate General further considered that non-compliance with a DSB recommendation or ruling could be a commercial policy option. However, it was clear that it was not a lawful option. Under WTO law, the legislative and executive bodies no longer had any discretion that could be reduced by recognizing WTO law to be directly applicable. He urged the Court to support the principle of legality after the expiry of the reasonable period allowed to comply, rather than the commercial option of non-compliance. The latter was a commercial policy option only because there was no means of enforcing WTO recommendations or rulings. This was bound up with their nature as instruments of international law. There was in principle no way of enforcing international law, and the Advocate General remarked pointedly that the position in Community law had in fact been the same before the introduction of (current) 260 TFEU on penalties which a Member State may incur for failure to comply with its obligations. Unenforceability was therefore no reason to disregard DSB recommendations and rulings.[182]

The Advocate General also took the view that recognizing the direct applicability of WTO law as a basis for a claim in damages did not reduce the discretion of the legislative and executive bodies in deciding how to implement a DSB recommendation. The end of an action for damages was not the abolition of a particular measure but compensation for damage caused. It did not therefore open the way for Biret to demand a particular form of conduct on the part of the Community in implementing DSB recommendations.[183]

As regards reciprocity, Alber AG considered that this was really a commercial issue, decked out in the legal trappings of a 'principle of reciprocity'. There appeared to be considerable doubt as to whether the Community's trading position might be weakened at all by recognizing the direct applicability of WTO law as a basis for a claim in damages.[184]

[181] N 166 above, paras 74–81 of the Opinion. [182] Ibid, paras 82–88.
[183] Ibid, paras 93–94. [184] Ibid, para 102.

In *Van Parys*, Tizzano AG agreed with the analysis by Alber AG in *Biret*.[185] He concluded that in a 'Community governed by law' DSB decisions had to be considered as a criterion of the legality of Community measures and that the Court consequently should not, on grounds of doubtful legal merit, give clear approval to legal arguments that would lead to the opposite conclusion.[186]

The legal effects of EU agreements: an assessment

The case law on the direct effect of international agreements concluded by the EU shows considerable openness towards international law, and a willingness to integrate those agreements into the EU legal order. It is true that the lack of direct effect of WTO law and of UNCLOS qualifies that openness, but it should be borne in mind that the great majority of agreements which have come before the Courts have been recognized as having direct effect; and are indeed effectively applied in litigation.

The case law nevertheless calls for a general assessment. A complete critique, though, could only be developed within the framework of a general theory about the relationship between EU law and international law—or even a theory on the relations between legal systems.[187] It is clear that the principles which the Court has developed are neither fully monist nor fully dualist. It is in any event doubtful that the concepts of monism and dualism continue to be very helpful,[188] as they supply only black and white answers to what is in fact a set of nuanced and diverse issues. One could also try to develop the critique on the basis of the concept of legal pluralism, which is currently the most developed concept for approaching relations between legal systems.[189] However, such an exercise is difficult to undertake within the scope of these few pages, and there are as yet few scholarly attempts to apply the concept of legal pluralism to the relationship between EU law and international law.

This critique is therefore more limited. It starts from the premiss that it is appropriate for the EU legal order to show great openness towards international law. That is appropriate in the light of: Article 216(2) TFEU; the basic principle that agreements concluded by the EU form an integral part of the EU legal order; and the EU's own origins. Indeed, one should not lose sight of the fact that the whole of the EU structure had, and continues to have, its basis in international treaties which, the Court recognized, had the capacity to create a new legal order. It would hardly

[185] N 152 above, paras 63–73 of the Opinion. [186] Ibid, para 73.

[187] For a valiant attempt at a theoretical construction, see R Holdgaard, *External Relations Law of the European Community—Legal Reasoning and Legal Discourses* (Wolters Kluwer, 2008).

[188] A von Bogdandy, 'Pluralism, direct effect, and the ultimate say: On the relationship between international and domestic constitutional law' (2008) International Journal of Constitutional Law 397.

[189] See e.g. N MacCormick, *Questioning Sovereignty* (OUP, 1999); N Walker, 'The Idea of Constitutional Pluralism' (2002) 65 MLR 317; M Maduro, 'Contrapunctual Law: Europe's Constitutional Pluralism in Action' in N Walker (ed), *Sovereignty in Transition* (OUP, 2003) 501.

be appropriate for EU law to develop an attitude of hostility towards other international treaties or agreements, which of course do not create a new legal order, but are none the less similar legal instruments. On the other hand, precisely because of the distinction between the EU's own new legal order and classic international law it is appropriate that direct effect should not be automatic, and that there may be agreements which, due to their nature and structure, cannot produce such effect. If that were not the case then agreements concluded by the EU would fully benefit from direct effect, and from its supremacy twin, in exactly the same way as 'internal' EU law. They would, effectively, be clothed with the imperial gowns of constitutionalism.

However, the limitations need to be at least internally and externally coherent. Internal coherence refers to the consistency in approach towards the direct effect of various agreements. Although every agreement is different, the criteria employed for determining direct effect should be broadly consistent, and should be applied consistently. External coherence refers to consistency with international law. As we have seen, the Court, in particular, when rejecting direct effect, makes an analysis of the nature and broad purpose of the agreement in question. That analysis must accurately reflect that agreement, also from a perspective of international law.

WTO law

The Courts' case law on the lack of direct effect of WTO law (including dispute rulings) has become less convincing over the years. This author has always defended the Court of Justice's reluctance to confer full direct effect on WTO law.[190] The core justification in *Portugal v. Council* for rejecting direct effect was that the EU's political institutions would lose the scope for manoeuvre which they currently have with respect to the implementation of WTO law, particularly in case of disputes with other WTO Members. The hands of those institutions would be much more tied than the hands of their US, Japanese, and other counterparts. Ultimately, the Court was unwilling to take that step of tying the hands of the EU's legislative and executive organs. This was the clear constitutional dimension of *Portugal v. Council*, and it went beyond the issue of reciprocity in international trade relations. The Court deferred to the EU legislature, in terms of respecting any specific policies, now or in the future, which may be challengeable under WTO law.[191]

Griller has argued that the Court was simply giving a licence to the EU institutions to violate WTO law, and that giving such a licence ran counter to current Article 216(2) TFEU.[192] This critique is, however, grounded in an approach towards compliance with WTO law which is too formal and places too much

[190] N 18 above and 'Judicial Enforcement of WTO Law in the European Union' (2002) 5 JIEL 83.

[191] Cf Cheyne (n 22 above) 272, who presages and defends this approach on the basis of the 'need to avoid unnecessary conflict with the political institutions in an area where the policy choices are so significant and the implications so diverse that it is not an area which is appropriate for judicial involvement'.

[192] Griller (n 68 above) 454 and 460–1.

faith in judicial enforcement. Judicial rulings are by no means the only or even the most appropriate method for ensuring that the EU (or any other WTO member) complies with its WTO law commitments. In *Portugal v. Council* the Court was merely saying that, as a rule, it would not act as a judicial enforcer of WTO law. It was essentially leaving it to the political institutions to determine the scope and meaning of the EU's obligations. That may well be the most appropriate course of action for a legal system such as that set up by the WTO Agreement, a legal system which is still fast evolving. It is vital to bear in mind that, as long as the WTO dispute-settlement organs have not reached a final ruling in a case, violations of WTO law are presumptive. As long as Geneva has not ruled against them, the EU's political institutions are entitled to argue that they do comply with WTO law. General direct effect would confer on the Courts the task of reviewing claims and arguments concerning violations, giving them the authority to judge compliance. It is likely that many cases could be brought in which private parties would invoke WTO law against EU acts or against acts of the EU Member States. There is little doubt that a majority of those would be cases which would have no counterpart in WTO dispute settlement, such that it would not be possible for the courts to rely on panel or Appellate Body rulings as specific authority for resolution of such cases. European courts, with the Court of Justice at the apex, might become day-to-day interpreters and enforcers of WTO law, with little or no guarantee that their rulings actually amounted to a correct interpretation of WTO law, or at least an interpretation with which the Appellate Body (the WTO's final judicial interpreter) and the WTO members (the ultimate interpreters of WTO law: see Article IX(2) WTO Agreement) would agree.[193]

Nor does direct effect guarantee full compliance. A WTO dispute may be brought against the EU in a case which was never submitted to the domestic courts. Or a case may first be brought before the European courts, and they may conclude that there is no violation, whereas WTO dispute settlement may come to a different view later on. One would then have a clash between, for example, the Court of Justice and the Appellate Body. That would not make matters any better for the faithful EU implementation of commitments.

The absence from the WTO's institutional constellation of a mechanism akin to the EU preliminary rulings procedure raises further issues.[194] Indeed, the question is whether in the current procedural matrices the direct effect of WTO law would actually contribute to the proper development of WTO law and of the WTO as such. As mentioned above, if the direct effect of WTO law were recognized there would be much domestic litigation in which parties would aim to rely on WTO law. Think only of TRIPs, with its potential impact on daily practice in intellectual

[193] Cheyne (n 22 above) 267–8. *Contra* J Pauwelyn, 'Europe, America and the "unity" of international law' in Wouters, Nollkaemper, and de Wet (n 68 above) 208–13.

[194] See also M Krajewski, *Verfassungsperspektiven und Legitimation des Rechts der Welthandelsorganisation (WTO)* (Duncker & Humblot, 2001) 63–7 and Rosas (n 68 above) 812.

property law. How many of the questions of law raised in such domestic proceedings would ever reach WTO dispute settlement? Very few, one may suspect. In those circumstances, which would be the methods for ensuring a more or less uniform interpretation of WTO law? Which would be the methods for avoiding the risk of domestic courts adopting interpretations which were completely out of touch with prevailing Geneva views and might therefore cause more harm than good?

Direct effect could also interfere with the rationale and operating method of WTO dispute settlement. It is fairly obvious that the Appellate Body has so far been a cautious and shrewd judicial operator, showing much awareness for the sensitivity of WTO law and taking care to gauge and calibrate the acceptability of its interpretations and rulings.[195] This has led to a marked case-by-case approach, focused more on leaving some scope for manoeuvre for future cases than on creating much legal certainty. Prime examples are the Appellate Body's approach to the concept of like products, central to WTO non-discrimination rules, and the concept of necessity under Article XX GATT, the general exceptions clause. In the case of like products the Appellate Body even goes so far as to use the image of an accordion to indicate that the concept can be stretched and squeezed.[196] This approach may be well suited to WTO dispute settlement, and it may be appropriate for the gradual development of WTO law through dispute settlement in a manner acceptable to the broad WTO membership. However, if there were direct effect, the WTO dispute-settlement organs would also need to keep an eye on the interpretation and application of WTO law by domestic courts. It could be very difficult to combine all that, for domestic courts are not well served by the degree of elaboration and sophistication which WTO dispute settlement appears to require.[197] For direct effect to work well, there would need to be much more clarity, precision, and conciseness.

There is therefore a good case against the general direct effect of WTO law, and where the Court in *Portugal v. Council* indicated that the EU's political institutions require room for manoeuvre, that can be read as an implicit reference to the above considerations. The Court does not seek to become the day-to-day judicial enforcer of WTO law.

However, in its more recent case law the Court has gradually returned to the *International Fruit Company* line of characterizing the GATT and the WTO as a perennial forum for negotiations, and as instruments of international law which are too flexible to be recognized as having direct effect[198]—as if the transition from GATT to the WTO, with the Copernican revolution of the dispute-settlement system, never happened. This fundamentally mischaracterizes the WTO, as will be

[195] Weiler (n 81 above); R Howse and E Tuerk, 'The WTO Impact on Internal Regulations—A Case Study of the Canada–EC Asbestos Dispute' in de Búrca and Scott (n 68 above) 304–6.

[196] WTO Appellate Body Report, *Japan—Taxes on Alcoholic Beverages*, WT/DS8/AB/R, WT/DS10/AB/R, and WT/DS11/AB/R, adopted 1 November 1996.

[197] Cf von Bogdandy (n 68 above) 31.

[198] The term 'flexibility' was not employed in *Portugal v. Council*, but has resurfaced in *FIAMM and Fedon* (n 20 above) para 130.

shown. Nor is the approach towards WTO dispute rulings justified by the general considerations for excluding direct effect, set out above.

WTO dispute decisions

The Court's analysis in *Portugal v. Council* of the WTO dispute-settlement system was justified, in the strict sense in which it was employed by the Court. The purpose of that analysis was simply to examine whether the WTO Agreement mandates direct effect.[199] The fact that the DSU envisages cases in which compliance with a dispute ruling is not forthcoming, and thus provides for remedies and mechanisms to secure such compliance (compensation and suspension of concessions), presupposes that WTO law does not require direct effect. If it did, and all WTO members accepted that WTO law was enforceable before their domestic courts, then there would arguably be no need for these international law mechanisms. However, by extending that reasoning in recent cases to non-compliance at the expiry of the reasonable time granted under WTO law, the Court has moved from a position in which WTO law is construed as not requiring direct effect—which is correct—to one in which compliance with WTO law is legitimately subject to perennial negotiations. That position, it is submitted, is an incorrect understanding of the dispute-settlement mechanism, and one which is not in accordance with international law principles.

The case against the Court's reading of the DSU was convincingly made by Alber AG in *Biret*. On balance, the relevant provisions of the DSU, even if couched in language and terms which are not wholly conclusive, leave little room for doubt that dispute rulings are binding, and that the mechanisms for ensuring such compliance, in those cases where it is not forthcoming, are simply temporary alternatives. But there is more. Looked at from a broader international law perspective, the Court puts the aim and function of the dispute-settlement mechanism on its head. In international law circles, the WTO dispute-settlement system is generally regarded as among the most sophisticated and advanced such systems in the international law universe. It is a system of compulsory jurisdiction (in itself rare), and in contrast with most other systems it contains at least some specific mechanisms to secure compliance. Suspension of concessions (often referred to as trade sanctions), in particular, offers members of the WTO at least some enforcement tool, even if it is a crude one, with many defects, to secure compliance by members failing to comply with dispute rulings. They are an attempt to respond to one of the greatest deficiencies of international law: its lack of enforcement. They are advanced by comparison with other sub-systems of international law, or with other international agreements, including agreements which the Court recognizes as having direct effect. This means, at least, that the WTO members sought to emphasize the need for compliance with dispute rulings when concluding the WTO Agreement. It is this emphasis which the Court effectively turns on its head, by characterizing it

[199] Cf Bourgeois (n 68 above) 109.

as an acceptance of perennial negotiations, and as weakening (if not denying) the binding character of WTO dispute decisions. The fact that WTO law provides for at least some mechanisms to secure compliance—some penalties for those breaking the law—is regarded as weakening the legal nature of the norms which are enforced.

It is true, as was mentioned, that the actual provisions of the DSU are not without ambiguity. There is more than those provisions, however. Under Article 31(3)(b) VCLT, 'any subsequent practice in the application of the treaty which establishes the agreement of the parties regarding its interpretation' shall be taken into account in the interpretation of treaties. What does that practice of the WTO members, together with the case law that has developed as part of that practice, tell us?

Pursuant to Article 21(5) DSU disagreements 'as to the existence or consistency with a covered agreement of measures taken to comply with the recommendations and rulings ... shall be decided through recourse to these dispute settlement procedures, including wherever possible resort to the original panel'. Such a compliance panel will look at the measures adopted to comply with an earlier ruling. A substantial number of WTO members—including the EU—have used this opportunity. A mere cursory examination of the panel reports adopted in such compliance cases shows that, routinely, (a) complainants claim that the defending party has failed to comply with the rulings and recommendations of the DSB, and (b) panels confirm or deny such claims, depending on the outcome of their substantive examination. Compliance panels may be appealed. The Appellate Body has not as yet squarely been asked whether rulings and recommendations of the DSB are 'binding'; WTO members simply accept that they are bound to comply. Nevertheless, the Appellate Body has been faced with several tangential issues and arguments, and its response to those arguments is straightforward and telling. In *EC—Bed Linen*, for example, the issue was whether it was possible, in a compliance case, to re-examine an unappealed finding by the original panel; a finding, therefore, adopted by the DSB. The Appellate Body's reply is worth quoting in full:

> ... in our view, an *unappealed* finding included in a panel report that is *adopted* by the DSB must be treated as a *final resolution* to a dispute between the parties in respect of the *particular* claim and the *specific* component of a measure that is the subject of that claim. This conclusion is supported by Articles 16.4 and 19.1, paragraphs 1 and 3 of Article 21, and Article 22.1 of the DSU. Where a panel concludes that a measure is inconsistent with a covered agreement, that panel shall *recommend*, according to Article 19.1, that the Member concerned bring that measure into conformity with that agreement. A panel report, including the *recommendations* contained therein, shall be *adopted* by the DSB within the time period specified in Article 16.4—unless appealed. Members are to *comply* with recommendations and rulings *adopted* by the DSB promptly, or within a reasonable period of time, in accordance with paragraphs 1 and 3 of Article 21 of the DSU. A Member that does not comply with the recommendations and rulings adopted by the DSB within these time periods must face the consequences set out in Article 22.1, relating to compensation and suspension of concessions. Thus, a reading of Articles 16.4 and 19.1, paragraphs 1 and 3 of Article 21, and Article 22.1, taken together, makes it abundantly clear that a panel finding which is not appealed, and which is included

in a panel report *adopted* by the DSB, must be accepted by the parties as a *final* resolution to the dispute between them, in the same way and with the same finality as a finding included in an Appellate Body Report adopted by the DSB—with respect to the particular claim and the specific component of the measure that is the subject of the claim. Indeed, the European Communities and India agreed at the oral hearing that both panel reports and Appellate Body Reports would have the same effect, in this respect, once adopted by the DSB.[200]

Even more straightforward is the position of the arbitrator in *EC—Chicken Cuts*. The arbitration award concerned the reasonable period of time for implementing the ruling in that case, which concerned the customs classification of chicken cuts. The EC argued that, in order to comply, it first needed to obtain a new decision by the World Customs Organization on the classification issue. The arbitrator was concerned that this could mean that implementation would become conditional on such a decision. In response, he stated:

It is axiomatic that alleged violations of the covered agreements must be redressed exclusively through the procedures set out in the DSU, providing for examination of such allegations by a panel and possibly the Appellate Body, and that, if violations are found and the relevant reports are adopted by the DSB, the respondent Member is obliged to implement promptly the recommendations and rulings of the DSB. These recommendations and rulings are *binding* on implementing Members, and give rise to an *obligation* to bring their WTO-inconsistent measures into conformity with their obligations under the covered agreements.[201]

The conclusions to be drawn from the above analysis are obvious. Adopted panel and Appellate Body reports create a clear, unconditional obligation to comply with the recommendations they contain (namely, for the responding party to bring its measures into conformity) within a reasonable period of time. If correct implementation is lacking, it is possible to agree on compensation, or to suspend concessions. These remedies, however, are not an alternative to compliance. Rather, they seek to induce compliance. The fact that these remedies exist should not be seen as in any way diminishing the obligation to comply, but as enhancing it. They show the importance that WTO Members attach to an effective and efficient system of dispute settlement.[202]

The Court's analysis of the dispute settlement is therefore misguided. However, in *FIAMM and Fedon* the Court has advanced a further argument against recognizing the direct effect of WTO dispute decisions: the apparently straightforward argument that, if WTO law as such does not have direct effect, WTO dispute decisions which simply apply such law cannot be relied upon either. Again, though, a different approach is called for. The Court's argument works to the extent that the

[200] Appellate Body Report, *EC—Bed Linen (Article 21.5—India)* paras 92–93, emphasis in the original.

[201] Award of the Arbitrator, *EC—Chicken Cuts*, para 55 (emphasis added). The arbitrator was James Bacchus, former Member and Chairman of the Appellate Body.

[202] Cf Bronckers (n 161 above) 616–18.

reasons for rejecting the direct effect of WTO law are equally valid for dispute decisions. It is not clear that that is the case. The political room for manoeuvre on which the Court based the lack of direct effect should no longer be protected in the face of an adverse WTO dispute ruling which establishes that the EU has violated WTO law. Where there is such an adverse ruling, allowing parties to rely on it does not turn the EU Courts into day-to-day enforcers of WTO law. Nor does it turn those Courts into adjudicators on merely presumptive violations of WTO law. Furthermore, the argument that there should continue to be room for political manoeuvre, even after an adverse ruling, and the expiry of the reasonable period, misunderstands the nature of WTO dispute settlement and violates the binding effect of dispute rulings. Ultimately, it is inconsistent with the core international law principle of *pacta sunt servanda*.

One hopes that this approach towards WTO dispute settlement is not transposed to other international agreements, least of all the ECHR, once the EU joins the Convention. The Court of Justice has stated, in *Opinion 1/91*,[203] that where an international agreement provides for its own system of courts, the decisions of that court would be binding on the EU institutions, including the Court of Justice. That principle should become practice. It is clear that, for this to happen, the Court needs to pass an important threshold, as it has never in its history accepted that it was bound by the decisions of another adjudicator. The Court should take that step, however, otherwise the autonomy of EU law risks turning into an undesirable form of autarchy.

UNCLOS: towards a rights-based approach?

In *International Fruit Company* the Court stated that GATT did not confer rights on citizens. The relationship between the concept of direct effect and the creation of 'rights' calls for some further exploration.

In the first edition of this monograph it was argued that there would be scope in the case law on the direct effect of international agreements for more analysis of whether an agreement confers rights. At that point the Court employed hardly any rights language. It had essentially transposed the 'internal' EU law approach towards direct effect of international agreements, with the proviso that the structure and nature of an agreement could preclude direct effect. That 'internal' EU law approach does not focus on whether a provision of EU law is intended to confer rights; the creation of rights is seen as a consequence of direct effect, which is very much the rule. The Court was obliged to adopt such an approach if it was to confirm the direct effect of E(E)C law, and of the Treaty in particular, for the simple reason that in its original form the Treaty had virtually no rights language. Direct effect was really a tool for the effective enforcement of Community law, and such effective enforcement was greatly enhanced by permitting private parties to rely on

[203] N 162 above.

provisions of Community law. This enlisting of the individual as an agent for the enforcement of Community law is well documented.[204]

One may have doubts as to whether the same approach should apply to international agreements. In view of the difference between the EU and the international legal order, the approach towards direct effect should arguably not only focus on the mere operational character of the rules in question (whether they are clear, precise, etc.), as this is essentially an enforcement approach. It would be useful to combine that with some measure of analysis of whether the provisions of an agreement confer rights. An example may illustrate this. From a perspective of direct effect and the creation of rights for private parties, the case law on the direct effect of provisions in agreements on non-discrimination and movement of workers, or rights of establishment, appears more convincing than the case law on the direct effect of the prohibition of 'measures having equivalent effect' in the free-trade agreement with Portugal. The decisions of the EC–Turkey association council on the treatment of Turkish workers, for example, are eminently suitable for direct effect as they are clearly intended to give rights to individuals.

It is trite to say that the individual is becoming an ever more important subject of international law.[205] The ICJ has recognized that an international agreement may directly confer rights on an individual.[206] This means that international law itself distinguishes between norms which confer such rights and those which do not. It is useful and appropriate for EU law to mimic that distinction, and to make it relevant to the direct-effect inquiry.[207] That is not to say that the rights-or-freedoms test should be the only one, but it should definitely occupy an important position.

The recent judgment in *Intertanko* placed the question of whether the agreement, *in casu* UNCLOS, conferred rights or freedoms on individuals in the centre of its analysis. In principle, that is to be applauded. Unfortunately, the application of the test is unpersuasive. The fact that UNCLOS appears to attach rights to ships does not, in the Court's conception, mean that it confers rights on individuals. The link between the rights of ships and those of individuals is severed by national law: it is the latter which grants nationality to a ship, and it is only through such nationality, conferred by the flag State, that a ship acquires rights under the convention. Those rights are not 'thereby conferred on the individuals linked to those ships, such as their owners'. This reasoning is formalistic. In the *LaGrand* case the ICJ decided that the Vienna Convention on Consular Relations conferred rights on individuals, but there too the prerequisite is that those individuals are nationals of

[204] See e.g. D Curtin and K Mortelmans, 'Application and Enforcement of Community Law by the Member States: Actors in Search of a Third Generation Script' in T Heukels (ed), *Institutional Dynamics of European Integration: Essays in honour of Henry G. Schermers—Volume II* (Martinus Nijhoff, 1994) 426–66.

[205] Cf A Peters, 'Membership in the Global Constitutional Community' in J Klabbers, A Peters, and G Ulfstein (eds), *The Constitutionalization of International Law* (OUP, 2009) 157–79.

[206] ICJ, *LaGrand (Germany v USA)* [2001] ICJ Rep 466, para 77.

[207] *Contra* Uerpmann-Wittzack (n 68 above) 140.

one of the parties to that convention. Nationality of individuals is equally conferred under a State's law, not directly by international law. Many international agreements confer rights on individuals or legal persons, such as companies, depending on nationality or place of incorporation. The latter may be a precondition for the exercise of international law rights, but that does not mean that it is a convincing basis for denying the existence of such rights. The Court appears to take an unduly narrow view of when an international agreement confers rights or freedoms.

That narrow view may have been inspired by two interlinked concerns. First, what has been unconvincing in the case law on the direct effect of international agreements is that the only agreements denied direct effect were GATT 1947 and the WTO Agreement. Up to *Intertanko* there were no other judgments in which the Court decided that the nature and broad logic of an agreement precluded direct effect. By reaching that conclusion for UNCLOS, the Court showed that GATT and WTO law were not a unique case; something which was increasingly hard to defend. Secondly, it is clear that the Court is very reluctant to accept broad challenges to EU legislation based on international law. One must always bear in mind that cases like *Intertanko* involve judicial review of general legislation. Such review is rarely successful, also in cases where international law is not in issue, and the challenge is based on the Treaties or on general principles of EU law. In substance, judicial review of general legislation is constitutional in nature, and the institutional balance between the legislature and the judiciary does not necessarily justify strict judicial review.

It is, however, questionable whether putting up formal obstacles, such as the lack of direct effect of an international agreement, is the right answer to constitutional preoccupations linked to institutional balance. There are other tools available, such as requiring a manifest breach of international law for a challenge to the legality or validity of an EU act to be successful. The same tool is employed for violations of general principles of EU law, such as the principle of proportionality.[208]

By excluding the direct effect of UNCLOS the Court has, for the second time, ruled that a vital multilateral agreement, often described with constitutional metaphors, cannot be relied upon in EU litigation. The Court's case law continues to show openness towards international law, but less so than before.

General international law

International law does not consist merely of international agreements. There are also general norms of international law, such as customary international law and general principles of law.[209] It is plain that the EU cannot take part in international treaty-making without respecting and applying general international law. The

[208] See e.g. Case C–58/08 *Vodafone and Others v. Secretary of State for Business, Enterprise and Regulatory Reform*, judgment of 8 June 2010, paras 51–71.

[209] See Art 38(1) ICJ Statute.

Court of Justice has therefore, without any difficulty, recognized that such general international law is binding on the EU. As with international agreements, however, that recognition does not of itself resolve all questions concerning the legal effects which such law may produce in the EU legal order. There is further case law in which the Courts have attempted to spell out those effects, even though there are fewer judgments than on the effects of agreements. This section analyses the various rulings and provides a general assessment.[210]

Early case law

In the well-known *Van Duyn* case, concerning exceptions to the free movement of workers, the Court referred to 'a principle of international law', namely that a State is precluded from refusing its own nationals the right of entry or residence, which the (then) EEC Treaty could not be assumed to disregard in the relations between Member States.[211] That was a very succinct statement, but it did at least express the Court's willingness to interpret the Treaty in accordance with rules of general international law. Such willingness was confirmed in *Ahlström v. Commission*, a challenge to a decision establishing that a number of non-Community undertakings had engaged in concerted practices to agree on prices of wood pulp in the Community, contrary to (current) Article 101 TFEU.[212] The Commission had applied the so-called effects doctrine, according to which Article 101 applies to anti-competitive practices which produce effects in the Community, even if the conduct itself takes place outside the Community. The applicants challenged the decision, *inter alia*, on grounds of breach of international law principles concerning a State's jurisdiction. Neither the Advocate General nor the Court dwelled at length on the effects of international law principles. Darmon AG none the less considered, after having identified the correct interpretation of Article 101 in the light of previous case law, that it was necessary to ascertain whether or not the interpretation was in conformity with the requirements and practice of international law.[213] The Court similarly examined arguments to the effect that the Commission decision was incompatible with public international law, but did not accept such arguments on their substance, thereby implicitly recognizing that Article 101 had to be interpreted in accordance with public international law.[214]

[210] For an in-depth study see Vanhamme (n 68 above); see also K Lenaerts and E de Smijter, 'The European Union as an Actor under International Law' (1999/2000) 19 YEL 122; J Klabbers, 'Re-Inventing the Law of Treaties: The Contribution of the EC Courts' (1999) 30 NYIL 45; PJ Kuijper, 'Customary international law, decisions of international organizations and other techniques for ensuring respect for international legal rules in Community law' in Wouters, Nollkaemper, and de Wet (n 68 above) 88–96; Uerpmann-Wittzack (n 68 above) 135–7.

[211] Case 41/74 *Van Duyn v. Home Office* [1974] ECR 1337, para 22.

[212] Joined Cases 89, 104, 114, 116, 117, and 125 to 129/85 *Ahlström v. Commission* [1988] ECR 5193.

[213] Ibid, Opinion of Darmon AG, para 18.

[214] Ibid, paras 15–23 of the judgment.

The Court was only a little more explicit on the precise effects of general international law in *Poulsen and Diva Corp.*[215] That case concerned the interpretation of a provision in a regulation on fisheries, effectively prohibiting the fishing of salmon and sea trout in certain regions of the high seas, as well as the retention on board, transshipment, landing, transportation, storage, selling, etc. of such fish. The provision was applied against a Panamanian vessel which had entered a Danish port. The case exemplified problems resulting from flags of convenience, as the captain and former owner of the vessel, as well as the crew, were all Danish, and as the vessel operated out of a Danish port. Several questions concerning the correct interpretation of the regulation were referred to the Court of Justice, most of them requiring an analysis of general international law. Indeed, as Tesauro AG pointed out, it was clear that a number of fundamental principles of general international law were at issue or, in any event, had to be closely scrutinized, namely: the freedom to fish on the high seas; navigation in the territorial waters of another State and the related right of innocent passage; the exercise by a coastal State of criminal jurisdiction over foreign vessels; the 'immunity' of a vessel that has taken refuge in a foreign port because it is in distress; and finally the respect to be paid to flags of convenience. The Advocate General was of the firm opinion that the regulation in question could not but be interpreted in conformity with the applicable rules of international law.[216] He carried out an extensive and learned analysis of the relevant principles of the law of the sea so as to arrive at the correct interpretation of the regulation. The Court took a similar approach, even if it did not in all respects follow the Advocate General's analysis. It did, however, also clarify the starting point of its interpretative act, which was that the Community must respect international law in the exercise of its powers and that, consequently, the relevant provision of the regulation had to 'be interpreted, and its scope limited, in the light of the relevant rules of the international law of the sea'.[217]

The Court's statement confirmed that EU legislation needs to be interpreted in accordance with principles or rules of general international law. It did not expressly address the question of whether an EU act could also be held unlawful or invalid on grounds of breach of such law. The statement was somewhat ambiguous in that it also mentioned that the scope of the regulation could be limited on the basis of international law, which could be interpreted in different ways. Also, one could argue that the logical consequence of the principle that the EU must respect international law in the exercise of its powers is that any failure to do so results in the unlawfulness of the act in question. However, as we have seen as regards international agreements, there may be further conditions: the Court recognizes that the EU must respect WTO law and UNCLOS, but it does not generally accept that breach of WTO law or of UNCLOS leads to a finding of unlawfulness.

[215] Case C-268/90 *Poulsen and Diva Corp.* [1992] ECR I-6019.

[216] Ibid, Opinion of Tesauro AG, para 4.

[217] Ibid, para 9 of the judgment.

Conclusion and suspension of agreements: *Opel Austria* and *Racke*

In *Opel Austria v. Council* the applicant challenged, before the CFI, a regulation withdrawing tariff concessions for imports of gearboxes from Austria.[218] The regulation was a reaction to aid granted by the Austrian government to Opel Austria which the Commission saw as contrary to the provisions of the 1972 free-trade agreement with that country. However, the Council adopted the regulation on 20 December 1993,[219] whereas it had on 13 December decided to conclude the EEA Agreement,[220] leading to the entry into force of the EEA Agreement on 1 January 1994. Article 10 of the EEA Agreement prohibited all customs duties and charges having equivalent effect, and Opel Austria argued that the withdrawal of tariff concessions was a violation of that provision. It was fairly obvious that, in substance, that was indeed the case, but the CFI faced the problem that it could not directly apply the EEA Agreement, because in the context of an application for annulment the legality of the contested measure had to be assessed on the basis of the facts and the law as they stood at the time when the measure was adopted. Since the EEA Agreement had not yet entered into force on 20 December 1993, it appeared as if the Court would be unable to review the regulation on grounds of violation of the agreement. Opel Austria also argued, however, that by adopting the regulation the Council had infringed a principle of public international law, i.e. the principle of good faith, according to which, pending the entry into force of an international agreement, the signatories to that agreement could not adopt measures which would defeat its object and purpose. The Court essentially agreed with that argument. It stated that the principle was a rule of customary international law whose existence was recognized by the ICJ and which was therefore binding on the Community. It referred to Article 18 VCLT as codifying the principle. It then recalled the sequence of events, pointing out that at the time of adoption of the regulation the Communities were aware of the date of entry into force of the EEA Agreement. The Court, in a second point, stated that the principle of good faith was the corollary in public international law of the principle of protection of legitimate expectations which formed part of the Community legal order: any economic operator to whom an institution had given justified hopes could rely on the latter principle. The Court concluded that, in a situation where the Communities had deposited their instruments of approval of an international agreement and the date of entry into force of that agreement was known, traders could rely

[218] N 98 above.

[219] Council Regulation 3697/93 withdrawing tariff concessions in accordance with Article 23(2) and Article 27(3)(a) of the Free Trade Agreement between the Community and Austria (General Motors Austria) [1993] OJ L343/1.

[220] Decision 94/1 on the conclusion of the Agreement on the European Economic Area between the European Communities, their Member States and the Republic of Austria, the Republic of Finland, the Republic of Iceland, the Principality of Liechtenstein, the Kingdom of Norway, the Kingdom of Sweden and the Swiss Confederation [1994] OJ L1/1.

on the principle of protection of legitimate expectations in order to challenge the adoption by the institutions, during the period preceding the entry into force of that agreement, of any measure contrary to the provisions of that agreement which was to have direct effect on them after it had entered into force. Consequently, the applicant was entitled to require a review of the legality of the contested regulation in the light of the provisions of the EEA Agreement which had direct effect after its entry into force.[221] The Court then established that Article 10 EEA had direct effect, and that it precluded the withdrawal of tariff concessions in issue. Accordingly, it annulled the regulation.[222]

In this judgment the CFI effectively recognized the force of customary international law. It none the less did not apply the principle of good faith on its own, but channelled it into the EU law principle of legitimate expectations. The correct reading of the judgment appears to be that, in the particular context of conclusion and entry into force of agreements which have direct effect, the international law principle of good faith is a component of the EU law principle of legitimate expectations. Private parties have an enforceable expectation that the EU will not act contrary to the principle of good faith. However, not every rule of general international law will come within such a category, and *Opel Austria* left open the question of whether EU acts could be annulled on grounds of breach of such general international law as such, in the absence of links with general principles (or other rules) of EU law.

Where *Opel Austria* concerned the conclusion and entry into force of an international agreement, the *Racke* case concerned the suspension and termination of such an agreement.[223] As the facts and legal context were rather complex it is appropriate to set them out in some detail. The case followed the suspension and termination of the 1983 co-operation agreement with Yugoslavia as a result of the break-up and war in that country in the early 1990s. The Community and its Member States attempted to play an active role in putting an end to the conflict, within the framework of what was then called European Political Co-operation (the predecessor of the CFSP), by, *inter alia*, contributing to a ceasefire agreement which was reached in The Hague in October 1991. When the ceasefire was not respected, the Community and its Member States issued a declaration appealing for compliance, and threatening to terminate the co-operation agreement if that did not happen. As the war continued, on 11 November 1991 the Community and its Member States adopted a decision suspending the agreement with immediate effect (the Suspension Decision[224]). The preamble to that decision stated that the pursuit of hostilities and their consequences on economic and trade relations constituted a radical change in the conditions under which the co-operation

[221] *Opel Austria* (n 98 above) paras 90–95. [222] See also Ch 8. [223] N 65 above.

[224] Decision 91/586 of the Council and the Representatives of the Governments of the Member States, meeting within the Council, suspending the application of the Agreements between the European Community, its Member States and the Socialist Federal Republic of Yugoslavia [1991] OJ L315/47.

agreement was concluded. On the same day the Council also adopted a regulation suspending the trade concessions provided for by the co-operation agreement, again with immediate effect and on the same grounds (the Suspension Regulation[225]). Two weeks later, on 25 November 1991, the Council denounced and terminated the co-operation agreement, pursuant to Article 60 of the agreement, which permitted denunciation with six months' notice.[226]

Whereas the definitive termination of the agreement fully complied with its provisions, the decision of immediate suspension had no specific basis in the agreement. Racke had imported wines from Kosovo into Germany, up to April 1992, several months after the suspension of the agreement, but none the less argued that those imports should benefit from the preferential rates of customs duty for which the co-operation agreement had provided. The case went to the *Bundesfinanzhof* (Federal Finance Court), which referred to the Court of Justice the question whether the Suspension Regulation was valid. The *Bundesfinanzhof* had doubts regarding the regulation's validity on grounds of international law, in particular the lawfulness of the unilateral suspension of the co-operation agreement. As the agreement did not provide for suspension, the Community decision had to be in conformity with customary international law rules on the suspension and termination of treaties, codified in the relevant provisions of the VCLT. Arguments focused on the rule of *rebus sic stantibus*, reflected in Article 62 VCLT. According to that provision, a fundamental change of circumstances which has occurred with regard to those existing at the time of the conclusion of a treaty, which was not foreseen by the parties, may not be invoked as a ground for terminating or withdrawing from the treaty, or for suspending its operation, unless: (a) the existence of those circumstances constituted an essential basis of the consent of the parties to be bound by the treaty; and (b) the effect of the change is radically to transform the extent of obligations still to be performed under the treaty. The *Bundesfinanzhof* had doubts whether the suspension of the co-operation agreement complied with those provisions. It reasoned that if the Suspension Regulation was invalid, the co-operation agreement had continued to apply, and that Racke was entitled to reduced customs duties on the basis of the direct effect of the relevant provision of the agreement (i.e. Article 22).

Jacobs AG distinguished the case from *Poulsen* and *Opel Austria*, in the sense that it was the first in which a Community regulation was sought to be declared invalid on the sole basis of an alleged violation of customary international law. He referred to *International Fruit Company*, where the Court had laid down the conditions for challenging the validity of a Community act on the basis of rules of international law.[227] He focused in particular on the second question, i.e. that the international

[225] Council Regulation 3300/91 suspending the trade concessions provided for by the Cooperation Agreement between the EEC and the Socialist Federal Republic of Yugoslavia [1991] OJ L315/1.

[226] Council Decision 91/602 [1991] OJ L325/23.

[227] *International Fruit Company* (n 9 above).

law rule in question had to be capable of conferring rights on citizens, and proceeded to examine whether that was the case for rules of customary international law. The Advocate General saw two sources of inspiration for finding an appropriate answer to that question, i.e. the Court's own case law on the direct effect of international agreements, and the approach in the legal systems of the Member States towards the effect of customary international law. From a comparative examination of those legal systems he concluded that they did attempt to give some effect to rules of customary international law but that they were cautious as to the effect of such rules on the validity of domestic legislation, and that there was no case, so far as could be seen, in any national court where an effect similar to that claimed by Racke had been recognized. As regards the Court's approach to the direct effect of agreements, the Advocate General inferred from the case law on the lack of direct effect of GATT that there were limits to the direct effect of agreements, and that an obstacle could lie in the overall purpose and nature of international law provisions. In the light of that, there also had to be limits to the effect of rules of customary international law relating to treaties, since the overall nature and purpose of the law of treaties was to lay down rules applying in the relations between States (and international organizations), and not to create rights for individuals. The Advocate General did note that there could be other types of rules of customary international law which intended to confer rights, for example rules of international humanitarian law. As regards the particular rules in issue, the Advocate General also pointed out that the notion of *rebus sic stantibus* was notoriously difficult and contested, and that it was therefore questionable whether the relevant provisions were sufficiently clear and precise to confer rights. There were thus good reasons for not allowing individuals to challenge Community acts on the basis of the law of treaties. None the less, Jacobs AG considered that such challenges could not be wholly excluded, for the following reasons. First, where an agreement had direct effect and created rights for individuals, the beneficiaries of such rights could have legitimate expectations as to the correct and proper implementation of the agreement, as was recognized in *Opel Austria*. To some extent those expectations could extend to the life itself of the agreement: where the agreement, as in *Racke*, provided for denunciation with six months' notice, it could be legitimate for an individual to expect that the agreement would not suddenly be suspended without due cause. Secondly, such entitlement to some measure of protection of legitimate expectation was further supported by the strength of the basic principle of the law of treaties, i.e. *pacta sunt servanda*; the stability of treaty relations required that the plea of fundamental change of circumstances be applied only in exceptional cases.[228]

In conclusion, the Advocate General was of the opinion that the Court should review only manifest violations of the law of treaties to the detriment of the individual concerned. Where there were such violations, there could be a breach of the

[228] Jacobs AG referred here to ICJ, *Gabčíkovo-Nagymaros Project (Hungary/Slovakia)* [1997] ICJ Rep 7, para 104.

Community law principle of the protection of legitimate expectations, and the breach of that principle, comporting at the same time a manifest violation of the law of treaties, could give rise to annulment of the Community act in issue, to a declaration of invalidity, or to a claim for damages. By allowing such review an appropriate balance was struck between the rights of the individual and the decision-making powers of the Community institutions. There had to be a relatively wide margin of discretion for those institutions to take decisions concerning the life of an agreement, in accordance with their powers under the Treaty, as it was only logical that this life should be primarily in the hands of the contracting parties, and as there was an important political dimension to the conclusion and termination of agreements which did not lend itself readily to judicial review.[229]

The Advocate General then proceeded to exercise such limited review, finding that there was indeed a fundamental change of circumstances, and that the Community institutions could reasonably consider that the effect of that change was such as radically to transform the extent of obligations still to be performed by the Community and its Member States. There was no point in continuing to grant preferences, with a view to stimulating trade, in circumstances where Yugoslavia was breaking up in a way which was strongly disapproved of by the international community.[230]

It is noteworthy that Jacobs AG, whilst first distinguishing *Racke* from *Opel Austria*, in the end applied a similar test to that of the CFI, combining the law of treaties with the principle of legitimate expectations. It is true that the CFI did not require a 'manifest' violation, but arguably the act in issue in *Opel Austria* constituted such a violation.

The Court of Justice adopted the test proposed by the Advocate General, but the reasoning through which it arrived at that test was different and, it must be said, not easy to follow. It took Article 22 of the co-operation agreement, which laid down the tariff preferences for imports of wines, as a starting point, by stating that the question whether the disputed regulation was valid having regard to customary international law had arisen incidentally in a dispute in which Racke claimed that Article 22 should be applied. The Court therefore first examined whether that provision had direct effect, finding that that was indeed the case. It then investigated whether an individual could challenge the validity under customary international law rules of the Suspension Regulation. It rejected arguments of the Council relating to the Suspension Decision, pointing out that it was only the validity of the regulation which was in issue. The Court then stated that, if the Suspension Regulation had to be declared invalid, the trade concessions granted by the agreement would remain applicable until the Community brought the agreement to an end in accordance with the relevant rules of international law. Thus, a declaration of invalidity would allow individuals to rely directly on the rights to preferential treatment granted by the agreement.[231]

[229] *Racke* (n 65 above) Opinion of Jacobs AG, paras 76–90.
[230] Ibid, paras 92–93.
[231] Ibid, paras 29–43 of the judgment.

The Court then referred to the Commission's doubts as to whether the relevant international law rules formed part of the Community legal order. The Court replied to that by referring to *Poulsen*,[232] and confirmed that the Community had to respect international law in the exercise of its powers, and was required to comply with the rules of customary international law when adopting a regulation suspending the trade concessions granted by an agreement. It followed that the customary international law rules concerning the termination and the suspension of treaty relations by reason of a fundamental change of circumstances were binding upon the Community institutions and formed part of the Community legal order.[233]

The Court subsequently returned to the point that Racke was incidentally challenging the validity of the regulation in order to rely upon rights which it derived from the agreement, and stated that, therefore, the case did not concern the direct effect of customary international law. It further pointed out that Racke was invoking fundamental rules of customary international law against the disputed regulation, which was adopted pursuant to those rules and deprived Racke of the rights under the agreement. In this respect the Court referred to the *Nakajima* judgment,[234] which it described as involving a comparable situation in relation to basic rules of a contractual nature. The Court then recalled the importance of *pacta sunt servanda*, as underlined by the ICJ. It concluded that, in those circumstances, an individual could rely on rules of customary international law. However, it added, because of the complexity of the rules in question and the imprecision of some of the concepts to which they referred, judicial review necessarily had to be limited to the question of whether the Council had made manifest errors of assessment concerning the conditions for applying those rules.[235]

On the substance, the Court's reasoning was similar to that of Jacobs AG, finding that there was no manifest violation of the law of treaties. The Suspension Regulation was therefore not considered invalid.

Recent case law

There have been a couple of further references to norms of customary and general international law, but they are not as significant as *Opel Austria* and *Racke*. *Greece v. Commission* was an action for annulment, involving a decision of the Commission to proceed to recovery of sums due by Greece in the framework of Greece's participation in building projects for the diplomatic mission of the Commission and of several Member States in Abuja, Nigeria. The project was based on memoranda between the Commission and the Member States involved, and one of Greece's pleas was that those memoranda had been infringed. When construing Greece's obligations under the memoranda, the CFI referred to the principle of good faith as

[232] N 215 above.
[233] *Racke* (n 65 above) paras 44–46.
[234] N 72 above.
[235] *Racke* (n 65 above) paras 47–52.

a rule of customary international law. It quoted Article 18 VCLT, which was also in issue in *Opel Austria*. As in that case, the Court noted that the principle of good faith was the corollary in public international law of the Community law principle of legitimate expectations.[236] Upon an analysis of the facts, the Court concluded that Greece had not acted in good faith in the process of implementing the memoranda. On appeal, the Court of Justice confirmed that the CFI had been entitled to invoke the customary international law principle of good faith.[237]

Rottmann v. Freistaat Bayern concerned an EU citizen, born in Austria and originally of Austrian nationality. In 1995 he transferred his residence to Munich (Germany), after having been heard in Austria on account of suspected serious fraud. In 1997, a national arrest warrant was issued against him in Austria. In 1998, he applied for German nationality, and during the naturalization procedure failed to mention the Austrian proceedings. His German naturalization had the effect of causing him to lose his Austrian nationality. When the German authorities learned of the Austrian proceedings, the Freistaat Bayern decided to withdraw the naturalization with retroactive effect, on the grounds that Dr Rottmann had not disclosed the judicial investigation in Austria, and had thereby obtained his German nationality by deception. He challenged that decision, and in those proceedings the question was raised of whether the decision should be scrutinized under EU law, since it had the effect of turning Dr Rottmann into a stateless person, thereby causing him to lose his status as an EU citizen.

The Court started its analysis by pointing out that, according to established case law, it was for each Member State, having due regard to Community law, to lay down the conditions for the acquisition and loss of nationality. Nevertheless, the fact that a matter fell within the competence of the Member States did not alter the fact that, in situations covered by EU law, the national rules concerned had to have due regard to the latter. The Court then determined that the decision in issue fell, by reason of its nature and consequences, within the ambit of EU law. It went on to state that the proviso that due regard must be had to EU law did not compromise the principle of international law that the Member States had the power to lay down the conditions for the acquisition and loss of nationality. It rather enshrined the principle that the exercise of that power was amenable to judicial review in the light of EU law. The Court then accepted that a decision withdrawing naturalization on grounds of deception could be compatible with EU law, since it corresponded to a reason relating to the public interest. To support that conclusion, the Court referred to the provisions of the Convention on the Reduction of Statelessness,[238] and of the European Convention on Nationality,[239] which permitted a person to be deprived of his nationality in cases of fraud. The conclusion was further in accordance with

[236] Case T–231/04 *Greece v. Commission* [2007] ECR II–63, paras 85–87.
[237] Case C–203/07P *Greece v. Commission* [2008] ECR I–8161, para 64.
[238] Done at New York on 30 August 1961; entered into force on 13 December 1975.
[239] Adopted under the aegis of the Council of Europe; entered into force on 1 March 2000.

the general principle of international law that no one is arbitrarily to be deprived of his nationality (see Article 15(2) of the Universal Declaration of Human Rights and Article 4(c) of the European Convention on Nationality). The decision to deprive Dr Rottmann of his German nationality could therefore in principle be legitimate. Whether it was so in practice depended on respect for the principle of proportionality. The application of that principle was left to the national court.[240]

In *Brita* the Court of Justice applied the principle of the relative effect of treaties (*pacta tertiis nec nocent nec prosunt*, see Article 34 VCLT) when determining the scope of the EC–Israel Association Agreement and of the EC–PLO Association Agreement, as regards products originating from the West Bank.[241]

Assessment

In a number of the above judgments, customary and general international law are used as providing a framework within which EU law needs to be interpreted and applied. *Ahlström*, *Poulsen*, and *Rottmann* come within that category. This is a significant use of international law, which is seen as constraining the EU and its Member States. In *Opel Austria* and *Racke*, on the other hand, the international law claims were directly targeted at EU acts. This calls for some further comments.

The basis on which the Court in *Racke* accepted that it should review the validity of the Suspension Regulation can be criticized. The Court twice emphasized that Racke's challenge to the regulation was merely incidental, and that Racke in fact relied on Article 22 of the co-operation agreement. The Court added that the case did not concern the direct effect of rules of customary international law. Yet when one compares the facts of and claims in *Racke* with, for example, those in *International Fruit Company*, it is difficult to find any material differences. The question which the *Bundesfinanzhof* referred to the Court of Justice concerned the validity of a regulation on imports into the Community, as in *International Fruit Company*. Both cases concerned the validity of a regulation under rules of international law. It is true that in *Racke* a finding of invalidity would have led to the further application of the provisions of the co-operation agreement, up to the point in time when the agreement was terminated. Again, however, the position in *International Fruit Company* was not dissimilar: if the regulation restricting imports of apples had been declared invalid, International Fruit Company would have benefited from the right to free importation under the then applicable Community law rules. Yet in *International Fruit Company* the Court required that the provisions of international law confer rights on citizens. It is thus submitted that, effectively, the *Racke* case was concerned with the direct effect of rules of customary international law, contrary to the Court's own assessment.

[240] Case C–135/08 *Janko Rottmann v. Freistaat Bayern*, judgment of 2 March 2010, paras 39–59.
[241] Case C–386/08 *Brita v. Hauptzollamt Hamburg-Hafen*, judgment of 25 February 2010, paras 39–58.

Nor is it clear why the Court refused to examine the Council's arguments relating to the Suspension Decision (in contrast to the Suspension Regulation). A finding of invalidity of the latter was obviously not sufficient for the further application of the co-operation agreement: that agreement was suspended by the Suspension Decision, and unless that decision was also invalid, the agreement was no longer in operation. The case therefore concerned the validity of both the regulation and the decision.

A further criticism is that the reference to *Nakajima* is unclear and unconvincing. The case did not concern the implementation of customary international law rules in the same way as *Nakajima* concerned the implementation of the GATT Anti-Dumping Code. If the passing reference in the preamble to the Suspension Decision and to the Suspension Regulation to a radical change of circumstances was sufficient to regard those instruments as triggering the principle of implementation, then the Court should have indicated and clarified that.

None the less, the outcome of the Court's reasoning and the test which it applied are satisfactory. Taken together, *Opel Austria* and *Racke* signify that the Courts are willing to exercise some measure of review of EU acts in the context of the entry into force, the suspension, and the termination of an international agreement concluded by the EU, if it is an agreement which has direct effect. As directly effective agreements confer rights on individuals, it is logical that there should be review of measures which affect the operation of those rights, even if such measures concern the life itself of an agreement. In its case law on the direct effect of international agreements the Court accepts that acts of the institutions, including legislative acts, need to comply with the provisions of a directly effective agreement. It would be awkward if decisions concerning the life itself of the agreement were not reviewable at all. Take an agreement which confers rights to free importation, such as the co-operation agreement with Yugoslavia. Those rights are fully enforceable, and private parties can challenge any EU (or national) acts which affect those rights. It would be awkward if, none the less, the Council could, at will and in violation of the law of treaties, suspend such an agreement, without those same private parties being able to challenge such suspension in any way. Review on the basis of the law of treaties is therefore a complement to the direct effect of agreements.

The Court is also right to limit review to manifest violations. As it pointed out in *Racke*, the law of treaties is complex and the relevant provisions of the VCLT are not very precise, leaving scope for argument as to their correct interpretation and application. And as Jacobs AG pointed out in connection with the *rebus sic stantibus* rule, there is an important political dimension which does not lend itself easily to judicial review. It is indeed appropriate for the judiciary to refrain from making an essentially political assessment as to whether there is a fundamental change of circumstances justifying suspension or termination of an agreement. It is thought proper for the courts to limit their interference to cases of manifest violation of the relevant international law rules.

Opel Austria and *Racke* concerned only the law of treaties, and the other judgments on general international law do not teach us much more about the effects of such law. There are therefore many questions which still need to be resolved. It is, however, submitted that the approach of Jacobs AG of investigating whether the purpose and nature of the rules at issue are such as to confer rights on citizens is correct. Rules of international humanitarian law, for example, should have direct effect, and it should be possible for private parties to challenge EU acts which violate such rules, if that were ever the case.

Agreements binding on the Member States

General issues

If this book were about the foreign affairs law of a State, there would be little need to discuss the status of international agreements to which that State has not consented, and which it has not ratified. Article 34 VCLT provides, in clear terms, that 'a treaty does not create either obligations or rights for a third State without its consent'. The EU, however, is an international organization composed of States who are themselves international legal persons, with full sovereignty (subject to the transfer of sovereignty to the EU), and who are very active treaty-makers. The Member States are bound by many treaties, conventions, and agreements. Some of those instruments bind all the Member States, the prime instance being the UN Charter. Others are limited to one or more Member States. Some of the instruments pre-date the creation of the EEC, or the relevant Member State's accession. Others were created when the relevant Member States were already in the EU.

This state of affairs creates some unique problems. There are of course many other international organizations, but none of them has anything like the broad law-making powers that the EU wields. The Member States have transferred large chunks of their sovereign powers to the EU. The laws which the EU produces have direct effect in national law, and prevail over any conflicting norms. As is well known, the EU law rule of primacy is absolute, and therefore in principle extends to conflicts between EU law and norms of national law resulting from an international agreement binding on a Member State. This creates a specific set of problems, in particular where the agreement is concluded with one or more non-member States. It is obvious that, under international law, an agreement between an EU Member State and a non-member State cannot be overridden by EU law.[242] On the one hand, the Member State is bound by EU law; on the other, it is bound by the international agreement. Within domestic law it needs to give priority to EU

[242] Again this follows from the principle embodied in Art 34 VCLT, and in its extension, Art 34 of the Vienna Convention on the Law of Treaties between States and International Organizations or between International Organizations.

law, due to the primacy rule, but that could trigger its international responsibility for failing to comply with its treaty obligations.

The drafters of the Treaties addressed only some of those problems. In what is currently Article 351 TFEU they attempted to regulate potential conflicts between EU law and agreements concluded by Member States prior to the creation of the EEC, or prior to their accession. The provision, further analysed below, permits a Member State to continue to respect obligations towards a non-member State under such an agreement, even in the face of conflicting EU law obligations. However, the Member State is also required to eliminate the incompatibility, for example by renegotiating or even terminating the international agreement.

The Treaties do not, however, address other important problems and questions. What about agreements concluded by a Member State after its EU accession? In so far as there is a conflict between such an agreement and EU law as it stood at the time the agreement was concluded, it is clear that the Member State acted contrary to EU law, and needs to comply with it. However, a Member State may also have concluded an agreement, for example in an area of shared competence, at a time when there was no EU legislation on the matter. If later on such legislation is enacted, and proves to be in conflict with such an agreement, does EU law simply prevail?

It is sometimes suggested that the rules and principles of Article 351 TFEU could, by analogy, be applied to such agreements. The case law none the less does not support such an extension of Article 351. Capotorti AG considered the point in *Procureur Général v. Arbelaiz-Emazabel*, a case concerning fisheries. He addressed the argument that the institutions' obligations under (current) Article 351 TFEU (see below) also applied to a later agreement, concluded before the Community exercised its powers in this area. He considered, though, that such a view conflicted with the wording of the first paragraph of (current) Article 351 TFEU and with the Court's case law. It seemed to him unacceptable, particularly since the provision was one of an exceptional nature, in so far as it ensured on a temporary basis the observance of obligations towards non-member States which were incompatible with Community law.[243]

A further question is whether the EU should itself avoid creating EU law which conflicts with the international commitments of Member States. It would be difficult to accept such a principle in any general sense, as extending to any treaty obligation of any Member State. For the EU to take all such obligations into account would probably create insurmountable problems for the EU legislative process, and would make it very difficult, if not impossible, to achieve the Treaties' objectives.

[243] Case 181/80 *Procureur Général v. Arbelaiz-Emazabel* [1981] ECR 2961, para 4 of the Opinion; for the same views, see Opinion of Van Gerven AG, para 17, in Case C–23/92 *Grana-Novoa v. Landesversicherungsanstalt Hessen* [1993] ECR I–4505. See also Case T–212/02 *Commune de Champagne and Others v. Council and Commission* [2007] ECR II–2017, para 168. But see Kokott AG in Case C-188/07 *Commune de Mesquer v. Total France* [2008] ECR I–4501, para 95, suggesting that a *mutatis mutandis* application of (current) Art 351 TFEU is conceivable.

What, however, about core international treaties and conventions, for instance those which count all the EU Member States among their contracting parties? Should such agreements not have some kind of special status, perhaps in the sense that the EU is under some obligation to avoid enacting legislation which conflicts with those agreements? Or could some agreements even be regarded as binding the EU?

The latter question has been answered in case law. The Court has accepted such binding effect in the case of one agreement only: the GATT of 1947, prior to the establishment of the WTO. In *International Fruit Company* the Court was asked to rule on the question of whether a trade regulation was invalid for violation of the provisions of GATT. The Court therefore had to examine whether GATT was binding on the Community, notwithstanding the fact that the Community had never formally become a Contracting Party. The Court's conclusion was positive, on the basis of a number of considerations.[244] When the EEC was established the Member States were GATT Contracting Parties. By concluding a treaty between them they could not withdraw from their obligations to third countries. On the contrary, their desire to observe GATT undertakings followed from the very provisions of the EEC Treaty and from their declarations in GATT. That intention was made clear in (current) Article 206 TFEU, which sought the adherence of the Community to the same aims as those sought by GATT, as well as by the first paragraph of (current) Article 351 TFEU on pre-EEC international commitments. The Community had assumed the functions inherent in the tariff and trade policy. By conferring those powers on the Community, the Member States showed their wish to bind it by the obligations entered into under GATT. Since the entry into force of the EEC Treaty and the setting-up of the common external tariff, the transfer of powers had been put into concrete form in different ways within the framework of GATT and had been recognized by the other Contracting Parties. The Community had appeared as a partner in tariff negotiations and as a party to all types of agreement within the framework of GATT. It therefore appeared that, in so far as under the EEC Treaty the Community had assumed the powers previously exercised by Member States in the area governed by GATT, the provisions of that agreement had the effect of binding the Community.

International Fruit Company established a kind of succession principle. It appears to be founded on the concept that a transfer of powers from the Member States to the EU also entails a transfer of the Member States' international obligations. It is indeed arguable that the Member States cannot confer powers on the EU which they themselves cannot exercise under international law.

However, the scope of that principle has remained very limited. The CFI applied it to the UN Charter in its judgments in *Yusuf* and *Kadi*,[245] but it is not clear

[244] N 9 above, paras 10–18.

[245] Case T–306/01 *Yusuf v. Council and Commission* [2005] ECR II–3353 and Case T–315/01 *Kadi v. Council and Commission* [2005] ECR II–3649.

whether the Court of Justice is willing to accept that the UN Charter is binding.[246] The *Kadi* litigation is analysed in a separate section below.

The Court of Justice has not accepted the application of this succession principle to a number of IMO conventions.[247] In *Intertanko*, analysed above as regards the lack of direct effect of UNCLOS, the claimants in the main proceedings also contended that there was a breach of Marpol 73/78, a convention to which all the Member States are parties, but not the EU.[248] The Court, however, declined to review the challenged directive in the light of the convention. It did not appear that the Community had assumed, under the EC Treaty, the powers previously exercised by the Member States in the field to which Marpol 73/78 applied, nor that, consequently, its provisions had the effect of binding the Community. Marpol 73/78 had to be distinguished from GATT 1947. It was not sufficient that all the Member States were parties to the convention. In the absence of a full transfer of powers previously exercised by the Member States to the Community, the latter could not, simply because all those States were parties to Marpol 73/78, be bound by the rules set out therein, which it had not itself approved. Since the Community was not bound by Marpol 73/78, the mere fact that the directive in issue had the objective of incorporating certain rules set out in that convention into Community law was likewise not sufficient for it to be incumbent upon the Court to review the directive's legality in the light of the convention. Admittedly, the powers of the Community had to be exercised in observance of international law, including provisions of international agreements in so far as they codified customary rules of general international law. None the less, it did not appear that the relevant Marpol provisions were the expression of customary rules of general international law. However, the fact that Marpol 73/78 was binding on the Member States was liable to have consequences for the interpretation of both UNCLOS and the provisions of secondary law falling within the field of application of customary international law. In view of the customary principle of good faith, which formed part of general international law, and of (current) Article 4(3) TEU, it was incumbent upon the Court to interpret those provisions taking account of Marpol 73/78.[249]

The Court thus attenuated the lack of binding effect of Marpol 73/78 by establishing a principle that the provisions of EU law in the fields covered by the convention have to be interpreted in the light of its provisions.

In *Commune de Mesquer*, on the consequences of the *Erika* tanker accident off the coast of Brittany, the Court adopted a similar approach towards the so-called Liability Convention and the Fund Convention.[250] The Community had not acceded

[246] *Kadi and Al Barakaat* (n 8 above) paras 305–307, where the Court spoke about the effects of the UN Charter as binding on the EU in hypothetical terms.

[247] See also Ch 7.

[248] International Convention for the Prevention of Pollution from Ships, signed in London on 2 November 1973, as supplemented by the Protocol of 17 February 1978.

[249] *Intertanko* (n 113 above) paras 47–52.

[250] N 243 above; see Ch 7.

to those instruments, and could not be regarded as having taken the place of its Member States, if only because not all of them were parties to the conventions.[251] Interestingly, Kokott AG was of the opinion that, notwithstanding the lack of binding effect of those conventions, the principle of consistent interpretation extended to them. It was clear that there was a broad political consensus for liability for oil pollution damage to be regulated by the conventions. They were ratified by nearly all Member States, and several non-binding Community instruments stated that oil pollution damage was subject to them. Furthermore, a departure by Community law from those conventions would encumber France and possibly other Member States with a conflict between their obligations under Community law and those under international law. The obligation of loyalty between the Community and the Member States required such conflicts to be avoided where possible. She also referred to a co-operation obligation imposed by Article 253(3) UNCLOS and to (current) Article 191(1) TFEU, which describes 'promoting measures at international level' as one of the EU's environmental policy objectives.[252] In *Commune de Mesquer* the Court did not discuss the principle of consistent interpretation, but it may be noted that the case ran in parallel with *Intertanko*, and that Kokott AG's Opinion was before the Court when it referred to the need to interpret EU law taking into account Marpol 73/78.

The restrictive approach towards the succession principle was again applied in *Bogiatzi*. That case concerned the interpretation of a regulation on air carrier liability in the event of accidents,[253] in connection with the so-called Warsaw Convention,[254] again a convention to which at the material time all the Member States had acceded. The Court examined whether the Community had, pursuant to the Treaty, assumed the powers previously exercised by the Member States in the field to which the Warsaw Convention applied, a convention which covered all international carriage by air of persons, baggage, and cargo. The Court established that the Community had adopted three regulations in the field to which the convention applied. However, an analysis of those regulations showed that they did not cover all the matters regulated in the convention. It followed that the Community had not assumed all the powers previously exercised by the Member States in the field to which the convention applied. The Community was therefore not bound.[255]

This case law shows that the Court is not easily willing to apply the succession principle of *International Fruit Company*. Although not a formal requirement, it would seem that the principle works only in areas in which the EU has exclusive competence. In other fields of EU activity, it will be rare for EU legislation to

[251] Ibid, para 85. [252] Ibid, paras 99–102 of the Opinion.

[253] Regulation 2027/97 [1997] OJ L285/1.

[254] Convention for the Unification of Certain Rules Relating to International Carriage by Air, signed at Warsaw on 12 October 1929, as amended by the four additional protocols signed at Montreal on 25 September 1975.

[255] Case C–301/08 *Bogiatzi v. Deutscher Luftpool and Others* [2009] ECR I–10185, paras 26–33.

regulate all the matters covered by a particular convention, as *Bogiatzi* appears to require. The scope for applying the succession principle is therefore likely to remain very limited. This means that there are many important international treaties and conventions which, though binding on all Member States, are not binding on the EU, even if it may be very active in the fields covered by those instruments. However, that would mean that, in effect, the succession principle could almost never be applied, in an area of shared competence, to broad-based, important, even foundational international instruments which are binding on the Member States. Indeed, the broader the coverage of such an instrument, the less likely it will be that literally all powers have been transferred to the EU, in the sense that there is EU legislation on all the matters covered by the instrument.

Such a narrow application of the succession principle makes little sense. It means that the EU is less likely to respect important international treaties and conventions. There is no conceivable rationale for such an approach. Clearly, the succession principle needs to be applied in such a manner that a middle way is found between the principle of respect for international law and the principle that the EU cannot be bound by any international agreement binding on any Member State. It is submitted that it is irrelevant, in finding such a middle way, whether or not the agreement comes within exclusive EU competence. What matters is (a) the importance and general recognition of the agreement, (b) its status as an agreement covered by Article 351 TFEU, and (c) the extent to which powers have been transferred in the matters covered by the agreement.

The Court has softened its rather uncompromising stance by recognizing that the principle of consistent interpretation applies. The precise operation of that principle remains to be clarified, though it is interesting to see that it is at least partly based on the duty of loyalty. It makes eminent sense to construe that duty as including a duty for the EU institutions to avoid obstructing the performance by Member States of their international obligations, again in particular where treaties or conventions are involved which are binding on all of them.

What should also be borne in mind is that there is one particular category of international agreements binding on all Member States which are, at least in some sense, binding on the EU, even if the succession principle clearly does not apply: treaties and conventions establishing fundamental rights. Indeed, those instruments have quasi-constitutional status, as they are a source for determining general principles of EU law.[256] Perhaps there is scope for further developing the notion of general principles of EU law, by allowing such principles to be formed also on the basis of certain international instruments outside the sphere of human rights protection.[257]

[256] See further I Butler and O De Schutter, 'Binding the EU to International Human Rights Law' (2008) 27 YEL 275.

[257] There are traces of such an approach in *Rottmann* (n 240 above). Note also that Art 78(1) TFEU provides that the 1951 Geneva Convention and the 1967 Protocol relating to the status of refugees, as well as other relevant treaties, are binding as regards the EU's asylum policy.

UN law: the *Kadi* judgment

There is little doubt that the UN Charter is the most significant international agreement binding on all Member States, but not concluded by the EU. Such conclusion is at any rate impossible without radical amendment of the Charter, which provides only for State membership (see Articles 3 and 4). The Charter clearly has constitutional-type features for the international legal system. Its character as a vital and central instrument for the conduct of international affairs finds expression in Article 103, which provides that in the event of a conflict between the obligations of the UN members under the Charter and their obligations under any other international agreement, their obligations under the Charter shall prevail. The importance of the Charter is not without recognition in the EU Treaties. (Current) Article 220 TFEU provides that the Union shall establish all appropriate forms of co-operation with the organs of the United Nations and its specialized agencies. (Current) Article 347 TFEU effectively permits Member States to derogate from their EU law obligations 'in order to carry out obligations . . . accepted for the purpose of maintaining peace and international security'. (Current) Article 351 TFEU applies to the Charter, which is a pre-accession agreement for all Member States, and therefore also enables the Member States to give effect to their Charter obligations. The Treaty of Lisbon has arguably strengthened the position of the Charter. Article 3(5) TEU, setting out the EU's objectives 'in its relations with the wider world', provides that the EU shall contribute 'to the strict observance and the development of international law, including respect for the principles of the United Nations Charter'.[258] Notwithstanding this recent strengthening, none of the above provisions define, with any degree of clarity or precision, the effects, in EU law, of the UN Charter or more broadly UN law. It is therefore for the EU Courts to determine those effects.

Those Courts have been confronted with UN Charter law mainly in the context of the EU's sanctions policies, which aim to implement UN Security Council resolutions. Those policies are analysed in more detail in Chapter 12. At this point, it may be sufficient to indicate that, in the light of its extensive competences in the sphere of trade and the provision of services, the EU became increasingly active in this field. That action was, uniquely, based on both the EU and EC Treaties, through the operation of the special provisions of (then) Articles 301 and 60 EC. Where the EU first adopted regulations imposing trade and economic embargos, pursuant to UN Security Council resolutions, it has more recently also become an actor in the field of counter-terrorism, among others through the adoption of regulations freezing the assets of persons suspected of supporting terrorism. Typically, the EC regulations which were adopted were mostly carbon copies of the UN Security Council resolutions to which they sought to give effect.

[258] This is confirmed by Art 21(1) TEU, which refers to 'respect for the principles of the United Nations Charter and international law' as a guiding principle for the Union's action on the international scene.

Yusuf and *Kadi* (Court of First Instance)

The issues set out above form the background to the important *Yusuf* and *Kadi* litigation.[259] *Yusuf v. Council and Commission* and *Kadi v. Council and Commission* were brought by persons suspected of supporting terrorism, and listed as such, not only in an EU common position, but also in an EC regulation freezing their assets.[260] The common position and the regulation reflected UN Security Council resolutions. The names of the persons involved were listed by the Sanctions Committee set up by those resolutions. The EC regulation faithfully followed the ebb and flow of the listing of persons and entities by the UN Committee. The applicants sought the annulment of the regulation, *inter alia*, on grounds of breach of fundamental rights. What follows does not set out the Court's full argument, which is lengthy, but concentrates on some of the crucial elements in the reasoning.

It is perhaps best to start with the CFI's conclusion on the question of judicial review on grounds of violation of fundamental rights. The Court considered that the challenged regulation fell outside the ambit of its judicial review powers, and that it had no authority to call in question, even indirectly, its lawfulness in the light of Community law.[261] This was remarkable of course, since the Court was not dealing with an EU common position, but with an EC regulation, clearly an act of the institutions in the sense of (current) Article 263 TFEU. The issue was indeed not whether an action for annulment could be brought. The issue was rather, in the Court's conception, that the regulation implemented and applied, in a Community context, resolutions of the Security Council.

In order to come to this remarkable conclusion the Court first considered the relationship between the international legal order under the UN Charter and the Community legal order. It opened that analysis by stating that, from the standpoint of international law, the obligations of the EU Member States under the UN Charter clearly prevailed over every other obligation of domestic law or of international treaty law, including their obligations under the EC Treaty.[262] That the Charter prevails over other international treaties is of course spelled out by the Charter itself (Article 103),[263] but the statement that it also prevailed over domestic law was more controversial. The CFI explained how this was the case: it simply followed from Article 27 VCLT, according to which a party could not invoke the provisions of its internal law as justification for its failure to perform a treaty.

The CFI then pointed out that this 'primacy', as it called it, extended to Security Council resolutions. It subsequently drew attention to (current) Articles 351 and

[259] N 245 above. The author should indicate that he was involved in the *Kadi* litigation, as a member of Mr Kadi's legal team on appeal before the Court of Justice and in *Kadi II*.

[260] Council Regulation 881/2002 [2002] OJ L139/9.

[261] References here and below are to *Yusuf* (n 245 above), here para 276.

[262] Ibid, para 231.

[263] Art 103 UN Charter reads: 'In the event of a conflict between the obligations of the Members of the United Nations under the present Charter and their obligations under any other international agreement, their obligations under the present Charter shall prevail'.

347 TFEU. The former provision permitted the Member States to give precedence to pre-EC treaty obligations; the latter recognized that a Member State could be called upon to take measures in order to carry out obligations it had accepted for the purpose of maintaining peace and international security. The Court concluded that, pursuant both to the rules of general international law and to the specific provisions of the Treaty, Member States could, and indeed had to, leave unapplied any provision of Community law that raised any impediment to the proper performance of their obligations under the UN Charter.[264]

The CFI subsequently admitted that the Community, not being a member of the United Nations, was not directly bound by the Charter as a matter of international law. The Court nevertheless held that the Community was bound, in the same way as its Member States, by virtue of the EC Treaty, as a matter of Community law. It developed a sophisticated reasoning, referring to the analogy with the *International Fruit Company* judgment, where the Court of Justice held that GATT was binding on the EEC,[265] to come to the conclusion that the Charter was also binding. The consequence was that, first, the Community could not infringe the obligations imposed on its Member States by the Charter or impede their performance and, secondly, that in the exercise of its powers it was bound to adopt all the measures necessary to enable its Member States to fulfil those obligations.

The CFI considered that it resulted from those considerations that there were structural limits on its judicial review capacity. It considered that the institutions, when adopting the regulation, acted under 'circumscribed powers', with the result that they had no autonomous discretion. Any review of the internal lawfulness of the contested regulation, especially having regard to the provisions or general principles of Community law relating to the protection of fundamental rights, would therefore imply that the Court was to consider, indirectly, the lawfulness of those resolutions. In that hypothetical situation, in fact, the origin of the illegality alleged by the applicant would have to be sought, not in the adoption of the contested regulation, but in the resolutions of the Security Council which imposed the sanctions. In particular, if the Court were to annul the contested regulation, although that regulation seemed to be imposed by international law, on the ground that that act infringed their fundamental rights which were protected by the Community legal order, such annulment would indirectly mean that the resolutions of the Security Council concerned, themselves infringed those fundamental rights. In other words, the applicants asked the Court to declare by implication that the provision of international law at issue infringed the fundamental rights of individuals, as protected by the Community legal order.[266]

This the CFI was not willing to do. It considered that it did not have jurisdiction to review the regulation on grounds of general principles of Community law.

[264] *Yusuf* (n 245 above) paras 234–240.

[265] N 9 above. [266] *Yusuf* (n 245 above) paras 266–267.

The Court, however, realized that, if it were to stop there, there would be no remedy whatsoever. In the end it found that there was scope for some measure of judicial review. The Court was empowered to check, indirectly, the lawfulness of the resolutions of the Security Council in question with regard to *jus cogens*, understood as a body of higher rules of public international law binding on all subjects of international law, including the bodies of the United Nations, and from which no derogation was possible.[267] What was the basis for this jurisdictional competence? Simply, the nature of *jus cogens* or peremptory norms under international law. If Security Council resolutions failed to respect *jus cogens*, however improbable that might be, they would bind neither the Member States of the United Nations nor, in consequence, the Community. The CFI then reviewed the applicants' arguments concerning the right to property, the right to be heard, and the right to an effective remedy. That section of the judgments need not be analysed here. The conclusion from the review was that there was no violation of *jus cogens*.[268]

The CFI's judgment was mostly criticized, including by this author.[269] Even though the case was clearly a hard one, most commentators considered that the effect of UN law could not be to trump the protection of fundamental rights, as required under EU law.

Kadi and *Al Barakaat* (Court of Justice)

On appeal the Court of Justice reversed the CFI's judgments, following the trenchant Opinion of Maduro AG. The starting point in his discussion of the relationship between the international legal order and the Community legal order was the landmark ruling in *Van Gend en Loos*, in which the Court affirmed the autonomy of the Community legal order. It considered that the Treaty had established a 'new legal order', beholden to, but distinct from the existing legal order of public international law. In other words, the Treaty had created a municipal legal order of trans-national dimensions, of which it formed the 'basic constitutional charter'. This did not mean, however, that the Community's legal order and the international legal order passed by each other like ships in the night. On the contrary, the Community had traditionally played an active and constructive part on the international stage. The application and interpretation of Community law was accordingly guided by the presumption that the Community wanted to honour its international commitments. The Community Courts therefore carefully examined the obligations

[267] Ibid, para 277.

[268] See e.g. the discussion on the right to a fair hearing, ibid, paras 304–331, in particular para 328.

[269] P Eeckhout, 'Community Terrorism Listings, Fundamental Rights, and UN Security Council Resolutions—In Search of the Right Fit' (2007) 3 European Constitutional Law Review 183. See also N Lavranos, 'UN sanctions and judicial review' in Wouters, Nollkaemper, and de Wet (n 68 above) 185; A Garde, 'Is it really for the European Community to implement anti-terrorism UN Security Council resolutions?' (2006) 65 CLJ 281.

by which the Community was bound on the international stage and took judicial notice of those obligations.[270]

Yet, the Advocate General continued, in the final analysis, the Community Courts determined the effect of international obligations within the Community legal order by reference to conditions set by Community law. He then referred to case law on the requirement that an agreement be adopted on a proper legal basis,[271] on the duty of loyal co-operation, and on compliance with general principles of Community law.[272] All these cases had in common that, although the Court took great care to respect the obligations that were incumbent on the Community by virtue of international law, it sought, first and foremost, to preserve the constitutional framework created by the Treaty. The relationship between international law and the Community legal order was governed by the Community legal order itself, and international law permeated that legal order under the conditions set by the constitutional principles of the Community. It followed that the appeal fundamentally turned on the question of whether the Community legal order accorded supra-constitutional status to measures that were necessary for the implementation of resolutions adopted by the Security Council.[273]

The Advocate General then discussed the relevance of the Court's *Bosphorus* judgment, which was interpreted differently by the parties.[274] The fact remained, however, that the Council, the Commission, and the United Kingdom had failed to identify any basis in the Treaty from which it could logically follow that measures taken for the implementation of Security Council resolutions had supra-constitutional status and were hence accorded immunity from judicial review. The United Kingdom suggested that such immunity could be derived from (current) Article 351 TFEU, in conjunction with the principle of loyalty in (current) Article 4(3) TEU. However, the Advocate General was not convinced by that argument.[275]

At first sight it might not be entirely clear how Member States would be prevented from fulfilling their obligations under the UN Charter if the Court were to annul the contested regulation. Indeed, in the absence of a Community measure, it would in principle be open to the Member States to take their own implementing measures, since they were allowed to adopt measures which, though affecting the functioning of the common market, might be necessary for the maintenance of international peace and security (see current Article 347 TFEU). None the less, the powers retained by the Member States in the field of security policy had to be exercised in a manner consistent with Community law. In the light of *ERT*,[276] it

[270] *Kadi and Al Barakaat* (n 8 above) paras 21–22 of the Opinion.

[271] Joined Cases C–317 and 318/04 *European Parliament v. Council (PNR)* [2006] ECR I–4721.

[272] Case C–122/95 *Germany v. Council* [1998] ECR I–973.

[273] *Kadi and Al Barakaat* (n 8 above) paras 23–25.

[274] Case C–84/95 *Bosphorus v. Minister for Transport, Energy and Communications, Ireland and the Attorney General* [1996] ECR I–3953. In that judgment, analysed in Ch 12, the Court had assessed whether a sanctions regulation against the FRY infringed fundamental rights and the principle of proportionality.

[275] *Kadi and Al Barakaat* (n 8 above) paras 26–29.

[276] Case C–260/89 *ERT* [1991] ECR I–2925.

could be assumed that, to the extent that their actions came within the scope of Community law, Member States were subject to the same Community rules for the protection of fundamental rights as the Community institutions themselves. On that assumption, if the Court were to annul the contested regulation on the ground that it infringed Community rules for the protection of fundamental rights, then, by implication, Member States could not possibly adopt the same measures without—in so far as those measures came within the scope of Community law—acting in breach of fundamental rights as protected by the Court. Thus, the argument based on (current) Article 351 TFEU was of indirect relevance only.[277]

The crucial problem with the argument raised by the United Kingdom, however, was that it presented (current) Article 351 TFEU as the source of a possible derogation from (then) Article 6(1) EU, according to which 'the Union is founded on the principles of liberty, democracy, respect for human rights and fundamental freedoms, and the rule of law'. The Advocate General saw no basis for such an interpretation of (current) Article 351 TFEU. It would potentially enable national authorities to use the Community to circumvent fundamental rights which were guaranteed in their national legal orders even in respect of acts implementing international obligations. This would plainly run counter to firmly established case law of the Court, according to which the Community guaranteed a complete system of judicial protection in which fundamental rights were safeguarded in consonance with the constitutional traditions of the Member States. The Advocate General referred, *inter alia*, to *Les Verts*, where the Court had stated that the European Community was a community based on the rule of law inasmuch as neither its Member States nor its institutions could avoid a review of the question whether the measures adopted by them were in conformity with the basic constitutional charter, the Treaty.[278] In short, the UK's reading of Article 351 TFEU would break away from the very principles on which the Union was founded, while there was nothing in the Treaty to suggest that the provision had a special status—let alone a special status of that magnitude—in the constitutional framework of the Community.[279]

The Advocate General further noted that the obligations under (current) Article 351 TFEU and the related duty of loyal co-operation flowed in both directions: they applied to the Community as well as to the Member States. This required Member States to exercise their powers and responsibilities in an international organization such as the United Nations in a manner that was compatible with the conditions set by the primary rules and the general principles of Community law. The Member States themselves, therefore, carried a responsibility to minimize the risk of conflicts between the Community legal order and international law.[280]

[277] *Kadi and Al Barakaat* (n 8 above) para 30.

[278] Case 294/83 *Les Verts v. European Parliament* [1986] ECR 1339, para 23.

[279] *Kadi and Al Barakaat* (n 8 above) para 31.

[280] Ibid, para 32.

If (current) Article 351 TFEU could not render the contested regulation exempt from judicial review, were there perhaps any other rules of Community law that could? The contention that the case concerned a 'political question', in respect of which even the most humble degree of judicial interference would be inappropriate, was untenable. The claim that a measure was necessary for the maintenance of international peace and security could not operate so as to silence the general principles of Community law and deprive individuals of their fundamental rights. This did not detract from the importance of the interest in maintaining international peace and security; it simply meant that it remained the duty of the courts to assess the lawfulness of measures that could conflict with other interests that were equally of great importance and with the protection of which the courts were entrusted.[281]

Certainly, extraordinary circumstances could justify restrictions on individual freedom that would be unacceptable under normal conditions. However, that should not induce us to say that 'there are cases in which a veil should be drawn for a while over liberty, as it was customary to cover the statues of the gods'.[282] Nor did it mean that judicial review in those cases should be only of the most marginal kind. On the contrary, when the risks to public security were believed to be extraordinarily high, the pressure was particularly strong to take measures that disregarded individual rights, especially in respect of individuals who had little or no access to the political process. Therefore, in those instances, the courts had to fulfil their duty to uphold the rule of law with increased vigilance. Thus, the same circumstances that could justify exceptional restrictions on fundamental rights also required the courts to ascertain carefully whether those restrictions went beyond what was necessary.[283]

The Advocate General further rejected the argument that the ECtHR relinquished its powers of review when a contested measure was necessary in order to implement a Security Council resolution. Even if that were the case, there remained important differences between the two courts. The task of the ECtHR was to ensure the observance of the commitments entered into by the contracting states under the Convention, which was designed to operate primarily as an interstate agreement which created obligations between the contracting parties at the international level. The EC Treaty, by contrast, had founded an autonomous legal order, within which States as well as individuals had immediate rights and obligations. The duty of the Court of Justice was to act as the constitutional court of the municipal legal order that was the Community. The ECtHR and the Court of Justice were therefore unique as regards their jurisdiction *ratione personae* and as regards the relationship of their legal system with public international law.[284]

The Advocate General, lastly, responded to the argument that the Court would be exceeding its proper function and be speaking on behalf of the international

[281] Ibid, paras 33–34.
[282] Translated from Montesquieu, *De l'Esprit des Lois*, Book XII.
[283] *Kadi and Al Barakaat* (n 8 above) para 35. [284] Ibid, paras 36–37.

community. Any repercussions on the international stage were the immediate consequence of the fact that, as the system governing the functioning of the United Nations stood, the only option available to individuals who wished to have access to an independent tribunal in order to obtain adequate protection of their fundamental rights was to challenge domestic implementing measures before a domestic court. Moreover, the legal effects of a ruling by the Court remained confined to the municipal legal order of the Community. To the extent that such a ruling would prevent the Community and its Member States from implementing Security Council resolutions, the legal consequences within the international legal order remained to be determined by the rules of public international law. While it was true that the restrictions which the general principles of Community law imposed on the actions of the institutions could inconvenience the Community and its Member States in their dealings on the international stage, the application of these principles by the Court was without prejudice to the application of international rules on State responsibility or to the rule enunciated in Article 103 of the UN Charter. The Council's contention that, by reviewing the contested regulation, the Court would assume jurisdiction beyond the perimeters of the Community legal order, was therefore misconceived.[285]

The Advocate General concluded that the CFI had erred in law, and that review in the light of fundamental rights was required. He then proceeded to examine the alleged breaches of fundamental rights, and found that the challenged regulation infringed the appellant's right to be heard, right to judicial review, and right to property.

The Court of Justice developed the following reasoning.[286]

First, the Community was based on the rule of law, inasmuch as neither its Member States nor its institutions could avoid review of the conformity of their acts with the basic constitutional charter, the EC Treaty, which established a complete system of legal remedies and procedures designed to enable the Court of Justice to review the legality of acts of the institutions.[287] Nor could an international agreement affect the allocation of powers fixed by the Treaties or, consequently, the autonomy of the Community legal system, observance of which was ensured by the Court by virtue of the exclusive jurisdiction conferred on it by (current) Article 19(1) TEU, jurisdiction that the Court had already held to form part of the very foundations of the Community.[288]

In addition, fundamental rights formed an integral part of the general principles of law the observance of which the Court ensured. It was also clear that respect for human rights was a condition of the lawfulness of Community acts and that measures incompatible with respect for human rights were not acceptable in the Community.[289]

[285] Ibid, paras 38–39. [286] Ibid, paras 281–326 of the judgment. [287] N 278 above.

[288] Opinion 1/91 [1991] ECR I–6079, paras 35 and 71, and Case C–459/03 *Commission v. Ireland* [2006] ECR I–4635, para 123 and case law cited.

[289] *Opinion 2/94 re Accession to the ECHR* [2006] ECR I–1759, para 34 and Case C–112/00 *Schmidberger* [2003] ECR I–5659, para 73 and case law cited.

It followed from all those considerations that the obligations imposed by an international agreement could not have the effect of prejudicing the constitutional principles of the EC Treaty, which included the principle that all Community acts had to respect fundamental rights, that respect constituting a condition of their lawfulness which it was for the Court to review in the framework of the complete system of legal remedies established by the Treaty.

The Court then referred to the nature of the review which it was asked to carry out, and its relationship with international law. It had to be emphasized that, in circumstances such as those of these cases, the review of lawfulness applied to the Community act intended to give effect to the international agreement at issue, and not to the latter as such. With more particular regard to a Community act which, like the contested regulation, was intended to give effect to a resolution adopted by the Security Council under Chapter VII of the Charter of the United Nations, it was not, therefore, for the Community judicature to review the lawfulness of such a resolution adopted by an international body, even if that review were to be limited to examination of the compatibility of that resolution with *jus cogens*. However, any judgment given by the Community judicature deciding that a Community measure intended to give effect to such a resolution was contrary to a higher rule of law in the Community legal order would not entail any challenge to the primacy of that resolution in international law. The Court had thus previously annulled a decision of the Council approving an international agreement after considering the internal lawfulness of the decision in the light of the agreement in question and finding a breach of a general principle of Community law, in that instance the general principle of non-discrimination.[290]

The next step in the reasoning was for the Court to consider whether, as the CFI held, as a result of the principles governing the relationship between the international legal order under the United Nations and the Community legal order, any judicial review of the internal lawfulness of the contested regulation in the light of fundamental freedoms was in principle excluded, notwithstanding the fact that such review was a constitutional guarantee forming part of the very foundations of the Community. In this respect, it first had to to be borne in mind that the European Community had to respect international law in the exercise of its powers.[291] Moreover, the powers of the Community provided for by (current) Articles 208 to 211 TFEU in the sphere of co-operation and development, had to be exercised in observance of the undertakings given in the context of the United Nations and other international organizations.[292] Such observance was required just as much in the sphere of the maintenance of international peace and security when the Community gave effect to resolutions adopted by the Security Council. In the exercise of that latter power it was necessary for the Community to attach special

[290] *Germany v. Council* (n 272 above).
[291] *Poulsen and Diva Navigation* (n 215 above) para 9.
[292] Case C–91/05 *Commission v. Council* [2008] ECR I–3651, para 65 and case law cited.

importance to the fact that, in accordance with Article 24 of the Charter, the adoption by the Security Council of resolutions under Chapter VII constituted the exercise of the primary responsibility with which that international body was invested for the maintenance of peace and security at the global level, a responsibility which included the power to determine what and who poses a threat to international peace and security and to take the measures necessary to maintain or restore them. When the Community drew up acts adopted on the basis of (then) Articles 60 and 301 EC whose object was to implement a resolution, the Community was to take due account of the terms and objectives of the resolution concerned and of the relevant obligations under the Charter relating to such implementation. Furthermore, for the purposes of the interpretation of the contested regulation, account had also to be taken of the wording and purpose of the resolution which that regulation was designed to implement.[293]

The Court then determined, however, that the above principles did not mean that judicial review was excluded, by virtue of either international or EU law. It had to be noted that the UN Charter did not impose the choice of a particular model for the implementation of resolutions adopted by the Security Council, since they were to be given effect in accordance with the procedure applicable in that respect in the domestic legal order of each member of the United Nations. The Charter left members free choice among the various possible models for transposition of those resolutions into their domestic legal order. It followed that it was not a consequence of the principles governing the international legal order under the United Nations that any judicial review of the internal lawfulness of the contested regulation in the light of fundamental freedoms was excluded by virtue of the fact that that measure was intended to give effect to a resolution of the Security Council adopted under Chapter VII of the UN Charter.

What was more, such immunity from jurisdiction for a Community measure like the contested regulation, as a corollary of the principle of the primacy at the level of international law of obligations under the Charter of the United Nations, could not find a basis in the EC Treaty. Admittedly, the Court had previously recognized that (current) Article 351 TFEU could allow derogations even from primary law, for example from (current) Article 207 TFEU on the common commercial policy.[294] It was true also that (current) Article 347 TFEU implicitly permitted obstacles to the operation of the common market when they were caused by measures taken by a Member State to carry out the international obligations it had accepted for the purpose of maintaining international peace and security. Those provisions could not, however, be understood to authorize any derogation from the principles of liberty, democracy, and respect for human rights and fundamental

[293] Case C–117/06 *Gerda Möllendorf ad Christiane Möllendorf-Niehuus* [2007] ECR I–8361, para 54 and case law cited.

[294] Case C–124/95 *The Queen, ex parte Centro-Com v. HM Treasury and Bank of England* [1997] ECR I–81, paras 56–61.

freedoms enshrined in (then) Article 6(1) EU as a foundation of the Union. Article 351 TFEU could in no circumstances permit any challenge to the principles that formed part of the very foundations of the Community legal order, one of which was the protection of fundamental rights, including the review by the Community judicature of the lawfulness of Community measures as regards their consistency with those fundamental rights.

Nor could an immunity from jurisdiction find any basis in the place that obligations under the Charter of the United Nations would occupy in the hierarchy of norms within the Community legal order if those obligations were to be classified in that hierarchy. (Current) Article 216(2) TFEU provided that agreements concluded under the conditions set out in that article were to be binding on the institutions of the Community and on Member States. Thus, by virtue of that provision, supposing it to be applicable to the Charter, the latter would have primacy over acts of secondary Community law. That primacy would not, however, extend to primary law, in particular to the general principles of which fundamental rights formed part.

That interpretation was supported by (current) Article 218(11) TFEU, which provided that an international agreement could not enter into force if the Court had delivered an adverse opinion on its compatibility with the Treaty, unless the latter had previously been amended.

The Court then rejected arguments in support of the CFI's finding, based on case law of the ECtHR. The Court responded that, as the ECtHR itself had noted, there existed a fundamental difference between the nature of the measures concerned in some of its recent decisions, with regard to which that court declined jurisdiction to carry out a review of consistency with the ECHR, and the nature of other measures with regard to which its jurisdiction would seem to be unquestionable.[295] While, in certain cases before it, the ECtHR had declined jurisdiction *ratione personae*, those cases involved actions directly attributable to the United Nations as an organization of universal jurisdiction fulfilling its imperative collective security objective, in particular actions of a subsidiary organ of the United Nations created under Chapter VII of the UN Charter or actions falling within the exercise of powers lawfully delegated by the Security Council pursuant to that chapter, and not actions ascribable to the respondent States before that court, those actions not, moreover, having taken place in the territory of those States and not resulting from any decision of the authorities of those States. By contrast, in paragraph 151 of *Behrami and Behrami v. France* and *Saramati v. France, Germany and Norway*, the ECtHR had stated that in the case leading to its judgment in *Bosphorus Hava Yollari Turizm ve Ticaret Anonim Şirketi v. Ireland*, concerning a seizure measure carried out by the authorities of the respondent State on its territory following a decision by one of

[295] *Behrami and Behrami v. France* and *Saramati v. France, Germany and Norway*, 2 May 2007, not yet published in the *Reports of Judgments and Decisions*, §151.

its ministers, it had recognized its competence, notably *ratione personae*, vis-à-vis the respondent State, despite the fact that the source of the contested measure was a Community regulation taken, in its turn, pursuant to a resolution of the Security Council. In the instant case it had to be declared that the contested regulation could not be considered to be an act directly attributable to the United Nations as an action of one of its subsidiary organs created under Chapter VII of the Charter of the United Nations or an action falling within the exercise of powers lawfully delegated by the Security Council pursuant to that chapter. In addition and in any event, the question of the Court's jurisdiction to rule on the lawfulness of the contested regulation had arisen in fundamentally different circumstances. As the Court had already noted, the review by the Court of the validity of any Community measure in the light of fundamental rights had to be considered to be the expression, in a community based on the rule of law, of a constitutional guarantee stemming from the EC Treaty as an autonomous legal system which was not to be prejudiced by an international agreement. The question of the Court's jurisdiction arose in the context of the internal and autonomous legal order of the Community, within whose ambit the contested regulation fell and in which the Court had jurisdiction to review the validity of Community measures in the light of fundamental rights.

The last set of arguments in support of the CFI's ruling which the Court considered, focused on whether it should defer to the Security Council's own re-examination procedure for terrorism listings. The Court pointed out that it had been maintained that, having regard to the deference required of the Community institutions vis-à-vis the institutions of the United Nations, the Court had to forgo the exercise of any review of the lawfulness of the contested regulation in the light of fundamental rights, even if such review were possible, given that, under the system of sanctions set up by the United Nations, having particular regard to the re-examination procedure which had recently been significantly improved by various resolutions of the Security Council, fundamental rights were adequately protected. According to the Commission, so long as under that system of sanctions the individuals or entities concerned had an acceptable opportunity to be heard through a mechanism of administrative review forming part of the UN legal system, the Court had not to intervene in any way whatsoever.

The Court's response was that it could be observed, first of all, that if in fact, as a result of the Security Council's adoption of various resolutions, amendments had been made to the system of restrictive measures set up by the United Nations with regard both to entry in the summary list and to removal from it, those amendments were made after the contested regulation had been adopted so that, in principle, they could not be taken into consideration in the appeals. In any event, the existence, within that UN system, of the re-examination procedure before the Sanctions Committee, even having regard to the amendments recently made to it, could not give rise to generalized immunity from jurisdiction within the internal legal order of the Community. Indeed, such immunity, constituting a significant derogation from the scheme of judicial protection of fundamental rights laid down by the EC Treaty, appeared unjustified, for clearly that re-examination procedure did not offer the guarantees of judicial protection. Although it was now open to any person or entity to approach the Sanctions Committee directly, submitting a request to be removed from the summary list at what was called the 'focal' point, the fact remained that the procedure before that Committee was still in essence diplomatic and intergovernmental, the persons or entities concerned having no real opportunity of asserting their rights and that Committee taking its decisions by consensus, each of its members having a right of veto. The Guidelines of the Sanctions Committee made it plain that an applicant submitting a request for removal from the list could in no way assert his rights himself during the procedure before the Sanctions Committee or be represented for that purpose, the government of his State of residence or of citizenship alone having the right to submit observations on that request. Moreover, those Guidelines did not require the Sanctions Committee to communicate to the applicant the reasons and evidence justifying his appearance in the summary list or to give him access, even restricted, to that information. Lastly, if that Committee rejected the request for removal from the list, it was under no obligation to give reasons.

The Court then arrived at its conclusion. It followed from the foregoing that the Community judicature, in accordance with the powers conferred on it by the EC Treaty, had to ensure the review, in principle the full review, of the lawfulness of all Community acts in the light of the fundamental rights forming an integral part of the general principles of Community law, including the review of Community measures which, like the contested regulation, were designed to give effect to the resolutions adopted by the Security Council under Chapter VII of the Charter of the United Nations.

The Court went on to examine whether Mr Kadi's and Al Barakaat's fundamental rights were violated, and found, like the Advocate General, that there was a breach of the rights of defence, in particular the right to be heard; of the right to effective judicial protection; and of the right to property.[296] The Court therefore annulled the regulation, but maintained its effects for three months, enabling the Council to remedy the violations. It is worth adding that the Commission re-listed Mr Kadi in December 2008, and that in *Kadi II* the General Court again annulled the listing, on the grounds of fundamental rights violations. As regards the reasoning of the Court of Justice in *Kadi and Al Barakaat*, analysed above, the General Court noted that doubts had been voiced in legal circles, but it also found that the appellate principle and the hierarchical judicial structure advised against the General Court revisiting points of law decided by the Court of Justice.[297]

[296] *Kadi and Al Barakaat* (n 8 above) paras 333–371.

[297] Case T–85/09 *Kadi v. Commission (Kadi II)*, judgment of 30 September 2010, paras 115–121.

Kadi: an assessment

The Court's analysis and findings in *Kadi* are to be applauded.[298] A superficial comparison with cases such as *Portugal v. Council*[299] and *Intertanko*[300] might lead to the conclusion that in *Kadi* the Court denied effect to a third important multilateral treaty, the UN Charter. However, the fundamental issue in *Kadi* was very different from the direct-effect questions concerning WTO law and UNCLOS. The effect which the CFI had given to UN resolutions was not the conferral of rights on private parties, or the inclusion of the Charter in the grounds for judicial review. It was in some sense exactly the opposite: the exclusion of judicial review in accordance with EU law standard criteria of respect for fundamental rights as general principles of EU law. In the CFI's conception the Charter had acquired supra-constitutional status, to use the words of Maduro AG. The Court of Justice rightly denied the Charter such a status.

The importance of *Kadi and Al Barakaat* is confirmed by the avalanche of academic commentary which it unleashed.[301] Most of this commentary focuses on the way in which the Court constructed the relationship between the EU legal order and UN Security Council Resolutions. Some of it is supportive of the judgment, but some of it also harshly critical.[302] The critique does not take aim at the outcome of the litigation. Rather, the Court is accused of disrespect for the central role which the UN Security Council plays in the international system; of excessive confirmation of the autonomy of EU law; indeed, even of being parochial and particularistic in its approach. Analogies are drawn with the *Medellin* decision of

[298] Compare with Eeckhout (n 269 above). [299] N 90 above. [300] N 113 above.

[301] See, *inter alia*, D Halberstam and E Stein, 'The United Nations, the European Union, and the King of Sweden: Economic sanctions and individual rights in a plural world order' (2009) 46 CML Rev 13; B Kunoy and A Dawes, 'Plate tectonics in Luxembourg: The *ménage à trois* between EC law, international law and the European Convention on Human Rights following the UN sanctions cases' (2009) 46 CML Rev 73; A Gattini, Annotation of *Kadi* (2009) 46 CML Rev 213; G de Búrca, 'The European Court of Justice and the International Legal Order after *Kadi*', Jean Monnet Working Paper 01/09, available at <http://centers.law.nyu.edu/jeanmonnet/papers/09/090101.pdf>; T Tridimas and J Gutierrez-Fons, 'EU Law, International Law and Economic Sanctions against Terrorism: The Judiciary in Distress?' (2008) 32 Fordham International Law Journal 660; S Griller, 'International law, human rights and the European Community's autonomous legal order: notes on the European Court of Justice decision in *Kadi*' (2008) 4 European Constitutional Law Review 528; G Harpaz, 'Judicial Review by the European Court of Justice of UN "Smart Sanctions" Against Terror in the *Kadi* Dispute' (2009) 14 EFA Rev 65; JHH Weiler, 'Editorial—*Kadi*: Europe's *Medellin*?' (2008) 19 EJIL 895; D Curtin, *Executive Power of the European Union—Law, Practices, and the Living Constitution* (OUP, 2009) 194–201; P De Sena and MC Vitucci, 'The European Courts and the Security Council: Between *Dédoublement Fonctionnel* and Balancing of Values' (2009) 20 EJIL 193; P Hilpold, 'EU Law and UN Law in Conflict: The *Kadi* Case' (2009) 13 Max Planck UNYB 141; T Tridimas, 'Terrorism and the ECJ; Empowerment and Democracy in the EC Legal Order' (2009) 34 ELR 103.

For an excellent overview of the literature see S Poli and M Tzanou, 'The *Kadi* Rulings: A Survey of the Literature' (2009) 28 YEL 533. See further the collection of articles in (2009) 28 YEL, under the heading 'Challenging EU Counter-Terrorism Measures before the Courts: An Assessment of the *Kadi* judgment', with contributions by M Cremona, E Cannizzaro, A Ciampi, G Gaja, N Lavranos, R Pavoni, M Scheinin, C Tomuschat, and F Fabbrini.

[302] See in particular de Búrca, Weiler, Halberstam and Stein (n 301 above) ibid.

the US Supreme Court,[303] even if that case was fundamentally different: it involved a denial of a form of rights protection offered through a decision of the ICJ, in the face of the execution of the death penalty. International law was argued to be a source for rights protection in *Medellin*, whereas the defendant institutions and intervening governments in *Kadi* sought to rely on international law to deny basic norms of rights protection. Furthermore, the two cases involved a fundamentally different use of international law, not just in the sense of being *pro* or *contra* the protection of fundamental rights. *Medellin* related to traditional questions about the 'self-executing' effect (in EU law terms 'direct effect') of international norms. In *Kadi* the institutions and intervening governments argued for a much more radical use of international law: one which would exclude the normal standards of judicial review under the EU's functional constitution.[304]

Some of the critique is based on broader, theory-oriented analyses of the relationship between the EU and international legal orders. As mentioned above, it is not the aim of this chapter to engage with the relevant theoretical concepts and constructs, such as monism and dualism, legal and constitutional pluralism, and constitutionalism. The author leaves this for another day. Rather, the aim here is to analyse the Court's preference for the EU version of the rule of law.

It is also not the aim of this chapter to offer a full account of the concept of the rule of law.[305] The term is used almost as a shorthand for fundamental principles and norms of a legal system. It is clear that questions related to the rule of law were in issue in *Kadi*; indeed the Court expressly referred to the concept when speaking about the requirement that all acts of the EU institutions be subject to judicial review.[306] On the other hand, those preferring greater respect for and emphasis on international law, also have in mind such fundamental principles and norms.

It is submitted that the choice in *Kadi* for the EU version of the rule of law was an obvious one. On a dispassionate reading, the Court simply confirmed established rules and principles concerning (a) judicial review, (b) the importance of fundamental rights, and (c) the relationship between international law and EU law. All acts of the institutions adopted under the EC Treaty (now the TFEU) are subject to judicial review.[307] All such acts need to comply with general principles of EU law, including fundamental rights.[308] When the EU acts under international law, for example by concluding an international agreement, the Treaties need to be respected (see all the judgments on external competence). The norms of an international agreement concluded by the EU need to be compatible with the EU Treaties, as the TFEU clarifies in Article 218(11).[309] A point which the *Kadi* judgment adds is that those

[303] US Supreme Court, *Medellin v Texas* 552 US 491 (2008).

[304] The term 'functional constitution' was used by the *Bundesverfassungsgericht* in its Lisbon Treaty judgment, see BVerfG, 2BvE 2/08 of 30 June 2009, para 231.

[305] In an EU context see A von Bogdandy, 'Founding Principles' in A von Bogdandy and J Bast, *Principles of European Constitutional Law* (2nd edn, Hart Publishing, 2010) 11.

[306] *Kadi and Al Barakaat* (n 8 above) para 281.

[307] *Les Verts* (n 278 above).

[308] See e.g. *Opinion 2/94* (n 289 above) para 34.

[309] *Germany v. Council* (n 272 above).

rules and principles extend to UN law, notwithstanding the primacy of the Charter under international law, embodied in Article 103 of the UN Charter.

Let us look at this point a little further. Most international law commentators are critical of the Court's silence on Art. 103. The only reference which the Court makes to that provision is an implicit one: 'any judgment given by the Community judicature deciding that a Community measure intended to give effect to . . . a resolution is contrary to a higher rule of law in the Community legal order would not entail any challenge to the primacy of that resolution in international law'.[310] There is no further analysis of the primacy rule. Nor is there in the Opinion of Advocate General Maduro. Is this not an approach which is too cursory, sweeping Article 103 under the carpet, as it were? As a matter of positive law, the answer to that question is negative.[311] It is difficult to see the relevance of Article 103 in the kind of proceedings leading to the judgment in *Kadi*. Article 103 addresses the obligations of the Members of the United Nations under the Charter (and the EU is not of course such a member), and provides that, in the event of a conflict with obligations under any other international agreement, the Charter prevails. Article 103 therefore speaks to the obligations of the EU Member States, but not to those of the EU. If one is serious about the autonomous nature of international organizations as international legal persons—and international law itself is most serious about that, see, for example, the International Law Commission's work on the responsibility of international organizations[312]—then as a matter of positive law it is difficult to see what effect Article 103 can have for the EU. Moreover, in *Kadi* the Courts were not looking at measures adopted by the EU Member States, which are of course bound by Article 103. They were scrutinizing an EC measure, adopted under the EC Treaty. It is the most basic principle of international law that a treaty needs to be respected. One cannot expect a court such as the Court of Justice, which by the EU Treaties is instructed to ensure that acts of the institutions are in conformity with those Treaties, to disregard that instruction simply on the basis of a provision in another treaty which, on its terms, does not apply.

The choice for the EU version of the rule of law was thus an obvious one, in the light of both EU and international positive law. Nevertheless, some of the critical commentators referred to above consider that the Court should have arrived at its result using a different route. They argue that the Court should have reviewed the EC regulation in issue, not on the grounds of EU protection of fundamental rights, but in terms of international human rights norms. They contend that the Court should have adopted the CFI's approach in *Kadi*, but that instead of limiting itself to *ius cogens*, the Court should have reviewed the EC regulation on the basis of customary and general international law norms of due process and of the UN-based human rights system.[313]

[310] *Kadi and Al Barakaat* (n 8 above) para 288.

[311] See further Eeckhout (n 269 above).

[312] See for an overview with further references <http://untreaty.un.org/ilc/summaries/9_11.htm>.

[313] See e.g. de Búrca (n 301 above) 47; Halberstam and Stein (n 301 above) 64–5.

One could call this the international version of the rule of law. Instead of anchoring its analysis in the EU version, the Court should have opted for the international rule of law. It is submitted, however, that this international version does not offer the straightforward route of the EU version, and would instead have been most precarious.

One may start by noting that the international version of the rule of law, applied to Security Council resolutions listing individuals as supporters of terrorism, would in any event have contained fundamentally conflicting elements. On the one hand, an argument could certainly be constructed to support a finding that the Security Council is bound by international human rights norms. On the other, it is equally clear that the Security Council has been given extensive powers, under Chapter VII of the UN Charter, to maintain peace and international security, and that it may exercise those powers with considerable discretion. Article 25 UN Charter confirms that Security Council resolutions are binding ('Members... agree to accept and carry out the decisions of the Security Council'). This, of course, is also an important dimension of the international rule of law. That fundamental tension at the heart of the international rule of law can only be resolved by means of a hard and contestable decision to give priority to international human rights norms over the powers of the Security Council. In so far as those human rights norms are considered to be based in customary international law, it is clear that they cannot override treaty norms. The powers of the Security Council are laid down in a treaty, the UN Charter, which not only overrides customary international law, but equally takes priority over all other treaties (Article 103 UN Charter). The latter point also means that it is impossible to argue that the UN Members should give priority to their obligations under UN human rights instruments such as the international covenants, over their obligation to accept and carry out Security Council resolutions under Chapter VII. All this considerably restricts the opportunities for applying international human rights law. The only route, it would appear, is an *ultra vires* argument: the Security Council's powers would need to be construed as limited, under the UN Charter itself, by the principles and purposes of the United Nations, which of course include the protection of fundamental rights. Those principles and purposes then need to be translated into enforceable norms of due process.[314]

Closely linked to those substantive problems is a procedural question. Even if it were accepted that the relevant resolutions violate fundamental rights norms binding the Security Council, and were thereby adopted *ultra vires*, there is the hurdle of permitting a court such as the Court of Justice, a 'regional' court overseeing the work of an international organization which is not even a UN Member, to make the relevant findings. The CFI was heavily criticized, on appeal,

[314] See further E. De Wet, *The Chapter VII Powers of the United Nations Security Council* (Hart Publishing, 2004) 191–204. See also the Commission's observations in *Kadi and Al Barakaat* (n 8 above) para 270.

for reviewing the resolution in the light of *ius cogens*. It was argued, with some justification, that it had no jurisdiction to conduct such a review.

The Court of Justice is criticized for not having opted for the precarious route of upholding the international version of the rule of law. If it had done so, it is argued, it would have made a contribution to the development of international human rights law, instead of emphasizing 'the particularism of Europe's fundamental rights'.[315] But imagine the criticism which this use of the international version, in preference over the European version of the rule of law, could have triggered. The Court would have been accused of arrogating to itself the power to rule on the validity of Security Council resolutions under international law, a branch of law in which it has limited expertise and no express jurisdiction. It would have been accused of transgressing its limited jurisdiction under the EU Treaties, and of operating as the world court of judicial review of UN Security Council resolutions. All this would have had to be done in the face of uncertain legal principles, and in the absence of clear precedent in international law. The Court would have been accused of fundamentally undermining the role and function of the Security Council: if the Court of Justice is entitled to review a resolution under international law, what would stop other domestic courts from doing the same? Is the international rule of law really assisted by decentralized judicial review, based in international law itself?

It is further submitted that the Court's choice of the EU version of the rule of law also serves the international rule of law, perhaps more so than would be the case if the Court had opted directly for the international version. It is undeniable that the Court's decision constitutes a challenge to the Security Council's listing policies, and that it can serve as a precedent in other jurisdictions. It is, however, a legitimate challenge, given how straightforward the case was when standard EU law principles of effective judicial protection were applied. It is also a much more modest challenge than one directly based in international law itself. Here one finds a legal system signalling that there are fundamental problems with simply implementing the relevant resolutions, because of fundamental rights concerns. The judgment enables the EU to start a dialogue with the Security Council about strengthening due process at the UN level.

That brings us to another dimension of the relationship between the EU and international legal systems: the dimension of dialogue. Several commentators contrast the Court's approach with the *Solange* principle, first established by the German *Bundesverfassungsgericht*.[316] Halberstam and Stein contend that the Court appeared to exclude ever deferring to the Security Council, even if that organ set up a satisfactory due process system for the listing of individuals. They deduce that

[315] de Búrca (n 301 above) 47.

[316] BverfG 29 May 1974, 37 Entscheidungen des Bundesverfassungsgerichts [BVerfGE] 271 (FRG), 2 CMLR 540 (*Solange I*); BverfG 22 Oct. 1986, 73 Entscheidungen des Bundesverfassungsgerichts [BVerfGE] 339 (FRG), 3 CMLR 225 (*Solange II*).

exclusion from the Court's analysis of the current Security Council re-examination process, which the Court found inadequate. They focus in particular on the statement that that procedure 'cannot give rise to generalised immunity from jurisdiction within the internal legal order of the Community'.[317] This author admits to being astounded by this construction of the Court's analysis. The fact that the Court engaged with the Commission's argument, in the sense of examining whether the current re-examination process guarantees effective judicial protection, surely suggests that a more satisfactory process at UN level could lead to a different conclusion. What the Court did in reply to the Commission's argument was not simply to reject the possibility that the EU system of judicial protection could ever defer to a UN mechanism for reviewing listings. Rather, the Court examined over a number of paragraphs whether the current UN system offered effective judicial protection, and unfortunately had to conclude that that was not the case.[318] It simply found that the UN re-examination procedure 'does not offer the guarantees of judicial protection'.[319] This is not a blanket refusal to defer; it is a refusal to defer in the light of the facts and circumstances of the case.[320]

De Búrca argues that the Court in *Kadi* 'eschewed the dialogic approach pioneered by the German constitutional court [in the *Solange* decisions] which engaged directly with the ostensibly conflicting international regime'.[321] Whilst there are surely differences between the *Solange* judgments and *Kadi*, they are, first of all, a result of the different issues and circumstances of the respective cases. The main contrast is that in *Solange* there was scope for a *judicial* dialogue. The *Bundesverfassungsgericht* was speaking to the Court of Justice. In the sphere of counter-terrorism, unfortunately, there is no judicial counterpart at international level. But more significantly, there are clearly strong elements of a dialogic approach also in the *Kadi* judgment. There is a section in which the Court points out that the Community must respect international law; that this includes observance of the undertakings given in the context of the United Nations; that the Community must attach special importance to the fact that Security Council resolutions constitute the exercise of the primary responsibility with which that international body is invested for the maintenance of peace and security at the global level; and that in drawing up measures to implement resolutions the Community is to take due account of the terms and objectives of the resolution concerned and of the relevant obligations under the UN Charter relating to such implementation.[322] Moreover, the section in which the Court analyses the current re-examination procedure in the United Nations, referred to above, must surely also be read as dialogic in nature. Indeed, the focus should not simply be on the section of *Kadi* focusing on whether the international norms in issue precluded the application of the normal mechanisms

[317] *Kadi and Al Barakaat* (n 8 above) para 321; Halberstam and Stein (n 301 above) 60.
[318] *Kadi and Al Barakaat* (n 8 above) paras 320–326. [319] Ibid, para 322.
[320] This is also confirmed by the analysis of the General Court in *Kadi II* (n 297 above) para 128.
[321] de Búrca (n 301 above) 49. [322] *Kadi and Al Barakaat* (n 8 above) paras 291–296.

of judicial review.[323] The Court went on to examine, in substantial detail, the violations of the rights of defence, the right to effective judicial protection, and the right to property.[324] Here again, the Court was receptive of arguments focused on the international dimension of the freezing measures and of the role of the Security Council. It pointed out, for example, that due to the Security Council origin of the listings, 'overriding considerations to do with safety or the conduct of the international relations of the Community and of its Member States may militate against the communication of certain matters to the persons concerned and, therefore, against their being heard on those matters'.[325] When analysing whether the restrictions of the right to property resulting from asset freezes were a disproportionate and intolerable interference, the Court again emphasized the important objectives which the Security Council was pursuing:[326]

> With reference to an objective of general interest as fundamental to the international community as the fight, by all means, in accordance with the Charter of the United Nations, against the threats to international peace and security posed by acts of terrorism, the freezing of the funds, financial assets and other economic resources of the persons identified by the Security Council or the Sanctions Committee . . . cannot per se be regarded as inappropriate or disproportionate.

Of course, none of these considerations led the Court to conclude that it was appropriate to set aside the normal mechanisms of judicial protection, or to conclude that the EU version of the rule of law had not been violated. But the Court surely cannot be accused of not having engaged with the relevant international norms and with the role and function of the Security Council. There is clearly a dialogue in the sense that the Court accepted that the challenged regulation was not simply an internal piece of EU legislation, but had to be looked at in its international context. The Court also accepted that this context may require a different approach towards EU judicial review. However, the Court considered that these factors could not justify the fundamental flaws of a system under which the assets of individuals are frozen, for an indefinite period, whilst disregarding the most basic norms of due process.[327]

In one respect, perhaps, the Court could have done a little more to stimulate dialogue. The due process principles and norms which it applied are of course not a purely home-grown part of the EU version of the rule of law. They find their origin in the constitutional traditions common to the Member States, and even more so in the ECHR. What the Court did not draw attention to was the fact that international human rights instruments, such as the UN-based International Covenant on Civil and Political Rights (ICCPR), also confirm due process requirements.

[323] Ibid, paras 280–330. [324] Ibid, paras 331–372. [325] Ibid, para 342. [326] Ibid, para 363.

[327] Cf M Kumm, 'The Cosmopolitan Turn in Constitutionalism: On the Relationship between Constitutionalism in and beyond the State' in JL Dunoff and JP Trachtman (eds), *Ruling the World? Constitutionalism, International Law, and Global Governance* (CUP, 2009) 287–8.

Indeed, the ECHR and the ICCPR are very similar human rights instruments, and it would have been relatively straightforward for the Court to find substantive confirmation of the EU version of the rule of law in the ICCPR. In fact that Covenant has already been referred to in the Court's case law as constituting a source of fundamental rights as general principles of Community law, since all the Member States are parties to the ICCPR.[328]

This was perhaps a missed opportunity in *Kadi*. However, a simple failure to mention, for example, the ICCPR does not mean that the Court's approach is particularistic, even 'parochial'.[329] It remains a fact that even if the ICCPR was not mentioned, the due process standards which the Court applied are very similar to those of international human rights law. There is nothing parochial about the EU version of the rule of law. Fundamental rights as they are understood in Europe stem from a universalist era, and have their roots in the international system of protection of human rights as it developed after World War II. Indeed, the Court has an inherently internationalist outlook when it defines and applies fundamental rights as general principles of EU law: any international treaty which has been signed up to by all EU Member States may be a source for those general principles.[330] This means that the EU version of the rule of law is in any event a close relative of the international version.

To sum up, the Court was right to employ the EU version of the rule of law, because this version offered the most straightforward and appropriate route for protecting the rule of law.

Agreements pre-dating accession

As was mentioned, when the EEC Treaty was drafted the negotiators realized that the new Treaty could entail obligations and commitments for the Member States which would turn out to be in conflict with other international law commitments of the Member States, in particular as they resulted from international agreements which were in force. In so far as such prior agreements had only the Member States themselves as parties, the new EEC Treaty would simply override them,[331] but the Treaty could not of course do likewise with agreements between a Member State and a third country. For the purpose of resolving problems of conflicting commitments the negotiators drafted (current) Article 351 TFEU:

> The rights and obligations arising from agreements concluded before 1 January 1958 or, for acceding States, before the date of their accession, between one or more Member States

[328] See e.g. Case C–244/06 *Dynamic Medien Vertriebs* [2008] ECR I–505, para 39 and Case C–540/03 *Parliament v. Council* [2006] ECR I–5769, para 37.

[329] de Búrca (n 301 above) 4.

[330] See further I Butler and O De Schutter, 'Binding the EU to International Human Rights Law' (2008) 27 Yearbook of European Law 275, who argue that the EU should go further down this route.

[331] See Art 30(4)(b) VCLT.

on the one hand, and one or more third countries on the other, shall not be affected by the provisions of the Treaties.

To the extent that such agreements are not compatible with the Treaties, the Member State or States concerned shall take all appropriate steps to eliminate the incompatibilities established. Member States shall, where necessary, assist each other to this end and shall, where appropriate, adopt a common attitude.

In applying the agreements referred to in the first paragraph, Member States shall take into account the fact that the advantages accorded under this Treaty by each Member State form an integral part of the establishment of the Union and are thereby inseparably linked with the creation of common institutions, the conferring of powers upon them and the granting of the same advantages by all the other Member States.

The concept of this provision is straightforward, in particular as regards the first two paragraphs. The first paragraph recognizes what is in effect an established principle of international law, whereas the second paragraph instructs the Member States to resolve any problems of incompatibility to which the application of that principle may give rise. The meaning of the third paragraph is less straightforward, and there appears to be no case law clarifying that meaning in any substantial way. The case law has concentrated on interpreting and applying the first two paragraphs, and is analysed below.[332]

First paragraph

Article 351 TFEU refers to agreements concluded before 1 January 1958, when the EEC Treaty entered into force, or, for acceding States, agreements concluded before their accession. The latter element was inserted by the Treaty of Amsterdam, reflecting the principle contained in all accession treaties. The clarification is useful and highlights the actual relevance of Article 351, which is much greater for acceding and recently acceded Member States than for the original six. The term 'agreements' refers to all types of international treaty obligations.[333]

Timing of agreements

The question of the date of birth of an agreement arose as regards the transition from the original GATT to the establishment of the WTO. That transition was regulated in the WTO Agreement, which refers to 'GATT 1947' and 'GATT 1994', and provides that they are legally distinct.[334] In *T. Port v. Council*[335] and *Banatrading v. Council*[336] the applicants sought damages from the Community, *inter alia*, on the

[332] See also Kaddous (n 22 above) 273–300; Lenaerts and de Smijter (n 210 above) 114–22.

[333] Case C-62/98 *Commission v. Portugal* [2000] ECR I-5171, para 43.

[334] See Art II(4) WTO Agreement, and the provisions of GATT 1994, as part of Annex 1A to the WTO Agreement.

[335] Case T-2/99 *T Port v. Council* [2001] ECR II-2093.

[336] Case T-3/99 *Banatrading v. Council* [2001] ECR II-2123.

ground that the Council had violated (current) Article 351 TFEU by adopting legislation on imports of bananas which was in breach of certain GATT provisions. The CFI pointed out that GATT 1994 had been concluded after the entry into force of the Treaty, and did not accept the argument that GATT 1994 replicated GATT 1947. It referred to the rule that both agreements were legally distinct, and cited with approval an earlier Opinion of Elmer AG.[337] The Advocate General considered that it followed from Article 59(1)(a) VCLT[338] that GATT 1994 had replaced GATT 1947 with effect from 1 January 1995. The WTO Agreement and GATT 1994 were concluded, as regards commercial policy, by the Community, which had exclusive competence for commercial policy. Accordingly, claims arising from GATT 1994 could be addressed only to the Community and not the various Member States. The Court added that obligations arising from GATT 1994 fell, not on the Member States, but on the Community.[339]

That reasoning is not wholly persuasive. From a formal point of view the Court is correct that GATT 1947 and GATT 1994 are legally distinct, but a large number of Member States' obligations were identical in both agreements, and were transferred as smoothly as possible from the old agreement to the new one. Nor is it correct that GATT 1994 obligations fall only on the EU. Both the EU and the Member States are founding members of the WTO, and as such bound by WTO law.[340] GATT 1994 provisions, such as Article III.2 on national treatment in matters of taxation, may affect national measures as much as EU measures. No allocation of obligations or commitments took place at the time of the conclusion of the WTO Agreement. The argument that the Member States have been bound, in a continuous way since 1947, by a number of GATT obligations is difficult to rebut. However, one also needs to determine the third country to which the Member States may be committed: in another *T Port* ruling the Court of Justice correctly pointed out that, in a case involving imports in 1995 of bananas from Ecuador, (current) Article 351 TFEU could not be relevant because Ecuador joined the WTO only in 1996.[341]

There was also a lot of debate on the timing of agreements, from the point of view of Article 351 TFEU, in the *Open Skies* cases.[342] Those cases concerned

[337] Joined Cases C–364 and 365/95 *T Port v. Hauptzollamt Hamburg-Jonas* [1998] ECR I–1023, para 16 of the Opinion.

[338] '1. A treaty shall be considered as terminated if all the parties to it conclude a later treaty relating to the same subject matter and: (a) it appears from the later treaty or is otherwise established that the parties intended that the matter should be governed by that treaty.'

[339] *T Port* (n 335 above) and *Banatrading* (n 336 above), respectively paras 78–82 and 73–76. In *OGT* (n 151 above) para 29, the ECJ also expressed doubts as to whether (current) Art 351 TFEU applied to GATT 1994.

[340] Cf *Hermès* (n 86 above) para 24.

[341] *T Port* (n 337 above) paras 62–63.

[342] Case C–466/98 *Commission v. UK* [2002] ECR I–9427; Case C–467/98 *Commission v. Denmark* [2002] ECR I–9519; Case C–468/98 *Commission v. Sweden* [2002] ECR I–9575; Case C–469/98 *Commission v. Finland* [2002] ECR I–9627; Case C–471/98 *Commission v. Belgium* [2002] ECR I–9681; Case C–472/98 *Commission v. Luxembourg* [2002] ECR I–9741; Case C–475/98 *Commission v. Austria* [2002] ECR I–9797; and Case C–476/98 *Commission v. Germany* [2002] ECR I–9855; see Ch 3.

bilateral air transport agreements between, on the one hand, a large number of Member States and, on the other, the United States. The Commission claimed that those agreements, the original versions of which pre-dated the Treaty or accession, but which had been renegotiated in 1995 and 1996, violated exclusive Community competence as well as the Treaty provisions on the right of establishment. The Court, for the most part, rejected the claim of exclusive competence, but held that provisions on national ownership and control of airlines were in breach of (current) Article 49 TFEU. The Court did not examine the Commission's alternative claim that the Member States in question had violated their obligations under (current) Article 351 TFEU. It did not feel the need to rule conclusively on the question of whether the renegotiations led to the existence of new agreements. It was satisfied that the renegotiations had led to new and significant international commitments and held in one of the judgments that, although (current) Article 351 TFEU applied to rights and obligations flowing from agreements concluded by Member States before the Treaty entered into force, it could not apply to amendments which Member States made to such agreements by entering into new commitments after the entry into force of the Treaty.[343]

Rights and obligations

The very first case on (current) Article 351 TFEU also concerned the relationship between GATT and Community law. The Commission claimed that customs duties which Italy applied to imports from other Member States violated the Treaty, and Italy sought to defend itself by invoking the provisions of the 1956 Geneva Protocol to GATT. The Court agreed with the Commission that the term 'rights and obligations' in (current) Article 351 TFEU referred, as regards the 'rights', to the rights of third countries and, as regards the 'obligations', to the obligations of Member States; by virtue of the principles of international law, by assuming a new obligation which was incompatible with rights held under a prior treaty, a State *ipso facto* gave up the exercise of these rights to the extent necessary for the performance of its new obligations. In matters governed by the EEC Treaty, that Treaty took precedence over agreements concluded between Member States before its entry into force, including agreements made within the framework of GATT.[344]

The Court thus confirmed from the outset that the first paragraph of (current) Article 351 TFEU only concerns the rights of third countries and the corresponding obligations of the Member States. Indeed, as Mischo AG stated in *Commission v. Portugal*, the provision is merely declaratory, an expression of the fundamental principle of *pacta sunt servanda*.[345] In relations between the Member States the Treaty

[343] *Commission v. Germany* (n 342 above) para 69.

[344] Case 10/61 *Commission v. Italy* [1962] ECR 1, para 10.

[345] *Commission v. Portugal* (n 333 above) Opinion of Mischo AG, para 56.

obligations automatically prevail over prior agreements, again in accordance with international treaty law,[346] as the Court often recalled.[347]

It is none the less not wholly excluded that, also in relations between Member States, it may be necessary for a Member State to respect obligations towards third countries. As Warner AG pointed out in *Henn and Darby*, a multilateral agreement concluded by Member States and third countries may create multilateral obligations between all the parties to it, so that third countries have a right to the observation of its provisions even in relations between Member States (e.g. in intra-Community trade).[348] International environmental agreements are often considered to create such multilateral obligations.[349]

A further question which arises concerns the position of private parties, who may have rights under a pre-accession agreement. It is clear that provisions in international agreements may confer individual rights.[350] Are such rights also covered by Article 351 TFEU? The Court of Justice touched upon this in *Burgoa*. The Court reasoned that the provision could not have the effect of altering the nature of the rights which might flow from the international agreements in question. It followed that that provision did not have the effect of conferring upon individuals who relied upon such agreements rights which the national courts of the Member States had to uphold. Nor did it adversely affect the rights which individuals might derive from such an agreement.[351] In other words, Article 351 TFEU is completely neutral as to any rights which individuals may have under the provisions of an international agreement concluded by a Member State before the entry into force of the Treaty.[352] For example, where a national legal order does not recognize the direct effect of such an agreement, individuals cannot invoke Article 351 TFEU to circumvent that non-recognition. As Capotorti AG pointed out in *Burgoa*, Community law does not require performance by a Member State of the agreements in question.[353]

On the other hand, the logic of this position, and indeed of Article 351 TFEU as an expression of principles of international law, is that private rights are also protected by the first paragraph. In other words, a private party which has rights

[346] See Art 30 VCLT.

[347] E.g. Case 121/85 *Conegate v. HM Customs & Excise* [1986] ECR 1007, para 25; Case 286/86 *Ministère public v. Deserbais* [1988] ECR 4907, para 18; Case 235/87 *Matteuci v. Communauté française of Belgium* [1988] ECR 5589, para 21; Case T–69/89 *RTE v. Commission* [1991] ECR II–485, paras 102–103; Case C–546/07 *Commission v. Germany*, judgment of 21 January 2010, para 44.

[348] Case 34/79 *R v. Henn and Darby* [1979] ECR 3795, 3833.

[349] Pauwelyn (n 193 above).

[350] E.g. *Lagrand* (n 206 above).

[351] Case 812/79 *Attorney General v. Burgoa* [1980] ECR 2787, para 10. See also J Klabbers, *Treaty Conflict and the European Union* (CUP, 2009) 129–30.

[352] In *OGT* (n 151 above) para 30, the Court of Justice recalled that the first para of (current) Art 351 TFEU does not confer rights; the CFI similarly held in *T Port* (n 335 above) para 83 and *Banatrading* (n 336 above) para 81, that the provision is not intended to confer rights on individuals, as required by the principles of non-contractual liability.

[353] *Burgoa* (n 351 above) Opinion of Capotorti AG, para 3.

under a pre-accession agreement is entitled to those rights, and the Member State is permitted to respect its corresponding obligation, even in the face of incompatible EU law. Bilateral investment treaties (BITs) involving a Member State offer an example of such agreements. Investors have certain rights, which are typically enforceable through arbitration, and there seem to be no good reasons for EU law not to respect those rights, when they are based on pre-accession investment treaties. It is moreover arguable that, in this respect, no distinction needs to be made between agreements between a Member State and a non-member State, and agreements between two Member States. There are indeed many investment treaties between Member States, one of which is usually a Central- or East-European country which concluded such a treaty before joining the EU. Under international law those treaties remain in force,[354] and investors should be able to enforce any rights they have as against the relevant Member State, even if that involves derogating from EU law.

It is true, however, that the Court of Justice has always upheld the principle that Article 351 TFEU cannot be applied in intra-Community relations. A recent example is the judgment in *Bogiatzi*, a case concerning the Warsaw Convention,[355] an agreement concluded by the Member States but not the EU, and an EU regulation on air carrier liability in the event of accidents. Ms Bogiatzi claimed compensation for the injury she suffered as a result of an accident while boarding a Luxair aeroplane. She based that claim on both the Warsaw Convention and the regulation, and questions were referred to the Court of Justice, the first of which was whether the convention came within the Court's jurisdiction. In connection with that question Luxair argued that the issue was really whether the national court should apply the convention, pursuant to (current) Article 351 TFEU. The Court simply responded by stating that it was settled case law that the provisions of an agreement concluded prior to the entry into force of the Treaty could not be relied on in intra-Community relations.[356] The judgment is not wholly conclusive, however, simply because the Court was not invited to consider whether Article 351 TFEU could also shield private rights. It was moreover not the person on whom the rights were conferred, Ms Bogiatzi, who attempted to rely on (current) Article 351 TFEU.

A further point is that Article 351 TFEU is inapplicable where an agreement allows, but does not require, a measure which appears to be contrary to EU law.[357]

Finally, it is hardly worth adding that the rights and obligations in question need to be still in force; developments in international law, for example in the form of the

[354] The 2004 Act of Accession does not expressly terminate or amend those agreements.

[355] Convention for the Unification of Certain Rules Relating to International Carriage by Air, signed at Warsaw on 12 October 1929, as amended by the four additional protocols signed at Montreal on 25 September 1975.

[356] *Bogiatzi* (n 255 above) paras 16–20. See also Case C–533/08 *TNT Expres Nederland v. AXA Versicherung*, judgment of 4 May 2010, para 52.

[357] Case C–324/95 *Evans Medical and Macfarlan Smith* [1995] ECR I–563 and Case C–124/95 *The Queen, ex parte Centro-Com v. HM Treasury and Bank of England* [1997] ECR I–81, para 60.

conclusion of further, incompatible international agreements by a Member State, may be such that an agreement concluded before the entry into force of the Treaty no longer produces effect.[358] An extensive application of this principle can be found in *Budějovický Budvar*. The question there was whether the Czech Republic had succeeded in the rights of the former Czechoslovak Socialist Republic under a bilateral convention between the latter and Austria. The Court made an extensive analysis of that international law question of State succession.[359]

Legal effects

The first paragraph of Article 351 TFEU provides that rights and obligations 'shall not be affected'. The effects of that provision were considered in cases concerning a French prohibition on nightwork for women. That prohibition implemented ILO Convention No 89, which France had concluded before the entry into force of the EEC Treaty. It was argued that the prohibition was contrary to Community law on sex equality. In *Stoeckel* the Court did not examine the effects of (current) Article 351 TFEU, and simply established a breach of Community law. However, Tesauro AG looked at the convention, but considered that it could not be relied upon because Community law did not require nightwork for women. It was open to France to prohibit all nightwork, thereby removing the discrimination, or else to denounce the convention.[360]

Two years later the issue was again before the Court in *Levy*, a case in which the referring court expressly inquired into the relationship between Convention No 89 and Community law. Again Mr Tesauro was Advocate General, but he took a slightly different line. He recalled that France should remove any incompatibility by either prohibiting all nightwork or denouncing the Convention. He then distinguished the second paragraph of (current) Article 351 TFEU, which was the basis for that obligation, from the first. He regarded the two paragraphs as separate, and considered that, as the French legislation stood, there was a clear conflict between a Community rule and an earlier contractual provision. That conflict was governed by the first paragraph of (current) Article 351 TFEU, according to which priority was to be given to the Member State's international obligations. The national court could not give precedence to Community law on the ground that France had not taken all the necessary steps to ensure that Community law was observed, because of the letter and spirit of (current) Article 351 TFEU: such a decision would lead to the penalization not only and not so much of the Member State concerned, but precisely of those non-member countries whose rights Article 351 TFEU was intended to protect.[361] Unfortunately, the Court did not engage with

[358] Case C–158/91 *Levy* [1993] ECR I–4287, paras 19–20.

[359] Case C–216/01 *Budějovický Budvar, národní podnik v. Rudolf Ammersin GmbH* [2003] ECR I–13617, paras 143–166.

[360] Case C–345/89 *Stoeckel* [1991] ECR I–4047, Opinion of Tesauro AG, para 11.

[361] *Levy* (n 358 above) Opinion of Tesauro AG, paras 6–8.

those issues, and simply left it to the referring court to determine which obligations the convention imposed and to ascertain to what extent its provisions constituted an obstacle to the application of Community law.[362]

The Opinion of Tesauro AG in *Levy* can be contrasted with the Opinion of Lenz AG in *Ministère public v. Asjes*, where he considered that a national court should examine whether the Member State in question had complied with the second paragraph of (current) Article 351 TFEU. If the conclusion was that it had not, the national authorities could not rely upon their unlawful omission to take measures against transport operators on the basis of pre-Treaty international commitments.[363]

On balance the approach by Tesauro AG is preferable. Were a national court to give precedence, on the basis of EU law principles, to EU law over a Member State's international obligations, the Treaty instruction of respect for international law embodied in Article 351 TFEU would not in effect be respected, and EU law would impose a breach of international law. The judgment in *Budějovický Budvar* appears to confirm this. The case, mentioned above, concerned the question of whether the Czech Republic had succeeded the Czechoslovak Socialist Republic. But the Court also spelled out the task of the national court, if the latter concluded that there was indeed such succession. The Court drew attention to the obligations of Austria under the second paragraph of (current) Article 351 TFEU. It followed that the national court had to ascertain whether a possible incompatibility between the Treaty and the bilateral convention could be avoided by interpreting that convention, to the extent possible and in compliance with international law, in such a way that it was consistent with Community law. If it proved impracticable to do so, it was open to Austria to take the appropriate steps, while, however, remaining obliged to eliminate any incompatibilities. It further noted that this could involve having to denounce the agreement. However, pending the success of one of the methods referred to in the second paragraph of (current) Article 351 TFEU, the first paragraph permitted the Member State to continue to apply the agreement in so far as it contained obligations which remained binding on that State under international law.[364]

A similar approach was taken in *Commission v. Austria*, a case involving the lawfulness, under Community law, of the prohibition of the employment of women in mining. The Commission claimed that this constituted a breach of Community law requirements of equal treatment of men and women. Austria, however, relied on Convention 45 of the ILO, a pre-accession agreement. Again the Court pointed out that Austria was under an obligation to remove the incompatibilities between that convention and Community law, and that this could require the denunciation of the convention. None the less, it had to be noted that the only occasion on which

[362] Ibid, para 21 of the judgment.

[363] Joined Cases 209 to 213/84 *Ministère public v. Lucas Asjes* [1986] ECR 1425, 1453.

[364] *Budějovický Budvar* (n 359 above) paras 168–172.

Austria could, following its accession to the EU, have denounced the convention in accordance with its rules was 30 May 1997. At that time the incompatibility with the relevant provisions of Community law had not been suficiently clearly established for that Member State to be bound to denounce the convention. The next opportunity for denunciation was to occur on the expiry of another ten years. It followed that, by maintaining in force the national provisions in issue Austria had not failed to fulfil its obligations under Community law.[365]

The approach of the two judgments is therefore to establish a close link between the two paragraphs of Article 351 TFEU. The opportunity to continue to invoke the first paragraph, and therefore to derogate from EU law, depends on whether the Member State in question should have established the incompatibility and had the opportunity to remedy it. Moreover, national courts are under a duty of consistent interpretation, and should therefore avoid establishing conflict between a pre-accession agreement and EU law.

In the context of the legal effects of the first paragraph of Article 351 TFEU one should also mention the division of judicial functions between the Court of Justice and national courts under the preliminary ruling system. The Court's jurisdiction under Article 267 TFEU is limited to interpreting EU law or ruling on its validity; it is not within the Court's province to interpret national law, or indeed a Member State's international commitments. In *Henn and Darby* Warner AG considered that where an international agreement had a bearing on a question referred to the Court, and no one suggested that the agreement was open to different interpretations, the Court could answer the question on the assumption that the agreement meant what it apparently said. But if there was dispute over the meaning of the agreement, the Court had to give alternative answers and leave it to the national court or tribunal to decide.[366] In *Levy*,[367] *Minne*,[368] *Centro-Com*,[369] and *Budějovický Budvar*[370] the Court each time left it to the referring court to determine the extent of the Member State's international obligations. It is none the less possible to read into the Court's ruling in *Centro-Com* some degree of scepticism as to whether there was actually a conflict between the Community law provisions and the international obligation.[371]

The legal effects of (current) Article 351 TFEU were also extensively discussed in the *Kadi* litigation, set out and analysed above. The Court clearly imposed limits on the scope of this Treaty provision, by stating that it could not be understood to authorize any derogation from the principles of liberty, democracy, and respect for human rights and fundamental freedoms enshrined in (then) Article 6(1) EU (currently reflected in Article 2 TEU). (Current) Article 351 TFEU could in no circumstances permit any challenge to the principles that formed the very foundations of

[365] Case C–203/03 *Commission v. Austria* [2005] ECR I–935, paras 57–64.
[366] *Henn and Darby* (n 348 above) 3853. [367] N 358 above, para 21.
[368] Case C–13/93 *Minne* [1994] ECR I–371, para 18. [369] N 254 above, para 58.
[370] N 359 above. [371] See Ch 12 for further details.

the Community legal order, one of which was the protection of fundamental rights. There was a difference here with other provisions of primary law, such as the Treaty provisions on the common commercial policy, which could be derogated from.[372] Maduro AG adopted a similar approach. He stated that a Member State, when acting within the scope of EU law, was always called upon to respect fundamental rights, as protected under EU law, and that (current) Article 351 TFEU could not disturb that obligation.[373] There may thus be situations where international obligations of a Member State have to give way to fundamental principles of EU law, notwithstanding the generally worded scope for derogations in Article 351 TFEU.

Obligations of the institutions

In *Burgoa* the Court, following Capotorti AG, clarified that, although the first paragraph of (current) Article 351 TFEU mentions only the obligations of the Member States, it would not achieve its purpose if it did not imply a duty on the part of the institutions of the Community not to impede the performance of the obligations of the Member States which stemmed from a prior agreement. However, that duty of the institutions was directed only to permitting the Member State concerned to perform its obligations under the prior agreement and did not bind the Community as regards the non-member countries.[374]

That principle was invoked in *T Port* and *Banatrading*,[375] where the applicants claimed that the violation of (current) Article 351 TFEU triggered the Community's non-contractual liability. As mentioned, the CFI first of all held that GATT 1994 constituted a new agreement. It further recalled that (current) Article 351 TFEU was not intended to confer rights, with the result that one of the conditions for non-contractual liability was not complied with.

Second paragraph

Incompatibilities

In some cases it may not be straightforward to establish an incompatibility between a pre-accession agreement and EU law. In a series of recent judgments the Court examined the incompatibility of BITs concluded by Member States prior to their accession with EU law.[376] What was notable was that the Commission did not claim that, as those agreements and EU law stood, there was as yet any substantive incompatibility. The argument was rather that those agreements, which all had so-called free-transfer clauses, could give rise to such an incompatibility if and when the Council decided to make use of its powers under certain Treaty provisions. The clauses typically guarantee the free transfer, without undue delay and in freely convertible

[372] N 8 above, paras 301–304. [373] Ibid, Opinion of Maduro AG, para 30.

[374] *Burgoa* (n 351 above) para 9. [375] Nn 335 and 336 above.

[376] Case C–205/06 *Commission v. Austria* [2009] ECR I–1301; Case C–249/06 *Commission v. Sweden* [2009] ECR I–1335; and Case C–118/07 *Commission v. Finland* [2009] ECR I–10889.

currency, of payments connected with an investment. They were thus in accordance with the free movement of capital, which extends to movements between Member States and third countries (see current Article 63 TFEU). However, under (current) Articles 64(2), 66, and (with amendments) 215 TFEU the Council was granted the power to restrict, in certain circumstances, the movement of capital and payments between Member States and third countries, including the movements covered by the transfer clauses in issue. The Commission was concerned that the investment treaties could hinder the Council in making use of that power.

Advocate General Maduro was of the opinion that the investment treaties in issue were not incompatible with the relevant EC Treaty provisions as such. Those provisions did not establish an exclusive Community competence; competence to adopt measures on the free movement of capital was shared with the Member States. To hold that the investment treaties were incompatible with the shared or concurrent powers which the Community had in this field would amount to making those powers exclusive.

The Advocate General nevertheless concluded that there was an incompatibility with Community law, namely with (current) Article 4(3) TEU, embodying the principle of loyalty. He drew an analogy with case law on directives whose period for transposition has not yet expired. He proposed that the Court rule that Member States were obliged to refrain from any measures liable seriously to compromise the exercise of Community competence. The Advocate General considered that this principle had been violated, particularly since some of the relevant Treaty provisions allowed the Community to adopt urgent measures. To do so could be made more difficult because of the transfer clauses in BITs.[377]

The Court's analysis was very brief. It described the powers of the Community to restrict, in certain specific circumstances, movements of capital and payments between the Member States and third countries. It then established that such measures had to be capable of being applied immediately—this was necessary to ensure their effectiveness. Such immediate application could extend to States with which Sweden and Austria have concluded investment treaties. The Court then concluded that there was an incompatibility between the Council's powers to adopt unilateral restrictive measures and the investment treaties—at least in so far as those treaties did not allow the Member States to exercise their rights and to fulfil their obligations under Community law and in so far as there was no international law mechanism to achieve the same result. Arguments by Sweden and Austria concerning the scope for renegotiation, suspension, or denunciation were rejected as insufficient to remove the incompatibility. The Court concluded by instructing the Commission and the Member States to adopt a common attitude—indeed the issue of transfer clauses is not limited to treaties concluded by Sweden and Austria, as all Member States are bound by treaties containing such clauses.[378]

[377] Ibid, Opinion of Maduro AG in *Commission v. Austria* and *Commission v. Sweden*.
[378] Ibid.

The judgments call for some comments. First, one hopes that the Court is not in these judgments establishing a broader principle that any international agreements concluded by the Member States, which may make the exercise of shared EU competences more difficult, are incompatible with EU law. That would indeed turn shared competences into exclusive ones. It cannot be right that the Member States are in breach of EU law whenever they conclude an international agreement in an area of shared competence, simply because at some later stage the EU may decide to adopt its own legislation, which may differ from the terms of the agreement. The judgments have to be read in the light of the particular legal context: the relevant Treaty provisions permit the EU to adopt urgent measures, and this may justify finding that any Member State agreements which would pose problems for the adoption and implementation of such measures are incompatible with the Treaties.

Secondly, the Court was very dismissive of the opportunities offered by treaty law to suspend or terminate the relevant treaties, if the need were to arise. Those opportunities were 'too uncertain in [their] effects'.[379] The Court's position was that, if and when the Council decided to take restrictive measures, nothing should stand in its way. International law obligations of the Member States should not form an obstacle of any kind. It is questionable whether this is the right approach to take towards an area of international law in which all the EU Member States are active. In *Intertanko*, analysed above, the Court suggested that, where all Member States were bound by an international agreement (in that case Marpol 73/78), the principle of loyalty had consequences for EC acts: it was then incumbent upon the Court to interpret such acts taking account of the agreement.[380] Should not the Council equally take account of international investment treaties binding the Member States when considering whether to take measures restricting capital movement?

Elimination

The second paragraph requires that the Member States take all appropriate steps to eliminate any incompatibilities. In most cases this will involve the renegotiation of the international agreement. Obviously, a Member State will need the co-operation of the third countries concerned. Such co-operation may be more or less forthcoming, depending on the interests of those countries or other factors. The ultimate question is therefore how a Member State needs to act where a third country is unwilling to renegotiate.

In *Lucas Asjes* Lenz AG remarked that, in such cases, the Member States were required to denounce the agreement,[381] and in *Stoeckel*[382] and *Levy*[383] Tesauro AG took the same view. The Court of Justice addressed the issue in two *Commission v. Portugal* cases.[384] Those cases concerned Portugal's obligations under a regulation

[379] *Commission v. Austria* (n 343 above) para 40. [380] N 113 above.

[381] *Lucas Asjes* (n 365 above) 1453. [382] N 360 above, para 11 of the Opinion.

[383] N 358 above, para 6 of the Opinion.

[384] *Commission v. Portugal* (n 333 above) and Case C–84/98 *Commission v. Portugal* [2000] ECR I–5215.

concerning freedom to provide services in the maritime transport sector.[385] The regulation provided that the Member States had to phase out or adjust cargo-sharing arrangements contained in existing bilateral agreements with third countries by a given date (Articles 3 and 4). The Commission claimed that Portugal had breached those obligations by neither adjusting nor denouncing agreements with Angola and with the Federal Republic of Yugoslavia. It did not therefore base its action on failure to comply with (current) Article 351 TFEU, but in its defence Portugal relied on that provision, arguing that the article required denunciation only exceptionally and in extreme circumstances. It further argued that, in the circumstances, denunciation would involve a disproportionate disregard of the interests linked to its foreign policy as compared with the Community interest.

Mischo AG considered that denunciation of a bilateral agreement could indeed be an act which governments found intrinsically repugnant, but the principle of uniform implementation of Community law carried with it requirements that should override the diplomatic interests of Member States. In his view it would be rather paradoxical if, having required Member States to ensure that Community law takes precedence even over their constitutional rules, case law should allow their diplomatic interests, the definition of which was very often somewhat vague, to prevail over that same law. It followed that denunciation was among the 'appropriate steps' required by the second paragraph of (current) Article 351 TFEU.[386]

The Court followed the Opinion. It recalled that the purpose of the first paragraph of (current) Article 351 TFEU was to make it clear, in accordance with the principles of international law, that application of the EC Treaty did not affect the duty of the Member State concerned to respect the rights of third countries under a prior agreement and to perform its obligations thereunder. It followed that Portugal had to respect in all cases the rights which Angola (and the Federal Republic of Yugoslavia—see the other case) derived from the contested agreement. However, that agreement contained a denunciation clause, so that denunciation would not encroach upon the rights which the other party derived from that agreement. Although the Member States had a choice as to the appropriate steps to be taken, they were nevertheless under an obligation to eliminate any incompatibilities existing between a pre-Community convention and the Treaty. If a Member State encountered difficulties which made adjustment of an agreement impossible, an obligation to denounce that agreement could therefore not be excluded. As regards the argument that such denunciation would involve a disproportionate disregard of the foreign policy interests of the Portuguese Republic as compared with the Community interest, it had to be pointed out that the balance between the foreign policy interests of a Member State and the Community interest was already incorporated in (current) Article 351 TFEU, in that it allowed a Member State not to apply a Community provision in order to respect the rights of third countries

[385] Council Regulation 4055/86 [1986] OJ L378/1.

[386] *Commission v. Portugal* (n 333 above) Opinion of Mischo AG, paras 60–61.

deriving from a prior agreement and to perform its obligations thereunder. The article allowed them to choose the appropriate means of rendering the agreement concerned compatible with Community law.[387]

The Court thus shows itself willing to accept that a Member State may face difficulties in removing incompatibilities with EU law, but ultimately, where the other party is intransigent, an agreement must be denounced. Foreign policy interests of the Member States cannot override that obligation, and a Member State cannot in principle argue that denunciation would be too harmful to those interests. That approach is also evident in the *Open Skies* cases,[388] where a number of Member States argued that the United States proved unwilling to renegotiate clauses on national ownership and control of airlines. The Court held that the Member States could simply not, when renegotiating the agreements, maintain in force a clause which infringed the rights of Community airlines arising from (current) Article 49 TFEU.[389] Particularly indicative is the Court's statement in *Commission v. Belgium* that the efforts made by Belgium in 1995 to eliminate the incompatibility of the clause with (current) Article 49 TFEU, however commendable, were clearly insufficient to disturb the finding of a breach of that Treaty provision.[390]

Those are the principles resulting from the case law. There is no suggestion that there may ever be cases where the EU itself is required to act so as to remove incompatibilities, for example by amending EU law. In practice, however, there may well be such instances. In political terms it may in some cases be preferable to take such action rather than requiring the Member States to renegotiate or denounce their international treaty obligations. Particularly where important multilateral agreements are involved, it may not always be possible to take the logic of Article 351 TFEU to its ultimate conclusion.

Conclusions

This chapter has extensively examined the various legal effects which different forms of international law produce in the EU legal order. The task of discovering and determining those effects has fallen almost exclusively on the Court of Justice. The case law in this area is very much the counterpart of the case law on the direct effect and supremacy of the Treaties and of internal legislation, the defining features of European constitutionalism. Because the Court had decided to set Community law, as a new legal order, apart from international law, it was forced to construct a relationship between those two legal systems. The Court was compelled to engage in judicial policy-making, as the E(E)C Treaty only provided that agreements concluded by the Community were binding, and contained no further instructions.

387 Ibid, paras 44–50 of the judgment.

388 N 342 above.

389 See e.g. *Commission v. Denmark* (n 342 above) para 134.

390 *Commission v. Belgium* (n 342 above) para 143.

One may surmise that this gave rise to tensions. On the one hand, the Court could give priority to the desire to affirm the new legal order by distinguishing it clearly from international law, which could be done by restricting the effects of international law in Community law. On the other, it seemed incongruous for a legal order which owed its very birth and existence to international law to become unreceptive to the latter.

After nearly forty years of case law one can certainly not conclude that the EU legal order is hostile towards international law. The lack of direct effect of GATT and WTO law has always occupied a central position in analyses and assessments of the Court's attitude towards international law, not unjustifiably in the light of the importance of those agreements, in particular for the Community and its policies. However, the general picture is positive.[391] The Court readily accepts that international agreements may have direct effect, and unless the structure and nature of the agreement preclude such effect, which hitherto is the case only for the GATT and the WTO Agreement, and for UNCLOS, the same criteria and reasoning apply as in the case of 'internal' EU law. The Court also accepts that there may be cases where effect needs to be given to general international law in ways which have hitherto not been customary (at least not in practice) in the legal systems of the Member States.[392]

This receptive attitude towards international law has an important political dimension. It reflects the EU's active and ever-growing involvement in international relations. Indeed, the EU has not in any way proved to be an inward-looking organization of States, however much one may feel inclined to criticize certain external (and internal) policies. On the contrary, it is an exporter of international co-operation—witness the very dense network of bilateral agreements with third countries and the very active involvement in multilateral negotiations and law-making. This is reflected in the current version of the TEU, which in Article 3(5), on the Union's objectives, provides that the Union 'shall contribute . . . to strict observance and development of international law, including respect for the principles of the United Nations Charter'.

The case law on the lack of direct effect of WTO law may seem a rather ugly blot on this general picture. However, it is not only, as was argued, justified in the current constellation; it is also of more limited scope than is often thought. The principles of consistent interpretation and of implementation permit that effect be given to WTO law in certain cases.

The lack of direct effect of WTO law is closely linked to the fact that the WTO has its own sophisticated system of dispute settlement—or better, its own judicial system. The evolution of the doctrine of direct effect of international law cannot be properly understood without involving the relations between the various judicial

[391] Contrary to evaluations in some of the literature, e.g., ibid, 129; M Cremona, 'External Relations and External Competence: The Emergence of an Integrated Policy' in P Craig and G de Búrca (eds), *The Evolution of EU Law* (OUP, 1999) 144.

[392] See the analysis by Jacobs AG in *Racke* (n 65 above).

actors. The international legal order is increasingly judicialized, and giving direct effect to an international agreement may involve submitting to the case law of an international court or tribunal. That may in effect be the biggest obstacle for greater receptiveness to international law. It is deplorable that the Court of Justice appears unwilling to consider the legal effects of WTO dispute decisions on their merits. There is room for debate as regards the direct effect of such decisions, but even in a case like *Ikea Wholesale*,[393] where it would have been straightforward to interpret the anti-dumping regulation in accordance with the Appellate Body's case law, the Court declined to accept that that case law produced any effect.

In the case of the Court of Justice, it is interesting to juxtapose the Court's relationship with two of the most significant international judiciaries from the perspective of EU law, i.e. the WTO's Appellate Body, and the ECtHR. There is no complete submission in either case, in the former on the ground of the lack of direct effect of WTO law, in the latter because the Community is not yet a party to the ECHR, partly owing to *Opinion 2/94*.[394]

This chapter also shows that the concept of direct effect itself, and its relationship with the various forms of actions and remedies which the Treaties offer, continue to be enigmatic. Over the last decade the Court has not attempted to keep the concept of direct effect nice and simple, either in the internal or the external sphere.[395] Perhaps this is unavoidable, but the effectiveness and coherence of the EU legal order none the less require clarity at this fundamental conceptual level. As was suggested in the first edition of this study, it is time to concentrate more on the question of whether a provision confers rights, or is intended to confer rights, on private parties. The EU citizen and the rights conferred on the citizen are becoming more central to the EU legal order. We should thus move away from focusing too closely on the abstract enforcement dimension of direct effect. Looking at the subject more from the rights angle would also permit a better connection with the system of remedies: where a directly effective right is recognized, there should be a remedy, following the treasured principle of English law, *ubi ius, ibi remedium*. In *Intertanko* the Court appeared to reason along those lines,[396] but unfortunately adopted a far too restrictive position.

The Court has therefore become less receptive towards international law. Of course, that statement also puts *Kadi and Al Barakaat* in the spotlight.[397] However, that judgment rejected a much more intrusive effect of international law than classic direct effect cases. The Court was surely right to deny that the UN Charter is capable of excluding judicial review of EU acts on the basis of the EU's very foundations, which include the protection of fundamental rights. No mature constitutional order is willing to accept such international law pre-eminence, in the absence of equivalent standards at the international level.

[393] N 126 above. [394] *Opinion 2/94 re Accession to the ECHR* [1996] ECR I–1759.
[395] Cf S Prechal, 'Does Direct Effect Still Matter?' (2000) 37 CML Rev 1047.
[396] N 113 above. [397] N 8 above.

Part III

Policies

10

Common commercial policy

Introduction

The common commercial policy is clearly the EU's most developed external policy. It was part of the essential arrangement of the European Economic Community, based as the Community was on a customs union (see old Article 23 EC), the GATT definition of which requires not only a common customs tariff on imports from third countries but also a common policy on other trade matters. As was analysed in Chapter 2, the EU's competence in external trade matters is exclusive, which means that, in principle, the policy is completely in the hands of the EU institutions, and the Member States have no powers in this field. In practice, though, this lack of national powers needs to be qualified. External trade policy interacts with general foreign policy, and to the extent that the Member States continue to have powers in that area, there is a frontier zone where the principle of exclusivity does not fully come into play. Also, the EU's common foreign and security policy affects the exercise of commercial policy powers in various ways.[1]

The common commercial policy none the less remains the centre-piece of the EU's external policies. Nearly all bilateral agreements which the EU concludes with third countries open with a chapter on trade, which is often the core of the bilateral relationship. That is so in particular because many of those agreements establish preferential trade relations (mostly free-trade areas), notwithstanding the non-discrimination principles of WTO law. Trade is also at the heart of the EU's 'external' legislation: as there has so far been only limited harmonization of Member States' policies on immigration and the movement of people across the EU's external borders, the regulation of imports and exports is where such external legislation is mainly located. Furthermore, the common commercial policy has a strong legal dimension, because of the extensive use, for about fifty years now, of various types of legal instruments. This is a long history of law-making, with a large measure of judicial overview owing to the European Courts' full jurisdiction in trade matters.

This chapter aims to conduct a survey of the main legal components of the policy, so as to complement the chapter on the EU's competences in this field, by

[1] See Ch 12.

giving some insights into the legal dimension of the practical operation of external trade policy.[2] The chapter consists of three general sections. The first briefly examines a few essential principles of the common commercial policy (there are not many). The second section provides an overview of the main legal instruments through which the policy is conducted, particularly at the internal, legislative level. The third section briefly discusses the actors of the common commercial policy, i.e. the institutions which are involved.

There are of course many other components of the common commercial policy which merit further study, such as the range and network of trade agreements with third countries, and the case law of the EU courts on judicial review of commercial policy measures. An in-depth and comprehensive legal analysis of the policy is, however, not possible within the scope of this study.

Principles

As was mentioned in Chapter 2, the TFEU does not contain much on what the common commercial policy should look like or how it should be conducted. Article 206 TFEU provides that, by establishing a customs union, the Union shall contribute, in the common interest, to the harmonious development of world trade, the progressive abolition of restrictions on international trade and on foreign direct investment, and the lowering of customs barriers. The common commercial policy should therefore generally be geared towards trade and investment liberalization, and should not simply be an instrument of trade protection. The wording of the article is aspirational, however, and the Court of Justice has refused to use it as a benchmark for the review of particular trade measures.[3]

Article 207 TFEU gives some description of the content of the common commercial policy. It states that the policy shall be based on uniform principles, particularly in regard to changes in tariff rates, the conclusion of tariff and trade agreements relating to trade in goods and services, and the commercial aspects of intellectual property, foreign direct investment, the achievement of uniformity in measures of liberalization, export policy, and measures to protect trade such as those to be taken in the event of dumping or subsidies. Again as analysed in Chapter 2, the Court has stated that this is a non-exhaustive enumeration. Article 207 also describes the procedure for adopting trade policy measures and for concluding agreements in this field.

In Article 207 the Treaty proclaims that the common commercial policy must be based on uniform principles. Uniformity, which is the substantive counterpart of the rule of exclusive Union competence, is indeed a core feature of the policy.

[2] See also I Macleod, ID Hendry, and S Hyett, *The External Relations of the European Communities* (OUP, 1996) ch 12.

[3] Case 112/80 *Dürbeck v. Hauptzollamt Frankfurt am Main-Flughafen* [1981] ECR 1095 para 44.

It is a notion which has given rise to some case law, which is analysed in the next subsection. From the case law on imports of goods one may further distill what may be called the principle of assimilation: once goods have been imported into the EU they fully benefit from the EU internal market. This is in fact as much a principle of the internal market as it is a principle of the common commercial policy, but it is none the less worth exploring a little further. The third subsection examines whether there is also a principle of non-discrimination in the EU's external trade relations.

The principle of uniformity

It is partly on the basis of the principle of uniformity that the Court in *Opinion 1/75* decided that the (then) Community's competence in trade matters was exclusive.[4] Not only should all essential rules concerning external trade be adopted by the EU, but they should also lay down a uniform regime for imports and exports. As was mentioned, this is required, at least to a large degree, by the provisions of Article XXIV GATT, which provide that a customs union must constitute a single customs territory where 'substantially the same duties and other regulations of commerce are applied by each of the members of the union to the trade of territories not included in the union'.[5] It is also required by the operation of the internal market. Due to the principle of assimilation (see below), all goods imported from third countries fully benefit from the internal market once they have cleared customs. That principle can function effectively only in the presence of a uniform external trade regime. If the common commercial policy were to lay down that a particular non-EU product cannot be imported into a particular Member State, but can be imported into some or all other Member States, then free circulation in the internal market could be used for the purpose of circumventing the prohibition on importation, and the differential policy would be defeated.

Despite the Treaty's insistence on uniformity which, according to the pre-Amsterdam version, had to be achieved by the end of the transitional period (1 January 1970), it took much longer before a satisfactory level of uniformity was reached. The customs union in a strict sense, i.e. the abolition of customs duties in trade between Member States and the adoption of the common customs tariff, was completed in the course of 1968. However, at the time the Member States continued to apply quantitative restrictions on imports of certain products from certain non-member countries, and the (then) Community proved unable either to abolish such quotas or to replace them with Community-wide quotas. The Community regulations on imports of goods simply recorded the existing quotas in their annexes,

[4] *Opinion 1/75 re Local Cost Standard* [1975] ECR 1355; see Ch 2.

[5] Art XXIV:8(a) GATT. On the interpretation of this phrase, see WTO Appellate Body, *Turkey—Restrictions on Imports of Textile and Clothing Products*, WT/DS34/AB/R, adopted 19 November 1999.

effectively providing for exceptions to the principle of uniformity as regards imports.[6] Quotas which Member States thus individually operated could not be circumvented by importing the goods in question into another Member State, so as to benefit from free circulation in the internal market, and to be marketed in the Member State with a quota: on the basis of (then) Article 115 EEC a Member State could be permitted by the Commission to control such so-called indirect imports.

The legality of that system was tested in the *Donckerwolcke* case.[7] A couple of Belgian firms had imported textiles into France, declaring that the goods originated from Belgium. An inquiry by the French customs authorities showed that the declaration was false, and that the true origin was Syria and Lebanon. Prosecution followed, and the case was referred to the Court of Justice to establish whether France could lawfully monitor indirect imports. The Court established the principle of assimilation, analysed in the next section. It then accepted that, notwithstanding the requirement in the Treaty that the common commercial policy be uniform by the end of the transitional period, the Member States could continue to apply the quotas in question, and that (then) Article 115 EEC could be used to authorize Member States to monitor indirect imports. However, the Court imposed a number of conditions on the operation of this system. One of those was that the measures of commercial policy adopted by the importing Member State (in other words, the quotas) were in accordance with the Treaty. As full responsibility in the matter of commercial policy was transferred to the Community, the Court stated, measures of commercial policy of a national character were permissible after the end of the transitional period only by virtue of a specific authorization by the Community.[8] *Donckerwolcke* thus clarified that the Member States could not autonomously maintain exceptions to uniform import rules. At the same time the judgment created authority for the Community to permit the Member States to adopt certain commercial policy measures which derogate from the principle of uniformity. Such authority is now confirmed in Article 2(1) TFEU.

The notion of a specific authorization is central to this effective exception to uniformity and to exclusive competence. The 1986 judgment in *Bulk Oil* showed that the authorization need not be too specific.[9] Since 1979 it had been UK policy to authorize the exportation of petroleum of UK origin only to Member States of the (then) Community, member States of the International Energy Agency, and countries with which there was 'an existing pattern of trade'. The case concerned a dispute over exports to Israel, which the United Kingdom did not authorize, and the question arose of whether such refusal was in accordance with the Community's commercial policy. At the time, Article 10 of the Community regulation on exports, which was adopted in 1969, excepted crude oil and petroleum oils from

[6] E.g. Council Regulation 288/82 on common rules for imports [1982] OJ L31/1.

[7] Case 41/76 *Donckerwolcke v. Procureur de la République* [1976] ECR 1921.

[8] Ibid, paras 31–32.

[9] Case 174/84 *Bulk Oil v. Sun International* [1986] ECR 559.

the principle of free exportation in Article 1 of the regulation.[10] Bulk Oil argued that the UK's policy was not specifically authorized by the Community, and that Article 10 did not amount to such an authorization, especially since the UK policy was adopted long after the entry into force of the regulation. The Court disagreed. It described Article 10 as limiting the scope of the principle of free exportation on a transitional basis with regard to certain products, until such time as the Council had established common rules applicable to them. It was therefore satisfied that Article 10 constituted a specific authorization permitting the Member States to impose quantitative restrictions on exports of oil to non-member countries, and there was no need to distinguish in that regard between previously existing quantitative restrictions and those which were subsequently introduced.[11] The judgment suggests that the notion of specificity does not relate to the precise national commercial policy measure in issue. It was sufficient for the Court that the regulation listed the products in question. The Court did, however, refer to the transitional character of the exception, thereby implying that there should be a common policy at some stage.

Bulk Oil provided authority for the view that the notion of specific authorization need not be interpreted too strictly. Around the same time the question arose of whether that notion also covered the organization of the Community's policy on imports of textile products, as it then stood. In that sector, too, there were national quotas on imports, but in contrast with policies for other products those quotas were laid down in Community regulations, which provided for a Community-wide quota, divided into national sub-quotas. In other words, here it was the Community regulation itself which created a non-uniform commercial policy. In the *Tezi* cases the Court none the less accepted that regime, too.[12] It characterized the regime as a step towards the establishment of a common commercial policy for the products concerned.

It was essentially the effort to complete the internal market by the end of 1992 which led to a more uniform common commercial policy, and which enabled the Community to abolish the remaining national quotas for imports of products such as textiles and clothing, Japanese cars, and bananas.[13] As the internal market required the abolition of all controls on intra-Community trade, it proved impossible to continue the application of (then) Article 115 EEC so as to control indirect imports. The remaining quotas were in any event of doubtful legality under GATT law, and the economic circumstances were such that the Member States were willing to agree to a common regime and to give up restrictions at national level. However, in the case of imports of bananas, the new Community regime led

[10] Council Regulation 2603/69 [1969] OJ Spec Ed (II) 590.

[11] *Bulk Oil* (n 9 above) paras 32–33.

[12] Case 59/84 *Tezi v. Commission* [1986] ECR 887 and Case 242/84 *Tezi v. Minister for Economic Affairs* [1986] ECR 933.

[13] See P Eeckhout, *The European Internal Market and International Trade—A Legal Analysis* (OUP, 1994) Chs 5 and 6.

to a prolonged trade war with the United States and other American countries and created serious friction within the EU.[14]

As there is now a common and uniform regime of imports and exports for nearly all products, the question arises to what extent the EU can still lawfully authorize the Member States to adopt commercial policy measures which derogate from the principle of uniformity. It is arguable that the Court's liberal approach to the notion of a specific authorization in the above case law was inspired by patience rather than principle. In its judgments the Court consistently mentioned the transitional character of the exceptions to uniformity. It is therefore submitted that the EU could not now authorize the Member States to adopt national restrictions on imports and exports in the same way as it could in the 1970s and 1980s. That applies in particular to restrictions for purely economic reasons.

However, the completion of the internal market and the corresponding completion of the common commercial policy did not lead to absolute uniformity in the conditions for imports and exports. All the basic regulations on imports and exports contain a provision permitting the Member States to adopt measures on non-economic grounds such as public policy, public security, and public health.[15] There thus remains scope for national measures directly affecting imports and exports.[16] The principle of uniformity is none the less a cornerstone of the common commercial policy, and the instruments of that policy need to be interpreted and applied in the light of the principle.[17]

The principle of assimilation

In the *Donckerwolcke* case the Court also established the principle of assimilation. The Court referred to (current) Article 28 TFEU, which provides that the Union shall comprise a customs union which shall cover all trade in goods between Member States. According to Article 28(2) the provisions adopted for the liberalization of intra-EU trade apply in identical fashion to products originating in Member States and to products coming from third countries which are in 'free circulation' in the EU. The Court further stated that products in free circulation were to be understood as meaning those products which, coming from third countries, were duly imported into any one of the Member States in accordance with the requirements laid down by (current) Article 29 TFEU. The Court then held that it appeared from Article 28 that, with regard to the free circulation of goods within the (then) Community, products entitled to free circulation were definitively and wholly

[14] For an in-depth analysis see F Breuss, S Griller, and E Vranes, *The Banana Dispute—An Economic and Legal Analysis* (Springer, 2003); see also U Everling, 'Will Europe Slip on Bananas? The Bananas Judgment of the Court of Justice and National Courts' (1996) 33 CML Rev 401.

[15] See the subsection on import and export regulations, below.

[16] See also Ch 12.

[17] See e.g. the common customs tariff below.

assimilated to products originating in Member States. The result of this assimilation was that the provisions of (current) Article 34 concerning the elimination of quantitative restrictions and all measures having equivalent effect were applicable without distinction to products originating in the Community and to those which were put into free circulation in any one of the Member States, irrespective of the actual origin of these products.[18]

The judgment established the principle of assimilation in strong terms, and appeared to leave no room whatsoever for any qualifications. It may in fact be noted that, a few years earlier, the Court delivered its seminal judgment on (current) Article 34 TFEU in the *Dassonville* case, which concerned trade in Scotch whisky between France and Belgium, at a time when the United Kingdom was not yet a Member State.[19] That, too, was therefore a case concerning third-country products in free circulation, even if the Court did not mention that factor in its analysis.

The *Donckerwolcke* judgment permitted one exception to the principle of assimilation, i.e. the application of (then) Article 115 EEC. Under that provision the Commission could authorize the Member States to derogate from the principle of free circulation to protect national measures of commercial policy (in practice import quotas: see the previous subsection). Article 115 was applied until 1993, when the EU managed to abolish the last remaining national import quotas on bananas. The provision has now been deleted.

It is remarkable that so few problems have arisen with the application of the principle of assimilation. In one respect, its precise contours remain to be determined for lack of case law. In the famous *Cassis de Dijon* judgment the Court of Justice established the rule that, as a result of (current) Article 34 TFEU, any product lawfully produced and marketed in a particular Member State was in principle entitled to free circulation within the (then) Community.[20] This is the rule of mutual recognition, a cornerstone of the internal market, not only in the context of case law on the free movement of goods, but also in that of harmonization of legislation. However, it is based on the idea that products are produced in one Member State, in accordance with the laws, regulations, or traditions of that Member State, and that other Member States should recognize that. How does that principle function in the case of third-country products, which were not produced in a Member State?

That question may be easier to resolve than it would seem. The principle of mutual recognition is in effect a convenient denominator for case law which in practice focuses not so much on the issue of whether a product was lawfully produced and marketed in a Member State, but simply examines whether or not any trade restrictions by the importing Member State are justified.[21] Under the case law on the free movement of goods there are two essential questions to be answered.

[18] *Donckerwolcke* (n 7 above) paras 14–18.

[19] Case 8/74 *Procureur du Roi v. Dassonville* [1974] ECR 837.

[20] Case 120/78 *Rewe v. Bundesmonopolverwaltung für Branntwein* [1979] ECR 649.

[21] P Eeckhout, 'The European Court of Justice and the Legislature' (1998) 18 YEL 19.

The first is whether a particular measure constitutes a restriction on trade within the meaning of Article 34 TFEU. If that is the case, the second question is whether the restriction can be justified on grounds of the so-called mandatory requirements or of Article 36 TFEU. That method of examination can be fully transposed to third-country products. All that is required is that the products are in free circulation.

Through the principle of assimilation, the common commercial policy displays openness towards trade with third countries. The internal market is not merely there for the benefit of EU products. Once goods have been imported, they can fully benefit from the internal market. There are of course various types of restrictions at the EU's external borders, but there are no further trade restrictions in the internal market other than those which also apply to EU products.

Towards a principle of non-discrimination?

The EU is a party to the WTO Agreement and is thus bound by GATT non-discrimination principles, in particular most-favoured-nation (MFN) treatment (prohibiting discrimination between third countries, members of the WTO) and national treatment (prohibiting discrimination against imported products). Those principles are clearly an important component of the common commercial policy, even if the EU makes extensive use of the scope under Article XXIV GATT to conclude preferential trade agreements establishing free-trade areas or customs unions, thereby derogating from the MFN principle. However, the GATT rules are not of themselves justiciable, as they do not have direct effect.[22] It is therefore, as a rule, not possible for private parties to enforce them.

That raises the question of the extent to which the principle of equal treatment or non-discrimination, as a general principle of EU law,[23] is relevant to, and can be enforced in the context of, the EU's external trade.[24] The Court of Justice has hitherto not been willing to accept that there is a requirement of equal treatment of third countries in the absence of specific provisions mandating such equal treatment. In *Faust v. Commission*, a case involving protective measures relating to imports of preserved mushrooms, the Court admitted that Taiwan appeared to have been treated less favourably than certain non-member countries. It stated, however, that there existed in the Treaty no general principle obliging the Community, in its external relations, to accord to non-member countries equal treatment in all respects. The Court also added that if different treatment of non-member countries was compatible with Community law, different treatment accorded to traders within the Community also had to be regarded as compatible with Community

[22] See Ch 9.

[23] On general principles of EU law see T Tridimas, *The General Principles of EC Law* (OUP, 1999).

[24] See for further analysis M Cremona, 'Neutrality or Discrimination? The WTO, the EU and External Trade' in G de Búrca and J Scott (eds), *The EU and the WTO—Legal and Constitutional Issues* (Hart Publishing, 2001) 151.

law, where that different treatment was merely an automatic consequence of the different treatment accorded to non-member countries with which such traders had entered into commercial relations.[25]

On the other hand, the Court of Justice does apply the principle of equal treatment to EU-based importers, even if it does not appear to do so in a very strict way. In the 1994 *Germany v. Council* case, concerning the regime for imports of bananas, the Court did not uphold the claim of unequal treatment of various categories of importers (called operators under the relevant rules), notwithstanding the grave effects of the system of import licence allocation on importers of so-called third-country bananas. The Court considered that the difference in treatment was justified in the light of the aims of the regulation, which were the integration of previously compartmentalized markets in the Community and the protection of Community and traditional ACP producers of bananas.[26] The judgment can be criticized on the ground that there was no strong link between treating operators differently, effectively giving one category of importers clear advantages, and the aims of the regulation. On proportionality grounds, the Court should have struck down the regulation for involving a greater measure of differential treatment than could be justified. Four years later, however, the Court did strike down further amendments to the banana regime, which aggravated the difference in treatment. The Community had concluded an agreement with a number of Latin American exporting countries so as to resolve the GATT dispute. That agreement provided for the allocation of export quotas to those countries, and introduced a system of export licences complementing the system of import licences. Again, however, a distinction was made between the different categories of operators, with those trading in Community and ACP bananas being exempted from the export licence system. The Court established that this difference in treatment had significant financial consequences for importers of third-country bananas, and that the further differential treatment could not be justified on the ground of maintaining an appropriate balance between the various categories of operators: the framework agreement had not disturbed the balance between them, and there was therefore no justification for the difference in treatment.[27]

Instruments

Conventional and autonomous instruments

There are basically two types of legal instruments which contain rules on external trade, adopted in the framework of the common commercial policy. Such rules may be included in bilateral or multilateral treaties or agreements between the EU and third countries (e.g. the WTO Agreement); and they may also flow from internal

[25] Case 52/81 *Faust v. Commission* [1982] ECR 3745, para 25.

[26] Case C–280/93 *Germany v. Council* [1994] ECR I–4973.

[27] Case C–122/95 *Germany v. Council* [1998] ECR I–973, paras 59–72; Joined Cases C–364 and 365/95 *T Port v. Hauptzollamt Hamburg-Jonas* [1998] ECR I–1023, paras 78–89.

EU legislation. This chapter does not offer a survey of the first category. Previous chapters have examined the procedure for concluding such agreements, the role of the courts, and the legal effects of international law rules. As was mentioned, trade policy is almost invariably at the heart of bilateral agreements between the EU and third countries. In many cases such agreements set up preferential trade relations, through the establishment of a customs union or a free-trade area, or in the context of development co-operation policy (the Cotonou Agreement and the Economic Partnership Agreements with ACP countries). The EU is, moreover, a key player in the WTO. The scale and scope of these conventional trade policies is such that their study would require an analysis of its own, which cannot be undertaken here.

This section concentrates on the EU's trade legislation. It may therefore appear to show only half the picture. However, most of the regulations discussed below are closely connected with the rules of certain agreements, in particular those of the WTO Agreement: they are based on those rules, they aim to implement them, or they contain procedures for starting dispute settlement at international level in connection with trade matters.

This section analyses only the main pieces of legislation on imports and exports of goods.[28] It does not cover services or intellectual property, and deals mostly with general rules, applying to all imports or exports. In specific agreements with third countries one may find derogations from those general rules. Such derogations are contained in bilateral agreements, or in multilateral agreements with groups of countries, such as the EEA Agreement and the Cotonou Convention. The provisions of agreements establishing a free-trade area or a customs union with specific third countries derogate from the Common Customs Tariff (CCT), in that there are as a rule no customs duties on imports of goods from such countries.

The scope for such derogations must be kept in mind, since agreements concluded by the EU are binding on the EU institutions and in principle prevail over EU legislation.[29] In many cases, however, the trade provisions of an agreement are implemented by way of internal legislation.

This section discusses the CCT; derogations from the CCT through the generalized system of preferences; instruments for applying the CCT; the general import regulations; the EU's anti-dumping and anti-subsidy policies; the so-called trade barriers instrument; and the EU's export policy.

Common Customs Tariff

The EU is based upon a customs union, which implies common customs duties on imports. The CCT was established by 1968, more than a year before the end of

[28] See also PJG Kapteyn and P VerLoren van Themaat, *Introduction to the Law of the European Communities* (3rd edn, by LW Gormley, Kluwer Law International, 1998) 1295–320.

[29] See Ch 9.

the transitional period of the original EEC Treaty. The CCT is genuinely uniform in character. There are no differences in customs duties according to the Member State of importation, and the requirement of uniformity is confirmed in the case law of the Court of Justice. The position here can be contrasted with the Court's acceptance of national quotas on imports, which benefited from a specific authorization (see above). In the *Generalized System of Preferences* case the Court examined whether it was permissible to divide tariff quotas (quotas involving reductions in customs duties) between the Member States. The Court emphasized that the CCT was intended to achieve an equalization of customs charges levied at the frontiers of the (then) Community on imports from non-member countries, in order to avoid any deflection of trade and any distortion of free internal circulation or of competitive conditions. The Court accepted that a scheme of national shares could be justified by administrative, technical, or economic constraints which precluded the administration of the quota on a Community basis. However, such a scheme had to include machinery to ensure that, until the overall Community quota was exhausted, goods could be imported into any Member State, even if that Member State's share of the quota was exhausted. It was not acceptable that, in such a situation, goods would have to bear customs duties at the full rate or would have to be re-routed via another Member State.[30] In other words, the scheme of national shares had to be purely technical, and economically and fiscally neutral. Moreover, with the development of information technology the need for national shares has disappeared, and tariff quotas are now fully administered at central EU level.

The current version of the CCT is found in Regulation 2658/87 on the tariff and statistical nomenclature and on the Common Customs Tariff.[31] That regulation contains both the so-called 'combined nomenclature' (CN) and the prevailing rates of duty. The CN is based on the International Convention on the Harmonized Commodity Description and Coding System, to which the EU is a party.[32] The CCT consists of autonomous and conventional rates of duty. The autonomous rates are the original rates as of 1968; the conventional rates are those negotiated in GATT, the so-called 'bound' duties. In practice, the latter are applied to all imports, including those from non-WTO members.[33] The current average MFN tariff is around 6.7 per cent.[34] There are, however, many derogations from the application of the conventional rates of duty set out in the CCT. The three most significant kinds of derogations are: (a) elimination of customs duties on imports from countries with which the EU concluded an agreement establishing a free-trade area or a customs

[30] Case 51/87 *Commission v. Council* [1988] ECR 5459, paras 6–9.

[31] [1987] OJ L256/1.

[32] Council Decision 87/369 concerning the conclusion of the International Convention on the Harmonized Commodity Description and Coding System and of the Protocol of Amendment thereto [1987] OJ L198/1.

[33] ELM Völker, *Barriers to External and Internal Community Trade* (Kluwer, 1993) 51.

[34] WTO, Trade Policy Review—European Communities, Report by the WTO Secretariat, WT/TPR/S/214, 2 March 2009, at 34.

union; (b) elimination of customs duties on imports from ACP countries, by virtue of the Cotonou Convention[35] and of Economic Partnership Agreements;[36] and (c) partial or full suspension of customs duties on imports from developing countries, covered by the GSP system (see below).

For imports of most agricultural products there are additional levies, besides the conventional rates of duty set out in the CCT. Various sets of rules apply to those levies, according to the type of common market organization concerned.

Lastly, other kinds of charges may be connected with the importation of goods into the EU. Such charges, imposed by the EU or by individual Member States, are generally indicated by the term 'charges having equivalent effect'. In intra-Community trade such charges are expressly prohibited (Article 30 TFEU). The Treaty does not contain such an express prohibition as regards imports from third countries. However, it is settled case law that no such charges may be applied by the Member States. In *Aprile v. Amministrazione delle Finanze dello Stato* the Court recalled the applicable principles.[37] The case involved a dispute between Aprile, a company in liquidation, and the Finance Department of Italy which refused to repay certain charges in respect of customs transactions. In previous judgments the Court had decided that those charges, in so far as intra-Community trade was involved, were collected in breach of Community law. The question arose of whether the same conclusion had to be reached for imports from the EFTA countries.

The Court first examined whether the Member States were entitled unilaterally to impose charges having equivalent effect in trade with non-member countries. It pointed to the function of the customs union of avoiding trade diversion and distortion of competition. It also stated that the common commercial policy implied that national disparities of a fiscal and commercial nature affecting trade with non-member countries had to be abolished. The Court then held that both the unicity of the Community customs territory and the uniformity of the common commercial policy would be seriously undermined if the Member States were authorized unilaterally to impose charges having equivalent effect to customs duties on imports from non-member countries. It followed that it was for the Community alone to determine the level of duties and taxes payable on products from those countries.[38]

In the second part of the judgment the Court determined the scope of the prohibition of charges having equivalent effect contained in agreements concluded with non-member countries or in Community regulations governing trade with such countries. There the Court considered that there was no reason to interpret such prohibitions differently from the prohibition of charges having equivalent effect

[35] [2000] OJ L317/3.

[36] See e.g. Economic Partnership Agreement between the CARIFORUM States, of the one part, and the European Community and its Member States, of the other [2008] OJ L289/3.

[37] Case C–125/94 *Aprile v. Amministrazione delle Finanze dello Stato* [1995] ECR I–2919.

[38] Ibid, paras 32–37. See also Case C–173/05 *Commission v. Italy* [2007] ECR I–4917, para 33.

in intra-Community trade. The agreements and regulations would be deprived of much of their effectiveness if the term 'charge having equivalent effect' contained in them were to be interpreted as having a more limited scope than the same term appearing in the Treaty.[39]

The judgment did not answer the question of how to interpret the prohibition on Member States introducing charges having equivalent effect in the absence of express provision in agreements or in EU regulations. It is, however, difficult to see any reasons for adopting a narrower interpretation of the concept in such a context.

Generalized tariff preferences

The system of generalized tariff preferences (GSP) was developed at the instigation of UNCTAD.[40] It is, however, an autonomous measure of the EU; there are no international agreements on such preferences, except for a decision of the GATT Contracting Parties which established that preferences in favour of developing countries are permanently compatible with GATT.[41] The EU system consists essentially of the full or partial reduction or suspension of the customs duties set out in the CCT with a view to facilitating the importation of certain products from developing countries. It was established for the first time in 1971. The current scheme is found in Regulation 732/2008, and follows a reform of the system initiated in 1994.[42] In the preamble to the 1994 regulation it was stated that the scheme should become more development-oriented, focusing on the poorest countries; that it should be complementary to GATT instruments and should foster the integration of developing countries into the world economy and the multilateral trading system; and that consequently preferences should be seen as a transitional measure. The current regulation makes provision for the removal of a country from the list of beneficiaries where the country is classified by the World Bank as a high-income country and fulfils certain other conditions.[43] It also incorporates the 'everything but arms' initiative, under which all quotas and duties on all products except arms from the world's forty-eight least-developed countries are eliminated.[44]

The GSP instrument also contains special incentive arrangements for sustainable development and good governance. Its preamble refers to the promotion of

[39] *Aprile* (n 37 above) paras 38–41.

[40] See further L Bartels, 'The Trade and Development Policy of the European Union' in M Cremona (ed), *Developments in EU External Relations Law* (OUP, 2008) 153–65.

[41] Decision of 25 June 1971 L/3545, BISD 18 Supp. (1972) 24.

[42] Council Regulation 732/2008 applying a scheme of generalized tariff preferences for the period from 1 January 2009 to 31 December 2011 and amending Regulations (EC) No 552/97, (EC) 1933/2006 and Commission Regulations (EC) 1100/2006 and (EC) 964/2007 [2008] OJ L211/1.

[43] Ibid, Art 3.

[44] See originally Council Regulation 416/2001 [2001] OJ L60/43; see Art 11 of Regulation 732/2008 (n 42 above).

sustainable development in developing countries as one of the objectives of the EU's development policy, and states that the common commercial policy must be consistent with and consolidate those objectives.

The regulation accordingly provides for special incentive arrangements. Those arrangements consist of a further reduction of customs duties, granted to countries which are considered vulnerable. Those countries must have ratified and effectively implemented a number of international conventions, and maintain ratification and implementation, and accept regular monitoring and review. The conventions are listed in an annex, and total twenty-seven. They are divided into two groups. The first is named 'Core human and labour rights UN/ILO Conventions', and refers to some of the main UN conventions on human rights and to the ILO conventions embodying the so-called core labour standards. The second group is named 'Conventions related to the environment and to governance principles', and lists the main multilateral environmental agreements as well as conventions dealing with narcotic drugs and corruption.

The success of those incentive arrangements has increased over the years, as the Commission has recognized sixteen countries as complying with the requirements.[45] The special incentive arrangements may be contrasted with the provisions on the temporary withdrawal of tariff preferences, which also refer to the core human and labour rights conventions.[46]

The GSP special incentive arrangements can be seen in the light of the overall objectives of EU external action, which emphasize the protection of human rights and the sustainable economic, social, and environmental development of developing countries (Article 21 TEU). They make access to trade preferences conditional upon compliance with non-trade policy requirements. There are, however, questions as to the compatibility of such conditionality with WTO law. In *EC—GSP* the WTO Appellate Body scrutinized an earlier version of the incentive arrangements under the provisions of WTO law regulating tariff preferences.[47] There is scope for debate as to whether the current regime is in conformity with the relevant rules of WTO law, which require that preferences need to respond to the development, financial, and trade needs of developing countries, and that there be a sufficient nexus between the preferences and those needs.[48]

Applying the CCT

The application of the CCT is left to national authorities, in conformity with the relevant provisions of Community law. Those provisions are the subject of an

[45] See Commission Decision 2008/938 [2008] OJ L334/90.

[46] Art 15(1)(a) of Regulation 732/2008 (n 42 above).

[47] WTO Appellate Body, *EC—GSP*, WT/DS246/AB/R, adopted 20 April 2004.

[48] L Bartels, 'The WTO Legality of the EU's GSP+ Arrangement' (2007) JIEL 869.

extensive body of technical legislation, mostly laid down in regulations. The basic instrument is Council Regulation 450/2008 establishing the Community Customs Code.[49] The Code contains, for example, rules on classification (where it refers to the CN contained in Regulation 2658/87), on valuation for customs purposes, and on the origin of products. Cases on the exact classification of products often end up in the Court of Justice, as a question of interpretation of the CN.[50] Again the principle of uniformity is essential, as can be illustrated by a few comments of Jacobs AG in *Neckermann Versand*, a case on the definition and classification of nightdresses. The referring court had mentioned the possibility of classifying goods on the basis of the generally accepted view on trade in the Member State of importation. That seemed to imply that the classification might vary depending on the point of entry into the customs territory of the (then) Community. The Advocate General thought it conceivable that a garment might, as a result of climatic and cultural differences in the Member States, be considered suitable for outdoor wear in one country but fit only for wearing in bed in another country. However, the very concept of a common customs tariff implied that goods imported into the Community should be subject to the same rate of duty regardless of the Member State of importation, and it was important to avoid using any criteria that might lead to a different classification depending on the country of importation. The Advocate General added that the suitability of a garment for wearing in bed had to be assessed in the light of the habits, not of one Member State, but of the Community as a whole. It could be difficult in practice for national authorities to make such an assessment, but the attempt had to be made.[51]

Rules of origin serve to identify the origin of products, with a view to determining the applicable customs regime. For imports subject to tariff preferences, for example in the context of a free-trade area, there are so-called preferential rules of origin, which are detailed and technical, and vary according to the country of exportation. For other purposes the general rules of origin apply. The most important provision is Article 36 of the Community Customs Code, according to which goods whose production involved more than one country shall be deemed to originate in the country where they underwent their last substantial transformation.[52]

Although for some products there are more specific rules, for most products origin has to be determined, in cases of doubt, on the basis of the above general rule. It goes without saying that that is not always an easy matter, and that it gives rise to litigation. Generally, the Court of Justice takes the view that origin should be determined on the basis of technical, and not economic, criteria. In one case,

[49] [2008] OJ L145/1.

[50] See the Opinion of Jacobs AG in Case C–338/95 *Wiener v. Hauptzollamt Emmerich* [1997] ECR I–6495, for an overview of the relevant principles of interpretation.

[51] Case C–395/93 *Neckermann Versand v. Hauptzollamt Frankfurt am Main-Ost* [1994] ECR I–4027, Opinion of Jacobs AG, para 14.

[52] Regulation 450/2008 (n 49 above).

involving the difficult issue of assembly operations, the Court also took the value added to the product in such operations into account.[53]

General import regulations

Regulation 260/2009 applies to most imports into the EU.[54] It contains the basic principle that imports are free, i.e. that they are not subject to any quantitative restrictions. The regulation also contains provisions on safeguard measures. They state under what conditions such measures may be taken, and effectively implement the WTO Agreement on Safeguards. The provisions are detailed and contain rules on the investigation procedure, where interested parties may have to be heard, and on how injury is to be established. The EU, however, does not often take safeguard action on the basis of those rules.

There is a separate regulation governing imports from a set of countries, mainly former Soviet Union republics, as well as North Korea and Vietnam,[55] a left-over of those countries' state-trading and non-market economy status. The regulation also provides for free importation.

Imports of most textile products are governed by Council Regulation 3030/93 on common rules for imports of certain textile products from third countries.[56] International trade in textiles has been subject to restrictions for decades, mostly within the framework of the Multi-Fibre Agreement. Those restrictions were phased out over a period of ten years, pursuant to the Agreement on Textiles and Clothing, which is part of the WTO Agreement.

Anti-dumping

Article VI GATT allows the GATT Contracting Parties to take action against dumping, defined as the practice 'by which products of one country are introduced into the commerce of another country at less than the normal value of the products'. Normal value is in principle the price for the like product when destined for consumption in the exporting country. Anti-dumping action may, however, be taken only where dumping causes or threatens to cause material injury to an established domestic industry, or materially retards the establishment of such an industry.

Such action consists of the levying of an anti-dumping duty (effectively a tax on imports). The current version of the basic EU legislation is contained in Council Regulation 1225/2009 on protection against dumped imports from countries

[53] Case 26/88 *Brother International v. Hauptzollamt Giessen* [1989] ECR 4253.

[54] Council Regulation 260/2009 on the common rules for imports [2009] OJ L84/1.

[55] Council Regulation 265/2009 on common rules for imports from certain third countries [2009] OJ L185/1.

[56] [1993] OJ L275/1.

not members of the European Community.[57] That regulation implements the new Anti-Dumping Code which resulted from the Uruguay Round negotiations, and which is part of the WTO Agreement. The regulation is very technical, and its application requires intimate knowledge of its provisions and of the accounting and pricing policies of companies. However, in practice it is those technicalities which may determine the outcome of proceedings. What follows is a short description of the main elements of an investigation.

To determine whether dumping has taken place one first needs to establish the *normal value* of the product.[58] For imports from market economy countries normal value is the price paid or payable, in the ordinary course of trade, by independent customers in the exporting country. For imports from non-market economy countries, however, different rules on normal value apply. The idea there is that the domestic prices in such a country are unreliable, and that therefore reference needs to be made to the prices in a market-economy country.

After establishing normal value one needs to establish the *export price*.[59] Once the normal value and the export price are established, they can be compared. That is no problem in those cases where domestic sales and exports take place under identical conditions, but in practice that is rarely the case. The regulation therefore provides that a fair *comparison* must be made.[60] After comparison, the *dumping margin* can be established.[61]

As mentioned, anti-dumping duties may be applied only if the dumping causes injury to the EU industry.[62] There are also rules on the *determination of injury* and a definition of the term 'EU industry'—normally the EU producers, as a whole, of the like products.[63]

Anti-dumping proceedings are as a rule initiated upon a written, substantiated complaint on behalf of the EU industry.[64] The Commission must examine the complaint, and take a decision on whether there is sufficient evidence to justify the initiation of an anti-dumping investigation. The Commission conducts this investigation,[65] which covers a period of not less than six months immediately prior to the start of the investigation. The Commission investigates whether over that period there was dumping and consequent injury. Interested parties have a right to be heard, and there are specific provisions on verification visits;[66] sampling;[67] non-co-operation by interested parties;[68] confidentiality;[69] and disclosure of essential facts and considerations on the basis of which measures are imposed.[70]

[57] [2009] OJ L343/51. See, *inter alia*, I Van Bael and J-F Bellis, *Anti-Dumping and other Trade Protection Laws of the EC* (3rd edn, CCH Editions, 1996); E Vermulst and P Waer, *EC Anti-Dumping Law and Practice* (Sweet & Maxwell, 1996); S Farr, *EU Anti-Dumping Law* (Palladian Law Publishing, 1998).

[58] Art 2(A).

[59] Art 2(B).

[60] Art 2(C).

[61] Art 2(D).

[62] The Regulation still refers to the 'Community', which is replaced in what follows by the EU.

[63] Art 3. [64] Art 5. [65] Art 6. [66] Art 16. [67] Art 17.

[68] Art 18. [69] Art 19. [70] Art 20.

In the course of the investigation the Commission may impose provisional anti-dumping duties, on the basis of a provisional establishment of dumping and injury.[71] Provisional duties are not immediately collected, but must be secured by a guarantee; they are collected when the investigation is completed, resulting in definitive anti-dumping duties. The latter are the outcome of a definitive finding of dumping and injury.[72] There is, however, no obligation for the EU to adopt duties upon such a finding. First, there is a measure of discretion in so far as it needs to be established whether such duties would be in the EU interest.[73] That interest is defined as including interests of the domestic industry and users and consumers, with special consideration for the need to eliminate the trade-distorting effects of injurious dumping and to restore effective competition. Secondly, the Commission may accept undertakings from the exporters relating to prices and exports.[74] The Commission is, however, under no obligation to do so, nor are the exporters required to enter into them.

Definitive anti-dumping duties may not exceed either the dumping or injury margin (the so-called lesser duty rule).[75] The duties are normally individualized for each supplier of dumped products, reflecting the fact that an anti-dumping investigation is in principle targeted at the pricing policies of individual exporters. Definitive duties expire after five years, but may be continued if the dumping and injury persist.[76]

Anti-dumping policy also offers an illustration of the EU's desire to respect WTO law, and to ensure that WTO dispute-settlement rulings are easily implemented. Council Regulation 1515/2001 concerns measures which may be taken following a WTO dispute-settlement report concerning anti-dumping or anti-subsidy matters.[77] It enables the Council to adopt, on a proposal from the Commission and by simple majority, any appropriate measures which may be required by a WTO ruling, either in a case involving a Community measure or in other cases.

Anti-subsidy

Action may also be taken by the EU against subsidized imports. As with anti-dumping, new basic legislation was adopted following the conclusion of the Uruguay Round. The current version is Council Regulation 597/2009 on protection against subsidized imports from countries not members of the European Community,[78] which implements the Agreement on Subsidies and Countervailing Measures, part of Annex 1A to the WTO Agreement. The structure of anti-subsidy investigations and action is similar to that of anti-dumping investigations. The EU does not, however, take anti-subsidy action very often.[79]

[71] Art 7. [72] Art 9. [73] Art 21. [74] Art 8. [75] Art 9(4), last sentence.
[76] Art 11. [77] [2001] OJ L201/10. [78] [2009] OJ L188/93.
[79] See further K Adamantopoulos and MJ Pereyra-Friedrichsen, *EU Anti-Subsidy Law and Practice* (Palladian Law Publishing, 2001); M Sanchez-Rydelski, *EG und WTO Antisubventionsrecht* (Nomos, 2001).

The trade barriers instrument

Part of the package of trade policy instruments adopted in December 1994 is Council Regulation 3286/94 laying down Community procedures in the field of the common commercial policy in order to ensure the exercise of the Community's rights under international trade rules, in particular those established under the auspices of the WTO.[80] That regulation is generally referred to as the trade barriers instrument. Under the regulation the EU industry has the right to lodge a complaint with the Commission as regards obstacles to trade that have an effect either on the EU market or on the market of a third country. In practice, the instrument is mainly used for channelling complaints concerning unfair trade practices in third-country markets which hinder market access. One of the innovations, compared to the previous instrument,[81] is that, where obstacles on the market of a third country are complained of, such a complaint may be lodged by a single EU enterprise which is affected. The regulation contains detailed rules on the examination procedure which needs to be followed if the Commission decides that the complaint contains sufficient evidence and that an examination is in the EU interest. If as a result of the examination it is found that action by the EU is necessary, the regulation allows the EU institutions to adopt any types of measures aimed at combating the obstacles to trade. Examples are: the suspension or withdrawal of concessions; the raising of customs duties or the introduction of a charge on imports; and the introduction of quantitative restrictions. However, such measures must be compatible with existing international obligations and procedures. The regulation does not therefore permit any action which would not be in full compliance with the EU's international commitments, particularly in the WTO. The regulation is clearly aimed at encouraging EU enterprises to trigger EU action in the WTO against foreign trade barriers.

Export policy

The Community also has legislation on exports to third countries. The general rules are contained in Council Regulation 1061/2009 establishing common rules for exports.[82] Article 1 of that regulation lays down the principle of freedom of exportation. There are basically two categories of exceptions. The first concerns petroleum products (see *Bulk Oil*, where the Court accepted that the Council could exclude petroleum products from the scope of the regulation[83]). Secondly,

[80] [1994] OJ L349/71. For further analysis see M Bronckers and N McNelis, 'The EU Trade Barriers Regulation Comes of Age' in A von Bogdandy, P Mavroidis, and Y Mény (eds), *European Integration and International Co-ordination—Studies in Transnational Economic Law in Honour of Claus-Dieter Ehlermann* (Kluwer Law International, 2002) 55.

[81] Council Regulation 2641/84 on the strengthening of the common commercial policy with regard in particular to protection against illicit commercial practices [1984] OJ L252/1.

[82] [2009] OJ L291/1.

[83] Art 9 and n 9 above.

there is Article 10 of the regulation, which is a copy of Article 36 TFEU. It has been invoked in the context of so-called strategic export controls.

It must also be noted that the EU has legislation on export controls of so-called dual-use goods, which can be used for both civil and military purposes.[84]

Actors

Before the entry into force of the Lisbon Treaty one could deal briefly with the role of the various institutions in the conduct of the common commercial policy. (Old) Article 133 EC mentioned only two institutions: the Commission and the Council. The long evolution towards greater involvement of the European Parliament in EU policy-making had not yet reached this important domain. Accordingly, the Treaty procedure was very simple: the Council acted, by qualified majority, on a proposal from the Commission. That procedure not only applied to the adoption of internal commercial policy acts, but extended to the negotiation and conclusion of international agreements. The Treaty did not even provide for mere consultation of the Parliament, the weakest form of parliamentary involvement.

There may have been a time when the technicality of commercial policy could justify this absence of parliamentary scrutiny. In today's societies, however, this approach can clearly not be maintained if there is to be even a semblance of democratic decision-making. This was realized by the members of the Convention on the Future of Europe, and the drafters of the Lisbon Treaty, who provided that the ordinary legislative procedure extends to the common commercial policy (see Article 207(2) TFEU). That is one of the important modifications to EU decision-making which the draft Constitution would introduce.

According to Article 207(2) TFEU the ordinary legislative procedure must be used for the adoption of regulations 'defining the framework for implementing the common commercial policy'. This language suggests that a distinction must be made between commercial policy regulations laying down general legislative provisions concerning trade policy, and the implementation and application of such provisions in specific cases. That distinction reflects the existing practice, for example as regards the trade defence instruments discussed above. In future, for example, amendments to the basic anti-dumping regulation will require action by the Parliament and the Council under the ordinary legislative procedure, but the adoption of specific anti-dumping regulations targeted at certain imports will not be subject to that procedure.

[84] The main instrument is Council Regulation 428/2009 setting up a Community regime for the control of exports, transfer, brokering and transit of dual-use items [2009] OJ L134/1.

At present, such specific regulations are adopted by the Council, acting under a special procedure.[85] That procedure probably needs to be regarded as one concerning the implementation of the basic regulation, in the meaning of Article 291 TFEU, paragraph 2 of which provides that: 'Where uniform conditions for implementing legally binding Union acts are needed, those acts shall confer implementing powers on the Commission, or, in duly justified specific cases . . . on the Council'. It would therefore seem that if the current procedure is to be maintained, it requires a specific justification.

The much greater involvement of the Parliament is not limited to the adoption of regulations defining the framework for implementing the common commercial policy. Since the ordinary legislative procedure now applies in this field, the Parliament's consent is required, pursuant to Article 218(6) TFEU, for the conclusion of international agreements on trade matters.[86]

At the time of writing it is too early to indicate the likely effects of the increased role of the Parliament on the EU's trade policy. In many nations outside Europe, trade policy is highly politicized and plays an important role in general public debate. In Europe this has not been the case, with the occasional exception. The conduct of trade policy has been a technical and bureaucratic affair, seldom capturing the political limelight. That may change, even if greater involvement of the Parliament does not in itself guarantee general debate and media attention.

The day-to-day conduct of the common commercial policy is none the less likely to remain a rather bureaucratic endeavour. Most of the technical expertise is located in the Commission, which has represented the Community and its Member States in GATT and then the WTO for decades, and which is the negotiator of international agreements. The Commission is assisted and supervised by an important committee of Member State representatives, previously called the 133 Committee (referring to the EC Treaty provision on the common commercial policy), now re-baptized as the Trade Policy Committee.[87] The committee is referred to in Article 207(3) TFEU, which provides that the Commission conducts trade negotiations 'in consultation with a special committee appointed by the Council' and must regularly report to that committee. The Trade Policy Committee also acts outside the framework of trade negotiations, much like other Council committees which are part of the EU's so-called comitology. An analysis of that system, which is undergoing substantial change pursuant to the entry into force of the Lisbon Treaty, is beyond the scope of this study.

In the past, the bureaucratic conduct of the common commercial policy has also been shrouded in secrecy, in particular as regards the role and work of the 133 Committee. This is exemplified by an attempt by World Wildlife Fund (WWF) to

[85] See Art 9(4) of Regulation 1225/2009 (n 57 above), providing for the adoption by the Council of a Commission proposal for definitive anti-dumping duties unless a simple majority in the Council rejects the proposal.

[86] See Ch 6.

[87] See Council document 16864/2009 of 1 December 2009.

obtain access to some of that Committee's documents, in particular a note submitted by the Commission on WTO negotiations after the failure of the Cancun WTO Ministerial Conference in 2003. The Council refused access to that document, on the ground that releasing it would seriously harm the EU's international economic relations with third countries and also thwart the EU's commercial interests. The WWF challenged that decision before the (then) Court of First Instance, but the application was rejected, the Court finding that the Council did not commit a manifest error of assessment, and was right to consider that disclosure of the note would have entailed the risk of undermining the public interest as regards international relations and the Community's financial, monetary, and economic policy, which was reasonably foreseeable and not purely hypothetical.[88] It is doubtful whether the current Trade Policy Committee will be able to maintain this secrecy or confidentiality, as it will need to interact, not just with the Commission, but also with the Parliament's Committee on International Trade.

Lastly, the EU courts often need to deal with cases involving commercial policy measures. The subject of judicial review of such measures deserves a brief, separate treatment.

Judicial review of commercial policy measures

It will be clear from the above that the EU's external trade policy is sophisticated, and that it is implemented through a myriad commercial policy measures. Such measures obviously affect a range of economic interests and actors—producers, importers, exporters, consumers. In many cases, the measures which the EU adopts have a specific and significant impact, creating strong incentives for judicial challenge. There is, as a result, a large body of case law on judicial review of commercial policy measures. Within the scope of this chapter it is not possible to offer a complete survey and analysis of this area of judicial review.[89] Instead, this section aims to offer some insights into some of the most important issues arising in this context.

Commercial policy measures, whether in the form of general legislation, such as the basic regulations on imports, exports, anti-dumping, etc., or in the form of more specific measures or even decisions, are subject to the general system of judicial review set up by the TFEU and applied by the EU courts. There are essentially three forms of action.

The first is the action for the annulment of an act of an EU institution (Article 263 TFEU). As is well known, and much debated, private parties ('natural or legal

[88] Case T-264/04 *WWF European Policy Programme v. Council* [2007] ECR II-911, para 41.

[89] For a case study concerning imports of Chinese toys see F Snyder, 'Judicial Review in the Age of Globalization: Chinese Toys in the European Court of Justice' in D O'Keeffe and A Bavasso (eds), *Judicial Review in European Union Law—Liber Amicorum in Honour of Lord Slynn of Hadley, Vol I* (Kluwer Law International, 2000) 651–64.

persons') could in the past bring such actions only against decisions addressed to them, or against a decision which, although in the form of a regulation or a decision addressed to another person, was of direct and individual concern to them. In practice, access to the courts turned on the notion of direct and individual concern, which was strictly interpreted.[90] As a result it was, generally speaking, not possible for private parties directly to challenge regulations, as they were not considered to be individually concerned by them. However, in the trade policy field there were significant exceptions to that rule. The courts have been willing to accept that anti-dumping regulations could be challenged by certain categories of affected economic operators. The reasoning underlying such acceptance was, however, based on the specific nature of anti-dumping measures, and could not readily be transposed to other commercial policy measures in the form of regulations, let alone general external trade legislation. It is useful to provide a brief overview of the principles established by the Court of Justice as regards standing in anti-dumping cases, before looking at the new provisions of Article 263, fourth paragraph, TFEU.

In *Allied Corporation and Others* the Court established that exporters affected by anti-dumping measures could bring an action for annulment.[91] The cases concerned provisional duties imposed by the Commission on exports of fertilizers by the applicants, who were expressly named in the regulation. The Court pointed out that anti-dumping measures were, as regards their nature and scope, of a legislative character, inasmuch as they applied to all the traders concerned, taken as a whole. None the less, the provisions of anti-dumping regulations could be of direct and individual concern to those producers and exporters who were charged with practising dumping. It was in particular clear from the provisions of the then applicable basic anti-dumping regulation that anti-dumping duties could be imposed only on the basis of findings resulting from investigations concerning the production and export prices of undertakings which had been individually identified. It was thus clear that measures imposing anti-dumping duties were liable to be of direct and individual concern to those producers and exporters who were able to establish that they were identified in the measures adopted by the Commission or the Council, or were concerned by the preliminary investigations. The Court added that there was no risk of duplication of means of redress since it was possible to bring an action in the national courts only following the collection of an anti-dumping duty which was normally paid by an importer residing within the Community, and since in the context of a reference it was for the Court of Justice alone to give a final decision on the validity of the contested regulations.[92]

The ruling of the Court in *Allied Corporation* signified that exporters would as a rule have standing to challenge anti-dumping duties affecting their exports. Indeed, anti-dumping investigations are normally conducted on the basis of the individual

[90] See most recently Case C–50/00P *UPA v. Council* [2002] ECR I–6677.
[91] Joined Cases 239 and 275/83 *Allied Corporation and Others v. Commission* [1984] ECR 1005.
[92] Ibid, paras 11–13.

pricing practices of companies which take part in the investigation and are named in the regulations.[93]

The Court also admitted actions for annulment brought by complainants, as became clear in the *Timex* case.[94] In issue were definitive anti-dumping duties on imports of mechanical wrist-watches originating in what was then the Soviet Union. The Council had adopted those duties following an investigation initiated by a complaint on behalf of Timex Corporation, among others. Timex considered the duties to be insufficient and brought an action for annulment. The Court repeated that anti-dumping measures were, in fact, legislative in nature and scope, inasmuch as they applied to traders in general, but that their provisions could nevertheless be of direct and individual concern to some of those traders. It was in this regard necessary to consider the part played by the applicant in the anti-dumping proceedings and its position on the market to which the contested legislation applied. The Court pointed out that the complaint had originated with Timex, and that Timex was heard during the procedure. It also referred to the fact that Timex was the leading manufacturer of mechanical watches and watch movements in the (then) Community and the only remaining manufacturer of those products in the Community. Furthermore, the conduct of the investigation procedure had been largely determined by Timex's observations and the anti-dumping duty had been fixed in the light of the effect of the dumping on Timex. The contested regulation was therefore based on the applicant's own situation. It followed that the contested regulation constituted a decision which was of direct and individual concern to Timex.[95]

For importers of dumped products, who actually pay the anti-dumping duties, matters were altogether different. The Court looked at the position of importers in general in the *Alusuisse* case.[96] The applicant imported orthoxylene as an independent importer, that is an importer who was not linked to a manufacturing or exporting company, from, *inter alia*, the United States and Puerto Rico. In the course of 1981, provisional and definitive anti-dumping duties were imposed on those imports. Alusuisse challenged the relevant regulations in an action for annulment. The Court stated that an action for annulment was not admissible in so far as it was directed against a regulation having general application, the test for distinguishing between a regulation and a decision being whether or not the measure in question had general application. It was therefore necessary to appraise the nature of the contested measures and in particular the legal effects which they were intended to produce or did in fact produce. The Court found that the measures in issue constituted—as regards independent importers who, in contrast to exporters,

[93] Among the exceptions are cases involving non-market economy countries, where no account is taken of individual companies' pricing practices: see e.g. P Eeckhout, 'European Anti-Dumping Law and China' (1997) 1 EIoP No 7; available at <http://eiop.or.at/eiop/texte/1997-007a.html>.

[94] Case 264/82 *Timex v. Council and Commission* [1985] ECR 849.

[95] Ibid, paras 12–16.

[96] Case 307/81 *Alusuisse v. Council and Commission* [1982] ECR 3463.

were not expressly named in the regulations—measures having general application, because they applied to objectively determined situations and entailed legal effects for categories of persons regarded generally and in the abstract. The Court rejected the argument that Alusuisse formed part of a closed category of traders, because a measure did not cease to be a regulation where it was possible to determine the number or even the identity of the persons to whom it applied at any given time, as long as it was established that such application took effect by virtue of an objective legal or factual situation defined by the measure in relation to its purpose. The Court also rejected the argument based on Alusuisse's participation in the procedure leading to the adoption of the duties: the distinction between a regulation and a decision could only be based on the nature of the measure itself and the legal effect which it produced, and not on the procedures for its adoption. The Court lastly pointed out that this was in conformity with the system of remedies provided for by (then) Community law, since importers could contest before the national court individual measures taken by the national authorities in application of the Community regulations. Alusuisse was therefore refused standing.[97]

Not all importers were refused standing. Those which were not independent but were associated with the exporters concerned were able to bring an action for annulment under certain circumstances, for example where their resale prices formed the basis for a constructed export price.[98]

As regards independent importers, the Court exceptionally admitted the action for annulment in *Extramet*, but that remains the sole instance of an independent importer being granted standing.[99] The admissibility of Extramet's action was clearly based on the specific, and exceptional, facts of the case, and there are no other examples of successful actions for annulment, in terms of standing, by independent importers.

Article 263, fourth paragraph, introduces a new standing test for 'a regulatory act': any natural or legal person may institute proceedings against such an act 'which is of direct concern to them and does not entail implementing measures'. Thus, for regulatory acts the requirement of individual concern has been removed. Anti-dumping regulations (as well as most other commercial policy measures of an implementing nature) are normally of direct concern and do not entail further implementing measures: Member State authorities simply need to apply the regulations. But are such regulations 'a regulatory act'? Unfortunately, that concept is nowhere defined in the Treaties. It has been argued that a distinction needs to be drawn between legislative acts, i.e. those acts adopted pursuant to the ordinary or a special legislative procedure, and other acts of a normative kind.[100] If that is correct,

[97] Ibid, paras 8–14.

[98] See e.g. Joined Cases C–305 and 160/87 *Neotype Techmashexport v. Commission and Council* [1990] ECR I–2945, paras 17–22.

[99] Case C–358/89 *Extramet Industrie v. Council* [1991] ECR I–2501.

[100] Cf M Dougan, 'The Treaty of Lisbon 2007: Winning minds, not hearts' (2008) 45 CML Rev 675.

anti-dumping regulations are clearly regulatory in nature, as would be a range of other implementing acts in the commercial policy field. The case law on lack of standing of independent importers may therefore no longer be valid under the provisions of the TFEU. It would indeed make sense to broaden standing to all persons who are directly concerned by commercial policy measures, other than general legislative regulations. To return to anti-dumping regulations, those are clearly of an administrative rather than legislative character. It is true that they lay down general rules on the duties to be levied on all imports of the dumped products, yet such general rules are only the end result of what is essentially an administrative process, focusing on the pricing policies of exporters and on the effects of dumped imports on EU producers, importers, and consumers. Indeed, the basic anti-dumping regulation recognizes that those are the various interests which need to be looked at and balanced, under the heading of EU interest.[101] It also recognizes that interested parties, including importers, have a right to be heard and to participate in the investigation.[102] It would be but a small step to accept that such recognition at legislative level of the various interests and interested parties needs to be transferred to the interpretation and application of Article 263 TFEU. It remains to be seen, however, how the EU courts will interpret the new provisions.

The restrictions on direct access or standing do not put general commercial policy measures beyond judicial review, which brings us to the second form of action. As such measures are typically implemented at the level of the Member States, where import and export transactions are administered, it is open to any affected economic operator to challenge such implementation before the competent national court or tribunal, on the basis that the EU measures are invalid. If such an operator manages to persuade that court or tribunal that there are indeed serious doubts as regards the validity of the EU measure, a reference will be made to the Court of Justice under Article 267 TFEU. The object of that reference is the question of whether the commercial policy measure, which may be of a legislative character, is valid.

The grounds for challenging the validity of EU acts by way of a preliminary reference are identical to those which may be advanced in an action for annulment,[103] so from that perspective there are no drawbacks to this alternative route for judicial review. There are, however, other disadvantages, which arguably result in the preliminary rulings procedure offering a less effective remedy than the action for annulment.[104] First, an economic operator may for various reasons find it difficult to locate and challenge a national implementing measure before a court in a Member State. The operator may even have to infringe the law so as to trigger some form of prosecution, in the context of which a challenge to the EU measure can be made, which is not a particularly attractive proposition. There may be difficulties in

[101] Art 21 of Regulation 1225/2009 (n 57 above). [102] Ibid, Art 6.

[103] M Brealey and M Hoskins, *Remedies in EC Law* (2nd edn, Sweet & Maxwell, 1998) 228.

[104] Cf Opinion of Jacobs AG in *UPA v. Council* (n 90 above).

obtaining standing before the competent court or tribunal. Secondly, the economic operator needs to be able to persuade the national court that the validity of the EU act is genuinely in doubt. It is indeed that court which has sole authority to decide that a reference needs to be made, and parties have no right to a reference. There may be cases where the operator is obliged to appeal against rulings declining the making of a reference, up to the highest court, which is obliged to refer in any case which turns on a point of EU law.[105] Thirdly, it may be more difficult to obtain interim measures, such as measures suspending the operation of the challenged EU act or legislation, and the national court is not particularly well placed to operate the balancing of interests which the decision on interim measures may require. Fourthly, and most significantly, because of its indirect character the preliminary rulings procedure is not well adapted to the challenge of commercial policy measures, particularly where such measures are fact-intensive and of an administrative character. The whole case before the Court of Justice will be defined by the order for reference, which may not always provide sufficient information. The proceedings are not adversarial (there is no exchange of written pleadings), and as a result the Court of Justice may not be in a good position to engage in a full investigation and review of all the facts and issues that may arise.

There is a third form of action which is available to an economic operator seeking judicial review: it may invoke the non-contractual liability of the Community (Articles 268 and 340 TFEU). The EU is obliged to compensate any damage resulting from wrongful behaviour, but in the case of rule-making it is only where there is a sufficiently serious violation of a rule intended to confer rights on private parties that compensation may be granted.[106] This means that a mere illegality will not always be sufficient, and there are very few examples of successful cases in this area.

Conclusions

The common commercial policy is clearly the most established and sophisticated external EU policy. This chapter has looked at a number of aspects, but is not complete. A comprehensive assessment would require all the bilateral and multilateral trade agreements which the EU has concluded to be examined. It would also require an in-depth study of WTO law, for such law is part and parcel of the EU law on external trade, and the WTO is the locus of further development of trade policy (and more than that) through its dispute-settlement system and through its rounds of multilateral negotiations. It would further require a more intense analysis

[105] See Art 267, third para, TFEU. For an example of a successful challenge to the validity of a commercial policy measure on a reference by a highest court (the German *Bundesfinanzhof* or Federal Finance Court), see Case C–24/90 *Hauptzollamt Hamburg-Jonas v. Werner Faust* [1991] ECR I–4905.

[106] Case C–352/98P *Laboratoires Pharmaceutiques Bergaderm v. Goupil* [2000] ECR I–5291.

of various trade policy instruments—in particular, but not only, of anti-dumping. One would need to look in detail at the highly complex subject of trade policy for agricultural products.

The survey and discussion in this chapter none the less lead to a couple of conclusions. At the level of institutional actors, it was remarkable that commercial policy remained for so long within the almost exclusive remit of the executive and of the Community's bureaucracy. Article 133 EC referred to the Council and the Commission only, and not to the Parliament. The technicality of many decisions further enhanced the powers of technocrats compared with those of elected politicians. There may have been certain advantages to this in terms of stability and rationality of decision-making, but they arguably did not outweigh the lack of democratic input. The Treaty of Lisbon rightly rectified this state of affairs, by fully involving the European Parliament through the extension of the legislative procedure to commercial policy.

The Courts are also important actors in the sphere of commercial policy, in contrast to other areas of EU external action, such as the Common Foreign and Security Policy (see Chapter 11). They hear many cases involving commercial policy measures, and interfere occasionally to ensure that adequate standards of legality are maintained. However, there may be scope for more intense scrutiny. When reading judgments involving some type of challenge to an EU commercial policy measure, and comparing them with rulings in cases involving 'internal' administrative acts (such as in competition law), one cannot escape the impression that the Courts are less inclined to assist private parties in the external trade field, some of which are of course companies which are identified as foreign rather than European. In addition, one should bear in mind the lack of direct effect of WTO law (Chapter 9), which also reduces the scope for judicial review.

At the level of autonomous commercial policy instruments there is limited scope for amendment or innovation owing to the obligations under WTO law. For example, it makes no sense to discuss the merits of anti-dumping policy solely within the EU. Such discussions need to take place at the global level. The only instrument which is less WTO-dependent is the GSP system, which only benefits from a general WTO imprimatur. The current system exemplifies the linkages between trade and non-economic policies which the EU is to some extent promoting, but again most of that debate needs to take place within the WTO.

11

Common Foreign and Security Policy

Introduction

In Chapter 5 the competences conferred upon the EU to conduct a foreign and security policy were analysed. That analysis revealed that the Common Foreign and Security Policy (CFSP) is to a large extent supplementary to the EU's other external policies, and that the actual terrain which it occupies consists mostly of forms of external action which cannot be undertaken under the TFEU, because there the necessary powers are lacking. In this chapter we return to the CFSP in order to take a closer look at the actual policies which the EU pursues. However, as this book focuses on the legal foundations of external relations, there is no attempt to review the CFSP from a pure policy perspective. That can be left to international relations and political science experts, many of whom have indeed scrutinized the CFSP.[1] Academic lawyers, by contrast, have in the past devoted less attention to the EU's foreign policy, but they are catching up.[2] That discrepancy is no coincidence. For a long time lawyers were at a loss when attempting to capture the CFSP in legal discourse. Law seemed to be kept out of the CFSP with a view to safeguarding its intergovernmental character and protecting it from supranational infection. The original TEU defined the objectives of the CFSP, and enabled the Council of Ministers to use legal instruments, in particular joint actions and common positions, but signally failed to clarify the nature and effect of those instruments. Even if the objective of their creation may have been to develop policy in a more systematic and formal way than under the preceding European Political Co-operation, as well as to reinforce the binding character of agreed policies,[3] the adoption of strong legal instruments was clearly not the primary objective.[4] The very terms 'joint action' and 'common position' did not evoke established legal instruments of either domestic, Community, or international law. The TEU provided that CFSP decisions were binding on the Member States, but it did not create any specific mechanisms

[1] See Ch 5, introduction.

[2] E.g. RA Wessel, *The European Union's Foreign and Security Policy—A Legal Institutional Perspective* (Kluwer, 1999); P Koutrakos, *Trade, Foreign Policy and Defence in EU Constitutional Law* (Hart Publishing, 2001) and *EU International Relations Law* (Hart Publishing, 2006) Ch 11; E Denza, *The Intergovernmental Pillars of the European Union* (OUP, 2002).

[3] S Keukeleire, *Het buitenlands beleid van de Europese Unie* (Kluwer, 1998) 181.

[4] Denza (n 2 above) 90.

of enforcement, other than supervision by the Council itself: the jurisdiction of the Court of Justice was not extended to CFSP matters, and the Commission was not made the guardian of the CFSP. The lack of Court jurisdiction also meant that little case law could develop on either the interpretation of certain TEU provisions or the effect of CFSP decisions. Could certain CFSP acts have direct effect? Does the principle of supremacy extend to the CFSP? The examination of such questions, interesting though they may be,[5] remained a matter of pure speculation in the absence of an ultimate judicial voice. Even on the very juridical nature of the EU, as distinct from the EC, it was almost impossible to determine the correct parameters of legal debate, let alone find some degree of consensus.

However, the actual conduct of policy does not have to be obstructed by lawyers' failure to apply their legal categories. A lot of practice developed under the CFSP, even if it rarely managed to capture the international political limelight. The CFSP practice, together with the Amsterdam, Nice, and Lisbon Treaty modifications, allow for more significant legal analysis than was possible when the TEU entered into force.

This chapter focuses on the instruments and actors of the CFSP (but largely leaves aside the Common Security and Defence Policy (CSDP)).[6] In the first part the various instruments which are at the EU institutions' disposal to enable them to conduct the CFSP are discussed, including the budgetary means. There is then an inquiry into the nature and legal effect of those instruments, on the basis not only of the TEU's language but also the actual content of CFSP acts. International agreements concluded on the basis of Article 218 TFEU are not covered, however, as the EU's treaty-making practice is discussed in previous chapters. Nor is there a specific analysis of the special case of what are now called restrictive measures (sanctions in common parlance) which may be adopted, pursuant to Article 215 TFEU, in conjunction with a CFSP decision: such sanctions will be given closer scrutiny in Chapter 12, on the connection between trade and foreign policy.

The second part of this chapter focuses on the role of the various institutions and authorities involved in CFSP decision-making. The Council and its various organs and agents—in particular the High Representative and the new European External Action Service (EEAS)—are the main players, but the analysis cannot be confined to them, in particular if one adopts a perspective of constitutionalism. Indeed, important questions of parliamentary and judicial scrutiny arise in connection with the CFSP, and require further examination.[7] Those questions

[5] On supremacy see CWA Timmermans, 'The Constitutionalization of the European Union' (2002) 21 YEL 9.

[6] On CSDP see e.g. Koutrakos, *EU International Relations Law* (n 2 above) ch 13; M Trybus and N White (eds), *European Security Law* (OUP, 2007); S Keukeleire and S MacNaughtan, *The Foreign Policy of the European Union* (Palgrave Macmillan, 2008) ch 7.

[7] See e.g. M Martín Martínez and I Lirola Delgado, 'Aspectos jurídico-constitucionales de la Accíon Exterior de la Unión Europea en el Tratado por el que se establece una Constitución para Europa: reformulación o reinvención?' in A Remiro Brotóns and I Blázquez Navarro (eds), *El futuro de la acción exterior de la Unión Europea* (tirant lo blanch, 2006) 29–33, 46–9.

are not unconnected with the issue of the legal nature and effect of CFSP acts. Depending upon the strength and depth of commitments entered into, and on the legal force and effects of decisions, those may become burning questions in a constitutional polity. It is from those angles that the role of the institutions is studied, and there is no attempt to offer a definitive institutional analysis, which would require a stronger interdisciplinary approach and would move us beyond external relations.

Instruments

Introduction and overview

Article 25 TEU provides that the EU shall conduct the CFSP by:

a) defining the general guidelines,
b) adopting decisions defining:
   (i) actions to be undertaken by the Union;
   (ii) positions to be taken by the Union;
   (iii) arrangements for the implementation of the decisions referred to in points (i) and (ii);

and by

c) strengthening systematic co-operation between Member States in the conduct of policy.

It may be useful to indicate how these provisions on the EU's CFSP instruments have evolved through the various Treaty amendments. The original version of the TEU did not contain the above enumeration as such. It spoke of systematic co-operation between the Member States and of the gradual implementation of joint actions in areas where the Member States had important interests in common (Article J.1(3)). Member States were to inform and consult one another, and the Council could define common positions to which national policies had to conform. Member States were also to co-ordinate their action in international organizations and at international conferences (Article J.2). The Treaty provided for a procedure for the adoption of joint actions, but did not define the concept itself (Article J.3). The original TEU appeared to have created some kind of halfway house between informal co-ordination of policies and the adoption of formal legal instruments with specific legal effects. CFSP acts were regarded as binding under international law,[8] but, as mentioned, no particular methods of enforcement were provided for. The lack of legal precision led to uncertainty and confusion, particularly as regards

[8] Denza (n 2 above) 55; M Eaton, 'Common Foreign and Security Policy' in D O'Keeffe and P Twomey (eds), *Legal Issues of the Maastricht Treaty* (Chancery Law, 1994) 222.

the distinction between joint actions and common positions, which became the core CFSP instruments.[9]

The Treaty of Amsterdam attempted to create more precision through an enumeration, in (then) Article 12 TEU, which included principles and guidelines; common strategies; joint actions; common positions; and systematic co-operation between Member States. It also offered some type of definition of joint actions (they 'address specific situations where operational action by the Union is deemed to be required': (old) Article 14(1) TEU) and of common positions (which 'define the approach of the Union to a particular matter of a geographical or thematic nature': (old) Article 15 TEU). It introduced common strategies, decided by the European Council, and 'to be implemented by the Union in areas where the Member States have important interests in common' (old Article 13(2) TEU).

The Treaty of Lisbon again modified the list of available instruments. Instead of having to use the peculiar concepts of 'joint actions' and 'common positions' the Council now simply adopts 'decisions'. It is to be noted that the legal concept of an EU 'decision' is modified by Article 288 TFEU: former Article 249 EC implied that decisions were by definition addressed to particular persons,[10] whereas Article 288 TFEU no longer requires a particular connection between a decision and an addressee, but also allows decisions of a general nature.[11] The use of decisions for the conduct of the CFSP also needs to be assessed in the light of the exclusion of legislative acts in the context of the CFSP (Articles 24(1) and 31(1) TEU). The scope of that exclusion, which was touched upon in Chapter 5, is further analysed below.

The replacement of joint actions and common positions with decisions does not mean that the distinction between actions and positions is abandoned. As set out above, Article 25 TEU speaks of decisions defining either actions to be undertaken or positions to be taken by the Union. That distinction is elaborated upon in Articles 28 and 29 TEU. The former provision addresses 'operational action', the latter concerns 'decisions which shall define the approach of the Union to a particular matter of a geographical or thematic nature'. As the CFSP decisions need to identify the TEU provisions on which they are based, the distinction between joint actions and common positions to some extent survives.

However, the post-Lisbon TEU removes 'common strategies' as a specific CFSP instrument. (Old) Article 13(2) TEU enabled the European Council to adopt common strategies. The ostensible purpose of common strategies was to create a general policy framework, in certain broader areas, leading to more coherent and unified CFSP actions. That idea is taken one step further by the current TEU, in the sense

[9] S Nuttall, *European Foreign Policy* (OUP, 2000) 186; E Decaux, 'Le processus de décision de la PESC: vers une politique étrangère européenne?' in E Cannizzaro (ed), *The European Union as an Actor in International Relations* (Kluwer, 2002) 42; Wessel (n 2 above) 129; G Edwards, 'Common Foreign and Security Policy' (1994) 14 YEL 545.

[10] 'A decision shall be binding in its entirety upon those to whom it is addressed.'

[11] 'A decision shall be binding in its entirety. A decision which specifies those to whom it is addressed shall be binding only on them.'

that, what are now called 'decisions of the European Council on the strategic interests and objectives of the Union' cover both CFSP and other areas of EU external action. Article 22 TEU, which follows the TEU provision setting out the EU's overall objectives as regards external action, contains the relevant provisions.

The analysis below focuses on those three types of formal decisions. Beyond those instruments, there are other types of CFSP acts, such as international agreements (see Chapter 6); European Council guidelines, statements, and declarations; and CFSP implementing decisions (Article 31(2) TEU), which are not further studied. The analysis also focuses on the exclusion of legislative acts, and on the budgetary rules.

Decisions on Union actions

Article 28(1) TEU defines the Council's powers to adopt decisions on actions (former joint actions), in the following terms:

> Where the international situation requires operational action by the Union, the Council shall adopt the necessary decisions. They shall lay down their objectives, scope, the means to be made available to the Union, if necessary their duration, and the conditions for their implementation.
>
> If there is a change in circumstances having a substantial effect on a question subject to such a decision, the Council shall review the principles and objectives of that decision and take the necessary decisions.

The remaining paragraphs of Article 28 TEU address the duties of the Member States with respect to decisions on actions, which 'shall commit the Member States in the positions they adopt and in the conduct of their activity' (paragraph 2). That obligation is fleshed out in Article 28(3), which provides:

> Whenever there is any plan to adopt a national position or take national action pursuant to a decision as referred to in paragraph 1, information shall be provided by the Member State concerned in time to allow, if necessary, for prior consultations within the Council. The obligation to provide information shall not apply to measures which are merely a national transposition of Council decisions.

Article 28(4) addresses 'cases of imperative need arising from changes in the situation and failing a review of the Council decision'; the Member States may then 'take the necessary measures as a matter of urgency having regard to the general objectives of that decision'. Further, Article 28(5) provides that, 'Should there be any major difficulties in implementing a decision as referred to in paragraph 1, a Member State shall refer them to the Council which shall discuss them and seek appropriate solutions', which 'shall not run counter to the objectives of the decision ... or impair its effectiveness'.

It is also worth mentioning that decisions on actions may be used to implement decisions on strategic interests and objectives adopted by the European Council, and that the Council generally acts by taking decisions 'on the basis of the general guidelines and strategic lines defined by the European Council' (Article 26(2) TEU).[12]

What can be learned from those Treaty provisions as regards the nature and legal effects of decisions on actions?[13] The definition of such decisions as instruments addressing specific situations where operational action is required does not shed much light on their legal nature. Operational action is not a legal term of art, and appears to allow for various types of decisions and provisions. The qualification that the decisions shall lay down their objectives, scope, means, duration, and conditions is not of much further assistance.

With respect to legal effects the Treaty language does emphasize that decisions on actions are binding on the Member States, or at least 'commit' them, as regards 'the positions they adopt and in the conduct of their activity'. The Treaty refers to national positions and national actions, not to national law. That appears to confirm that joint actions are not intended to be used as a legislative instrument; that we should not look at joint actions from the perspective of the relationship between EU and domestic *law*, but rather from the perspective of political statements and action. As mentioned before, it is not clear whether doctrines such as direct effect and supremacy can extend to CFSP acts.

The Treaty does not provide that decisions on actions also commit the EU institutions—in particular the European Commission, which is responsible for much external 'action' under the TFEU. The absence of such a provision is no doubt linked to the relationship between the former pillars, and the tension between supranationalism and intergovernmentalism. As discussed in Chapter 5, the Commission is concerned that CFSP decisions may interfere with its powers and prerogatives under the TFEU. The Commission is none the less under an obligation, together with the Council, and assisted by the High Representative, to ensure the consistency of the EU's external activities as a whole (Article 21(3) TEU).

In the light of the lack of Treaty precision as regards the nature and effects of decisions on actions, it may be useful to take a closer look at the actual practice (including of course the practice under the former version of the TEU as regards joint actions). It is clear from that practice that decisions on actions are in many respects the key vehicle of the CFSP.[14] It is in particular interesting to investigate what types of 'operational action' the Council undertakes. Joint actions and decisions on actions have concerned a wide range of acts and activities. They provide for financial expenditure and transfers.[15] They involve sending missions, from election

[12] Wessel (n 2 above) 119 reports that in an initial phase, joint actions used to be based on European Council guidelines, but that this is no longer the practice.

[13] See also, as regards the pre-Lisbon practice, A Dashwood, 'The Law and Practice of CFSP Joint Actions' in M Cremona and B De Witte (eds), *EU Foreign Relations Law—Constitutional Fundamentals* (Hart Publishing, 2008) 53.

[14] Cf E Paasivirta, 'The European Union: From an Aggregate of States to a Legal Person?' (1997) 2 *The Hofstra Law & Policy Symposium* 51.

[15] E.g. Joint Action 2004/494 on European Union support to the establishment of the Integrated Police Unit in the Democratic Republic of Congo (DRC) [2004] OJ L182/41.

observers to military personnel, consisting mostly of persons seconded by the Member States.[16] They have provided for diplomacy, consultations, démarches, representation, and conferences.[17] Joint actions have instructed the Member States to take various forms of action, up to the adoption of legislation (including sanctions)[18] and the ratification of international conventions.[19] They may set up institutions and centres with legal personality.[20]

The ill-defined nature of joint actions and decisions on actions therefore appears to permit virtually any type of government activity, with the exception of general normative action creating rights and obligations for citizens. It is only in the latter sense that joint actions and decisions on actions can be said to be non-legislative, and in material terms a number of joint actions do have legislative effect, albeit through legislative action which the Member States are instructed to take. This broad juridical scope of joint actions and decisions on actions needs to be borne in mind when considering the involvement of the various institutions. In particular, from a perspective of constitutionalism, the question arises of whether the current standards of parliamentary and judicial supervision of decisions on actions are satisfactory.

Decisions on Union positions

Article 29 TEU provides:

> The Council shall adopt decisions which shall define the approach of the Union to a particular matter of a geographical or thematic nature. Member States shall ensure that their national policies conform to the Union's positions.

Article 29 TEU does not spell out the effects of these decisions on the Member States. However, Article 34 TEU, concerning action in international organizations and at international conferences, describes some of the Member States' obligations: 'They shall uphold the Union's positions in such forums' (Article 34(1)).[21] The Treaty is thus equally taciturn on the nature and legal effects of decisions on actions and on positions, and academic literature in fact agrees that the distinction with decisions on actions is unclear in either theory or practice.[22] Other than that

[16] E.g. Council Decision 2010/279 on the European Union Police Mission in Afghanistan (EUPOL AFGHANISTAN) [2010] OJ L123/4.

[17] E.g. Joint Action 2007/805 appointing a European Union Special Representative to the African Union [2007] OJ L323/45.

[18] E.g. Joint Action 2000/401 concerning the control of technical assistance related to certain military end-uses [2000] OJ L159/216. In recent years, however, that practice appears to have been abandoned.

[19] E.g. Joint Action 96/588 on anti-personnel landmines [1996] OJ L260/1.

[20] E.g. Joint Action 2008/550 establishing a European Security and Defence College (ESDC) and repealing Joint Action 2005/575 [2008] OJ L176/20.

[21] See also the provisions of Art 34(2) TEU as regards the work of the UN Security Council.

[22] E.g. Nuttall (n 9 above) 186; Decaux (n 9 above) 42–3 (both addressing the former joint actions and common positions).

the emphasis appears to be on political positions rather than operational action, there is little that one can derive from the Treaty language. As can be seen from the above discussion of decisions on actions, the latter in practice have also involved the adoption of political positions, although in recent years that practice appears to have been abandoned.

What does the practice as regards common positions and decisions on positions show? They have broadly concerned the following activities and positions:

- restrictive measures, including economic and financial sanctions, often in implementation of UN Security Council resolutions, and in combination with EC regulations based on Articles 301 and 60 EC—now based on Article 215 TFEU, including also other sanctions, in particular travel bans and visa restrictions, and arms trade restrictions; [23]
- objectives, priorities, and activities towards specific third countries; [24]
- broad policy documents on general international problems, for example human rights and good governance in Africa; [25] conflict prevention, management, and resolution in Africa; [26] terrorism; [27]
- support for democratic and peace processes; [28]
- conflict prevention and non-proliferation; [29]
- policy towards the international criminal courts and tribunals; [30] and
- temporary reception in Member States of particular persons. [31]

As can be seen, the range of subjects addressed through common positions and decisions on positions is as wide as that covered by joint actions and decisions on actions, and many subjects are similar, if not identical. There are, however, a number of differences in the content of the respective measures, and they have become more pronounced in recent years. Common positions and decisions on positions do not involve financial expenditure and transfers, the sending of missions, or the establishment of institutes or centres. Those are therefore clearly forms of 'operational action'

[23] E.g. Council Decision 2010/232 renewing restrictive measures against Burma/Myanmar [2010] OJ L105/22.

[24] E.g. Common Position 2002/830 on Rwanda and repealing Common Position 2001/799 [2002] OJ L285/3.

[25] Common Position 98/350 concerning human rights, democratic principles, the rule of law and good governance in Africa [1998] OJ L158/1.

[26] Common Position 2001/374 concerning conflict prevention, management and resolution in Africa [2001] OJ L132/3.

[27] Common Position 2001/930 on combating terrorism [2001] OJ L344/90.

[28] E.g. Common Position 2003/319 concerning European Union support for the implementation of the Lusaka Ceasefire Agreement and the peace process in the Democratic Republic of Congo (DRC) and repealing Common Position 2002/203 [2003] OJ L115/87.

[29] E.g. Common Position 2001/869 on participation by the EU in the Korean Peninsular Energy Development Organization (KEDO) [2001] OJ L325/1.

[30] E.g. Common Position 2003/444 on the International Criminal Court [2003] OJ L150/67.

[31] Common Position 2002/400 concerning the temporary reception by Member States of the EU of certain Palestinians [2002] OJ L138/33.

for which a decision on a position is not the appropriate instrument. Common positions and decisions on positions have increasingly concerned all kinds of restrictive measures. Again one can say that the instrument is non-legislative because it does not directly regulate rights and obligations of citizens. Indirectly, however, and in a substantive sense, common positions and decisions on positions do have legislative character. This is particularly the case for restrictive measures, which acquire binding force through implementation, either under the TFEU, where the measures come within Article 215 TFEU, or by the Member States (mostly visa and travel bans, and restrictions on trade in military material and technologies).

A good example of a common position with strong legislative purpose is the common position on combating terrorism.[32] Under Article 1 the wilful provision or collection of funds for terrorist purposes shall be criminalized. Article 2 concerns the freezing of funds held by terrorists. Article 8 provides that terrorists shall be brought to justice and that terrorist acts shall be established as serious criminal offences. Pursuant to Article 9 Member States must afford one another and third States assistance in connection with criminal investigations or proceedings. Article 10 requires that the movement of terrorists or terrorist groups be prevented by effective border controls. Article 14 provides that the Member States shall become parties as soon as possible to the relevant international conventions and protocols. These are just a number of examples of the kind of provisions that decisions on positions may contain. As with decisions on actions, the questions of parliamentary involvement and judicial supervision arise.

Decisions on strategic interests and objectives

Articles 22(1) and 26(1) TEU define the role of the European Council in the conduct of the CFSP. Article 22(1) provides that: 'On the basis of the principles and objectives set out in Article 21, the European Council shall identify the strategic interests and objectives of the Union'. It further provides that the relevant decisions:

> ... shall relate to the common foreign and security policy and to other areas of the external action of the Union. Such decisions may concern the relations of the Union with a specific country or region or may be thematic in approach. They shall define their duration, and the means to be made available by the Union and the Member States.

Article 26(1) TEU further provides that the European Council shall identify the Union's strategic interests, and determine the objectives of and define the general guidelines for the CFSP.

As was mentioned, the ostensible purpose of decisions on strategic interests and objectives (former common strategies) is to create a general policy framework, in

[32] Common Position 2001/930 (n 27 above).

certain broader areas, leading to more coherent and unified CFSP actions. Indeed, the extension of this instrument to other areas of EU external action follows that same logic. The European Council is clearly an important actor in CFSP matters, and in EU external action generally. Nearly every European Council meeting devotes considerable time to international affairs and external relations, and the Presidency Conclusions invariably contain policy statements and guidelines for further EU action.

There is, however, also a significant institutional and decision-making dimension to decisions on strategic interests and objectives. Pursuant to Article 31(2) TEU the Council acts by qualified majority 'when adopting a decision defining a Union action or position on the basis of' such a European Council decision, by way of derogation from the standard unanimity requirement. Throughout the inception and life of the CFSP there has been intense debate about the voting rules in the Council. Unanimity is regarded as safeguarding national sovereignty, whereas qualified majority is advanced as indispensable for effective decision-making. This debate took place at Amsterdam and in the Convention on the Future of Europe. Decisions on strategic interests and objectives are thus also akin to a form of ceasefire in the constitutional politics of the EU as regards voting rules in CFSP matters.[33]

The broad, inclusive nature of decisions on strategic interests and objectives raises questions concerning their relationship with TFEU policies. As with decisions on actions and positions, the Treaty does not clarify whether the EU institutions are bound by them when acting within the framework of the TFEU. Again this is left to the consistency requirement for which the Council, the Commission, and the High Representative are responsible.

The first common strategies adopted concerned Russia, Ukraine, and the Mediterranean region.[34] They were thus geographical in character. They were also broad in terms of subject matter, addressing overall policy towards the countries concerned, and making reference to the entire gamut of external policies, conducted by the EU, by the Member States, *and* by the (then) EC. Those common strategies did not, however, contain strict instructions for the Community; the European Council rather 'call[ed] on the Council, the Commission and Member States', to 'review, according to their competencies and capacities, existing actions, programmes, instruments, and policies to ensure their consistency with this Strategy'.[35]

Nor did they contain operational legal provisions, in contrast to joint actions and common positions. It is further notable that the three common strategies followed

[33] S Peers, 'Common Foreign and Security Policy' (1997) 17 YEL 546 suggests that this was the real purpose of introducing common strategies; A Dashwood, 'External Relations Provisions of the Amsterdam Treaty' in O'Keeffe and Twomey (eds) (n 8 above) 212 speaks of the primary purpose.

[34] Common Strategy 1999/414 on Russia [1999] OJ L157/1; Common Strategy 1999/877 on Ukraine [1999] OJ L331/1; and Common Strategy 2000/458 on the Mediterranean region [2000] OJ L183/5.

[35] E.g. Common Strategy 1999/414 (n 34 above), Instrument and Means, Section 2.

rather than preceded significant Community policies and instruments. In the cases of Russia and Ukraine the strategies made ample reference to the partnership and co-operation agreements with those countries,[36] whereas the strategy on the Mediterranean region expressly built 'on the Euro-Mediterranean partnership established by the Barcelona Declaration and its subsequent *acquis*'.[37]

The common strategies instrument was not highly praised. The former High Representative for the CFSP, Mr Solana, produced a critical report arguing that the common strategies were rhetorical and descriptive of existing instruments.[38] In academic literature, too, one finds criticism: common strategies were said to equal joint actions, but adopted by the European Council, and it was argued that the EU none the less remained the prisoner of divided competences.[39] According to Denza, however, an overview of existing and projected programmes was presentationally helpful for the country or region concerned as well as for those working in a narrow area of the Council or the Commission. By formulating policy and objectives agreed unanimously by the Member States, they opened the way to co-ordinated implementing decisions (by qualified majority within the Second Pillar). The practice was for each incoming presidency to draw up a work programme for each common strategy, and in these documents the allocation between pillars and legal bases was made clear.[40]

Those three common strategies have now expired, and since 2003 the European Council has not formally adopted new strategies which were published in the EU Official Journal. However, the Presidency Conclusions report five more 'strategies', which are referred to in various joint actions and common positions. They are the European Security Strategy;[41] the Strategy against Proliferation of Weapons of Mass Destruction;[42] the Strategy on Small Arms and Light Weapons;[43] the Counter-terrorism Strategy;[44] and 'The EU and Africa: Towards a Strategic Partnership'.[45] In substance, those strategies appear to conform to the way in which the current TEU describes decisions on strategic interests and objectives. The reason for not formally adopting them as (then) common strategies may relate to the fact that each of those strategies also involved external action outside the scope of the CFSP.

[36] Agreement on partnership and co-operation establishing a partnership between the European Communities and their Member States, of one part, and the Russian Federation, of the other part [1997] OJ L327/3 and Partnership and co-operation agreement between the European Communities and their Member States, and Ukraine [1998] OJ L49/3.

[37] Common Strategy 2000/458 (n 34 above) Part I, para 4.

[38] Europe Documents, No 2228; see Denza (n 2 above) 292.

[39] Decaux (n 9 above) 34–5, 37–40.

[40] Denza (n 2 above) 292–3.

[41] 12 Dec 2003, Council Doc 78367.

[42] 10 Dec 2003, Council Doc 15708/03.

[43] 17 Oct 2005, Council Doc 13066/05.

[44] 30 Nov 2005, Council Doc 14469/4/05 REV 4.

[45] 14 Dec 2005, Council Doc 15702/1/05 REV 1.

The exclusion of legislative acts

It is useful, at this point of the analysis, to examine the express exclusion of legislative acts in the context of the CFSP. Remarkably, the TEU twice contains exactly the same phrase, 'The adoption of legislative acts shall be excluded', in Articles 24(1) and 31(1). This exclusion was touched upon in Chapter 5, but there is scope for further observations concerning its meaning and effect. The analysis needs to be conducted in the light of CFSP practice, in particular as regards (former) joint actions and positions and (current) decisions on actions and positions.

The reference to 'legislative acts' finds its origins in the ill-fated Constitution for Europe, which would have introduced a general distinction between legislative and non-legislative acts.[46] Under its provisions, European decisions were labelled as non-legislative acts. The legislative acts encompassed European laws, and such an act was defined as a legislative act of general application, binding in its entirety and directly applicable in all Member States; and European framework laws, which were described as a legislative act binding, as to the result to be achieved, upon each Member State to which it was addressed, but leaving to the national authorities the choice of form and methods. The Constitution for Europe did not in terms exclude the adoption of legislative acts in the framework of the CFSP, but as it only allowed the adoption of CFSP decisions (as does the current TEU), it was obvious that legislative acts were excluded.

The current versions of the TEU and the TFEU are not of course identical to the Constitution for Europe. The Treaty of Lisbon largely abandoned the concepts of legislative and non-legislative acts, keeping the existing instruments of regulations, directives, decisions, recommendations, and opinions (Article 288 TFEU). However, it kept the denomination of ordinary and special 'legislative' procedures for the adoption of EU legal acts (Article 289(1) and (2) TFEU). All of those procedures involve at least the Parliament and the Council. Moreover, the TFEU specifies that 'Legal acts adopted by legislative procedure shall constitute legislative acts' (Article 289(3) TFEU).

The exclusion of legislative acts for the conduct of the CFSP could simply be understood, in accordance with the above TFEU provisions, as confirming that the ordinary or special legislative procedures do not apply to CFSP decision-making. However, such a straightforward reading is difficult to justify in the light of the principle of effective Treaty interpretation. Indeed, it is most clear from the TEU provisions on CFSP decision-making that CFSP decisions are not adopted in accordance with either the ordinary or a special legislative procedure, as the Parliament is not involved. There was therefore no need to confirm, twice, that legislative acts are excluded: the provisions on decision-making already implied such an exclusion.

[46] See Arts I-33 to I-35.

A purely formal reading of the exclusion of legislative acts is thus unpersuasive. There are, moreover, strong arguments in support of a more substantive reading[47]—a reading which excludes general normative action in the framework of the CFSP.

The first argument is based on the democratic principles underpinning the EU, as now set out in Articles 9 to 12 TEU. Article 10, in particular, describes how the functioning of the Union shall be founded on representative democracy. It points out that citizens are directly represented at Union level in the European Parliament, and that Member States are represented in the European Council and the Council by their (heads of) governments, themselves democratically accountable to either their national Parliaments or their citizens. Article 10(3) confirms that every citizen shall have the right to participate in the democratic life of the Union and that decisions—a concept clearly used in a generic sense—shall be taken as openly and as closely as possible to the citizen.

As the European Parliament has no direct say in CFSP matters (see further below), the CFSP decisions benefit from only one type of representative democracy: through Member State representation in the European Council and the Council. It could well be argued that this explains the exclusion of legislative acts, understood as general normative action. The latter clearly affects European citizens directly, and should therefore only result from decision-making involving the Parliament, which directly represents those citizens. Regulations and directives adopted under the TFEU involve such general normative action, even if directives are not directly applicable and require national implementation: they are nevertheless binding as to the results, which more often than not encompass creating rights and obligations for EU citizens (as well as other persons subject to EU jurisdiction). CFSP decisions should not involve that kind of normative action. Such an understanding of representative democracy justifies a reading of the exclusion of legislative acts for the conduct of the CFSP which precludes general normative action, in particular action which purports to create rights and obligations.

A second argument in support of such a reading is derived from the principle that the Union is founded on the rule of law (Article 2 TEU).[48] In the conception of the Court of Justice, that principle implies that all acts of the institutions are subject to review as regards their conformity with the basic constitutional charter, the (then) EC Treaty.[49] Clearly, the exclusion of the Court's jurisdiction over CFSP decisions (see below) constitutes a breach in this foundational principle. However, it is a breach which is more tolerable if general normative action is excluded in the context of the CFSP.

[47] Cf A Türk, *The Concept of Legislation in European Community Law—A Comparative Perspective* (Kluwer Law International, 2006) 77–185; K Lenaerts and M Desomer, 'Simplification of the Union's Instruments' in B de Witte (ed), *Ten Reflections on the Constitutional Treaty for Europe* (RSCAS, 2003) 110–11.

[48] Cf R Gosalbo Bono, 'Some Reflections on the CFSP Legal Order' (2006) 43 CML Rev 347, where he states that the principle of the rule of law is applicable to the CFSP.

[49] Case 294/83 *Les Verts v. European Parliament* [1986] ECR 1339, para 23, as confirmed in Joined Cases C–402 and 415/05P *Kadi and Al Barakaat v. Council and Commission* [2008] ECR I–6351, para 281.

There are signs that the Court itself shares such a conception. In *Segi* it was confronted with a challenge, by way of an action in damages, against a common position listing Segi, a Basque group, as a terrorist organization. The common position was based on the pre-Lisbon TEU provisions concerning CFSP (Second Pillar) and concerning Police and Judicial Co-operation in Criminal Matters (Third Pillar). Segi's listing was in fact characterized as a Third Pillar act. The case had first been brought to the (then) Court of First Instance (CFI), which had established that the then TEU did not provide for an action in damages against the institutions, and therefore dismissed the application. On appeal, the Court of Justice could only confirm that finding. However, as to whether this finding was in conformity with the right to effective judicial protection, the Court made the following analysis. The background to this analysis is that, at the time, the Court had some jurisdiction for Third Pillar measures: it could hear actions for annulment brought against framework decisions and decisions, and references from national courts on the interpretation and validity of framework decisions and decisions, but it could not hear such actions or references as regards common positions.

The Court first admitted that the system of remedies as regards the Third Pillar was less extensive than that under the (then) EC Treaty. Nevertheless, the appellants could not validly argue that they were deprived of all judicial protection. As was clear from (then) Article 6 TEU, the Union was founded on the principle of the rule of law and it respected fundamental rights as general principles of Community law. It followed that the institutions were subject to review of the conformity of their acts with the treaties and the general principles of law, just like the Member States when they implemented the law of the Union. Here it was to be noted that (then) Article 34 TEU provided that the Council could adopt acts varying in nature and scope. Under Article 34(2)(a) TEU the Council could 'adopt common positions defining the approach of the Union to a particular matter'. A common position required the compliance of the Member States by virtue of the principle of the duty to co-operate in good faith, which meant in particular that Member States were to take all appropriate measures, whether general or particular, to ensure fulfilment of their obligations under EU law. However, a common position was not of itself supposed to produce legal effects in relation to third parties. That is why, in the system established by the then TEU, only framework decisions and decisions could be the subject of an action for annulment before the Court of Justice. The Court's jurisdiction, as defined by Article 35(1) TEU, to give preliminary rulings also did not extend to common positions but was limited to rulings on the validity and interpretation of framework decisions and decisions, on the interpretation of conventions established under Title VI, and on the validity and interpretation of the measures implementing them.

Article 35(1) TEU, in that it did not enable national courts to refer a question to the Court for a preliminary ruling on a common position but only a question concerning the acts listed in that provision, treated as acts capable of being the subject of such a reference for a preliminary ruling all measures adopted by the Council and intended to produce legal effects in relation to third parties. Given that the procedure enabling the Court to give preliminary rulings was designed to guarantee observance of the law in the interpretation and application of the Treaty, it would run counter to that objective to interpret Article 35(1) TEU narrowly. The right to make a reference to the Court of Justice for a preliminary ruling therefore had to exist in respect of all measures adopted by the Council, whatever their nature or form, which were intended to have legal effects in relation to third parties. As a result, it had to be possible to make subject to review by the Court a common position which, because of its content, had a scope going beyond that assigned by the TEU to that kind of act. Therefore, a national court hearing a dispute which indirectly raised the issue of the validity or interpretation of a common position adopted on the basis of Article 34 TEU, and which had serious doubts whether that common position was really intended to produce legal effects in relation to third parties, would be able, subject to the conditions fixed by Article 35 TEU, to ask the Court to give a preliminary ruling. It would then fall to the Court to find, where appropriate, that the common position was intended to produce legal effects in relation to third parties, to accord it its true classification, and to give a preliminary ruling.[50]

The Court thus displayed a willingness to review the use of common positions under the then Third Pillar, and considered that such common positions were precluded from producing legal effects in relation to third parties. That was the justification, and indeed the condition, for its exclusion of jurisdiction to be justified.

Those considerations can easily be transposed to current CFSP decisions. The only justification, and indeed a condition, for the exclusion of the Court's jurisdiction is that CFSP decisions cannot produce legal effects in relation to third parties. The amended TEU and TFEU recognize this, because the Court does have jurisdiction, pursuant to Article 275 TFEU, to review 'the legality of decisions providing for restrictive measures against natural or legal persons adopted by the Council on the basis of Chapter 2 of Title V of the Treaty on European Union' (the CFSP chapter). This exception confirms the principle that, in a Union governed by the rule of law, all acts of the institutions producing legal effects in relation to third parties must be reviewable. It does not, on the other hand, imply that general normative action is permitted under the CFSP. Article 275 TFEU talks about restrictive measures against natural or legal persons, and clearly recognizes that such decisions are adopted in the context of the CFSP. However, such restrictive measures do not of necessity involve general normative action. They may be in the nature of administrative decisions concerning individual cases.

General normative acts can therefore only be adopted under the TFEU, where the Court has full jurisdiction. The exclusion of legislative acts for the conduct of the CFSP, thus understood, is the counterpart of the exclusion of the Court's jurisdiction.

[50] Case C–355/04P *Segi v. Council* [2007] ECR I–1657, paras 50–54.

It should furthermore be noted that, pursuant to current Article 40 TEU, it would be open to the Court to advance such an understanding of the nature and indeed limitations of CFSP acts, and to police it. Article 40 clarifies that the CFSP shall not affect the procedures and the extent of the powers of the institutions for the exercise of Union competences under the TFEU. Clearly, if the treaties are to be read as precluding CFSP decisions from producing legal effects in relation to third parties by way of general normative action, such acts being reserved to decision-making under the TFEU, then this concerns the procedures and the powers of the institutions for the exercise of Union competences under the TFEU.

The conclusion at this point, on the basis of the EU's democratic principles and of the principle of the rule of law, is that the exclusion of legislative acts for the conduct of the CFSP is to be understood as an exclusion of general normative action producing legal effects in relation to third parties. If that conclusion is correct, two further questions arise. First, what is the scope of this limitation; what kind of acts does it preclude? Secondly, does the current CFSP practice conform to the limitation?

As regards the first question, clearly, a CFSP decision cannot contain general provisions producing legal effects in relation to third parties which are directly applicable in the Member States. In other words, they cannot have an effect equal to that of general regulations adopted under the TFEU. This appears to imply that CFSP decisions cannot have direct effect, and that the principle of the primacy of EU law does not extend to them, at least not in the meaning normally attributed to those concepts in EU law. Indeed, direct effect means that, of its own force, a provision of EU law has effect in national law. The principle of primacy means that such a provision prevails over any inconsistent national law. Unavoidably, a general act which has such effects in and on national law will produce legal effects in relation to third parties. It is therefore arguable that the exclusion of legislative acts for the conduct of the CFSP implies that CFSP acts do not have direct effect and do not prevail over national law.

That may not be the end of the matter, however. CFSP decisions (or former joint actions and common positions) do not in terms purport to have direct effect or to prevail over inconsistent national law. They do not define their legal effects. The TEU itself only clarifies that the Member States are under an obligation to comply. It is the Member States which are bound by the CFSP decisions (also pursuant to the duty of sincere co-operation in Article 4(3) TEU—see further the Court's statements on the binding nature of Third Pillar common positions in *Segi*, as set out above). Is that sufficient for the purpose of the exclusion of legislative acts? Since CFSP decisions do not of themselves have any effect in and on national law, are they, by definition, not legislative acts? It is submitted that that would be an approach which is too formal. The analogy with directives comes to mind. Directives are not directly applicable in the laws of the Member States, but need to be transposed. Nevertheless, most directives clearly have a strong legislative scope. They purport to produce legal effects for third parties, subject to their transposition into national law, which in any event, as a matter of law, is a foregone conclusion: Member States need to achieve the directive's result and are under an obligation to transpose. CFSP decisions, even if equally binding, are not permitted to have legislative scope. They cannot, to use a non-hypothetical example, provide that Member States need to ensure that acts of terrorism shall be established as serious criminal offences. The exclusion of legislative acts must extend to the normative content of the decisions in issue. An analysis of that content cannot be avoided on the mere basis that a CFSP decision is only binding on the Member States and is not as such directly applicable.

Does CFSP practice conform to those limitations?[51] It is not clear that it does. In particular the practice as regards restrictive measures stands out as a cause for concern. Decisions on restrictive measures (formerly common positions) contain detailed and extensive provisions which, in substance, have a normative content.[52] The best example is the latest decision (at the time of writing) concerning Iran.[53] That decision involves restrictions on imports and exports; on technical assistance; on investment; on financial services; on the transfer of funds; on the entry into and transit through the Member States of listed persons; and on the freezing of funds. It is true that such decisions are usually implemented, at least in part, by means of regulations adopted under Article 215 TFEU. That, however, does not mean that the CFSP decisions have no legislative scope, or that such scope is justified. Not all aspects of the relevant CFSP decisions acquire a TFEU counterpart: restrictions on the sale and export of arms, and on the entry and transit of persons, are never incorporated in the Article 215 regulations (or their Articles 301 and 60 EC predecessors). Moreover, even if one were to accept that the principle of the exclusion of legislative acts is somehow remedied by also taking action under the TFEU, the CFSP decisions ought not to be as detailed as they usually are, for then the TFEU regulations constitute a mere transposition of what is effectively CFSP legislative action.

Budget

Many CFSP joint actions involve considerable expenditure, and the question therefore arises of how financing is organized. When the TEU was negotiated it was not envisaged that the EU, as distinct from the (then) EC, would require its own budget and financial resources. Article J.11 of the original TEU provided that administrative expenditure was to be charged to the EC budget. As regards operational expenditure, the Treaty left two options: either the Council decided unanimously that

[51] Dashwood (n 13 above) 54 and 64 notes that certain pre-Lisbon joint actions had legislative purposes 'presumably as the least inappropriate instrument available'.

[52] Cf Gosalbo Bono (n 48 above) 364.

[53] Council Decision concerning restrictive measures against Iran and repealing Common Position 2007/140 [2010] OJ L195/39.

such expenditure was to be charged to the EC budget, in which case the relevant EC Treaty provisions were applicable, or it could determine that such expenditure be charged to the Member States, where appropriate in accordance with a scale to be decided. It may be noted that the first option effectively implied a measure of communitarization, as the Commission and the Parliament have significant powers and functions in relation to the budget.

These financial arrangements were criticized from the outset as showing that the EU lacked any financial autonomy, and in practice they soon proved to be divisive and time wasting.[54] The lack of automatic financial cover for CFSP decisions either led to prolonged wrangling or even prevented action.[55] The financing option created tension between the objective of keeping the CFSP intergovernmental and the concern to spare national budgets.[56] Gradually the practice moved towards the systematic use of the EC budget, but this in itself did not solve the issue of which institution would control the decision to finance a joint action, or who would control and oversee implementation.[57] In 1997, the Parliament, the Council, and the Commission concluded an inter-institutional agreement on provisions regarding the financing of the CFSP.[58] This agreement provided that CFSP expenditure was to be regarded as non-compulsory. It arranged for an overall structure of CFSP financing in the EC budget, with a particular CFSP chapter to be subdivided into certain categories. Transfers within the chapter were to be allowed, but any additional overall CFSP expenditure that proved necessary during the year was to be agreed under an urgent procedure. In the event of disagreement between the Council and Parliament, an ad hoc concertation procedure was to be set up to expedite agreement, and the Parliament extracted significant commitments on information and consultation.[59]

The Treaty of Amsterdam amended the TEU provisions on CFSP financing, effectively confirming actual practice. (Old) Article 28(3) TEU modified the provisions on operational expenditure, by providing that operational expenditure was to be charged to the EC budget, except for such expenditure arising from operations having military or defence implications and cases where the Council acting unanimously decided otherwise.

In the meantime the above inter-institutional agreement had been replaced by the (general) inter-institutional agreement on budgetary discipline and improvement of the budgetary procedure,[60] but without material modification of the arrangements on CFSP expenditure. (Current) Article 41 TEU confirms this approach. However, it also makes room for the Council to establish specific

[54] Denza (n 2 above) 57.

[55] J Monar, 'The Financial Dimension of the CFSP' in M Holland (ed), *Common Foreign and Security Policy—The Record and Reforms* (Pinter, 1997) 34.

[56] Wessel (n 2 above) 98; Nuttall (n 9 above) 265.

[57] Peers (n 33 above) 542.

[58] [1997] OJ C286/80.

[59] See also Peers (n 33 above) 544.

[60] [1999] OJ C172/1.

procedures for guaranteeing rapid access to appropriations in the Union budget for the urgent financing of initiatives within the framework of the CFSP, and in particular for the preparatory activities for CSDP tasks (see Articles 42(1) and 43 TEU). Such preparatory activities which are not charged to the Union budget shall be financed by a start-up fund made up of Member States' contributions.

The most notable dimension of the CFSP financing saga is that it has led to greater Commission and Parliament involvement in CFSP matters than that for which the TEU expressly provides (see also below).[61]

Actors

European Council

The role and function of the European Council in EU policy-making are ever increasing. That is also the case with the CFSP. The original TEU referred to the European Council in the last part of the CFSP title. Article J.8(1) confined the role of the European Council to defining the principles of, and general guidelines for, the common foreign and security policy. The Treaty of Amsterdam enhanced the European Council's position and input, by enabling it to adopt common strategies and to decide an EU common defence, as the ultimate outcome of the EU's defence policy.[62] The Lisbon Treaty further modified the nature of the European Council by turning it into a formal EU institution (Article 13(1) TEU). Its task is to provide the Union with the necessary impetus for its development and to define the general political directions and priorities thereof. It cannot, however, exercise legislative functions (Article 15(1) TEU). The institutionalization is strengthened by the creation of the office of the President of the European Council (Article 15(5) TEU).

As the European Council has been re-baptized as an EU institution in its own right, it has been granted specific powers, in particular as regards the CFSP. Reference has already been made to Article 22(1) TEU, which enables the European Council to take decisions on the Union's strategic interests and objectives, encompassing both the CFSP and other areas of external action. Article 26(1) TEU builds on that power, by providing that the European Council shall identify the Union's strategic interests, and determine the objectives of and define the general guidelines for the CFSP, including for matters with defence implications. Furthermore, if international developments so require, the President of the European Council shall convene an extraordinary meeting of the European Council in order to define the

[61] And see the Interinstitutional Agreement between the European Parliament, the Council and the Commission on budgetary discipline and sound financial management [2006] OJ C139/1, in particular paras 42–43.

[62] Dashwood (n 13 above) 212.

strategic lines of the Union's policy in the face of such developments. Article 31(1) determines that the European Council acts unanimously. As regards the CSDP, Article 42(2) provides that this policy 'will lead to a common defence, when the European Council, acting unanimously, so decides'.

As mentioned above, at every European Council meeting a substantial amount of time is devoted to international affairs and external action, and Presidency conclusions invariably contain long passages on the EU's external policies, which indeed serve as guidelines for the daily work of the other institutions, in particular the Council. Council CFSP decisions regularly refer to the European Council's deliberations, although there does not appear to be a fixed pattern. The common strategies instrument has been less frequently used (see above), and it is not yet clear whether the new instrument of European Council decisions on strategic interests and objectives will form a significant contribution to policy-making, and whether it effectively increases the European Council's involvement.

However, the European Council's most important role is probably at constitutional and institutional level. For example, one of the most significant CFSP developments over the years has been the construction of the CSDP, which forms part of the CFSP, but with a clear, separate identity. This process has been driven by the European Council, in an attempt to strengthen the EU's crisis-management and conflict-prevention capabilities. The construction of the CSDP required significant institutional action, and it is at the level of the European Council that decisions were taken to convert the Political Committee into a Political and Security Committee; to create a European Union Military Committee (EUMC); and to set up a European Union Military Staff Organization (EUMS).[63]

The European Council President also has a role to play in the conduct of the CFSP. Article 15(5) TEU provides that the President 'shall, at his or her level and in that capacity, ensure the external representation of the Union on issues concerning its common foreign and security policy, without prejudice to the powers of the High Representative of the Union for Foreign Affairs and Security Policy'. It is not wholly clear what is meant by the phrase 'at his or her level and in that capacity'. Clearly, there is no dearth of actors who may represent the EU externally: the European Council President and the High Representative, but also the Commission as regards non-CFSP issues (see Article 17(1) TEU), as well as the EEAS and the Union delegations.[64]

Council

The Council is by far the most important institution for the conduct of the CFSP. Whereas policy-making under the TFEU is characterized by a strong division of powers between the Council, the Commission, and the Parliament,

[63] Nice Presidency Conclusion, Annex IV; see <http://ue.eu.int/en/Info/eurocouncil/index.htm>.
[64] Cf J-C Piris, *The Lisbon Treaty—A Legal and Political Analysis* (CUP, 2010) 208.

requiring constant co-operation between those institutions, the Council clearly dominates the CFSP. However, more than in any other area the Council is not merely the meeting of members of national governments. As the Council's functions in CFSP matters are to a large extent executive, many of its acts require a lot of further activity of different types, i.e. institutional, diplomatic, and military. Also, the preparation of Council decisions requires a strong administrative framework. In performing its functions the Council is therefore served by other actors, bodies, and organs. It will of course need to interact closely with the High Representative and with the EEAS, which are discussed in a separate subsection, below. Accordingly, this subsection first addresses the Council's powers under the relevant Treaty rules, it then looks at decision-making within the Council, and lastly discusses those other actors within the Council framework.

Powers

Article 24(1) TEU provides, in general terms, that the CFSP shall be defined and implemented by the European Council and the Council. Article 26(2) TEU further provides that the Council shall frame the CFSP and take the decisions necessary for defining and implementing it on the basis of the general guidelines defined by the European Council. The Council must also, with the High Representative, ensure unity, consistency, and effectiveness of action by the Union. Articles 28 and 29 TEU lay down the provisions on, respectively, decisions on Union actions and on Union positions (see above). Article 30 provides that any Member State, the High Representative, or the High Representative with the Commission's support, may refer any question relating to the CFSP to the Council and may submit to it initiatives or proposals. The Council, together with the European Council, is also the forum where Member States consult one another 'on any matter of foreign and security policy of general interest in order to determine a common approach' (Article 32). A further power of the Council is to appoint, on a proposal of the High Representative, a special representative with a mandate in relation to particular policy issues (Article 33 TEU).

The Council may also conclude international agreements with one or more States or international organizations (see Chapter 6). Lastly, the Council shall, in accordance with Article 16 TFEU (on data protection), adopt a decision laying down the rules relating to the protection of individuals with regard to the processing of personal data by the Member States when carrying out activities which fall within the scope of the CFSP (Article 39 TEU). This provision confirms that data protection must be maintained throughout the Union's activities, and completes the competences under the TFEU to provide for such protection.[65]

[65] Cf Joined Cases C–317 and 318/04 *European Parliament v. Council and Commission (PNR)* [2006] ECR I–4721.

Decision-making

Article 31 TEU contains the provisions on Council decision-making in CFSP matters. The rule is unanimity. There is one qualification to that rule, so-called constructive abstention, and three exceptions, where the Council decides by qualified majority.

Article 31(1) provides that the Council acts unanimously. There is, however, room for a Member State to abstain. The Treaty clarifies that, when abstaining in a vote, any member of the Council may qualify its abstention by making a formal declaration. It provides that in that case the member in question shall not be obliged to apply the decision, but shall accept that the decision commits the Union. In a spirit of mutual solidarity, that Member State shall refrain from any action likely to conflict with or impede Union action based on that decision, and the other Member States shall respect its position. However, no decision can be adopted where the Member States qualifying their abstention represent at least one-third of the Member States comprising at least one-third of the population of the Union.

This mechanism of constructive abstention is unique in Council decision-making under the Treaties. It is clearly intended to lower, in some cases, the high hurdle of unanimous decision-making. Whether, however, it has much practical relevance is unclear. In 2001, Peers reported that the mechanism had never been used,[66] and this appears not to have changed in the meantime, as far as joint actions and decisions on actions, and common positions and decisions on positions, are concerned.

Since the Treaty of Nice there have been three types of decisions which the Council adopts by qualified majority, pursuant to Article 31(2) TEU:

- when adopting a decision defining a Union action or position on the basis of a European Council decision relating to the Union's strategic interests and objectives;
- when adopting any decision implementing a decision defining a Union action or position;
- when appointing a special representative in accordance with Article 33.

The Treaty of Lisbon has inserted a further instance of Council qualified majority voting:

- when adopting any decision defining a Union action or position, on a proposal which the High Representative has presented following a specific request from the European Council, made on its own initiative or that of the High Representative.

Moreover, the TEU now enables the European Council to extend the cases of qualified majority voting: it may unanimously adopt a decision stipulating that the Council shall act by a qualified majority in other cases (Article 31(3)).

[66] Peers (n 33 above) 537.

There are, however, two exceptions to the use of qualified majority (Article 31(4) TEU). First, it does not extend to decisions having military or defence implications. Secondly, every member of the Council has a kind of veto right:

If a member of the Council declares that, for vital and stated reasons of national policy, it intends to oppose the adoption of a decision to be taken by qualified majority, a vote shall not be taken. The High Representative will, in close consultation with the Member State involved, search for a solution acceptable to it. If he does not succeed, the Council may, acting by a qualified majority, request that the matter be referred to the European Council for decision by unanimity.

Hitherto, qualified-majority voting primarily took place as regards the implementation of joint actions and decisions on actions, and common positions and decisions on positions.[67] There is also an example of a joint action being adopted by qualified majority on the basis of a common strategy.[68]

It is obvious that the rule of unanimity may make it difficult for the EU to develop common policies on matters of general interest. For example, if one examines the joint actions and common positions of 2002 and of the first half of 2003, one finds no trace of the conflict in Iraq, which will come as no surprise to all those who have followed the events in question. The Member States simply could not reach a consensus on their attitude towards the Iraqi regime. Whether, however, the EU is ripe for more extended use of qualified-majority voting in the most sensitive areas of international politics is another matter.

Other actors

The Council is chaired by the High Representative, whose powers are described below. The Council and the EU institutions are, in general, greatly assisted by committees consisting of national representatives, often from national administrations (so-called comitology).[69] The most important of those committees is Coreper, the Committee of Permanent Representatives of the Member States. Its role is described in Article 16(7) TEU and Article 240(1) TFEU as preparing the work of the Council and as carrying out the tasks assigned to it by the Council. Coreper is active throughout the work of the Council, but in CFSP matters there is a second committee, originally called the Political Committee and since the Treaty of Nice the Political and Security Committee (PSC), in order to reflect increasing activity in the field of security and defence. Article 38 TEU describes the role of the PSC:

Without prejudice to Article 240 of the [TFEU], a Political and Security Committee shall monitor the international situation in the areas covered by the common foreign and security policy and contribute to the definition of policies by delivering opinions to the Council at

[67] Ibid, 538–9. [68] Joint Action 1999/878 establishing an EU Co-operation Programme for Non-Proliferation and Disarmament in the Russian Federation [1999] OJ L331/11.

[69] See in general M Andenas and A Türk (eds), *Delegated Legislation and the Role of Committees in the EU* (Kluwer Law International, 2000); C Joerges and E Vos (eds), *EU Committees: Social Regulation, Law and Politics* (Hart Publishing, 1999).

the request of the Council or of the High Representative . . . or on its own initiative. It shall also monitor the implementation of agreed policies, without prejudice to the powers of the High Representative.

Within the scope of this Chapter, the Political and Security Committee shall exercise, under the responsibility of the Council and the High Representative, the political control and strategic direction of crisis management operations referred to in Article 43.

The Council may authorize the Committee, for the purpose and for the duration of a crisis management operation, as determined by the Council, to take the relevant decisions concerning the political control and strategic direction of the operation.

In the literature the Political Committee has been described as the backbone of foreign policy co-ordination since the inception of European Political Co-operation.[70] It has also been noted that there have been power struggles between Coreper and the Political Committee, and that co-ordination between them is not straightforward.[71]

The second and third paragraphs of Article 38 TEU were inserted by the Treaty of Nice, and were immediately applied in the EU's military operations in the former Yugoslav Republic of Macedonia (FYROM) and Congo. Both joint actions contained provisions reflecting the language of those paragraphs, and they conferred on the PSC the powers to amend the operation plan, the chain of command, and the rules of engagement.[72] That has remained the practice for EU military and other missions.

Commission

Upon a mere reading of the TEU the Commission's role in CFSP matters appears strictly limited. Indeed, the Commission is hardly ever mentioned in the TEU chapter on the CFSP. Article 27(3) TEU provides that the Commission has to give its consent to the Council decision establishing the EEAS, and that the EEAS shall also comprise Commission officials. Article 30 TEU enables the High Representative, either on his or her own, or 'with the Commission's support', to refer any question relating to the CFSP to the Council.

That is all the Treaty provides for. The actual role of the Commission is, however, much more extensive. Because the High Representative is at once also a Commission Vice-President, there is an institutional link with the conduct of the CFSP. Of course, the High Representative, when acting within the scope of the CFSP, has no responsibilities towards the Commission and takes no instructions from it. However, the CFSP is but one segment of the EU's overall external action. As discussed in other chapters, the CFSP cannot be dissociated from external action

[70] Peers (n 33 above) 551.

[71] Nuttall (n 9 above) 245 *et seq.*; Edwards, 'Common Foreign and Security Policy' (1993) 13 YEL 499; Wessel (n 2 above) 79.

[72] Art 4(1) Joint Action 2003/92 [2003] OJ L34/26 and Art 7(1) Joint Action 2003/423 [2003] OJ L43/5.

under the TFEU, where the Commission generally plays a much more important role. It negotiates most of the international agreements which the EU concludes. It represents the EU for matters coming within the scope of the TFEU, such as trade, where it acts for the EU in the WTO. The Commission is also very active in the area of development co-operation, other forms of co-operation with third countries, humanitarian aid, and external environmental policies. All of those policies need to be co-ordinated with the CFSP, and the fact that the High Representative has been made a member of the Commission is precisely intended to ensure such co-ordination, and will thereby contribute to associating the Commission with the CFSP.

Even in strict CFSP matters the role of the Commission is more extensive than it may appear at first sight. Under Article 317 TFEU it is the Commission that implements the budget, and, as analysed above, that budget is increasingly used to finance the CFSP. Decisions on Union actions requiring expenditure therefore invariably refer to the Commission as the institution responsible for implementing the policy in question. Indeed, some joint actions, which were limited to financial support for a particular cause or country, referred almost exclusively to the Commission.[73]

In practice, therefore, the Commission is represented at all levels in the CFSP structure.[74] The Commission has also made use of its right to make proposals to the Council (modified now as a right to support a proposal by the High Representative), and some of those have been accepted (even if in much modified form).[75]

High Representative

The Treaty of Lisbon has introduced the office of the High Representative of the Union for Foreign Affairs and Security Policy, a major institutional innovation in the sphere of external action.[76] It has its origin in the Constitution for Europe, and the original name of EU Minister for Foreign Affairs indicates the ambition of the Treaty drafters. It is clear from the work of the Convention on the Future of Europe that this so-called double-hatted office was introduced mainly to ensure coherence and efficiency between the various institutions and actors.[77] Indeed,

[73] E.g. Joint Action 1999/878 (n 68 above).

[74] Wessel (n 2 above) 91.

[75] Peers (n 33 above) 540.

[76] See also Piris (n 64 above) 243–9; J Wouters, D Coppens, and B De Meester, 'The European Union's External Relations after the Lisbon Treaty' in S Griller and J Ziller (eds), *The Lisbon Treaty—EU Constitutionalism without a Constitutional Treaty?* (Springer-Verlag, 2008) 150–6; C Kaddous, 'Role and Position of the High Representative of the Union for Foreign Affairs and Security Policy under the Lisbon Treaty' in Griller and Ziller (above) 206; D Curtin, *Executive Power of the European Union—Law, Practices, and the Living Constitution* (OUP, 2009) 100–103.

[77] European Convention, Final Report of Working Group VII on External Action, CONV 459/02, at 4–5.

because of the constitutional and institutional gap between the CFSP and other areas of EU external action, the EU had developed parallel administrations, in the Council and the Commission, dealing with external policies. Previous chapters have illustrated the scope for inter-institutional strife to which this gap gave rise. As was analysed in Chapter 5, the Treaty of Lisbon in no sense removes the special character of the CFSP and its awkward relationship with other EU external policies. Instead, it attempts to create an institutional bridge, through the office of the High Representative and indeed the creation of the EEAS. It remains to be seen whether that institutional bridge will be effective in reducing inter-institutional tension and conflict, or whether the creation of a new office and a new institution, the EEAS, will increase the scope for infighting.

The new office of the High Representative has its own pedigree. For some time there had been a growing desire to put a face to the CFSP through the appointment of a distinguished politician responsible for moving the CFSP forward and for representing the EU in CFSP matters. The Treaty of Amsterdam thus created the position of High Representative for the CFSP, occupied by Mr Solana, who was at the same time Secretary-General of the Council. The creation of that position was already an important development.[78] Whereas the (old) TEU described his or her role as that of assisting the rotating Presidency of the Council, the practice in the context of implementing joint actions went further. They did not, as a rule, provide for an important role for the Presidency, but instead conferred powers on the High Representative and on the PSC. In the EU's military operations, the role of the PSC was preponderant. In other matters there was a more important role for the High Representative.

The new office of the High Representative builds on that practice. However, the powers of the High Representative are much more extensive than those of her pre-Lisbon predecessor. An analysis of the provisions of the TEU referring to the High Representative show that there are, broadly speaking, five types of powers (understood in a broad sense as encompassing responsibilities and duties).

The first is a power to make proposals. Article 18(2) TEU, which speaks about the office in general terms, provides that the High Representative shall contribute by his proposals to the development of the CFSP. Further provisions refer to more specific rights of proposal. Article 22(2) TEU, concerning European Council decisions on the Union's strategic interests and objectives, provides that the High Representative and the Commission may submit joint proposals. Article 27(1) instructs the High Representative to contribute, through his proposals, towards the preparation of the CFSP. Along the same lines, Article 30(1) provides that the High Representative may refer any question relating to the CFSP to the Council. More specific rights of proposal concern the appointment of a special representative with a mandate in relation to particular policy issues (Article 33 TEU), and the setting-up of a start-up fund for the urgent financing of CFSP initiatives (Article 43(3) TEU).

[78] Decaux (n 9 above) 20.

The second power is that of chairing the Foreign Affairs Council (Article 27(1)). Part of that power is the right to convene extraordinary Council meetings, in an emergency (Article 30(2)). There is no further indication of the role of the chair, but it is clear in any event that it is an important one, if only because the chair sets the agenda.

The third power is one of implementation and supervision. Article 18(2) TEU already indicates that the High Representative 'shall conduct the Union's [CFSP]'. Article 24(1) similarly provides that the CFSP 'shall be put into effect' by the High Representative (and by the Member States), a phrase which is repeated in Article 26(3) TEU. Similarly, Article 27(1) provides that the High Representative shall ensure the implementation of the decisions adopted by the European Council and the Council.

A further indication of what implementation of the CFSP involves is given by Article 24 TEU. That provision determines that the CFSP must be conducted within the framework of the (general) principles and objectives of external action, and that the policy must be based on the development of mutual political solidarity among Member States, the identification of questions of general interest, and the achievement of an ever-increasing degree of convergence (Article 24(2)). The Member States must support the Union's policy actively and unreservedly in a spirit of loyalty and mutual solidarity and must comply with Union action; they must also work together to enhance and develop their mutual political solidarity and refrain from any action contrary to the Union's interests or likely to impair its effectiveness as a cohesive force in international relations (Article 24(3)). The provision ends by stating that the Council and the High Representative 'shall ensure compliance with these principles' (also Article 24(3); see also Article 26(3) TEU).

There is therefore also a supervisory and enforcement role for the High Representative, to some degree similar to the role which the Commission has, in other areas of EU policy, 'to ensure the application of the Treaties' (Article 17(1) TEU). However, in contrast with the Commission, the High Representative has no legal means to ensure Member State compliance with the CFSP, such as the opportunity to bring an action before the Court of Justice. It remains to be seen whether the limited political instruments in the hands of the High Representative will be sufficient for this purpose.

The High Representative also supervises the special representatives which may be appointed (Article 33 TEU). In the context of the CSDP tasks referred to in Article 43(1) TEU (joint disarmament operations, humanitarian and rescue tasks, military advice and assistance tasks, etc.), the High Representative shall ensure co-ordination of the civilian and military aspects of such tasks.

Lastly, under the heading of implementation and supervision one may also refer to the High Representative's duty regularly to consult the European Parliament on the main aspects and the basic choices of the CFSP and to inform it.

A fourth power—or duty in fact—concerns the Holy Grail of ensuring consistency in the EU's external action. Article 18(4) indicates that the fact that the

High Representative is also one of the Commission's Vice-Presidents, responsible for Commission responsibilities in external relations, is aimed at ensuring such consistency. Article 21(3) TEU again emphasizes the need for consistency between the different areas of external action and between these and other EU policies, and instructs the Council and the Commission, assisted by the High Representative, to ensure that consistency and to co-operate to that effect.

A fifth power concerns the external representation of the EU as regards the CFSP, and co-ordination of external action by the Member States. Article 27(2) provides that the High Representative shall represent the Union for CFSP matters, and that he shall conduct political dialogue with third parties on the Union's behalf and shall express the Union's position in international organizations and at international conferences. Furthermore, Article 34(1) instructs the High Representative to organize the co-ordination of Member States' action in international organizations and at international conferences. Article 34(3) envisages that the High Representative will be invited to present the Union's position before the UN Security Council, when that position concerns a subject which is on the Security Council's agenda.

As can be seen, this is a tremendous range of powers and responsibilities. There can be serious doubts as to whether one person could ever accomplish all of those tasks. The High Representative is of course assisted, in particular by the EEAS, which was in the process of being set up at the time of writing. Delegation of some of the High Representative's functions will no doubt take place. Nevertheless, the combination of participation in the Commission's work, the chairing of the Foreign Affairs Council, and the external representation of the EU would seem to be a very tall order indeed.

European External Action Service

Article 27(3) TEU provides that the High Representative shall be assisted by a European External Action Service (EEAS), which shall work in co-operation with the diplomatic services of the Member States and comprise officials from relevant departments of the General Secretariat of the Council and of the Commission, as well as staff seconded from national diplomatic services of the Member States.[79] The article further provides that the organization and functioning of the EEAS shall be established by a decision of the Council, acting on a proposal of the High Representative after consulting the European Parliament and after obtaining the consent of the Commission. As with the office of the High Representative, the idea is clearly to bridge the gap between the Commission and Council departments responsible for

[79] See also Wouters, Coppens, and De Meester (n 76 above) 156–60; S Vanhoonacker and N Reslow, 'The European External Action Service: Living Forwards by Understanding Backwards' (2010) 15 EFA Rev 1.

external action. However, the inclusion of diplomatic staff from the Member States also shows that this new EU diplomatic service is intended to build on and work in close co-operation with national administrations.

The EEAS was set up in July 2010 by Council decision,[80] after an intense negotiation between the various institutions. It is beyond the scope of this overview to provide a full analysis of its genesis. It will no doubt take some time to see what the effects of the creation of this EU 'Foreign Office', 'State Department', or 'Ministry for Foreign Affairs' will be on EU external action and what kind of role it may come to play.

The EEAS is set up as 'a functionally autonomous body of the European Union, separate from the General Secretariat of the Council and from the Commission with the legal capacity necessary to perform its tasks and attain its objectives' (Article 1(2) of the decision). It is placed under the authority of the High Representative (Article 1(3)) and is made up of a central administration and of the Union delegations to third countries and to international organizations (Article 1(4)). The inclusion of Union delegations is not as such provided for in the Treaties: Article 221 TFEU simply provides that Union delegations in third countries and at international organizations shall represent the Union, and that they shall be placed under the authority of the High Representative. However, it clearly makes institutional sense to integrate the Union delegations with the Brussels 'Foreign Office'.

As regards staff, the EEAS comprises officials and other servants of the EU, including personnel from the diplomatic services of the Member States appointed as temporary agents (Article 6(2)). As regards the Council, the departments and staff transferred are those covering the CFSP and the CSDP. As regards the Commission, the transfer includes nearly the entire Directorate-General (DG) for External Relations and parts of the DG for Development. This reflects to some extent the Commission portfolio of the current High Representative, which is limited to external relations. The Commission continues to have its own DGs for Development; Enlargement; Humanitarian Aid and Civil Protection; and Trade.

The task of the EEAS is, first of all, to support the High Representative (a) in fulfilling his or her CFSP and CSDP mandate; (b) in his or her capacity as President of the Foreign Affairs Council; and (c) in his or her capacity as Vice-President within the Commission (Article 2(1) of the EEAS decision). However, the EEAS shall also assist the President of the European Council, the President of the European Commission, and the Commission in the exercise of their respective functions in the area of external relations (Article 2(2)). When fulfilling those tasks, the EEAS must also co-operate with a range of institutions and actors. It must support, and work in co-operation with, the diplomatic services of the Member States, as well as the General Secretariat of the Council and the services of the Commission, in order to ensure consistency between the different areas of the Union's external

[80] Council Decision 2010/427 establishing the organisation and functioning of the European External Action Service [2010] OJ L201/30.

action and between those areas and its policies (Article 3(1)). The EEAS and the Commission services must consult each other on all matters relating to EU external action, except on matters covered by the CSDP. The EEAS must also extend appropriate support and co-operation to the other institutions and bodies of the Union, in particular to the European Parliament (Article 3(4)). The preamble to the EEAS decision emphasizes that the Parliament will fully play its role in the external action of the Union, including its functions of political control as provided for in Article 14(1) TEU, as well as in legislative and budgetary matters.

The EEAS decision also contains specific provisions on EU delegations. Such delegations shall comprise EEAS staff and, where appropriate for the implementation of the Union budget (which is a Commission responsibility) and Union policies other than those under the remit of the EEAS, Commission staff (Article 5(2)). The delegations therefore serve both the EEAS and the High Representative, on the one hand, and the Commission, on the other. This is exemplified by the provision which enables not only the High Representative and the EEAS to give instructions to heads of delegations, but also the Commission, 'in areas where the Commission exercises the powers conferred upon it by the Treaties' (Article 5(3)). Moreover, the Union delegations 'shall have the capacity to respond to the needs of other institutions of the Union, in particular the European Parliament, in their contacts with the international organizations or third countries to which the delegations are accredited'.

Parliament

Under the terms of the TEU the Parliament's role in the conduct of the CFSP is very limited.[81] Article 36 TEU addresses that institution:

> The High Representative ... shall regularly consult the European Parliament on the main aspects and the basic choices of the common foreign and security policy and inform it of how those policies evolve. He shall ensure that the views of the European Parliament are duly taken into consideration. Special representatives may be involved in briefing the European Parliament.
>
> The European Parliament may ask questions of the Council or make recommendations to it and to the High Representative. Twice a year it shall hold a debate on progress in implementing the common foreign and security policy, including the common security and defence policy.

The above provisions limit the High Representative's consultation duty to 'the basic choices', and do not provide for a right of consultation on all Council CFSP acts. The Parliament has the right to ask questions and make recommendations, but

[81] It may be noted that national parliaments may also, through Conference of Community and European Affairs Committees of Parliaments of the European Union, debate CFSP matters, pursuant to Protocol No 1 on the role of national parliaments; see Piris (n 64 above) 13.

there could hardly be any doubt that a democratically elected legislature has those rights anyway, whether or not confirmed in the Treaty.

The Parliament is none the less very active in CFSP matters; it exercises considerable influence, and the Council follows many of its views and recommendations.[82] It also manages to have a say in CFSP decisions through its budgetary powers (see above). As most CFSP operational expenditure is charged to the EU budget, the Parliament is automatically involved. As described above, an inter-institutional agreement contains further provisions on budgetary matters. Given that CFSP expenditure is classified as non-compulsory, the Parliament has the right to amend the draft CFSP budget.[83] Commentators agree that the budget has been a vital means for the Parliament to gain a wider role in the CFSP.[84] It is none the less the case that the Parliament has no formal legislative or decision-making powers in CFSP matters, and that the Council is not truly accountable before the Parliament. CFSP power is clearly concentrated in the executive.

Court of Justice

The Court of Justice and the General Court have but limited jurisdiction in CFSP matters.[85] Article 24(1) TEU provides that the Court of Justice of the European Union (which comprises both the Court of Justice and the General Court as well as specialized courts—see Article 19(1) TEU) shall not have jurisdiction with respect to the CFSP provisions, with the exception of its jurisdiction to monitor compliance with Article 40 TEU and to review the legality of certain decisions as provided for by the second paragraph of Article 275 TFEU.

The Court's jurisdiction under Article 40 TEU was analysed in Chapter 5. It was noted there that the Court must delimit the CFSP from other EU policies, and that such delimitation must focus on respect for the applicable Treaty procedures and powers of the institutions for the exercise of the respective EU competences. Article 275 TFEU, on the other hand, provides:

> The Court of Justice of the European Union shall not have jurisdiction with respect to the provisions relating to the common foreign and security policy nor with respect to acts adopted on the basis of those provisions.
>
> However, the Court shall have jurisdiction to monitor compliance with Article 40 of the Treaty on European Union and to rule on proceedings, brought in accordance with the conditions laid down in the fourth paragraph of Article 263 of this Treaty, reviewing the legality

[82] Denza (n 2 above) 337.

[83] PJG Kapteyn and P VerLoren van Themaat, *Introduction to the Law of the European Communities* (3rd edn, by LW Gormley, Kluwer Law International, 1998) 227.

[84] Edwards (n 72 above) 13; Wessel (n 2 above) 99.

[85] See also M-G Garbagnati Ketvel, 'The Jurisdiction of the European Court of Justice in Respect of the Common Foreign and Security Policy' (2006) 55 ICLQ 77; G De Baere, *Constitutional Principles of EU External Relations* (OUP, 2008) 177–200.

of decisions providing for restrictive measures against natural or legal persons adopted by the Council on the basis of Chapter 2 of Title V of the Treaty on European Union.

This provision constitutes an innovation. The Court is now capable of hearing actions for the annulment of CFSP decisions providing for restrictive measures against natural or legal persons. Before Lisbon, the Court's jurisdiction was limited to regulations adopted under Articles 60 and 301 EC seeking to implement CFSP common positions. The famous *Kadi and Al Barakaat* judgment came about pursuant to that jurisdiction.[86] That jurisdiction remains of course intact, in the sense that the Court may review restrictive measures which are implemented under the successor to Articles 60 and 301 EC, i.e. Article 215 TFEU, paragraph 2 of which also allows the Council to adopt restrictive measures against natural or legal persons and groups or non-State entities. However, Article 275, second paragraph, clearly extends the Court's jurisdiction to hear actions for annulment—but not, for example, actions in damages or preliminary rulings cases—concerning CFSP acts entailing restrictive measures against natural or legal persons. As indicated in Chapter 5 and above in this chapter, CFSP decisions on Union positions often contain such restrictive measures which have no counterpart under the TFEU, such as restrictions on entry and transit of certain persons. The Court's jurisdiction now extends to such measures, which implements and confirms the principle of the rule of law.

There are further ways in which CFSP acts are subject to Court jurisdiction. First, it is arguable that the Court has full jurisdiction as regards international agreements which include CFSP matters. Such agreements are concluded on the basis of Article 218 TFEU, and are therefore acts adopted, in part, on the basis of the TFEU, and not exclusively on the basis of the TEU's provisions on the CFSP. This argument finds support in Article 218(11) TFEU, concerning requests for an Opinion (see Chapter 8), which makes no distinction according to the subject matter of an agreement. It would follow that actions for the annulment of a decision to conclude a CFSP agreement, and preliminary references on the interpretation and effects of such agreements, are within the Court's jurisdiction.

Secondly, the EU law rules and principles on transparency and access to documents extend to all Council documents, including those which come within the scope of the CFSP. The (then) Court of First Instance decided this in *Svenska Journalistförbundet*, and the ruling has since been confirmed.[87] This does not, however, mean that access must be granted to all CFSP documents. The current regulation on access to documents provides for exceptions where disclosure would undermine the protection of the public interest as regards, *inter alia*, public security, defence and military matters, and international relations (Article 4(1)).[88] The Courts none

[86] N 49 above.

[87] Case T–174/95 *Svenska Journalistförbundet v. Council* [1998] ECR II–2289, para 81 and Case T–14/98 *Hautala v. Council* [1999] ECR II–2489, para 42; see further A Tomkins, 'Transparency and the Emergence of a European Administrative Law' (1999/2000) 19 YEL 231.

[88] Regulation 1049/2001 of the European Parliament and of the Council regarding public access to European Parliament, Council, and Commission documents [2001] OJ L145/43.

the less show willingness to construe the principle of access to documents broadly, by applying the principle of proportionality and obliging the institutions to grant partial access where only parts of a document are protected.[89]

The jurisdiction of the Court has therefore been expanded by the Lisbon Treaty, but continues to be limited. According to Denza, there were essentially two reasons for the exclusion of jurisdiction in the original TEU. The first related to the nature of CFSP instruments, which were short term in character, potentially both wide-ranging and sensitive, and which were not designed to establish a permanent framework of mutual legal obligations. Measures to enforce compliance were not envisaged. The insistence on the continuation of ultimately sovereign policies, together with the need for speed in the resolution of differences, meant that the conditions for the judicial resolution of disputes did not exist. The second reason concerned the nature and record of the Court, whose rulings in the sphere of external relations laid much more emphasis on the integrationist purpose of the Treaties and less on presuming a minimum derogation from individual sovereign powers. There was concern that doctrines such as that of exclusive external powers might find their way into the CFSP.[90]

The case for limited Court jurisdiction in CFSP matters is not persuasive. In a Union governed by the rule of law there ought to be no acts of the institutions which are outside the Court's jurisdiction.

Conclusions

The analysis of the actors and instruments of the CFSP shows that this policy continues to be in a somewhat precarious state, from a legal and institutional perspective. There is a range of legal instruments, but they are ill-defined and the practice does not bring much clarity. The precise legal effects are uncertain, be it in relation to the Member States, to the EU institutions, or to individuals. The institutional lacuna of lack of Court jurisdiction has prevented authoritative clarification. The overall institutional arrangements are complex, with a variety of actors with uncertain remits, including the President of the European Council, the High Representative, the EEAS, Coreper, and the PSC, and with more subcutaneous involvement by the Commission and the Parliament through the linkages with, respectively, TFEU policies and the EU budget. In the eyes of the general public the CFSP is not credited with much success. This is partly due to lack of knowledge about its achievements, but one can indeed doubt whether the current constitutional framework is conducive to effective policy-making, even if one disregards the flagship unanimity/majority issue.

[89] Curtin (n 76 above) ch 8.

[90] Denza (n 2 above) 312.

The Treaty of Lisbon aimed to bring relief by homogenizing the institutional framework. The creation of the High Representative, heading a unified EEAS, appeared to make sense. The previous existence of parallel central administrations in the Council and the Commission was bound to be unproductive and to lead to turf battles rather than effective policy-making. There is, however, a risk that, instead of simplifying matters, the new framework has merely created a set of new institutional actors, and may not lead to greater inter-institutional harmony.

However, it is at the level of parliamentary involvement and judicial scrutiny that much remains to be done. Here, unfortunately, the Treaty of Lisbon made only limited progress. The current state of affairs, it is submitted, is unacceptable in a polity governed by the rule of law. CFSP policies show signs of significant expansion, in particular in their natural terrain of security and defence policies. There are now a string of decisions on actions involving military operations. The analysis above reveals, moreover, the many different objects of CFSP decisions in particular, some of which appear to have indirect legislative scope. All these policies are excessively dominated by the executive. The focus of debate should not continue to be the well-worn battle between supranationalism and intergovernmentalism, but should turn to issues of accountability. The latter is clearly no luxury in times when the EU is involved in military operations and the war against terrorism. The exclusion of legislative acts, introduced by the Lisbon amendments, is to be taken seriously.

Parliamentary and judicial scrutiny is fortunately not as limited as the Treaty language suggests. In legal terms the scope of the CFSP is restricted to areas not covered by the TFEU (see Chapter 5). The Parliament has impact through its budgetary role, and the Court has jurisdiction as regards restrictive measures (see also Chapter 12). That is not, however, sufficient. There is no reason in principle to exclude CFSP policies from full parliamentary involvement and judicial scrutiny, even if there are difficult questions in terms of finding room for executive discretion. The exercise of arranging for such involvement and scrutiny would force the EU polity to come to terms with the reality of the attempt to construct a meaningful and workable CFSP. The often lofty ideals and objectives of CFSP policies need to be matched with strong constitutionalism.

12

Sanctions policy

Introduction

It is one of the hallmarks of the EU's external relations that external economic policy and foreign policy are constitutionally separated, the first always having been at the very core of supranational integration and the second forming the subject of evolving, but still on the whole intergovernmental, co-operation. Chapters 2 and 5 examined the interface between trade policy and foreign policy from the angle of the respective competences of the EU under the TFEU and under the TEU. Chapter 10 looked briefly at the EU's import and export regulations, which are the legal cornerstones of external trade. Particularly as regards exports, the analysis in that chapter was limited to the general export regulation, which provides for the freedom to export. Yet it is obvious that exports may be a sensitive issue from a foreign and security policy perspective. As certain parts of the world are rather unstable and as certain countries' regimes are considered a threat to international peace and security, exports need to be monitored and controlled. Such controls do not of course cover armaments alone, which are to some extent outside EU competence,[1] but also so-called dual-use goods which can be used for both civil and military purposes. Such goods are normally traded, and as such are fully covered by the common commercial policy, but because they are sensitive their exportation is controlled under specific legal instruments which are based on foreign and security policy considerations.[2]

Next to such export controls, there is another obvious instance of a foreign policy instrument which directly affects trade, both imports and exports: embargo measures, or, to use the common EU law term, economic sanctions, which are adopted to force a State or regime to modify its behaviour.[3] It is in those areas of export controls and economic sanctions that the artificiality of the dichotomy between trade policy and foreign and security policy first became apparent. Other instruments of trade policy are of course also influenced by foreign policy considerations, but then at a general and aggregate level. Export controls and

[1] See Art 346(1)(b) TFEU.

[2] See Council Regulation 428/2009 setting up a Community regime for the control of exports, transfer, brokering and transit of dual-use items [2009] OJ L134/1.

[3] See Ch 11.

economic sanctions, however, are specific trade policy *instruments* which are exclusively employed for foreign policy *objectives*. In legal terms, this tension between instrument and objective connects those areas with exclusive EU competence under the common commercial policy, with the CFSP, and with the Member States' autonomous powers over foreign policy. Export controls and economic sanctions are located in a border area between trade policy and foreign policy where it is difficult, if not impossible, to draw clear boundaries. To take the image a little further, one could say that they are in a no man's land between the front lines of the supranational and the intergovernmental.

In recent years, moreover, there has been a shift from broad economic sanctions, such as trade embargos, to so-called smart sanctions, which focus on targeting those at the heart of political regimes which are considered objectionable. The shift towards such smart sanctions was partly inspired by concerns over the widespread negative effects of general embargos, which are too blunt an instrument. The shift means that sanctions policy has become increasingly orientated towards specific individuals, associations, and companies. It operates mainly by providing for travel bans and asset-freezing measures. The latter instrument has also been extensively employed, since 9/11, in the field of counter-terrorism. In turn, that has led to a large and ever-growing body of case law, as a result of private parties facing such asset freezes seeking judicial assistance to defrost sanctions. Chapter 9 looked in detail at the *Kadi* litigation, which put the relationship between UN law—in particular UN Security Council resolutions—and EU law in issue. However, *Kadi* also concerned questions of competence and of human rights protection, and there is a string of other rulings in which various aspects of EU sanctions policy have been considered.

The EU's sanctions policies therefore offer an excellent case study of the evolving interaction between external policies under the TFEU, and the CFSP, as well as national foreign policy. In the light of the above-mentioned constitutional dichotomy, it will come as no surprise that practice in this area has given rise to a series of legal developments, and has thrown up a number of issues and questions. This chapter aims to address the most significant ones. It shows that there is considerable evolution in these areas, generally towards more developed common policies. Indeed in the area of sanctions we have moved from Member State action, through the use of the common commercial policy, in conjunction with decisions in the framework of European Political Co-operation, to a specific legal basis in the EC Treaty, and now in the TFEU, for the adoption of sanctions, based on decisions taken within the CFSP. Sanctions policies also exemplify the difficulties associated with achieving consistency in the EU's external relations. They concern the interaction between the supranational and the intergovernmental, and their study may reveal the extent to which fears of encroachment upon the *acquis communautaire* and supranational integration mechanisms are warranted.[4]

[4] See Ch 5 on consistency of external action.

This chapter does not offer a comprehensive analysis of sanctions policies and of the fast expanding case law;[5] instead, it aims to focus on some of the essential legal issues which are central to the themes of this book. It starts with a short review of the history of EC/EU involvement, followed by an analysis of questions of competence. It then turns to what has become the central judicial concern in this area, namely the protection of fundamental rights. The chapter further looks at some selected questions of interpretation and application of sanctions instruments, and concludes with an analysis of the question whether, or to what extent, the Member States continue to have autonomous legal capacity to adopt sanctions.

A short history

It took until the 1980s before a pattern of EC involvement in the adoption of economic sanctions developed. Previously the Member States defended their powers to proclaim sanctions under the so-called Rhodesia doctrine, which was based on (current) Article 347 TFEU. The doctrine provided that Member States were deemed free to implement economic sanctions serving political aims against a third country under national rules justified on the basis of Article 347.[6] The prevailing view was that economic sanctions were beyond the scope of the common commercial policy.[7] In the early 1980s, European Political Co-operation (EPC), the predecessor to the CFSP, developed. This provided the basic institutional preconditions for a culture of consultation,[8] within which it became possible to adopt sanctions regulations on the basis of (current) Article 207 TFEU. The first such sanctions were directed against the Soviet Union, following the declaration of martial law in Poland.[9] In the same year the Council adopted sanctions against Argentina, for the first time expressly mentioning discussions in the context of EPC in the preamble.[10] That became the established practice: sanctions were based on (current) Article 207 TFEU, and referred to preceding discussions in the framework of EPC as the political source for their adoption.[11] Commentators agree that this

[5] See C Eckes, *EU Counter-Terrorist Policies and Fundamental Rights—The Case of Individual Sanctions* (OUP, 2009); see also C Murphy, *The European Union Rule of Law in the 'War on Terrorism'*, PhD, King's College London, 2010; P Koutrakos, *EU International Relations Law* (Hart Publishing, 2006) ch 12.

[6] Art 347 TFEU provides: 'Member States shall consult each other with a view to taking together the steps needed to prevent the functioning of the internal market being affected by measures which a Member State may be called upon to take in the event of serious internal disturbances affecting the maintenance of law and order, in the event of war, serious international tension constituting a threat of war, or in order to carry out obligations it has accepted for the purpose of maintaining peace and international security'.

[7] P Koutrakos, *Trade, Foreign Policy and Defence in EU Constitutional Law* (Hart Publishing, 2001) 58.

[8] Ibid, 63–64.

[9] Council Regulation 596/82 [1982] OJ L72/15.

[10] Council Regulation 877/82 [1982] OJ L102/1.

[11] PJ Kuijper, 'Trade Sanctions, Security and Human Rights and Commercial Policy' in M Maresceau (ed), *The European Community's Commercial Policy after 1992: The Legal Dimension* (Kluwer, 1993) 390.

movement towards Community involvement was mainly the result of a concern to ensure the effective and uniform imposition of sanctions, rather than constituting a principled recognition of Community competence.[12] Regulations could be adopted relatively smoothly on the basis of the then Treaty provisions on the common commercial policy, as a Commission proposal and a qualified majority in the Council were sufficient. They are directly applicable in all the Member States and automatically override all inconsistent national law.

This practice was codified in (then) Article 301 EC, introduced by the TEU:

> Where it is provided, in a common position or in a joint action adopted according to the provisions of the Treaty on European Union relating to the common foreign and security policy, for an action by the Community to interrupt or to reduce, in part or completely, economic relations with one or more third countries, the Council shall take the necessary urgent measures. The Council shall act by a qualified majority on a proposal from the Commission.

A corresponding provision extended this approach to the movement of capital and payments. Article 60 EC provided:

> 1. If, in the case envisaged in Article 301, action by the Community is deemed necessary, the Council may, in accordance with the procedure provided for in Article 301, take the necessary urgent measures on the movement of capital and on payments as regards the third countries concerned.
>
> 2. Without prejudice to Article 297 and as long as the Council has not taken measures pursuant to paragraph 1, a Member State may, for serious political reasons and on grounds of urgency, take unilateral measures against a third country with regard to capital movements and payments. The Commission and the other Member States shall be informed of such measures by the date of their entry into force at the latest.
>
> The Council may, acting by a qualified majority on a proposal from the Commission, decide that the Member State concerned shall amend or abolish such measures. The President of the Council shall inform the European Parliament of any such decision taken by the Council.

As can be seen, those provisions spoke in general terms of interrupting or reducing economic relations. In practice the sanctions based on them initially included trade embargos, prohibiting imports and exports; financial sanctions, banning transfers of funds, lending, or investment; and sanctions regarding means of transport or transport services.[13] Most EU sanctions implemented UN Security Council resolutions. They were, in accordance with the above provisions, preceded by 'political' decisions under the CFSP.[14]

These initial policies led to case law in the 1990s. *Bosphorus* concerned the EU implementation of a UN Security Council resolution imposing a trade and transport embargo against the Federal Republic of Yugoslavia (Serbia and

[12] Koutrakos (n 5 above) 64. [13] Ibid, 69. [14] Common positions: see Ch 11.

Montenegro).[15] The Court of Justice was faced with questions of interpretation and of compatibility with fundamental rights, in particular the right to property. *Ebony Maritime* and *Centro-Com* concerned the same set of sanctions, and also involved questions of interpretation and scope.[16] In *Centro-Com*, moreover, issues of EC and national competence were also raised, as analysed in Chapter 2.

Sanctions policy then gradually shifted towards smart sanctions, and from 9/11 became a central tool of counter-terrorism policy. That policy is of course not confined to the EU's external action, but aims to combat terrorism generally, both inside and outside Europe. Nevertheless, the EU institutions continued to base regulations providing for the freezing of assets of individuals and groups or associations suspected of supporting terrorism, on (then) Articles 301 and 60 EC. However, because of the limits imposed by the wording of those provisions—'to interrupt or to reduce . . . economic relations with one or more third countries'—it was considered necessary to add (then) Article 308 EC as a legal basis. Indeed, the link between the individuals and associations concerned and third countries was particularly tenuous in the case of sanctions against those suspected of supporting Al-Qaida. There continued to be a link, of course, with CFSP decisions, as well as with UN Security Council resolutions. However, as regards the latter a dichotomy developed. The Security Council developed its own practice of listing named individuals, groups, or associations, and part of the EU's policy has been simply to copy those lists into EU regulations.[17] Such mere copying was found to be in breach of the EU's fundamental rights standards in *Kadi and Al Barakaat*.[18] Other EU listing regulations are autonomous in the sense that they are not based on UN listings, but on decisions adopted and information supplied by EU Member States.[19]

The EU's competence to target individuals who are not connected with a third country was challenged in *Kadi*, but without success, as will be seen below. The Courts accepted that (then) Article 308 EC could supplement Articles 301 and 60 EC so as to allow the sanctions involved. It is not inconceivable that in reaching that decision the Courts took into account that the Treaty of Lisbon aimed to broaden the scope of EU sanctions policy. Article 215 TFEU now provides:

[15] Case C–84/95 *Bosphorus v. Minister for Transport, Energy and Communications, Ireland and the Attorney General* [1996] ECR I–3953.

[16] Case C–177/95 *Ebony Maritime and Loten Navigation v. Prefetto della Provincia di Brindisi and Others* [1997] ECR I–1111; Case C–124/95 *The Queen, ex parte Centro-Com v. HM Treasury and Bank of England* [1997] ECR I–81.

[17] See Council Regulation 881/2002 imposing certain specific restrictive measures directed against certain persons and entities associated with Usama bin Laden, the Al-Qaida network and the Taliban, and repealing Council Regulation (EC) 467/2001 prohibiting the export of certain goods and services to Afghanistan, strengthening the flight ban and extending the freeze of funds and other financial resources in respect of the Taliban of Afghanistan [2002] OJ L139/9.

[18] Joined Cases C–402 and 415/05P *Kadi and Al Barakaat v. Council and Commission* [2008] ECR I–6351.

[19] See in particular Council Regulation 2580/2001 on specific restrictive measures directed against certain persons and entities with a view to combating terrorism [2001] OJ L344/70.

1. Where a decision, adopted in accordance with Chapter 2 of Title V of the Treaty on European Union, provides for the interruption or reduction, in part or completely, of economic and financial relations with one or more third countries, the Council, acting by a qualified majority on a joint proposal from the High Representative of the Union for Foreign Affairs and Security Policy and the Commission, shall adopt the necessary measures. It shall inform the European Parliament thereof.

2. Where a decision adopted in accordance with Chapter 2 of Title V of the Treaty on European Union so provides, the Council may adopt restrictive measures under the procedure referred to in paragraph 1 against natural or legal persons and groups or non-State entities.

3. The acts referred to in this Article shall include necessary provisions on legal safeguards.

The current sanctions practice therefore continues to straddle the CFSP and the policies and acts adopted under the TFEU. It consists of both smart sanctions against particular third-country regimes, as well as counter-terrorism measures. The practice is that CFSP decisions lay down the overall sanctions—or 'restrictive measures', as they are officially labelled. Part of those sanctions is then translated, as it were, into regulations adopted on the basis of Article 215 TFEU. However, sanctions involving travel bans and exports of arms are confined to the CFSP decision.[20]

Competence issues

Chapter 2 looked at case law delimiting the scope of the common commercial policy in relation to measures with a foreign or security policy dimension. The *Centro-Com* judgment concerned economic sanctions, and the Court did not accept the UK argument that the Member States were entitled, pursuant to their national competence in the field of foreign and security policy, to adopt measures which interfered with the operation of the Community regulations imposing a trade embargo on Serbia and Montenegro. The Member States could not treat national measures whose effect was to prevent or restrict the export of certain products as falling outside the scope of the common commercial policy on the ground that they had foreign and security objectives.[21]

Centro-Com pre-dated the practice under Articles 301 and 60 EC, based on the combination of CFSP measures with EC regulations. The *Kadi* litigation enabled the EU Courts to consider this special relationship between the TEU and the EC Treaty. As mentioned above, the extension of the sanctions to individuals had led the institutions to include Article 308 EC (current Article

[20] See e.g. Council Decision concerning restrictive measures against Iran and repealing Common Position 2007/140/CFSP [2010] OJ L195/39.

[21] N 16 above; see Ch 2.

352 TFEU) as the legal basis. However, that provision referred to the objectives of the Community, not to those of the EU under the TEU provisions on the CFSP.[22]

The Court of First Instance (CFI) nevertheless accepted the use of Article 308.[23] It considered that Articles 60 and 301 EC were wholly special provisions, in that they contemplated situations in which action by the Community proved necessary to achieve, not one of the objects of the Community, but rather a CFSP objective. Under those provisions, action by the Community was in actual fact action by the Union. The Court then referred to the requirement of consistency in (then) Article 3 TEU. It pointed out that, just as all the powers provided for by the EC Treaty could be proved insufficient to attain one of the EC objectives, so the powers under Articles 301 and 60 could be insufficient to attain a CFSP objective. There were therefore good grounds for accepting that recourse to the additional legal basis of Article 308 EC was justified for the sake of the consistency requirement, when Articles 301 and 60 did not give the Community institutions the power necessary, in the field of economic and financial sanctions, to act for the purpose of attaining the objective pursued by the Union and its Member States under the CFSP.[24]

On appeal, the Court of Justice modified that reasoning, whilst also accepting that sanctions against individuals could be adopted on the basis of Articles 60, 301, and 308 EC. The Court did not accept that the bridge between the EC and the CFSP extended to Article 308 EC. This would have allowed the adoption of Community measures concerning not one of the objectives of the Community but one of the TEU objectives. This ran counter to the wording of Article 308 EC. Furthermore, the coexistence of the Union and the Community as integrated but separate legal orders, and the constitutional architecture of the pillars, constituted considerations of an institutional kind militating against any extension of the bridge to articles of the EC Treaty other than those with which it explicitly created a link. Also, Article 308 EC, based on the principle of conferred powers, could not serve as a basis for widening the scope of Community powers beyond the general framework created by the provisions of the EC Treaty as a whole and, in particular, by those defining the tasks and activities of the Community. However, that did not mean that the measures were adopted on the wrong legal basis. The contested regulation, inasmuch as it imposed restrictive measures of an economic and financial nature, plainly fell within the ambit *ratione materiae* of Articles 60 and 301 EC. The Court distinguished this material scope of those provisions from their personal scope. Since Articles 60 and 301 EC did not provide for any express or

[22] Article 352(4) TFEU now expressly provides that the article cannot serve as a basis for attaining objectives pertaining to the CFSP.

[23] See also P Koutrakos, 'Legal Basis and Delimitation of Competence in EU External Relations' in M Cremona and B De Witte (eds), *EU Foreign Relations Law—Constitutional Fundamentals* (Hart Publishing, 2008) 188–197.

[24] Case T–315/01 *Kadi v. Council and Commission* [2005] ECR II–3649, paras 124–128. See also Case T–306/01 *Yusuf v. Council and Commission* [2005] ECR II–3353.

implied powers of action to impose such measures on addressees in no way linked to the governing regime of a third country, that lack of power could be made good by having recourse to Article 308 EC. Inasmuch as they provided for Community powers to impose restrictive measures of an economic nature in order to implement actions decided on under the CFSP, Articles 60 and 301 EC were the expression of an implicit underlying objective, namely, that of making it possible to adopt such measures through the efficient use of a Community instrument. That objective could be regarded as constituting an objective of the Community for the purpose of Article 308 EC. Nor did implementing restrictive measures of an economic nature go beyond the general framework created by the provisions of the EC Treaty as a whole, because such measures by their very nature offered a link to the operation of the common market. The Court then pointed to effects on trade, the free movement of capital and payments, and the right of establishment in the internal market.[25]

The finding in *Kadi and Al Barakaat* that Article 308 EC was capable of extending the application of Articles 301 and 60 to individuals who were not linked to the governing regime of a third country, clearly put some strain on the principle of conferred powers.[26] However, the entry into force of the Treaty of Lisbon has removed that strain, through the introduction of Article 215(2) TFEU, which permits restrictive measures against natural or legal persons and groups or non-State entities. Not all questions of competence have been resolved, though. In the field of counter-terrorism the combined application of the (then) TEU and the EC Treaty was aided by the presence of the Third Pillar, Police and Judicial Co-operation in Criminal Matters. Indeed, the EU listings in this field include persons and organizations residing both in and outside the EU. As regards the autonomous EU listings at least, the applicable common position containing such listings was based on both the Second and Third Pillar provisions of the TEU.[27] From that perspective, the place of residence of the persons concerned did not matter. In so far as the measures targeted EU-based supporters of terrorism, they formed part of internal co-operation policy in criminal matters. In so far as they targeted persons and organizations located outside the EU, they were part of the CFSP. However, the TEU provisions on the Third Pillar were removed and, with amendments, incorporated in the TFEU. There is at present a specific TFEU provision, Article 75, on, *inter alia*, the freezing of funds to combat terrorism. It provides:

Where necessary to achieve the objectives set out in Article 67, as regards preventing and combating terrorism and related activities, the European Parliament and the Council, acting

[25] *Kadi and Al Barakaat* (n 18 above) paras 197–230. It may be noted that a third position, with equal result, was defended by Maduro AG.

[26] Cf T Tridimas, 'Terrorism and the ECJ; Empowerment and Democracy in the EC Legal Order' (2009) 34 ELR 106.

[27] Common Position 2001/931 on the application of specific measures to combat terrorism [2001] OJ L344/93.

by means of regulations in accordance with the ordinary legislative procedure, shall define a framework for administrative measures with regard to capital movements and payments, such as the freezing of funds, financial assets or economic gains belonging to, or owned or held by, natural or legal persons, groups or non-State entities.

The Council, on a proposal from the Commission, shall adopt measures to implement the framework referred to in the first paragraph.

The acts referred to in this Article shall include necessary provisions on legal safeguards.

This provision is recorded as the successor to Article 60 EC. However, in contrast with that provision it is not located in the chapter on capital and payments,[28] but forms part of the general provisions on the Area of Freedom, Security, and Justice. Nor is it premised on a link with the TEU provisions on the CFSP. It is also more specific than Article 215(2) TFEU, in two ways: it is dedicated to preventing and combating terrorism and related activities; and it concerns specifically the freezing of funds, financial assets, or economic gains, not generally 'restrictive measures'. The law-making procedure is different, in that the Parliament is involved, acting in accordance with the ordinary legislative procedure, as regards the framework for specific administrative measures in this field.

This raises novel questions of how to delimit the scope of Articles 75 and 215(2) TFEU. At the time of writing, those questions are submitted to the Court in an action brought by the Parliament against the amendments by Regulation 1286/2009 to Regulation 881/2002.[29] The Parliament contends that Article 75 should be the legal basis, rather than Article 215(2). A full analysis of the issues in this case is beyond the scope of this chapter. It is nevertheless clear that there are some strong arguments in support of the use of Article 75, rather than Article 215(2), in the case of asset-freezing measures in the sphere of counter-terrorism. Article 75 specifically refers to terrorism as well as to freezing measures. The measures concerned include persons residing in the EU, making the use of decisions adopted under the CFSP rather awkward. If the Court were to go along with the Parliament, the scope of Article 215(2) TFEU would become restricted to smart sanctions against natural or legal persons associated with a third-country regime, whereas Article 75 would need to be employed for counter-terrorism purposes.

Other questions arise, post-Lisbon, about the interaction between CFSP decisions and regulations adopted under Article 215 TFEU. In *Kadi* the Court of Justice spoke of the TEU and the EC as constituting integrated but separate legal orders. The General Court further explored those concepts in *Bank Melli Iran*, a case involving sanctions against an Iranian bank considered to be involved in activities of nuclear proliferation. The Court accepted that Articles 301 and 60 EC formed

[28] This stands in contrast with Art III-160 of the Constitution for Europe, materially identical to Art 75 TFEU, which was located in the capital and payments chapter.

[29] Case C–130/10 *European Parliament v. Council*, pending. See Notice in [2010] OJ C134/26; Regulation 881/2002 (n 17 above); Council Regulation 1286/2009 amending Regulation (EC) No 881/2002 imposing certain specific restrictive measures directed against certain persons and entities associated with Usama bin Laden, the Al-Qaida network and the Taliban [2009] OJ L346/42.

a bridge between the pillars, but emphasized the limits of that image. Even if an action by the Community under Articles 60 and 301 EC gave effect to one of the objectives of the Union, it was nevertheless undertaken on the basis of the Community pillar. The lawfulness of the relevant measures had to be assessed in relation to the conditions laid down by the rules of that pillar, including the appropriate voting rule (qualified majority). Therefore, the CFSP common position which triggered the adoption of the regulation in issue in *Bank Melli Iran* did not form a legal basis for that regulation. The existence of a common position or joint action previously adopted in the sphere of the CFSP was simply a condition laid down by Article 301 EC.[30]

That is the correct approach, but it again illustrates the awkward relationship between the pillars, which the Treaty of Lisbon has not modified. The CFSP decision does not as such bind the institutions when acting under the TFEU. At most, there is the requirement of consistency, further discussed in Chapter 5.

Chapter 5 also analysed the provisions of Article 40 TEU, which aim to delimit the CFSP from policies pursued under the TFEU, and vice versa. Moreover, in Chapter 11 it was argued that the exclusion of legislative acts for the pursuit of the CFSP ought to be understood in substantive terms as prohibiting normative action purporting to create rights and obligations for third parties. If that argument is correct, the present practice gives rise to concerns over its conformity with the Treaties. The use of smart sanctions is proliferating, and some CFSP decisions are clearly legislative in nature. A good example is the July 2010 Council Decision concerning restrictive measures against Iran.[31] That decision contains detailed, prescriptive, and prohibitory provisions, on such issues as export and import restrictions (Articles 1 to 3); restrictions on the financing of certain enterprises (Articles 5 to 7); restrictions on financial support for trade (Article 8); restrictions in the financial and transport sectors (Articles 9 to 18); restrictions on admission of certain persons (Article 19); and provisions on the freezing of funds and economic resources (Article 20). To give just one example of a provision with clear legislative scope: Article 6(a) provides that 'the granting of any financial loan or credit to enterprises in Iran that are engaged in the sectors of the Iranian oil and gas industry . . . or to Iranian or Iranian-owned enterprises engaged in those sectors outside Iran' shall be prohibited. If the exclusion of legislative acts within the framework of the CFSP is to be understood in the manner contended for in Chapter 11, such CFSP decisions violate the relevant TEU provisions.

The current practice also raises questions under Article 40 TEU. The Iranian sanctions extend to trade in goods and services; investment; capital movement and payments; transport; and the admission of persons to the territories of the Member States. The EU has competences, under the TFEU, to legislate in all those areas. As regards their content, the Iranian sanctions are clearly within the

[30] Case T-390/08 *Bank Melli Iran v. Council* [2009] ECR II-3967, paras 44–47.

[31] [2010] OJ L195/39.

scope of the TFEU. Their aim, by contrast, is one of foreign and security policy. It is not clear, however, that that is sufficient to bring them within the scope of the CFSP. If the Court's case law on the scope of the common commercial policy in relation to trade restrictions for foreign or security policy purposes is anything to go by, that objective is not sufficient (see Chapter 2). The practice could further be defended on the ground that, whenever 'restrictive measures' are adopted with foreign and security policy objectives, the TEU provisions on the CFSP are the correct legal basis. Article 215 TFEU could be referred to in aid of such an approach. However, such a reading of the relationship between the CFSP and the EU's competences under the TFEU is not in its effects much different from accepting that an act comes within the scope of the CFSP on the sole basis that it pursues foreign and security policy objectives. The concept of 'restrictive measures' is so broad as to encompass virtually all legislative measures pursuing such objectives.

The exclusion of legislative acts and Article 40 TEU could instead be read and applied in such a way that the CFSP does not encroach on EU competences conferred under the TFEU. The CFSP decisions on restrictive measures ought to be confined to expressing the basic principles and consensus underpinning such measures, whilst leaving the legislative detail to be determined under the relevant decision-making procedures of the TFEU.

Protection of fundamental rights

Economic and other sanctions are measures which do not simply affect countries or regimes. They have immediate effects, often of a stark nature, on a person's or a company's economic activities. Those effects may be such that people's very lives are disrupted or even jeopardized. It is therefore not surprising that the kind of sanctions on which this chapter focuses are often challenged from a human rights perspective. Such challenges are not confined to the level of policy-making. They may also take the form of legal action. EU sanctions, too, are not immune from attack on grounds of human rights violations, as many recent cases have shown. Such human rights challenges to sanctions raise complex issues. Fundamental rights are protected as general principles of EU law, they are binding on the EU institutions, and the Court strikes down legal acts which violate such rights. In the case of sanctions, however, there is usually a strong political dimension, particularly where the sanctions implement Security Council resolutions. Challenges to EU sanctions may in effect be challenges to Security Council decisions, as private parties are not in a position to bring legal actions against Security Council decisions as such. At the level of international law it is not clear whether there is a hierarchical relationship between human rights law and action by the Security Council to maintain peace and international security, in the sense that one would trump the other. The discussion is in any event fairly theoretical, as there are no effective means for challenging

Security Council decisions.[32] The issue therefore becomes, as it were, decentralized. Within a municipal legal order giving effect to Security Council resolutions, decisions need to be taken as to the relationship between fundamental rights protection and economic and other sanctions.

The autonomous sanctions which the EU adopts are of course also subject to review on grounds of violations of fundamental rights. Often, however, the EU's autonomy is limited. For example, one branch of EU decisions freezing the assets of those suspected of supporting terrorism is generally based on a UN Security Council resolution, but the latter does not identify the relevant persons, groups, or associations. For that purpose, the EU acts draw upon judicial and other measures adopted at national level.[33] Some of the smart sanctions which the EU adopts are, by contrast, wholly autonomous, in that they are not predicated on a UN resolution or on Member States' laws or measures.[34]

Even the mildly informed reader will be aware that the central litigation in this area culminated in the judgment of the Court of Justice in *Kadi and Al Barakaat*, where the Court decided that, notwithstanding the UN origin and basis of certain listings, the EU law version of fundamental rights protection required review of the measures as to their compliance with the right to be heard, the right to effective judicial protection, and the right to property.[35] The judgment was extensively analysed in Chapter 9, as regards the relationship between UN law and EU law. There have been many more cases, however, in which a breach of fundamental rights was argued. This section aims to provide a succinct and selective overview.

Bosphorus

The *Kadi* litigation was not the first in which a sanctions regulation, implementing a UN Security Council resolution, was challenged before the Court of Justice. In *Bosphorus* the Court had to interpret and review a sanctions regulation.[36] In implementation of UN Security Council resolutions the Council had adopted Regulation 990/93 concerning trade between the EEC and the Federal Republic of Yugoslavia (Serbia and Montenegro; hereafter, FRY).[37] The sanctions were a reaction to the conflict in the former Yugoslavia, particularly in Bosnia-Herzegovina. They extended to means of transport: Article 8 of the regulation provided that all vessels, freight vehicles, rolling stock, and aircraft in which a majority or controlling interest was held by a person or undertaking in, or operating from, the FRY had to be impounded by the competent authorities of the Member States. That wording was in substance identical to the relevant passage in the Security Council

[32] N Angelet, 'Protest against Security Council Decisions' in K Wellens (ed), *International Law: Theory and Practice—Essays in Honour of Eric Suy* (Martinus Nijhoff, 1998) 277.

[33] Regulation 2580/2001 (n 19 above).

[34] See e.g. Common Position 2002/145 concerning restrictive measures against Zimbabwe [2002] OJ L50/1.

[35] N 18 above.

[36] N 15 above.

[37] [1993] OJ L102/14.

resolution.[38] Bosphorus Airways was a Turkish air charter company, which in 1992 had leased two Boeing aircraft from Yugoslav Airlines (JAT). They were so-called dry leases, meaning that Bosphorus Airways provided the cabin and flight crew and had full day-to-day operational control and direction of the aircraft. The leases were themselves not in breach of the sanctions, the agreement between Bosphorus Airways and JAT was entirely *bona fide*, and Bosphorus Airways operated the aircraft for its charter operations, flying between Turkey and various EU Member States as well as Switzerland. JAT had no further involvement whatsoever with the use of the aircraft or the management and direction of Bosphorus Airways. In April 1993, one of the aircraft was flown to Dublin Airport for the purpose of maintenance. At that point the Irish authorities impounded the aircraft, in implementation of Article 8 of the sanctions regulation. They acted after having consulted the UN Yugoslavia Sanctions Committee, which took the view that the aircraft came within the scope of the resolution and therefore had to be impounded. In subsequent proceedings the Irish Supreme Court referred to the Court of Justice the question of whether an aircraft such as that in issue was covered by Article 8 of the regulation.

The Turkish charter company argued that the impounding of its aircraft was contrary to legal certainty, proportionality, and respect for fundamental rights. Jacobs AG considered that this part of Bosphorus Airways' claim raised an important issue, which led him to examine it in some detail. The company specifically referred to the right to peaceful enjoyment of property and to the right to pursue a commercial activity, which had both been recognized as fundamental rights by the case law of the Court of Justice. Jacobs AG analysed the right to property as protected under Article 1 of the First Protocol to the ECHR. He carefully examined the relevant case law of the ECtHR, and established that the type of interest which Bosphorus Airways had in the impounded aircraft was covered by the ECHR. Article 1 recognized that States were entitled to control the use of property in accordance with the general interest, but a fair balance had to be struck between the demands of the general interest of the community and the requirements of the protection of the individual's fundamental rights. There were no decisions of the ECtHR dealing specifically with the impounding of assets in implementation of international sanctions, but there were judgments in which the ECtHR recognized that confiscation could be justified as a measure of enforcement against an innocent owner. The Advocate General then analysed the case law of the Court of Justice on the right to property, and referred to the statement in *Hauer* that it was necessary to identify the aim pursued by the disputed regulation and to determine whether there was a reasonable relationship between the measures provided for by the regulation and the aim pursued by the Community.[39] Jacobs AG concluded that the essential question was whether the obvious interference with Bosphorus Airways' possession of the aircraft was

[38] Resolution 820 (1993), para 24.

[39] Case 44/79 *Hauer v. Land Rheinland-Pfalz* [1979] ECR 3727, para 23.

a proportionate measure in the light of the aims of general interest which the sanctions regulation sought to achieve. The Advocate General recognized that the impounding of the aircraft was a severe restriction on the exercise by Bosphorus Airways of its property rights, a restriction difficult to distinguish, in its effects, from a temporary deprivation. On the other hand, it was also obvious that there was a particularly strong interest in enforcing embargo measures decided by the UN Security Council. Indeed it was difficult to think of any stronger type of public interest than that of stopping a civil war as devastating as the one which engulfed the former Yugoslavia, and in particular Bosnia-Herzegovina. Unavoidably, the sanctions decided by the international community to put pressure on the FRY affected property rights, including those of innocent economic operators. In that respect Bosphorus Airways was in no way in a unique position, as many others were likely to have suffered severe losses from the embargo measures. That did not mean that any type of interference with the right to property should be tolerated. In the case in issue, however, the Advocate General considered that the decision to impound the aircraft on the ground that it was owned by an undertaking in the FRY could not be regarded as unreasonable, in the light of the aims of the sanctions regulation (see above). He lastly examined the alleged drastic financial and commercial effects of the decision to impound. He pointed out that the financial consequences might vary (a lessee might simply be able to cancel the agreement and lease another aircraft), and did not in any case think that it was possible to set aside a general measure such as the sanctions regulation because of the financial consequences which it could have in a particular case. But even if it were relevant to take account of the losses allegedly incurred, the Advocate General did not think that the principle of proportionality would be infringed, in view of the importance of the public interest involved.[40]

The Court of Justice was more concise in its analysis, but in essence concurred with the reasoning of its Advocate General. It referred to settled case law that the fundamental rights invoked by Bosphorus Airways were not absolute and their exercise could be subject to restrictions justified by objectives of general interest pursued by the Community. It then pointed out that any measure imposing sanctions had, by definition, consequences which affected the right to property and the freedom to pursue a trade or business, thereby causing harm to persons who were in no way responsible for the situation which led to the adoption of sanctions. Moreover, the importance of the aims pursued by the regulation at issue was such as to justify negative consequences, even of a substantial nature, for some operators. The Court then sketched the aims and justifications of the sanctions. It concluded that, as compared with an objective of general interest so fundamental for the international community, which consisted of putting an end to the state of war in the region and to massive violations of human rights and humanitarian international law in the Republic of Bosnia-Herzegovina, the impounding of the aircraft in

[40] *Bosphorus* (n 15 above) Opinion of Jacobs AG, paras 49–66.

question, which was owned by an undertaking based in or operating from the FRY, could not be regarded as inappropriate or disproportionate.[41]

The judgment in *Bosphorus* was severely criticized for failing to protect fundamental rights. Canor argued that the Court should have interpreted the sanctions regulation in a manner which afforded protection to Bosphorus Airways' right to property. She deplored the fact that the Court dissociated the question of how to interpret the notion of 'interest' in the sanctions regulation from the issue of fundamental rights protection. In her view, the text of the regulation was not as clear as the Court portrayed it, the notion of interest being sufficiently vague to be open to interpretation. Accordingly, it should have been interpreted in such a way that it did not apply to the kind of interest which JAT had in the leased aircraft, over which it did not have day-to-day control, and which could not therefore be used to evade or circumvent the sanctions. The Court should have given precedence to the rights of the innocent lessee.[42]

This critique may appear attractive if one focuses on the particular facts of the case. However, were the approach which Canor advocated to be generalized, the protection afforded to the right to property would be liable to undermine the entire sanctions regime. It is obvious that, in itself, the impounding of the aircraft in question was unlikely to have contributed much to the sanctions. But the same reasoning would be valid for many instances of application of the various sanctions. A specific small import or export transaction, though clearly prohibited under the trade embargo, would also not in itself undermine that embargo. Yet it needed to be prohibited because the sanctions could only be effective through their aggregate effect. Similarly, the EU agent of such a specific transaction could be as innocent as Bosphorus Airways. If, then, Bosphorus Airways' challenge had been successful, it could have opened up a channel for a flood of litigation, undermining the entire sanctions regime.

The *Bosphorus* case then made its way to the ECtHR, which decided that the EU system of fundamental rights protection was equivalent to that of the ECHR, and that there was no manifest deficiency in the way the Court (and the Advocate General) had reviewed the sanctions regulation in issue.[43]

Yusuf and *Kadi*

Bosphorus Airways concerned a general (transport) embargo affecting an innocent company. It pre-dated the era of smart sanctions and of asset-freezing measures targeted at supporters of terrorism. The latter practice developed after 9/11, and triggered the (then) CFI's judgments in *Kadi* and *Yusuf and Al Barakaat*.[44] Those cases

[41] Ibid, paras 21–26 of the judgment.

[42] I Canor, '"Can Two Walk Together, Except They be Agreed"—The Relationship Between International Law and European Law: The Incorporation of United Nations Sanctions Against Yugoslavia Into Community Law Through the Perspective of the European Court of Justice' (1998) 35 CML Rev 137–87.

[43] ECtHR, *Bosphorus Hava Yolları Turizm ve Ticaret Anonim Şirketi v. Ireland* [GC], no. 45036/98, ECHR 2005-VI.

[44] N 18 above.

involved persons and an association listed by the UN Security Council, shortly after 9/11. They challenged their listings in actions for annulment, which the CFI rejected. As analysed in Chapter 9, the Court decided that it could not apply the normal standards of judicial review, in light of the UN origin of the listings. Such review would constitute an indirect review of the UN resolutions in the light of Community law, and that could not be justified either on the basis of international law or on the basis of Community law. The Court nevertheless considered that it was empowered to check, indirectly, the lawfulness of the resolutions in question with regard to *jus cogens*, understood as a body of higher rules of public international law binding on all subjects of international law, including the bodies of the United Nations, and from which no derogation was possible.[45] The Court proceeded to review the listings on that basis, effectively adopting a broad concept of *jus cogens*, as incorporating certain human rights standards emanating from the Universal Declaration of Human Rights and the International Covenant on Civil and Political Rights. However, even when employing such a broad concept the Court did not establish a violation of norms of *jus cogens*, as regards the right to property and the principle of proportionality, the right to be heard, and the right to effective judicial protection.

OMPI **and** ***PMOI***

Before looking at the appeal before the Court of Justice, it may be useful to explore the way in which the (then) CFI reviewed the EU's autonomous system for freezing the assets of persons or groups supporting terrorism. In the *OMPI* and *PMOI* cases the Court adopted a radically different approach from that taken in *Yusuf* and *Kadi*.[46] In issue in those cases were various successive listing decisions targeting the *Organisation des Modjahédines du peuple d'Iran* (or People's Mojahedin Organization of Iran; hereafter, PMOI), an Iranian resistance organization. The origin of the decisions lay, initially, in a decision by the UK Home Secretary to include the applicant in the list of organizations proscribed under the Terrorism Act 2000. The PMOI brought various actions against that decision at national level, which were eventually successful. It also challenged the EU listings, again with success. The evolving set of facts and national and EU decisions was large and complex, and as a result the judgments of the CFI are too extensive to be fully analysed here. One of the main findings was that the exclusion of the normal standards of judicial review, as identified in *Yusuf* and *Kadi*, did not extend to the *PMOI* cases, since the organization had not been listed by the United Nations. The Court was therefore prepared fully

[45] *Kadi* (n 24 above) para 226.

[46] Case T–228/02 *OMPI v. Council* [2006] ECR II–4665; Case T–256/07 *PMOI v. Council (PMOI I)* [2008] ECR II–3019; and Case T–284/08 *PMOI v. Council (PMOI II)* [2008] ECR II–3487. See also G della Cananea, 'Return to the due process of law: the European Union and the fight against terrorism' (2007) 32 ELR 895.

to examine the applicant's arguments relating to the lack of a sufficient statement of reasons; the breach of the right to a fair hearing, the rights of defence, and the right to effective judicial protection; and the misapplication of the burden of proof and manifest error in assessing the evidence.

The essence of the applicant's successive claims was that it was not a terrorist organization, since it had renounced all use of violence, and that this was confirmed in successful judicial challenges in the UK courts. The Council, however, had refused to give effect to those challenges, as it had continued to list the organization, and had ultimately sought to rely on a judicial inquiry against certain of the organization's members in France.[47] In *PMOI I* the Court noted that the UK Proscribed Organizations Appeal Commission (OPAC), a judicial authority, had established that the Home Secretary's decision to proscribe the PMOI had been 'perverse'. The EU Council, however, had completely disregarded the OPAC decision, and had simply noted that the Home Secretary had launched an appeal against it, even if that appeal could not extend to the findings of fact that the PMOI had disarmed in 2003 and had not sought to recreate any form of structure that was capable of carrying out or supporting terrorist acts. The Council's disregard amounted to a statement of reasons which was obviously insufficient to provide legal justification for continuing to freeze the applicant's funds.[48] In *PMOI II* the Court was even more scathing. It described how the Council, subsequent to the unsuccessful appeal by the Home Secretary against OPAC's decision, had relied on a judicial inquiry opened by the anti-terrorist Prosecutor's office of the Tribunal de Grande Instance of Paris, in order to continue to list the PMOI. The Court found that neither the information contained in the contested decision, its statement of reasons and the letter of notification, nor even the material contained in the Council's two answers to the Court, complied with the applicable requirements of proof. The Council had not provided the Court with any precise information or material in the relevant file which indicated that the French judicial inquiry constituted, in respect of the applicant, a decision meeting the definition in Article 1(4) of Common Position 2001/931.[49] The Council had further refused to release certain information to the Court, on the basis that the French authorities had claimed that that information was confidential. The Court pointedly noted that this did not explain why the production of the relevant information or material in the file to the Court would have violated the principle of confidentiality, whereas their production to the members

[47] See *PMOI II* (n 46 above).

[48] *PMOI I* (n 46 above) paras 167–187.

[49] *PMOI II* (n 46 above) paras 56–57. Art 1(4) provides: 'The list in the Annex shall be drawn up on the basis of precise information or material in the relevant file which indicates that a decision has been taken by a competent authority in respect of the persons, groups and entities concerned, irrespective of whether it concerns the instigation of investigations or prosecution for a terrorist act, an attempt to perpetrate, participate in or facilitate such an act based on serious and credible evidence or clues, or condemnation for such deeds... For the purposes of this paragraph "competent authority" shall mean a judicial authority, or, where judicial authorities have no competence in the area covered by this paragraph, an equivalent competent authority in that area' (n 27 above).

of the Council, and thus to the governments of the twenty-six other Member States, had not. In any case, the Council was not entitled to base its fund-freezing decision on information or material in the file communicated by a Member State, if the said Member State was not willing to authorize its communication to the Community judicature whose task was to review the lawfulness of the decision.[50] It may be noted that the judgment in *PMOI II* was handed down on the day following the oral hearing, which is extremely rare, if not unique, in the practice of the Court.

Those are some of the specific flaws which led to the annulments in *PMOI I* and *II*. It is, however, also useful to discuss the nature of the judicial review which the Court carried out in those cases. In *PMOI I*, the Court analysed that question as follows. As regards the EU's autonomous listing decisions, the relevant legislation made it clear that such listings had to be based on precise information or material in the relevant file which indicated that a decision had been taken by a competent authority.[51] The procedure therefore took place at two levels, one national, the other Community. Verification that there was the requisite decision of a national authority was an essential precondition for the adoption, by the Council, of a decision to freeze funds. The principle of loyal co-operation (current Article 4(3) TEU) entailed, for the Council, the obligation to defer as far as possible to the assessment conducted by the competent national authority, at least where it was a judicial authority, in particular in respect of the existence of 'serious and credible evidence or clues' on which its decision was based. Nevertheless, the Council did not act under circumscribed powers, and enjoyed discretion in assessing the reasons why the person concerned had to be listed and his or her funds frozen. The prime consideration for the Council had to be its perception or evaluation of the danger that, for want of such a measure, the funds might be used to fund or prepare acts of terrorism. The discretion for the Council was broad, but that did not mean that the Court was not to review the interpretation made by the Council of the relevant facts. The Community judicature had to establish whether the evidence relied on was factually accurate, reliable, and consistent. It also had to ascertain whether that evidence contained all the relevant information to be taken into account in order to assess the situation and whether it was capable of substantiating the conclusions drawn from it. However, when conducting such a review, it could not substitute its own assessment of what was appropriate for that of the Council. In addition, the review of observance of certain procedural guarantees was of fundamental importance. These included the obligation for the competent institution to examine carefully and impartially all the relevant elements of the individual case and to give an adequate statement of reasons for its decision.[52]

[50] *PMOI II* (n 46 above) paras 69–73.
[51] See Art 1(4) of Common Position 2001/931 (n 27 above).
[52] *PMOI I* (n 46 above) paras 130–139.

Kadi and Al Barakaat

The *OMPI* and *PMOI* litigation thus showed that, as regards autonomous counter-terrorism listings, the CFI exercised intense judicial review. Was the same type of review going to be employed for EU listings which were based on UN resolutions, and on specific listings by the UN Security Council's Sanctions Committee? In *Kadi and Al Barakaat* the Court of Justice decided that the immunity from jurisdiction which the CFI had established for such listings constituted an error in law. It therefore examined the listings of Mr Kadi and of Al Barakaat in the light of EU law principles of respect for fundamental rights.

In *Kadi*,[53] Maduro AG noted that the respondent institutions advocated a type of judicial review that was at heart very similar to the approach taken by the CFI under the heading of *jus cogens*. Their argument was that the case raised a 'political question', and that the Court was not in a position to deal adequately with such questions: the matters at issue were of international significance, and Court intervention might upset globally co-ordinated efforts to combat terrorism. In contrast with the Security Council, the courts were ill equipped to determine which measures were appropriate. Maduro AG disagreed with such a conception. It was true that the Court ought not to be institutionally blind, and had to be mindful of the international context and conscious of its limitations. Where possible, it had to recognize the authority of institutions, such as the Security Council, that were established under a different legal order than its own and that were sometimes better placed to weigh the fundamental interests at stake. However, the Court could not, in deference to the views of those institutions, turn its back on the fundamental values that lay at the basis of the Community legal order and which it had the duty to protect. Respect for other institutions was meaningful only if it could be built on a shared understanding of those values and on a mutual commitment to protect them.[54]

The fact that the measures at issue were intended to suppress international terrorism should not inhibit the Court from fulfilling its duty to preserve the rule of law. In doing so, rather than trespassing into the domain of politics, the Court was reaffirming the limits that the law imposed on certain political decisions. Especially in matters of public security, the political process was liable to become overly responsive to immediate popular concerns, leading the authorities to allay the anxieties of the many at the expense of the rights of a few. That was precisely when courts had to get involved, in order to ensure that the political necessities of today did not become the legal realities of tomorrow. There was therefore no reason for the Court to depart from its usual interpretation of the fundamental rights that had been invoked by the appellant.[55]

[53] Maduro AG delivered separate but substantively identical Opinions in *Kadi* and in *Al Barakaat*. References here are to the *Kadi* Opinion (n 18 above).

[54] Ibid, paras 43–44.

[55] Ibid, paras 45–46.

The Advocate General then turned to the facts of the case. The problem facing the appellant was that all of his financial interests within the Community had been frozen for several years, without limit of time and in conditions where there appeared to be no adequate means for him to challenge the assertion that he was guilty of wrongdoing. Clearly, the indefinite freezing of someone's assets constituted a far-reaching interference with the peaceful enjoyment of property. The consequences for the person concerned were potentially devastating, even where arrangements were made for basic needs and expenses. This underscored the need for procedural safeguards which required the authorities to justify such measures and demonstrate their proportionality, not merely in the abstract, but in the concrete circumstances of the given case. The prevention of international terrorism did not *ipso facto* relieve the authorities of the requirement to demonstrate that the restrictions were justified in respect of the person concerned.[56]

The institutions, Maduro AG continued, had not afforded any opportunity to the appellant to make known his views on whether the sanctions against him were justified and whether they should be kept in force. The existence of a de-listing procedure at the level of the UN offered no consolation in this regard. The processing of any de-listing request was purely a matter of intergovernmental consultation, and the de-listing procedure did not provide even minimal access to the information on the basis of which the decision was made to include the petitioner in the list. One of the crucial reasons for which the right to be heard had to be respected was to enable the parties concerned to defend their rights effectively, particularly in legal proceedings. The Advocate General then looked at the right to effective judicial protection, which held a prominent place in the firmament of fundamental rights. It was unacceptable in a democratic society to impair the very essence of that right. The appellant had been listed for several years, and still the Community institutions refused to grant him an opportunity to dispute the grounds for his continued inclusion. They had, in effect, levelled extremely serious allegations against him and had, on that basis, subjected him to severe sanctions. Yet they entirely rejected the notion of an independent tribunal assessing the fairness of these allegations and the reasonableness of the sanctions. There was a real possibility that the sanctions might be disproportionate or even misdirected, and might nevertheless remain in place indefinitely. The Court had no way of knowing whether that was the case in reality, but the mere existence of that possibility was anathema in a society that respected the law.[57]

The Court followed the Opinion. It opened its analysis by stating that, in the case, the rights of the defence, in particular the right to be heard, and the right to effective judicial review of those rights were patently not respected. The Court referred to the principle of effective judicial review as a general principle of Community law. In this instance, the effectiveness of judicial review, which it had to be possible to apply to the lawfulness of the grounds on which the name of a person

[56] Ibid, para 47. [57] Ibid, paras 51–53.

or entity was included in the list, meant that the Community authority in question was bound to communicate those grounds to the person or entity concerned, so far as possible, either when that inclusion was decided on or, at the very least, as swiftly as possible after that decision in order to enable that person or entity to exercise their right to bring an action. Observance of that obligation was necessary both to enable the persons concerned to defend their rights in the best possible conditions and to decide, with full knowledge of the relevant facts, whether there was any point in their applying to the Community judicature, and to put the latter fully in a position in which it could carry out the review of the lawfulness of the Community measure in question.[58]

As regards the rights of defence, and in particular the right to be heard, the Court then established that the Community authorities could not be required to communicate the grounds for the listing before the name of a person or entity was entered. Such prior communication would be liable to jeopardize the effectiveness of the freezing of funds and resources. The measures, by their very nature, had to take advantage of surprise and apply with immediate effect. Nor were the Community authorities bound to hear the appellants before their names were included. In addition, overriding considerations to do with safety or the conduct of the international relations of the Community and of its Member States could militate against the communication of certain matters to the persons concerned and, therefore, against their being heard on those matters. However, that did not mean, with regard to the principle of effective judicial protection, that restrictive measures such as those imposed by the contested regulation escaped all review by the Community judicature once it had been claimed that the act laying them down concerned national security and terrorism. In such a case, it was none the less the task of the Community judicature to apply techniques which accommodated, on the one hand, legitimate security concerns about the nature and sources of information taken into account in the adoption of the act concerned and, on the other, the need to accord the individual a sufficient measure of procedural justice. The inevitable conclusion was that neither the regulation nor the common position to which it referred provided for a procedure for communicating the evidence justifying the inclusion of the names of the persons concerned in the list, and for hearing those persons, either at the same time as that inclusion or later.[59]

The Court next pointed out that the Council at no time informed the appellants of the evidence adduced against them. Because the Council neither communicated to the appellants the evidence used against them nor afforded them the right to be informed of that evidence within a reasonable period after those measures were enacted, the appellants were not in a position to make their point of view known to advantage. Therefore, the appellants' rights of defence, in particular the right to be heard, were not respected. In addition, the appellants were also unable to defend their rights with regard to that evidence in satisfactory conditions

[58] Ibid, paras 334–337 of the judgment.

[59] Ibid, paras 338–345.

before the Community judicature, so that their right to an effective legal remedy had also been infringed. That infringement had not been remedied in the course of the actions which the appellants had brought. The Court could not, therefore, do other than find that it was not able to undertake the review of the lawfulness of the contested regulation, with the result that it had to be held that, for that reason too, the fundamental right to an effective legal remedy had not been observed.[60]

The Court subsequently examined whether, in the case of Mr Kadi, there was a breach of the right to property. That right was not absolute, but had to be viewed in relation to its function in society. Consequently, the exercise of the right could be restricted, provided that those restrictions in fact corresponded to objectives of public interest pursued by the Community and did not constitute, in relation to the aim pursued, a disproportionate and intolerable interference, impairing the very substance of the right. Applying that test, the Court first found that the freezing measure in issue constituted a temporary precautionary measure which was not supposed to deprive the persons concerned of their property. It did, however, undeniably entail a restriction of the exercise of Mr Kadi's right to property that, moreover, had to be classified as considerable, having regard to the general application of the freezing measure and to the fact that it had been applied to him since 20 October 2001. Was that restriction justified?[61]

According to the case law of the ECtHR, there had to exist a reasonable relationship of proportionality between the means employed and the aim sought to be realized. The Court had to decide whether a fair balance was struck. In so doing, the Court recognized that the legislature enjoyed a wide margin of appreciation. As the Court of Justice had already held in *Bosphorus Airways*, the importance of the aims pursued by a Community act was such as to justify negative consequences, even of a substantial nature, for some operators. With reference to an objective of general interest as fundamental to the international community as the fight by all means, in accordance with the UN Charter, against the threats to international peace and security posed by acts of terrorism, the freezing of the funds, financial assets, and other economic resources of the persons identified by the Security Council or the Sanctions Committee as being associated with Usama bin Laden, members of the Al-Qaeda organization, and the Taliban, could not *per se* be regarded as inappropriate or disproportionate. The Court also drew attention to the exemptions from the regime for basic expenses, and to the procedure for periodic re-examination by the Sanctions Committee. It therefore had to be found that the restrictive measures constituted restrictions of the right to property which could, in principle, be justified.[62]

However, the Court then went on to examine whether, when the regulation was applied to Mr Kadi, his right to property was respected in the circumstances of the case. It was to be borne in mind in this respect that the applicable procedures also had to afford the person concerned a reasonable opportunity of putting his case to the competent authorities. The contested regulation, by contrast, was

[60] Ibid, paras 346–351. [61] Ibid, paras 354–359. [62] Ibid, paras 360–366.

adopted without furnishing any guarantee enabling Mr Kadi to put his case to the competent authorities, in a situation in which the restriction of his property rights had to be regarded as significant, having regard to the general application and actual continuation of the freezing measures affecting him. Therefore, in the circumstances of the case, the imposition of the freezing measures constituted an unjustified restriction of his right to property.[63]

The Court therefore annulled the regulation in so far as it applied to Mr Kadi and to Al Barakaat. However, the annulment with immediate effect would have been capable of seriously and irreversibly prejudicing the effectiveness of the restrictive measures, because in the interval preceding its replacement by a new regulation Mr Kadi and Al Barakaat might have taken steps seeking to prevent measures freezing funds from being applied to them again. Furthermore, it could not be excluded that, on the merits of the case, the listings might prove to be justified. The Court therefore decided to maintain the effects of the regulation for three months, to allow the Council to remedy the infringements.[64]

Kadi II

The judgment of the Court of Justice, though clearly central to the whole litigation, was not the end of the *Kadi* saga. It was not, in contrast with what the Court suggested, the Council which re-listed Mr Kadi; that was done by the Commission, which followed a procedure whereby it communicated to Mr Kadi a 'summary of reasons' for the listing, which had been obtained from the UN Security Council. It allowed Mr Kadi to respond to that summary, which he did in an attempt to disprove the allegations which it contained. The Commission then decided that it was not satisfied with the response, and re-listed Mr Kadi, who brought a new action for annulment leading, at the time of writing, to the judgment of the General Court in *Kadi II*.[65]

The Court started by setting out some of the facts, including Mr Kadi's assertions that he was placed on the Sanctions Committee's list at the request of the United States without any independent scrutiny or assessment by the UN of the allegations made against him by the United States. Mr Kadi had also pointed out that a number of the allegations were manifestly false, and that the US authorities had relied on a number of newspaper articles, including one written by a journalist who was later found to have fabricated stories and had been forced to resign.[66]

[63] Ibid, paras 367–370.

[64] Ibid, paras 373–376. *Kadi and Al Barakaat* has been confirmed in Case T–318/01 *Othman v. Council and Commission* [2009] ECR II–1627; Joined Cases C–399 and 403/06P *Hassan v. Council and Commission and Ayadi v. Council* [2009] ECR I–11393; and Case C–550/09 *Criminal Proceedings against E and F* [2010] ECR I–xxx.

[65] Case T–85/09 *Kadi v. Commission*, judgment of 30 September 2010. The summary of reasons is reproduced at para 50.

[66] Ibid, paras 75–78.

The Court then examined the appropriate standard of review in the case before it. It pointed out that the Court of Justice had rejected the immunity from jurisdiction for the review of a regulation implementing a UN resolution. It described how the reasoning of the Court was not uncontested 'in legal circles', and found that those criticisms were not entirely without foundation. However, the appellate principle governing the relationship between the General Court and the Court of Justice, and the hierarchical structure which was its corollary, generally advised against the General Court revisiting points of law which had been decided by the Court of Justice—*a fortiori* when the latter was sitting in Grand Chamber composition.[67]

The Commission, the Council, and the intervening governments had again contended that there could only be a limited form of judicial review. The Court rejected that, however, stating that if that approach were followed there would be no effective judicial review of the kind required by the Court of Justice in *Kadi*, but rather a simulacrum thereof. The task of the General Court was to ensure 'in principle the full review' of the lawfulness of the contested regulation in the light of fundamental rights, without affording any immunity from jurisdiction. That had to remain the case, at the very least, so long as the re-examination procedure operated by the Sanctions Committee clearly failed to offer guarantees of effective judicial protection. The Court then established that even if an Ombudsperson had been appointed to be involved with the re-examination of UN listings, there was still no independent and impartial body responsible for hearing and determining actions against individual decisions taken by the Sanctions Committee. In those circumstances, the review carried out by the Community judicature could be regarded as effective only if it concerned, indirectly, the substantive assessments of the Sanctions Committee itself and the evidence underlying them.[68]

The Court then examined how the Court of Justice had set out the scope and intensity of review in *Kadi and Al Barakaat*. The review extended to the lawfulness of the grounds on which the measure was founded, and to ascertaining whether the contested act was well founded and whether it was vitiated by any defect. The review also had to extend not only to the apparent merits of the measure but also to the evidence and information on which the findings made in the measure were based. The Court pointed out that the UN's own Monitoring Team had also understood the judgment in *Kadi* in that way. It further found that the Court of Justice had drawn on the reasoning of the CFI in *OMPI*, and therefore determined that the appropriate standard of review was the same as that elaborated in the *OMPI* and *PMOI* litigation (see above). The Community judicature had to establish that the evidence relied on was factually accurate, reliable, and consistent, but also had to ascertain whether that evidence contained all the relevant information and whether it was capable of substantiating the conclusions drawn from it. However, it was not its task to substitute its own assessment of what was appropriate for that of the competent institution. Judicial review extended to the assessment of the facts and the

[67] Ibid, paras 112–121. [68] Ibid, paras 123–129.

circumstances relied on, and to the evidence and information on which that assessment was based. The General Court also had to ensure that the rights of defence were observed; that the requirement of a statement of reasons was satisfied; and that any overriding considerations relied on exceptionally by the competent Community institution in order to justify disregarding those rights were well founded. In the current context, review was all the more essential because it constituted the only procedural safeguard ensuring that a fair balance was struck between the need to combat international terrorism and the protection of fundamental rights. It was not possible to raise objections that the evidence and information used by the competent Community institution were secret or confidential. Although the ECtHR recognized that the use of confidential information could be necessary when national security was at stake, that did not mean, in that Court's view, that national authorities were free from any review by the national courts simply because they stated that the case concerned national security and terrorism.[69]

The General Court did not stop at this overview of the relevant principles, drawn from previous case law. It stated that the above considerations had to be supplemented by certain considerations based on the nature and effects of fund-freezing measures such as those at issue in *Kadi II*, viewed from a temporal perspective. Such measures were particularly draconian for those who were subject to them. All of the applicant's funds and other assets had been indefinitely frozen for nearly ten years. The Court referred to a recent UK Supreme Court judgment in *Ahmed and Others*, where that court took the view that it was no exaggeration to say that persons designated in this way were effectively 'prisoners' of the State.[70] The General Court even noted that it might be asked whether it was now not time to call into question the finding according to which the freezing of funds was a temporary precautionary measure which, unlike confiscation, did not affect the very substance of the right of the persons concerned to property in their financial assets but only the use thereof. In the scale of a human life, ten years in fact represented a substantial period of time and the question of the classification of the measures in question as preventative or punitive, protective or confiscatory, civil or criminal seemed now to be an open one. In support of that perspective, the Court referred to an opinion of the UN High Commissioner for Human Rights.[71] In any event, as regards the appropriate standard of judicial review, the Court concluded that the principle of a full and rigorous judicial review was all the more justified given that the freezing measures had a marked and long-lasting effect on the fundamental rights of the persons concerned.[72]

[69] Ibid, paras 132–146.

[70] *Her Majesty's Treasury (Respondent) v. Mohammed Jabar Ahmed and Others (Appellants), Her Majesty's Treasury (Respondent) v. Mohammed al-Ghabra (Appellant)* and *R (on the application of Hani El Sayed Sabaei Youssef) (Respondent) v. Her Majesty's Treasury (Appellant)* [2010] UKSC 2, paras 60 and 192.

[71] United Nations High Commissioner for Human Rights, report to the General Assembly of the United Nations of 2 September 2009, entitled 'Report . . . on the protection of human rights and fundamental freedoms while countering terrorism', document A/HRC/12/22, point 42.

[72] *Kadi II* (n 65 above) paras 148–151.

The Court then focused on the applicant's pleas concerning rights of defence and effective judicial protection. It found that Mr Kadi's rights of defence had been 'observed' only in the most formal and superficial sense, as the Commission in actual fact considered itself strictly bound by the Sanctions Committee's findings and therefore at no time envisaged calling those findings into question in the light of the applicant's observations. The Commission failed to take due account of the applicant's comments, and did not grant him even the most minimal access to the evidence against him. No balance was struck between his interests and the need to protect the confidential nature of the information in question. In those circumstances, the few pieces of information and the imprecise allegations in the summary of reasons appeared clearly insufficient to enable the applicant to launch an effective challenge to the allegations against him. That was the case, taken as a particularly telling but in no way unique example, of the allegation, not otherwise substantiated and thus irrefutable, that the applicant was a shareholder in a Bosnian bank in which planning sessions against a US facility in Saudi Arabia 'may have' taken place.[73]

The Court then referred to a contemporaneous judgment of the ECtHR, in *A. and Others v. United Kingdom*, on the sort of material which needed to be made available to a detainee suspected of terrorist acts.[74] Applying criteria identical to those used by the ECtHR to the facts of *Kadi II*, it was clear that the applicant was not in a position to mount an effective challenge to any of the allegations against him, given that all that was disclosed to him was the summary of reasons. It was also telling that the Commission had made no real effort to refute the exculpatory evidence advanced by the applicant in the few cases in which the allegations against him were sufficiently precise to permit him to know what was being raised against him. It followed that the regulation was adopted in breach of the rights of defence.[75]

Moreover, the fact that the applicant had an opportunity to be heard by the Sanctions Committee in the re-examination procedure did not remedy that breach. The violation of rights of defence also led to an infringement of his right to effective judicial review, an infringement which had not been remedied in the course of the action. The General Court could not, therefore, do other than find that it was not able to undertake a review of the lawfulness of the regulation, with the result that it had to be held that, for that reason too, the applicant's fundamental right to effective judicial review had not been observed. As a last point, the Court distinguished the UN-based listings from the autonomous fund-freezing regime in issue in the *OMPI* and *PMOI* litigation, where there was a two-tier procedure, one national, the other Community, and where the rights of the defence were in the first place effectively safeguarded as part of the national procedure. It was precisely

[73] Ibid, paras 171–175, quotation marks in the original.

[74] ECtHR, judgment of 19 February 2009, not yet published in the *Reports of Judgments and Decisions*.

[75] *Kadi II* (n 65 above) paras 176–179.

those safeguards of the rights of the defence that existed at national level, subject to effective judicial review, which relieved the Community institutions of any obligation to provide fresh safeguards at Community level in relation to the same subject matter. In contrast to that autonomous regime, the UN-based regime was characterized by an absence of any safeguards of the rights of defence at the level of the procedure before the Sanctions Committee.[76]

In *Kadi II* the General Court displayed considerable frustration with the response of the Commission to *Kadi and Al Barakaat*. The statements that Mr Kadi's rights of defence had been 'observed'—with the quotation marks in the original—only in the most formal and superficial sense and that, if the institutions' concept of judicial review were adhered to, there would be no more than a simulacrum of judicial review, are witness thereto. It is further remarkable that the Court was willing to consider the nature of freezing measures which had been in place for nearly ten years, by suggesting that they may be regarded as punitive, and therefore of a criminal character. If that finding were confirmed, it would of course have enormous consequences for the determination of the appropriate due process standards.[77]

The CFI (now the General Court) exercised less strict judicial review in cases involving smart sanctions against Iran and Burma (Myanmar). In cases brought by an Iranian bank and its UK subsidiary, the Court refused to strike down the freezing measures, pointing out that the Council had broad discretion as regards the determination of whether the bank was involved in nuclear proliferation activities. It has to be noted, though, that in neither of those cases was that involvement directly challenged by the applicant.[78] In the context of sanctions against Burma the Court rejected the action brought by the son of a Burmese businessman, whose assets had been frozen because of his father's association with the Burmese regime. The Court accepted that the Council could rightly consider that those in charge of major businesses under the military regime in Myanmar could be treated as persons associated with that regime. As regards their family members, it could be presumed that they benefited from the functions exercised by those businessmen, but that presumption could be rebutted if an applicant successfully demonstrated that he did not have a close link with the businessman who was part of his family.[79] The Court also highlighted the contrast with freezing measures targeted at supporters of terrorism. In a case such as *Tay Za*, the restrictive measures were directed at the Myanmar regime. Instead of imposing a general embargo against that country, the Council had provided for targeted, selective sanctions and had enumerated the categories of persons and entities specifically covered by the restrictive measures. It was not

[76] Ibid, paras 180–187. As a final point, the Court found an infringement of the principle of proportionality, on the basis of the infringements it had already established: see paras 192–195.

[77] The same Court, but a different chamber, had summarily rejected the criminal character of the freezing of funds in *Bank Melli Iran* (n 30 above) para 111.

[78] Joined Cases T-246 and 332/08 *Melli Bank Plc v. Council* [2009] ECR II-2629 and *Bank Melli Iran* (n 30 above).

[79] Case T-181/08 *Pye Phyo Tay Za v. Council*, judgment of 19 May 2010, paras 65–68.

therefore the activities of the persons and entities concerned which justified the restrictive measures, but their membership of a certain general category of persons and entities having a function or position in the State which was the subject of the sanctions. In the case of sanctions against a third country specifically applying to an individual there were, therefore, no proceedings initiated against that individual for the purposes of the *OMPI* litigation. The process which culminated in the adoption of such sanctions did not constitute, in respect of the persons listed, proceedings in the course of which they could, as individuals, have sanctions imposed on them. A regulation which contained such sanctions was a general legislative act even if the persons concerned were identified by name. It was true that such a regulation adversely affected them directly and individually and that they were entitled to bring an action to challenge it. However, in a legislative procedure culminating in the adoption of sanctions against a third country which applied to certain categories of its nationals, the rights of the defence were not applicable to them. For the establishment of such a regulation, individuals did not have rights of participation, even if they were individually concerned.[80]

Those findings mark a considerable contrast between counter-terrorism and smart sanctions. *Tay Za* was under appeal at the time of writing, and it remains to be seen whether the Court of Justice upholds what looks like a fundamental difference in the approach towards judicial review.[81]

Interpretation and application

Sanctions regulations are acts open to interpretation by the Court of Justice. National authorities are required to implement and apply the regulations, and as the latter affect private companies engaged in trade, or providing transport or financial services, and individuals listed as well as those dealing with them, it is hardly surprising that the precise scope or application of the regulations may be disputed, giving rise to litigation. National courts may be confronted with issues of interpretation or even validity, and may refer questions to the Court of Justice under Article 267 TFEU. A number of such cases have come before the Court, and they show the kind of issues to which sanctions regulations may give rise. This subsection looks at case law on how to interpret and apply sanctions regulations. The Court has had to grapple: with the required method of interpretation of the terms of sanctions regulations, in particular where they find their origin in UN Security Council resolutions; with the territorial scope of such regulations; with sanctions and penalties applied by the Member States; with the application of the exceptions for which the regulations provide; and with their relationship with other instruments of EU law, in particular the general export regulation.[82]

[80] Ibid, paras 122–123. [81] Case C-376/10 P.

[82] Council Regulation 1061/2009 establishing common rules for exports [2009] OJ L291/1.

Sanctions against the FRY

The facts of *Bosphorus* are set out above.[83] When the Irish authorities impounded the aircraft, in implementation of Article 8 of the sanctions regulation, they acted after having consulted the UN Yugoslavia Sanctions Committee, which took the view that the aircraft came within the scope of the resolution and therefore had to be impounded. Bosphorus Airways then applied to the High Court in Dublin for judicial review. The High Court quashed the decision on the ground that the aircraft was not one in which a majority or controlling interest was held by a person or undertaking in or operating from the FRY. It considered that the aim of the sanctions regulation was to operate as a punishment, deterrent, or sanction against the people or government of the FRY, and that the type of interest referred to in Article 8 had to have been intended to identify a situation in which the person in or operating from the FRY could exercise a decision-making function in relation to the use on a day-to-day basis of the asset in question. Any other construction was both unreal and unjust, and the aim of the regulation was not to punish or penalize peoples or countries who had not in any way caused or contributed to the tragic events in Yugoslavia. The Irish Minister then appealed to the Supreme Court, which referred to the Court of Justice the question whether an aircraft such as that in issue was covered by Article 8 of the regulation.

Jacobs AG took the text of Article 8 as a starting point, and considered that it left little room for doubt. The term 'interest' was very broad, encompassing all types of property interest, and most other language versions of the regulation referred to the notion of property, instead of interest. As JAT continued to be the exclusive owner of the aircraft in question, Article 8 on its wording clearly applied. This conclusion was further strengthened by the requirement of uniform interpretation, to which the preamble to the regulation expressly referred. The issue was therefore whether there were any compelling reasons to interpret the regulation in a way which appeared to depart from its wording. The Advocate General examined that question in the light of the context and the objects of the regulation, which were the Security Council resolutions which it aimed to implement. He pointed out that the term 'majority or controlling interest' was reproduced verbatim from Resolution 820 (1993). He did not agree with the reasoning of the Irish High Court that the purpose of the relevant provision of the resolution was to deprive the FRY of recourse to the aircraft which could be used to transport goods in breach of the applicable trade embargo. It was not excluded that the Security Council had intended to go further, requiring the freezing of assets abroad. Jacobs AG was of the opinion that it was much more difficult to divine the precise purpose of a Community measure implementing a Security Council resolution than it would normally be to ascertain the purpose of an ordinary Community measure, because of the involvement of the intentions of the Security Council, an organ composed

[83] N 15 above.

of many diverse States acting in highly charged political circumstances. He agreed with the Commission that the aim of the measure could also be to prevent persons or undertakings in the FRY from recovering means of transport temporarily outside their control. He also found support for his view in other provisions of the resolution. The Advocate General lastly examined the weight of the opinion of the Yugoslavia Sanctions Committee, which had led to the impounding of the aircraft. He considered that due regard should be given to that opinion, but that it could not be regarded as binding, if only because such an effect was not provided for in the resolution, at least as regards the issue in question.[84]

The Court largely adopted the reasoning of Jacobs AG. Nothing in the wording of the regulation suggested a distinction between ownership and control. The regulation had to be interpreted in the light of its context and aims, which included the UN resolutions. The wording of the resolution confirmed its application to any aircraft which was the property of a person or undertaking in the FRY, and confirmed that actual control was not required. The word 'interest' could not, on any view, exclude ownership as a determining criterion; the conjunction with the word 'majority', moreover, clearly implied the concept of ownership. Other language versions of the regulation confirmed this. The Court also stated that the impounding contributed to restricting the exercise by the FRY and its nationals of their property rights, and was thus consistent with the aim of the sanctions, namely to put pressure on the FRY. By contrast, the use of day-to-day operation and control as the decisive criterion could jeopardize the effectiveness of the strengthening of the sanctions, as it would allow the FRY or its nationals to evade application of those sanctions through the mere transfer of day-to-day operation and control of means of transport.[85]

The *Bosphorus* case established a number of important principles. Sanctions regulations, in particular those adopted in implementation of UN Security Council resolutions, must be interpreted literally, in the light not only of their own wording but also of that of the corresponding resolution. Uniform interpretation is clearly paramount, as it is one of the main rationales for EU involvement in the adoption of sanctions. There is therefore little deference to the views of national authorities, including national courts.

In the subsequent case of *Ebony Maritime* the same Regulation, 990/93, was in issue.[86] The facts were a little more spectacular than those of *Bosphorus*. In April 1994, the *Lido II*, a tanker flying the Maltese flag and owned by Loten Navigation Company Ltd, a Maltese company, left the Tunisian port of La Skhira bound for Rijeka, Croatia, with a cargo of petroleum products and motor spirit. The cargo was owned by Ebony Maritime, a Liberian company. At some point, when the vessel was in the Adriatic, the master sent out distress signals,

[84] *Bosphorus* (n 15 above) Opinion of Jacobs AG, paras 31–47.
[85] Ibid, paras 8–18 of the judgment.
[86] N 16 above.

because the *Lido II* began to take on water in the engine room. Stating that he was unable to contain the leak, he set course towards the Montenegrin coast, which was nearest. Before the *Lido II* entered Yugoslav territorial waters, thus still being in international waters, a NATO/WEU helicopter landed on its deck and a Dutch military squad took control of the vessel, which was towed to Brindisi and placed at the disposal of the Italian authorities. The *Prefetto* (Prefect) of Brindisi decided to arrest the vessel and confiscate its cargo, in implementation of the sanctions laid down in Italian law for breach of the trade embargo. The companies involved brought proceedings before the competent Italian courts, and the Consiglio di Stato (Council of State) referred several questions to the Court of Justice.

The first issue in the case was whether Regulation 990/93 actually applied to the facts. The United Kingdom and France argued that it did not. They referred to Article 11, according to which the regulation applied within the territory of the Community and in any aircraft or vessel under the jurisdiction of a Member State, and to any person elsewhere who was a national of a Member State and any body elsewhere which was incorporated and constituted under the law of a Member State. The argument was that, as both Ebony Maritime and Loten Navigation were non-Community companies, as the *Lido II* flew the Maltese flag, and as it was taken control of when in international waters, none of the connecting criteria was present. The Court did not agree. It referred to Article 9, read in conjunction with Article 1(1)(c), and Article 10 of the regulation, according to which the competent authorities of the Member States were required to detain, pending investigations, all vessels and cargoes suspected of having breached the prohibition of entry into the territorial sea of the FRY for purposes of trade, and were permitted to confiscate vessels and cargoes once an infringement had been established. It followed from the wording of those provisions that the detention and confiscation measures applied to all vessels, irrespective of flag or ownership. Nor was the application of those measures subject to the condition that the breach of the sanctions should take place within Community territory—in any case the prohibition on entry into the territorial sea of the FRY could be breached only outside Community territory. Since under Article 11 the regulation applied within the whole territory of the Community, Articles 9 and 10 were applicable once vessels were within the territory of a Member State and thus under the territorial jurisdiction of that State. That interpretation was borne out by the wording and purpose of Resolution 820 (1993), paragraph 25 of which expressly provided that all vessels suspected of violations that were found in the territory of a State had to be detained and, where appropriate, forfeited to that State.[87] Again the Court largely adopted the reasoning of Jacobs AG, who in addition pointed out that the regulation needed to be interpreted so as to make the sanctions provided for by the resolution fully effective. He also considered that the regulation was not thereby given an interpretation

[87] Ibid, paras 15–21.

conflicting with rules or principles of international law, such as the principle of the freedom of the high seas, expressed in Articles 87 and 92 of the Convention on the Law of the Sea.[88] Measures adopted by the Security Council under Chapter VII of the UN Charter were binding on all UN member States (Article 25), and in the event of conflict between obligations under the Charter and under any other international agreement the former prevailed (Article 103).[89]

The second issue in *Ebony Maritime* arose because the *Lido II* had been taken over by NATO/WEU forces before its actual entry into the territorial waters of the FRY. The legal question was whether Article 1(1)(c) and (d) of the regulation prohibited only the actual entry of commercial traffic into the territorial sea of the FRY or whether it also prohibited conduct occurring in international waters which gave good reason for the belief that the vessel concerned was on course for that territorial sea for purposes of commercial traffic.[90] The Court noted that the prohibition on entry was introduced pursuant to Resolution 820 (1993), which was designed to reinforce the sanctions imposed against the FRY. In order to guarantee that those sanctions would be effective, it was deemed vital to prevent all commercial traffic in Yugoslav waters. The Court considered that effective prevention of all such traffic implied that the prohibition should apply not only to actual entries, but also to attempted entries by vessels in international waters. Any other interpretation would risk rendering the prohibition ineffective. The prohibition in Article 1(1)(d) of any activity the object or effect of which was to promote the entry of any commercial traffic into the FRY's territorial sea confirmed that a breach of the sanctions could result from conduct occurring in international waters.[91] In line with the broad territorial scope of the regulation, the Court thus opted for a broad interpretation of the prohibitions which it laid down, so as to ensure the effectiveness of the sanctions.

The third issue in *Ebony Maritime* was whether the Italian authorities were entitled to confiscate the cargo of the *Lido II*. There was some confusion about the actual wording of the regulation, because of differences in the various language versions. But the Court also addressed further issues. The companies involved argued that the confiscation ran counter to the principle of *nulla poena sine culpa*, in that no proof of fault on the part of the owner of the cargo was required, thereby implying

[88] Done at Montego Bay on 10 December 1982, 21 ILM 1261 [1998] OJ L179/3.

[89] *Ebony Maritime* (n 16 above) paras 21 and 27.

[90] Art 1(1)(c) and (d) provided:

> 1. As from 26 April 1993, the following shall be prohibited:
>
> ...
>
> (c) the entry into the territorial sea of the Federal Republic of Yugoslavia (Serbia and Montenegro) by all commercial traffic;
>
> (d) any activity the object or effect of which is, directly or indirectly, to promote the transactions mentioned under (a), (b) or (c);
>
> ....

[91] *Ebony Maritime* (n 16 above) paras 22–27.

a system of strict criminal liability. They further contended that it was contrary to the principle of proportionality for the owner of the cargo to be penalized in the same way as the owner of the vessel, regardless of their respective degrees of involvement. The Court replied to those arguments by first referring to the basic principle that the Member States were required to take all measures necessary to guarantee the application and effectiveness of Community law. While the choice of penalties remained within their discretion, they had to ensure in particular that infringements of Community law were penalized under conditions, both procedural and substantive, which were analogous to those applicable to infringements of national law of a similar nature and importance and which, in any event, made the penalty effective, proportionate, and dissuasive. The Court then pointed out that it had already accepted that a system of strict criminal liability penalizing breach of a regulation was not in itself incompatible with Community law.[92] It was for the national court to determine whether the penalty of confiscation complied with the above principles and, in particular, whether it was dissuasive, effective, and proportionate. In making that determination, the national court had to take account, in particular, of the fact that the objective pursued by the regulation, which was to bring to an end the state of war in the region concerned and the massive violations of human rights and humanitarian law in the Republic of Bosnia-Herzegovina, was one of fundamental general interest for the international community.[93] The Court thus again hinted at the overriding concern for making the sanctions effective.

The third case involving sanctions against the FRY, *Centro-Com*,[94] concerned payment for authorized exports of medical products. The applicable sanctions regulation at the time of the facts was Regulation 1432/92,[95] which gave effect to UN Security Council Resolution 757 (1992). Article 1(b) of the regulation prohibited all exports to Serbia and Montenegro, but Article 2(a) exempted exports of commodities and products intended for strictly medical purposes and foodstuffs notified to the UN Yugoslavia Sanctions Committee. Article 3 subjected such exports to a prior export authorization, to be issued by the competent authorities of the Member States. Centro-Com was an Italian trading company, specializing in the supply of pharmaceutical goods. After having obtained the approval of the Sanctions Committee and the prior authorization of the Italian authorities required by Article 3 of the regulation, Centro-Com exported from Italy, between 15 October 1992 and 6 January 1993, fifteen consignments of pharmaceutical goods and blood-testing equipment to two wholesalers in Montenegro. Payments for those exports were to be debited from a bank account held by the National Bank of Yugoslavia with Barclays Bank, London. Under the applicable UK law implementing the financial

[92] See Case C–326/88 *Anklagemyndigheden v. Hansen* [1990] ECR I–2911, para 19.

[93] *Ebony Maritime* (n 16 above) paras 28–39.

[94] N 16 above; see also Ch 2.

[95] Council Regulation 1432/92 prohibiting trade between the European Economic Community and the Republics of Serbia and Montenegro [1992] OJ L151/4.

sanctions against Serbia and Montenegro (which were not covered by the sanctions regulation[96]), the Bank of England could authorize such payments, and indeed authorized them for eleven of the fifteen consignments. However, following reports of abuse of the authorization procedure established by the Sanctions Committee, such as misdescription of goods and unreliability of the documents issued, or apparently issued, by that Committee, the UK Treasury decided to change its policy. Henceforth, payment from Serbian and Montenegrin funds held in the United Kingdom for exports of goods exempt from the sanctions, such as medical products, was to be permitted only where those exports were made from the United Kingdom. One of the main reasons for the new policy was to enable the UK authorities to exercise effective control over goods exported to Serbia and Montenegro so as to ensure that the goods exported actually matched their description and that no debiting of accounts held with British banks was authorized for payments for non-medical or non-humanitarian purposes. In implementation of this new policy, the Bank of England did not permit Barclays Bank to transfer funds to Centro-Com in payment of the four remaining consignments. Centro-Com challenged that decision before the High Court, which refused its application, and in the appeal proceedings the Court of Appeal referred a couple of questions to the Court of Justice. The question which is of interest here was, in substance, whether the above UK policy on the release of funds was compatible with the Community's common commercial policy, as implemented by the sanctions regulation.

The Court considered that that question raised two problems. The first concerned the relationship between measures of foreign and security policy, such as those intended to ensure effective application of Resolution 757 (1992), on the one hand, and the common commercial policy, on the other. When analysing this problem the Court discussed the scope of the common commercial policy, as examined in Chapter 2. The United Kingdom argued that the measures in issue had been taken by virtue of its national competence in the field of foreign and security policy and that performance of its obligations under the Charter and under the resolutions of the United Nations fell within that competence. The Court accepted that the Member States retained competence in the field of foreign and security policy, but also emphasized that national competences had to be exercised in a manner consistent with Community law. The Member States could not treat national measures, the effect of which was to prevent or restrict the export of certain products, as falling outside the scope of the common commercial policy on the ground that they had foreign and security objectives.[97]

The second problem concerned the scope of the common commercial policy and of the relevant measures adopted pursuant to (then) Article 113 EEC. Here the Court analysed the precise meaning and effect of the combined provisions of the sanctions regulation and of Regulation 2603/69 establishing common rules for

[96] The regulation was adopted on the basis of (then) Art 113 EEC.
[97] *Centro-Com* (n 16 above) paras 23–30.

exports (the export regulation then in force).[98] The latter provided for a principle of free exportation, but allowed for exceptions on grounds of public policy or public security. The Court construed the general prohibition of exports in the sanctions regulation as a derogation from the principle of free exportation in the export regulation. However, in so far as the sanctions regulation permitted exports of medical products, such exports remained subject to the common system provided for by the export regulation. As Article 1 of that regulation prohibited quantitative restrictions on exports, the question arose of whether restrictions on the release of funds held at a bank could constitute such a quantitative restriction.[99]

The Court replied to that question with the following reasoning. It noted that Article 1 of the export regulation implemented the principle of freedom to export at Community level and therefore had to be interpreted as covering measures adopted by the Member States whose effect was equivalent to a quantitative restriction where their application could lead to an export prohibition. National measures by a Member State preventing the release of Serbian and Montenegrin funds as payment for goods that could be legally exported to Serbia and Montenegro unless those goods were exported from its own territory, constituted a restriction on the payment of the price of the goods which, like the supply of goods, was an essential element of an export transaction. Such measures were equivalent to a quantitative restriction, since their application precluded the making of payment in consideration of the supply of goods dispatched from other Member States, and thus prevented such exports.[100]

The further question which then arose was whether the requirement that the authorized exports take place from UK territory was justified on grounds of public security, and could benefit from the exception in Article 11 of the export regulation. The United Kingdom argued that, having regard to the difficulties involved in applying the system of authorizations issued by the Sanctions Committee, that requirement was necessary in order to ensure that the sanctions imposed by Resolution 757 (1992) were applied effectively, since it allowed the UK authorities themselves to check the nature of goods exported to Serbia and Montenegro. Jacobs AG was of the opinion that the general question of whether the UK policy was justified did not need to be resolved, since the specific decision in issue did not in any event comply with the principle of proportionality. When the Treasury changed the policy, Centro-Com had already exported to Montenegro, having obtained the approval of the Sanctions Committee as well as an Italian export authorization. In those circumstances the refusal to release payment could not serve the objective of an effective implementation of the export ban, since the exports had already taken place.[101] The Court, however, went further, and addressed the general question of justification. It first noted that the concept of public security within the meaning of Article 11 of the export regulation covered both a Member State's internal security and its

[98] [1969] OJ Spec Ed (I) 170. [99] *Centro-Com* (n 16 above) paras 31–39.
[100] Ibid, paras 40–42. [101] Ibid, Opinion of Jacobs AG, para 71.

external security and that the risk of a serious disturbance to foreign relations or to the peaceful coexistence of nations could affect the external security of a Member State. Therefore, a measure intended to apply sanctions imposed by a resolution of the UN Security Council in order to achieve a peaceful solution to the situation in Bosnia-Herzegovina, which formed a threat to international peace and security, fell within the exception provided for by Article 11 of the export regulation. However, a Member State's recourse to Article 11 ceased to be justified if Community rules provided for the necessary measures to ensure protection of the interests enumerated in that article. The sanctions regulation, which was designed to implement, uniformly throughout the Community, certain aspects of the sanctions imposed by the UN Security Council, laid down the conditions on which exports of medical products to Serbia and Montenegro were to be authorized (i.e. notification to the Sanctions Committee and export authorization by a Member State). In those circumstances, measures regarding the release of funds such as those adopted by the United Kingdom could not be justified, since effective application of the sanctions could be ensured by other Member States' authorization procedures, as provided for in the sanctions regulation, in particular the procedure of the Member State of exportation. The Member States had to place trust in each other with regard to the check made by the competent authorities of the Member State from which the products in question were dispatched. There was nothing in the case to suggest that the system of export authorizations had not functioned properly. Finally, it had to be borne in mind that, since Article 11 of the export regulation formed an exception to the principle of freedom to export, it had, on any view, to be interpreted in a way which did not extend its effects beyond what was necessary for the protection of the interests which it was intended to guarantee. Less restrictive measures were possible here, such as resorting to administrative collaboration with the authorities of other Member States. The Court therefore concluded that the UK policy was contrary to the combined provisions of the sanctions regulation and of the export regulation.[102]

The judgment in *Centro-Com* strongly enhanced the status and effect of EC sanctions regulations and external trade rules. On the issue of competence, even if the Court recognized that the Member States retained powers in the field of foreign and security policy and that the sanctions regulations constituted implementation of political decisions in the framework of EPC, it none the less emphasized that the Member States needed to comply with the various commercial policy instruments, including sanctions regulations. The political subordination to foreign policy decisions was not matched by any form of legal subordination.[103] As regards the interpretation of the various provisions in the sanctions regulation and in the export regulation, it is first of all noteworthy that the Court had no qualms about fully applying the principle of freedom of exportation resulting from Article 1 of

[102] *Centro-Com* (n 16 above) paras 44–53 of the judgment. [103] See also Ch 2.

the export regulation to exports authorized under the sanctions regulation. Secondly, the Court interpreted the principle of free exports broadly, as encompassing measures regarding payment for export. Thirdly, and most significantly, it did not accept recourse to the public security exception in Article 11 of the export regulation, on the ground that the sanctions regulation occupied the field. In this respect the judgment followed the general approach towards the relationship between free trade and free movement principles in the internal market, exceptions thereto, and Community harmonization. It is indeed established case law that exceptions to free movement can no longer be relied upon where the Community has harmonized the relevant laws and regulations of the Member States.[104] In *Centro-Com* the Court not only extended that approach to external trade; it did so in what was, from the perspective of national sovereignty, a most sensitive area. Notwithstanding the fact that the Member States were required, under international law, to abide by the UN Charter and by Security Council resolutions, and that they retained competence in the area of foreign and security policy, they could no longer act outside the EC law framework once a comprehensive sanctions regulation had been adopted. Jacobs AG summed up the position in stark terms. He considered that the UK's argument on national competence in the field of foreign and security policy appeared to suggest that the Member States had more leeway in interpreting, applying, or supplementing Community acts which had a foreign or security policy dimension than they had in respect of other Community acts. He rejected that view. The interpretation of a Community act depended on its objectives, its terms, and its context. The fact that it had a foreign or security policy dimension could therefore have an impact on its interpretation, but it did not in principle mean that the Member States had more leeway.[105]

Counter-terrorism sanctions

Those judgments dating from the 1990s have been followed by more recent cases concerning counter-terrorism sanctions. *Möllendorf* related to the Al-Qaida sanctions, implemented under Regulation 881/2002.[106] The case concerned the sale, in Germany, of land and buildings to a partnership of three buyers, one of whom was subsequently listed in the regulation. Although the sellers had been paid, the sale had not been fully completed, in the sense that, at the time of the listing decisions, it had not yet been finally registered in the *Grundbuch* (the Land Register). The German authorities refused to proceed with that registration in the light of the EU listing of one of the buyers, and the *Kammergericht* (Higher Regional Court)

[104] Case 5/77 *Tedeschi v. Denkavit* [1977] ECR 1555, para 35.

[105] *Centro-Com* (n 16 above) para 43 of the Opinion.

[106] Case C–117/06 *Gerda Möllendorf and Christiane Möllendorf-Niehuus* [2007] ECR I–8361. Regulation 881/2002 (n 17 above).

of Berlin referred questions to the Court of Justice, inquiring whether that refusal constituted the correct application of the sanctions regulation.

The Court started its analysis by establishing that the essential question was whether, in the circumstances of the case, final registration of transfer of ownership in the Land Register implied that an economic resource was made available, directly or indirectly, to designated persons so as to enable them to obtain funds, goods, or services within the meaning of Article 2(3) of the regulation. The sellers had argued that a resource was not made available when there was an economic balance between the consideration given and the consideration received. The Court rejected that interpretation. The prohibition was framed in particularly broad terms, as evidenced by the use of the words 'directly or indirectly'. In addition, the expression 'made available' had a wide meaning: rather than denoting a specific legal category of act, it encompassed all the acts necessary under the applicable national law if a person was effectively to obtain full power of disposal in relation to the property concerned. Final registration in the Land Register constituted such an act, since it was only after final registration that the buyer had the power not only to mortgage the property, but also and above all to transfer title to that property. It was precisely acts of that kind which the regulation sought to prohibit, since they enabled the designated person to obtain funds, goods, or services. Account also had to be taken of the wording and purpose of Resolution 1390 (2002), which the regulation was designed to implement. The broad and unambiguous terms of the resolution confirmed that the regulation applied to any mode of making available an economic resource. If the sellers' argument were accepted, it would be necessary to determine on the facts of each case whether there was a true economic balance, with the attendant risk that the prohibition might be circumvented, and presenting difficult problems of interpretation. Even if there were an economic balance, the possibility remained that the asset obtained by the designated person could offer better prospects for value enhancement.[107]

The Court then considered whether the fact that the transaction had been commenced prior to the listing could modify its finding. It emphasized that the regulation had to be applied with immediate effect, including to ongoing transactions. That followed from the objectives of the regulation, and from the fact that there was no express exception for completing the kind of transaction in issue.[108]

Nor could issues relating to legal requirements for the sellers to repay the sale price to the buyers affect the Court's finding. That repayment benefited from an exception under Article 2a(4)(b) of the regulation, provided that the relevant funds were frozen. Questions about how to proceed with this repayment, given that the buyer was a member of a partnership, could equally not affect the interpretation of the regulation, and had to be resolved under national law.[109]

[107] Ibid, paras 45–59. [108] Ibid, paras 61–66. [109] Ibid, paras 67–73.

The Court lastly examined an alleged infringement of the right to property, not as regards the designated person, but in relation to indirect effects of the obligation to repay, arising under national law, for the other persons involved. Again the Court pointed out that any resulting disproportionate infringement of the right to property could not have an effect on the interpretation of the regulation. That question was a matter of national law and could not be examined in the context of a reference for a preliminary ruling. However, the Court also pointed out that, in accordance with settled case law, the requirements flowing from the protection of fundamental rights within the Community legal order were also binding on Member States when they implemented Community rules, and that consequently they were bound, as far as possible, to apply the rules in accordance with those requirements.[110]

In *Möllendorf* the Court again interpreted a sanctions regulation in a strict way, as it did in the FRY cases, analysed above. However, in one of the most recent sanctions cases, *M and Others*, the Court was more lenient.[111] The case originated in the United Kingdom, where the Treasury had taken the view that the sanctions extended to social security and social assistance benefits paid to the spouses of designated persons. It considered that such payments came within the scope of Article 2(2) of Regulation 881/2002, which prohibited the making available of funds, directly or indirectly, to, or for the benefit of, a designated person. Because the sums in question could be used to cover the basic needs of the households to which the designated persons belonged, such as the buying of food for a communal meal, they were, in the Treasury's opinion, made indirectly available for the benefit of those persons. A group of spouses had challenged the Treasury's interpretation, and the case had gone to the (then) House of Lords, which referred it to the Court of Justice, not without itself expressing the opinion that such an intrusive regime was not required by the regulation.

The Court first attempted to resolve the issue before it by means of a textual interpretation of the regulation. However, the various language versions were so different that this did not yield a clear result. It was therefore necessary to interpret by reference to the purpose and the general scheme of the rules of which the provision in issue formed part. In addition, account also had to be taken of the wording and purpose of Resolution 1390 (2002), which the regulation was designed to implement. However, the various language versions of the resolution were also divergent. The Court therefore turned to the purpose and general scheme of the legislation. It established that the objective was to prevent designated persons from having at their disposal any financial or economic resources, in order to impede the financing of terrorist activities. It followed that the objective of the freezing of funds was to stop those persons having access to economic or financial resources, whatever their nature,

[110] Ibid, paras 74–78.

[111] Case C-340/08 *The Queen on the application of M and Others v. Her Majesty's Treasury*, judgment of 29 April 2010.

that they could use to support their terrorist activities. Thus, the measure freezing economic resources applied only to those assets that could be turned into funds, goods, or services capable of being used to support terrorist activities. However, in the cases in the main proceedings the interpretation by the Treasury was not based on any danger whatsoever that the funds in question might be diverted in order to support terrorist activities. The funds were not handed over to the designated persons, and were used by the spouses to meet the essential needs of their households. It was hard to imagine how those funds could be turned into means that could be used to support terrorist activities, especially as the benefits at issue were fixed at a level intended to meet only the strictly vital needs of the persons concerned. Accordingly, Article 2(2) did not apply to the payment of social security or social assistance benefits in circumstances such as those in issue in the main proceedings.[112]

The Court found support for that interpretation in the principle of legal certainty, which required that the legislation—which in this case was sanctioned, at the national level, with criminal penalties—be clear and precise. A different construction from that which the Court had reached would pose the danger of engendering legal uncertainty, in particular with reference to triangular situations in which funds were made available, directly or indirectly, not to a designated person but to someone else to whom the designated person was more or less closely connected and in which the latter indirectly derived some benefit from those funds.[113]

In terms of the balance between the intergovernmental and the supranational, the above case law on the interpretation and application of sanctions regulations thus strongly confirms the full scope and effect of supranational legal instruments. Their adoption may be conditioned on prior political decisions, but once adopted the regulations in question need to be uniformly interpreted and applied (*Bosphorus*, *Möllendorf* and *M and Others*); they need to be effective (*Bosphorus* and *Ebony Maritime*); they have broad territorial scope (*Ebony Maritime*); sanctions and penalties by Member States need to be effective, proportionate, and dissuasive (*Ebony Maritime*); and the Member States cannot freely decide how to enhance their effectiveness by imposing further requirements which do not conform to the regulations themselves (*Centro-Com* and *M and Others*).

Sanctions by the Member States

It is clear from the above analysis that the EU has extensive powers to adopt sanctions. The practice is that virtually all Security Council resolutions imposing sanctions are followed by a CFSP decision, triggering sanctions regulations adopted on the basis of the TFEU. In effect, therefore, the EU occupies the field.

[112] Ibid, paras 38–63. [113] Ibid, paras 64–66.

The question none the less arises of whether there remains scope for action by the Member States in this area. There are several angles to that question.

First, it is obvious that the Member States are under an obligation to implement and apply sanctions regulations adopted by the EU. The Member States need to provide for effective, proportionate, and dissuasive penalties, and they are generally required to take all measures necessary to make the sanctions effective. Even if regulations are directly applicable in all the Member States, this requirement of effectiveness will lead to various forms of legislative and executive activity at national level. However, the *Centro-Com* judgment shows the limits of what action a Member State is entitled to take to ensure the effectiveness of the sanctions.[114] Derogation from the terms of the applicable regulations is not permitted.

Secondly, what is the position where there are no EU sanctions regulations, or where a particular aspect of sanctions is not regulated at EU level? Is the EU's competence under the TFEU to adopt sanctions exclusive? That is clearly not the case, since restrictive measures are not listed in Article 3 as an area of exclusive competence. Also, the reference to a prior decision under the CFSP suggests that EU competence under the TFEU is conditional. That is a further compelling argument against exclusivity: if there is no CFSP sanctions decision, for example because there is no unanimity, the EU cannot adopt sanctions regulations. Surely this signifies that the Member States, which as the Court recognized remain competent in the area of foreign and security policy,[115] have the power to adopt sanctions. However, the position changes if one takes into account the EU's common commercial policy, which comes within exclusive competence.[116] Economic sanctions at national level cannot in principle be decreed in breach of EU competence in trade matters. Therefore, where a Member State seeks to adopt trade restrictions, let alone a trade embargo, it needs to comply with EU trade legislation.[117] So much follows from *Centro-Com*, where the Court verified whether the UK policy on the release of funds in payment of authorized export transactions complied with the relevant sanctions regulations *and* with the EU export regulation. The Court was unequivocal, both in that case and in the *Werner* and *Leifer* judgments:[118] measures whose effect is to prevent or restrict the export (or, by analogy, the import) of certain products cannot be treated as falling outside the scope of the common commercial policy on the ground that they have foreign policy and security objectives, and national foreign and security policy measures have to respect the provisions adopted by the EU in the field of the common commercial policy. That does not, however, mean that there is no scope whatsoever for national economic sanctions affecting trade. The basic commercial policy instruments all contain an exception for public security, and in *Werner* and *Leifer* the Court accepted that a Member State

[114] N 16 above. [115] Ibid. [116] Ch 2.

[117] Cf K Lenaerts and E De Smijter, 'The United Nations and the European Union: Living Apart Together', in Wellens (ed) (n 32 above) 449.

[118] Case C–70/94 *Werner v. Germany* [1995] ECR I–3189; Case C–83/94 *Leifer and Others* [1995] ECR I–3231; see Ch 2.

could control exports on the basis of that exception. It did not interpret the public security exception too strictly, as it was satisfied that the German legislation in issue, which not only referred to external security but also to the peaceful co-existence of nations and to Germany's external relations, came within it. On that basis, it would be open to a Member State to adopt trade restrictions or an embargo on the ground that this is required from the perspective of public security.

As regards capital movements, Article 65(1)(b) TFEU allows the Member States to take measures which are justified on grounds of public policy or public security. The observations above on the public security exceptions in the framework of the common commercial policy can therefore be extended to financial sanctions restricting the movement of capital and payments, both within the EU and in relations with third countries. The Member States are in principle entitled to restrict financial movements to or from third countries if that is necessary on grounds of public security.

A third angle is the provision of Article 347 TFEU, which refers to measures that a Member State may be called upon to take in the event of serious internal disturbances affecting the maintenance of law and order, in the event of war, or of serious international tension constituting a threat of war, or in order to carry out obligations it has accepted for the purpose of maintaining peace and international security. In *Kadi and Al Barakaat*, however, the Court did not accept that the effect of that provision was to trump the EU's human rights standards (see Chapter 9). The provision could not have the effect of rendering a regulation which sought to implement a Security Council resolution adopted for the purpose of maintaining peace and international security immune from the Courts' jurisdiction.

Article 347 can, however, also be relied upon in the event of serious internal disturbances, war, or serious international tension constituting a threat of war. There has been one case in which a Member State has invoked those exceptions in order to justify a trade embargo. The break-up of Yugoslavia in the early 1990s led to the formation of a number of new States, including the Former Yugoslav Republic of Macedonia (FYROM). Greece strongly objected to the use of the name Macedonia, which it regarded as part of its own cultural patrimony, and complained that the FYROM promoted the idea of a unified Macedonia. After a series of further developments, interventions, and negotiations, culminating in the official recognition of the FYROM by a number of EU Member States and by the United States, Greece adopted a trade embargo against its neighbour. In February 1994, it unilaterally prohibited trade, in particular via the port of Thessaloniki, in products originating in, coming from, or destined for the FYROM, and imports into Greece of products originating in or coming from that Republic. It was clear that the embargo was in breach of the applicable EC law rules and instruments on trade with the FYROM. Greece relied on (current) Article 347 TFEU, and the Commission immediately brought an action under (current) Article 348 TFEU, which, by derogation from Articles 258 and 259, allows the Commission or any Member State to bring the matter directly before the Court of Justice if it considers that a Member State is making improper use of the powers provided for in Articles 346 and 347.

The Court never ruled on the Commission's action because the case was withdrawn after Jacobs AG delivered his Opinion, which therefore represents the only judicial authority.[119] The Advocate General first examined whether there were 'serious internal disturbances affecting the maintenance of law and order'. He took as a starting point that the situations covered by (current) Article 347 were 'wholly exceptional',[120] as evidenced by the fact that they permitted suspension of all the ordinary rules governing the common market. He therefore considered that the provision envisaged a situation verging on a total collapse of internal security. In his opinion Greece had clearly failed to establish that in the absence of the trade embargo against the FYROM, civil disturbances would have taken place on such a scale that the means at its disposal for maintaining law and order would have been insufficient. Greece had made only vague and unsubstantiated assertions about massive demonstrations. The Advocate General therefore rejected the idea that Greece could rely on that particular ground in Article 347.

Jacobs AG next considered whether Greece could invoke the notions of war or serious international tension constituting a threat of war. He considered that this question was far more complex and raised the fundamental issue of the Court's power to exercise judicial review in such cases. Whilst it was plain that the Court had power to review the legality of action taken by a Member State under this heading, the scope and intensity of such review were severely limited on account of the nature of the issues raised. There was a paucity of judicially applicable criteria, he argued, that would permit the Court, or any other court, to determine whether serious international tension existed and whether such tension constituted a threat of war.[121] That is a theme which runs through the whole Opinion. The Advocate General reiterated it when he looked at the Commission's argument that the action taken by Greece was likely to increase tension and thus adversely affect the internal and external security of Greece: that was very much a political assessment of an eminently political question, and there simply were no juridical tools of analysis for approaching such problems.[122] He also returned to the point when he examined whether Greece had made 'improper use' (see Article 348) of the powers provided for in Article 347. Again, if a Member State considered, rightly or wrongly, that the attitude of a third State threatened its vital interest, its territorial integrity, or its very existence, it was for the Member State and not for the Court of Justice to determine how to respond to that perceived threat, and there were no judicial criteria by which such matters could be measured. It was difficult to identify a precise legal test for determining whether a trade embargo was a suitable means of pursuing a political dispute between a Member State and a third country.[123]

Another theme which runs through the Opinion is that the question of whether there was international tension constituting a threat of war had to be looked at, not

[119] Case C-120/94 *Commission v. Greece* [1996] ECR I-1513.

[120] See Case 222/84 *Johnston v. Chief Constable of the Royal Ulster Constabulary* [1986] ECR 1651.

[121] *Commission v. Greece* (n 119 above) Opinion of Jacobs AG, paras 50–51.

[122] Ibid, para 59. [123] Ibid, para 65.

from some outside objective perspective, but from the subjective point of view of the Member State concerned. War was by nature an unpredictable occurrence and the transition from sabre-rattling to armed conflict could be swift and dramatic.[124]

If the matter was looked at from Greece's subjective point of view and if due weight was attached to the geopolitical environment and the history of ethnic strife, border disputes, and general instability that had characterized the Balkans for centuries, then it could not be said that Greece was acting wholly unreasonably by taking the view that the tension between itself and the FYROM bore within it the threat—even if it was long term and remote—of war.[125] The Advocate General also referred to case law of the ECtHR, according to which issues of national security were primarily a matter for the appraisal of the authorities of the State concerned.[126]

The Advocate General also stressed, perhaps to some degree in contrast to his other Opinions on trade and foreign policy,[127] that Article 347 recognized that foreign policy remained essentially a matter for the individual Member States, and that the Member States retained ultimate responsibility for their relations with third States. Notwithstanding the co-operation pursued within the framework of the provisions introduced by the Single European Act and the TEU, it was still for each Member State to decide in the light of its own interests whether to recognize a third State and on what footing to place its relations with such a State.[128] Articles 347 and 348 recognized that the autonomy left to Member States in the field of foreign policy was in stark contrast to the integration achieved in the field of economic and commercial policy, and they attempted to define the outer limits of the autonomy left to the Member States in the field of foreign policy.[129]

Jacobs AG also considered that there were no indications that Greece had made improper use of its powers in the sense of affording protection, instituting discrimination, or taking disproportionate action. As regards proportionality, he pointed out that the effect on the common market was the appropriate benchmark. As the embargo affected a tiny percentage of the total volume of Community trade and was unlikely to have any perceptible impact on the competitive situation in the Community, there was clearly no breach of the principle of proportionality.[130] Accordingly, the Advocate General proposed that the Commission's action be dismissed.

The Opinion of Jacobs AG in the *FYROM* case is the EU judicial text which came closest to establishing some kind of political question doctrine within the framework of EU constitutional law.[131] The emphasis on severely limited judicial

[124] Ibid, paras 54 and 52.
[125] Ibid, para 56.
[126] Ibid, para 55.
[127] Canor (n 42 above) 166.
[128] *Commission v. Greece* (n 119 above) Opinion of Jacobs AG, para 64.
[129] Ibid, para 66.
[130] Ibid, paras 69–72.
[131] It is perhaps no coincidence that Jacobs AG cited TM Franck, *Political Questions/Judicial Answers* (Princeton University Press, 1992).

review, on the paucity of judicially applicable criteria, and on the eminently political character of the issues involved may create an impression of judicial abdication in the face of a Member State's claims under Article 347. The Advocate General also referred to similar approaches under German, UK, and ECHR law in support of judicial deference. However, the general language used does not perhaps completely match the type of review actually undertaken. Jacobs AG was surely right to point out that wars may flare up rather unexpectedly, and that a lot, if not everything, depends on the perception in the countries involved. The serious tension between Greece and the FYROM was undeniable, as was the history of ethnic violence and conflict in the Balkans. On the facts, therefore, judicial deference and acceptance were clearly warranted, and the Advocate General took great care in examining and reflecting on those facts. It is moreover doubtful whether such highly charged political issues can in any way be resolved by a judicial ruling.

The approach by Jacobs AG is warranted in the case of war, a situation which in any event will rarely be in doubt, or serious international tension constituting a threat of war. It should not be extended to the other grounds for Member State action, i.e. serious internal disturbances and obligations to maintain peace and international security. Indeed, the Advocate General clearly distinguished the case of serious internal disturbances, swiftly discarding Greece's claim based on that limb of Article 347 as being unsubstantiated, and emphasizing that those disturbances should verge on a complete internal collapse. As regards obligations to maintain peace and international security, which were not at issue in the *FYROM* case, the observation that there are few judicially applicable criteria would clearly be incorrect. Determining the extent of a Member State's international obligations surely requires some degree of legal analysis which a court is perfectly capable of carrying out, even if there may be a margin of political appreciation.

The Advocate General also emphasized national competence as regards foreign and security policy. Here one wonders whether the emphasis has not shifted in the meantime. It is undeniable that there has been more movement towards common action in this area, not just in practice but also at constitutional level.[132] From that angle one should ask the question whether today, if a Member State were to find itself in a situation such as that of Greece, and the case were to come before the Court, that Member State should not have to prove that it has sufficiently attempted to follow the CFSP route, by involving the EU as a whole in negotiations aimed at reducing international tension. If a Member State can derogate from any of its common market obligations (effectively any of its Treaty obligations), then it is not excessive to require that Member State first to exhaust the EU political and diplomatic mechanisms and channels. The Court could exercise at least some review of that process.

The *FYROM* case was, fortunately, highly exceptional. More significant questions arise, for legal practice, as regards the role for Member State action in the field

[132] See the strengthening of CFSP through the successive Treaty amendments.

of smart actions and counter-terrorism listings. As mentioned above, the EU has largely occupied the field here. However, it is clear that the Courts exercise strict review, in particular as regards counter-terrorism listings. The *Kadi* litigation shows that it is not impossible for there to be an ultimate annulment of a listing by the EU Courts, without further appeal, or maintenance of the effects of the regulation, or a re-listing by the EU institutions. If that listing reflects a UN listing, what is the position of and scope for action by the Member States, who continue to be bound by the Security Council resolution? Are the Member States entitled to maintain the listing, notwithstanding annulment? It may in this respect be noted that a number of Member States have adopted legislative measures directly aimed at implementing Resolution 1333 (2000) in national law, which therefore coexist with Regulation 881/2002.[133]

Prior to the Court of Justice's judgment in *Kadi and Al Barakaat*, there seemed little doubt that the Member States were entitled to rely on Article 351 TFEU (as well as Article 347) to continue to honour their international obligations under the UN Charter. An EU listing might be annulled, it seemed, without this leading to a de-listing at national level. However, certain statements by the Advocate General and the Court in *Kadi and Al Barakaat* have cast doubt on whether that is the correct legal position.

Maduro AG developed the following reasoning when considering the relevance of (current) Article 351 TFEU. At first sight, he stated, it could not be entirely clear how Member States would be prevented from fulfilling their obligations under the UN Charter if the Court were to annul the contested regulation. Indeed, in the absence of a Community measure, it would in principle be open to the Member States to take their own implementing measures, since they were allowed, under the Treaty, to adopt measures which, though affecting the functioning of the common market, could be necessary for the maintenance of international peace and security (current Article 347 TFEU). None the less, the Advocate General continued, the powers retained by the Member States in the field of security policy had to be exercised in a manner consistent with Community law. In the light of the Court's ruling in *ERT*,[134] it could be assumed that, to the extent that their actions came within the scope of Community law, Member States were subject to the same Community rules for the protection of fundamental rights as the Community institutions themselves. On that assumption, if the Court were to annul the contested regulation on the ground that it infringed Community rules for the protection of fundamental rights, then, by implication, Member States could not possibly adopt the same measures without—in so far as those measures came within the scope of Community law—acting in breach of fundamental rights as protected by the Court. Thus, the argument—advanced by the United Kingdom—was of indirect relevance only.[135]

[133] *Ahmed and Others* (n 70 above), referred to in *Kadi II* (n 65 above) para 36.
[134] Case C-260/89 *ERT* [1991] ECR I-2925.
[135] *Kadi and Al Barakaat* (n 18 above) Opinion of Maduro AG, para 30.

These statements suggest that the annulment of an individual listing, on grounds of the violation of EU standards of fundamental rights protection, binds the Member States, in the sense that they cannot maintain that listing, even on national law grounds, and for the purpose of honouring their international obligations. As long as they are acting within the scope of EU law, they are bound by EU human rights standards, and Articles 347 and 351 TFEU do not permit any derogation from those standards. One presumes that the annulment of an individual listing does not take that listing outside the scope of EU law.

The Court appeared to confirm this, where it established that (current) Articles 347 and 351 TFEU could not be understood to authorize any derogation from the principles of liberty, democracy, and respect for human rights and fundamental freedoms enshrined in Article 6 TEU as a foundation of the Union. (Current) Article 351 TFEU could in no circumstances permit any challenge to the principles that formed part of the very foundations of the Community legal order, one of which was the protection of fundamental rights, including the review by the Community judicature of the lawfulness of Community measures as regards their consistency with those fundamental rights.[136]

These are possibly the furthest-reaching statements by the Court in *Kadi and Al Barakaat*. Textually, there is only limited support for the distinction which the Court made between those provisions of the (then) EC Treaty from which a Member State could derogate on the basis of (current) Article 351 TFEU (the Court referred to current Article 207 TFEU on the common commercial policy), and those foundational provisions, like Article 6 TEU, which do not tolerate derogation—even, apparently, to comply with UN Charter obligations. The distinction confirms the strong constitutional reading of the Treaties in *Kadi and Al Barakaat*. Certain basic values are of such a fundamental character that no other provisions in the EU legal system are capable of allowing derogations from them.

Conclusions

The analysis in this chapter shows that there is a host of legal issues in the field of sanctions policy, owing to the constitutional separation which characterizes the EU's external action. In these conclusions it is not possible to return to all those issues. Partly because of 9/11, economic and financial sanctions are no longer exclusively geared towards countries, but increasingly focus on individuals. Sanctions adopted under the CFSP also move in the direction of putting pressure on regimes through action against individuals (so-called smart sanctions). The Treaty of Lisbon reflected these developments, by the insertion of Article 215 TFEU.

Recent cases have therefore been increasingly concerned with the confrontation between human rights law and the executive world of foreign and security

[136] Ibid, paras 303–304 of the judgment.

policy. The courts have had to face up to the delicate and sensitive task of striking the right balance between the various competing interests. They have rightly rejected a political-question doctrine in EU law and have not exaggerated judicial deference. They have not abdicated judicial review on the mere basis of the political sensitivity of the issues. Judicial intervention has not been denied on the ground that measures have their origin in a UN resolution. Domestic courts, in our case both the EU Courts and national courts, effectively offer the only opportunity for judicial review of such measures. In the absence of such review, sanctions are pure executive acts, and no matter what type of foreign and security policy interests are at stake, it cannot be accepted in an organization based on the rule of law that executive acts which strongly affect people's lives are not subject to any effective judicial scrutiny.

There may be inherent difficulties in exercising judicial review, such as the essentially political nature of certain assessments, the complexity of facts, the secret character of sources of information, etc. Those difficulties cannot be denied, yet courts should face up to them in the light of the importance of their task and position in these matters.

Index